Painting Fantasy with GOUACHE

TUTORIALS, TIPS, AND TRICKS FROM PROFESSIONAL PAINTERS

3dtotal Publishing

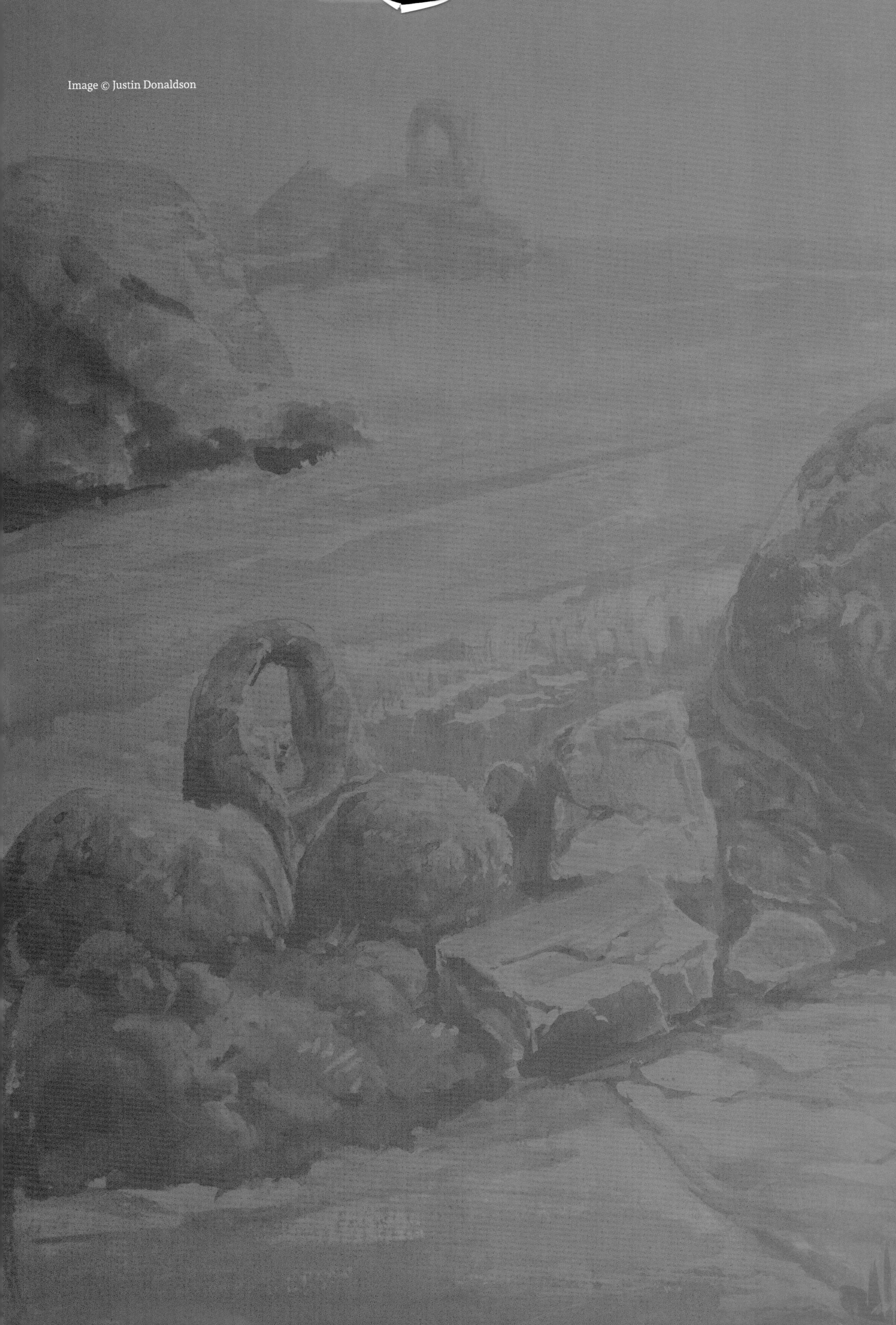

Painting Fantasy with
GOUACHE

TUTORIALS, TIPS, AND TRICKS FROM PROFESSIONAL PAINTERS

3dtotal Publishing

3dtotalPublishing

Correspondence: **publishing@3dtotal.com**
Website: **store.3dtotal.com**

Painting Fantasy with Gouache: Tutorials, tips, and tricks from professional painters © **2025, 3dtotal Publishing**. All rights reserved. No part of this book can be reproduced in any form or by any means, without the prior written consent of the publisher. All artwork, unless stated otherwise, is copyright of the featured artists. All artwork that is not copyright of the featured artists is marked accordingly.

Every effort has been made to ensure the credits and contact information listed are present and correct. In the case of any errors that have occurred, the publisher respectfully directs readers to **store.3dtotal.com/pages/information** for any updated information and corrections.

First published in the United Kingdom, 2025, by 3dtotal Publishing.

Address: 3dtotal.com Ltd,
29 Foregate Street, Worcester,
WR1 1DS, United Kingdom.

Soft cover ISBN: 978-1-915992-16-1

Printed and bound in Shanghai, China by KS Printing.

Visit **store.3dtotal.com** for a complete list of available book titles.

Editor: Marisa Lewis
Designer: Matthew Lewis
Lead Editor: Samantha Rigby
Lead Designer: Joseph Cartwright
Studio Manager: Simon Morse
Managing Director: Tom Greenway

Cover artwork © individual artists as credited throughout the book.

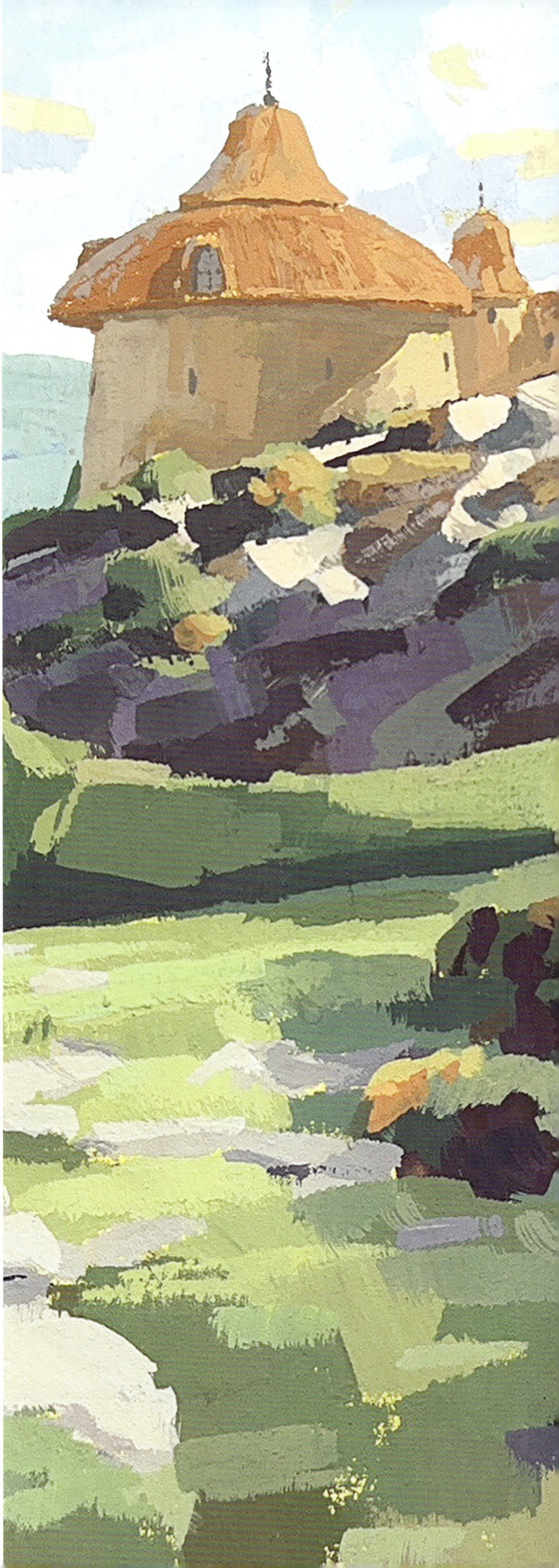

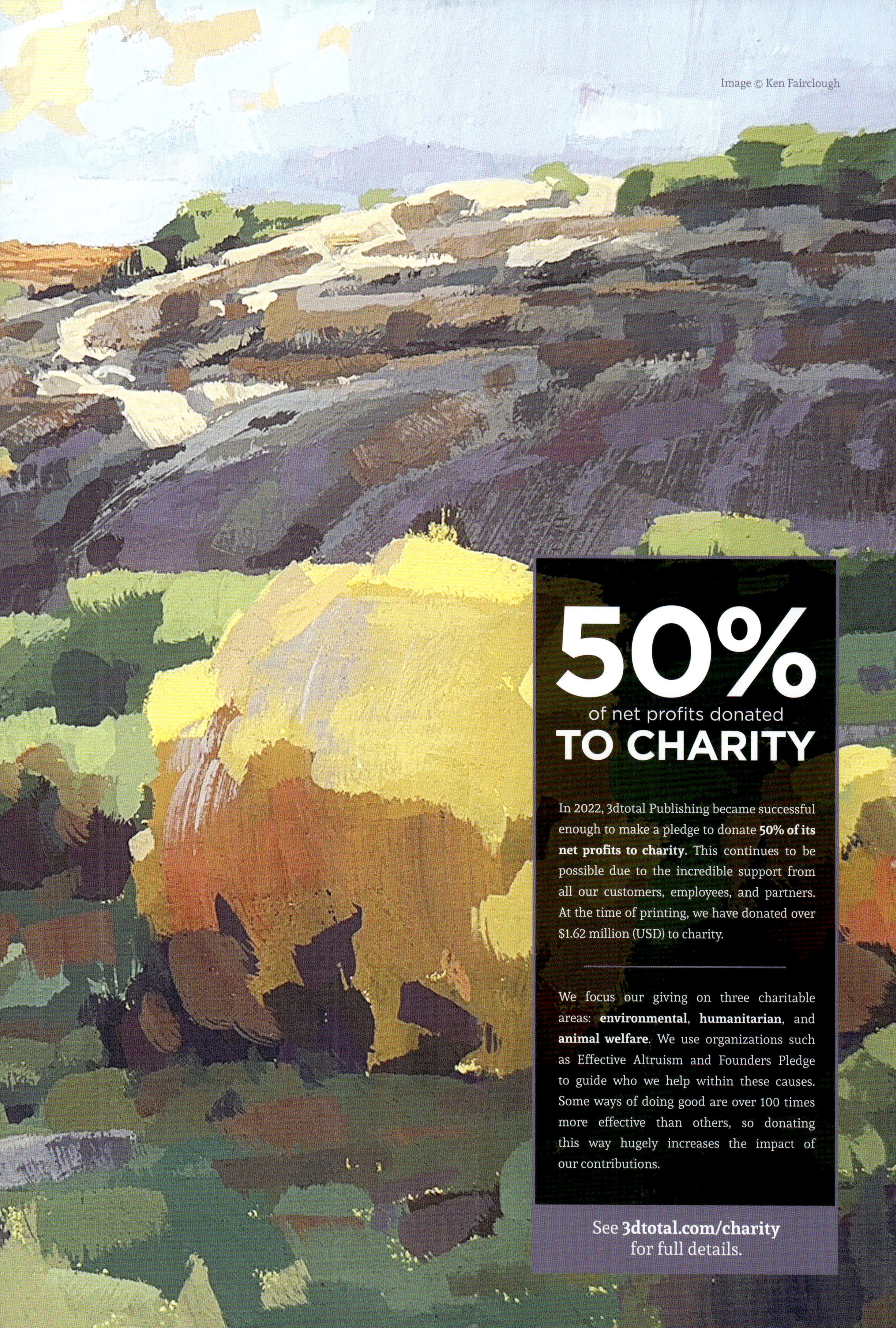

Image © Ken Fairclough

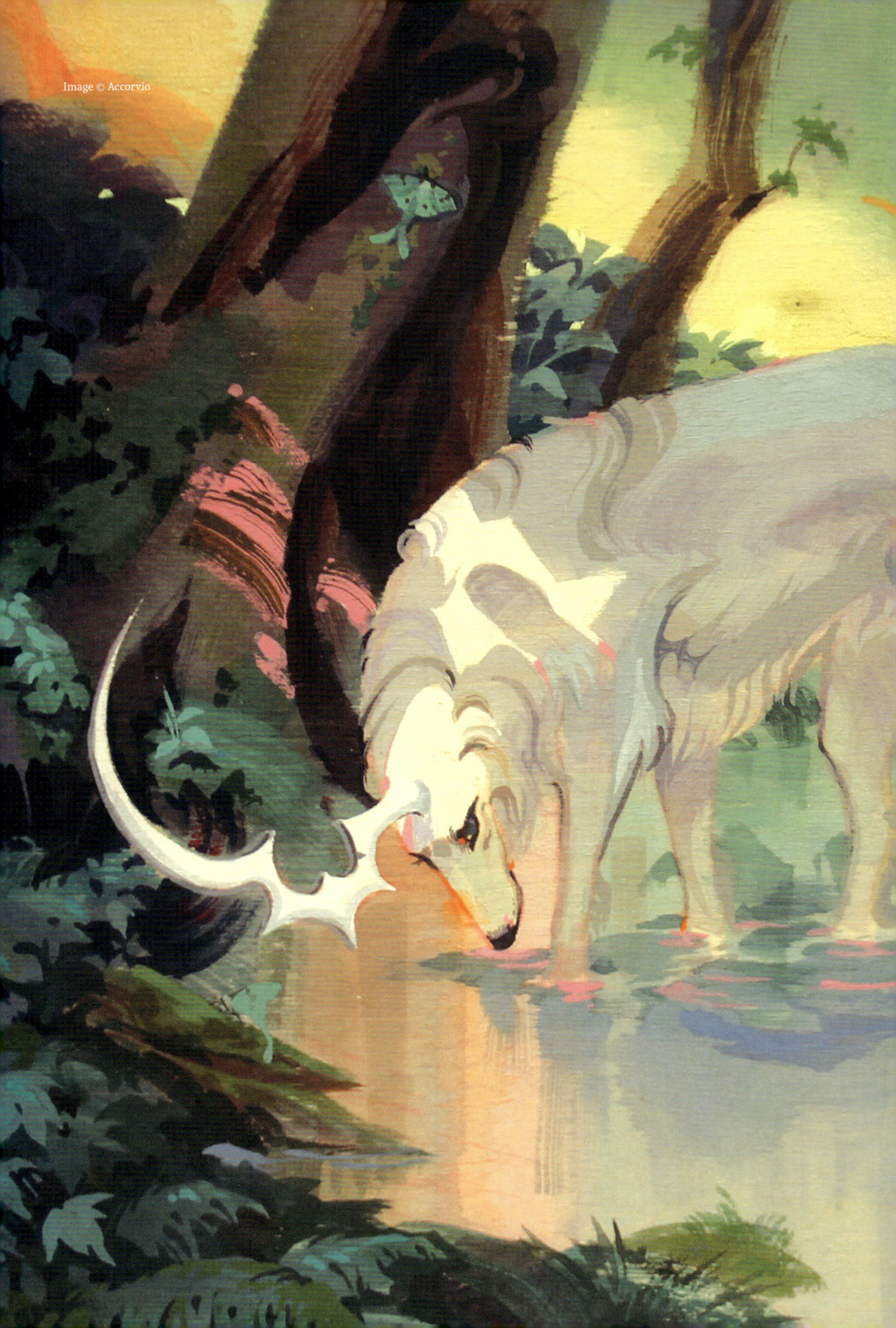

Image © Accorvio

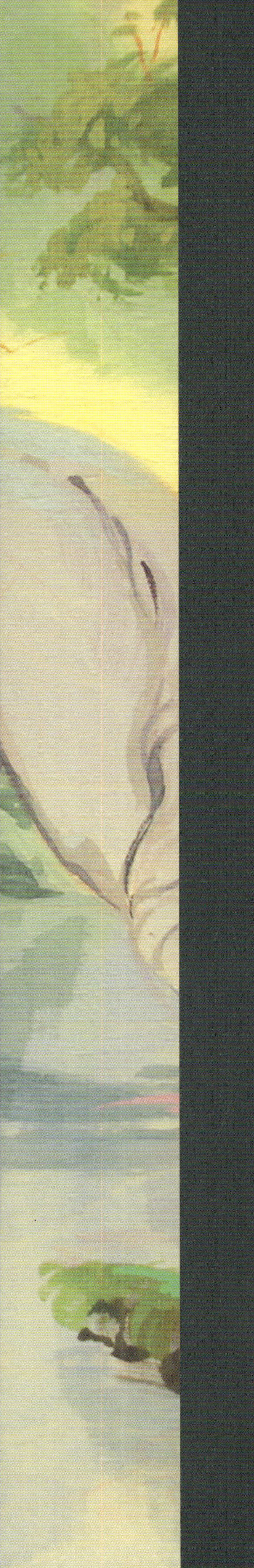

The CONTENTS

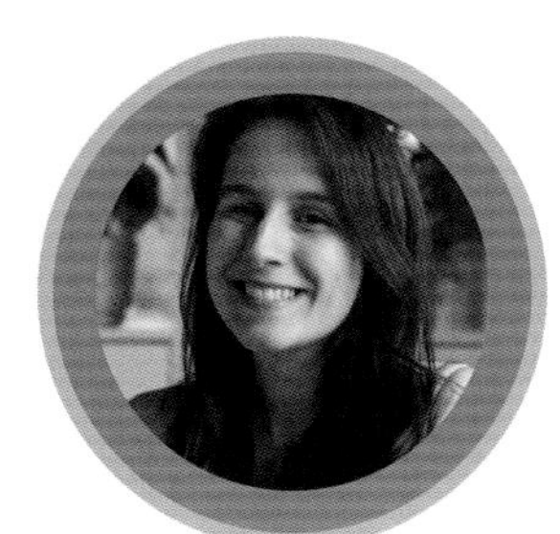

Luisa J. Preißler
FOREWORD

For over a decade, I dedicated my career to painting fantastical worlds – creating digital art for book covers, trading cards, and games. Photoshop became my playground; a space where I could bring bold colours and epic stories to life. But as any creative soul knows, the itch to explore new tools and media is impossible to resist. It's hardwired into who we are. For me, that itch had a name: gouache.

I was drawn to its bold, punchy colours – the kind of vibrancy I loved in digital art but could now bring to life on paper. Gouache had a reputation for being versatile, forgiving, and capable of producing striking contrasts. I didn't know much about it, but that didn't stop me. I jumped in head first, thrilled by the possibilities.

The beginning was, predictably, messy. My first attempts were far from masterpieces, but each brushstroke taught me something new. Within weeks, I started to find my rhythm. What I discovered was a medium that offered the best of both worlds: the spontaneity and texture of traditional art with the methodical layering I'd mastered in digital painting. It gave me the freedom to build an image slowly, correcting and refining as I went.

Gouache quickly became my new creative obsession. Its versatility opened up endless possibilities: I could play with transparent washes or lay down opaque, striking strokes of colour. Mistakes weren't the end of the world – they were just another step in the process, easily adjusted with a bit of water or a fresh layer of paint. And speaking of water, I loved how fast gouache dried. Unlike oils, I didn't have to wait days (or weeks) for a piece to be ready. Gouache gave me results that were both quick and deeply satisfying.

For my new work, nature became my muse. Painting lush greenery, blooming flowers, and quiet landscapes gave me a chance to slow down and rediscover the beauty around me. And there's something undeniably magical about holding a finished painting in your hands, imperfections and all.

Whether you're a seasoned artist itching for a fresh challenge or a total beginner curious to try something new, gouache has a lot to offer. It's a medium that thrives on experimentation, rewards patience, and encourages you to embrace happy accidents along the way.

Let me invite you to grab your brushes and dive in – gouache has a way of turning simple ideas into something vibrant and alive.

Luisa J. Preißler

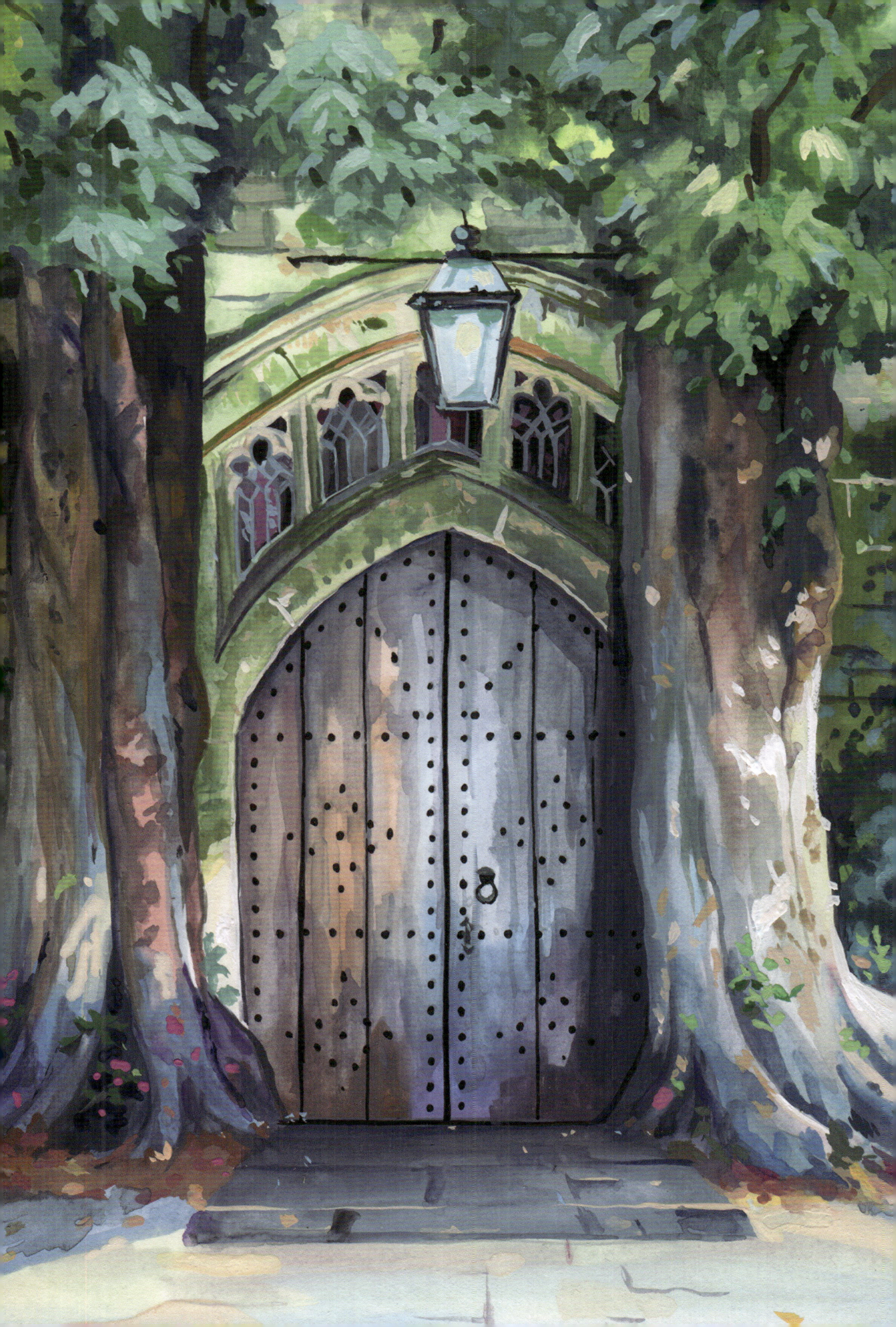

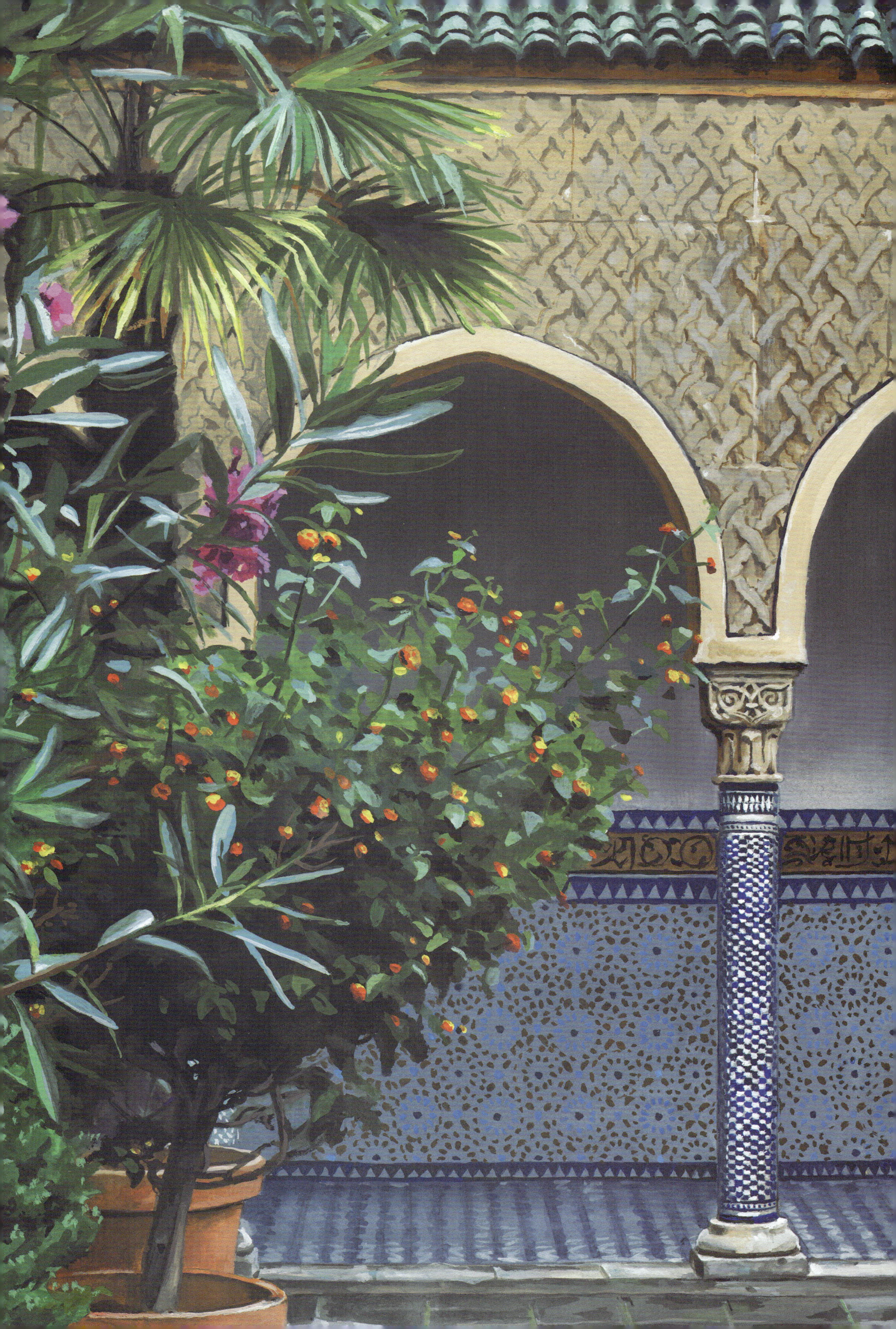

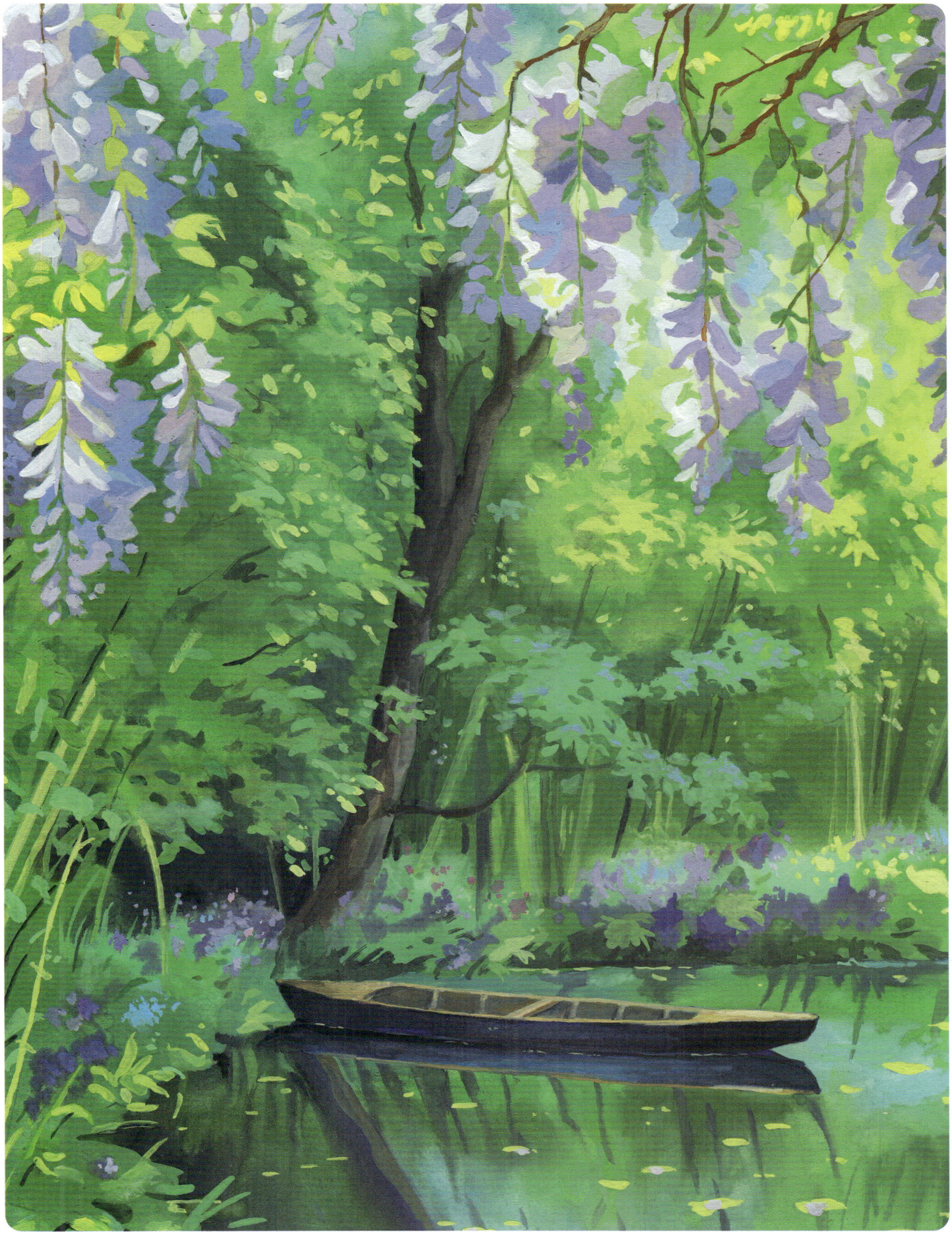

Gardens of the World (left) and *Monet's Boat* (above) © Luisa J. Preißler

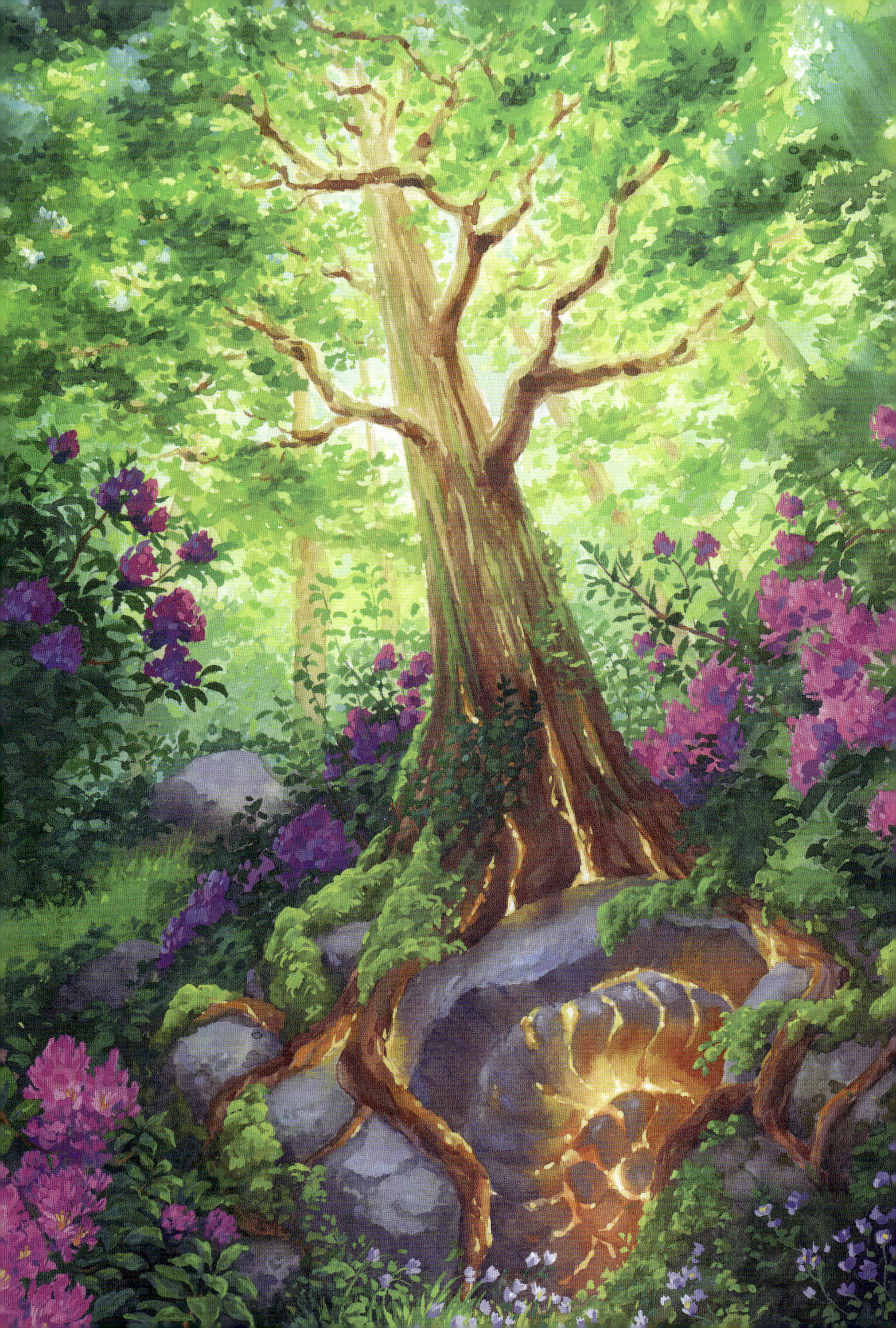

How to
USE THIS BOOK

Gouache is a versatile, underrated medium among paints. Thicker than watercolour and cheaper than oils, it has long been a favourite of landscape painters on the go and illustrators or designers needing bold, fast-drying colour. Used by such historic icons as Edgar Degas and Henri Matisse, gouache is still popular in the present day, especially among digital artists who want a break from their screens to paint outdoors or reconnect with traditional media. Wherever you're coming from, if you're at the start of your gouache journey, this book is a good place to begin.

In the **Introduction** (page 14), Justin Donaldson will instruct you in the basics of gouache, covering fundamental tools, terms, and techniques. His practical demos will begin training your eye for colour, value, and opacity, before you start inventing fantasy scenes.

The step-by-step **Tutorials** (page 76) show how professional gouache painters create fantasy-themed artwork in a range of beautiful styles. It's best to work through these projects in sequence to build up your confidence and familiarity with the medium.

On page 184 is the **Gallery** of inspiring portfolio work from the tutorial artists, followed by a **Glossary** of useful terms on page 219.

Remember that patience and developing your knowledge of colour and light are the keys to success. Practise mixing different colours from scratch and compare how they look with different amounts of water on different types of paper. Paint indoors and out, if you can. Paint from observation and imagination. Don't be put off by mistakes, as gouache can be a very forgiving medium for beginners.

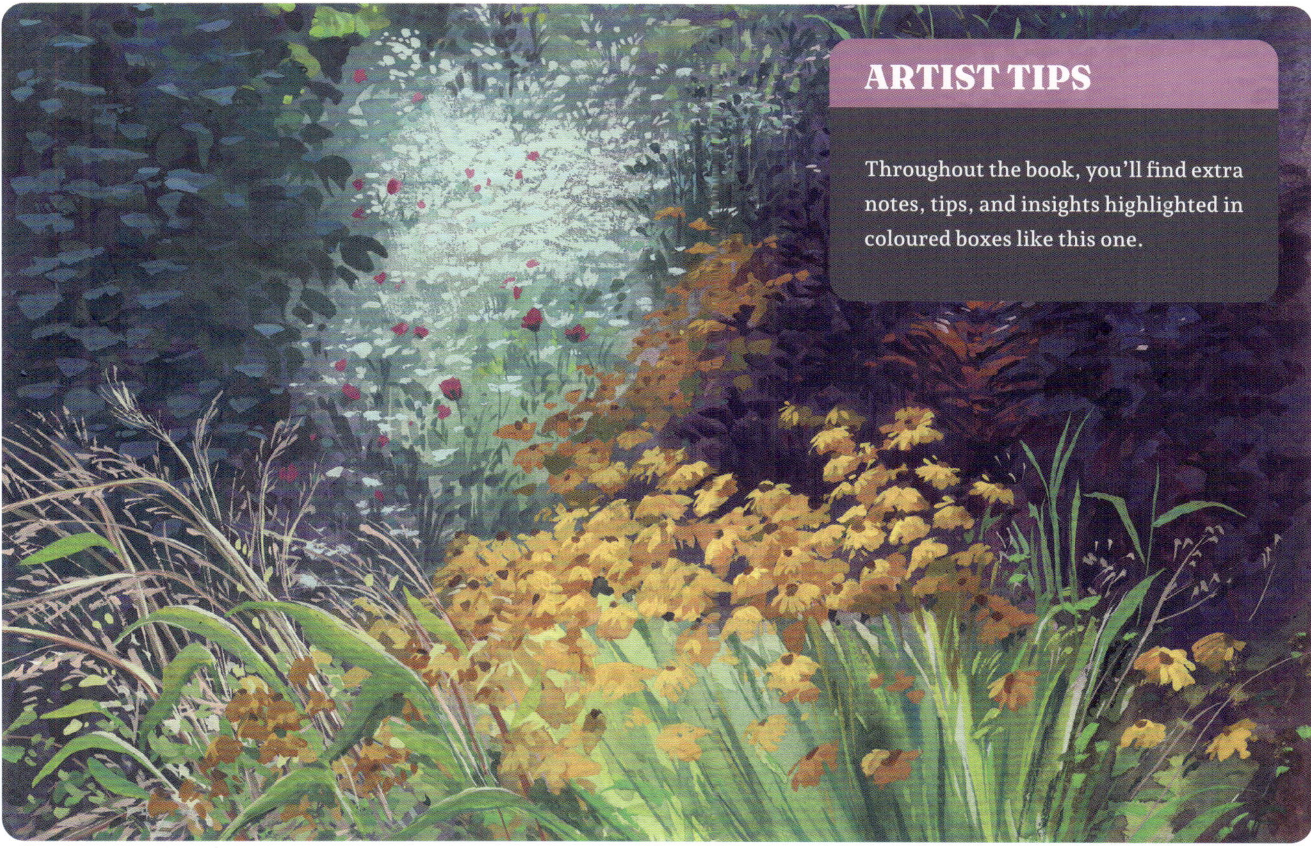

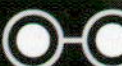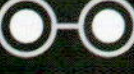

Justin Donaldson

INTRODUCTION

Before you can begin painting fantastical gouache scenes, it is important to know some fundamentals: essential tools, common terminology, useful techniques, and the importance of observation and life study for tackling any subject. In this introductory chapter, painter and educator Justin Donaldson will share his must-know basics of gouache painting.

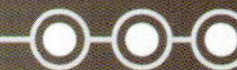

WHAT IS GOUACHE?

Gouache is a water-based paint that has been used by artists for centuries. The term 'gouache' was first used in France in the 18th century to describe a type of paint made from pigments bound in water-soluble gum, similar to watercolour, but with added white pigment to make it opaque. Gouache uses more binder than watercolour, and various amounts of inert pigments, such as chalk, are added to boost opacity. It can form a thicker layer of paint on the paper surface, preventing the paper (or previous layers) from showing through.

WHY USE GOUACHE?

There are many reasons you might choose to use gouache, but let me start by telling you why I keep using it:

- **Gouache is really portable.** You don't need a fancy set-up or lengthy clean-up in order to get full use of it.

- **It dries quickly.** This means that you can apply many layers very quickly and create a painting fast. You can close your sketchbook pretty soon after finishing without worrying about smearing paint.

- **It has very little body.** This means that you can build up many, many layers without adding superfluous texture.

- **It dries matte.** This means it scans and photographs really well without any glare.

The downside of gouache is that, because it is reflective when wet and matte when dry, its physical appearance changes during the drying process. Generally, you'll notice that the dark colours get lighter and the light colours get darker. Before you get too concerned, let me assure you that you can learn to predict what your paint is going to look like once it dries, and you won't have to think about this value shift any longer.

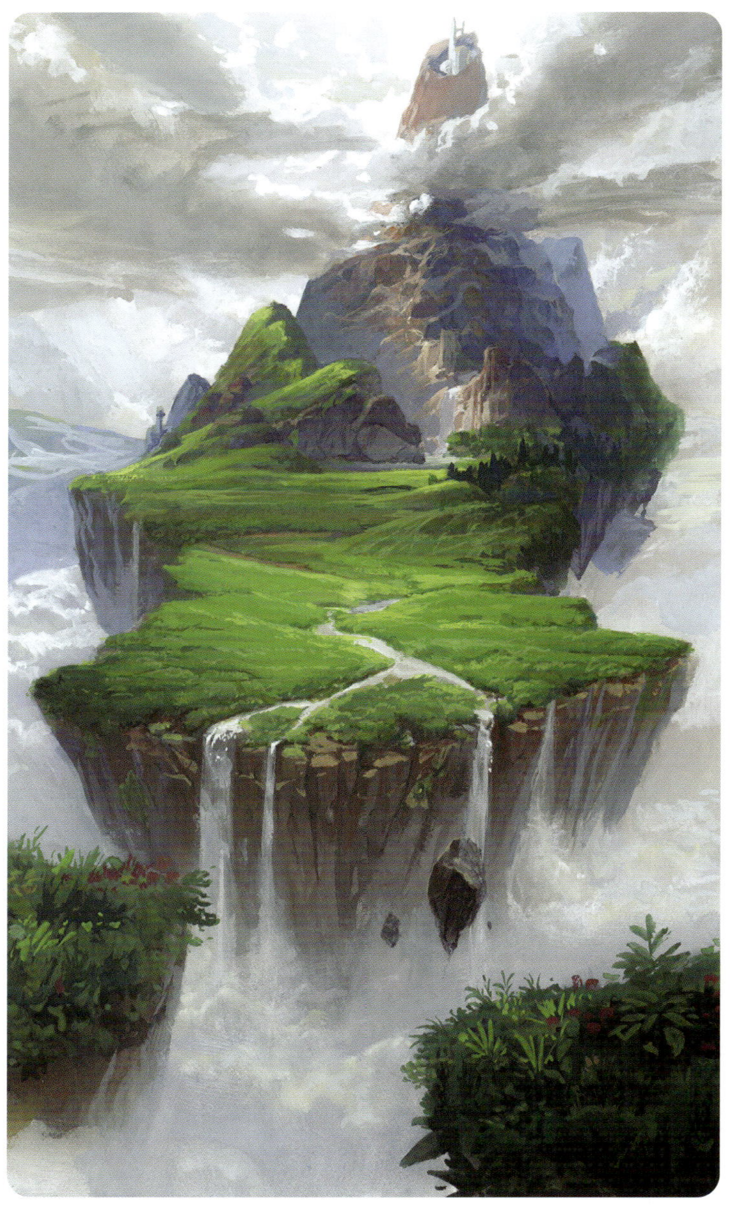

Floating Islands

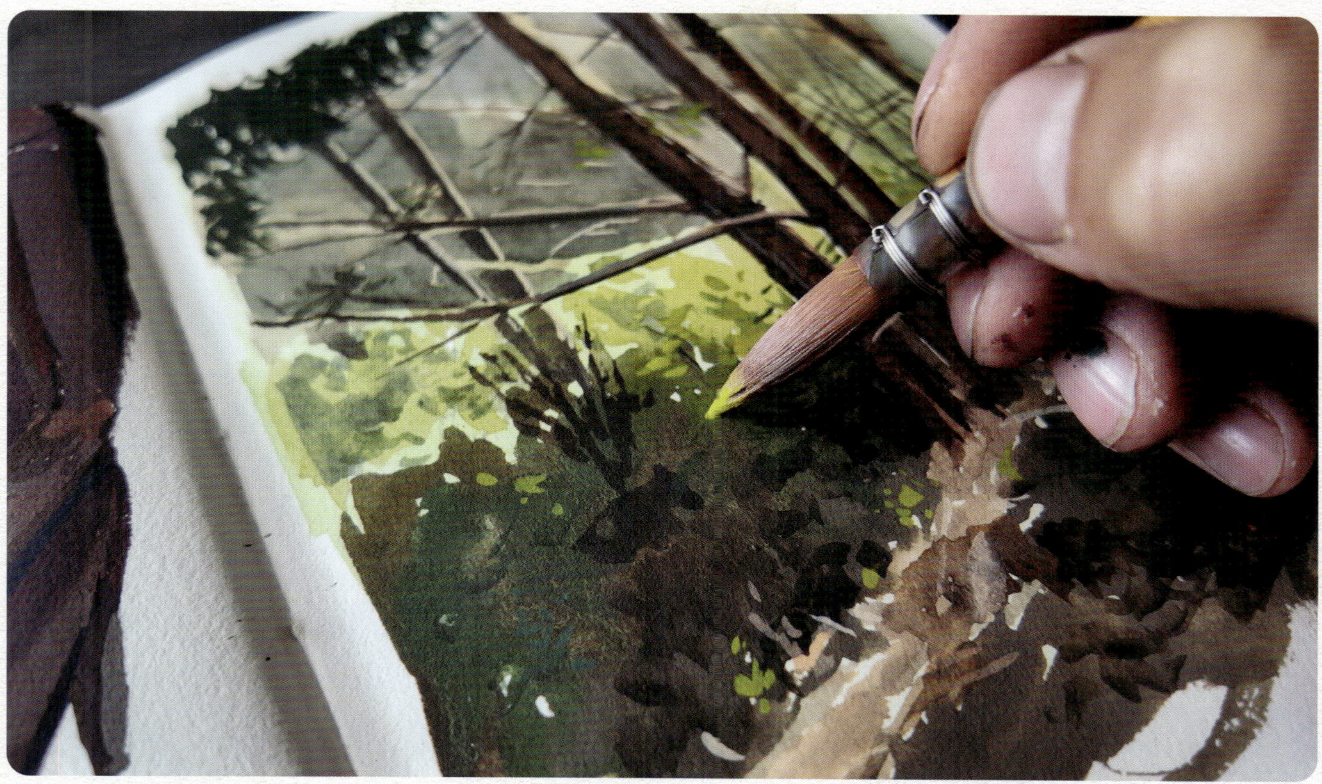

This piece was painted impromptu while sitting on the grass on a beautiful day, and when I was done I closed my sketchbook and took a walk; everything I need for my painting can fit into a bag, without weighing me down or taking a great deal of time to set up

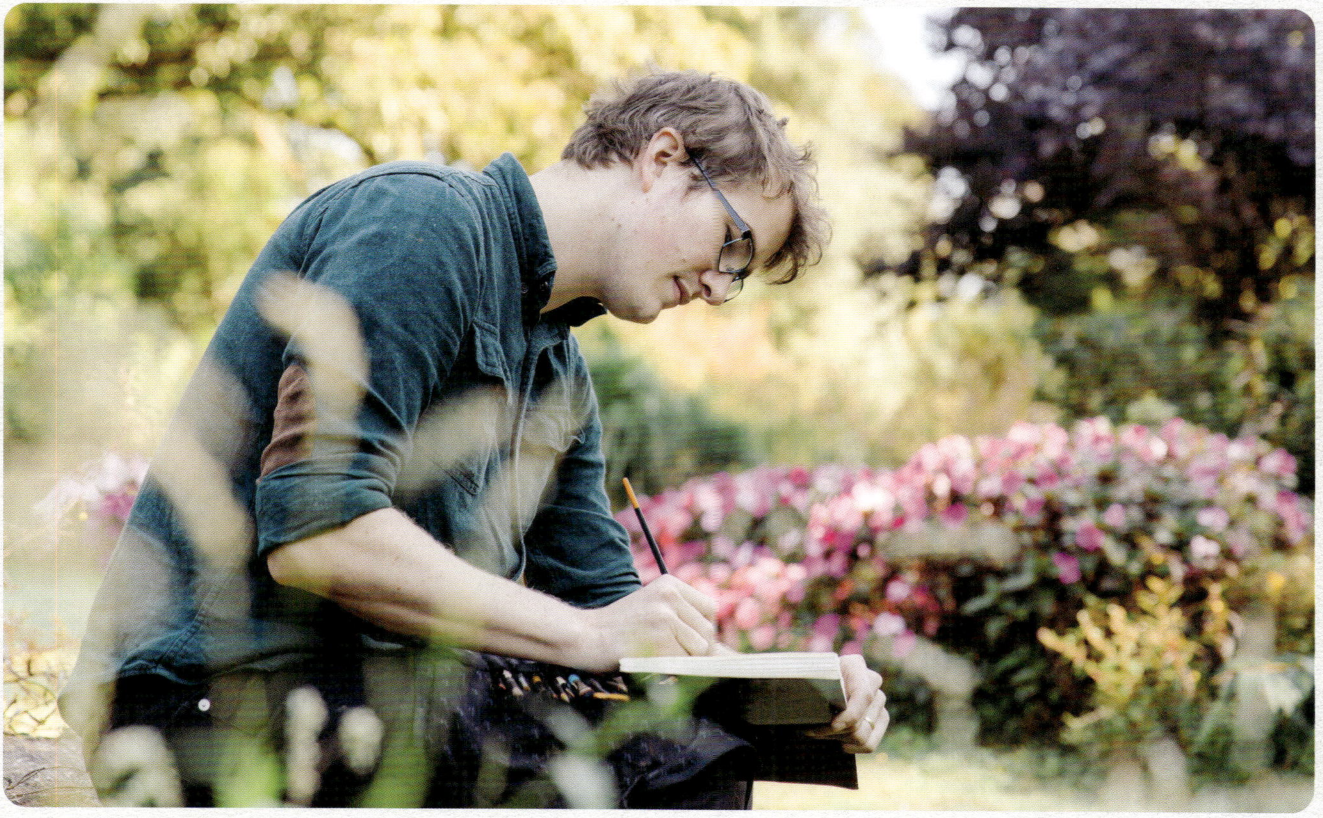

Painting with gouache doesn't require a big set-up

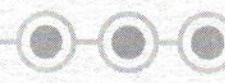

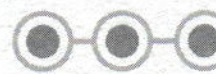

ESSENTIAL TOOLS

What do you need to get started? These are my essential tools. Some things may come and some may go, but these are always at the core of my set-up.

PAINTS

After a long time using gouache, I have realized the best approach is to get a small number of high-quality paints rather than a large number of cheap paints. The high-quality paints will last longer, do what you want, and lead to a lot less struggle. This is especially true if you are trying to do more advanced techniques. The basic colours below will enable you to mix a wide range of hues.

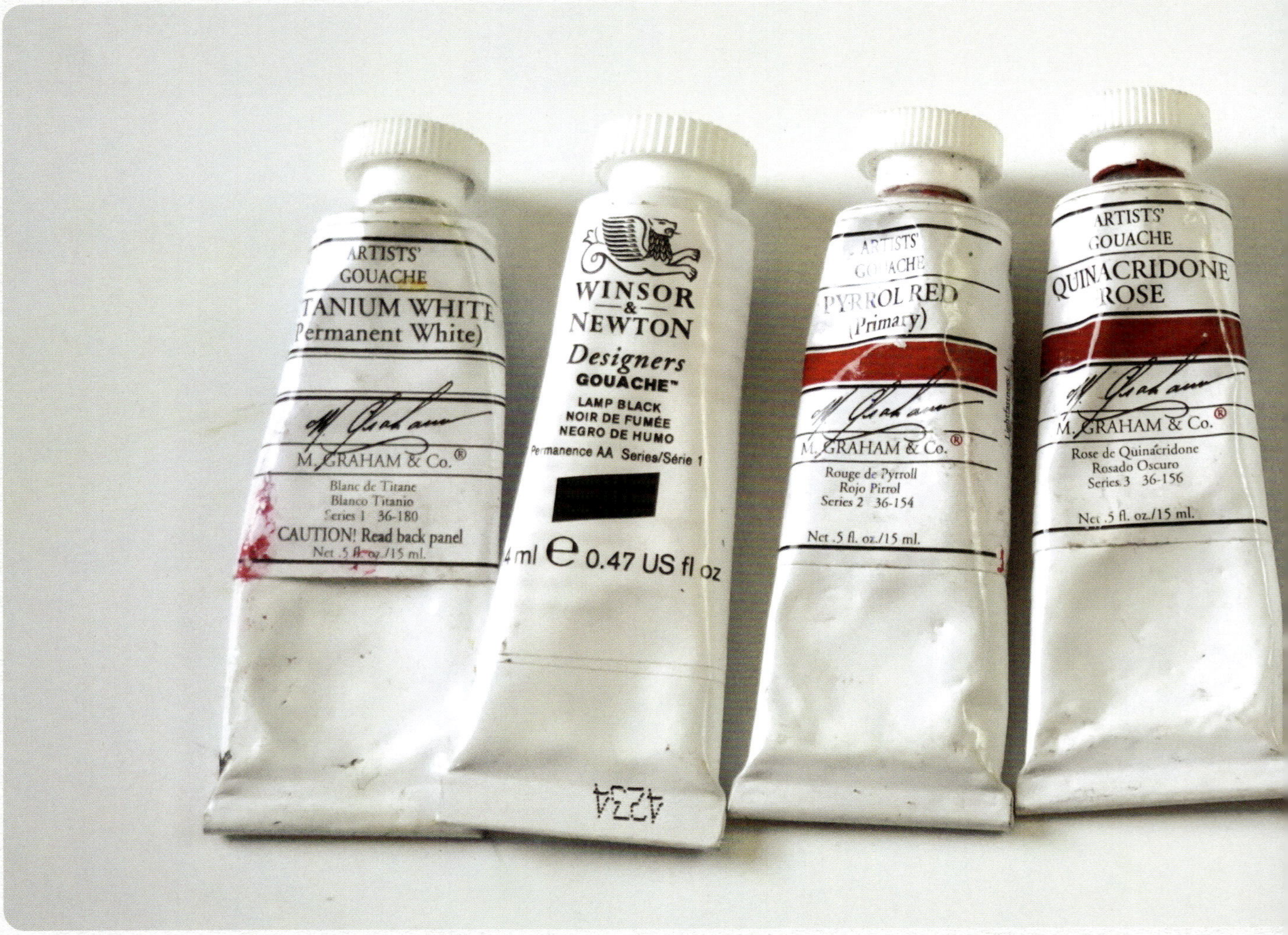

White, black, and some good-quality primary colours are a strong starting point for your collection

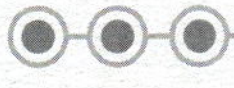

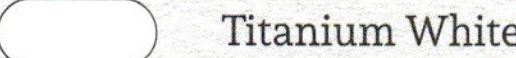 Titanium White

Lamp Black

Pyrrol Red

Quinacridone Magenta, Quinacridone Rose, or Alizarin Crimson

Primary Cyan, Cerulean Blue, or Phthalo Blue

Ultramarine Blue or Prussian Blue

Hansa Yellow

Cadmium Yellow

A NOTE ON JELLY GOUACHE

Please note that if you are looking to use jelly gouache, you'll find that it is much less diverse in the consistencies you are able to achieve. I wouldn't recommend using it if you are serious about following along with the demonstrations in this book – it is essentially a different medium with a similar name.

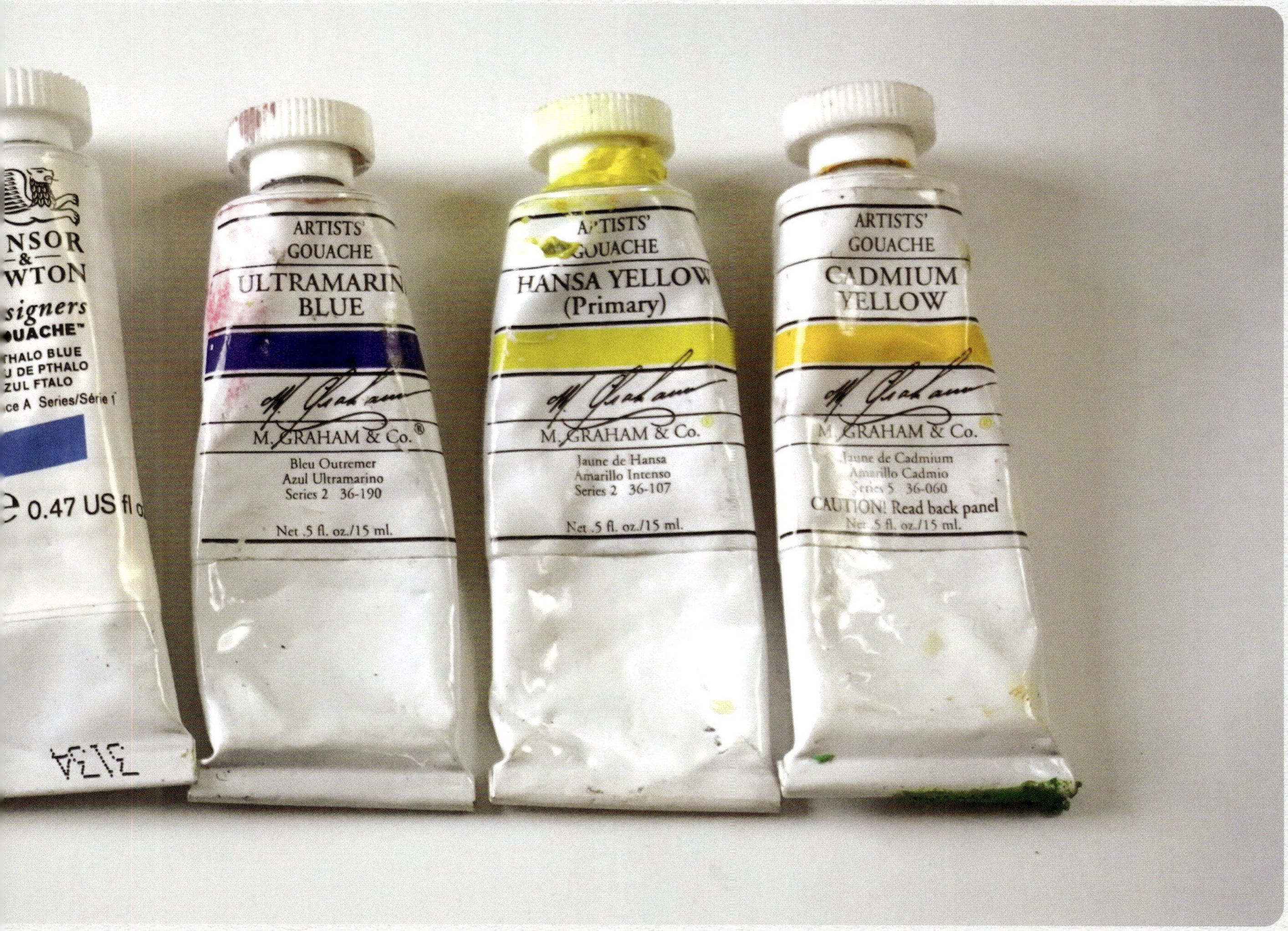

CHOOSING BRUSHES

Brushes are great and it's a lot of fun to try out a large variety but, of all the materials to consider, I believe brushes may matter least. Pay for good paint, pay for good paper ... then go and find a brush somewhere! Jokes aside, here are the brushes I find myself coming back to, and here is what I look for in a brush.

Does it spring back to its shape? If it doesn't, then you'll find it hard to predict how the brushstroke is going to come out, and will have to continuously manage the brush.

Is it soft? A soft brush will often allow easier control and a higher variety of brushstrokes. A firmer-bristled brush, like those often used in oil painting, will give a more direct but less diverse set of brushstrokes.

BRUSH TYPES

These are some essential brushes for your toolkit:

- **Small rounds** are a great staple for getting small detail.

- **Medium rounds** are great for holding a good amount of paint and creating a range of shapes.

- **1" flats** are great for covering large spaces in a very even fashion.

These are more specialized brushes that may occasionally be useful:

- **Oval mop brushes** and **extra-soft flats** aren't always good for direct painting onto paper, but are fantastic for softening edges as you paint, or for smoothing out a technical gradient.

- **Squirrel brushes** hold a lot of water and paint at their base, and so are brilliant for large washes or painting with lots of fluid. They also come to a fine point that can allow for very delicate and refined brushstrokes, as long as they aren't too loaded with fluid.

- **Large wide flats** are great for creating large fluid effects in the initial stages, or else creating large planes.

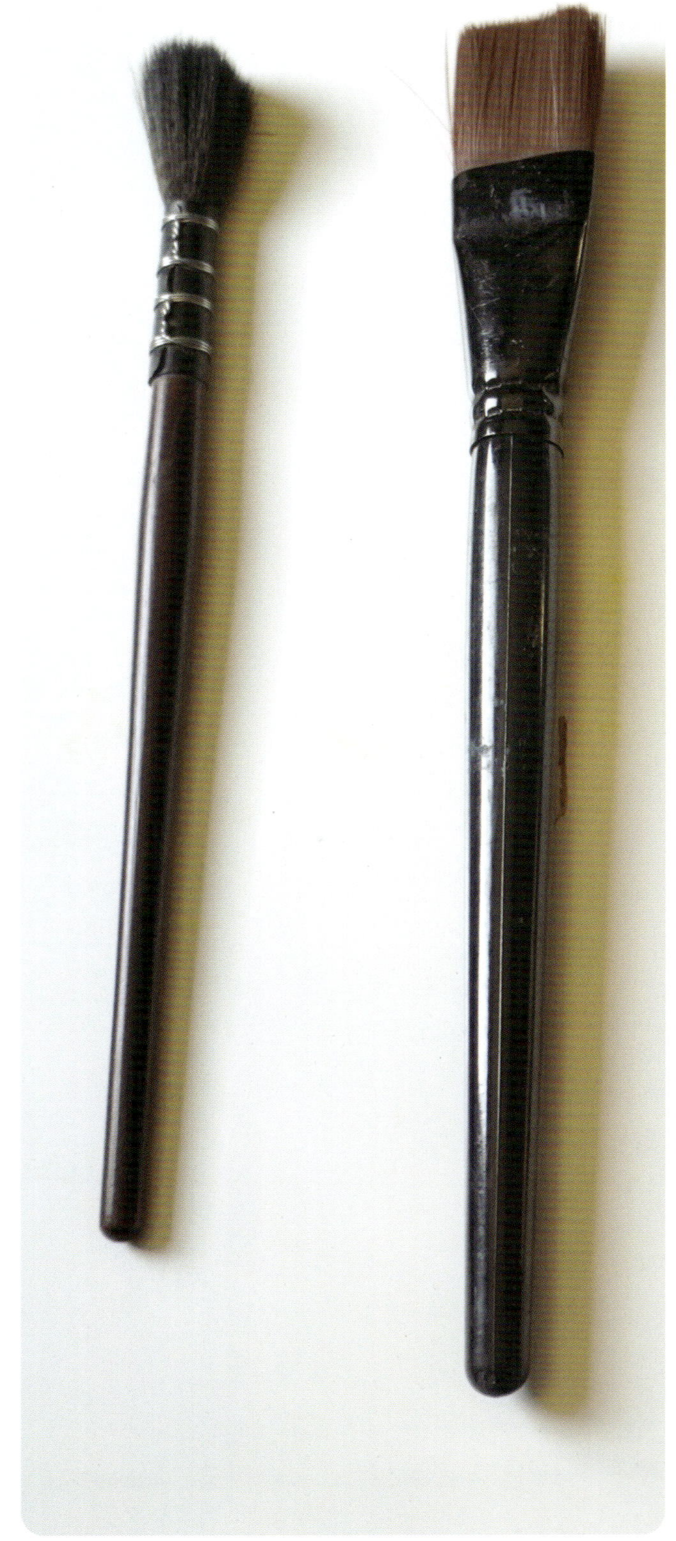

The brushes currently in my bag, from left to right: medium round, 1" flat, 1" extra-soft flat, small round, and sizes 0 and 4 from 'Series 304' by Rosemary & Co

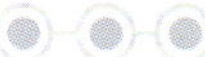

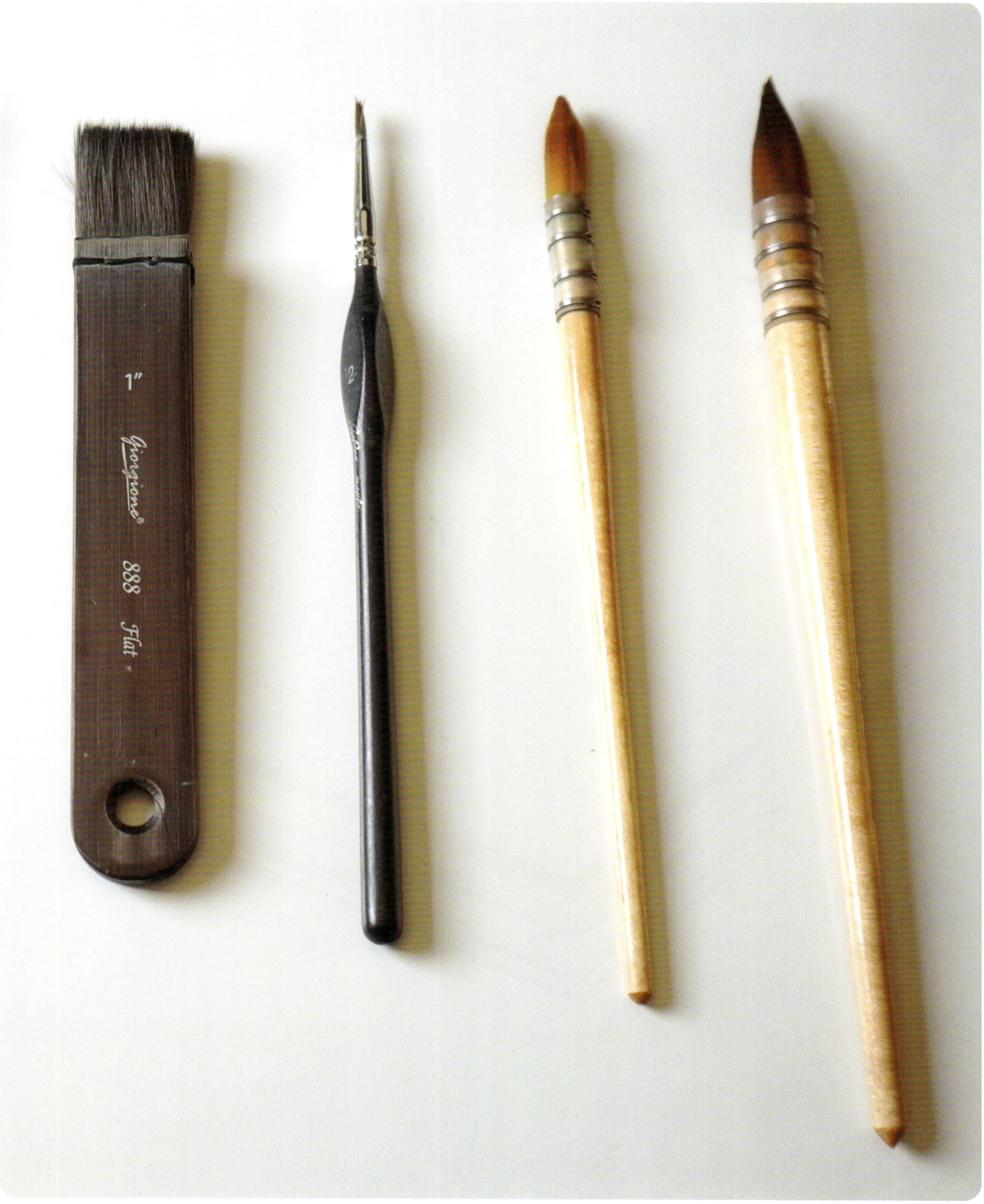

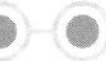

MIXING SURFACE

As you begin learning gouache, I recommend using a 'stay-wet' palette for mixing your paints. This is a small palette with a sponge to which you can apply moisture, with a semi-permeable layer on top that allows the water to seep through and keep your paints wet. This not only extends the paints' working time, but also allows them to keep the same value (because, as you'll quickly find, gouache changes value as it dries). You'll need to adjust the amount of water you place in the palette to keep it from being either too dry or too wet.

When choosing a mixing surface in general, your choices will typically be plastic or enamel. Plastic is obviously cheap and easy to find, but will result in the paint 'beading up' when used with lots of water, making it harder to see the colours you've mixed. You can gently scour the plastic with fine sandpaper in order to break up the surface enough to allow the paint to pool. An enamel palette will not cause beading, so it's much easier to look at and see what your paint is doing.

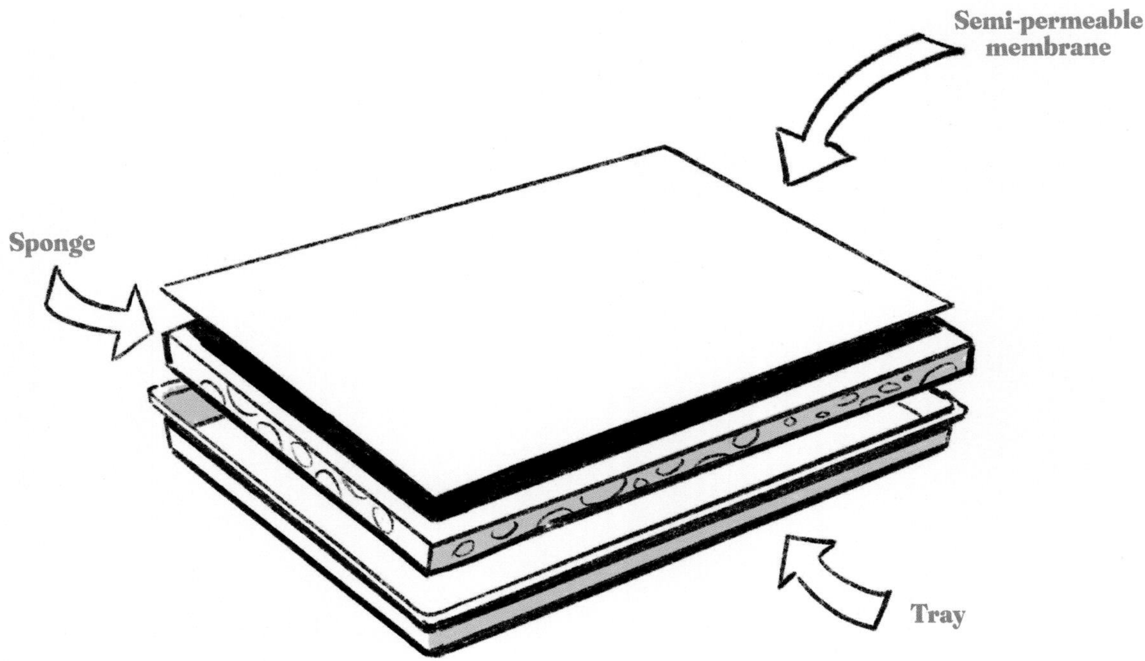

A stay-wet palette is a great option for newcomers to gouache

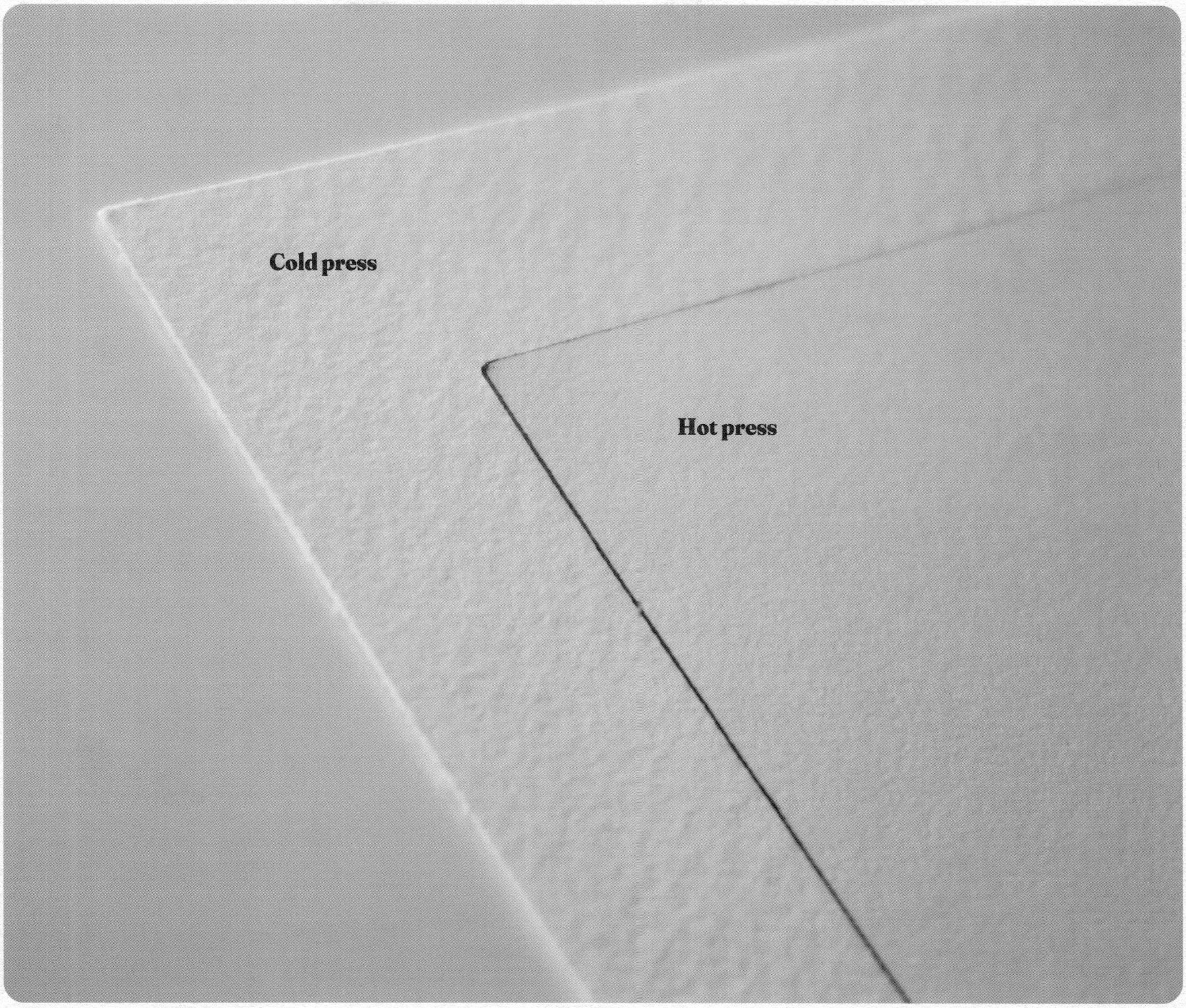

Cold-press paper is coarse and hot-press paper is smooth

PAPER

Paper is another area where it's worth getting good material. If you are painting relatively dry you can get away with using almost any kind of watercolour paper or watercolour sketchbook. However, when you start to use a lot of water and rely on water-heavy effects, it's time to upgrade to 100% cotton paper, which is more durable. Watercolour paper is typically found in two types: cold-press and hot-press.

- **Cold-press paper** is what you envisage when you think of watercolour paper. It is generally decently thick and has a good amount of texture. This rougher paper does some amazing things when creating texture effects with paint.

- **Hot-press paper**, on the other hand, is a lot smoother. You will find that this more refined surface is great for painting hard edges, smooth lines, and technical gradients.

Paper thickness, or 'weight', is measured in pounds or grams. Whichever texture you choose, aim for a weight of 352 gsm (130 lb) or greater. The thicker (heavier) the paper, the less you will have to deal with the paper warping as you apply paint. There are some more advanced techniques to help with this, which we'll talk about on page 64, but paper weight will always be a factor. If you truly dislike buckling, go for a 638 gsm (300 lb) paper.

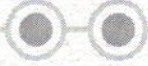

CARE AND CLEAN-UP

One of the big advantages to using gouache is that care and clean-up are very easy compared to other mediums. Because the paint is water-soluble, you can simply use water to clean the paint from brushes or tabletops. The paint reactivates, so it doesn't matter how long it's been around – just add enough warm water and you will find that it scrubs off. The biggest thing you need to be aware of is that some pigments are more staining than others, so there are some colours that will be harder to clean if you drop your paints onto the carpet.

To care for your brushes, bathe them in warm water to get rid of any excess paint.

To care for your paintings, I recommend using clear plastic bags to store and ship them. The binding agent in some gouache can weaken after too much reactivation, and I have found that if two paintings rub together, there will be transfer of dried pigment from one painting to the other. However, if you protect them with plastic, this won't happen.

To display your paintings, I find the best way is under museum glass. This is a glass that has its glare reduced significantly and can protect your artwork from UV light.

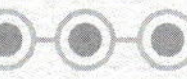

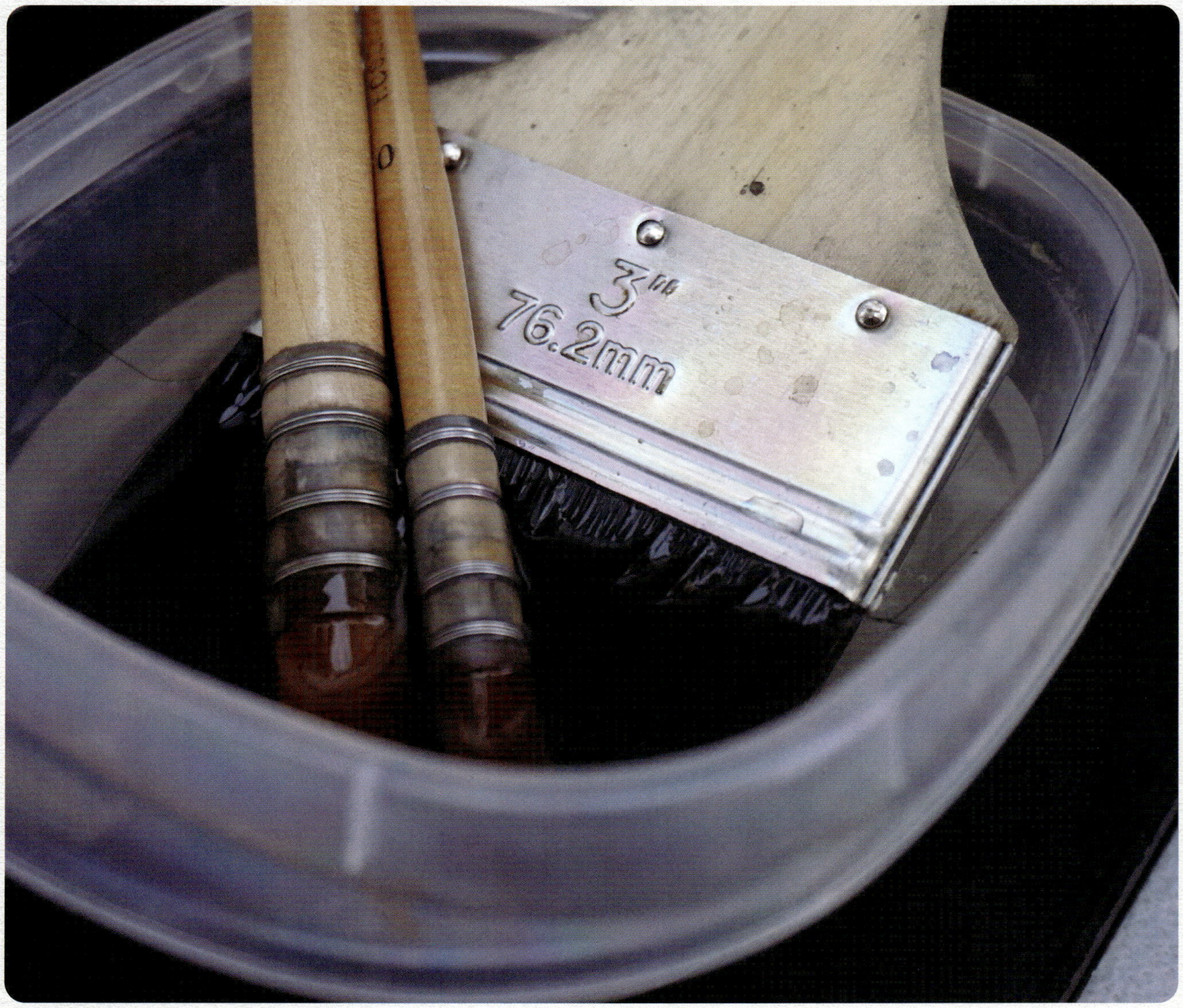

Warm water is sufficient to keep your brushes clean

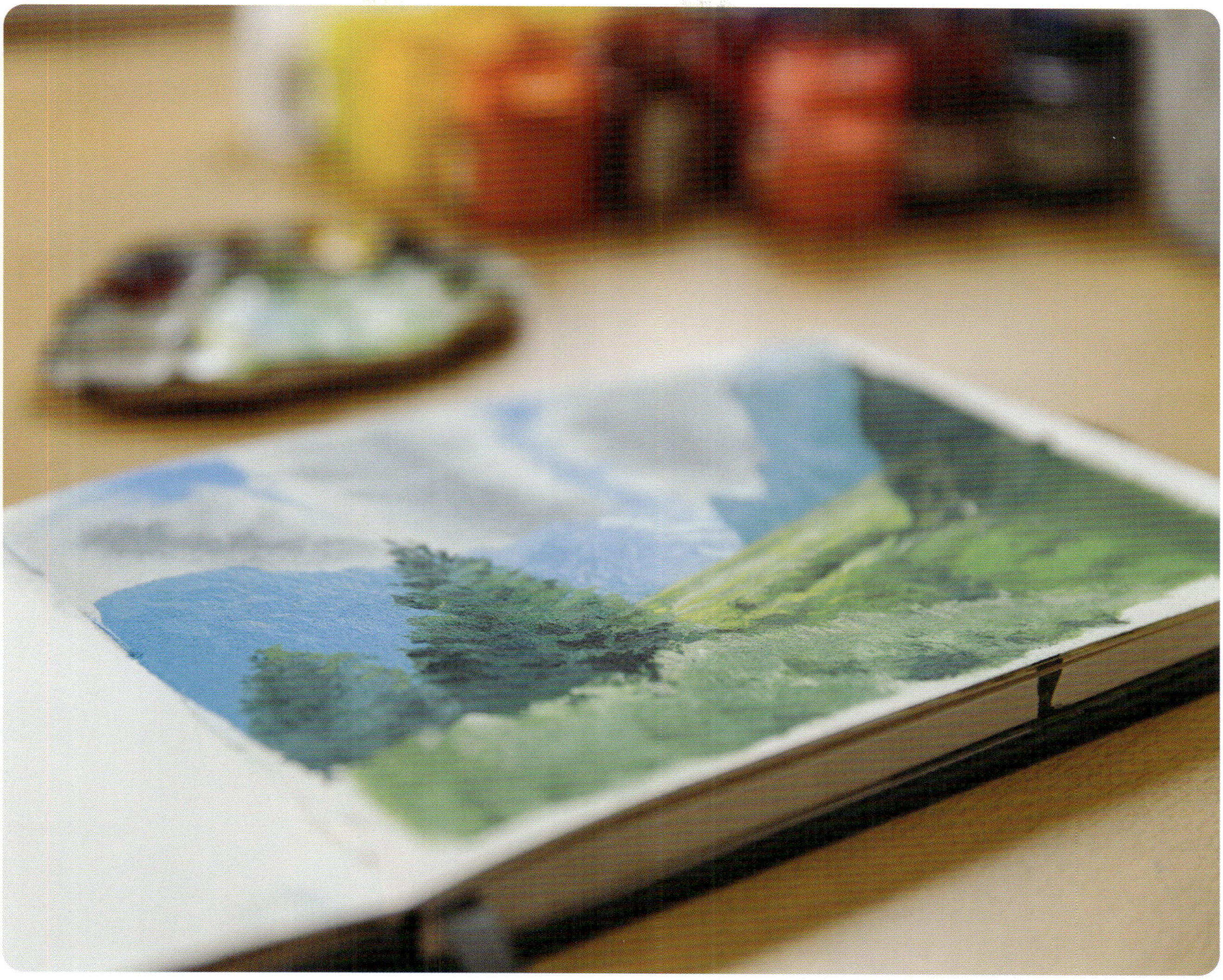

A sketchbook of watercolour paper is a great format for portability and storage, but be mindful of painted pages rubbing together

'REACTIVATION'

Throughout this book you'll see artists refer to 'reactivating' paint. This just means dry paint becoming wet and malleable again through the application of liquid, allowing your brush to pick it up or blend it further. Depending on the result you're aiming for, reactivating your paint can be a drawback or a desirable effect.

GLOSSARY

Don't forget to check the glossary section for other commonly used terminology that may occur throughout this book's tutorials. You can find it on page 219, towards the back of the book.

BASIC TECHNIQUES

In this section I'll cover a few basic skills that every aspiring gouache artist must conquer in order to get their gouache badge. While there are no right and wrong ways to paint with gouache, there are some benchmark skills that will help you gain control over the medium.

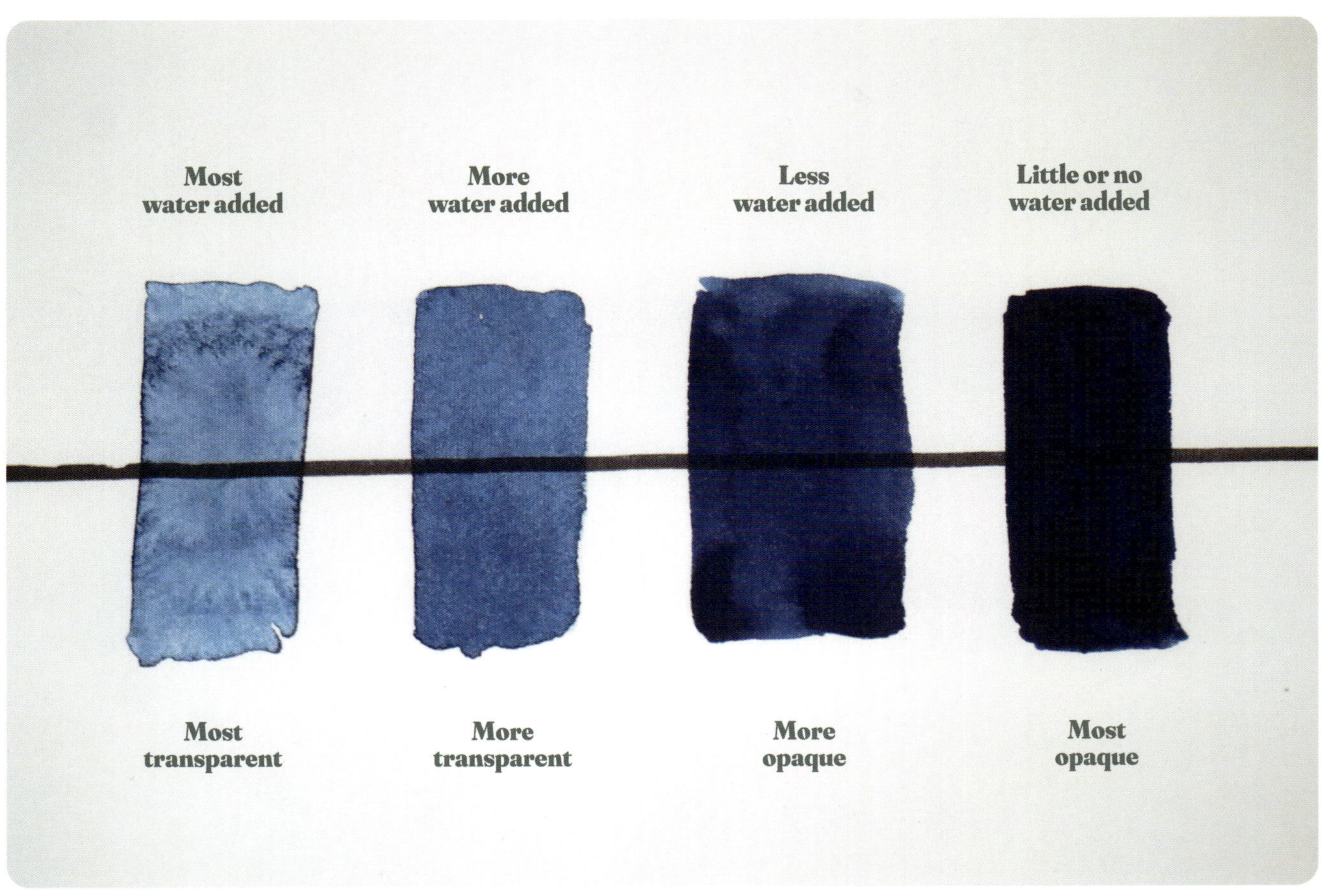

A transparent swatch (left) versus an opaque swatch (right)

OPAQUE PAINTING

The first benchmark is the ability to **paint opaquely.** This means that when you paint, the gouache has a thick enough consistency that you can't see what's underneath – be that paper or the previous layer of paint. You can see above how that might appear, with different mixes of gouache and water painted over black pen. You'll test this yourself on page 30.

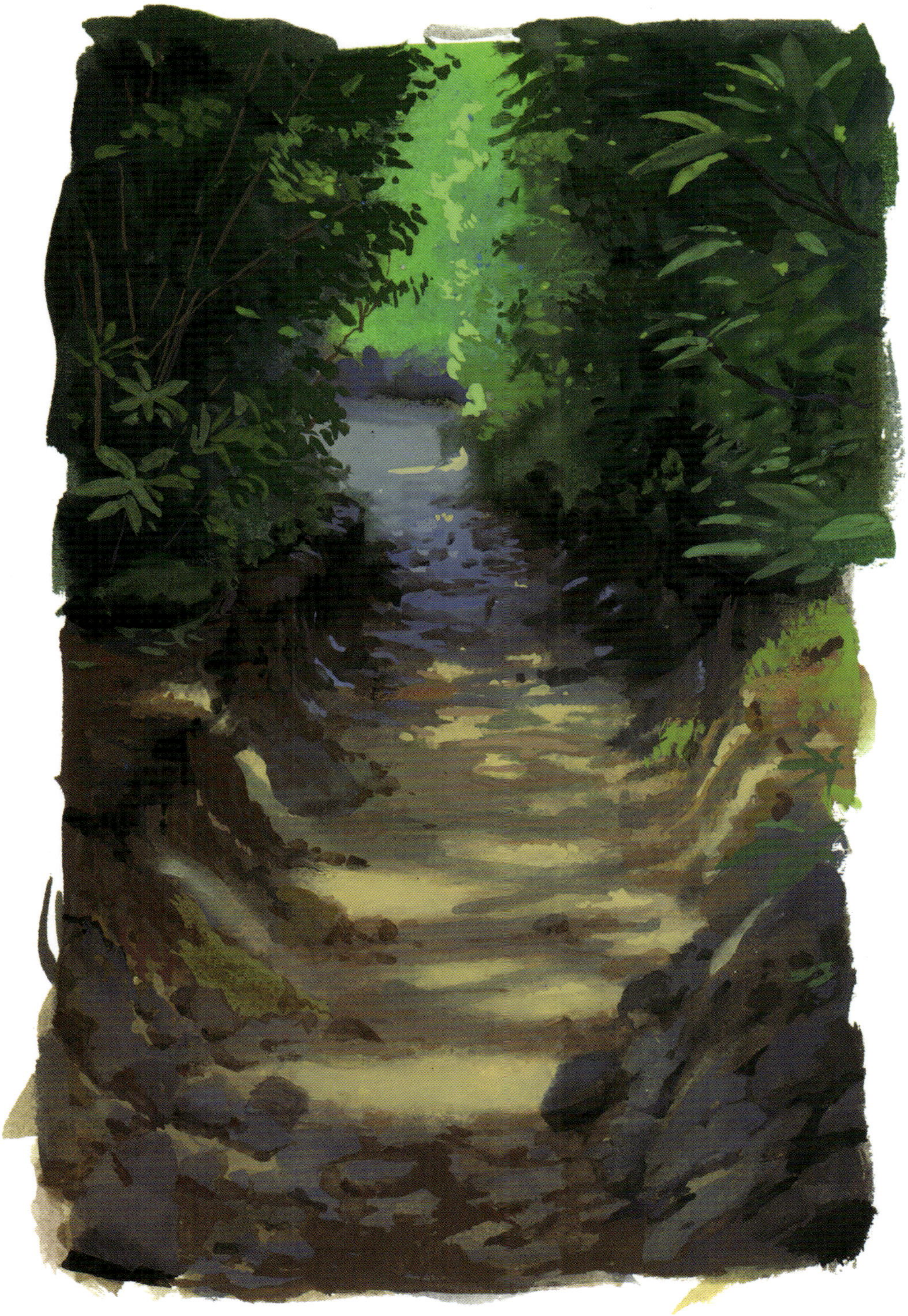

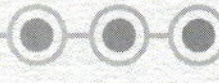

Sun-dappled Path. Opaque gouache creates bold, richly coloured shapes, like the stones, leaves, and highlights in this painting

MASTERING WATER

In the world of gouache, water is king. Learn what the water does and you'll learn how to predict and control the paint. If there is one thing you should put down this book to do, it's this: learn how to navigate water in your painting. Large amounts, equal amounts, small amounts. How does it affect your coverage? How does it change the transparency and value (light or dark) of the end result? Changing the amount of water you are using to achieve your goal is the one skill that will unlock gouache for you.

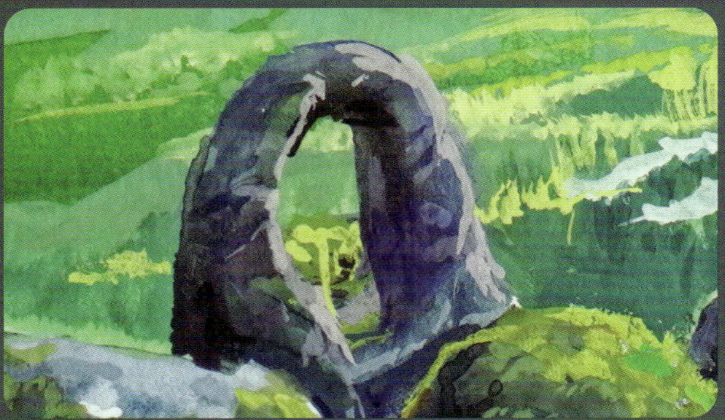

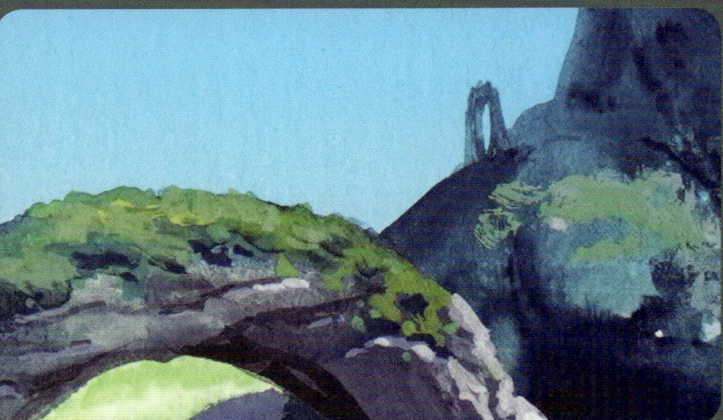

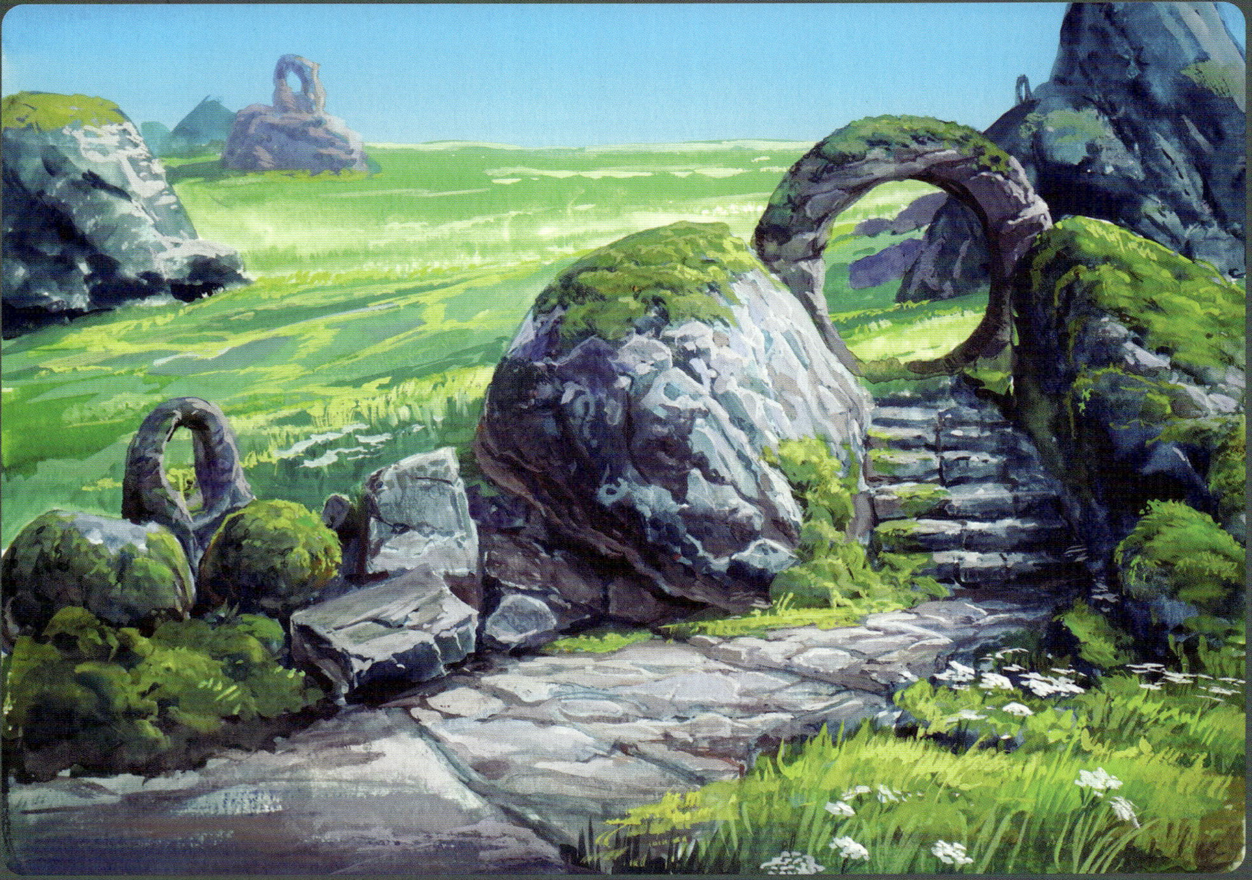

Rock Formations

GAUGING OPACITY

There are no rules to follow when it comes to choosing whether to paint transparently or opaquely, but crossing between the two when painting will change your outcome quite significantly. This is why learning to control opacity is the first benchmark of gouache skill. Once you can consistently get enough paint and enough water to cover the layer underneath, you have mastered the art of painting opaquely. But how do we know if our paint will be transparent or opaque?

One good way to judge is to look at the fully loaded brush, as shown below. If you can't see the colour of the bristles through the paint, then you are likely close to painting opaquely. If you can see through the paint on the brush, you'll probably be able to see through the paint once it's on the paper.

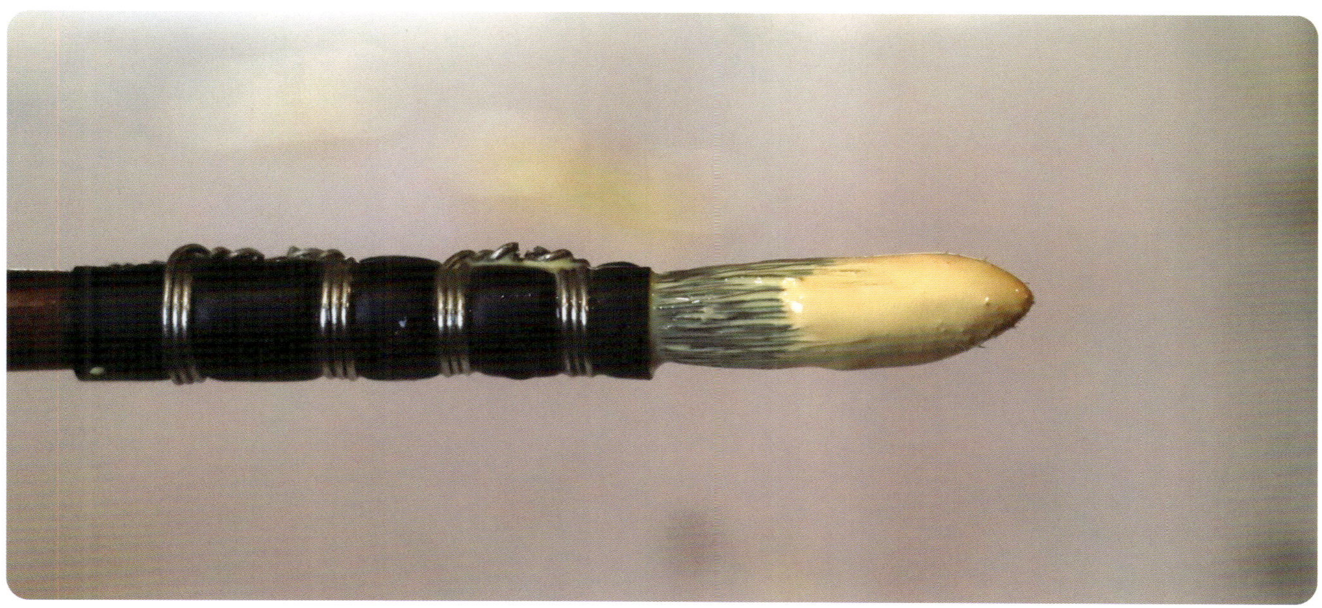

If you can't see the bristles through the paint, you will likely have a highly opaque brushstroke

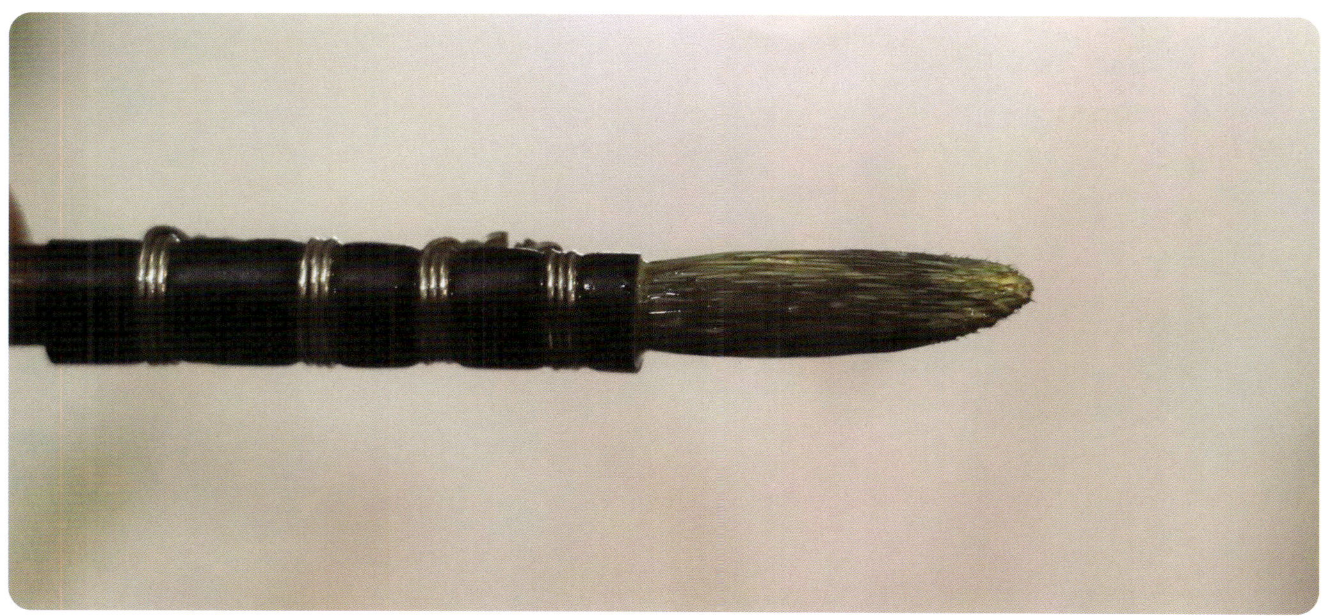

If you can see the bristles through the paint, your stroke will appear transparent on the paper

Chunky paint straight out of the tube will give you brilliant opacity, but will require a lot of paint to cover large areas

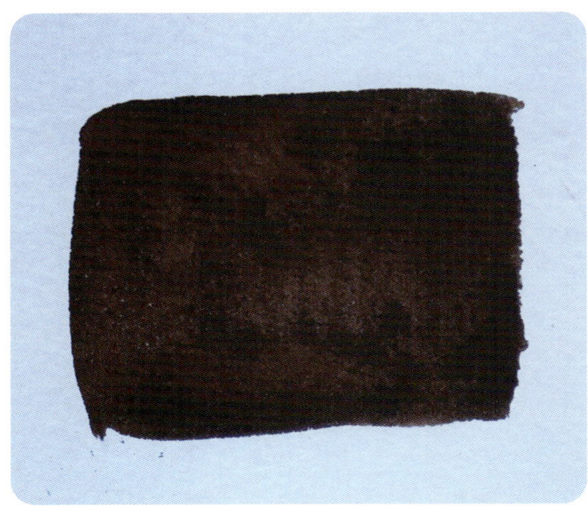

Adding a bit of water will allow you a similar value and extra texture, while being able to cover more paper

Adding lots of water allows you to cover a large area very easily, and shows the colour of the paper through the paint

TESTING ON PAPER

Let's test this out in practice. Try painting with some gouache directly from the tube (top left). You'll notice that it's thick, opaque, and results in very chunky brushstrokes. This creates rich colour but makes covering a large area potentially very difficult.

Next, try painting with gouache mixed with a bit of water (middle left). You'll find it allows you a very similar value, depending on how light or dark the paint is, while covering a larger area. You'll also gain a hint of extra texture.

As you add more water, you'll get to a point where the paint becomes transparent, and you'll be able to see the colour of the paper or underlying paint through it. Try that next by adding a considerable amount of water to your paint (bottom left). While it covers a large area very easily, you'll find the paint has become lighter and the texture more pronounced. The paint will be thin enough that the white of the paper further illuminates the paint. Don't think that this is a bad thing – it merely gives you more to think about and work with when you are using gouache.

TRANSPARENT PAINTING

This brings us to our second benchmark skill: **transparent painting**. If you want to paint in a watercolour-like fashion, you can load extra water into the paint and gain some brilliant textures and large coverage. As mentioned on the previous page, if you can see the colour of the bristles through the paint on your brush, then you'll be able to see through the paint once it's down on paper. Let's see what that would look like in more detail below.

Painting transparently in a direct fashion (below, top) will leave marks in every place your brush touches. You can use this to your advantage. However, sometimes you'll want a smoother effect (below, bottom), enabling you to create large transparent areas of paint without the brushstrokes. This is achieved using the bead method, which we'll cover next.

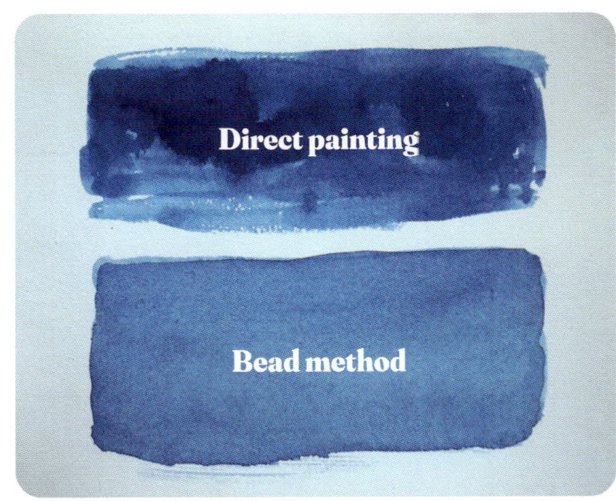

Two different approaches to transparent painting

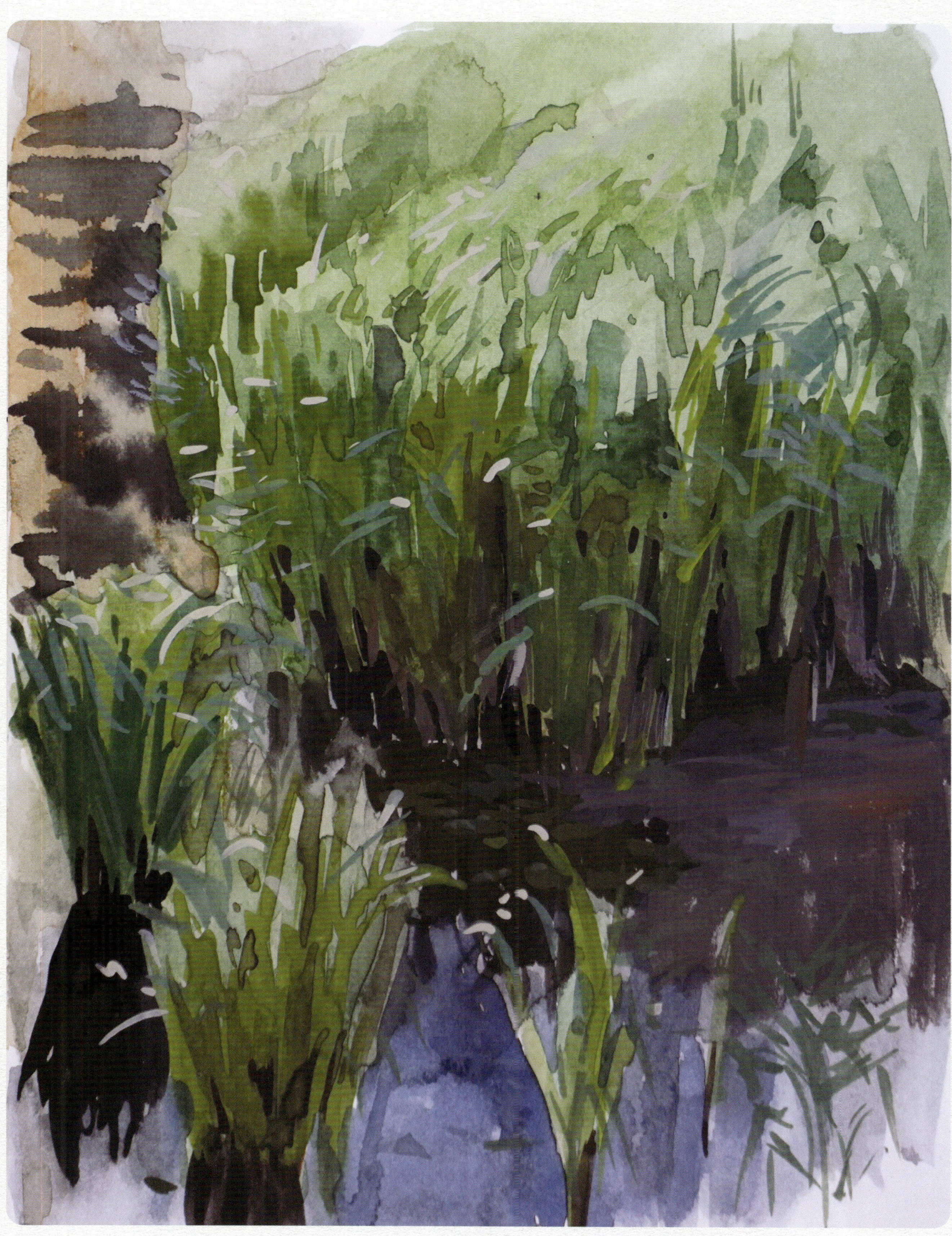

Reeds. Transparent gouache can be used more like watercolour, employing the brightness of the paper to create highlights

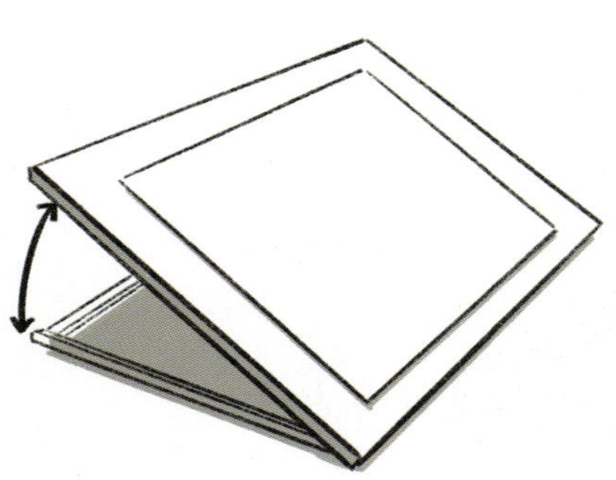

An angled surface is the key to using this method

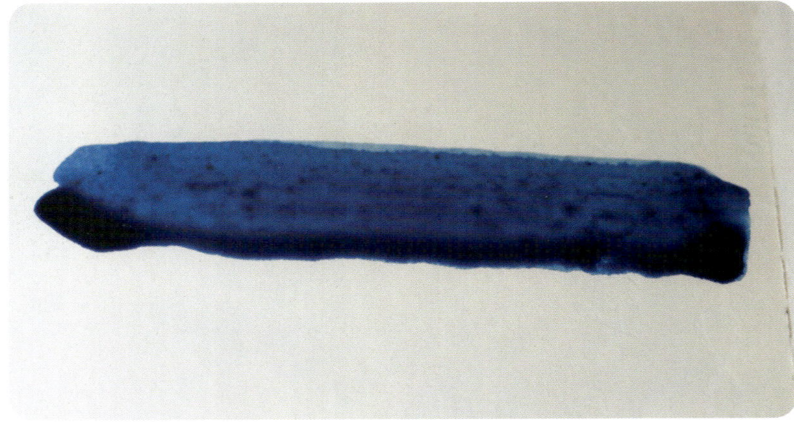

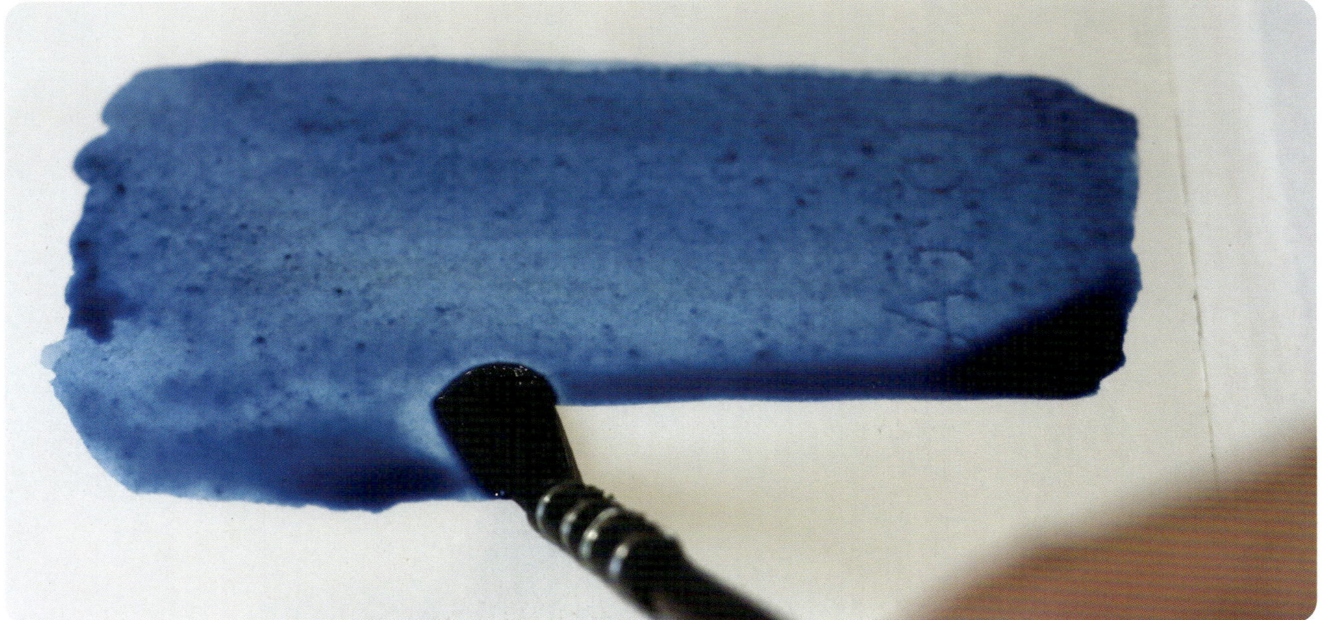

The bead method with transparent gouache

THE BEAD METHOD

Painting directly with a high quantity of transparent paint will result in a lot of your brushstrokes being visible. In order to achieve consistent, soft, large areas of transparent colour instead, it's best to use **the bead method**. This technique requires three things: enough paint, enough water, and the assistance of gravity. Water needs somewhere to go, and if you tilt your painting surface, it will move in one direction rather than spreading everywhere. This results in a very consistent layer of paint.

With your watery colour mix, paint onto a tilted surface so that any extra liquid runs to the bottom of the brushstroke. This gathered droplet is the 'bead'. If this bead doesn't form, make sure you've used enough water and that your surface is tilted enough.

So long as that bead remains wet, you can continue to add paint through the area, and gravity will continue to assist the water down, so you can extend your paint in any direction. This skill might take a few attempts to get right, but once you've mastered it, you can use it to create amazing smooth areas that don't have brushstrokes all over them. Again, there's nothing wrong with having visible brushstrokes, but we want the freedom to choose how our paint looks!

This idea is easiest to master using transparent paint, because it's easier to see the bead when it's darker than the paint above it, but it's possible to achieve with opaque gouache too, as shown on the opposite page.

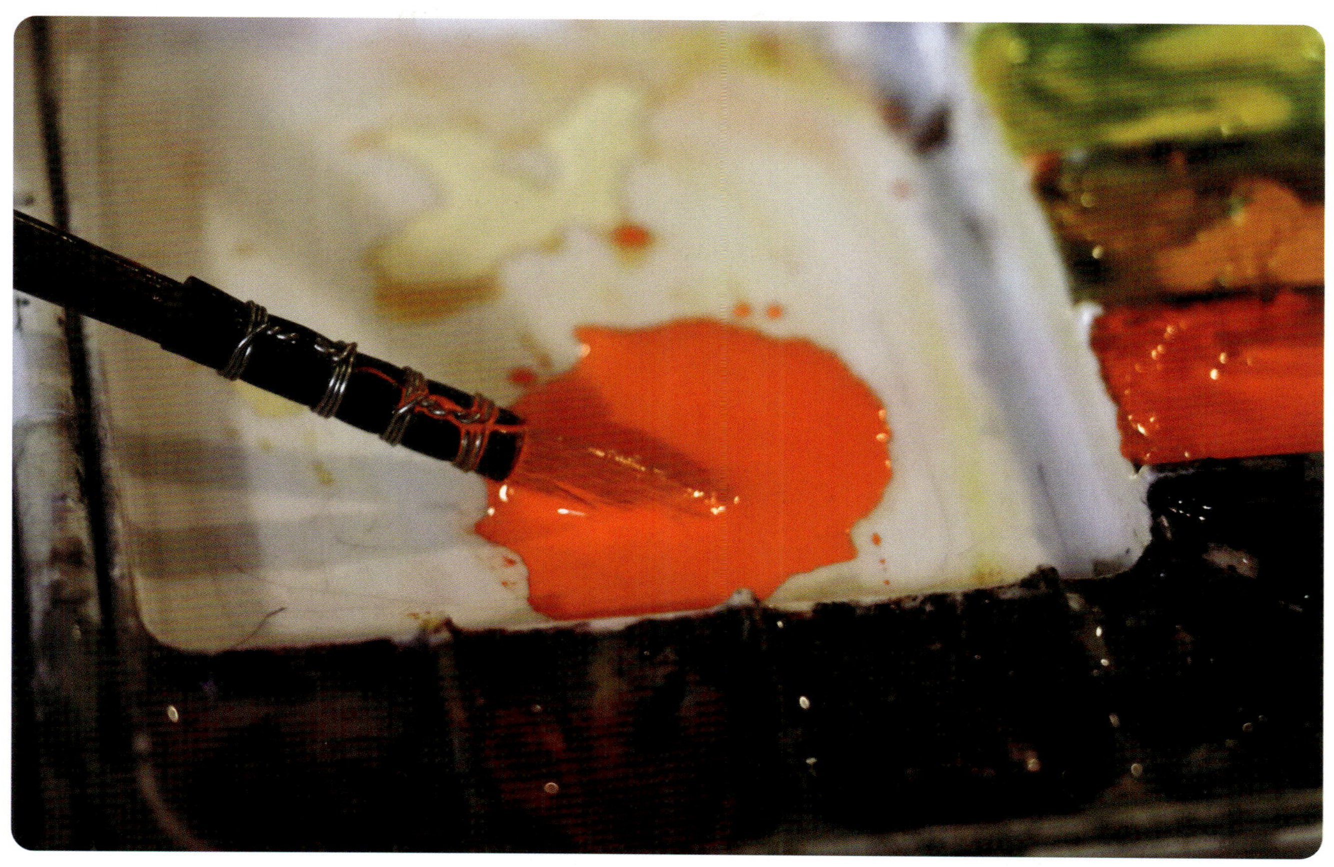

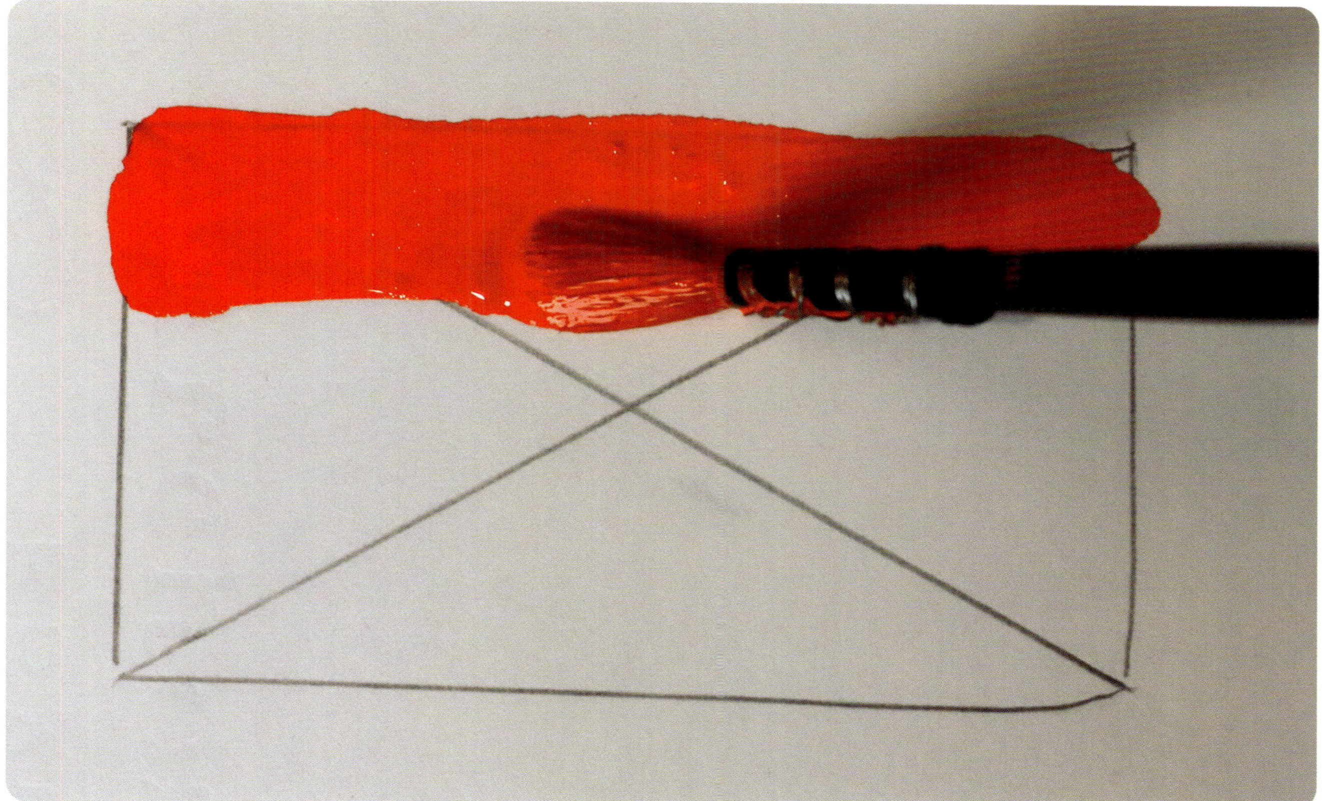

The bead method with opaque gouache is still possible, but the bead will be slightly harder to see

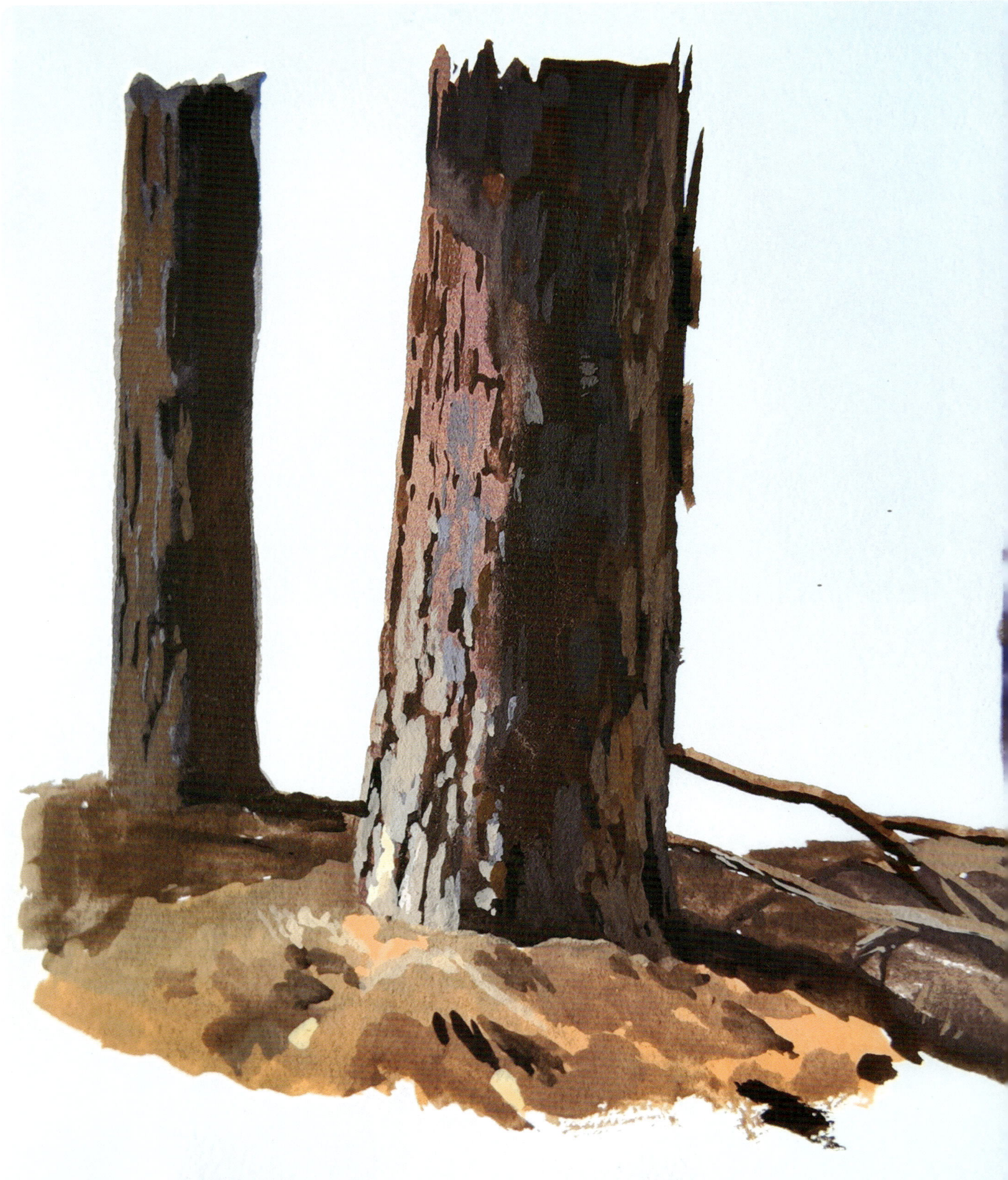

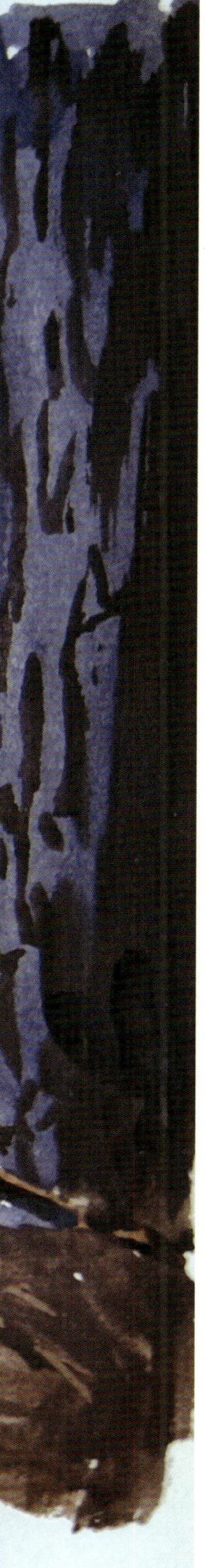

LAYERING SKILLS

One of the great strengths of gouache is its ability to layer well and layer quickly. Let's take a look at the things you should be considering as you layer with gouache. While these methods aren't the only way to paint, they are a great way to get a feel for how to layer without any problems at all.

1. Be brief. When you paint into wet paint, you get softer edges, the mixing of layers, and the merging of paint. The less time you take to apply a new layer of paint, the less time it will take to reactivate the previous layer and merge your two layers together, if that's the effect you are aiming for.

2. Be patient. Conversely, if you want separation between layers, wait until the layer below is fully dry before placing a new one. I can't tell you how many times I've seen a student be a little too impatient and decide to add a whole new layer before the painting was dry – or even done so myself! If you do this, you'll spend twice as long trying to fix things. I promise it's worth the wait if you want to create a new, clean, separate layer.

3. Use more paint than the previous layer. Starting with thin layers means you are less likely to reactivate or pick up those earlier layers as you paint. If you start with thin layers and slowly get thicker, you are setting yourself up for a great layering experience. Thicker paint has less water in it, meaning you are also using less moisture that might reactivate the lower layers.

If these all sound simple, it's because they are! Simple doesn't always mean easy but, truly, any problems that you encounter with layering will most likely come from a breakdown in one of these three practices.

NO SCRUBBING!

To 'scrub' is to push your brush back and forth vigorously over a single area. This forcefully reactivates your previous layer and often results in the paint lifting away. The opposite of scrubbing, and generally a good idea when layering, is a brushstroke that touches the paper only enough to do exactly what it needs to do. The brush should pass over the area once and be done. Don't feel bad if you don't get there immediately, but have the goal in mind.

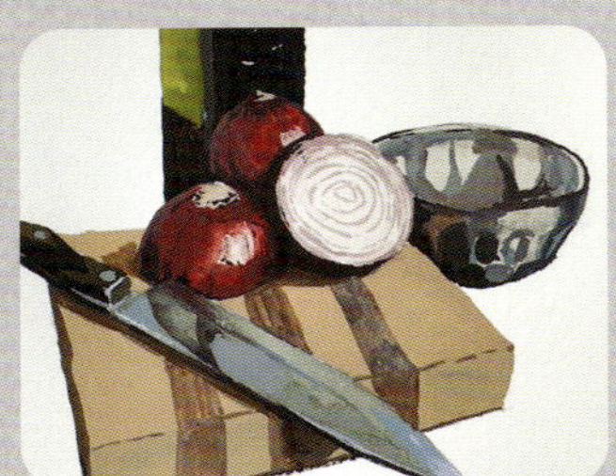

Exercise: STILL-LIFE PAINTING

Let's put these ideas into practice, starting with an observational still life. We'll discuss it more later, but creating fantasy-themed paintings starts with reality. Everyone you know who paints from their imagination does so only to the degree to which they have studied real life. Luckily, productive life studies can be done using any objects you have around.

01. REFERENCE

This is my reference scene. You can paint along with it if you like, or set up a similar scene with household objects of your own. Note how it contains different shapes, colours, and materials. Before we begin the painting itself, we'll be making a small three-value study. The goal of painting a value study is to see how simple shapes and values can create the majority of the illusion of three dimensions. It's also simple enough that you can take things from everyday life, organize them, and change them to whatever fantasy-themed idea you like. A bottle of oil can become a potion. A knife can become a dagger. An onion can become a poisoned apple!

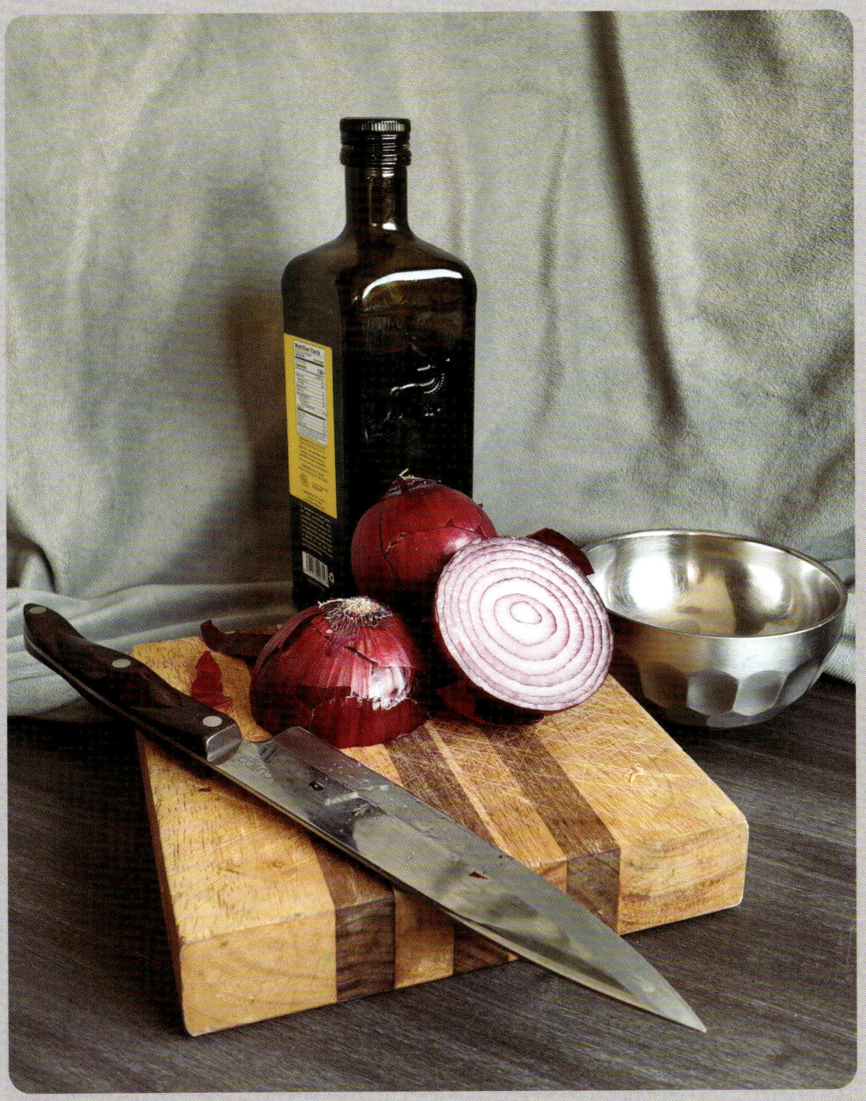

01. My practice scene contains a range of everyday objects with different colours and textures

02. VALUE STUDY

To create the value study, we'll experiment with an idea called 'painting through'. This means you are going to leave the highlights, but anything darker than that will receive a translucent wash of light grey value, using the bead technique mentioned on page 32.

Be patient and allow that layer to dry, then lay down a medium-grey value in the same fashion, painting through the mediums and darks but leaving out the light areas. Let this layer dry as well. Finally you can lay down the major darks, painting only those areas.

This is a quick and easy way to check your painting. If the image doesn't work at this stage, chances are it will fall apart when you start to add colour and separate its elements into finer points of value. But now that you have a strong basis established, you can move on to flat colour.

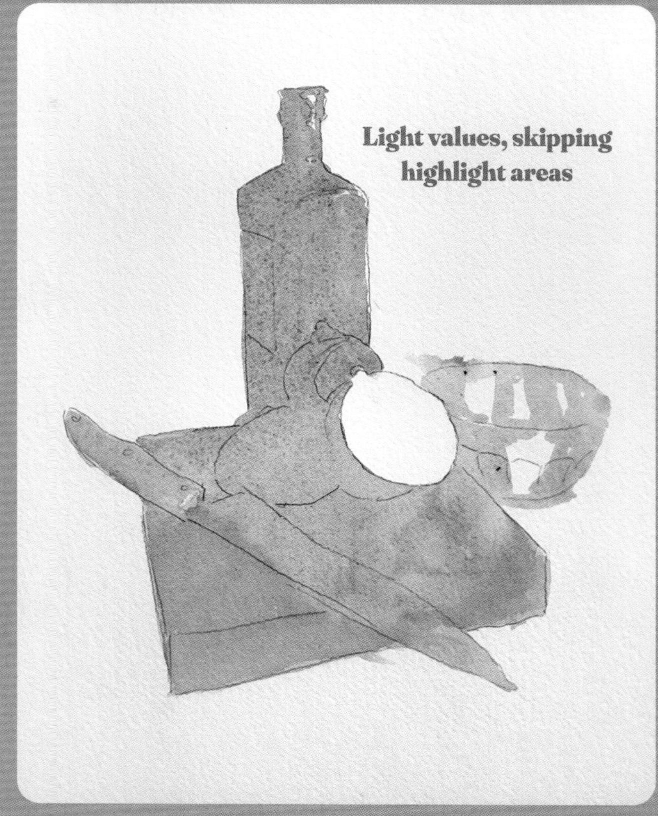

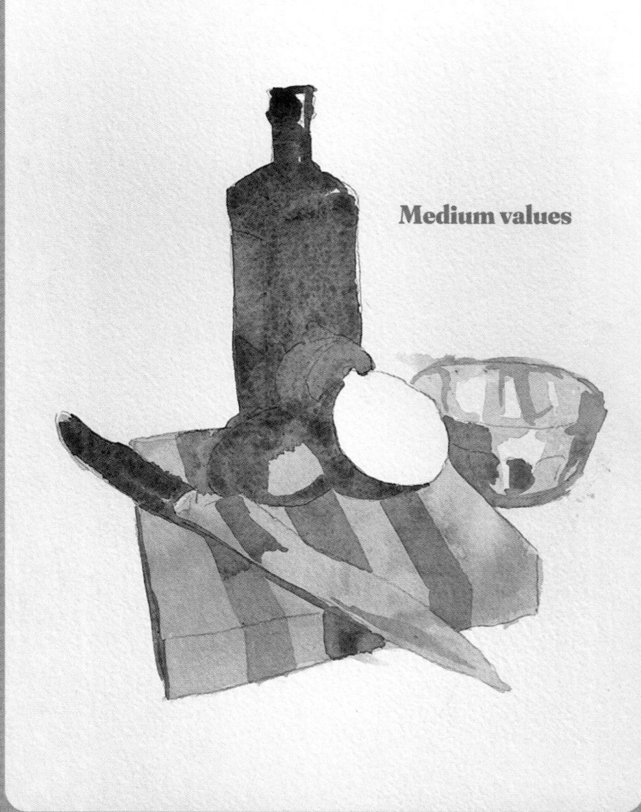

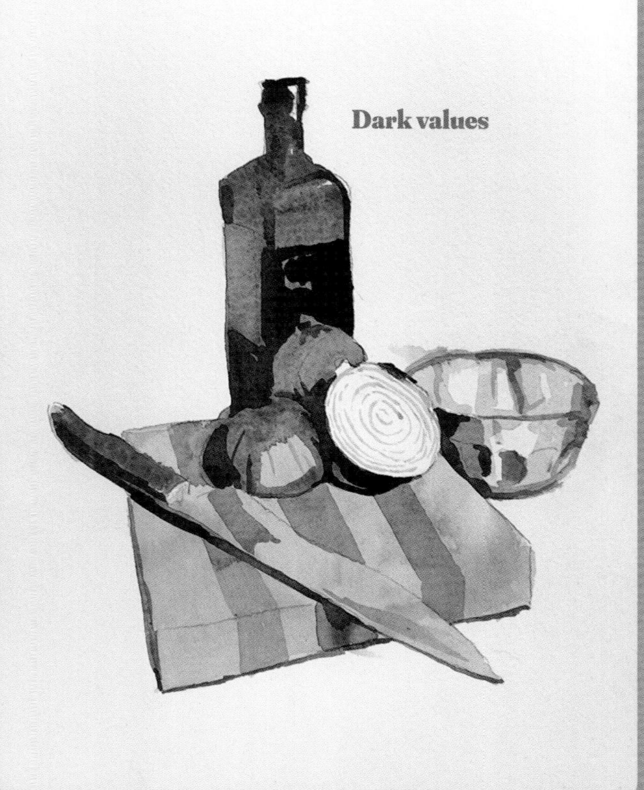

02. Painting through a three-value study

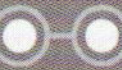

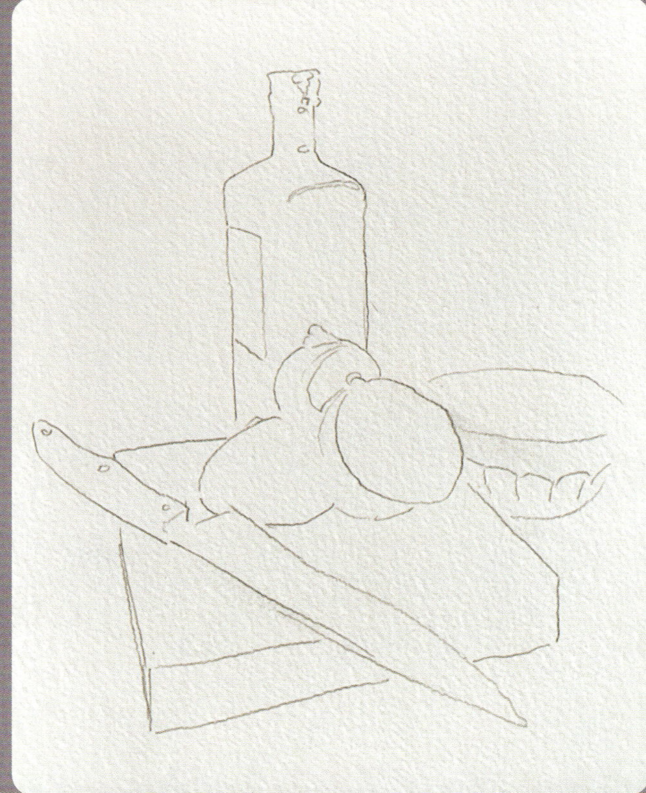

03. Sketch the clean, simple shapes of your still-life scene

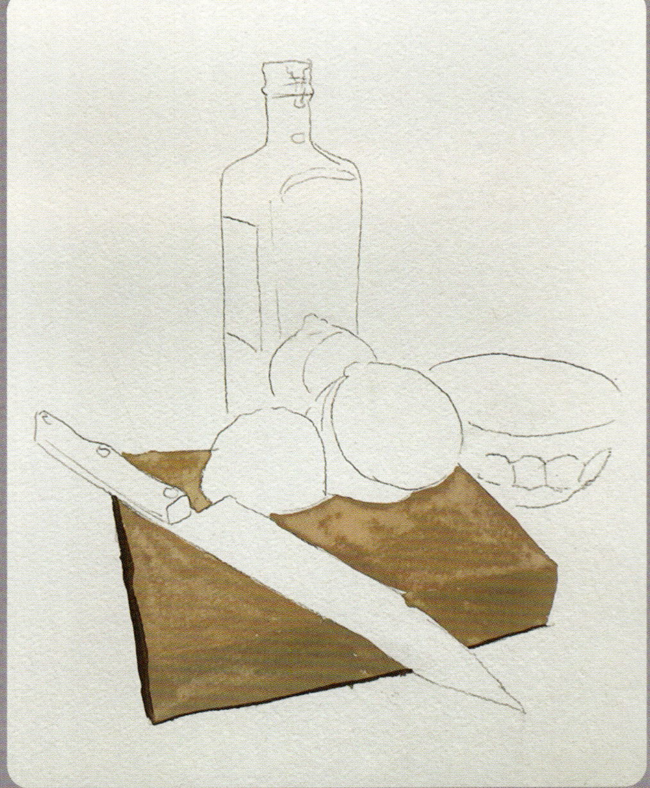

04. Paint the light wood and wait for it to dry

03. UNDERDRAWING

Next you need a solid underdrawing. You'll be painting thickly enough to cover these lines, so you won't be able to see this drawing later, but focus on getting some clear shapes early on. This will make it easier to rework the interiors later, if needed. Do this with a pencil on a fresh piece of thick watercolour paper.

04. LIGHT TONES

Start by painting some of the light tones with lots of thick paint. In this case, I start with the wooden block. Since gouache dries quickly, if you want to have a soft or organic edge quality between areas, it can be helpful to paint those areas one after another. The edge can be manipulated while still a little wet. You can also see in this image that half the paint is dry, but half is still wet and appears quite dark. Refrain from trying to fix the colours while they are in this patchy, half-dry state. Wait until the paint is all dry before you try to determine if it's working or not.

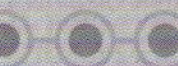

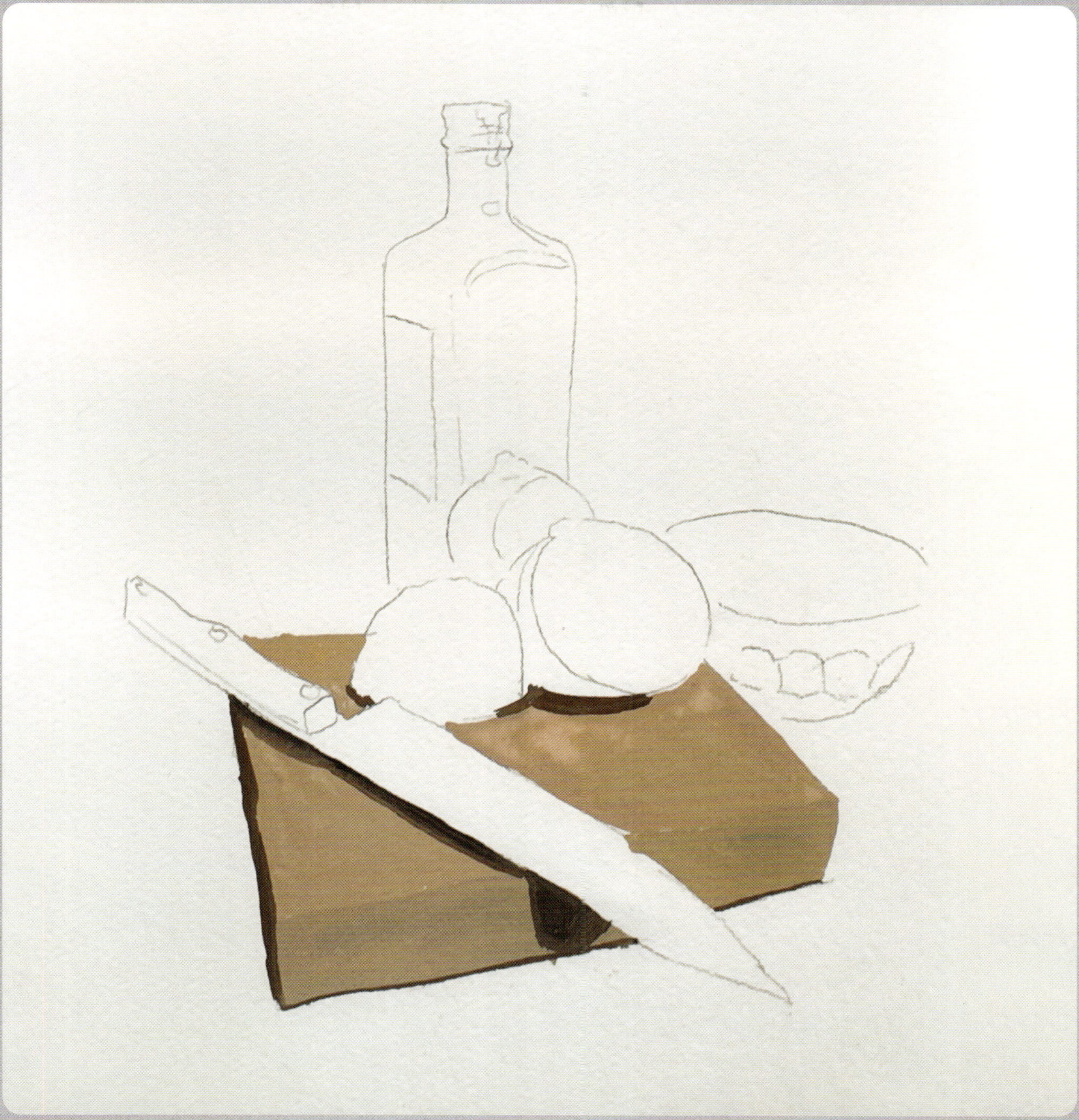

05. Once the paint is dry, add dark, solid shadows under the objects

05. OBJECT SHADOWS

Once the previous layer is dry, you can add some shadows into the areas already established in the value study. These small shadows might seem simple, but they are a big factor in ensuring the objects look like they are physically sitting in the scene and not floating.

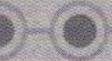

06. MAIN COLOURS

Now you can start adding in colour. As gouache dries its colour and value shifts, so it's important to add our main 'colour notes' early. You can alter them if you need to, as they dry or afterwards. Since the colour intensity will shift, you might find it helpful to make the maroon of the red onions a little more intense than in reality. That way, when the paint dries, it'll dry to a natural-looking intensity.

06a. This swatch looks patchy because it's still half wet; the colour will even out and darken as it dries

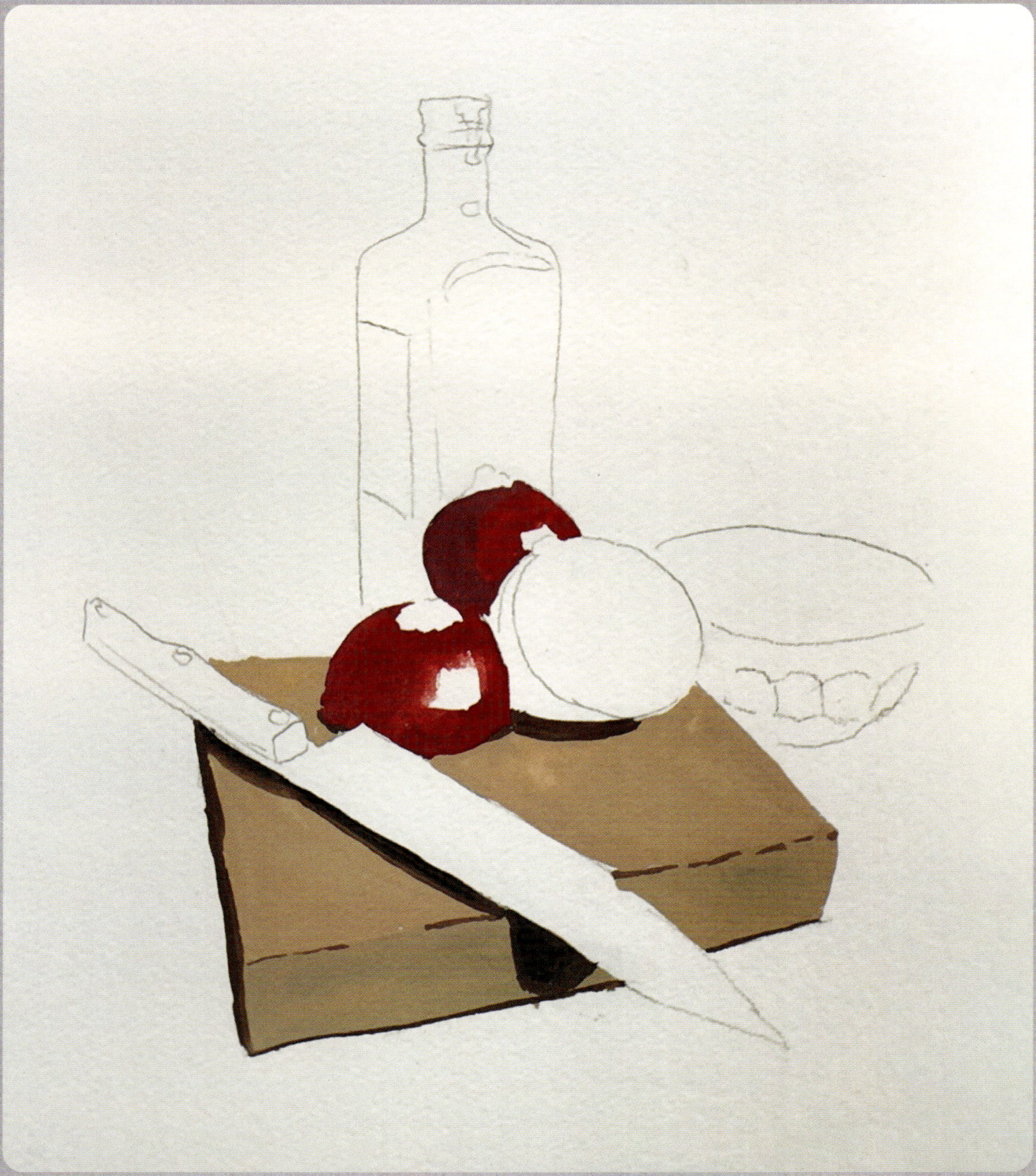

06b. Keep gouache's value shifts in mind when you apply colours

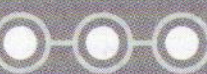

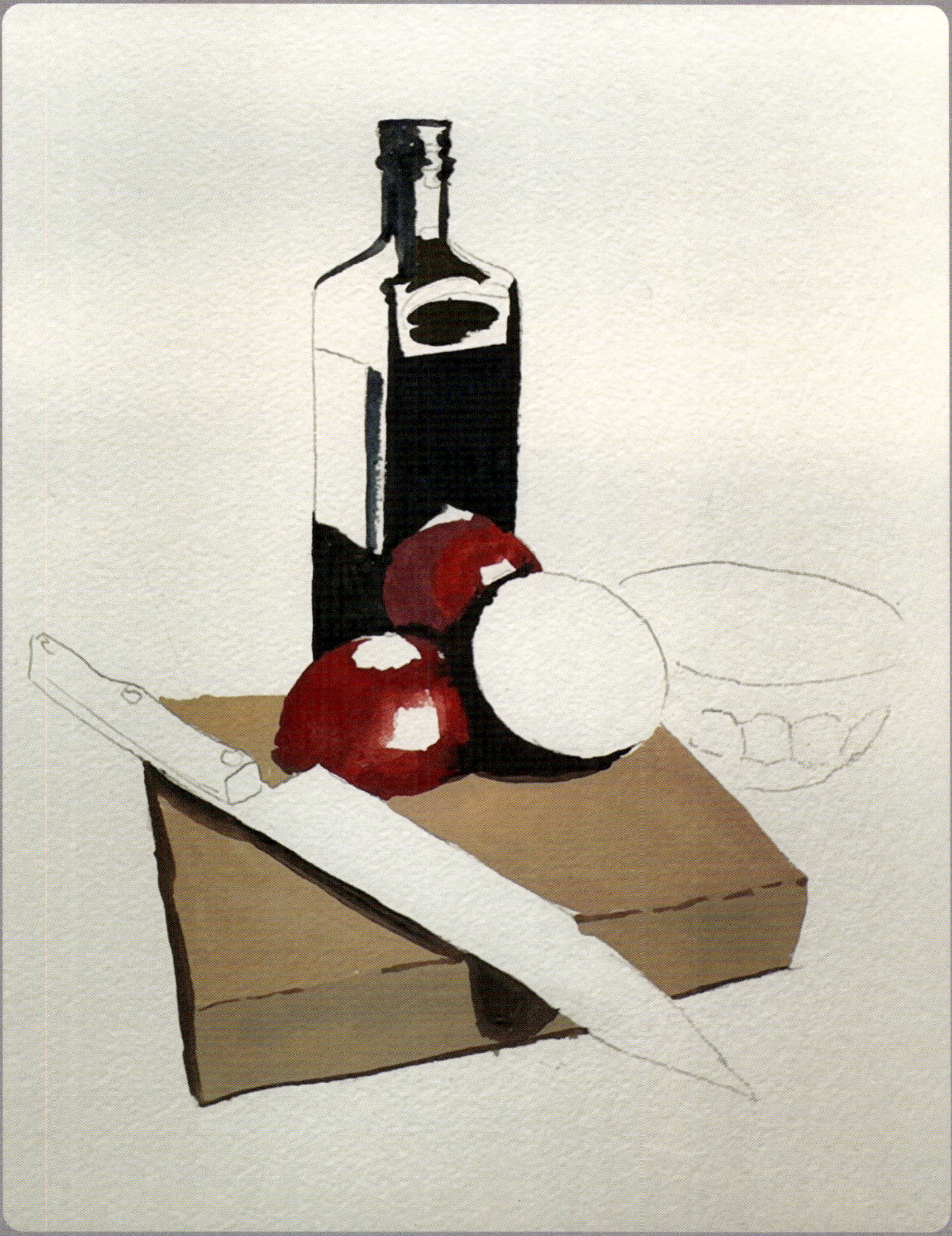

07. Note how the wet shadow blends from one onion to the others

07. DARK COLOURS

Now you can bring in some of the darks – the darkest green sides of the glass bottle and brown shadow of the onion. Even though this exercise has focused on big, flat pieces of colour so far, you can see that the shadows of my foremost onion have bled into the wet red of the onion on the left, creating a softer edge. The more you can learn to predict how the paint and water will act, the better at painting with gouache you will be. This kind of interaction allows you to create soft transitions without having to paint forcefully.

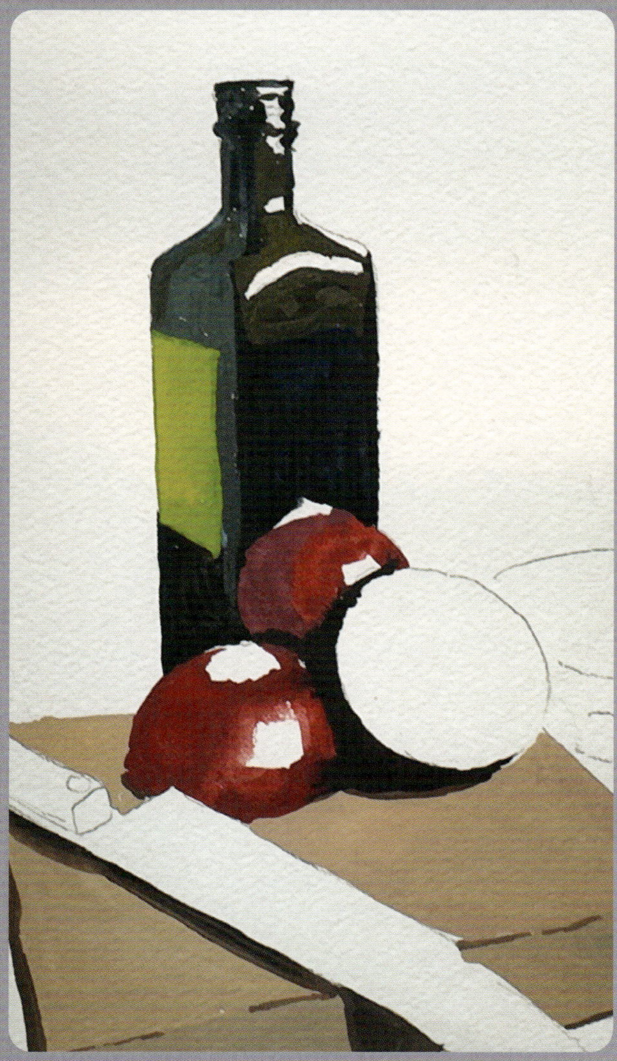

08. Flesh out the bottle with hues that are a little lighter

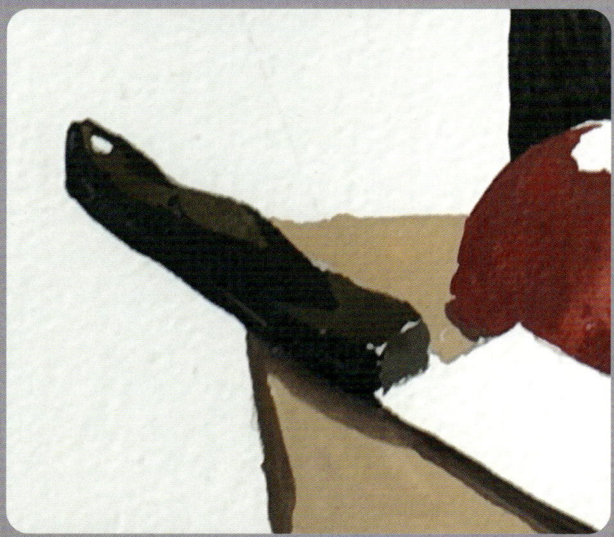

09. Create highlights by leaving thin,
translucent areas that show the white paper

08. EXPANDING COLOURS

Now that you've established the darkest darks, you can lighten up and make sure you're keeping a sense of colour, even in the shadows. A slightly lighter blue-green side gives depth to the glass bottle, and the yellow label brings a pop of brighter colour. Colour and value are relative; the truth of this is doubly evident when you're using gouache and find that its values shift as they dry. This stage is still all about putting in your best guesses. You can come back and fine-tune the colours when you have the whole image covered.

09. KNIFE HANDLE

Next you can paint the knife handle. You can see that I have left the highlights out instead of painting the whole handle and layering light on top. While it is possible to layer light over dark, you will find it easier to control your lights when painting thinly on top of white paper, rather than using white paint over dark paint, which may shift darker than intended. Both strategies are very useful, but in this instance try working with the former.

10. REMAINING AREAS

In this pass (pictured right), we use our gouache almost like watercolour, adding lots of water and painting thinly to establish a sense of colour in the areas that have been blank to this point. The bowl, the knife blade, and the ends of the onions receive light layers of colour. To do this, use the bead method that you used for the value study, but this time with colour instead of just black paint.

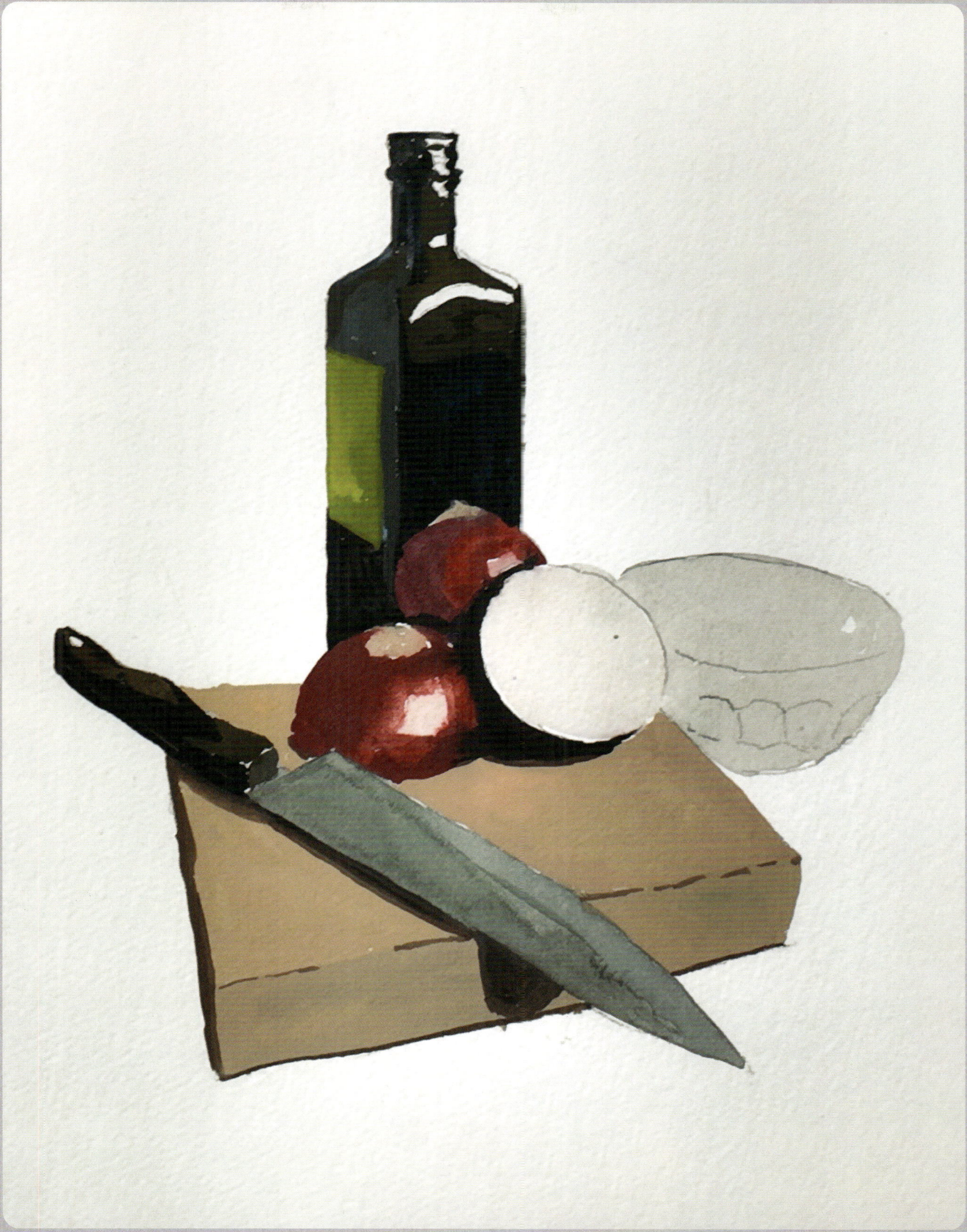

10. Fill out the last few objects with light colour

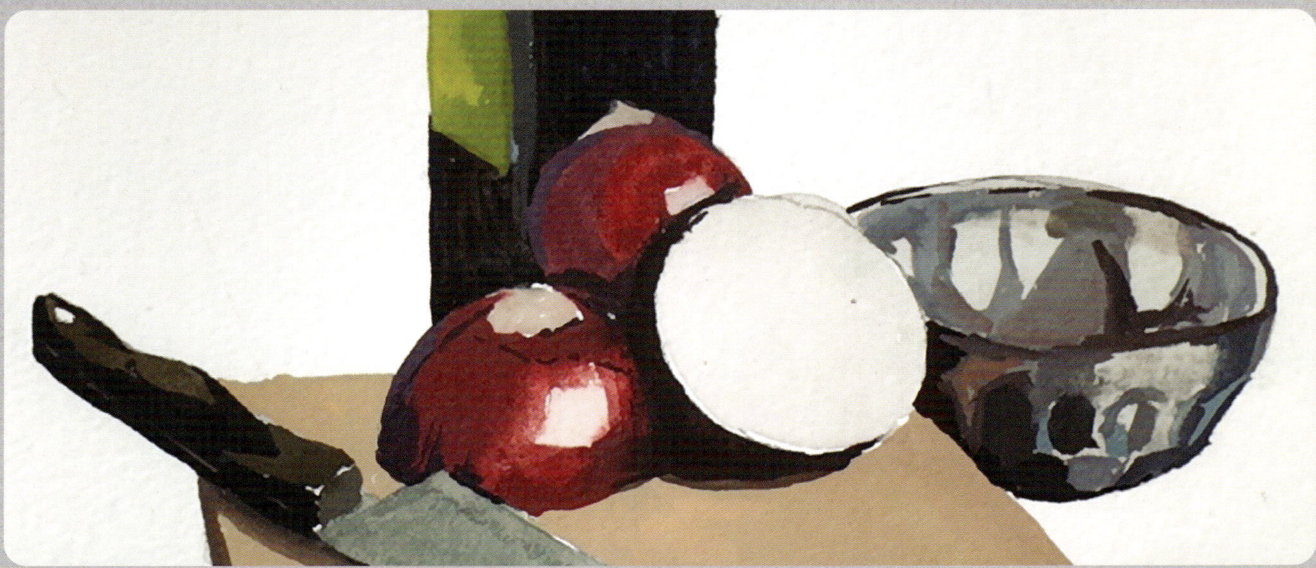

11. Start wrapping up the scene with smaller details

11. ADDING DETAILS

Now you can come in with details to fine-tune the areas you have established. This means adding darks to the onion skins and reflections to the bowl. The biggest things to remember with layering are to wait for the layer below to dry and to be brief. The less time your brush spends on the paper, the less likely it will be that you reactivate the layer below and muddy your colours.

12. FINISHING TOUCHES

Now you're close to finishing. Add the small details, reflections, and textures with thick paint. In my case, I add details on the knife handle and blade, light glinting off the bottle, the rings and ends of the onions, and patterns on the wooden board. When we are learning to paint, it's good to paint small studies and objects that are directly in front of us, because they can easily be broken down into simple shapes and clear colours. Once you get comfortable with these, you can move on to grander and more expansive scenes that will rely more on texture and depth.

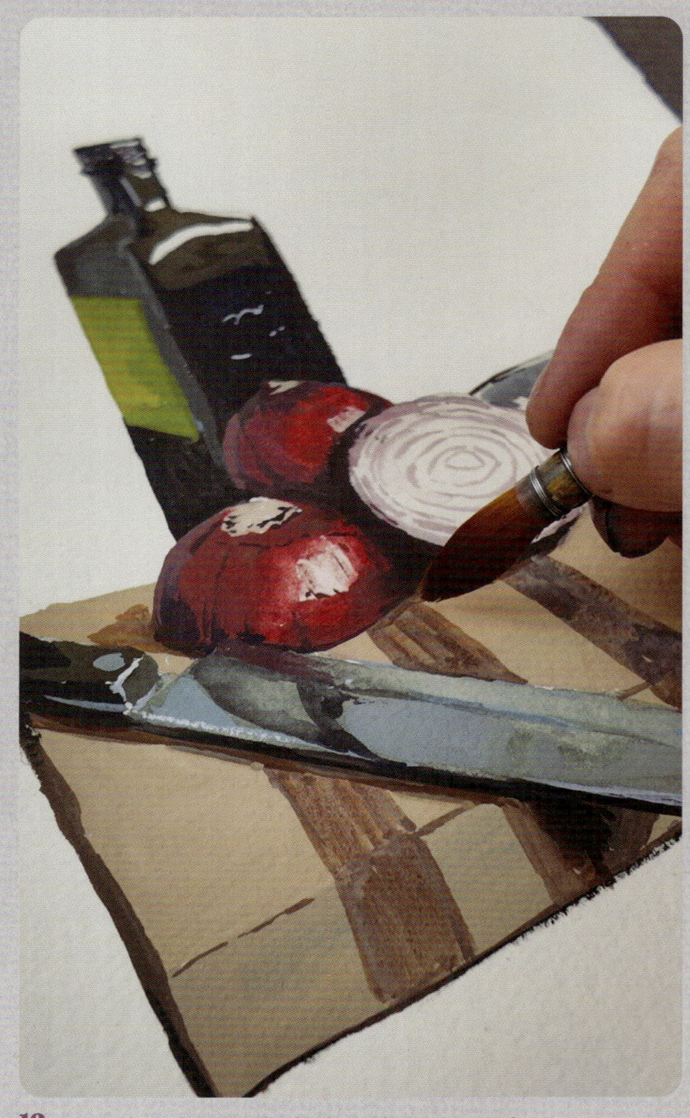

12. Add the finest details and highlights with opaque gouache

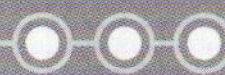

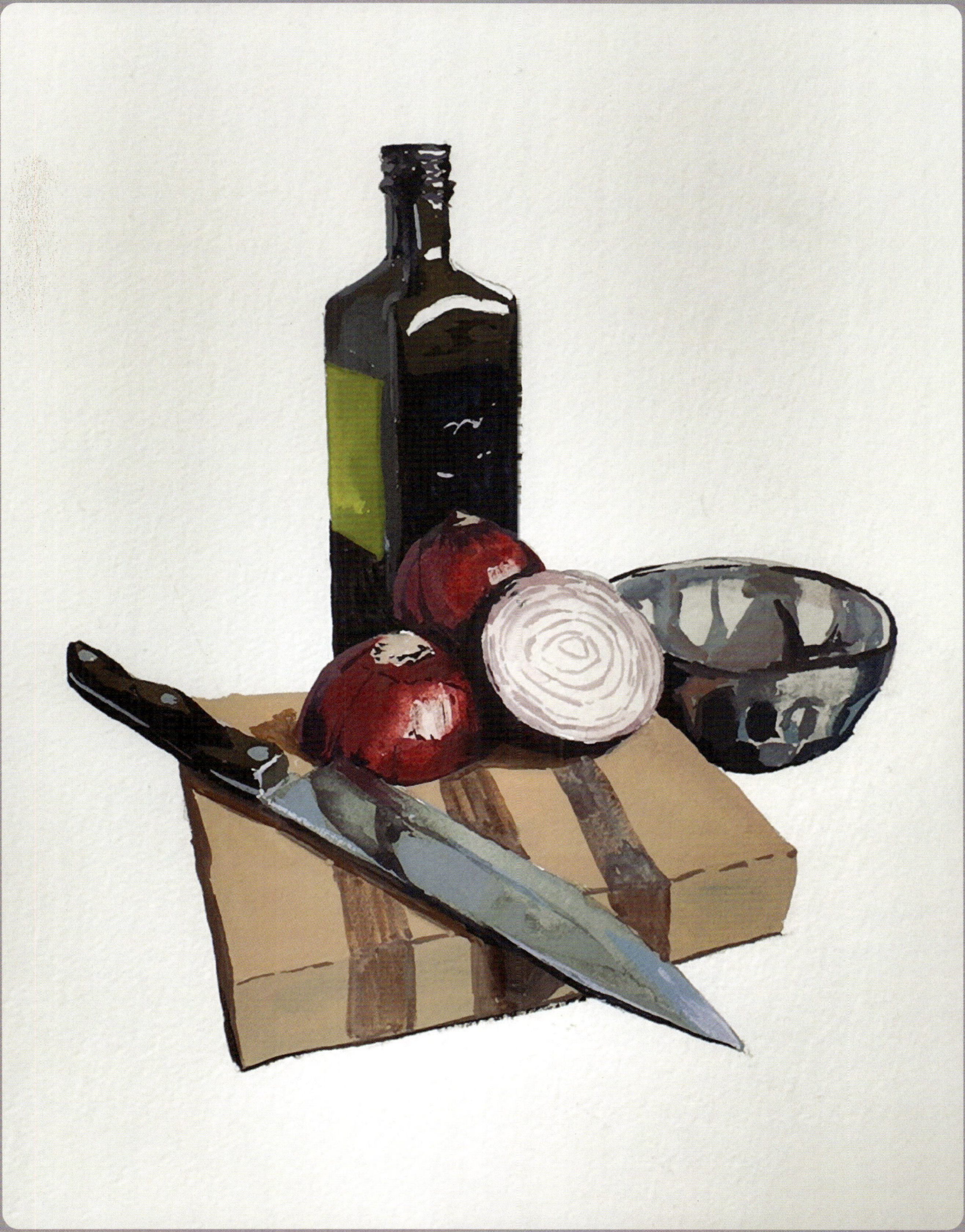

The finished study. Try setting up and studying small scenes of your own – the possibilities are endless!

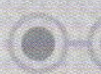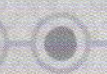

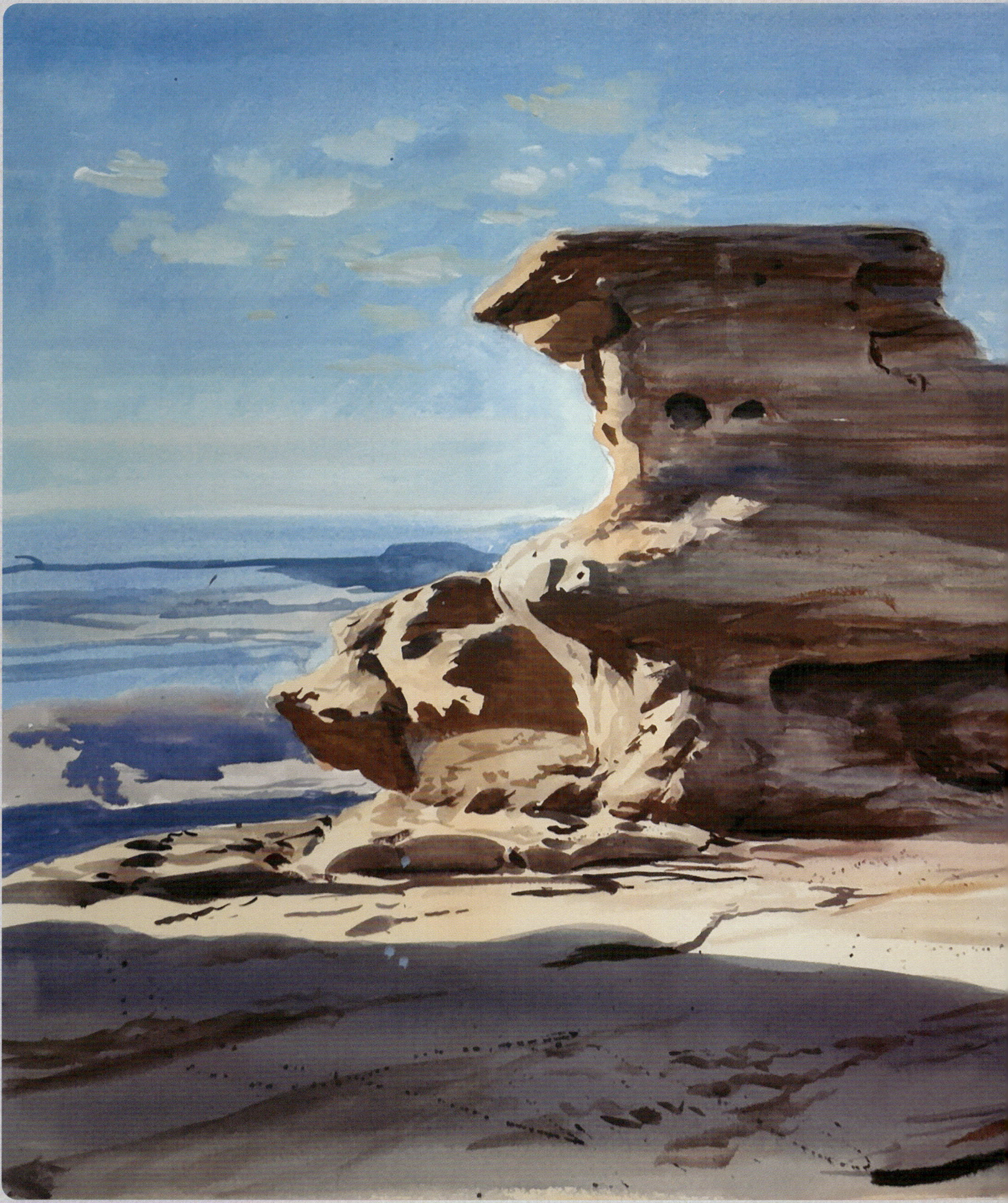

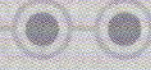

Dead Horse. Developing your eye for values will help you paint anything, anywhere!

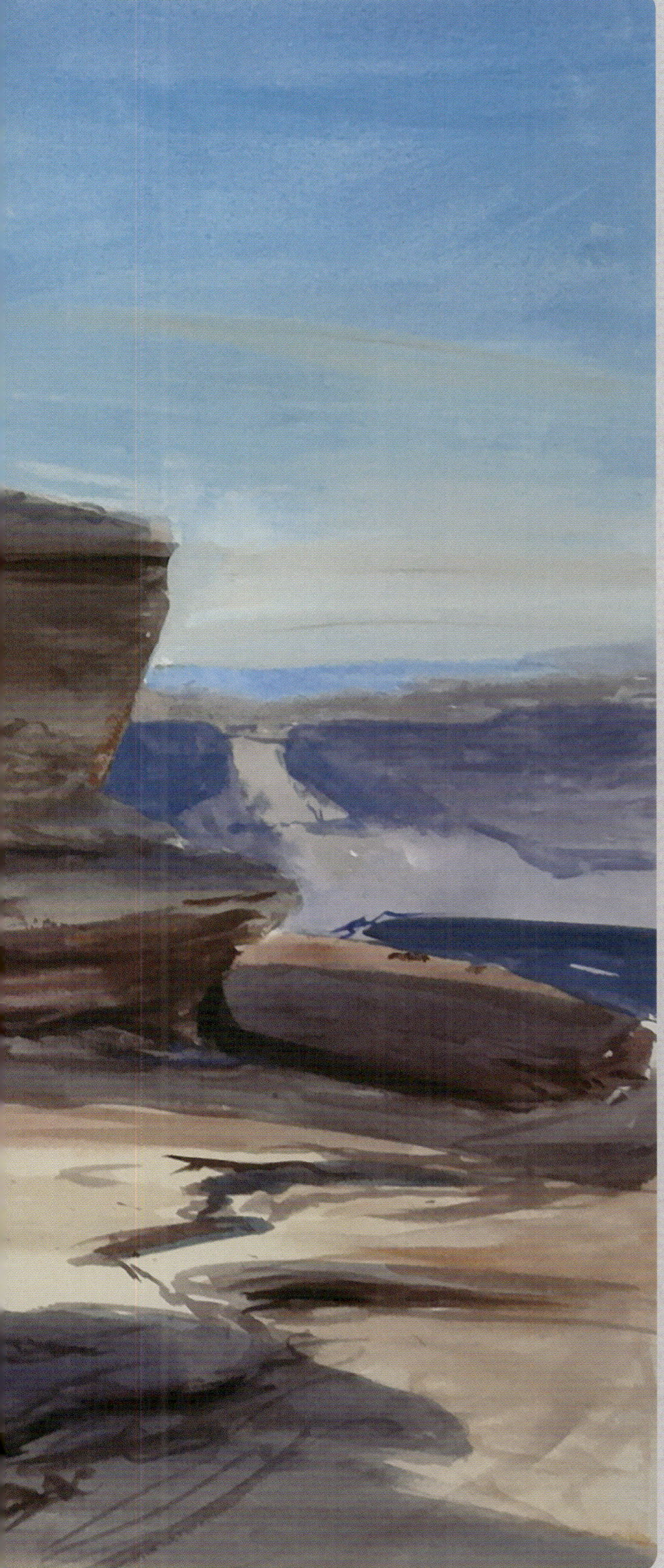

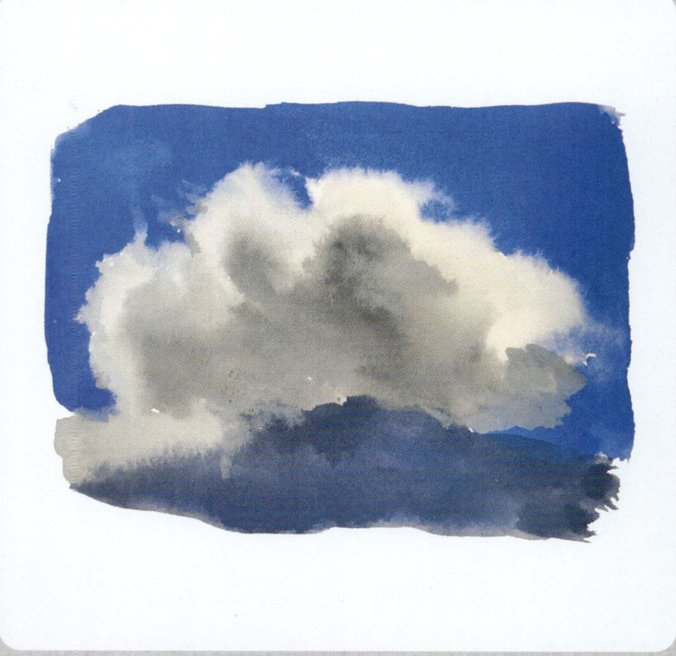

Bleeding wet edges will allow you to achieve soft, organic effects such as the fluffiness of this cloud

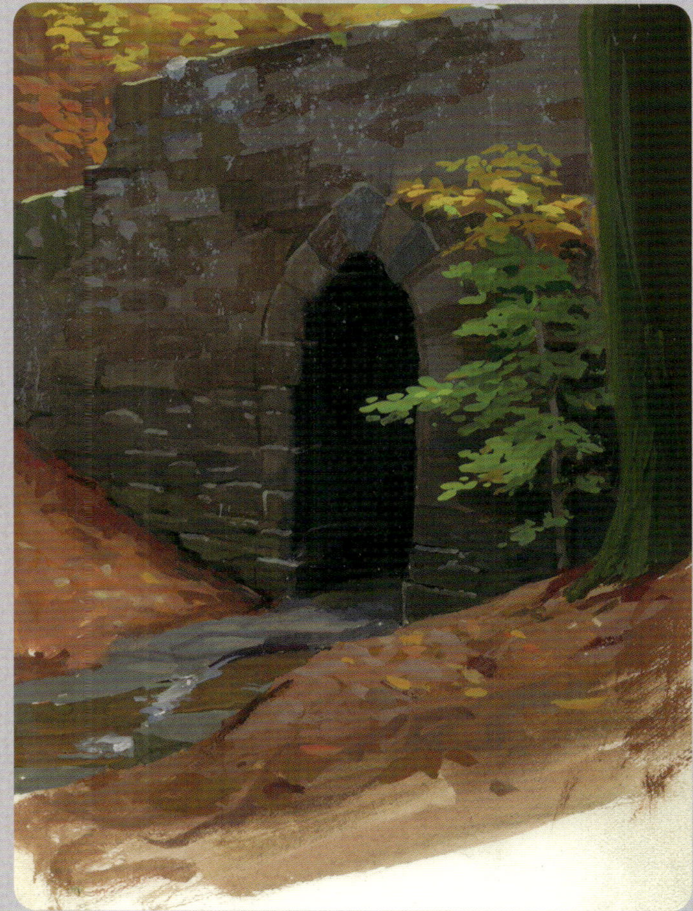

Save finer details for last, using a small brush with thick paint

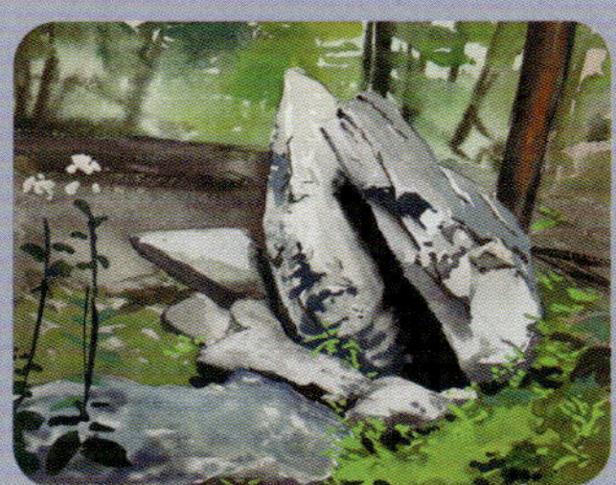

Exercise:
NATURE PAINTING, THIN TO THICK

Let's explore a technique I mentioned briefly in the layering overview on page 35. This is a method I call 'thin to thick' and it's a great way to get used to layering in gouache. For this demo, in contrast to the last one, we'll step from indoors to outdoors and paint a woodland scene with natural lighting, a background, and lots of organic textures. We'll start painting with thin gouache, almost like watercolour, and get progressively thicker with each new layer. As always, it's worth mentioning that there is no right or wrong way to paint with gouache. Every different set of ideas is worth playing with and adopting into your painting vocabulary. The more tools you have in your belt, the more versatile you will be, and the more you'll be free to paint whatever you like, however you like.

01. VALUE STUDY

Again, begin with a value study of the scene. This uses the same 'paint through' technique shown on page 37, limiting the values to white, light, medium, and dark in order to see if you can paint simply and still get a powerful image. With this established, you can move on to using colours.

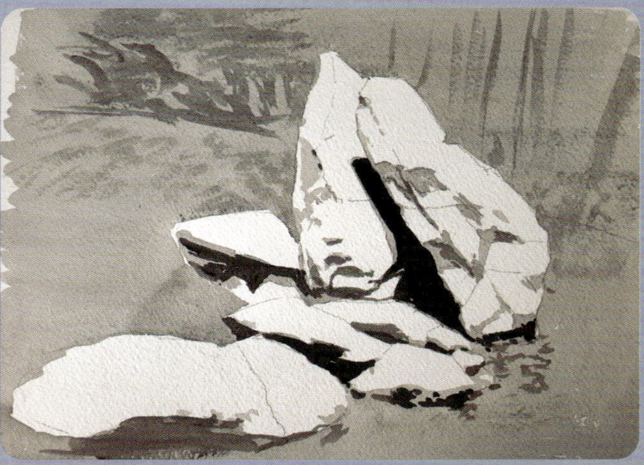

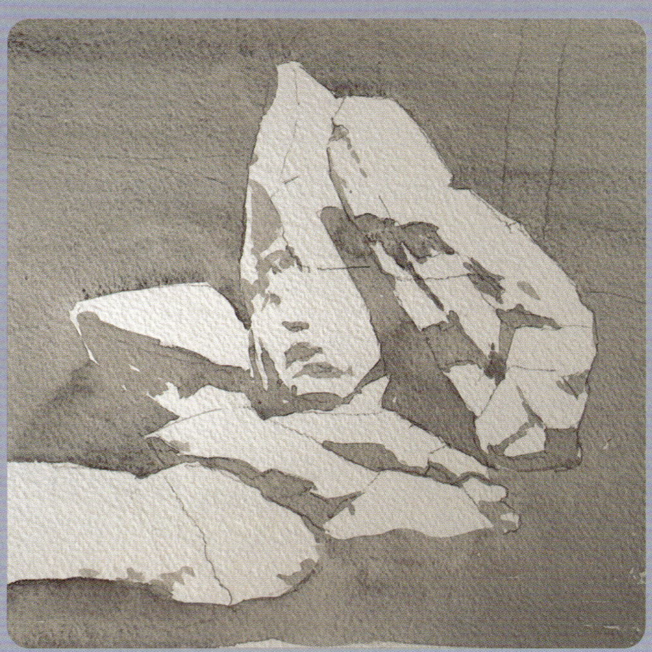

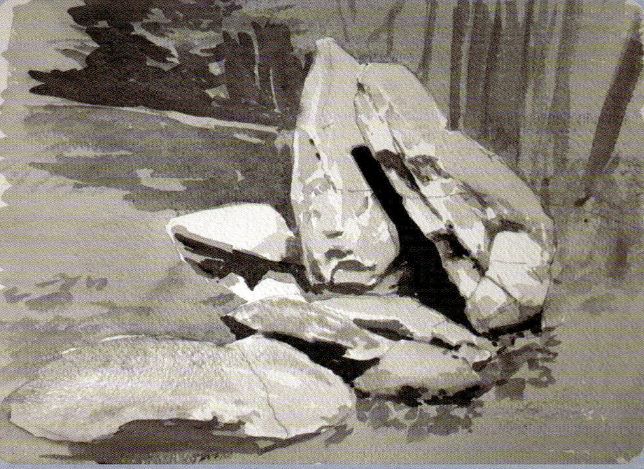

01. Begin with a quick study using minimal values

02. TRANSPARENT BEAD

Now redraw the pencil sketch on a fresh piece of paper. Use the transparent bead method outlined on page 32 to work through the light values on the main rock, giving it a warm grey tone.

Because you are painting thinly with lots of water, you can easily layer on top of these parts later in order to create details.

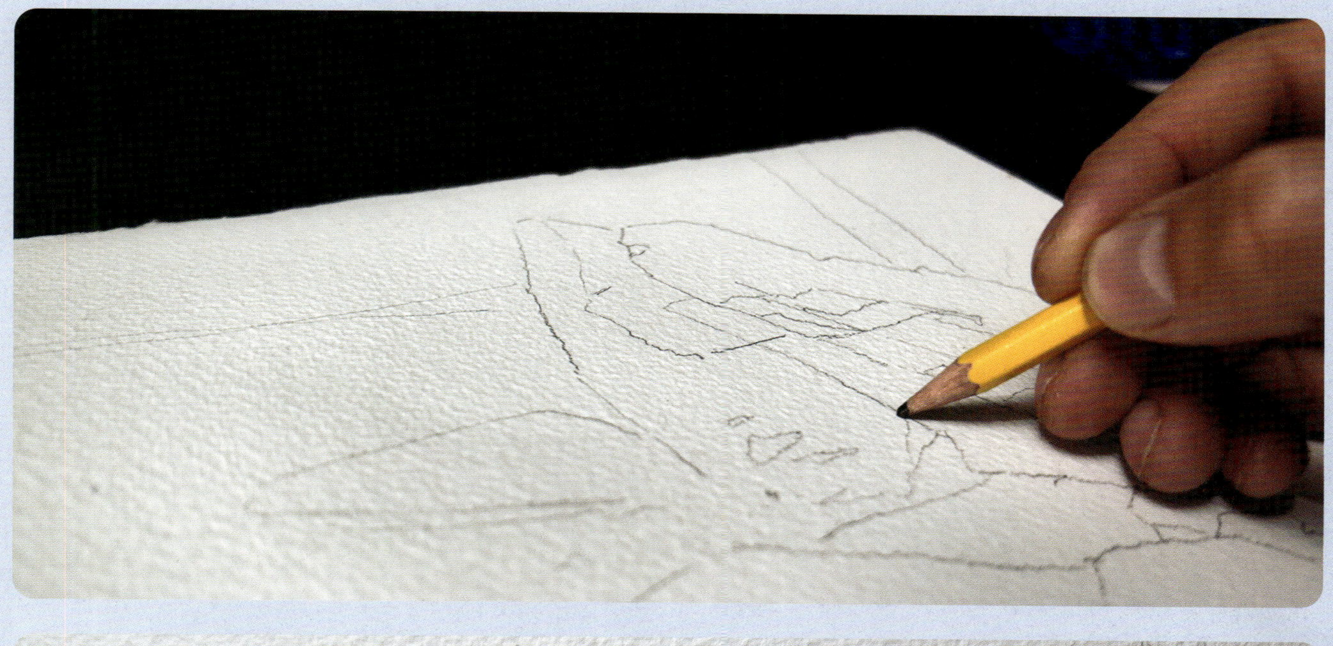

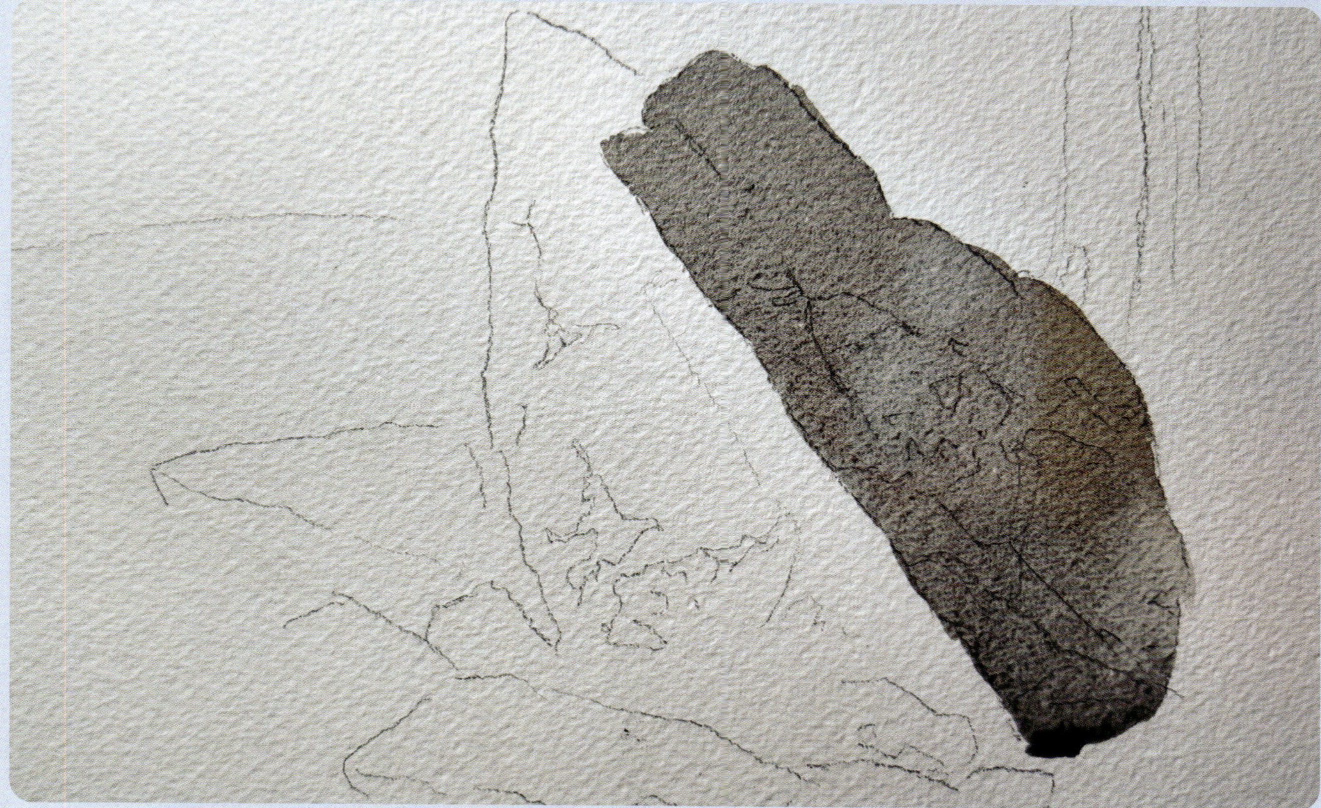

02. Begin painting the rocks using thin paint and the bead method

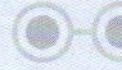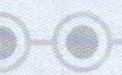

03. COLOUR VARIATIONS

As you work through the other rocks in a similar fashion, look out for colour variations and accentuate them. Remember that when you are using lots of water with gouache, the colour's intensity will reduce when it dries, so it's worth pushing the colours a little here. In the end, they will all appear like small, subtle changes in the grey of the rock. Continue this throughout all the rocks and let them dry.

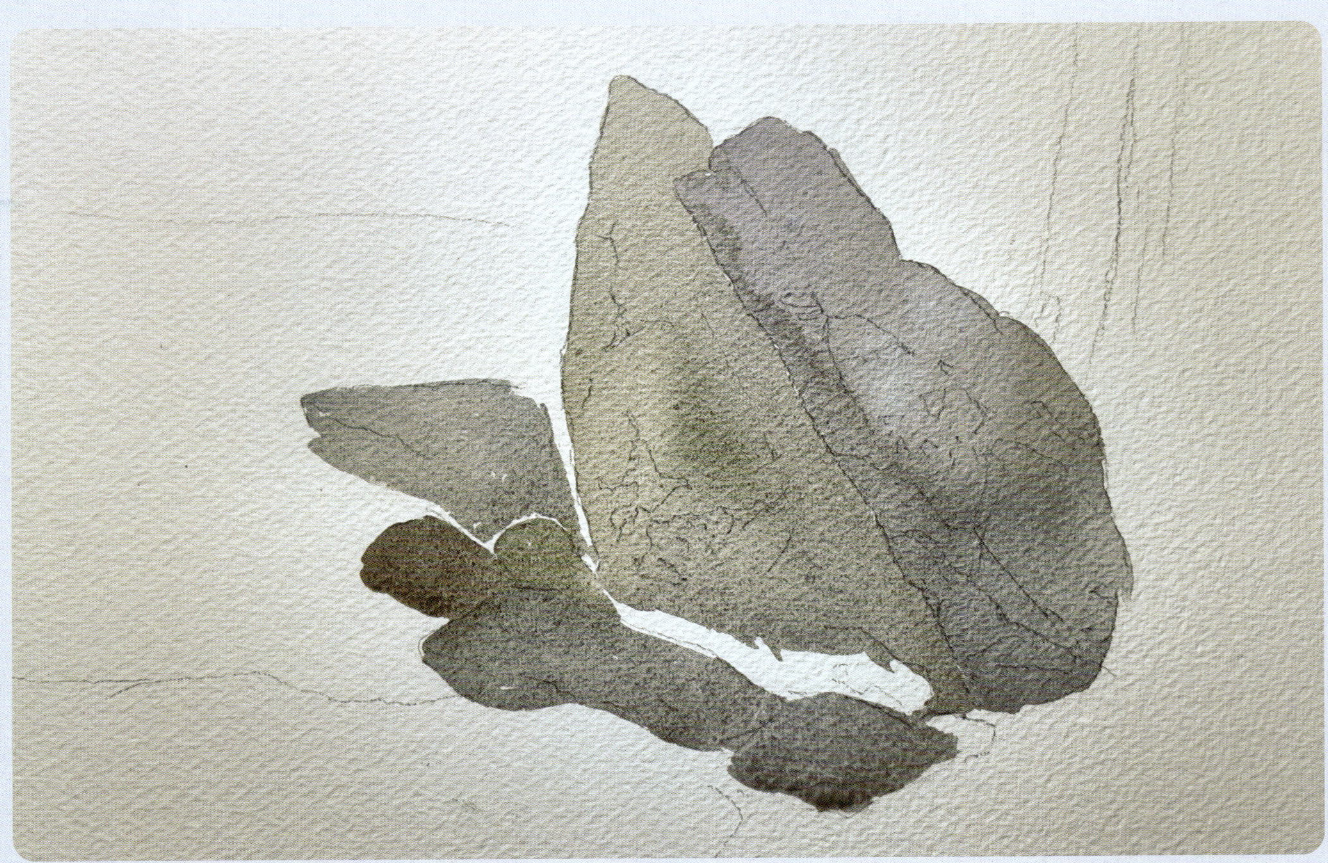

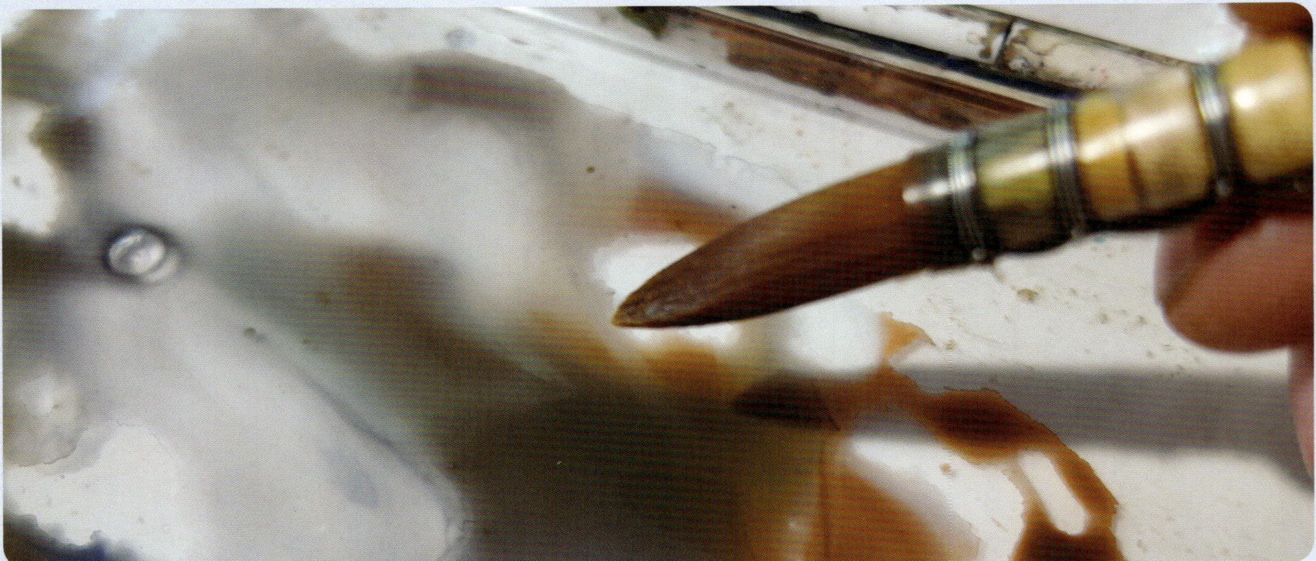

03. Add colour variation to the rocks using plenty of water

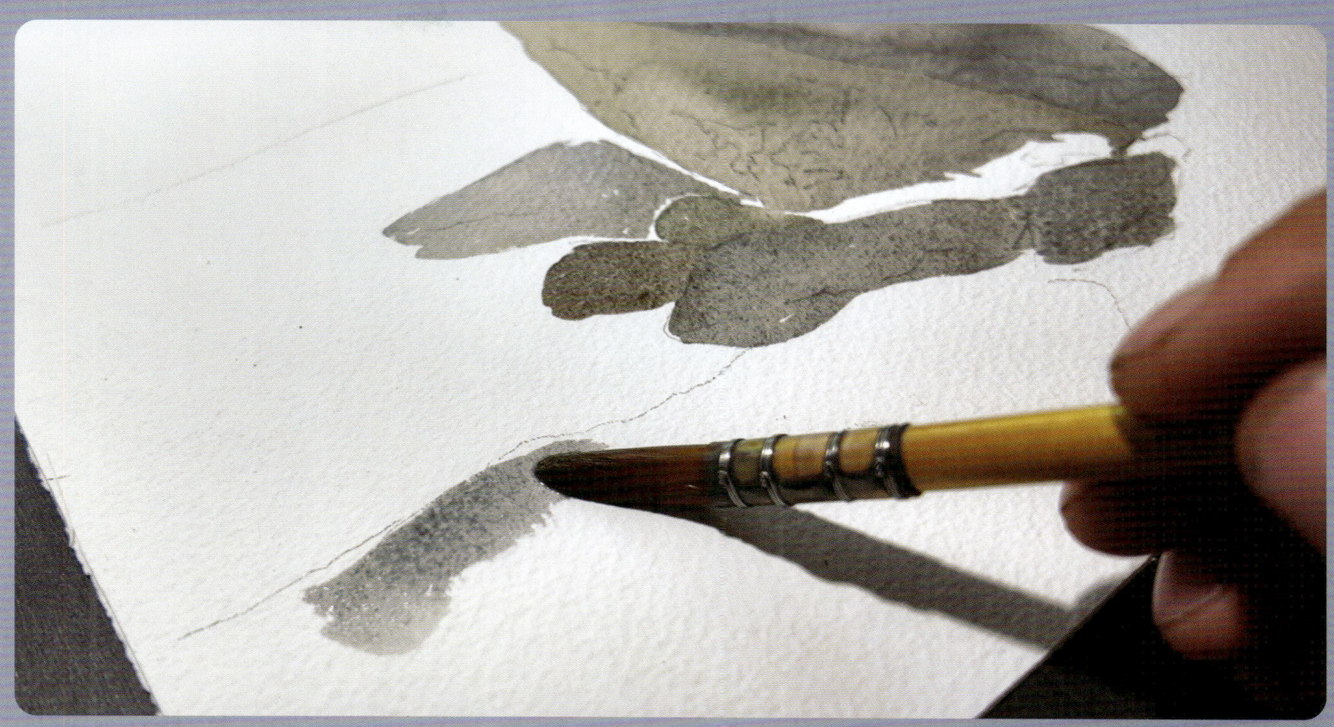

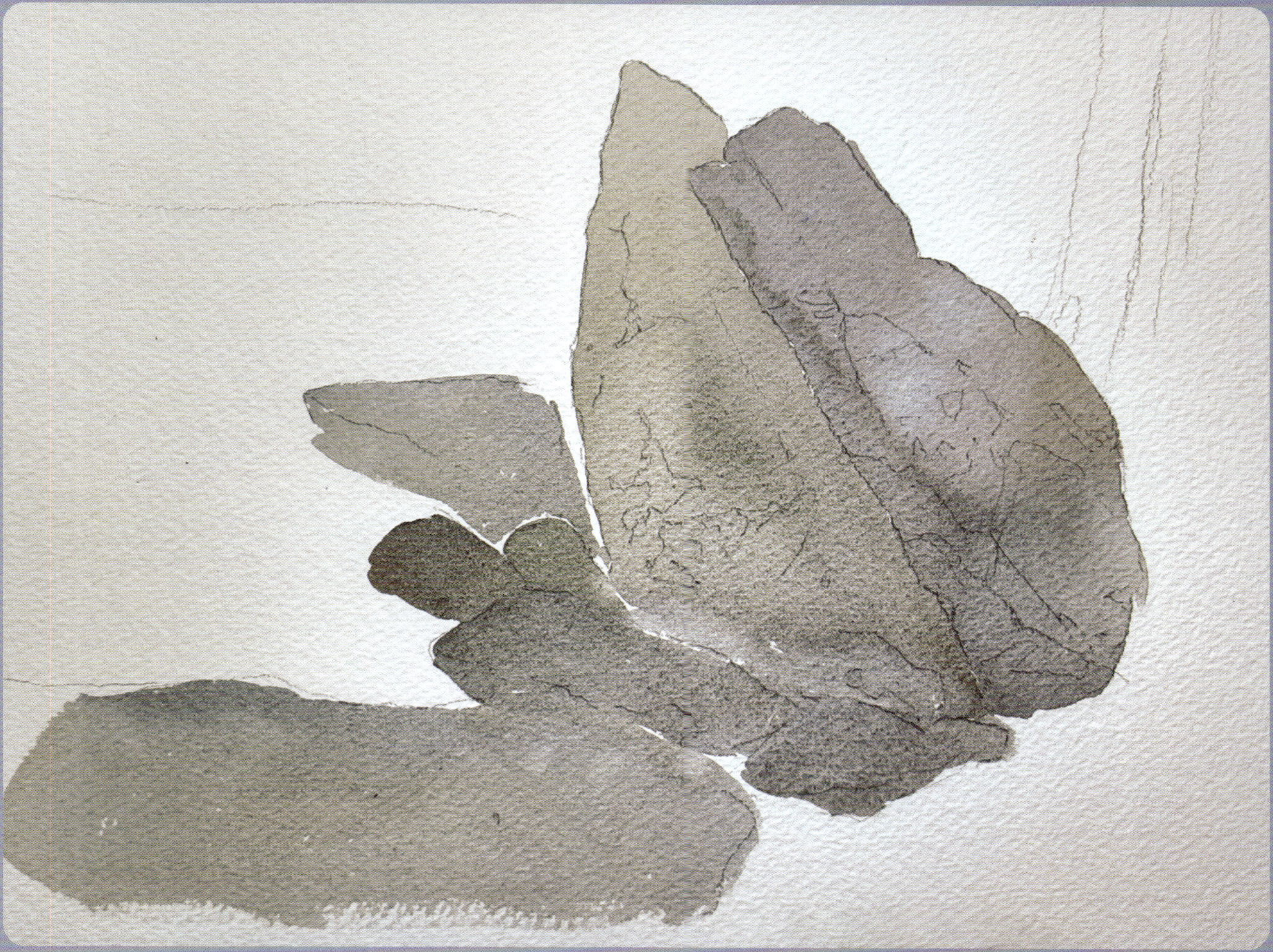

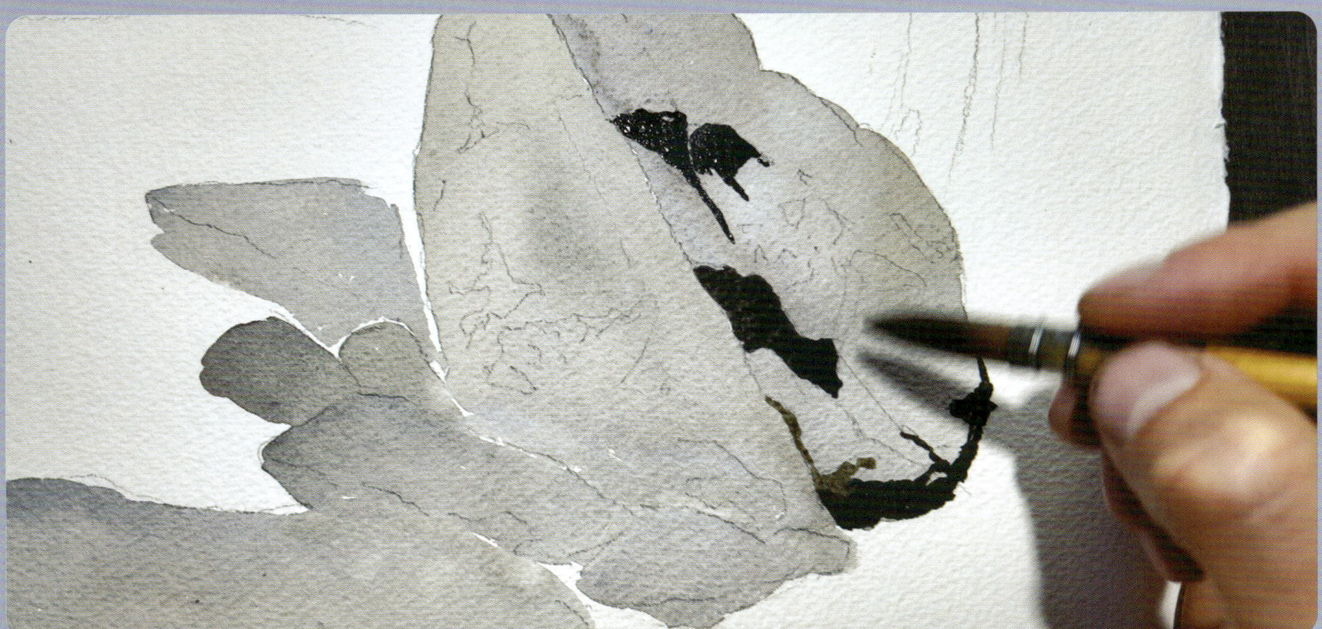

04. Add dark shadows and move on quickly to the next step!

04. THICK SHADOWS

Now you can start adding shadows using nice thick paint. Because you used a thin layer underneath, you shouldn't have to worry too much about reactivating the previous layer – there isn't much there to reactivate! Paint in some dark grey-green crevices in the rock, and be sure to move on to the next step before your paint dries.

05. SOFTENING SHADOWS

While the previous brushwork is still wet, load a new brush with some water only. Run this across the edges of the shadow that appear to be softer on the rock – the side where it's curving away from the light source. This change in edge quality will go a long way in giving the rock a three-dimensional feel.

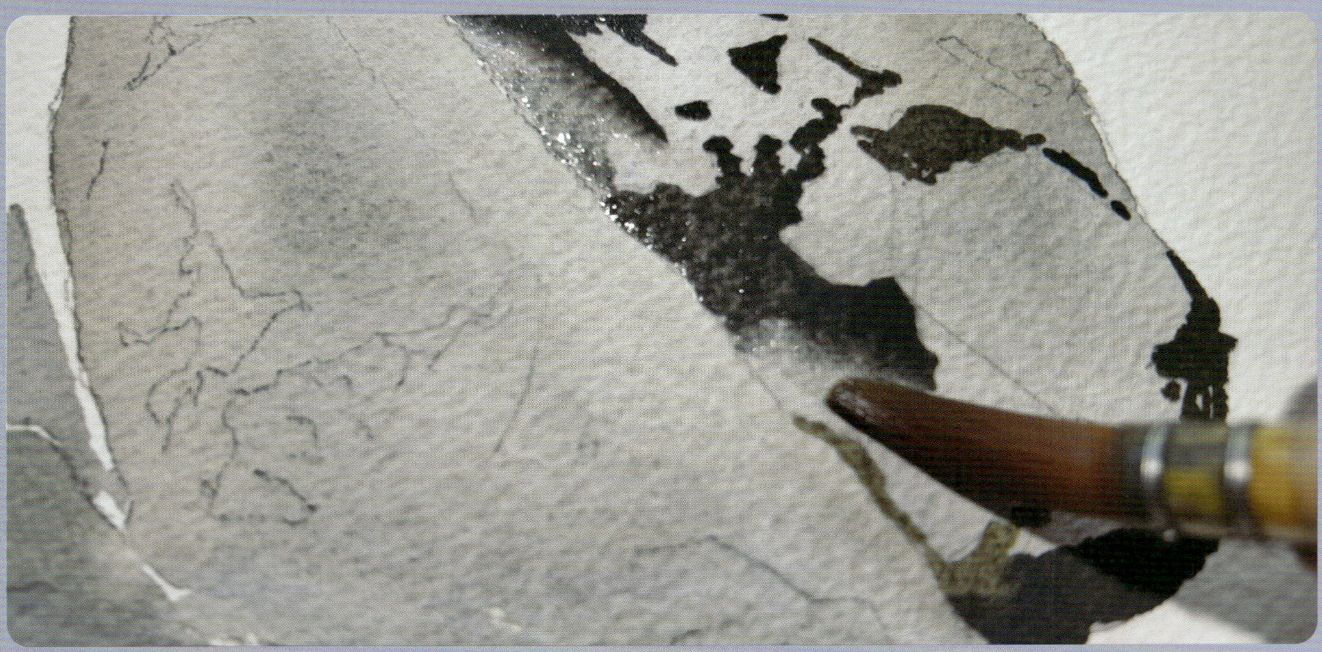

05. Use a clean brush and water to make a softer edge

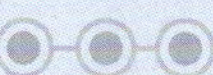

06. PAINTING ONTO WATER

Now you'll continue using water to soften the edges of an area of paint, but in the reverse order of the previous step. This time lay down a wide, moderately wet brushstroke of water to the left side of the rock, where there'll be the soft edge of a shadow. Paint over this area with your shadow colour, which will create a shadow with a hard edge on the right side and a soft edge on the other, where it spreads out into the water. Allow this layer to dry.

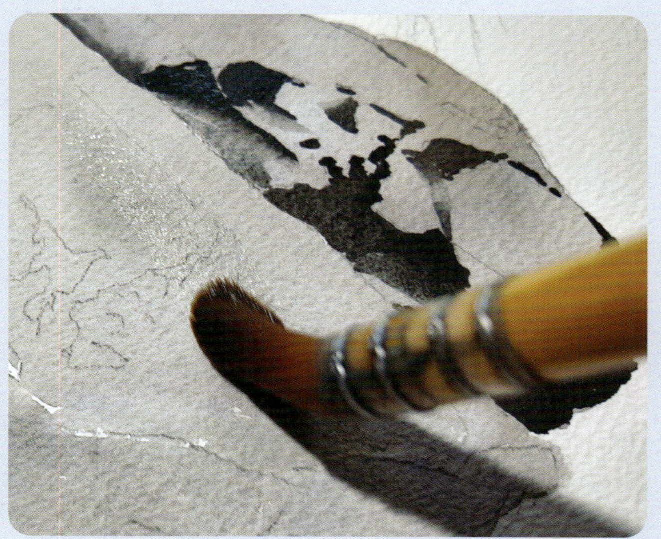

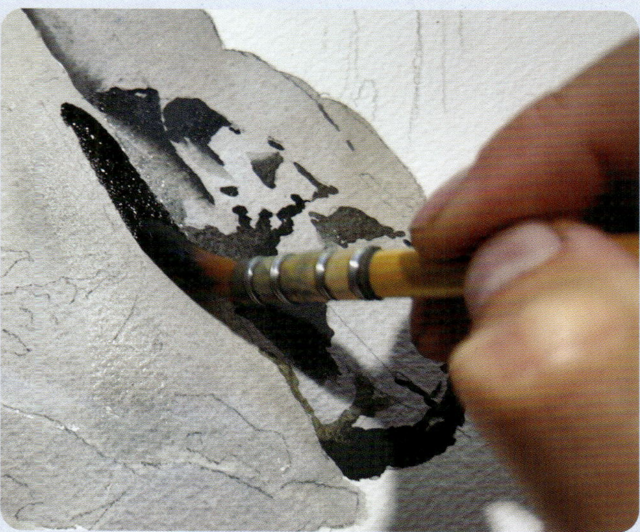

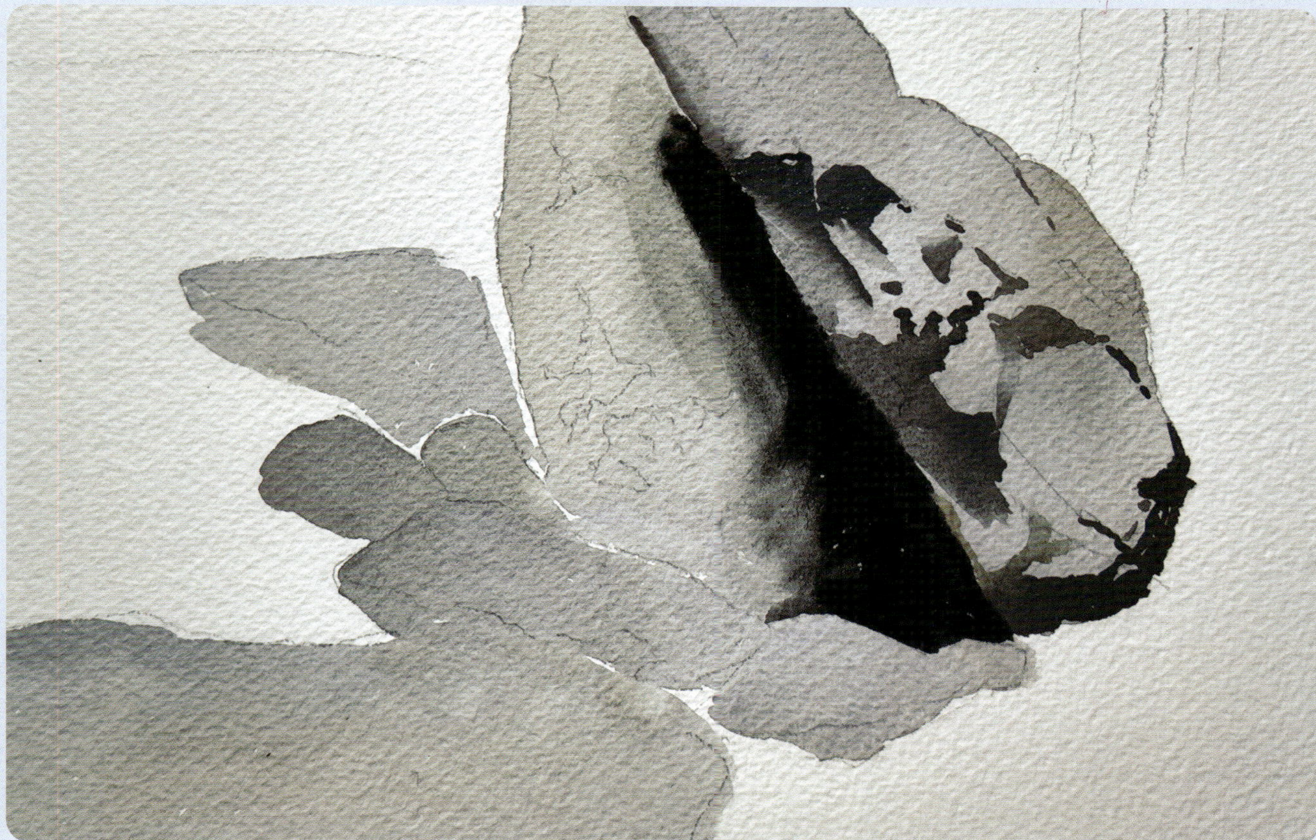

06. Use water strategically to spread and soften your brushstrokes

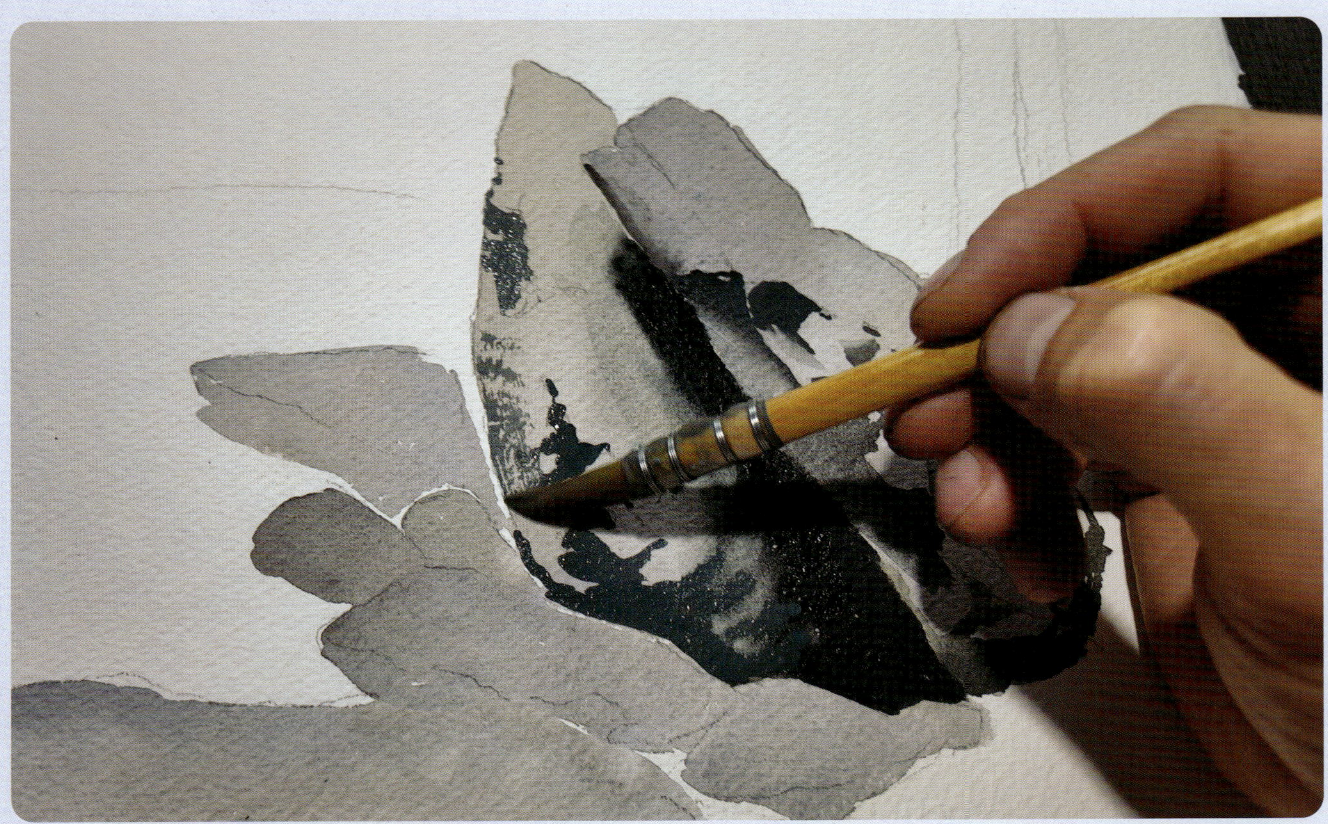

07. DRY BRUSHING

Let's throw in another technique: dry brushing. The left side of this rock has some solid shadows, but then some areas are more textural and hard to define. Put some grey paint onto the brush, then place the first few brushstrokes onto a paper towel or spare piece of paper. The brush will start to produce texture rather than a solid stroke of paint. You can then use this brush on the rock in order to produce a rough, textured effect. Once that's done, return to using darker, wetter paint to add shadows to the smaller rocks.

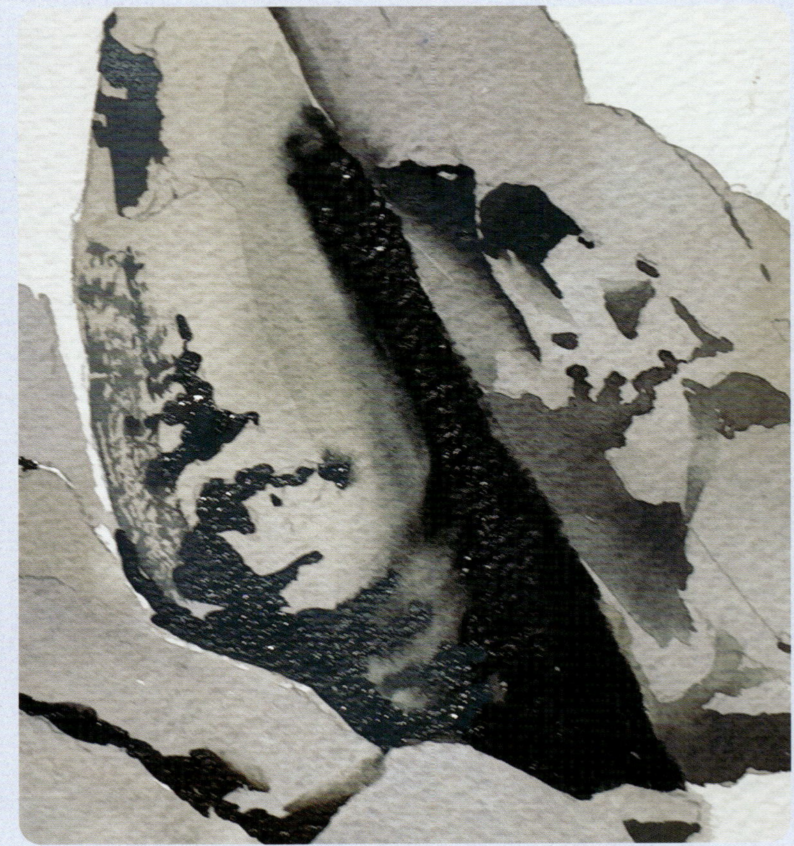

07. Create rough textures with dry brushing

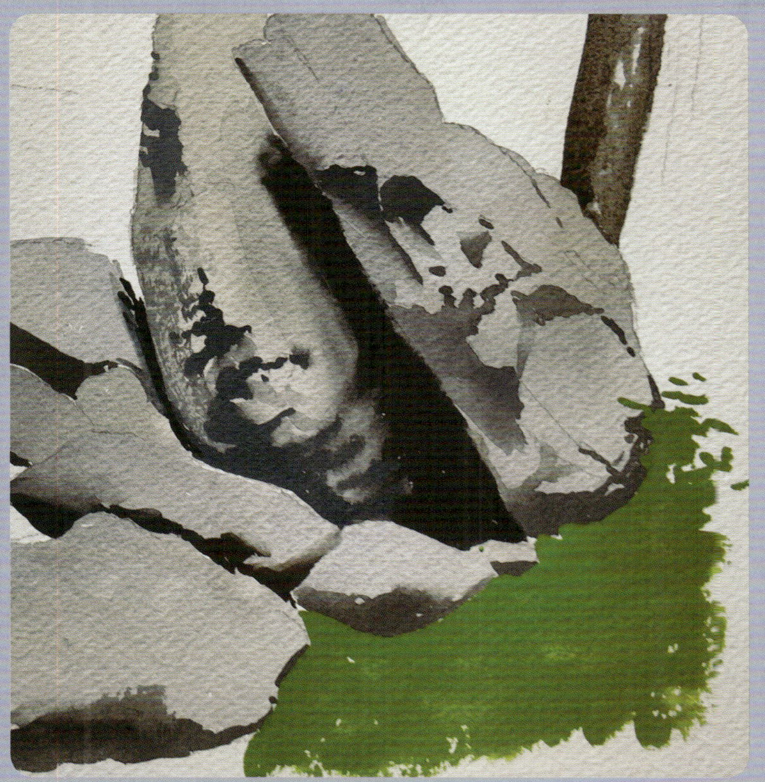

08. GRASSY GROUND

Up to this point you have focused on the rocks in order to keep things clean and simple, but now you can move on and start to paint the surrounding context. Use some thick paint with a moderate amount of water to create some grass in the foreground. Then add a darker green into that mixture, all while it's still wet. This will give a varied, organic feel to the grass. You aren't trying to create detail at the moment, just laying the groundwork for later detail. Use a desaturated brown to add a nearby tree trunk on the right.

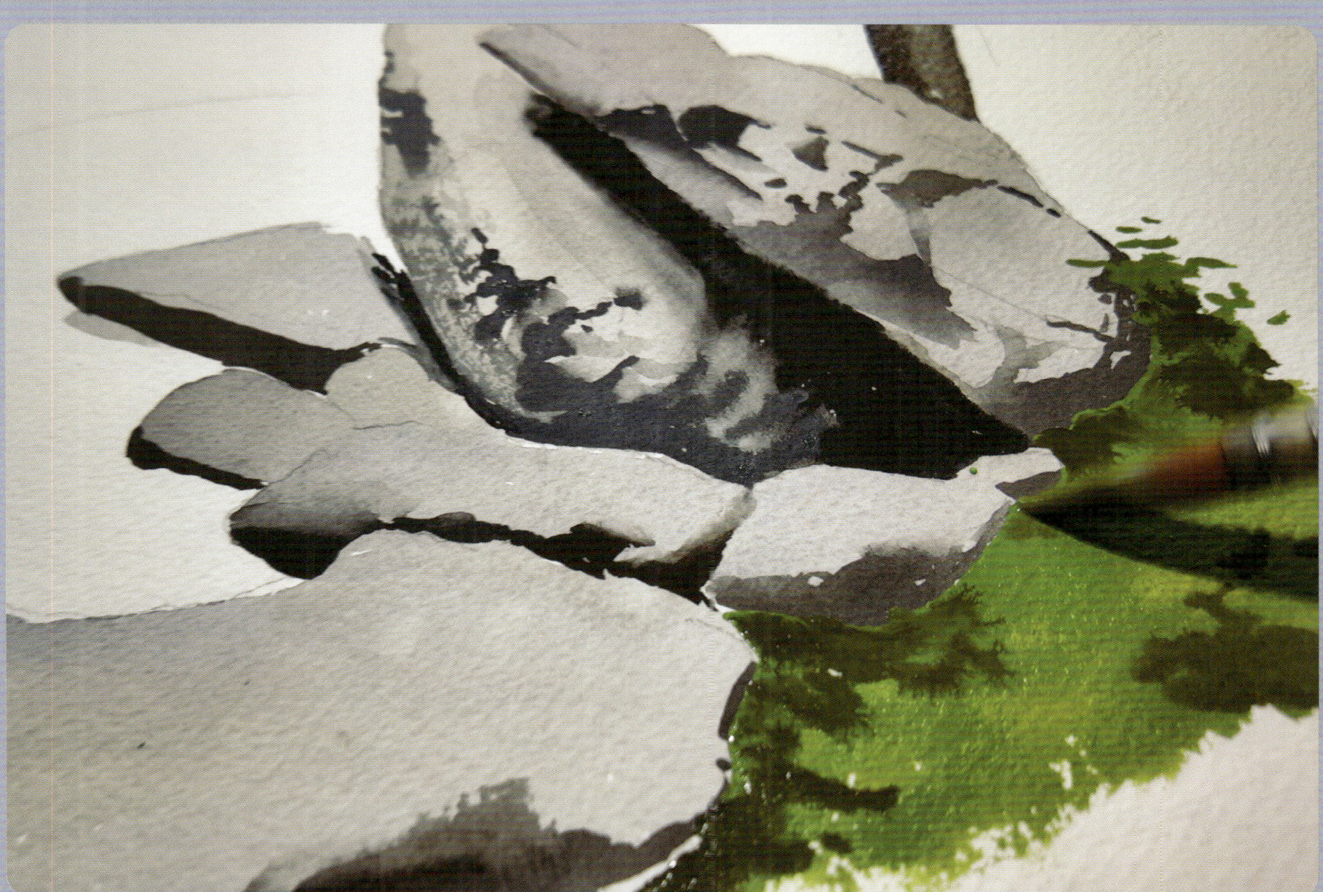

08. Use two shades of green to loosely paint some grass

09. ROUGH BACKGROUND

Using a thin mix with plenty of water, like watercolour, continue adding context by painting the ground and trees in the back. Because you are using gouache, you can always use thicker paint to add more detail on top later, so don't be afraid to generalize at this point. In the foreground, leave an empty area for a pool of water beside the rocks.

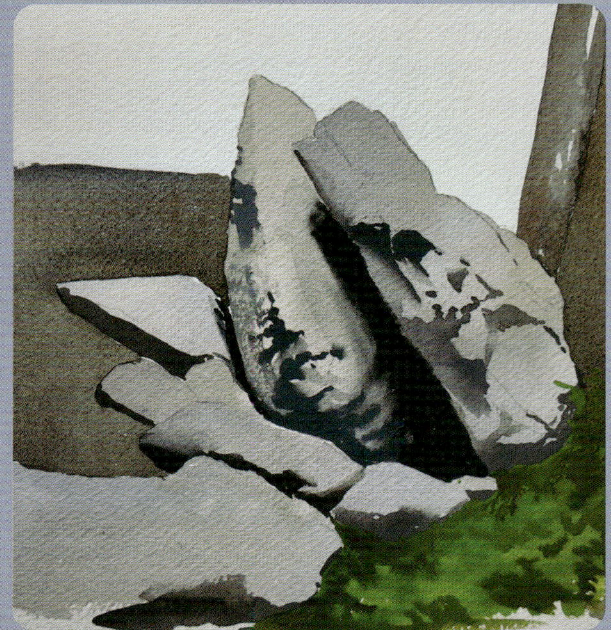

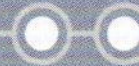

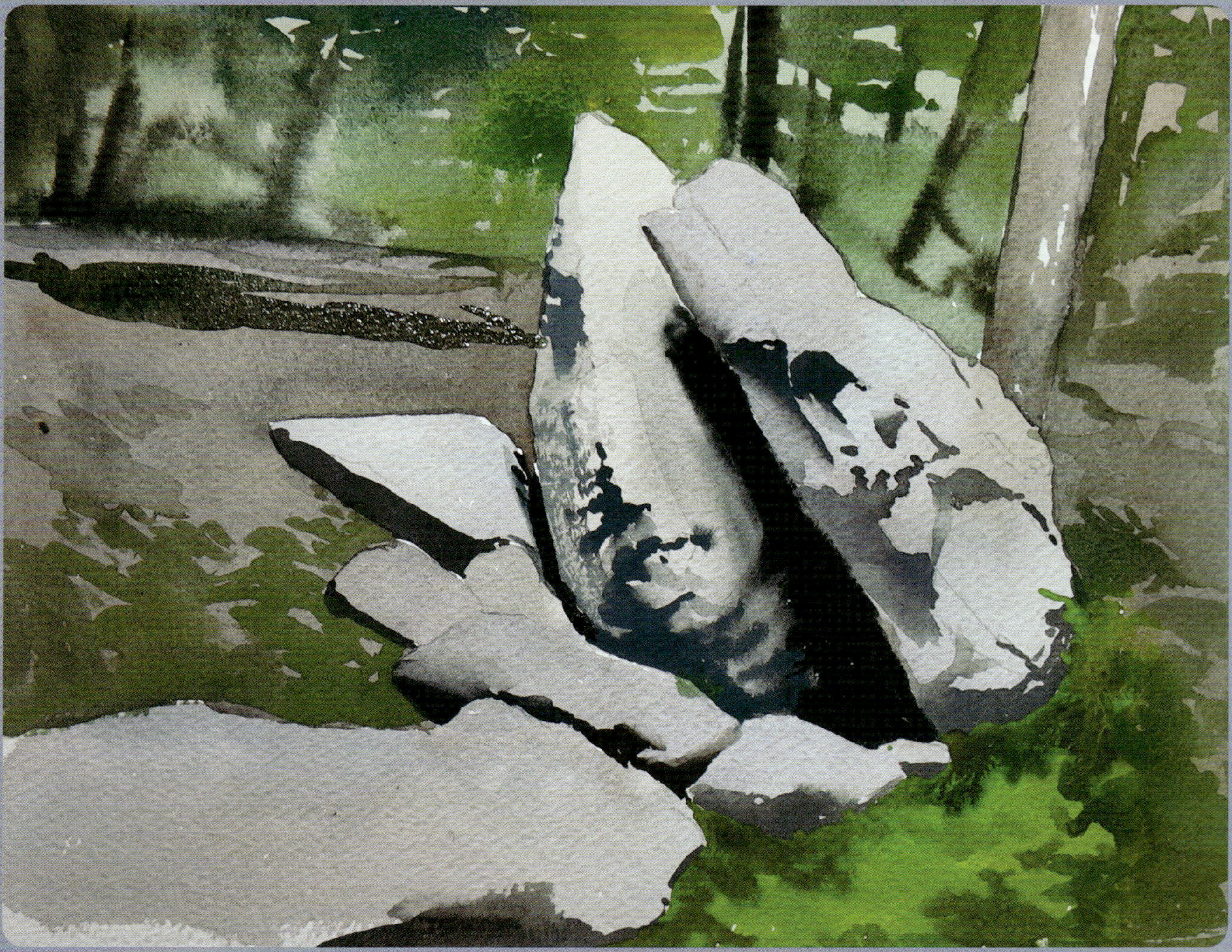

09. Paint in the ground and background – note how the values change as they dry

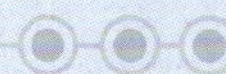

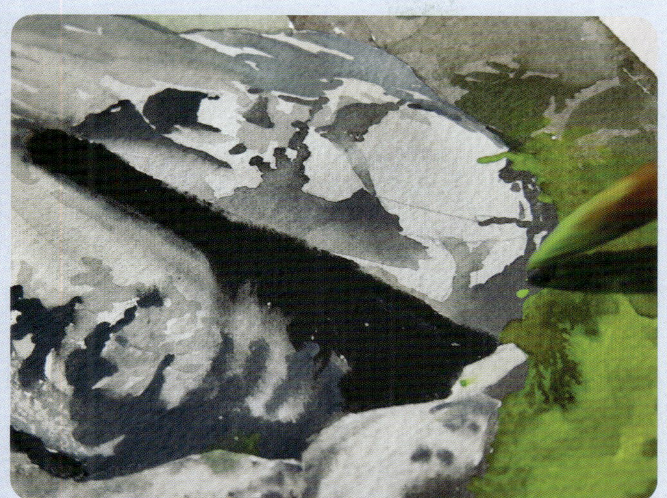

10. FINISHING TOUCHES

Fill out the pool of water using the same wet-to-dry approach as the rocks, starting with thin, watery layers and finishing off with some dry-brushed ripples against the stones. Then, using progressively thicker paint, go around the painting adding individual leaves and any extra details within the background, rock formations, and foreground foliage. This is the stage I like to call 'coverage' – everything is painted and now you get to balance out the elements, add more details, and change anything you might need or want to change. The work has been done and play has begun!

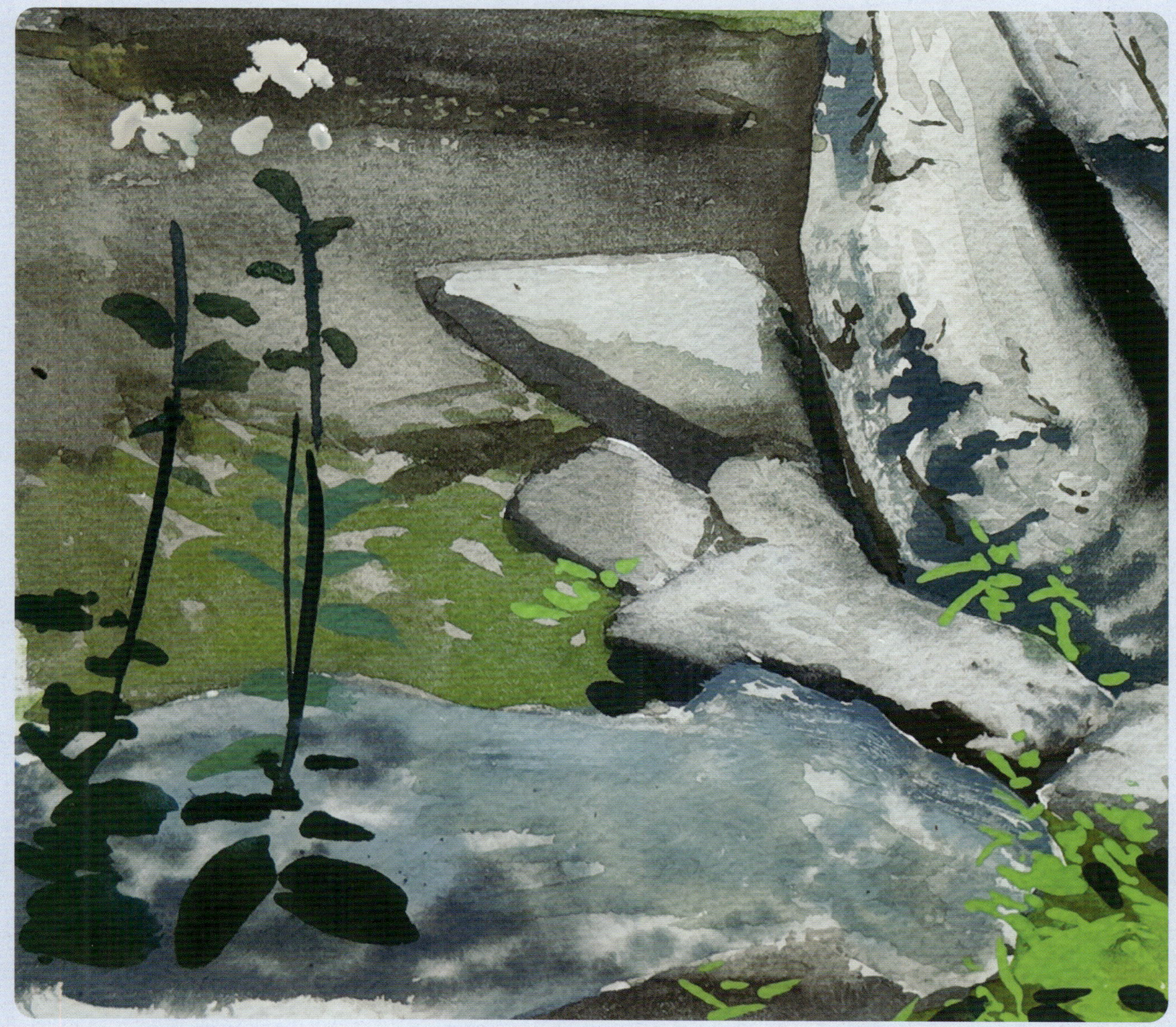

10. Use your thickest paint for foliage details and final touches

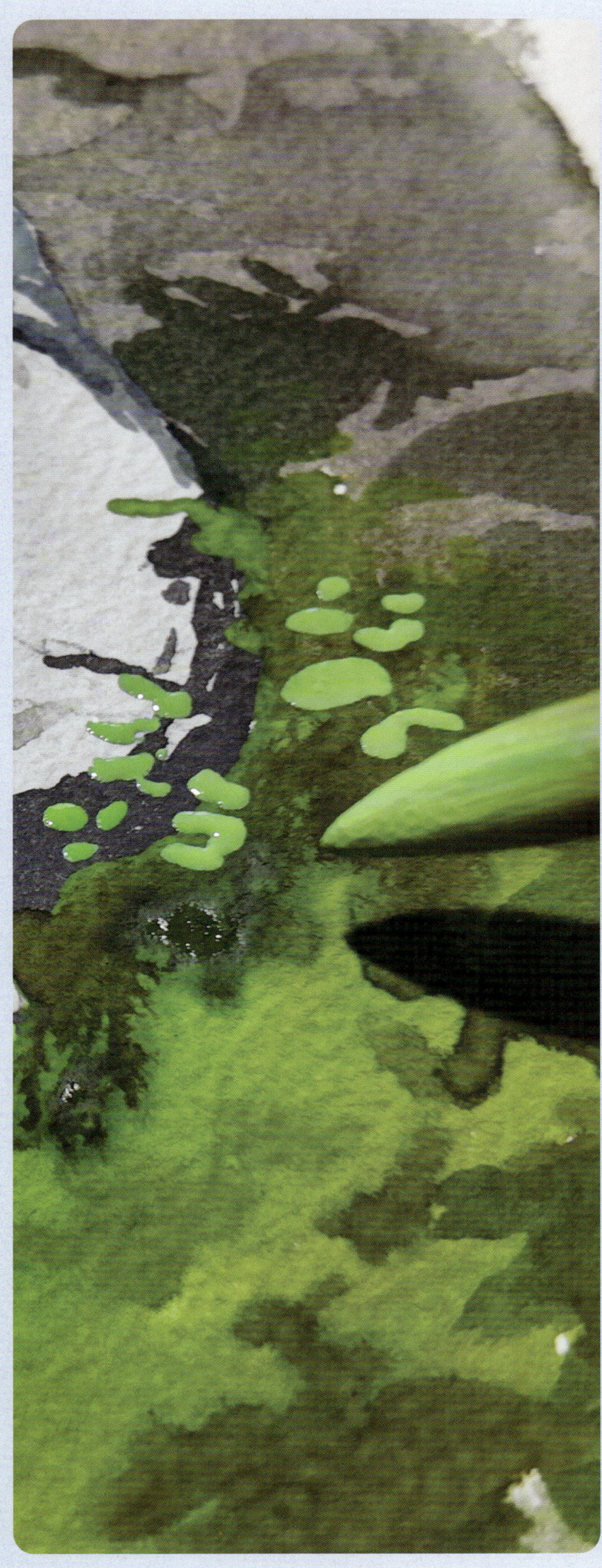

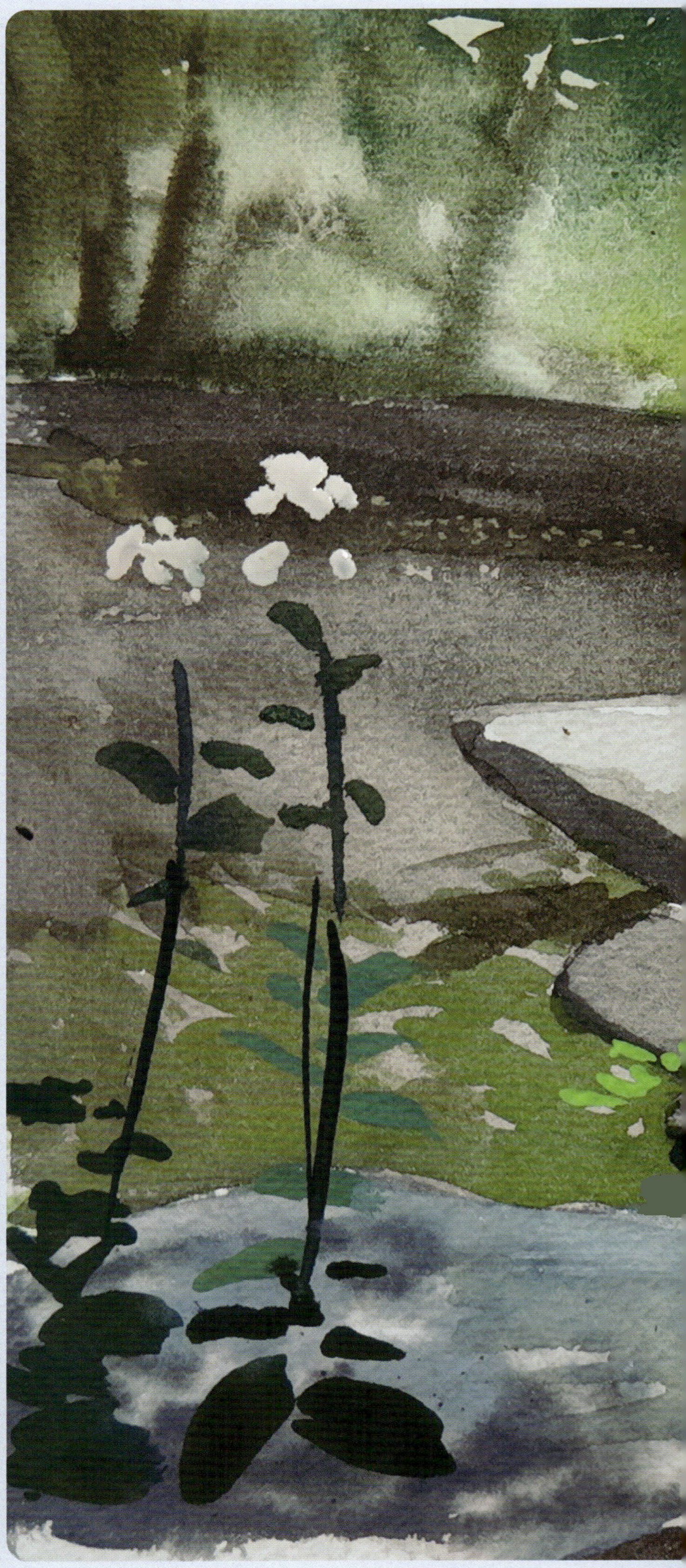

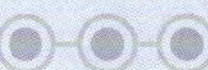

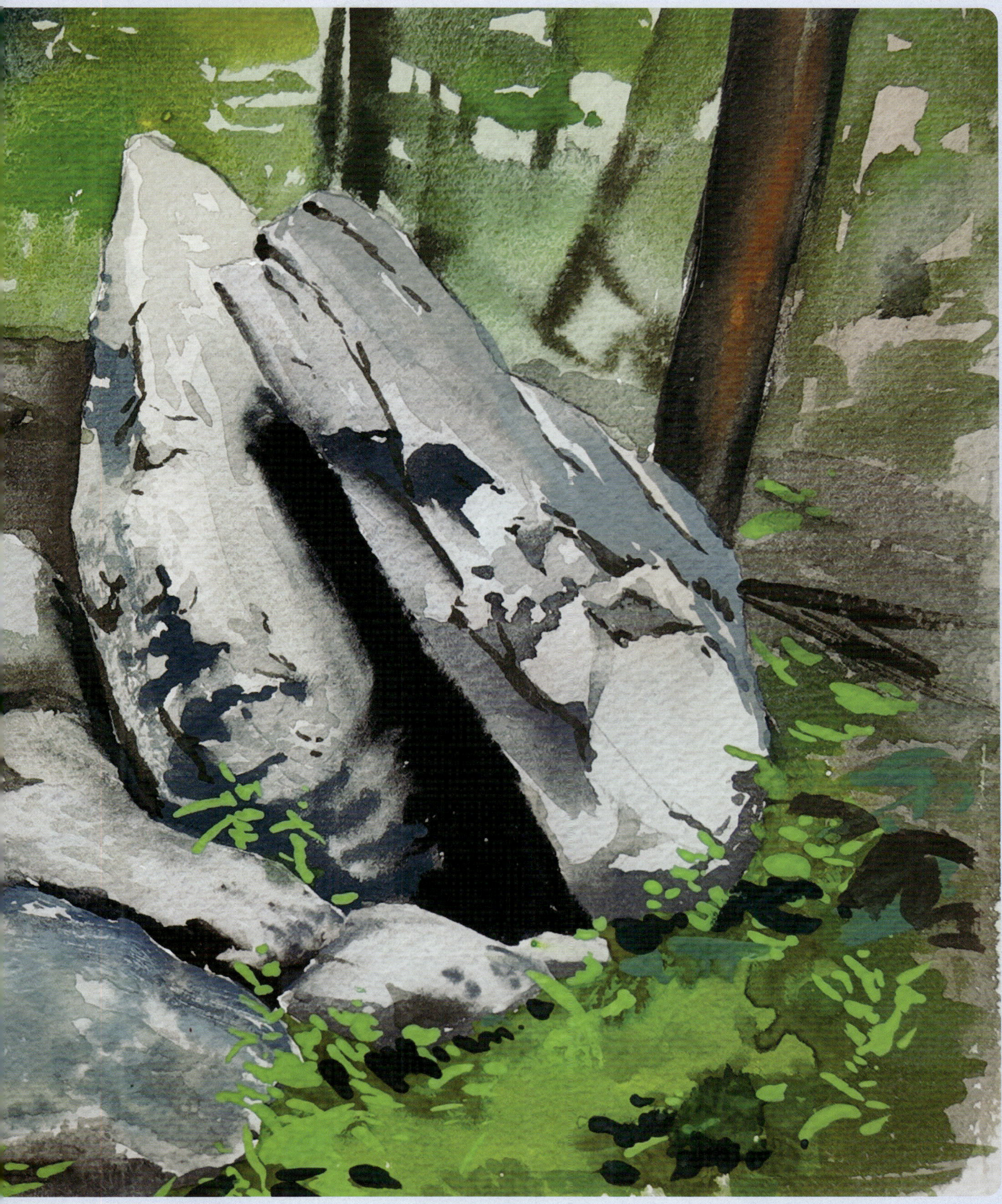

The finished study feels spontaneous, natural, and organic

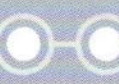

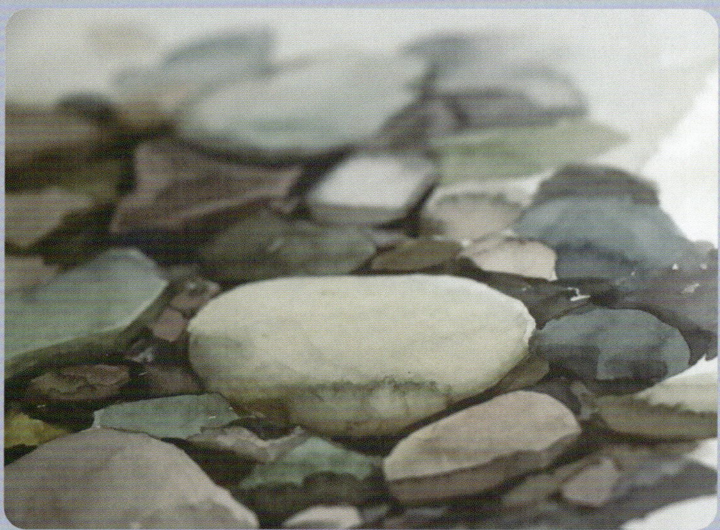

A sketchbook allows you to gather inspiration and study directly from nature

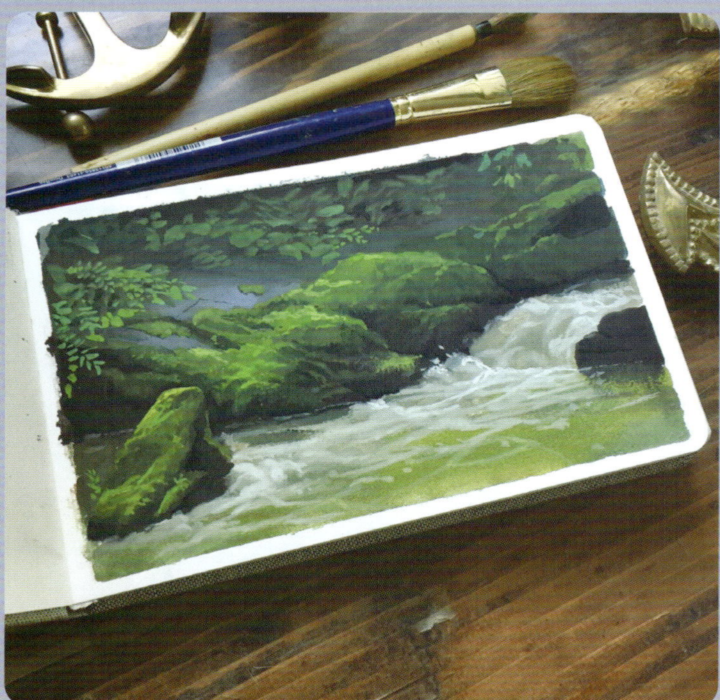

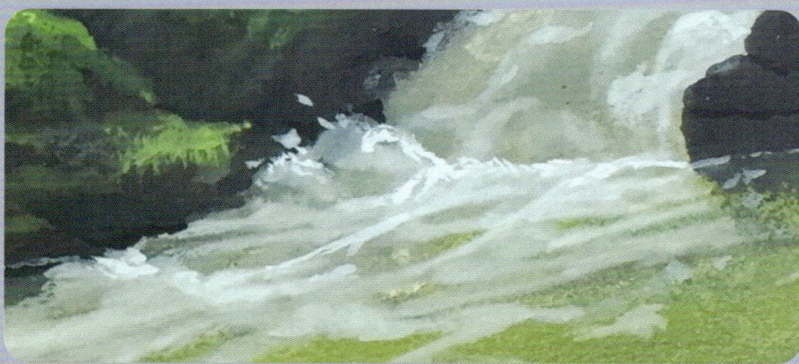

When painting ponds, lakes, and rivers, study how their surfaces are affected by reflections or lack thereof

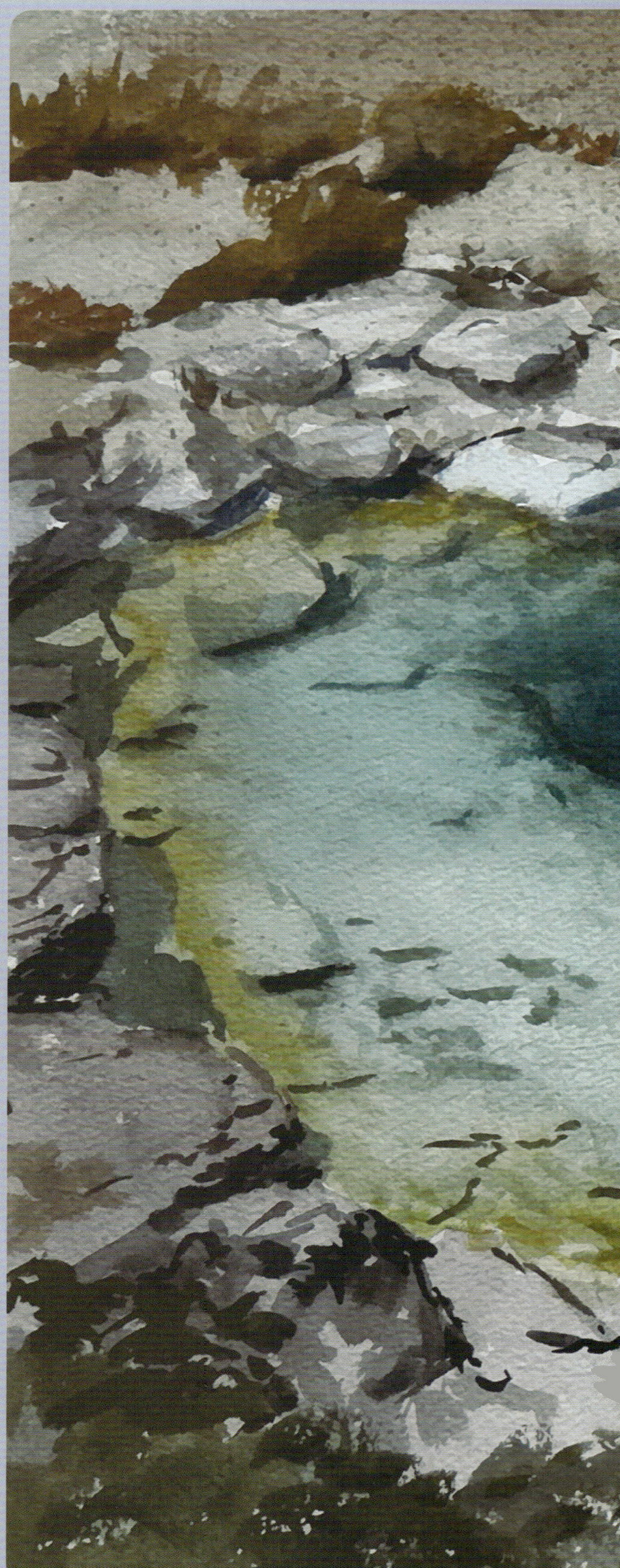

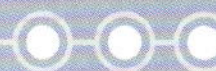

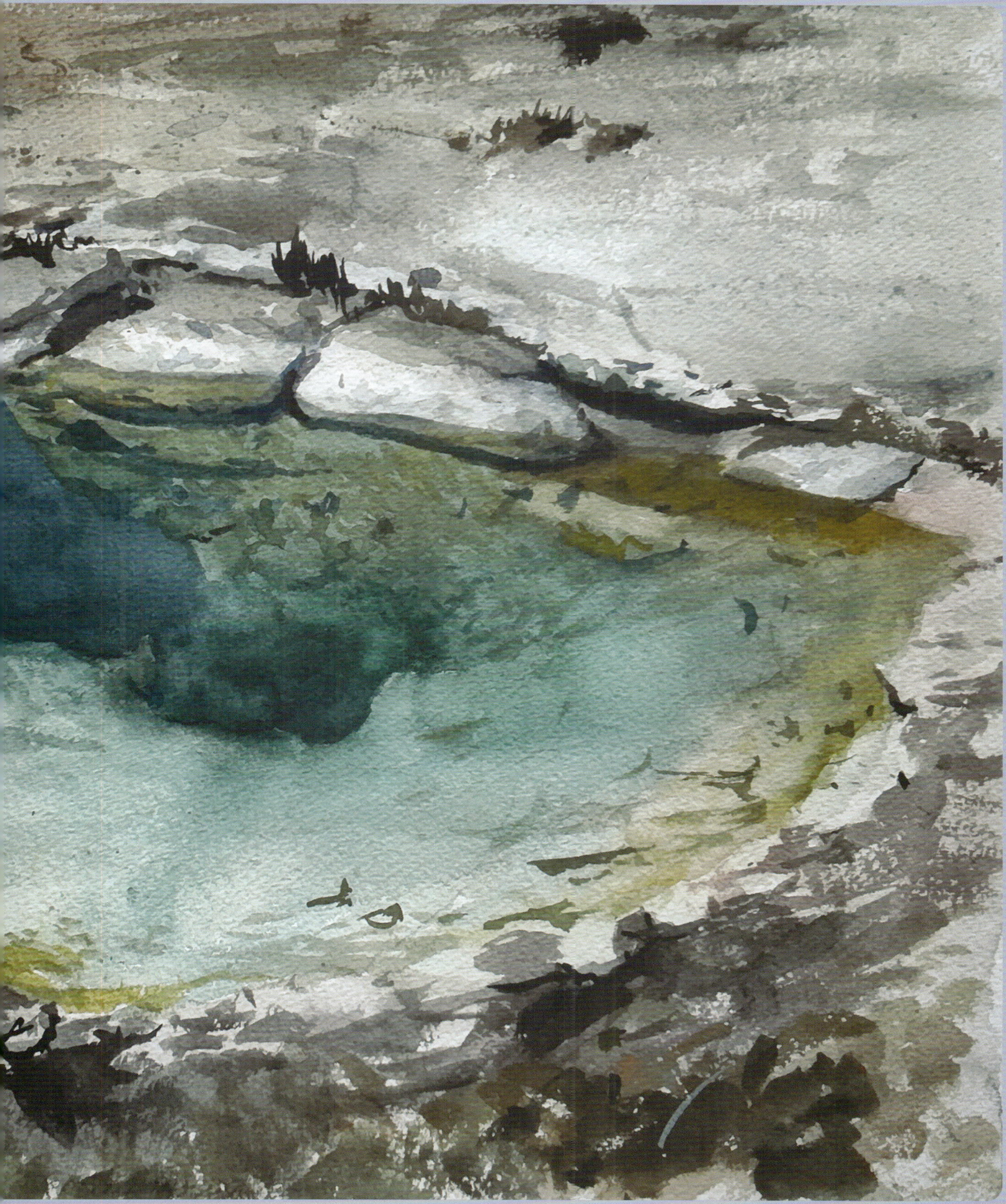

You can clearly see the difference between transparent and opaque coverage in this study of a clear pool

PAINTING WET TO DRY

Let's now talk about some more difficult ideas to integrate. We touched on a few of these in the second exercise, but we'll look at them more thoroughly now. This is our chance to explore the idea of 'wet to dry'. No matter what we do, whether we are painting a single stroke or a whole scene, our work will go from being wet to dry. The more comfortable you are with how this affects your work, the better equipped you'll be to master the paint.

Gouache is naturally inclined towards hard edges and hard transitions, but if you paint into an area of paper or paint that is still wet, you will get a much softer edge. The more water, the softer the edge. Conversely, the drier the paint or surface, the harder the edge or transition will be.

A WET-TO-DRY SCENE

This approach works on a stroke-by-stroke basis (painting one stroke, and then another into it) and on a whole-painting basis, where the whole painting might go from being wet to being dry – as the one below did.

Falls was started on entirely wet paper, with the focus first being on the soft transitions in the waterfall. As the paper dried, the harder transition of rocks and textures were added in. You can test out this method with the simple experiment on pages 64 and 65.

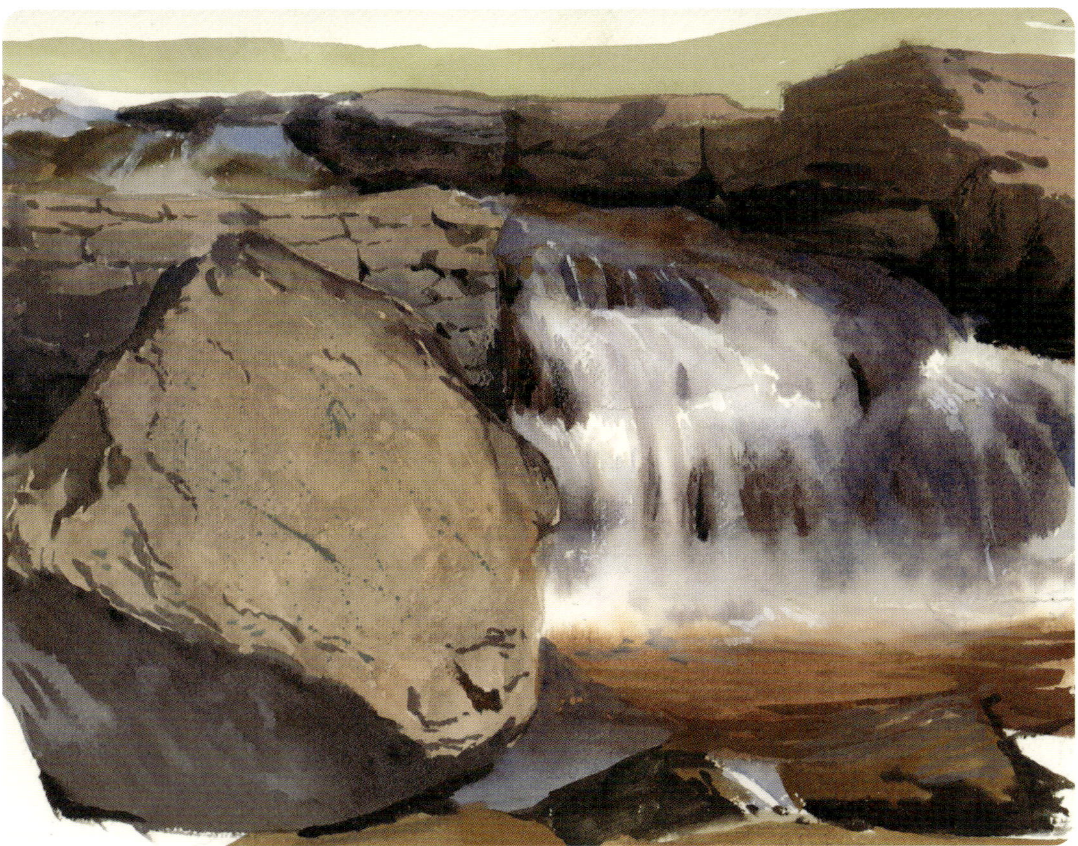

Falls is a good example of a piece painted from wet to dry

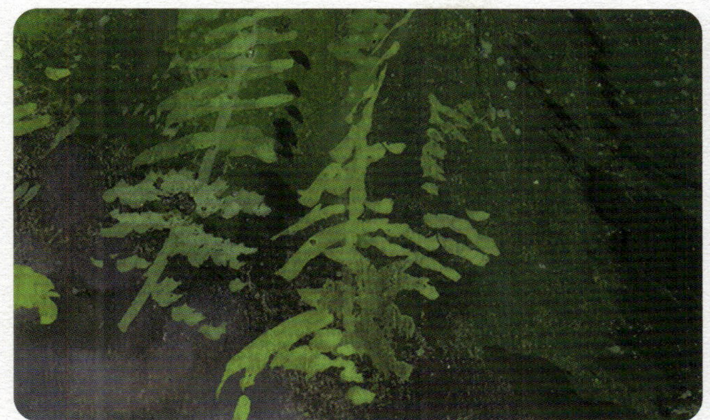

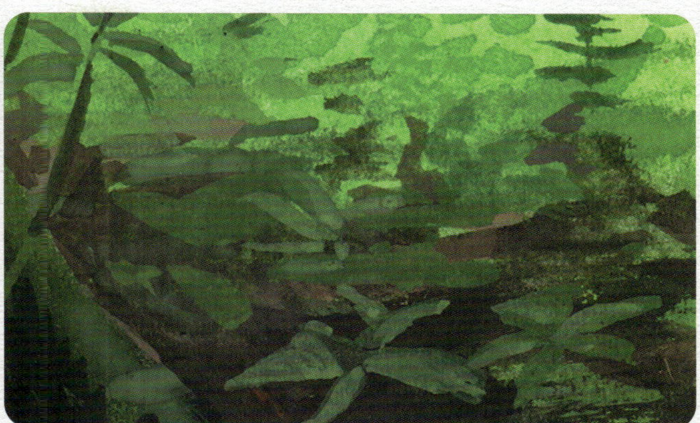

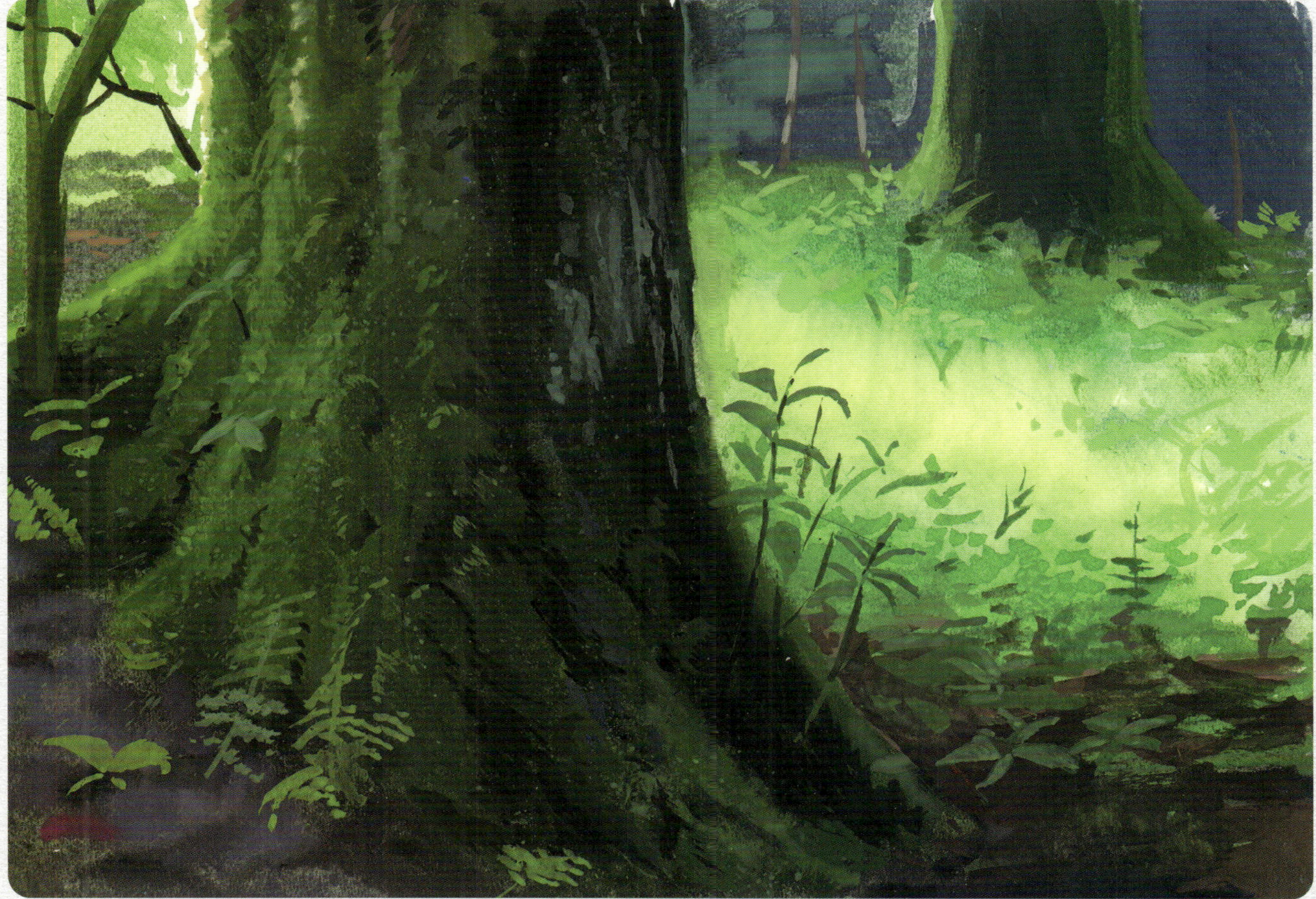

Combine the wet-to-dry paper approach with thin-to-thick paint application

FROM SOFT TO SOLID

In the painting above, I achieved a beautiful 'out of focus' feeling by painting wet to dry. I wet both sides of the paper with a brush and clean water. At first I didn't paint any details, just the big, soft movements of foliage in the background and the general form of the tree. As the paper started to dry, I moved into using thicker paint to get more solid statements of form and shape.

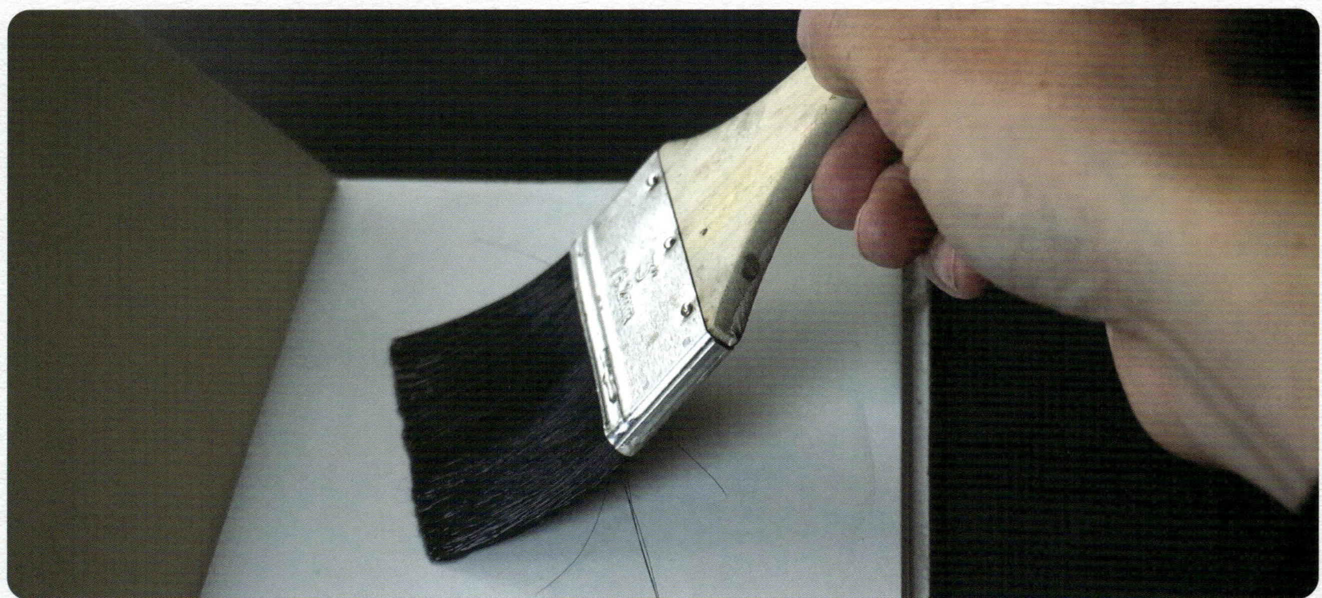

01. Use a large brush and clean water to wet both sides of the paper

01. PREP THE PAPER

Start by wetting the paper with clean water, starting on the back side and then wetting the front. Paper warps when water is unevenly distributed – the overly wet areas will bloat and the dry parts won't, which results in buckling. Wetting both sides of the paper evenly is very important for this reason.

02. WET SHEEN

Don't start painting until the reflective sheen on the paper has disappeared. In the image below you can see the heavy sheen of freshly wet paper – reflections in the water that's still sitting on top of the page. Once the page is wet but no longer reflective, you can start to paint.

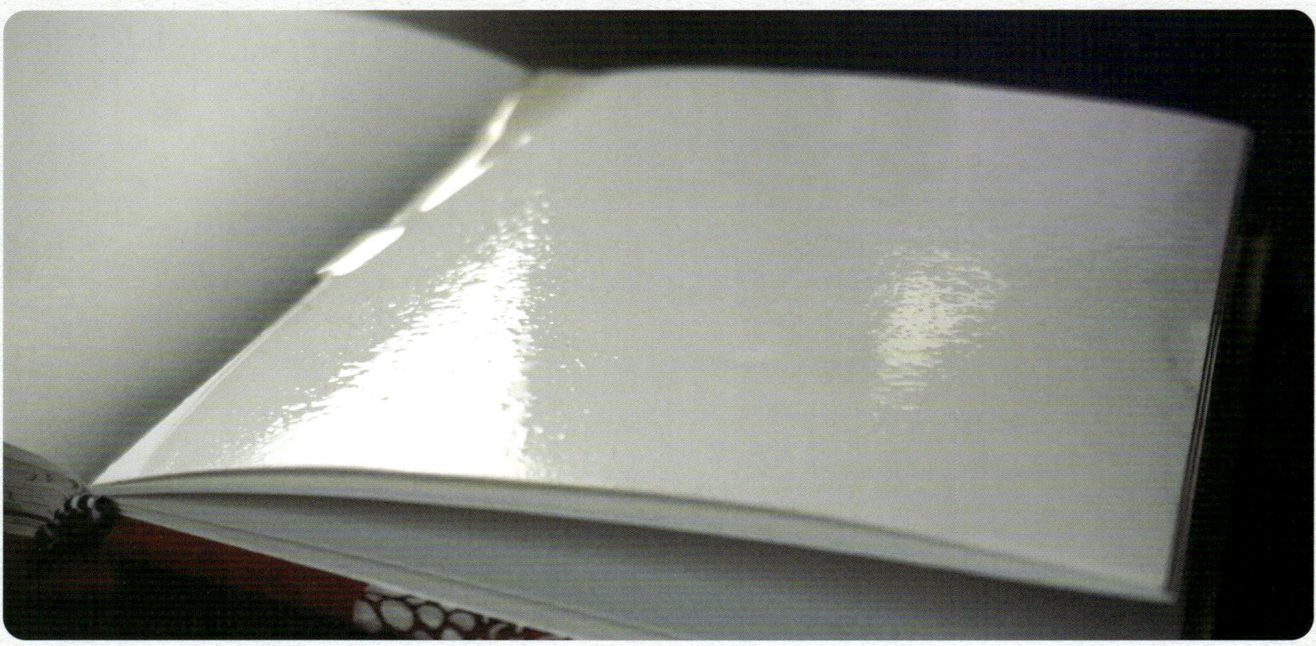

02. Shiny wet paper isn't ready for painting on

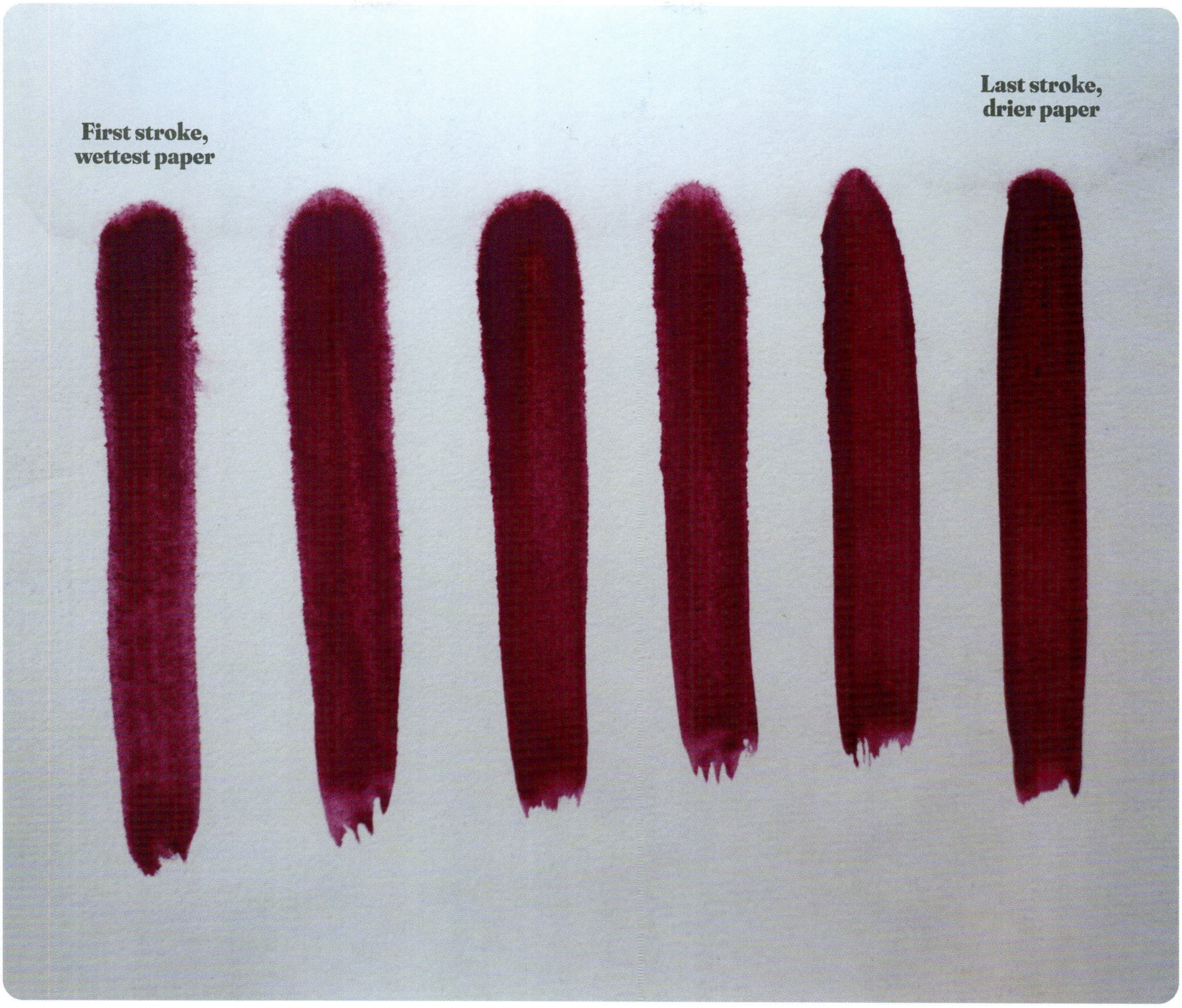

03. Brushstroke texture changes as the paper dries

03. STROKE COMPARISONS

Next, create a series of single brushstrokes, one minute apart, until the paper is dry. Use the same colour and try to use the same amount of paint each time. What you'll see is that the first brushstrokes (on the left side, above) end up with softer edges, then the drier the paper gets, the harder the edges become (towards the right). You can use this idea to help create edge variation and focus within your paintings.

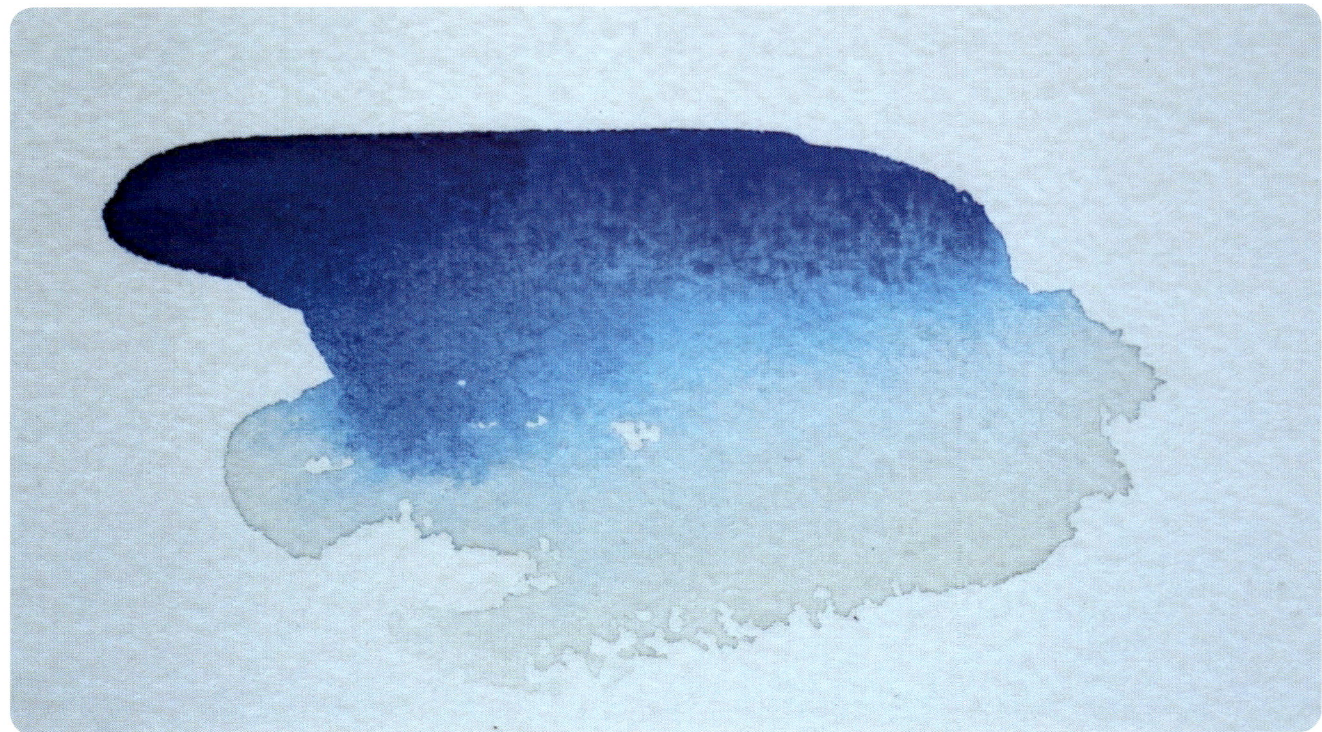

Use clean water to disperse a hard edge

SOFTENING AN EDGE

Now let's look at doing this on an individual brushstroke level. Any single brushstroke, like this hard-edged blue one, will go from wet to dry and enable us to change its edge quality. At some point in the drying process, take a brush loaded only with clean water and run it across the edge of the brushstroke. If you catch the paint early in the drying process, you'll get an edge like this, where the paint is dispersed in a dramatic fashion. You can wait until later in the process to soften up an edge, as we did in step 06 of the nature-painting demo (page 53).

WET-ON-WET COLOUR

Instead of using water, you can use a second colour to paint 'wet on wet' – the process is the same. You'll see the same softening of edges as the colours are laid side by side. The longer you wait between applying colours, the harder the resulting edges; the sooner you paint, the softer the mixed edge between will be.

I used this idea in this painting below. The tree was catching the last light of the sun, so I placed down the golden yellow of the tree first. Then, while it was still a little wet, I placed the darker green to create the soft transition from light to shadow.

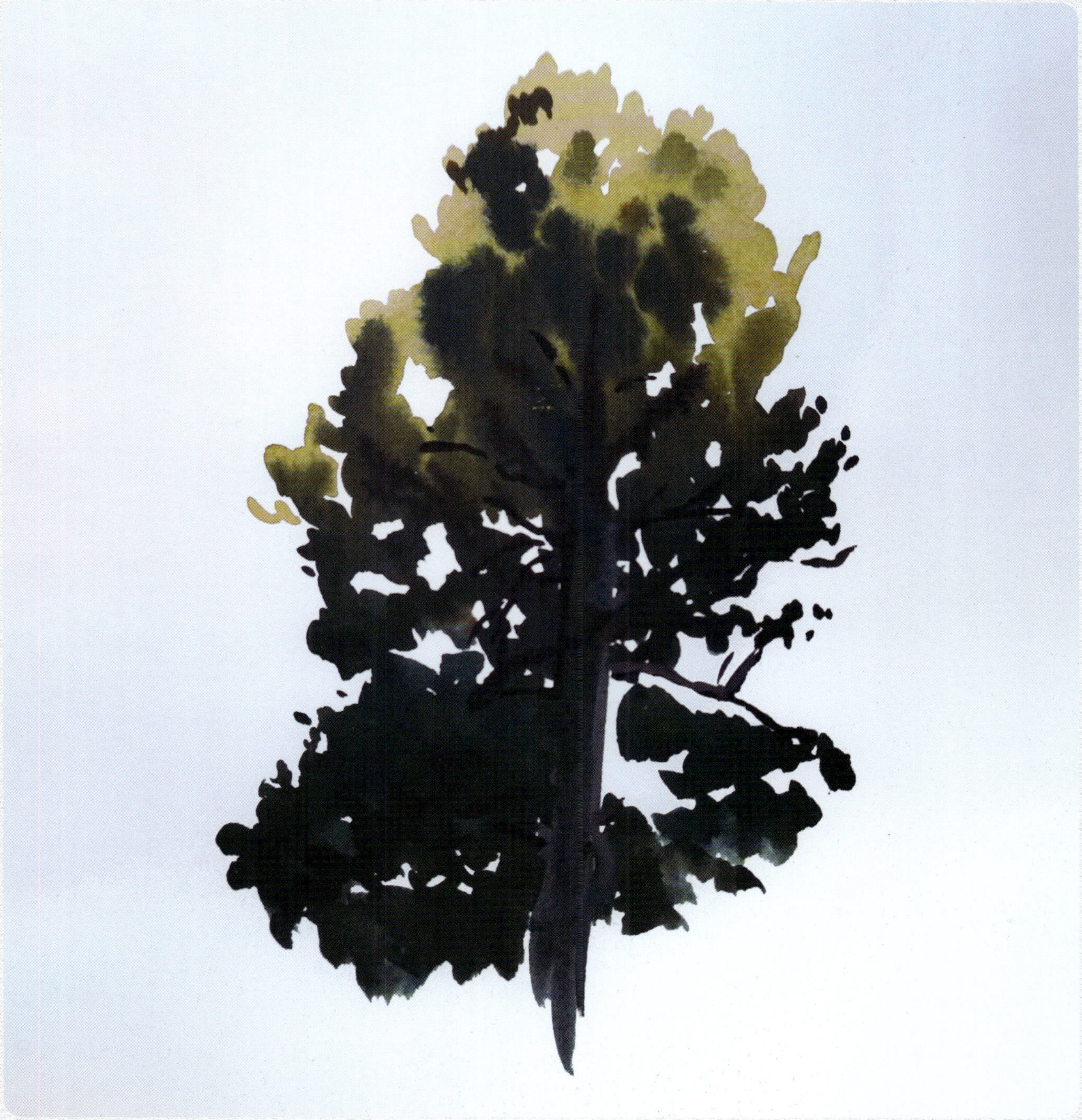

Try softening with a second colour instead of only water

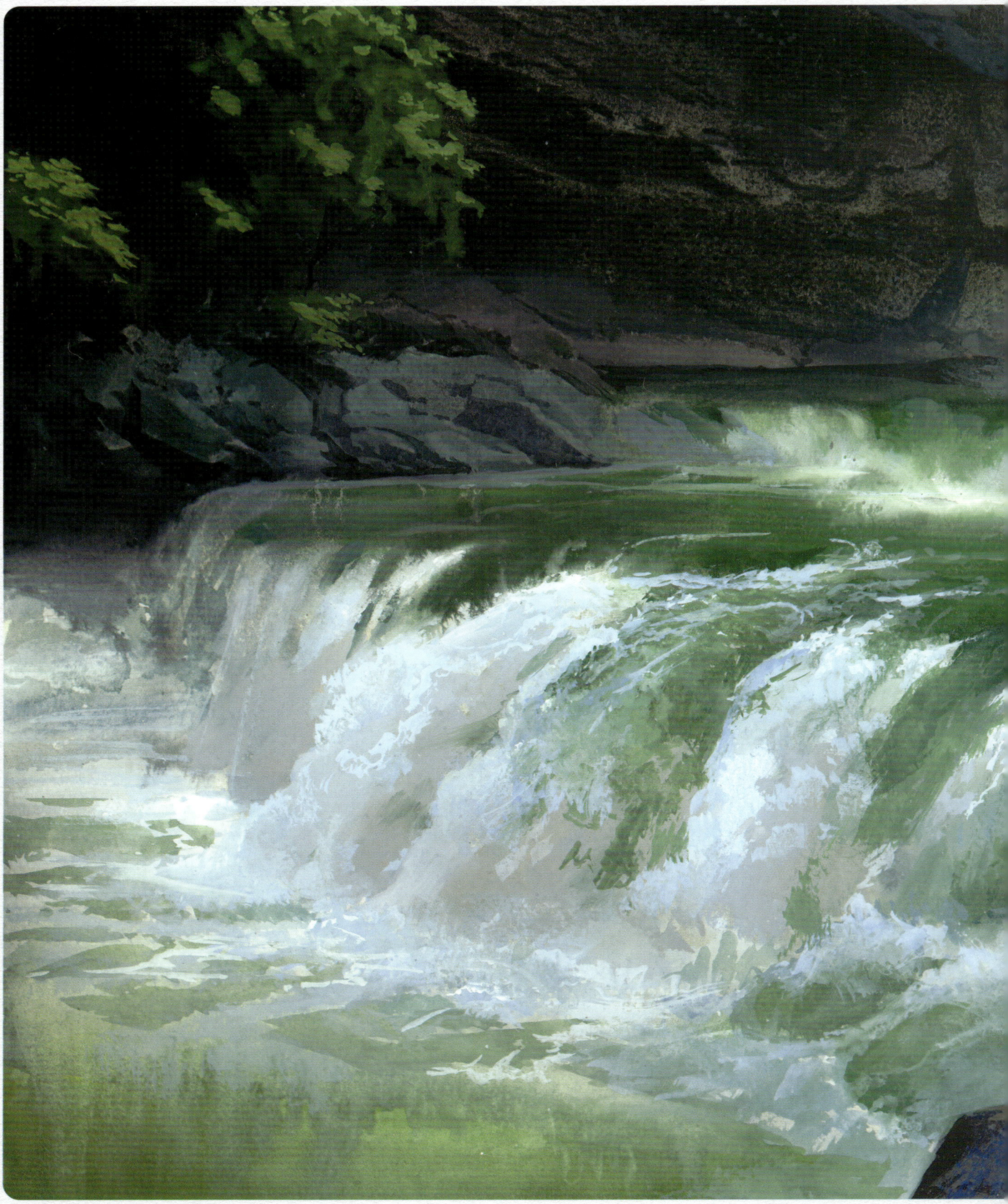

Start from the large, soft areas before narrowing down

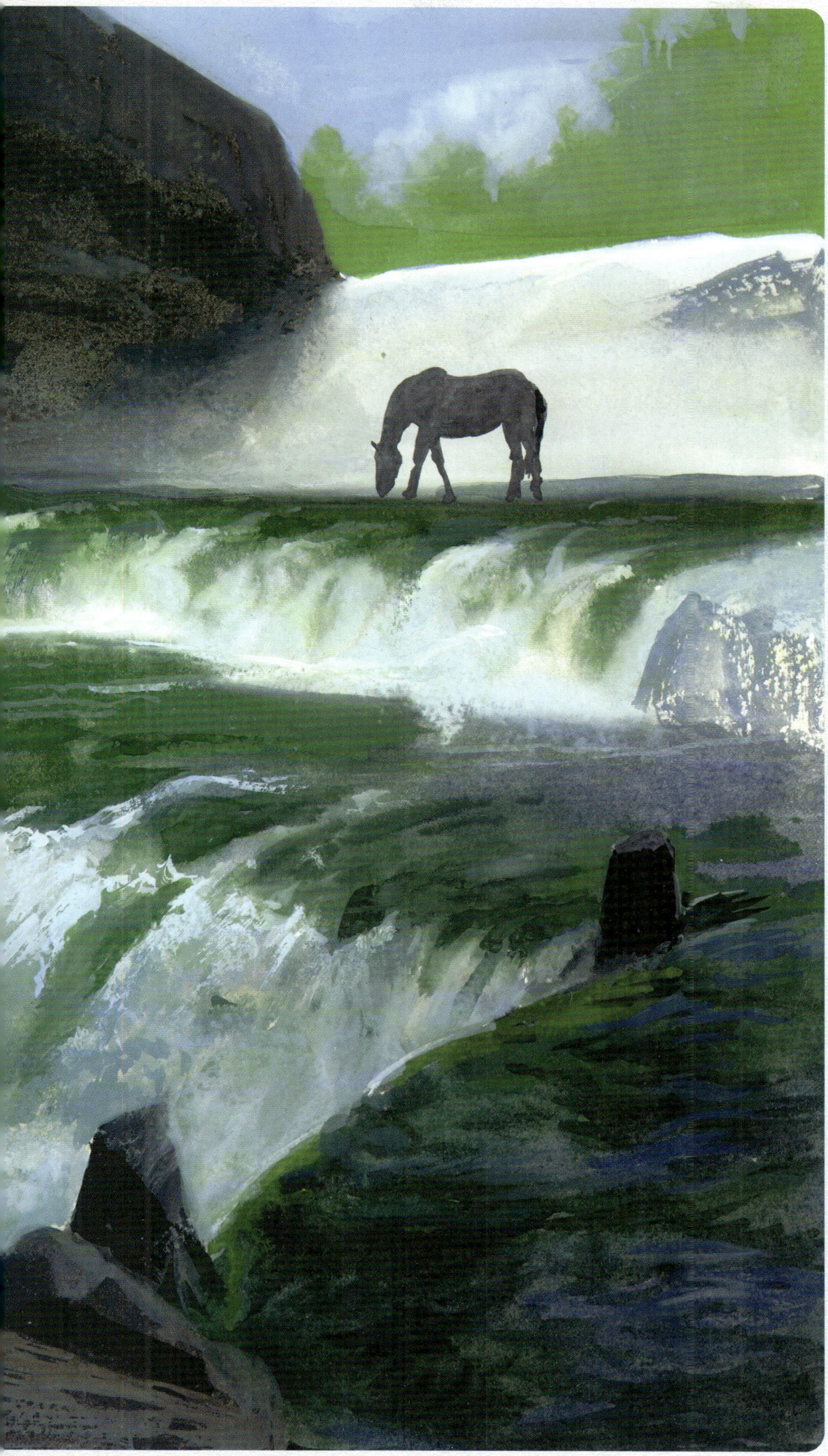

LARGER PAINTINGS

This is a large gouache painting where I used the wet-to-dry method. Using lots of water *and* lots of paint at the same time means you can have soft transitions without the painting feeling like a transparent watercolour. Start with the areas that you know will have soft transitions (such as the foam in the waterfalls). Focus on the large shapes and slowly, as everything dries, get more specific and work on smaller details.

HEAVY LAYERING

This painting relied on a different idea – 'layering and loading'. It was a dry time of year and the paint was drying *very* quickly, so when I put a stroke down, that was it. No blending, no soft transitions. Instead I added interest by leaning into what the paint was doing – allowing for lots of dry texture and heavy layering, and letting the previous layer shine through where the thick paint allowed. As for 'loading', I loaded the paintbrush with multiple colours at the same time to evoke the feeling of leaves and needles scattered on the floor.

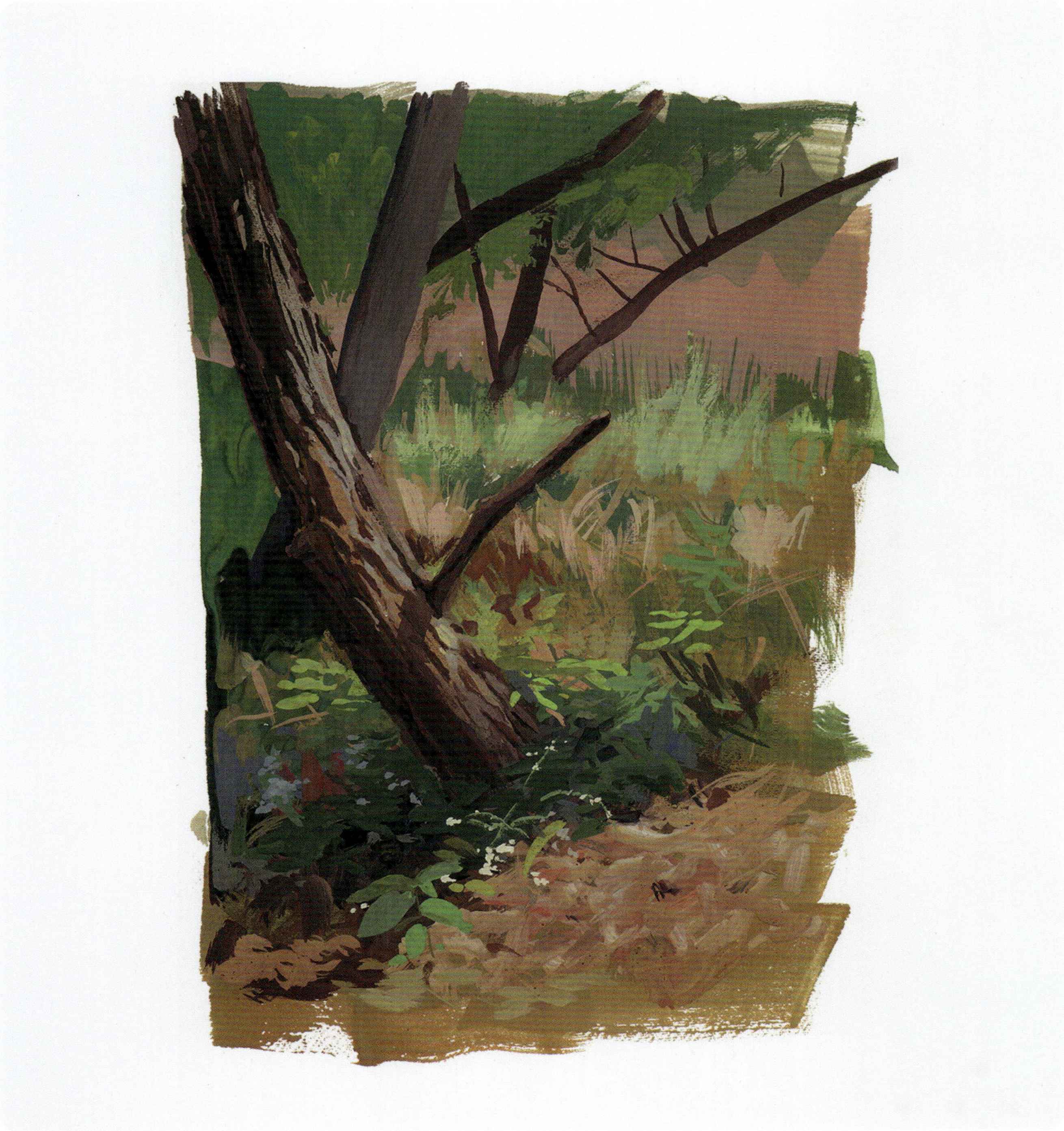

These thick, dry layers are often made with a brush loaded with multiple colours

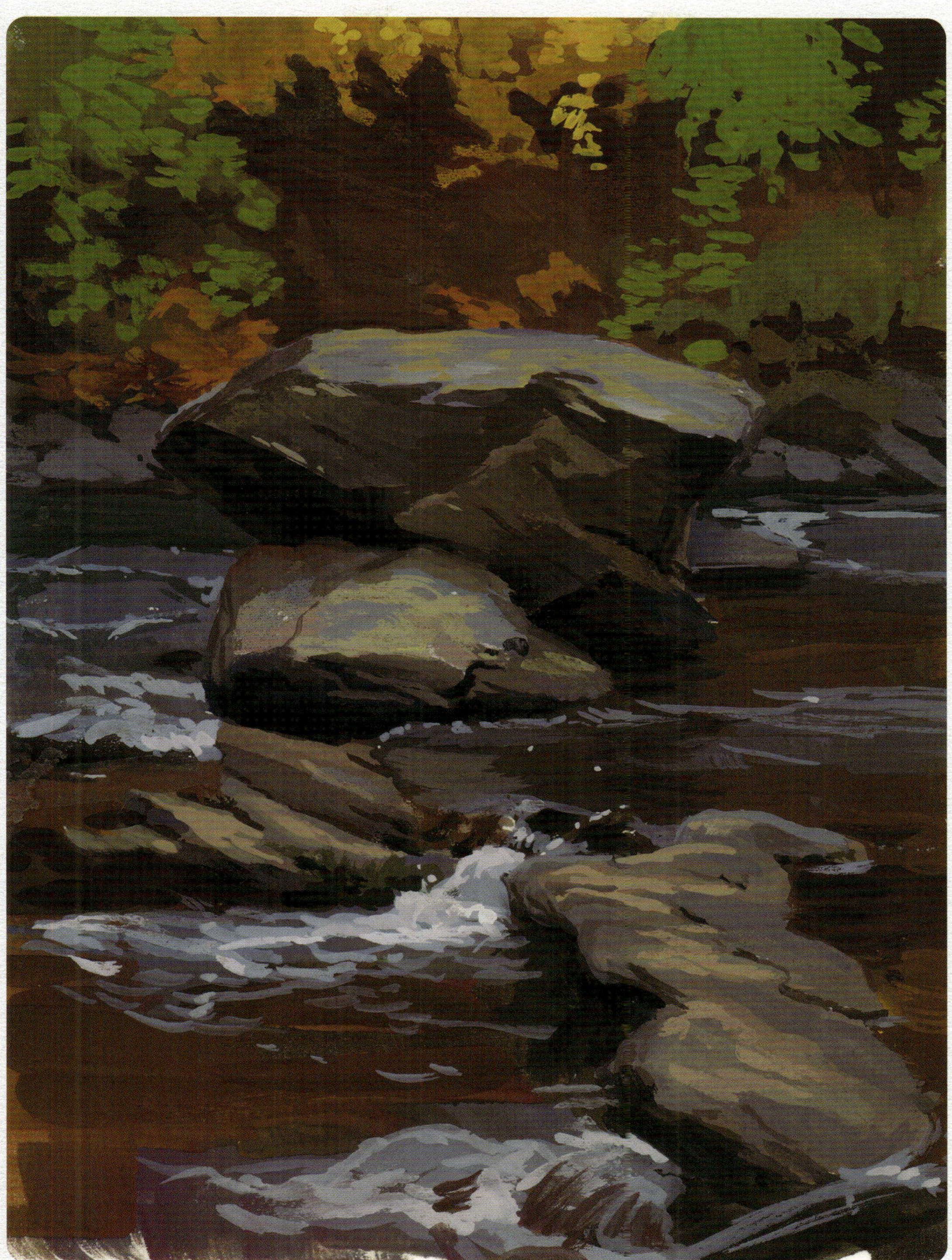

Observe reality and follow what the paint wants to do

PAINTING IS A CONVERSATION

Here's my last word on advanced techniques. No single technique will save you or make your art great. Rely on observation, even when working from imagination (more on that in a minute). And finally, lean into what the paint wants to do. If there is a fight between you and the paint, the paint will win. Painting is a three-way conversation between you, your subject, and your paint. It's not a monologue.

PAINTING FROM THE IMAGINATION

One sentiment that you might come across is that painting from the imagination and painting from life are two separate and distinct acts. While on the surface this might appear true, it doesn't take long to realize that those who have the ability to draw and paint from their imagination have only been able to do so following a thorough and sincere study of nature. Your most direct path towards fluency in painting from your imagination is to study what's in front of you. My favourite approach to this is to follow a three-step method: deconstruction, reconstruction, and synthesis.

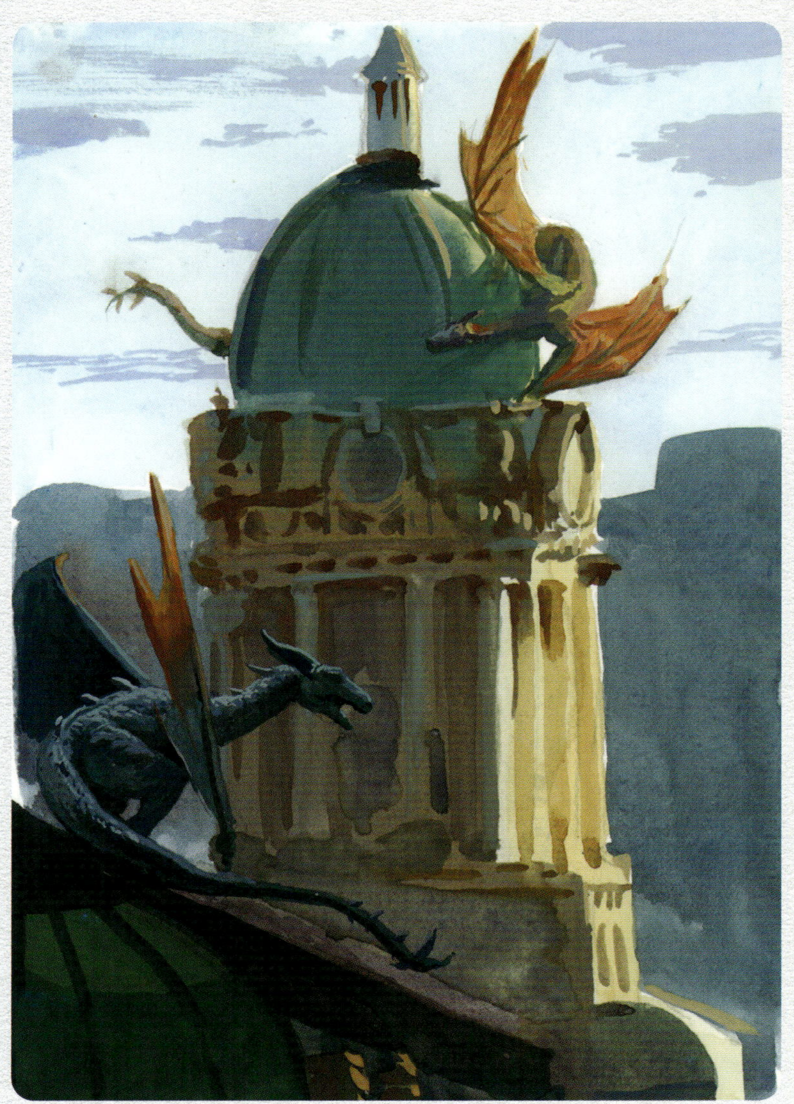

You can take the ordinary and make it extraordinary by adding just a few fictional elements

DECONSTRUCTION

First, break down a few scenes that you might like to paint. This is an observational act. Sit and absorb everything in front of you. You might be itching to move on to painting or drawing it all out, but just sit. You will see more than you could imagine.

RECONSTRUCTION

Reconstruct those scenes so that you get a real practical feel. This is where you take out your paint and start to note things down visually. The better you are at practical skills, such as colour-matching and drawing, the easier this step will be for you.

SYNTHESIS

Create something new using the principles and elements you have been studying. Take a forest and make it twice as large. Take a mountain and put a castle on it. Synthesis requires a really strong sense of lighting. If there is one thing that needs to be cohesive throughout your new painting, it's the lighting. Get the lighting right and you can make the viewer believe the most unbelievable things. You will see that everything we do, even while being full of magic and fantasy, is grounded in reality.

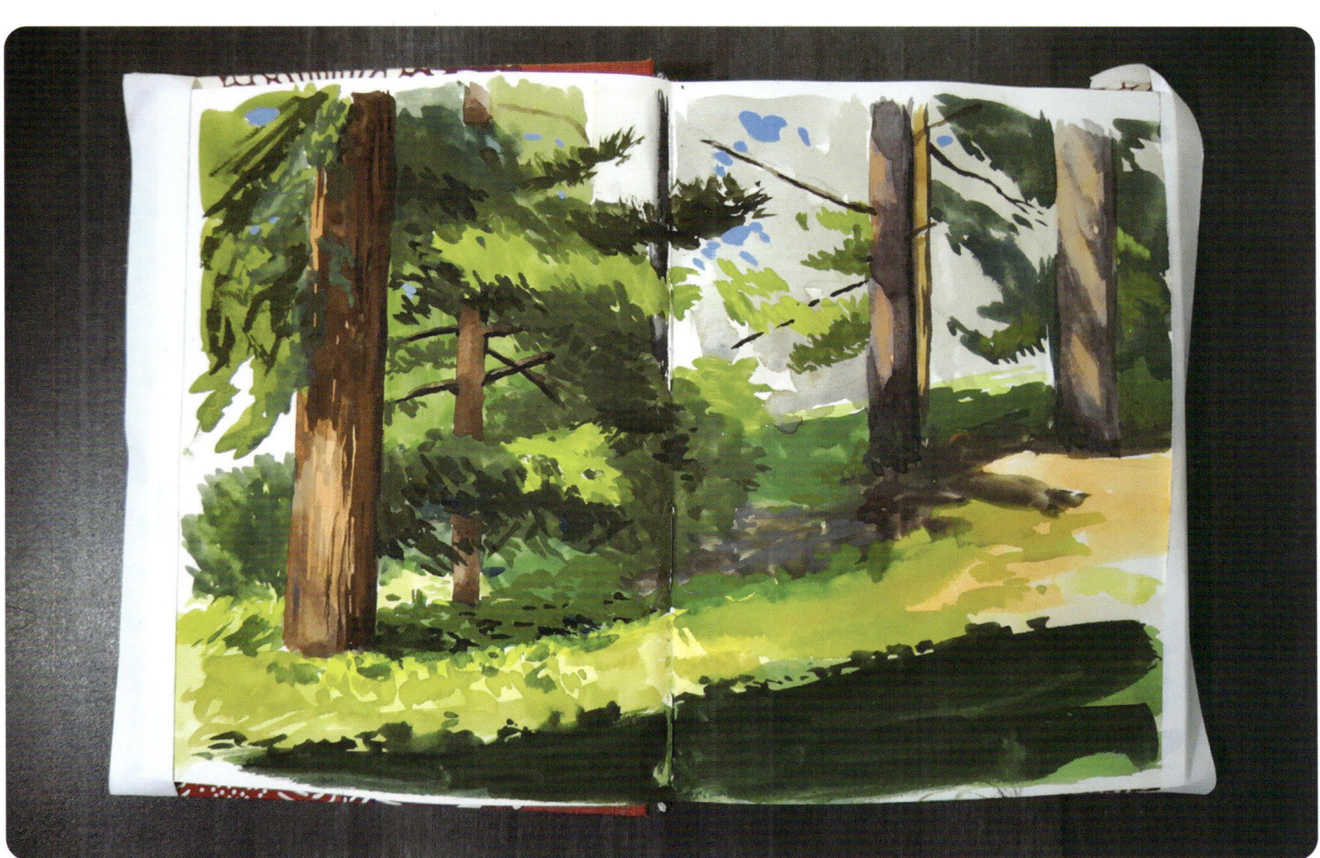

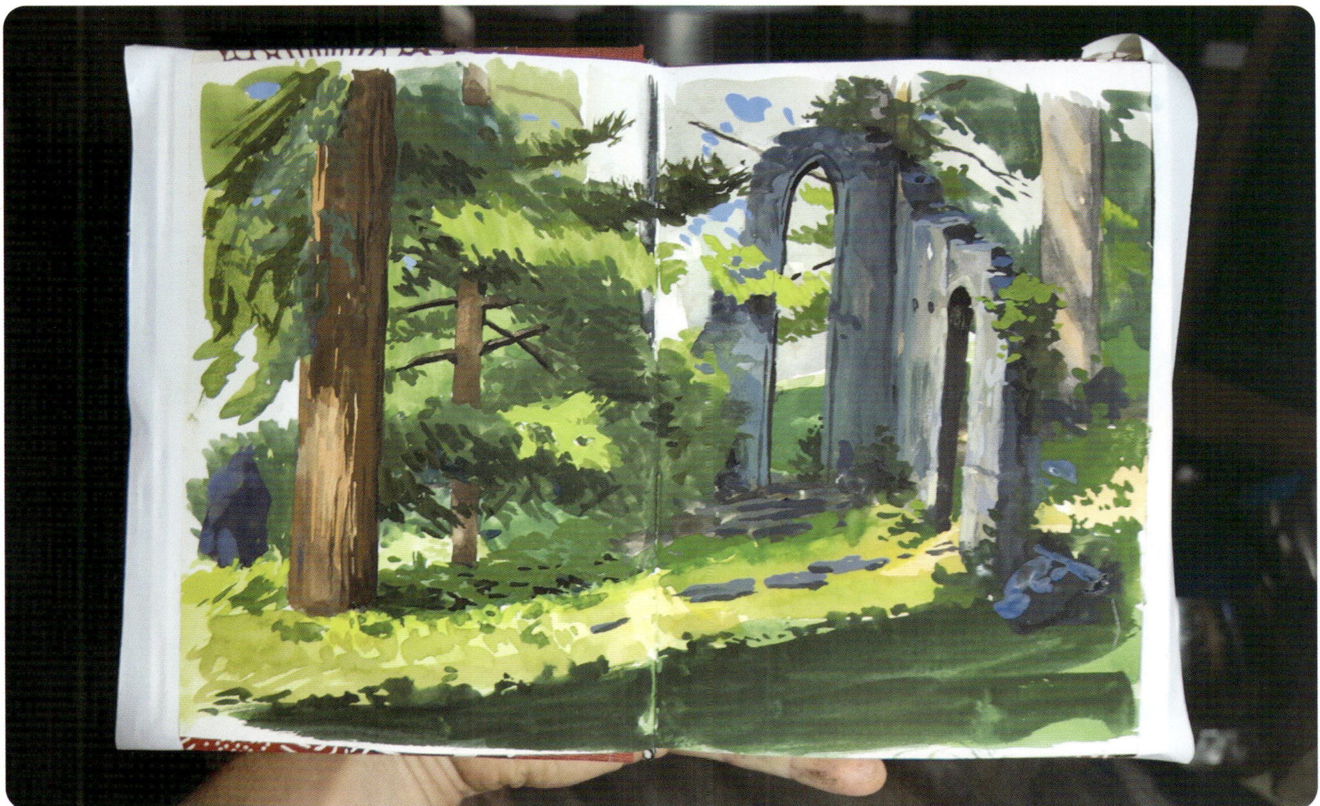

Here's an example of taking a nature study and using it as a basis for a fictional scene – the mysterious ruins were added later!

AUTHENTICITY OVER ORIGINALITY

Ironically, fantasy has always been used as a medium in which to tell the truth. When we are using our art to communicate, we are looking to find things that are important to us, for whatever internal or external reasons we might have, and to communicate them in ways we expect others to be able to understand. If I were to give you something entirely original, you wouldn't like it, because it would be completely unrelatable to you. You wouldn't understand what it is you see. Thus in our pursuit to increase our ability to better communicate the wild and brilliant fantasy, we must take reality and amplify it.

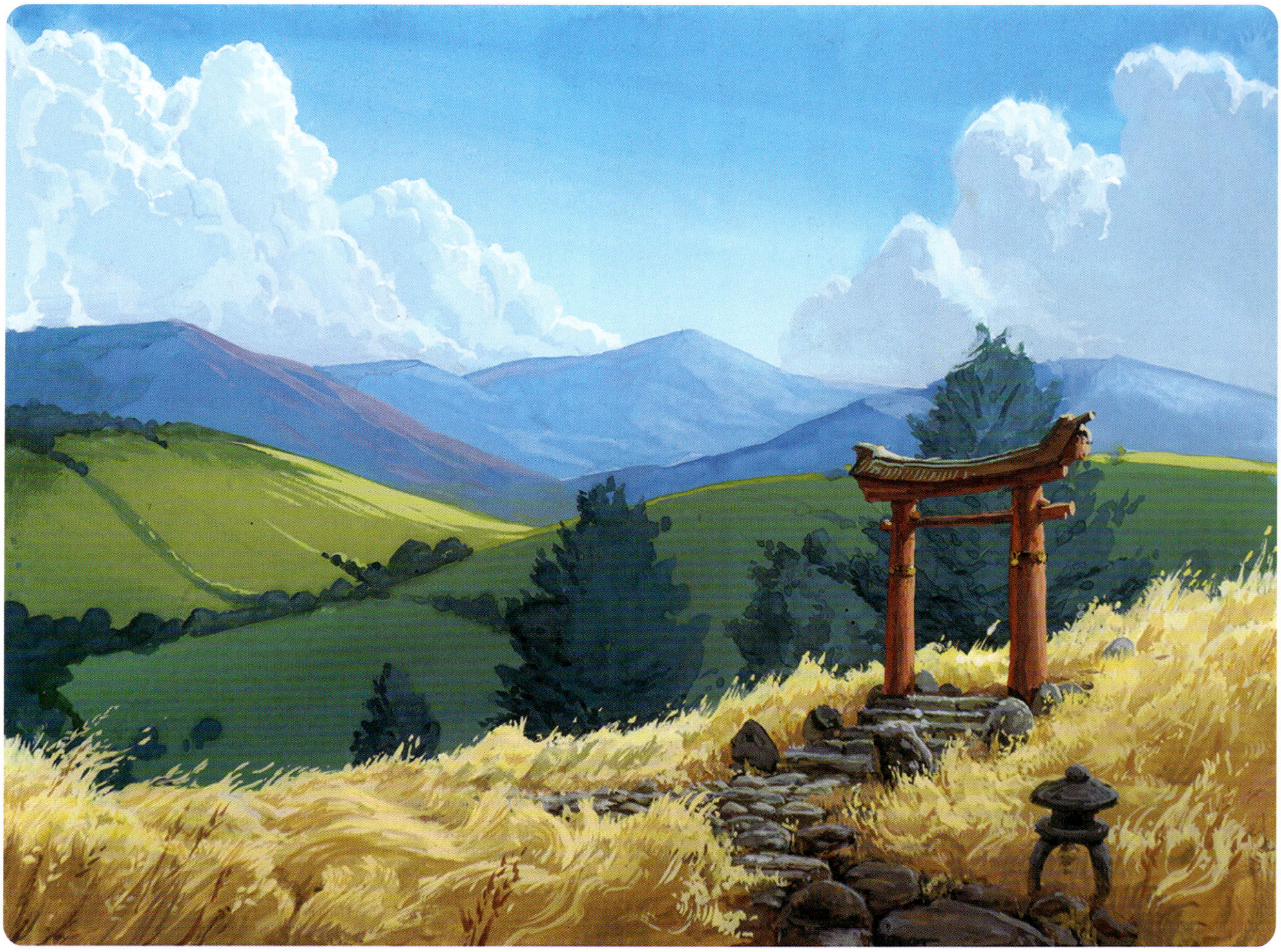

Torii. Find the most interesting parts of reality and multiply them

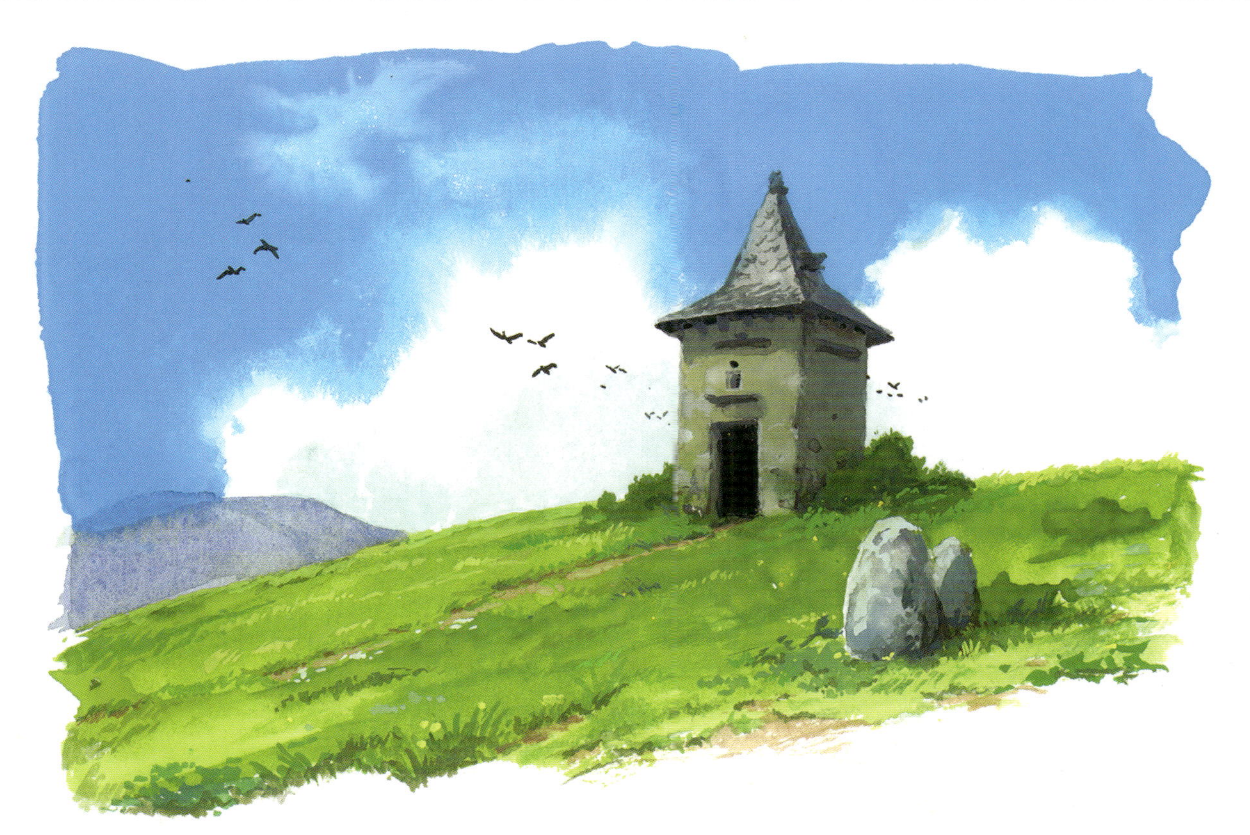

Hut. Take something simple and make it moody

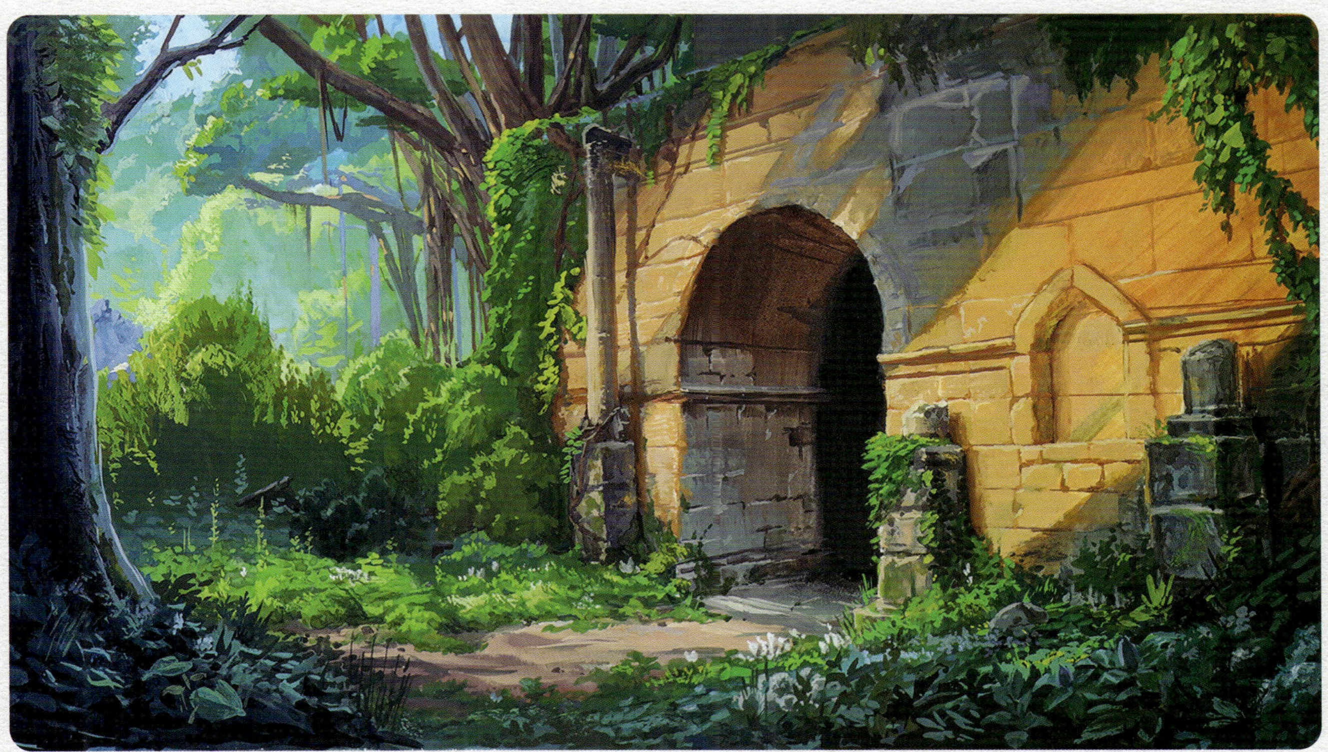

Doorway to Somewhere. Create scenes from your imagination by combining the things you love most

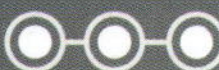

TUTORIALS

Now that you are acquainted with the essentials of gouache, it's time to try your hand at some more complex projects. In the following chapters, six talented professional painters will share their process for creating a fantasy scene with gouache. These will include fully imagined scenes, plein air-inspired landscapes that put a twist on real references, and paintings on white paper, black paper, and even wooden board. Each artist will guide you step by step through their unique personal process, from rough sketches to final images.

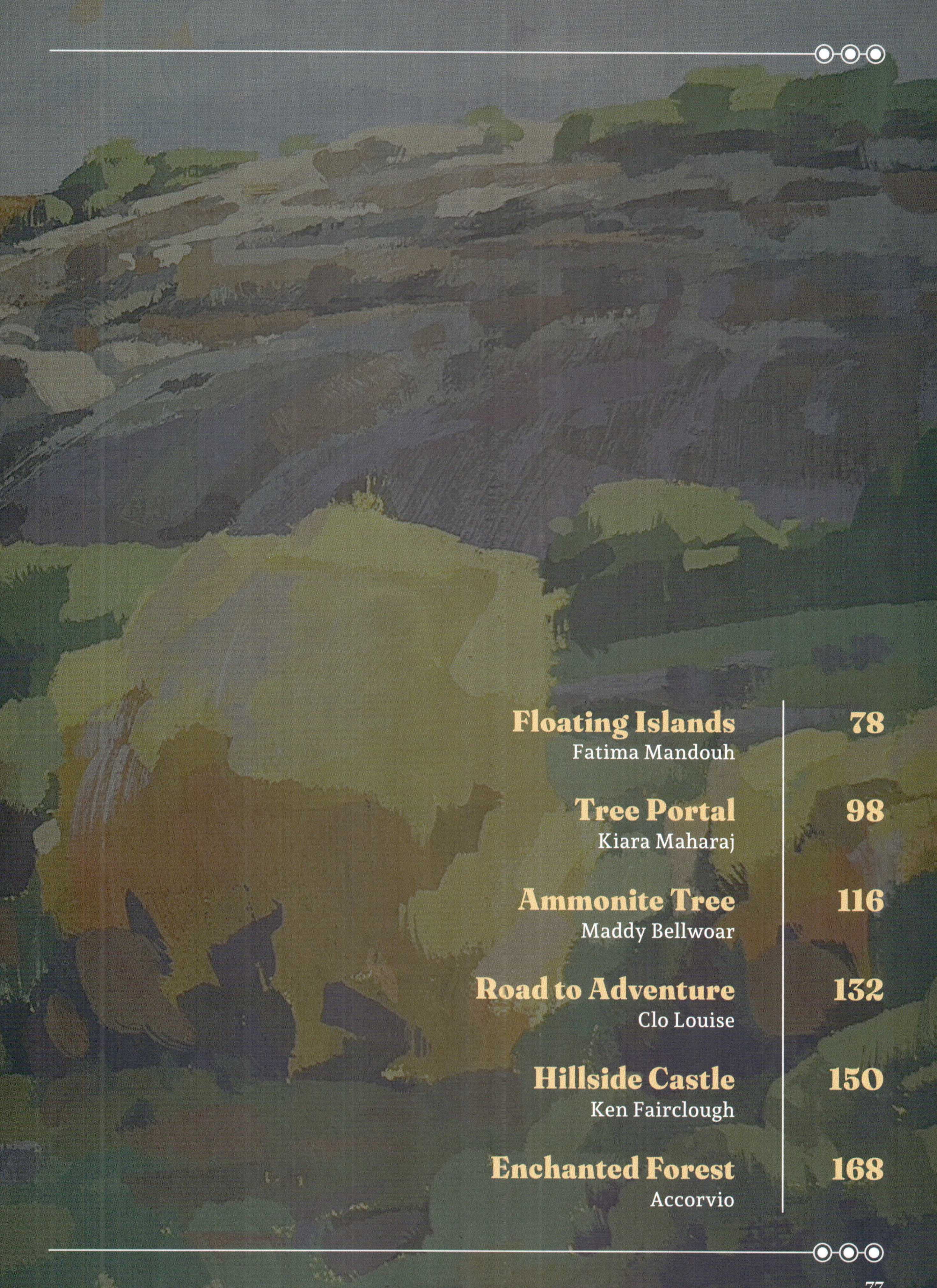

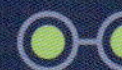

Final image © Fatima Mandouh

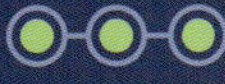

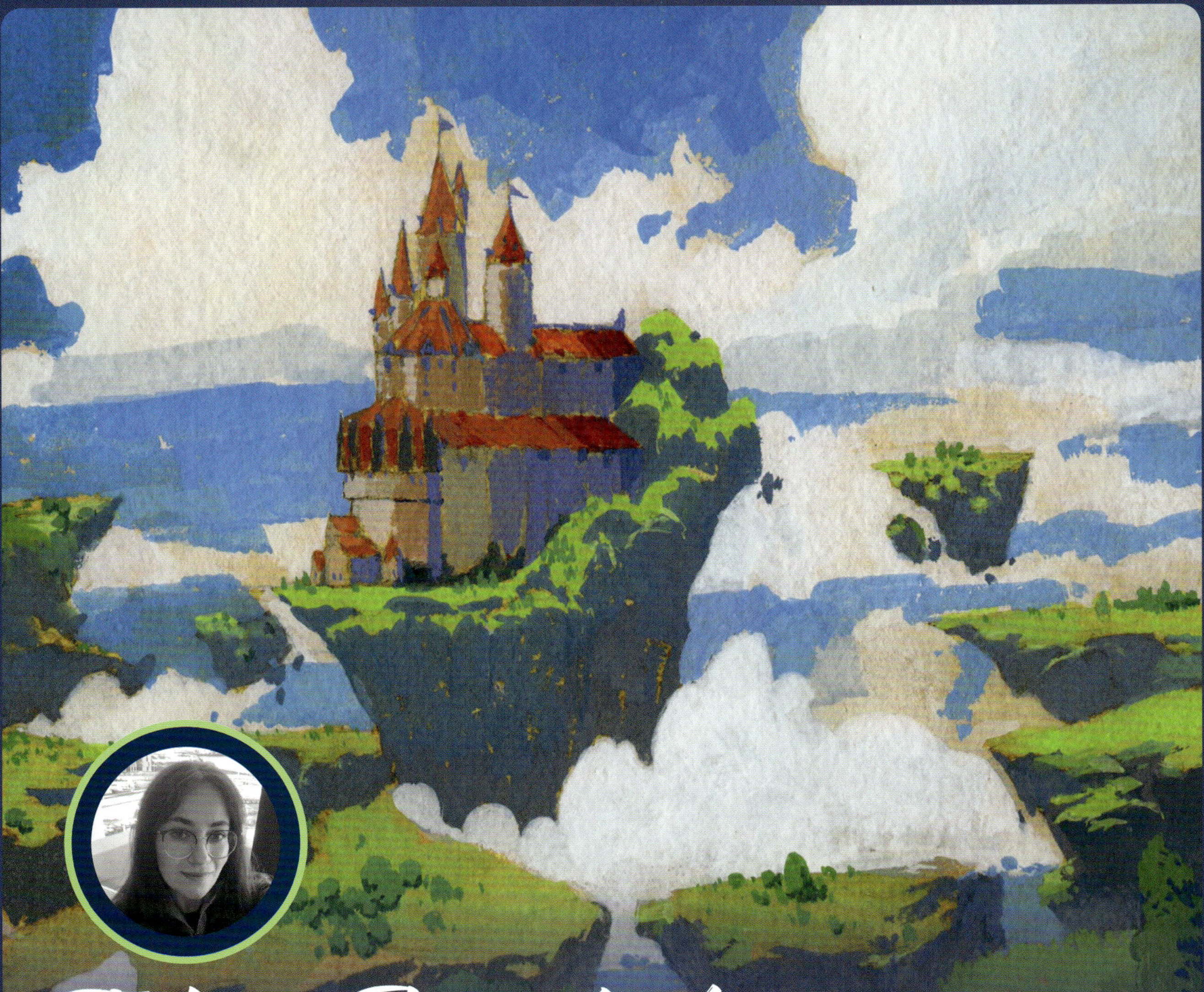

Fatima Mandouh

FLOATING ISLANDS

In this tutorial, I'll show you how to paint a breathtaking landscape of floating rocks and a grand castle suspended in the sky. The scene will capture a magical atmosphere, with dramatic rock formations hovering in the air and a majestic castle at the centre, surrounded by the vast, serene, cloudy sky. The whole scene will have a dreamy, otherworldly vibe. I love working with gouache because it's so versatile and produces such vibrant results. It can seem a bit intimidating at first, but my goal is to show you how fun and forgiving it can be!

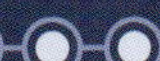

I'll be using a set of M. Graham & Co. primary colours plus black and white. Azo Yellow is a bright yellow similar to Cadmium Yellow Light, but slightly less opaque; Naphthol Red is a warm-toned red similar to Cadmium Red Light, but also less opaque. I'll use a bit of Yellow Ochre watercolour to create a translucent base, but you can substitute diluted Yellow Ochre gouache or mix a dark yellow using your gouache primaries and lots of water.

COLOUR LIST

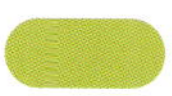 Azo Yellow

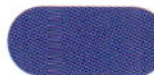 Cobalt Blue

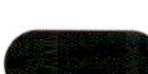 Ivory Black

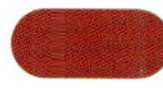 Naphthol Red

 Titanium White

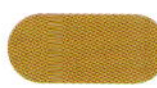 Yellow Ochre (watercolour or gouache)

TOOLKIT

- **Watercolour paper**
  11" × 15", 400 gsm (150 lb)

- **Rag or paper towel**

- **Mixing tray**

- **Jar of water**

- **Spray bottle**

- **Pencil**
  (for sketching)

- **Painter's tape**

- **Stapler**

- **Matte fixative spray**

BRUSHES

Princeton Velvetouch Chisel Blender brushes
Sizes 6 & 8

Princeton Select Artiste Flat Shader brushes
Sizes 2, 4, & 8

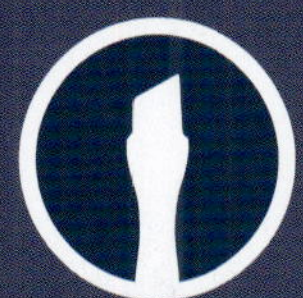
Princeton Select Artiste Angle Shader brush
¼"

01.

These are the materials I will be using for this project. I'll be painting on a sheet of St. Armand's handmade Dominion paper, which is cold-press cotton-rag paper with torn edges, but any similarly heavy paper will work well. Feel free to adjust based on your own tools and personal preferences – it's important to choose what works for you.

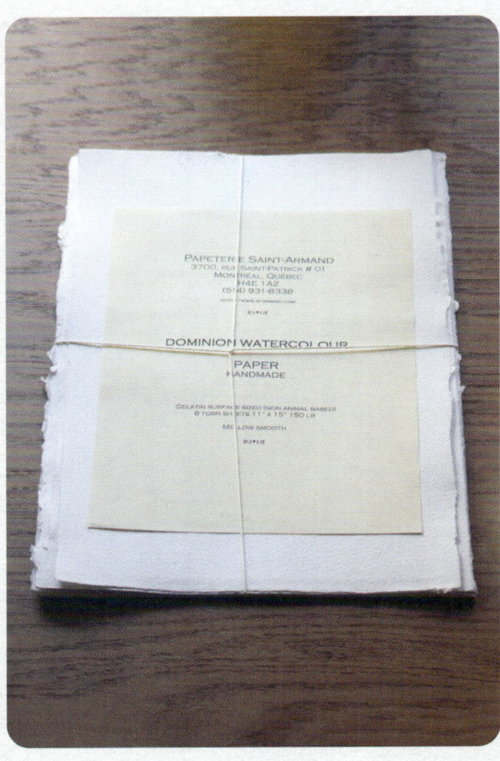

01a. St. Armand cotton-rag paper

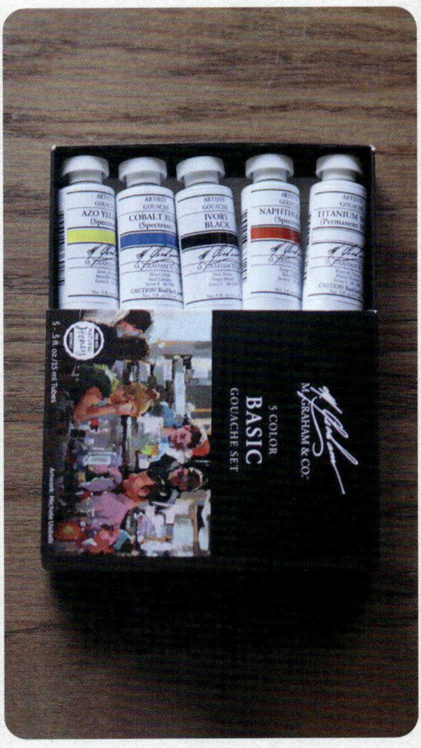

01b. Five essential gouache colours

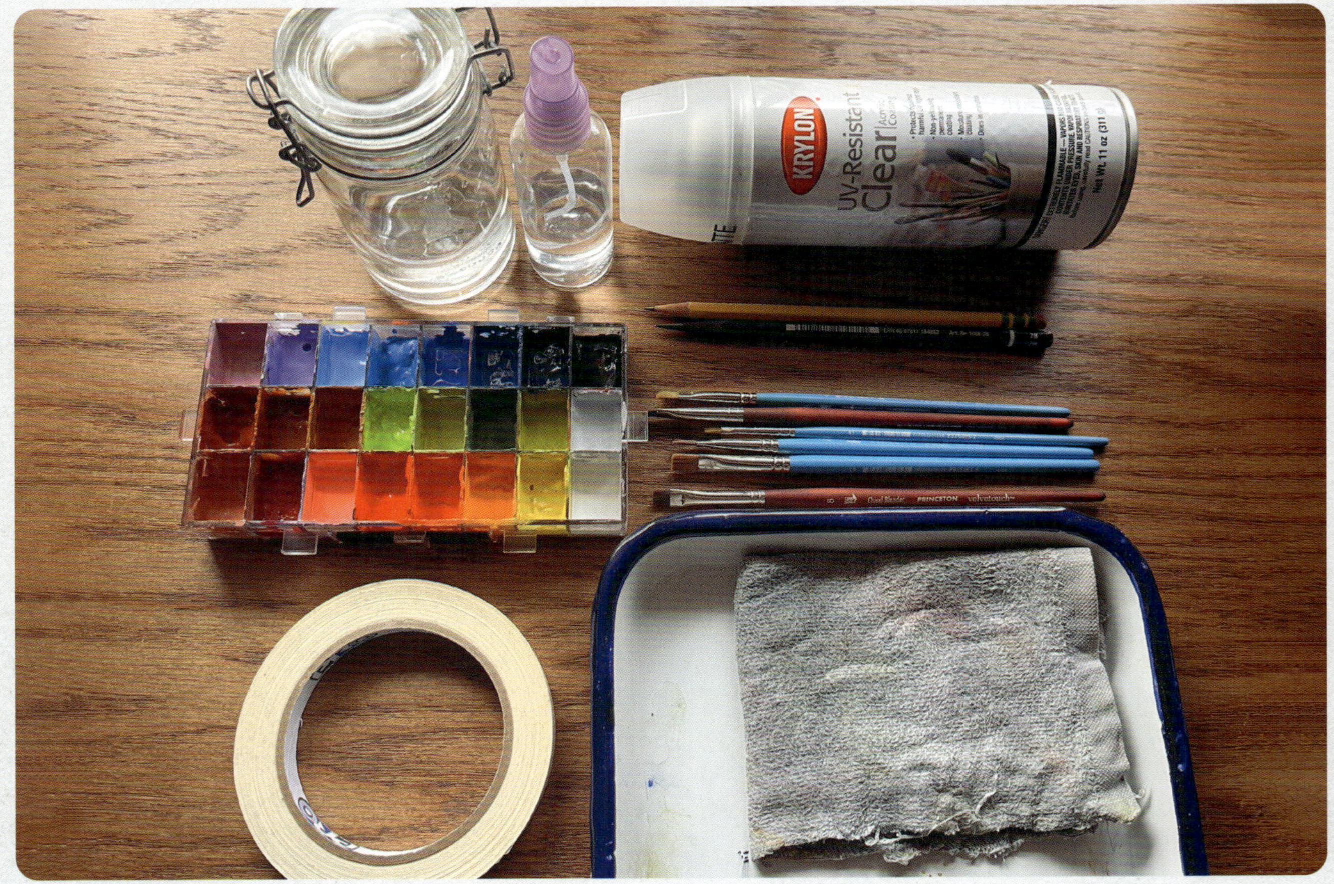

01c. All the other tools I'll be using for this painting

02a. Staple the wet paper to your painting surface

02.

I begin by stretching the watercolour paper, which involves soaking it in water to allow the fibres to expand and relax. After five minutes, secure the paper to your board using staples and let it dry completely to prevent curling while working with wet paints. Once the paper is ready, create a border using painter's tape, sectioning off the area in which you'll paint the scene.

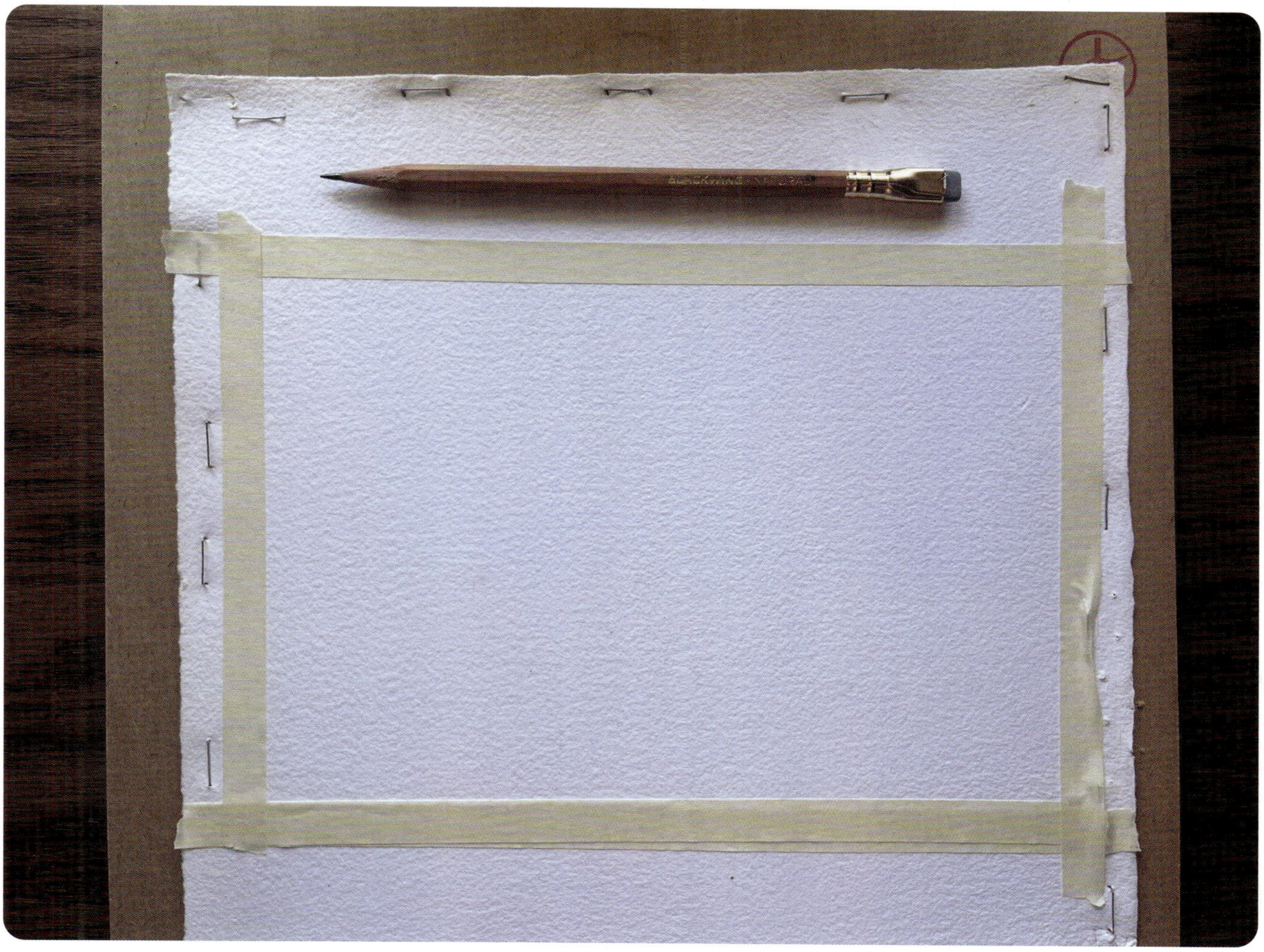

02b. The stretched and dried paper, ready for painting

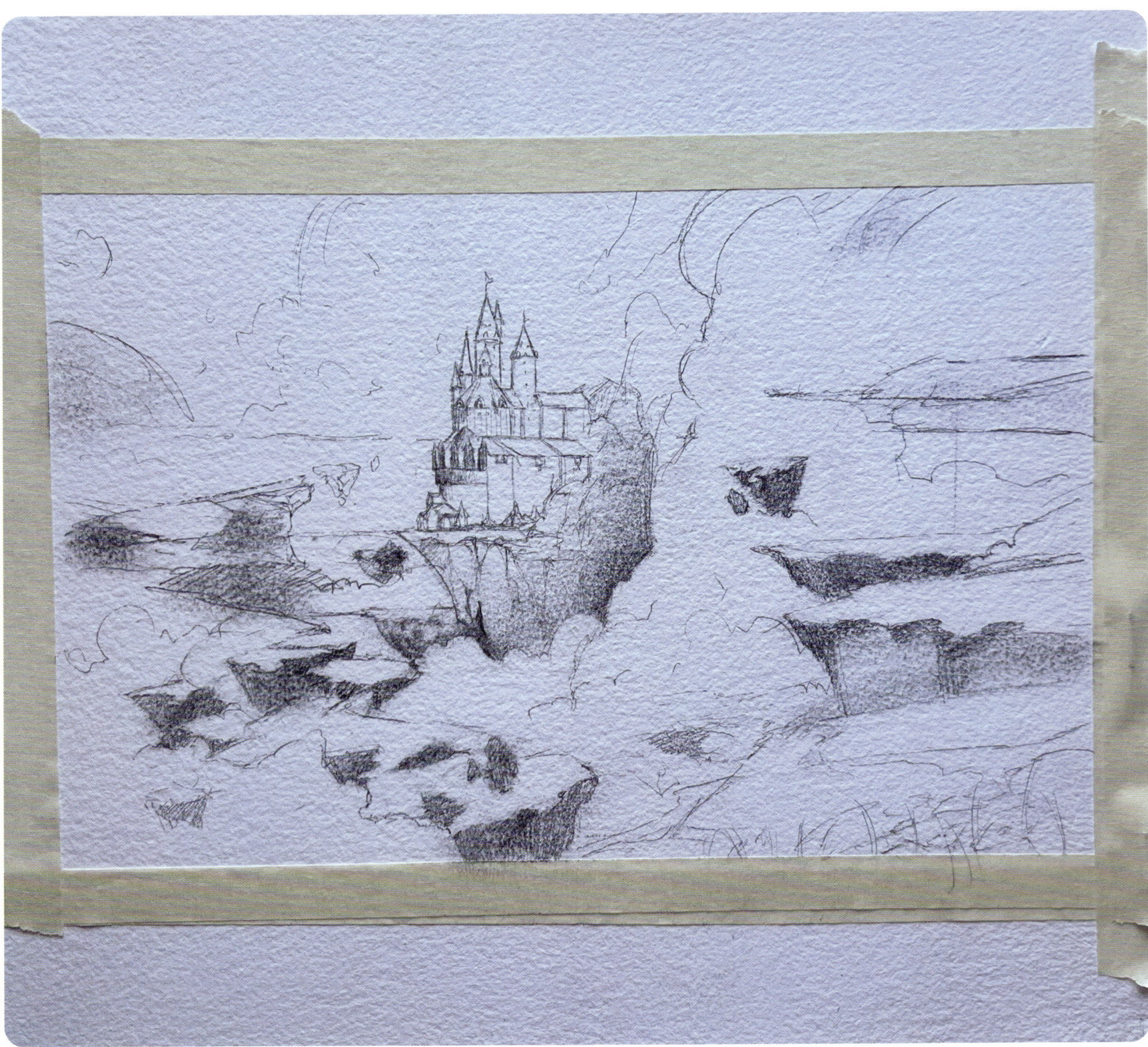

03. The pencil sketch with some rough shading, ready to be painted over

03.

The scene will be grand and fantastical, featuring magical elements that float around the composition. I use a pencil to roughly sketch out the scene, ensuring I have a clear idea of the layout. It's crucial to map out your composition before painting, as this helps you plan your layers effectively and avoid working blindly. This initial step provides a solid foundation, making it easier to build depth and bring your vision to life as you progress.

04.

Once the sketch is complete, tone the paper with a translucent colour. For this, I'll use Yellow Ochre watercolour, but you can also use gouache with lots of water to achieve a wash like this. A pure white background can feel overwhelming to paint on, especially if you plan to use any white paint, and this yellow tone will help you see your lighter colours more clearly. I apply the paint with my largest flat brush and then let the watercolour dry completely. After it's dry, I lightly spray it with a coat of matte fixative. This step is crucial, as it creates a barrier between paint layers, reducing issues like over-blending and damage to the paper. Allow the fixative to dry fully before continuing.

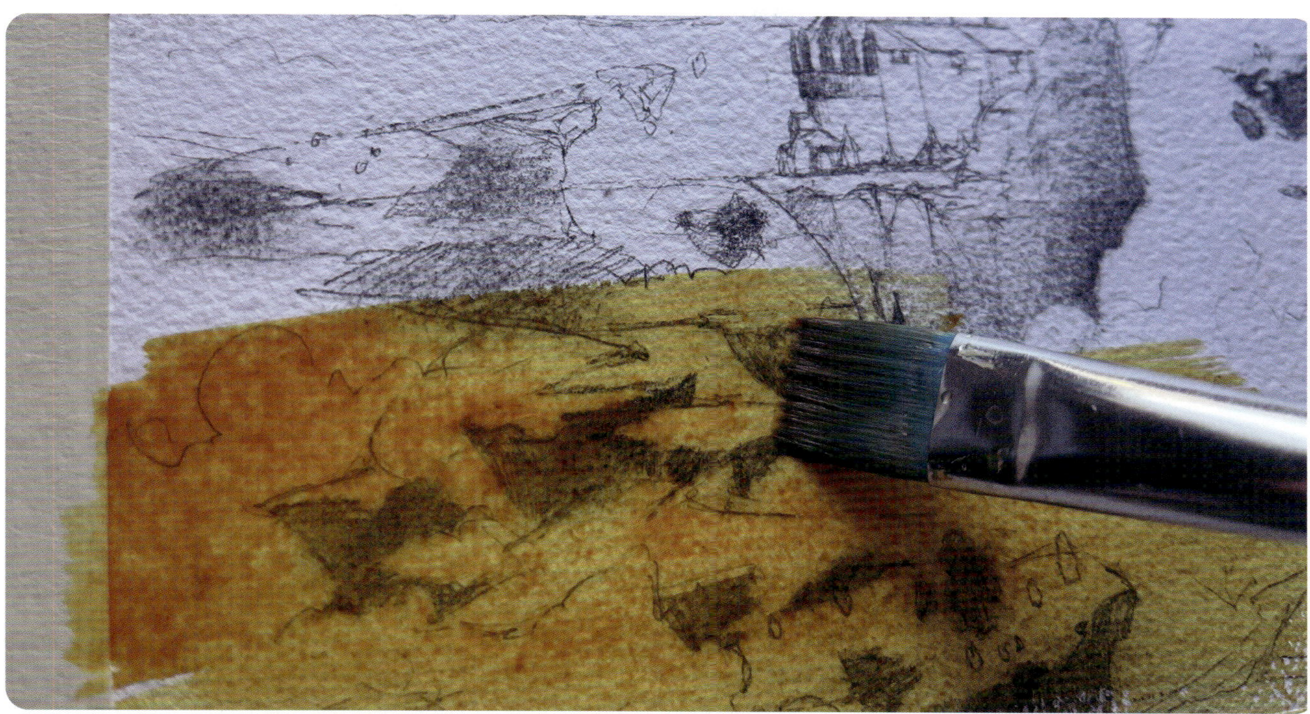
04a. Covering the white page will make it easier to judge your colours

04b. A Yellow Ochre wash is a strong base to start from

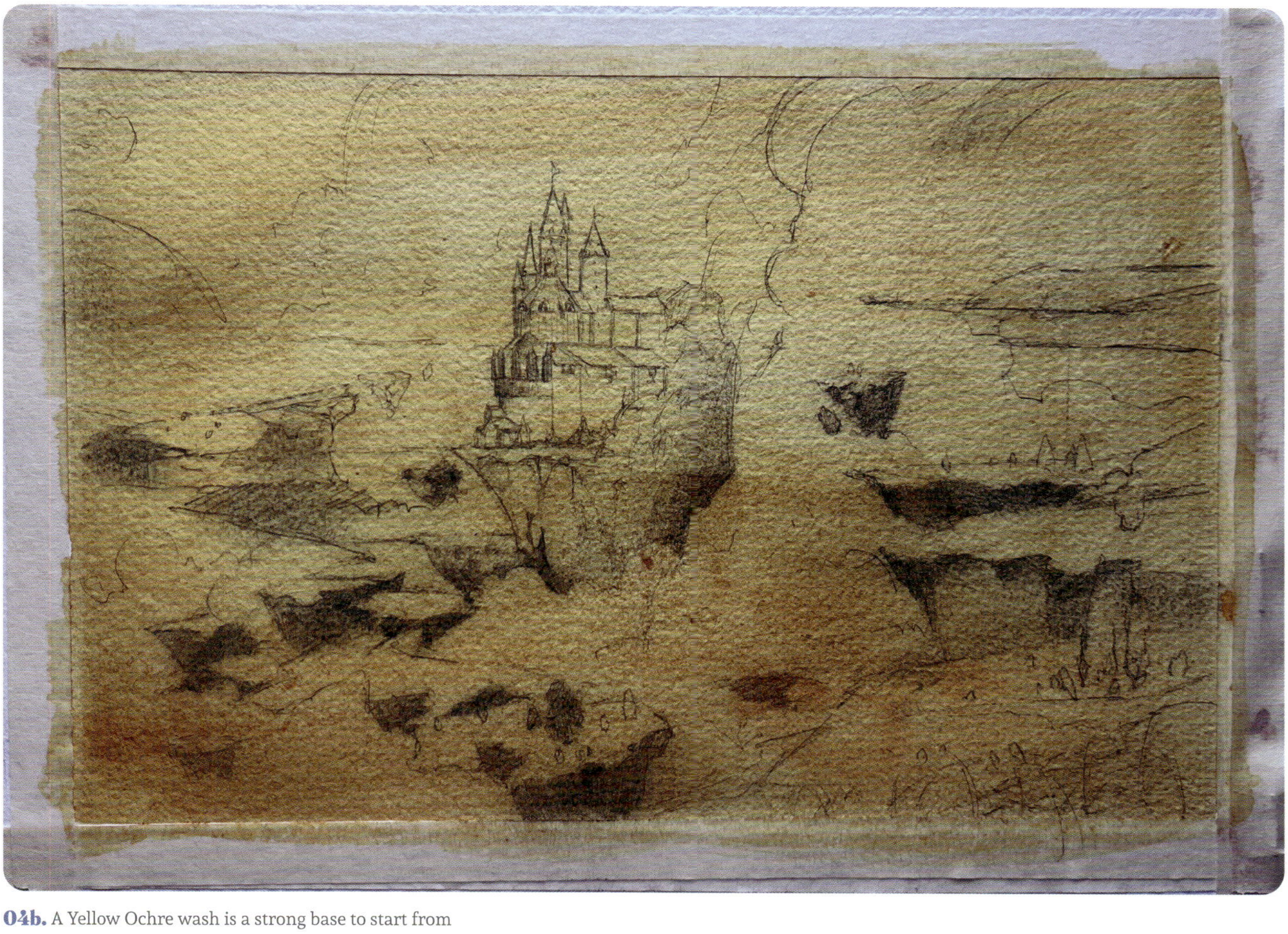

05.

I typically like to start my landscapes from the farthest point. In this case, I start with the sky, using a slightly warm-tinted white to roughly indicate where my clouds will appear. There's no need to start doing any kind of heavy rendering; you only want flat colours and basic shapes for the beginning. Don't be scared to apply paint because you can easily cover up mistakes in the coming steps.

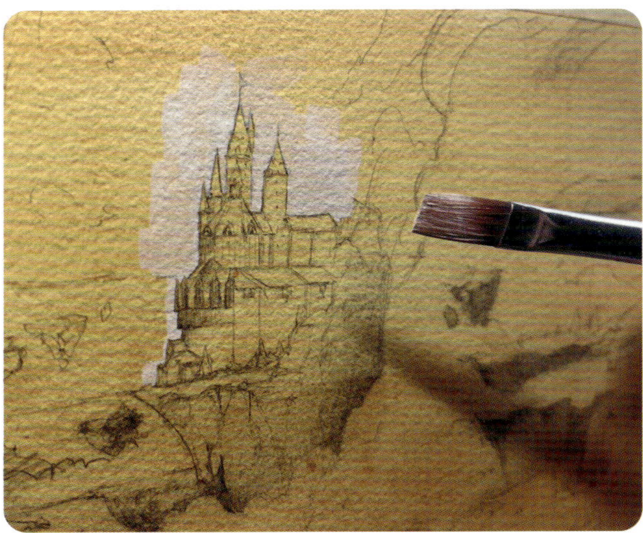

05a. Begin using white to build up rough cloud shapes

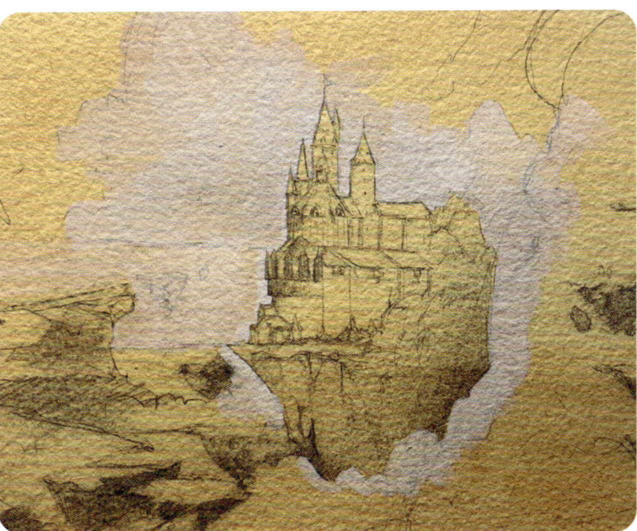

05b. Don't render the clouds in detail at this stage

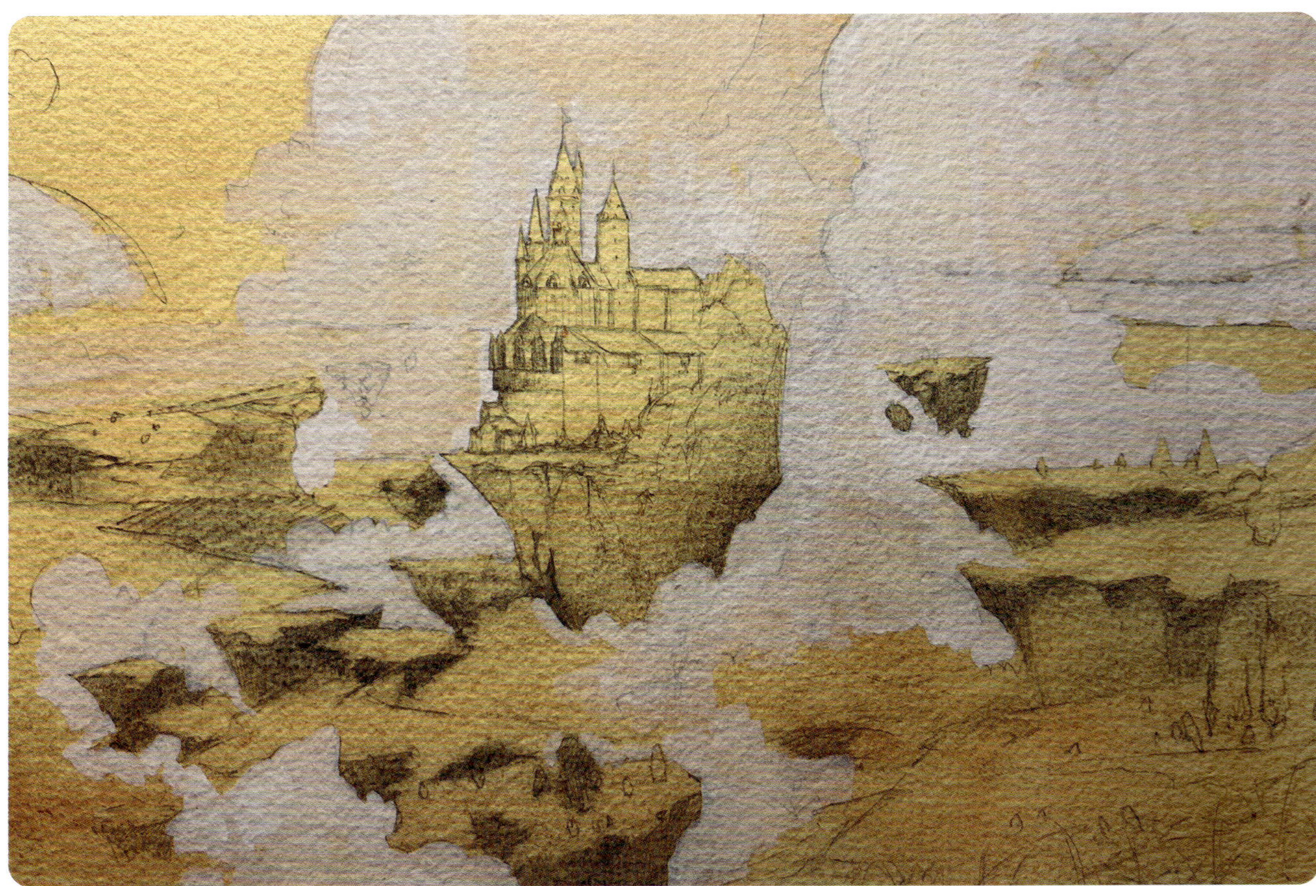

05c. The cloud formations are now roughly blocked out

06a. Begin blocking out the castle with flat colours

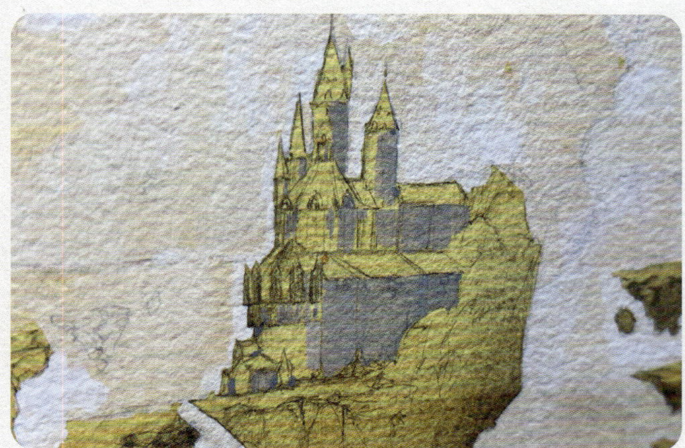

06b. Use a grey tone for the shadow sides of the castle

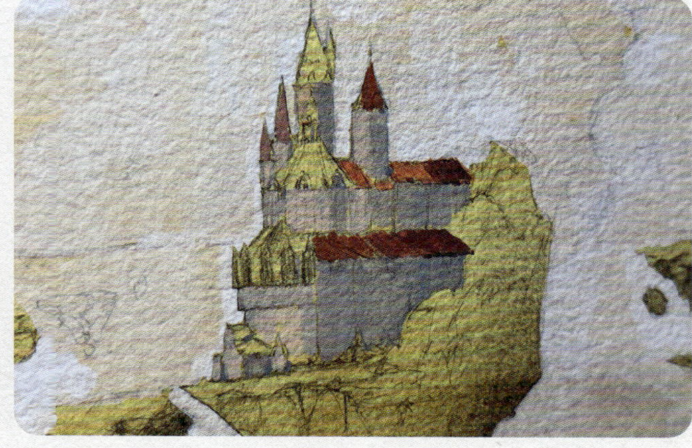

06c. Add a light grey for the warmly lit side, and reddish rooftops

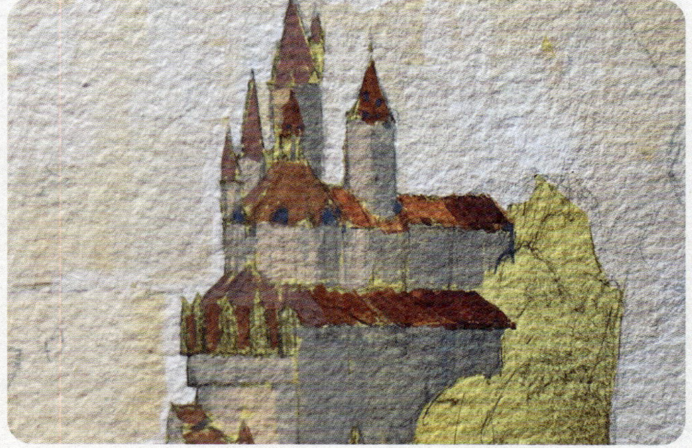

06d. Block out the smaller towers and turrets

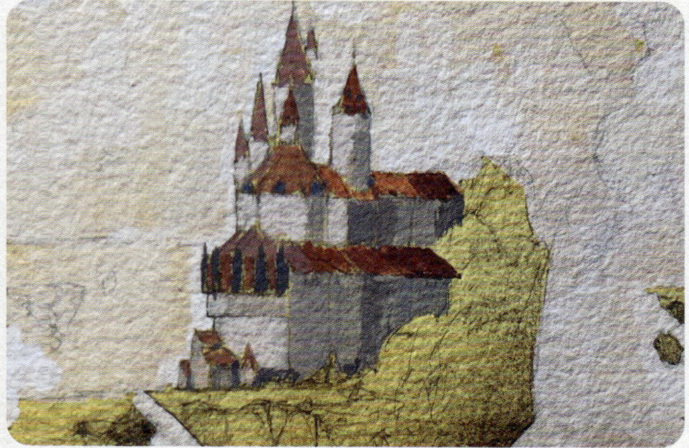

06e. Save the lightest grey highlights for last

06.

In this step, I focus on laying down flat colours to establish the base of the castle. Using bold, flat strokes, I concentrate on building the geometry and structure of the castle without worrying about intricate details. This approach helps create a strong foundation and clearly defines the forms and proportions of the castle. By starting with simple, confident strokes, you can ensure the composition remains balanced and ready for additional layers and refinement later.

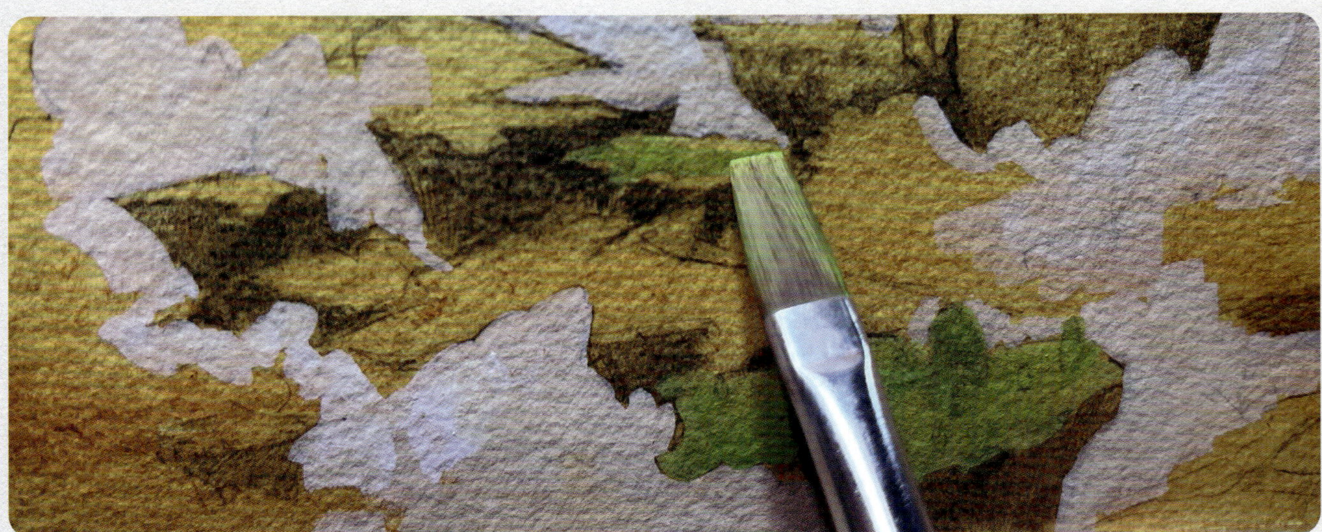

07a. Use a light yellow-green to begin adding grass

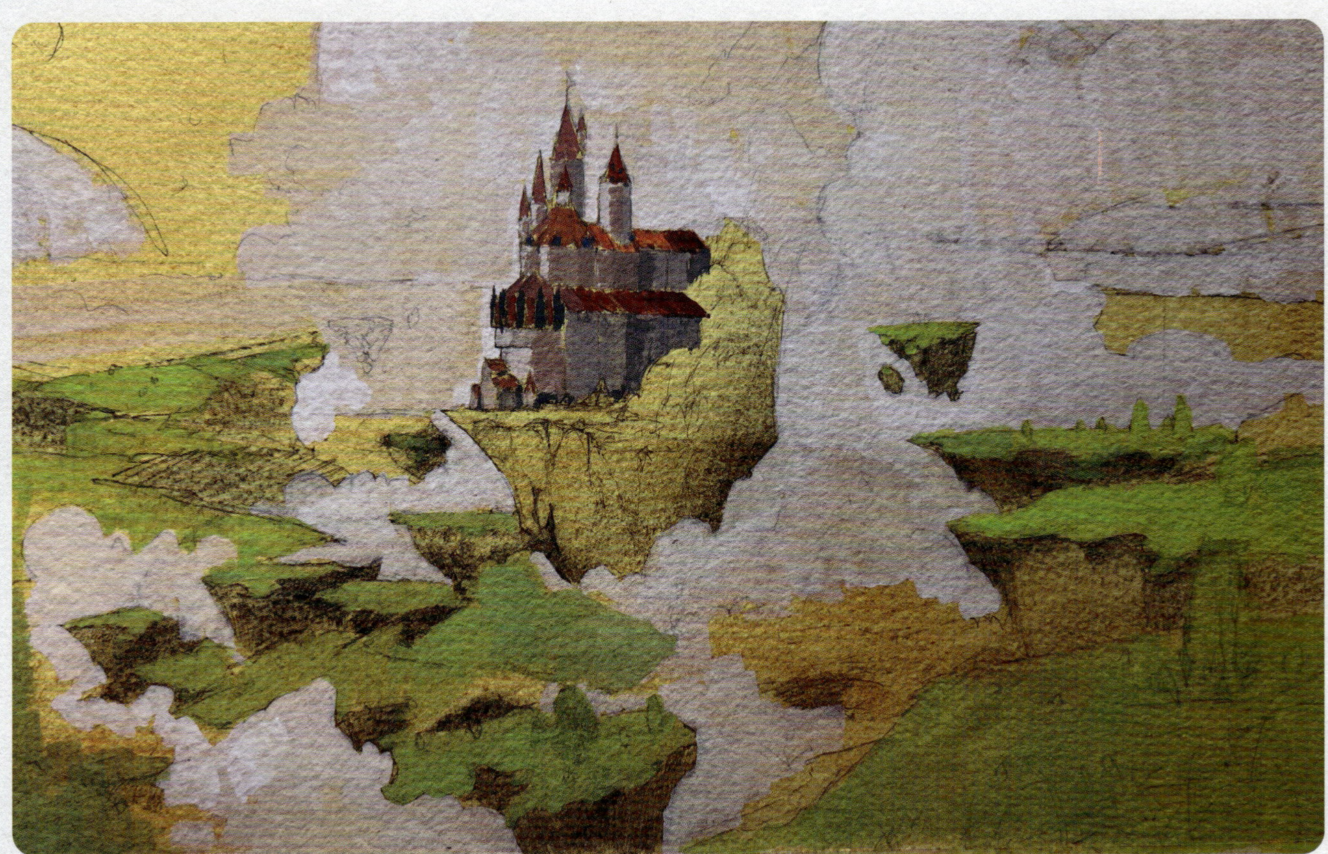

07b. Block out the bright grassy tops of all the floating rocks

07.

Next I mix a bright yellow-green and begin using it to lay down the foundation for the grass. Starting with lighter tones allows me to create a base that I can gradually build upon with darker shades later. This technique helps to maintain depth and dimension in the painting, as the lighter colours peek through and add vibrancy to the finished piece. By working from light to dark, you ensure a balanced progression that enhances the overall richness of the grass.

08.

Next I start blocking out the visible surfaces of the rocks, focusing on capturing their form and structure. To create depth and a sense of aerial perspective, I use blue hues, which help convey the illusion of distance and atmosphere. This technique adds a subtle coolness to the rocks, making them recede naturally into the background. By carefully blocking in these areas with colour, you'll create a strong base that enhances the atmosphere of the composition.

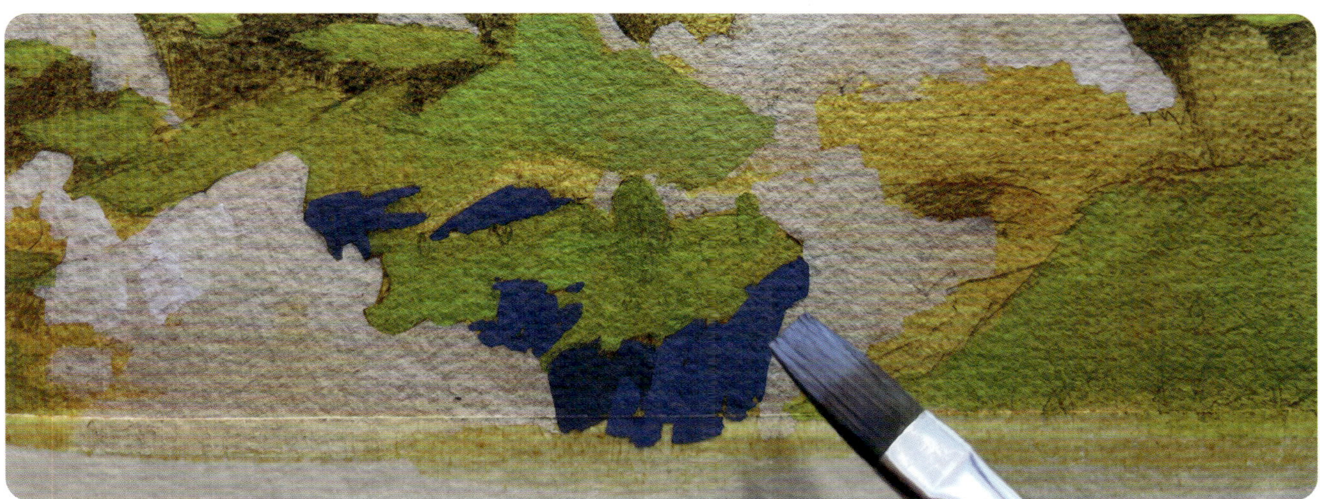

08a. Use a blue tone for the shadowy undersides of the rocks

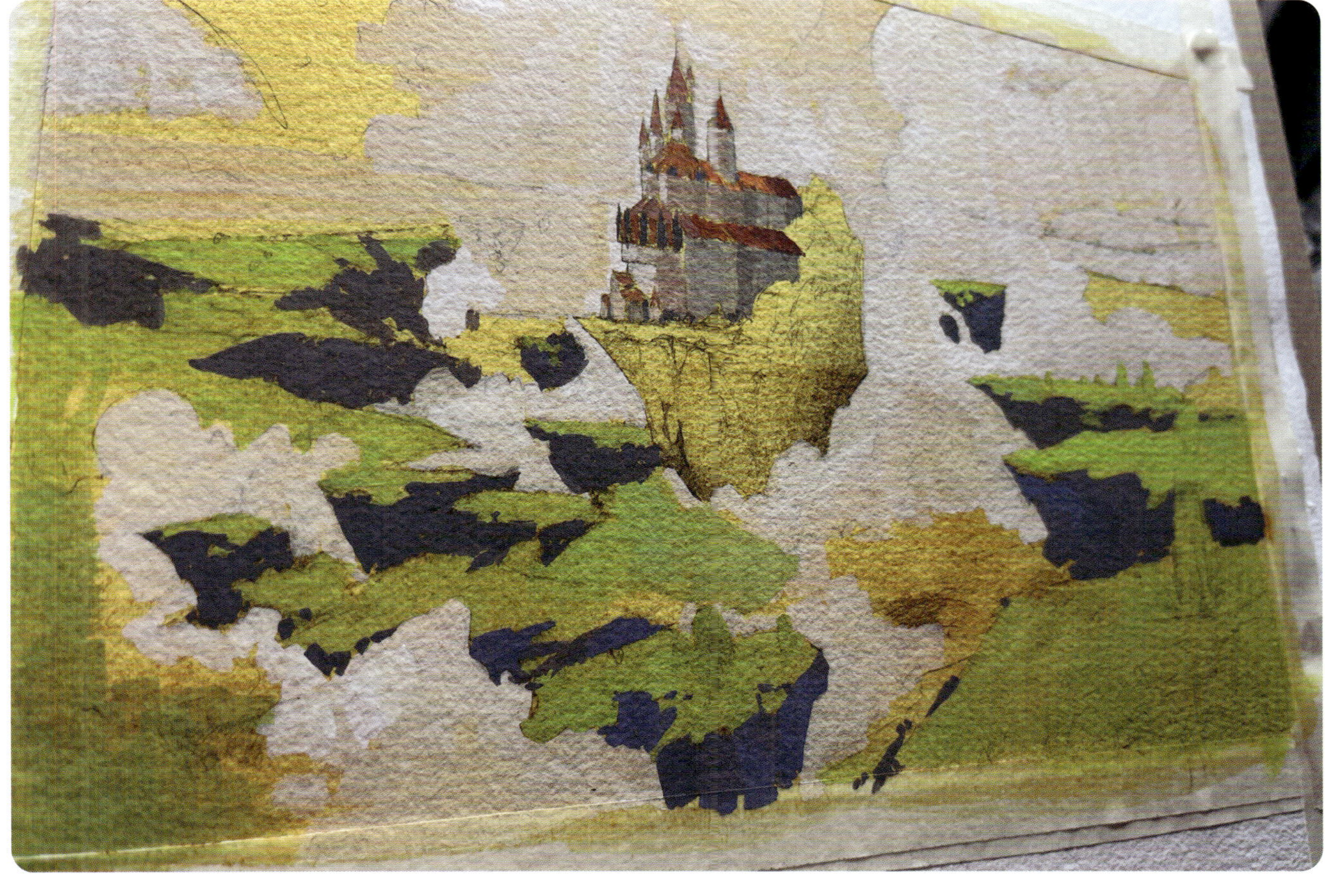

08b. The scene so far, with most of the land masses roughly blocked out

09.

Whenever I paint skies, I focus on simple shapes that complement the composition. After the clouds dry, I use a flat brush with light blue paint to 'sculpt' the final cloud shapes. I do this for a few reasons: to prevent unnecessary colour mixing, as gouache is water-soluble, and to ensure that the lightest colours are painted first. If white is applied over solid blue, it mixes and dulls the colours, and you'll want to keep the cloud shapes sharp and bold. Additionally, you can incorporate cooler grey tones beneath the clouds to suggest light and shadow.

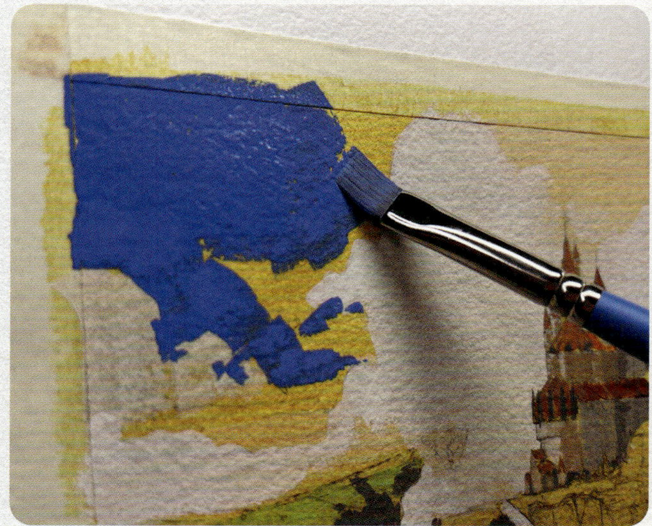

09a. Painting the sky after the clouds ensures the clouds stay crisp and light

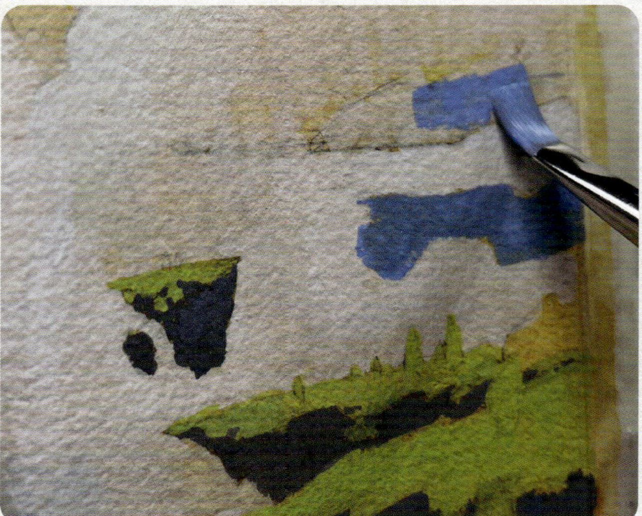

09b. Fill out the blue sky areas across the whole scene

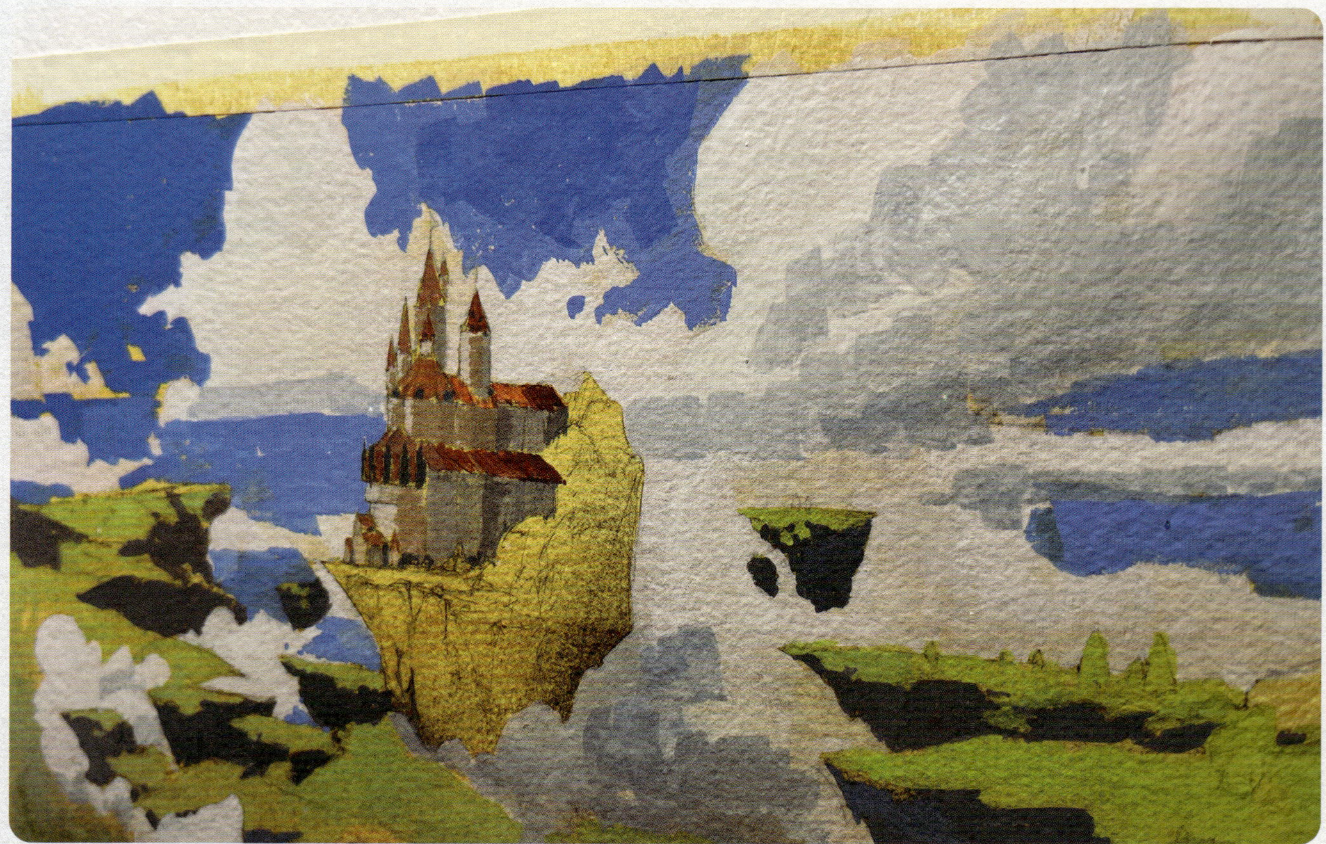

09c. Use a light, cool grey to shade the undersides of the clouds

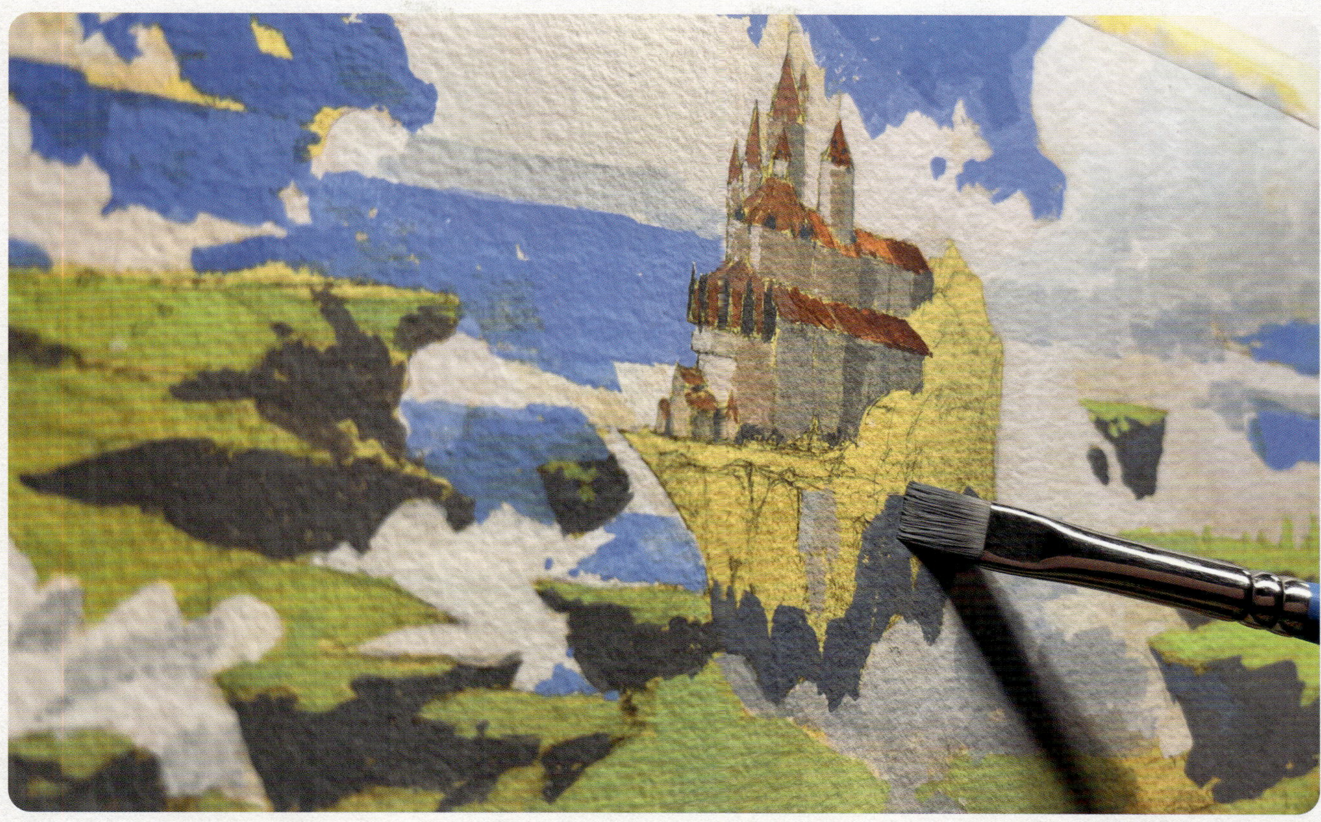

10a. Block out the castle rock, starting with the grey sides

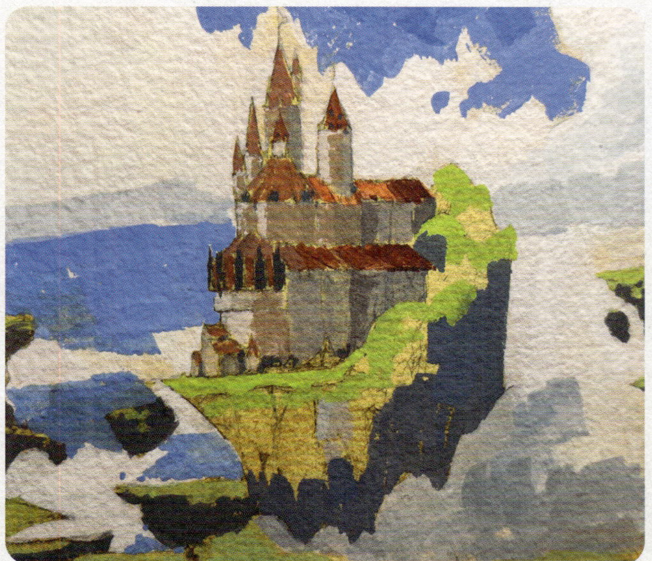

10b. Add the grassy green shapes on top

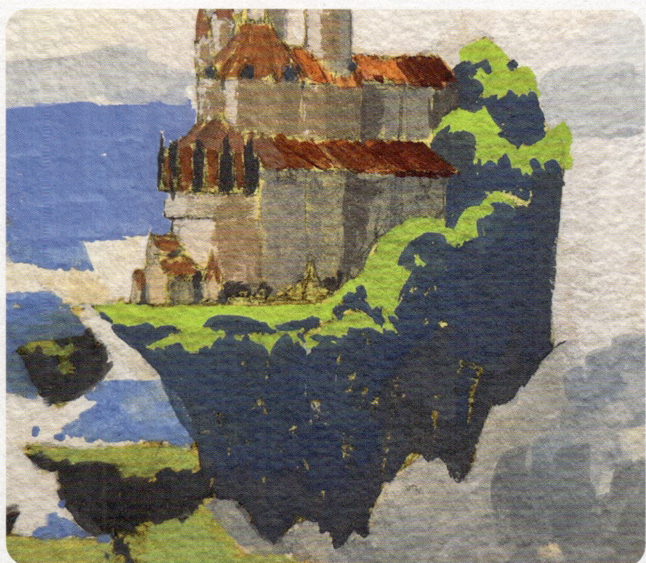

10c. The castle's island fully blocked out

10.

In this step, I block in the rock structure that supports the castle. This method is similar to the cloud technique, allowing me to build the foundational shapes before refining the details. By establishing the rock's form first, I can then 'sculpt' around the surrounding green areas of grass with more precision. This layered approach ensures the elements integrate seamlessly into the composition, while also providing a clear base for adding texture in later stages.

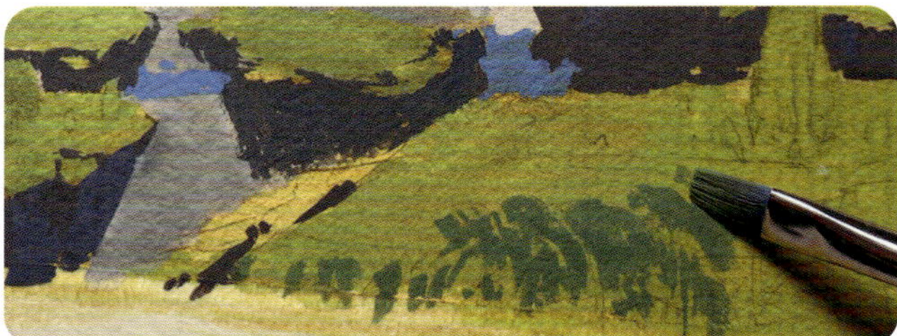

11a. Begin painting more grass and foliage in the foreground

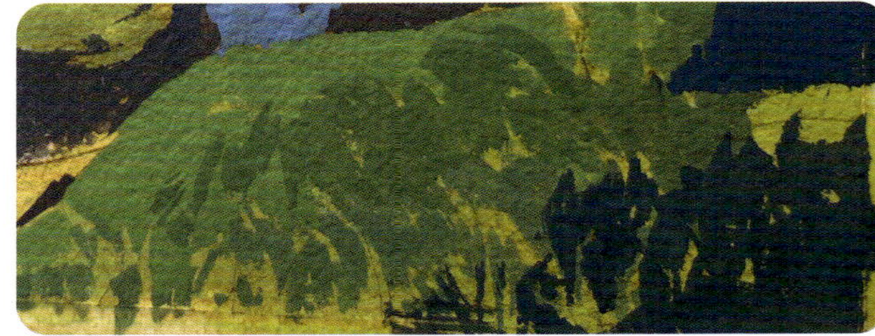

11b. Building up layers of value creates more depth

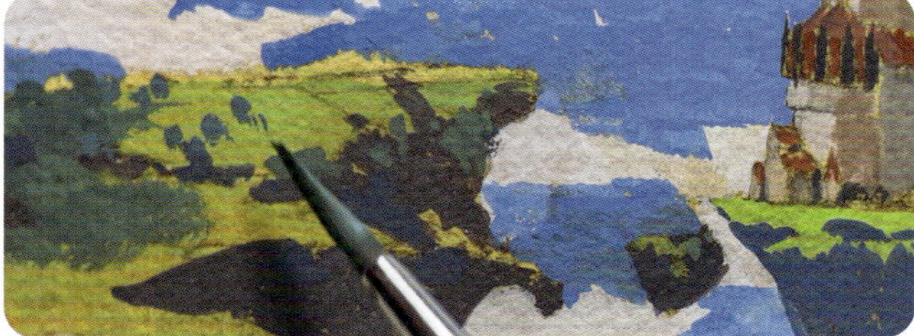

11c. Continue adding small strokes and dabs of green in the background

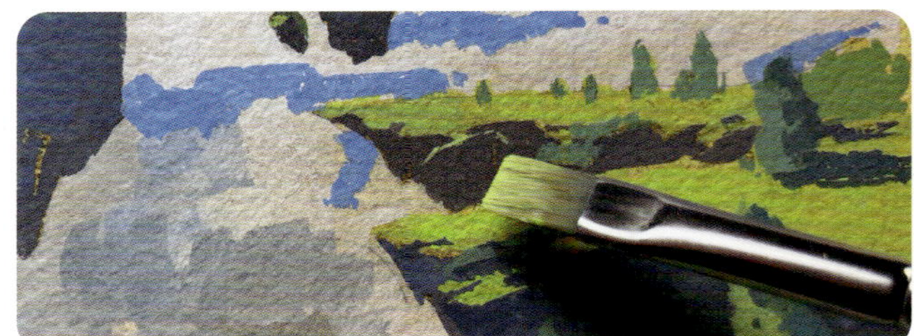

11d. Create simple tree shapes with little dabs of your brush

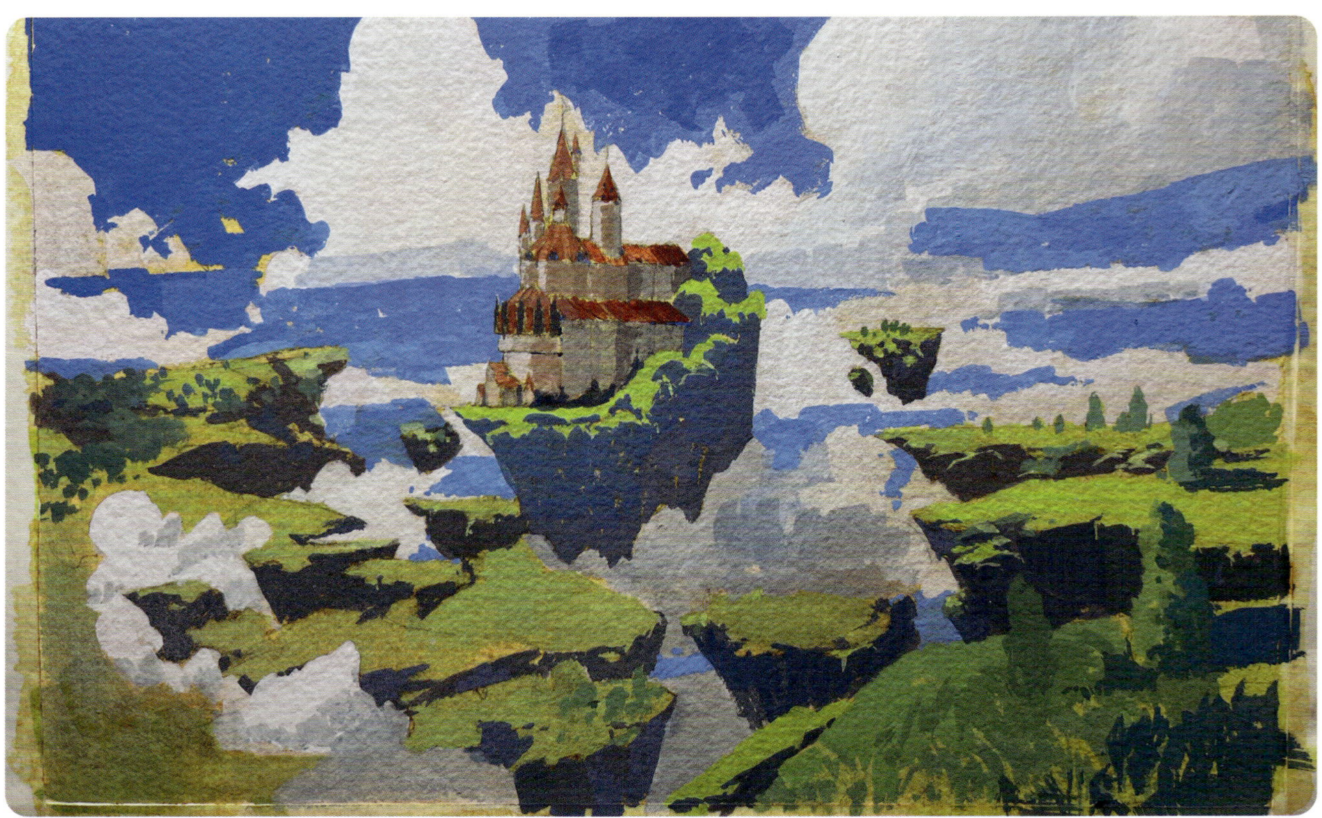

11e. The landscape now feels much more rich and alive

11.

Now that most of the foundational block-ins are done, it's time to focus on adding the details that will really bring the scene to life. I start by adding things like grass, foliage, and textures to the rocks, using smaller brushes or the narrow edges of my flat brushes.

These little touches help define the composition and make it feel more complete. By layering these elements carefully, you ensure they blend smoothly with the base layers, giving the painting a cohesive and dynamic feel. This step adds richness and character to the piece.

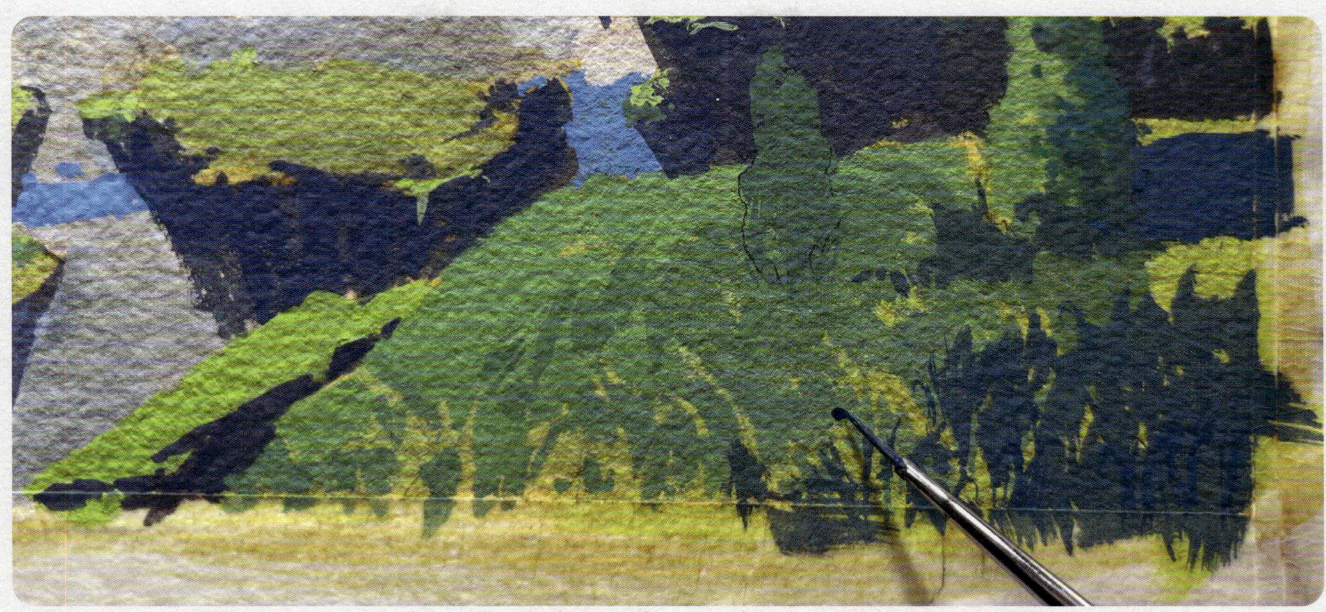

12a. Return to the foreground with a small brush to add finer details

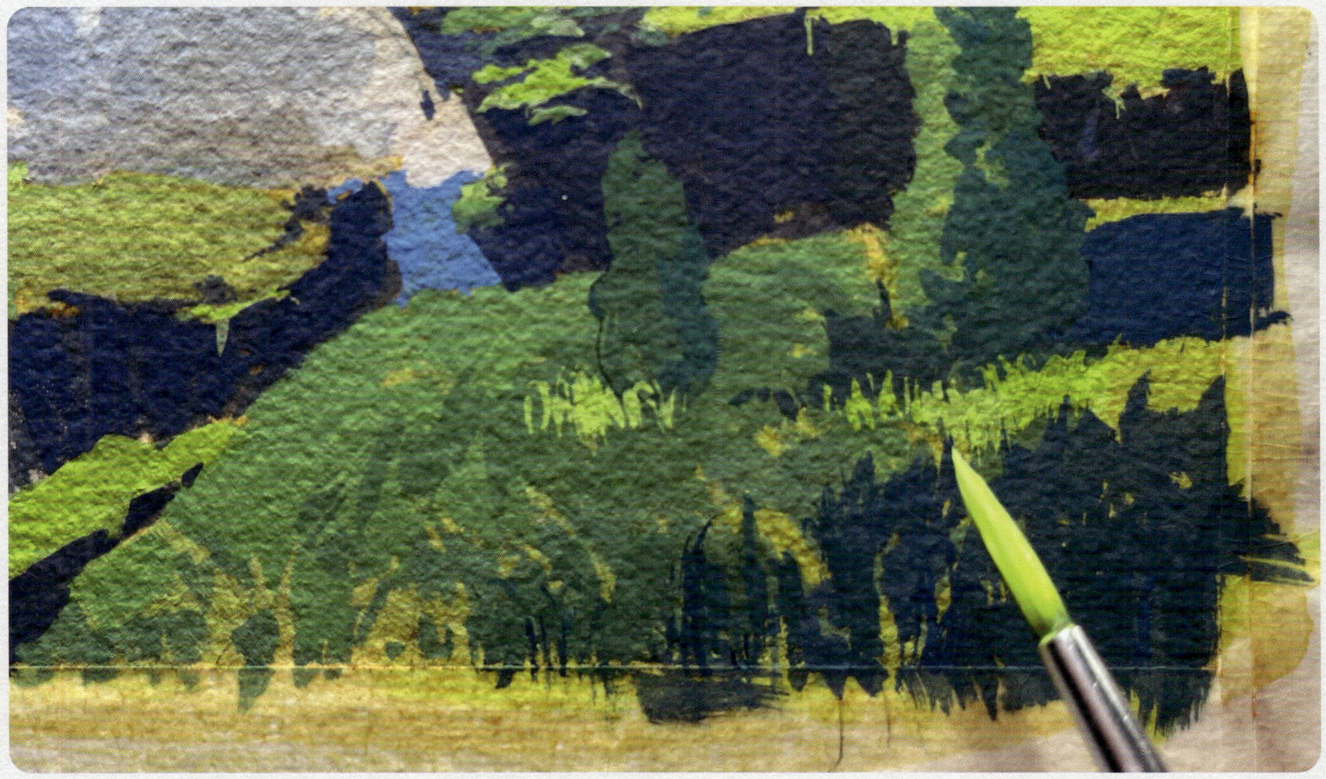

12b. Fine blades of light and dark grass will make the foreground pop!

12.

In this step, concentrate on the patch of land in the foreground, as it should feature more descriptive details compared to elements in the distance. To achieve this, emphasize stronger shadows on the trees and add more defined textures to the patches of grass, so they appear closer to the viewer. These intentional details help create a stronger focal point in the foreground, making it more visually engaging.

13.

As mentioned earlier, the painting is starting to look more complete, so now you can revisit areas you worked on previously to add more structure and refinement. Add additional trees in the distance, incorporating subtle shadows to enhance their presence without overwhelming the scene. For the sky, use thicker layers of white paint to fill in areas of the clouds that appeared too sheer, creating a fuller and more balanced look. These adjustments really make the scene come to life!

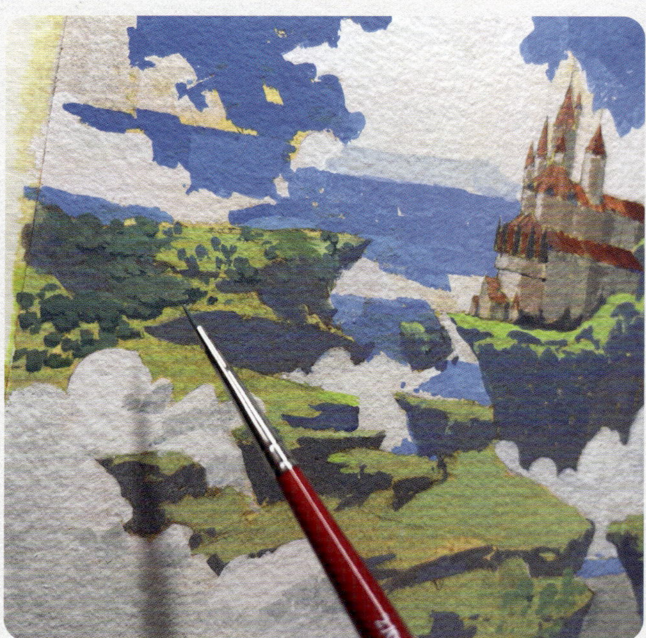

13a. Go back over the background to add small refinements

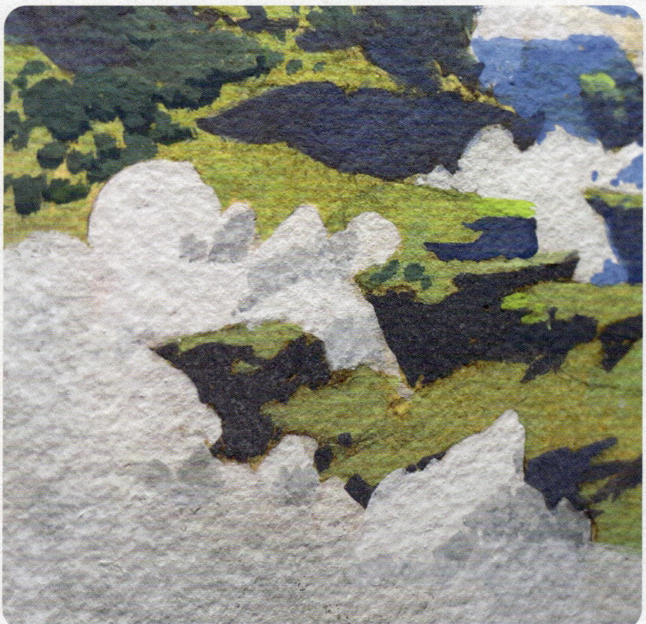

13b. Firm up the opacity of the white clouds in the foreground

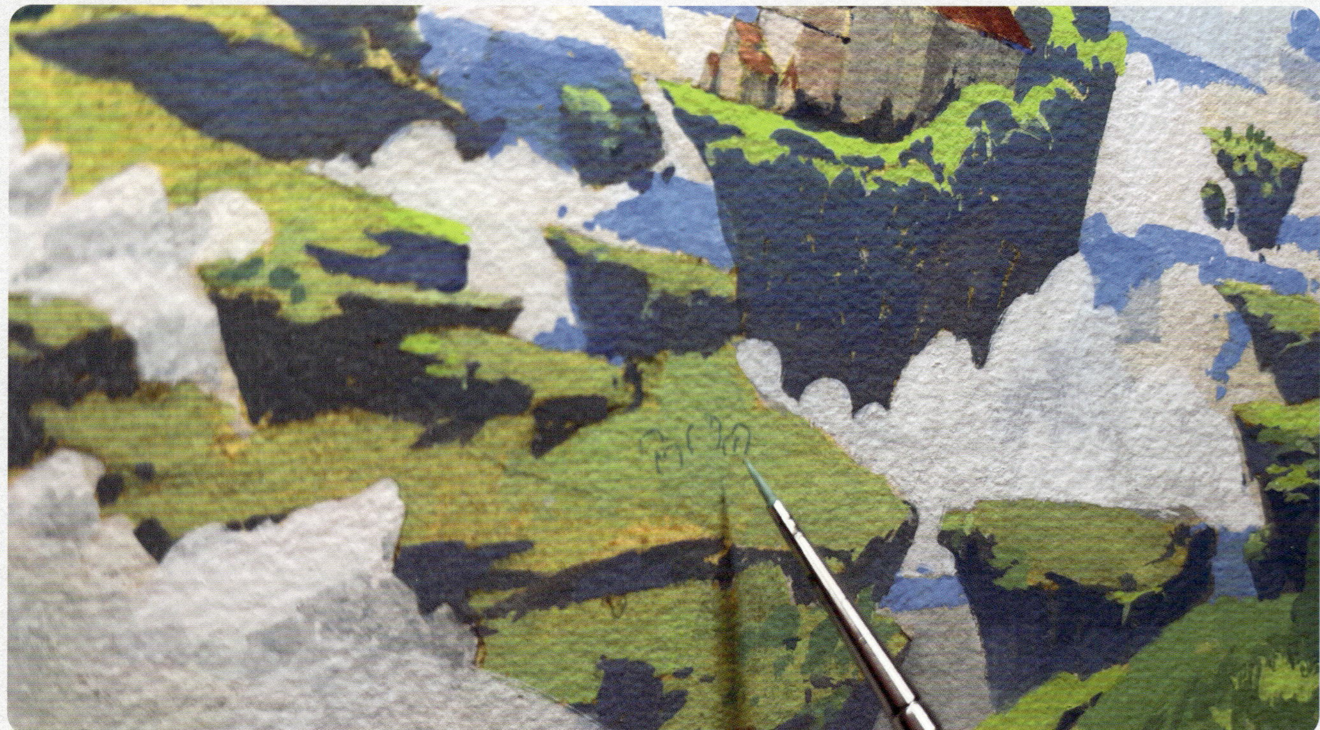

13c. Go over the nearer islands to add little trees and foliage details

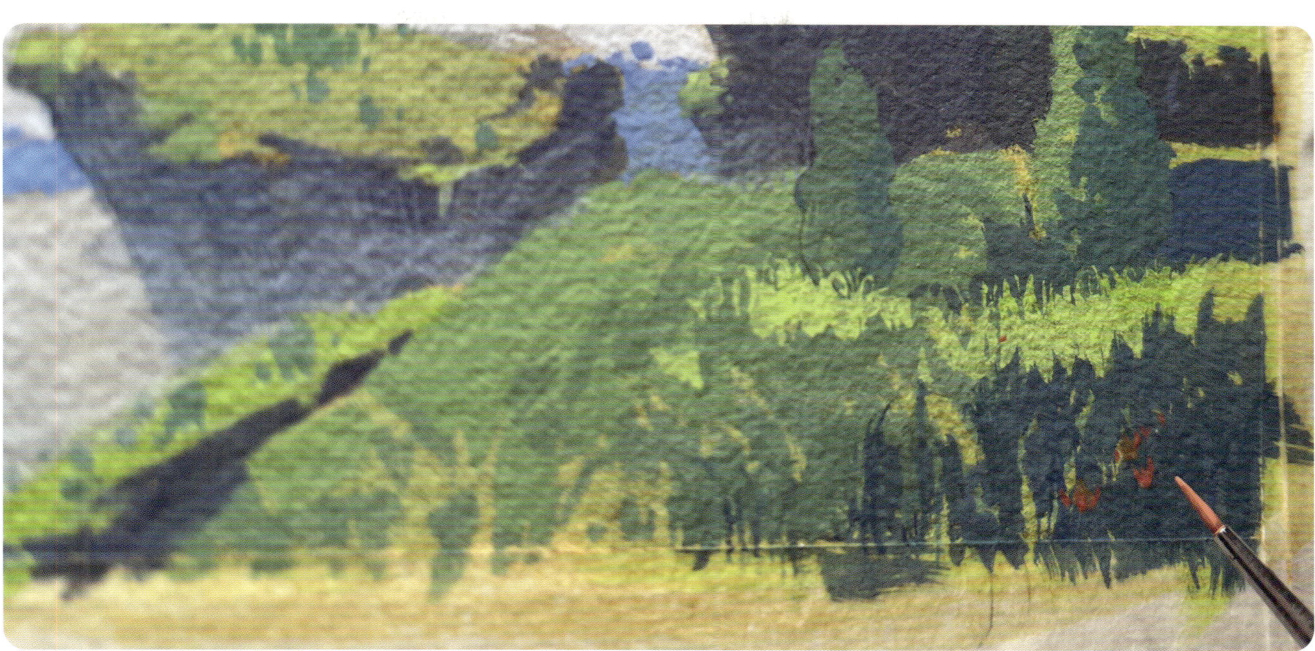

14a. More detail will make the foreground feel 'closer' to the viewer

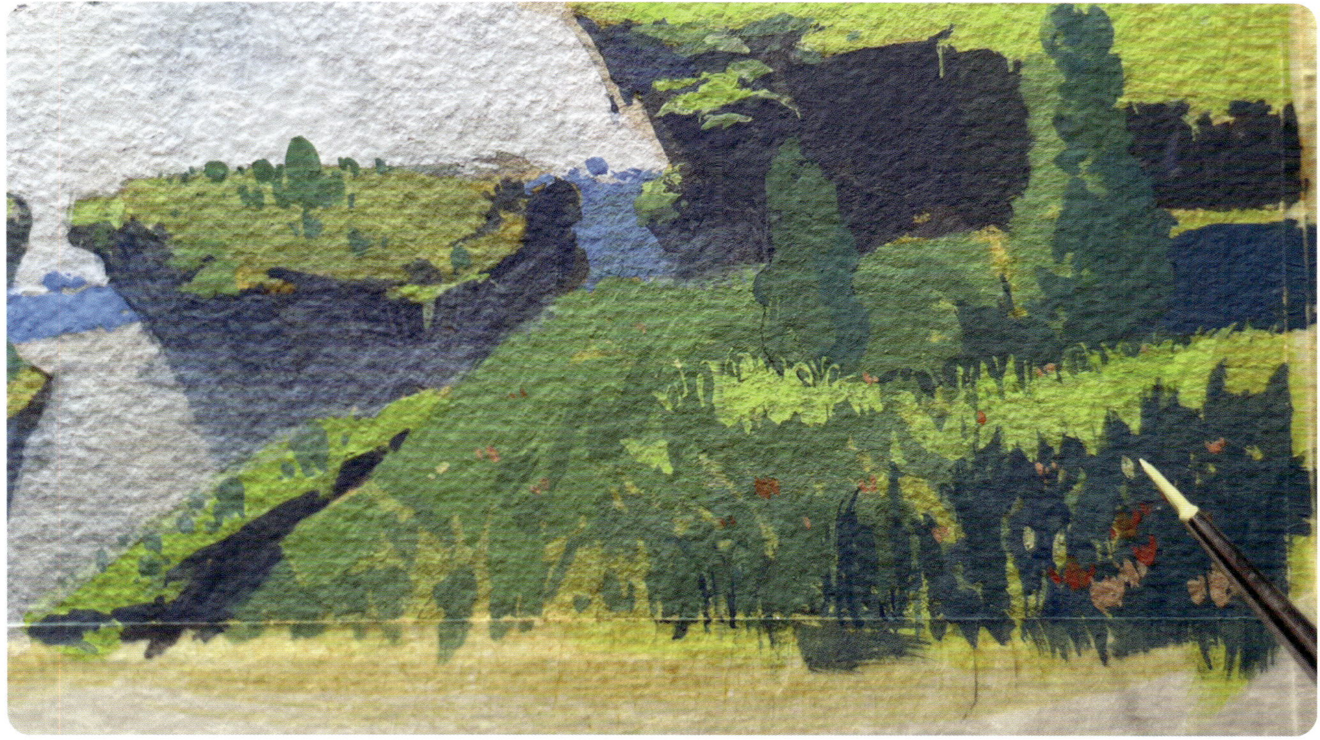

14b. Add nearby flowers by painting tiny dabs of red and orange

14.

The foreground could use a bit more life, so I add some extra flowers and plants using my finest brush. These small additions make the scene feel more balanced and add a little extra charm to the overall composition. As I work on these finishing touches, I also go back to the distant pieces of land and repaint the rocks to give them more aerial perspective, using cooler tones to help them recede into the background. You can see here how the lowest floating rock now has more misty atmosphere around it.

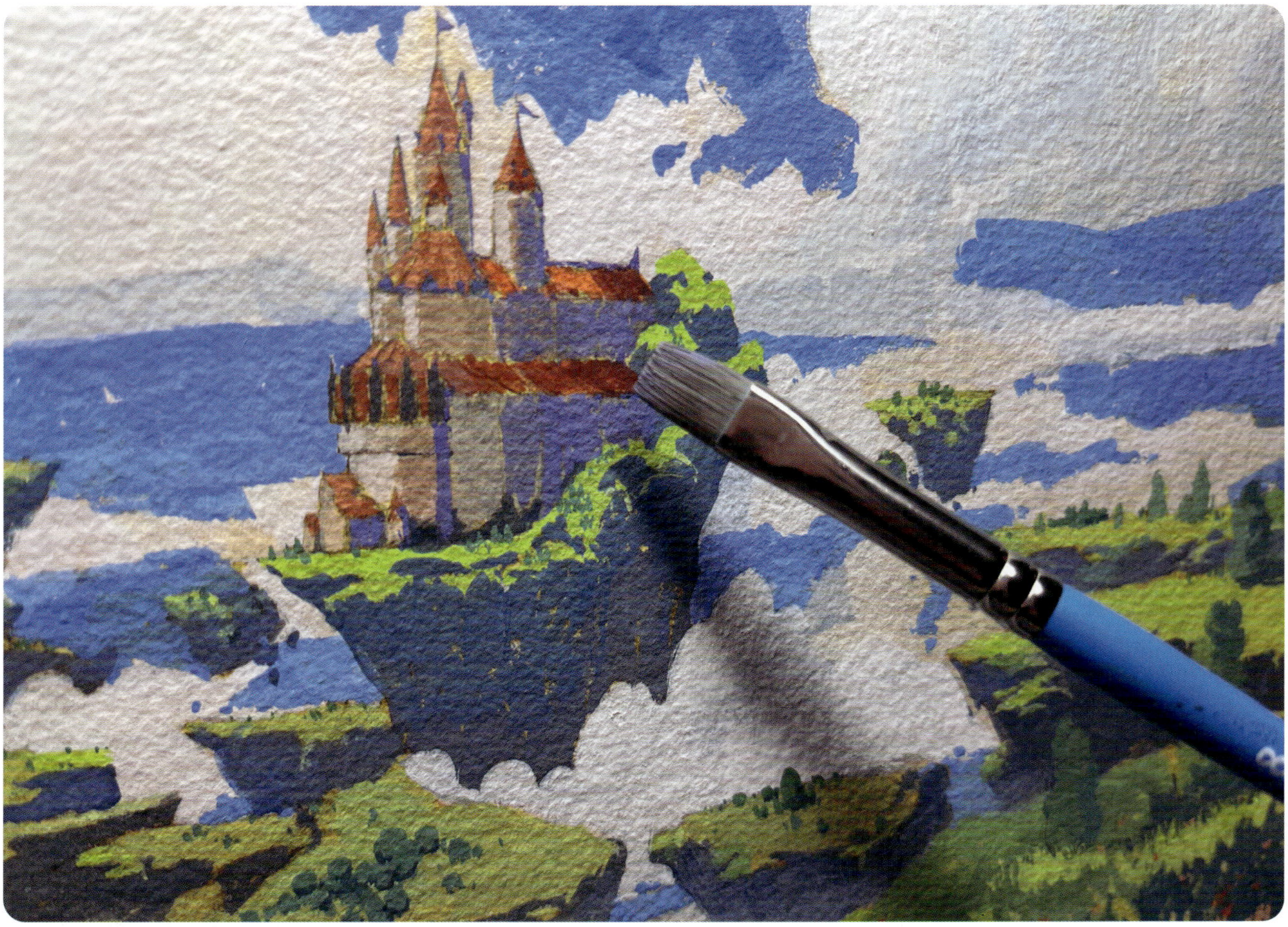

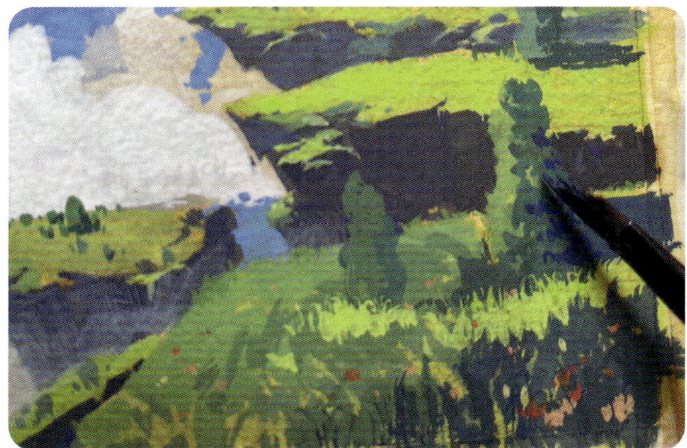

15a. The castle is the focal point, so check over it again before you finish the piece

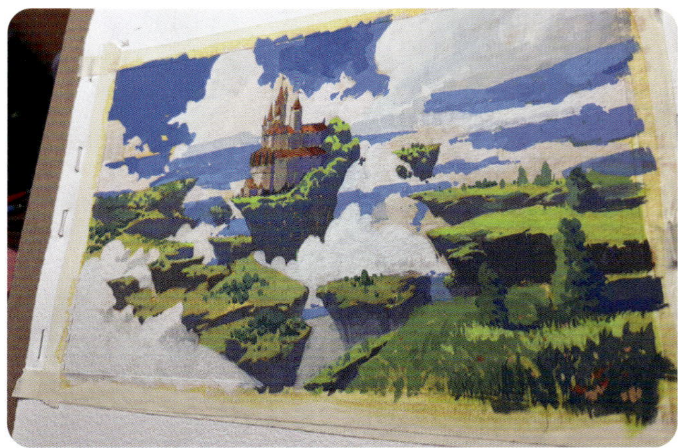

15b. A few cool, dark shadows help finish up the foreground

15c. Step back and leave the finished piece to dry!

15.

For the finishing touches, I add cooler tones to the castle to give it more of an atmospheric feel. I also make the shadows bolder, keeping them simple and not overloading them with detail. The great thing about the castle being in the distance is that you don't need to add too much information – it works better when it's kept subtle. This approach keeps the focus on the overall composition while still making the castle feel like part of the scene.

16.

Peel away the tape to reveal the finished piece! This is the most satisfying part, where you can finally see all your hard work neatly framed. It's always exciting to see the clean edges and how everything comes together. However, be sure to peel the tape carefully, as it can sometimes stick to the paper and cause damage. Take your time with this step to ensure the paper stays intact and your painting looks crisp and polished.

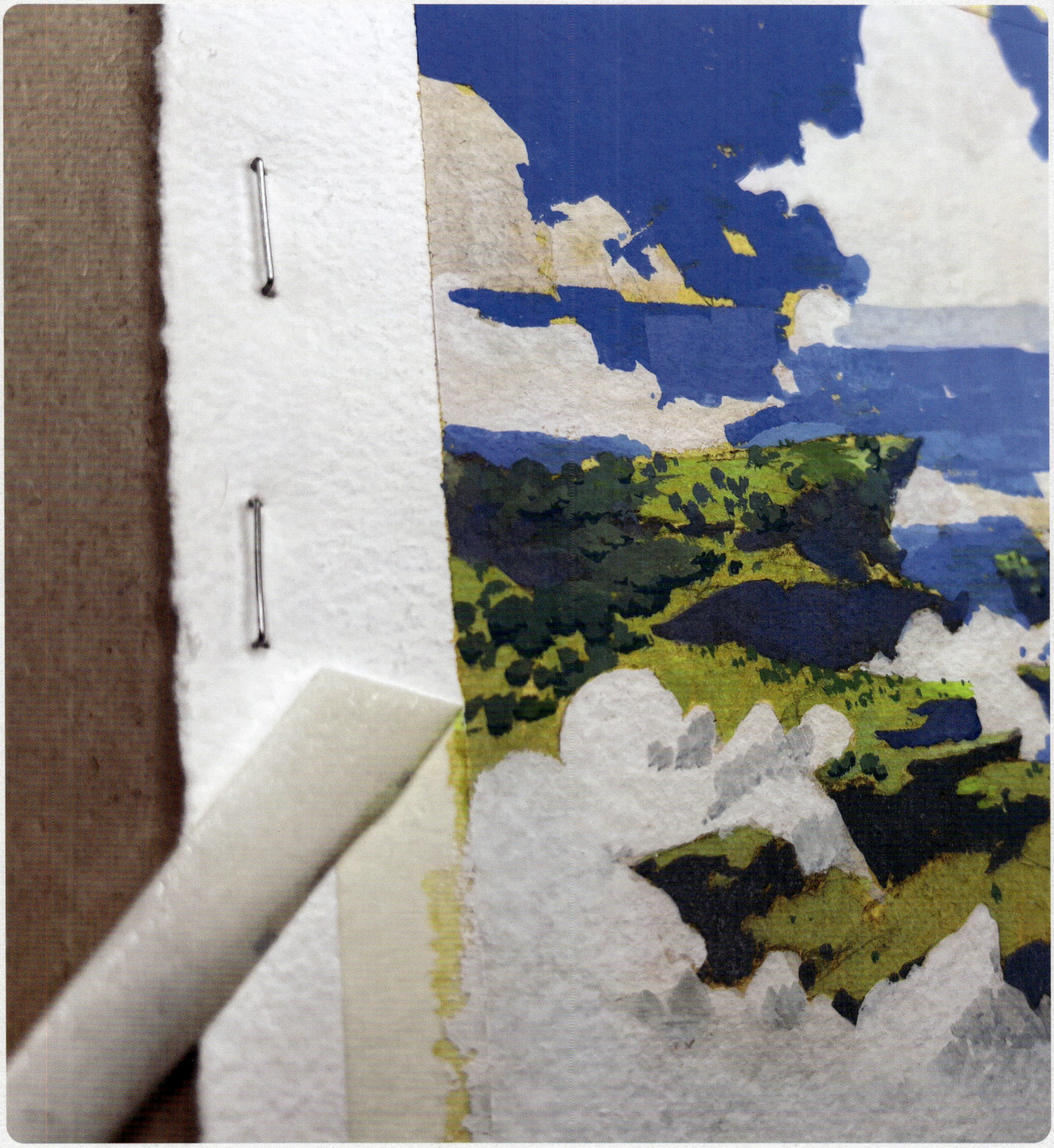

16. Carefully peel the tape off the finished painting

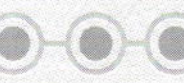

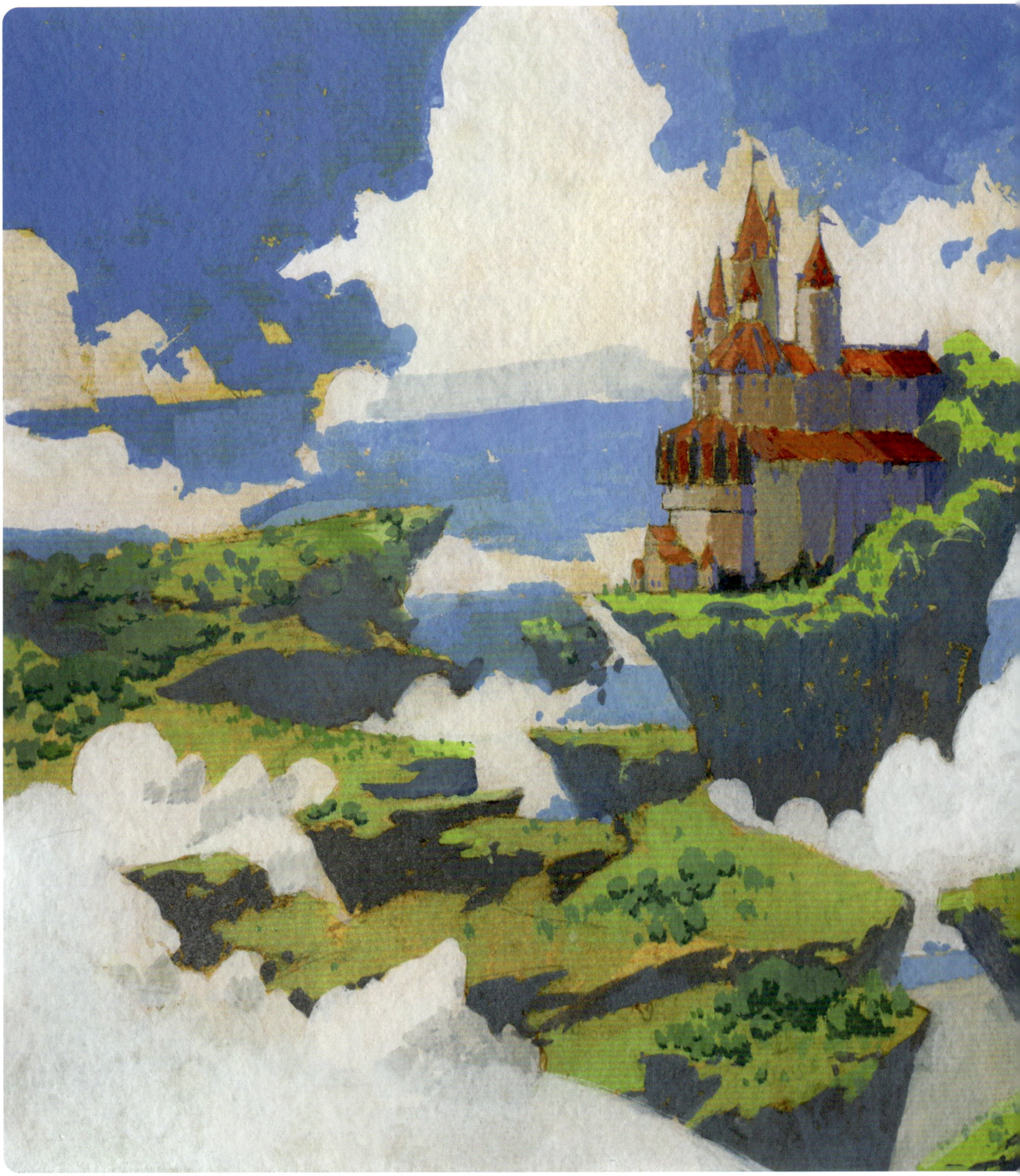

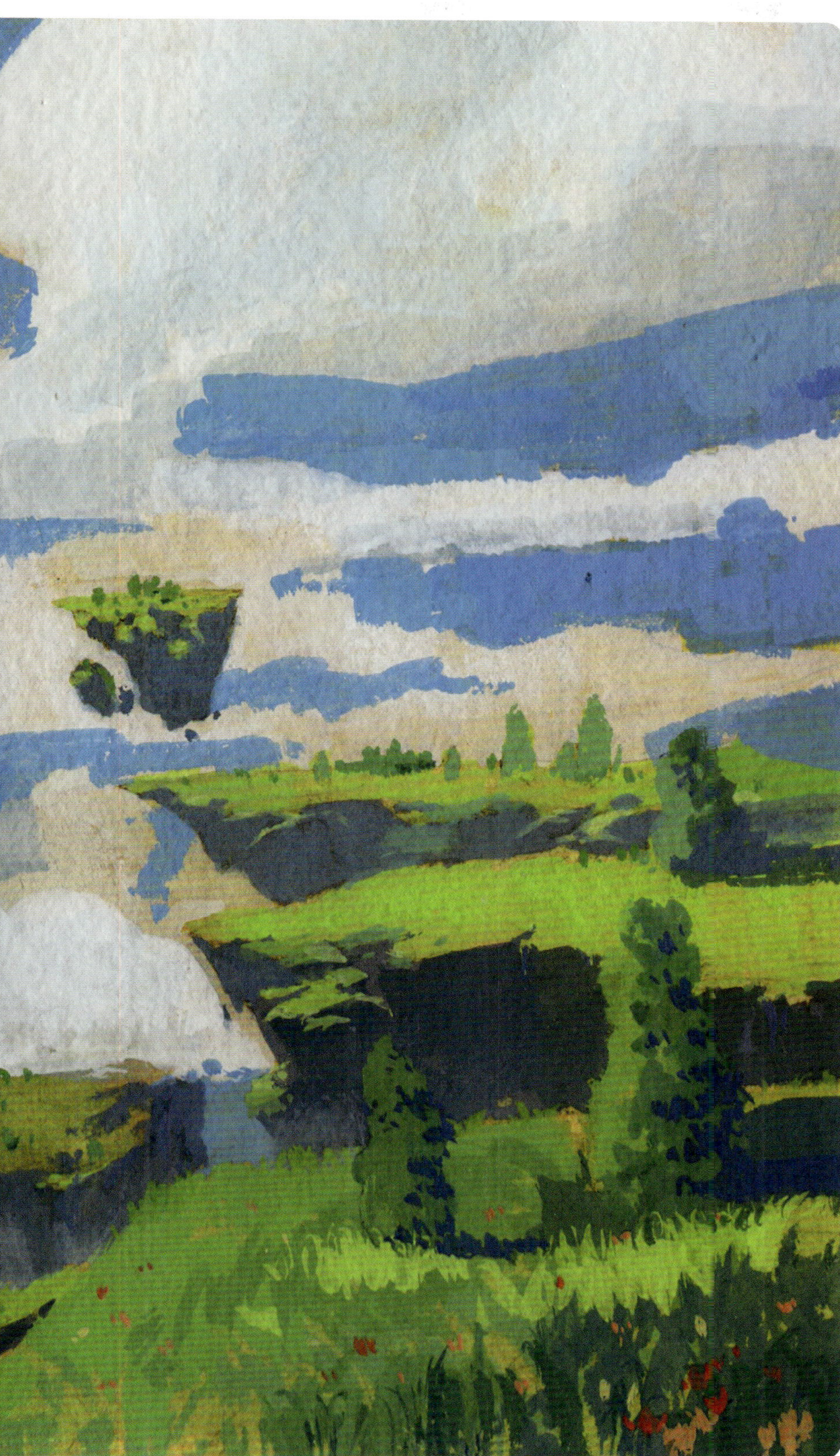

CONCLUSION

I'm really pleased with how this painting turned out – it truly reflects my style and brings life and beauty to a subtle, fantasy-inspired landscape. The most important lesson for me when painting natural scenes is to simplify as much as possible. Too much detail can overwhelm the composition, so it's essential to keep things balanced. I believe gouache is the perfect medium for practising simple environments and honing composition skills. These colours are some of my favourites, and I hope my work resonates with anyone who enjoys bright, lively scenes like I do.

Final image © Fatima Mandouh

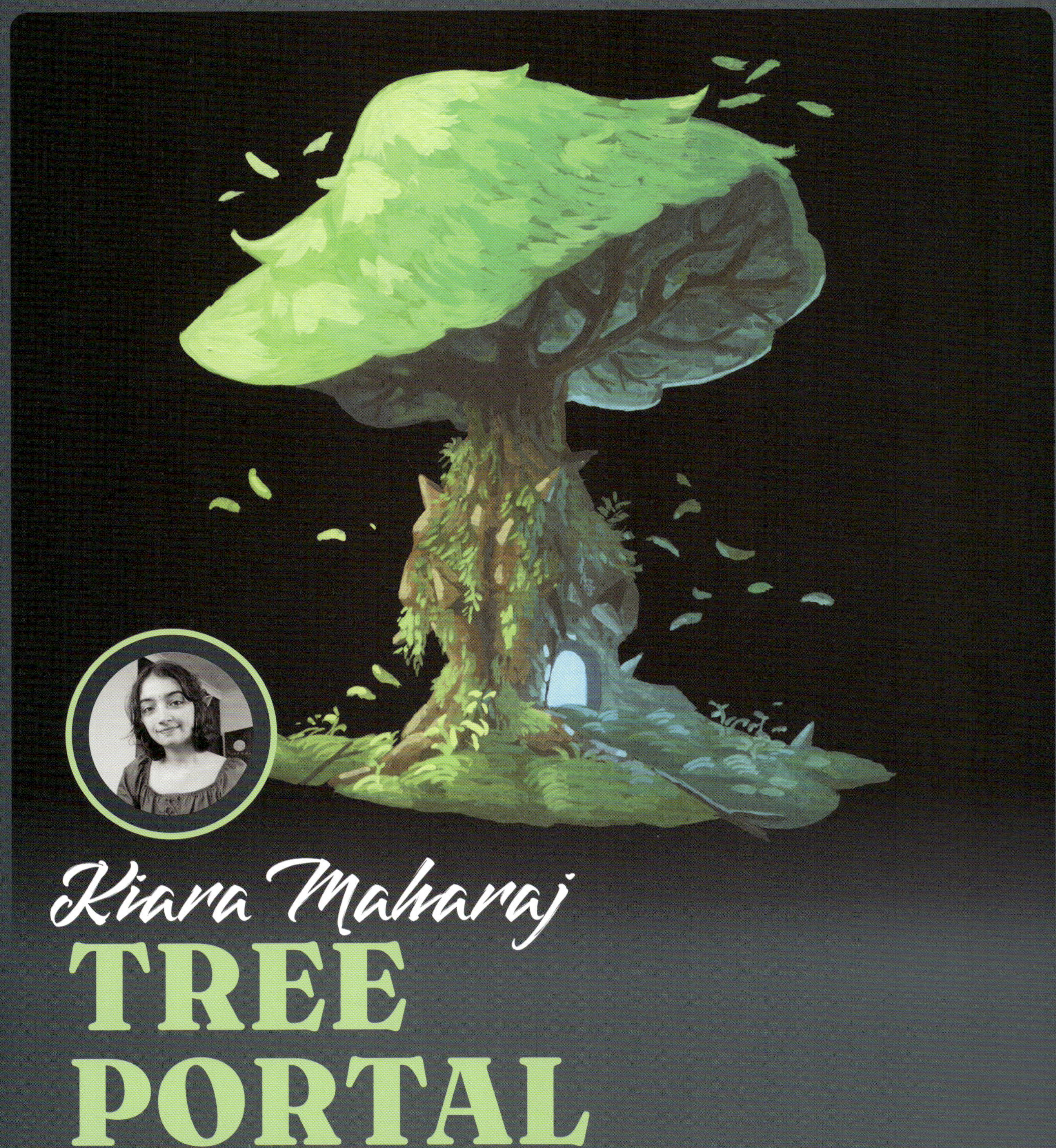
Final image © Kiara Maharaj

Kiara Maharaj

TREE PORTAL

In this tutorial I'm going to paint a tree portal with dynamic lighting: a magical door set within the bark of a tree, emitting blue light, while the sun warmly shines on its leafy canopy. This style of scene with two light sources is my favourite to paint, especially using gouache on black paper, because of the quiet and mysterious feeling it evokes. I am so excited to guide you through the magic of the black page – from sketching on black paper, to mixing colours, to creating dynamic lighting, and tips and tricks I've learned throughout the years of using this medium.

TOOLKIT

- **Thick black paper** 300 gsm (110 lb)

- **Regular white printer paper**

- **HB pencil**

- **Blue pencil** (optional)

- **Palette**

- **Jar of water**

- **Spray bottle of water**

- **Tissue paper** (to clean brushes)

BRUSHES

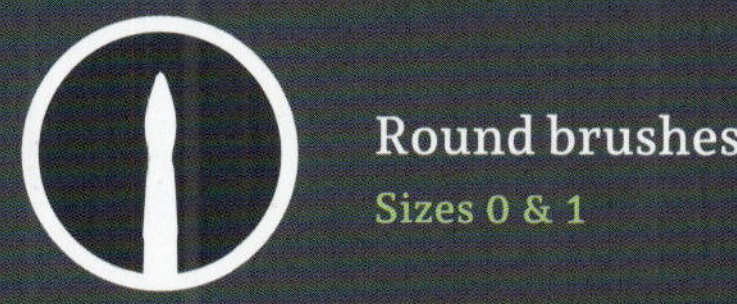

Round brushes Sizes 0 & 1

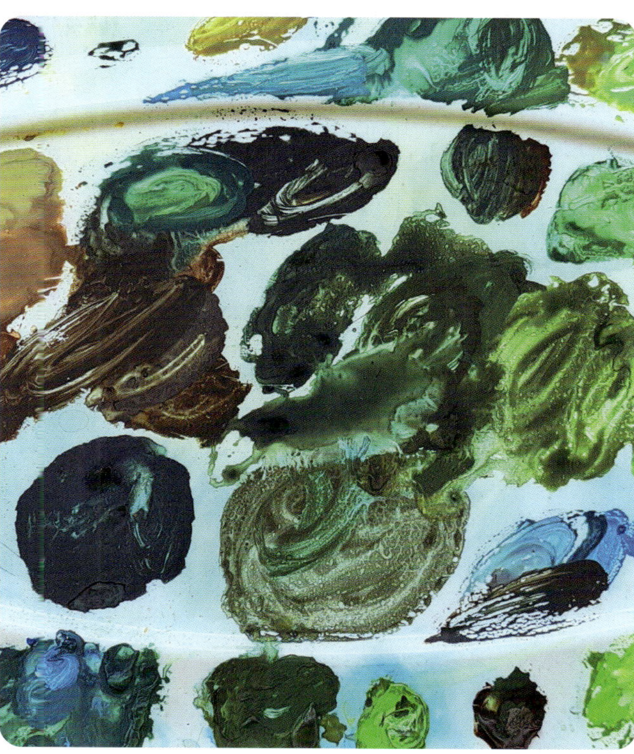

This colour selection includes a couple of greens and browns for painting the tree trunk and foliage, blue and yellow to create different lighting temperatures, and black and white for mixing and creating a range of values. I like to include Viridian, a strong blue-green, as it fits well between the blue and green hues.

COLOUR LIST

- Burnt Sienna
- Burnt Umber
- Cascade Green
- Viridian
- Cerulean Blue
- Hansa Yellow Light
- Lamp Black
- Spring Green
- Titanium White

01.

First and foremost, before you paint or draw or create anything, you have to organize your workspace and the supplies you're going to use. I like to use black paper that is at least 300 gsm (110 lb), so I can paint lots of layers without the paper warping or buckling. Avoid painting with black paper in direct sunlight; I have found that no matter how good the paper quality, black paper in direct sunlight always gets damaged and buckles in the heat.

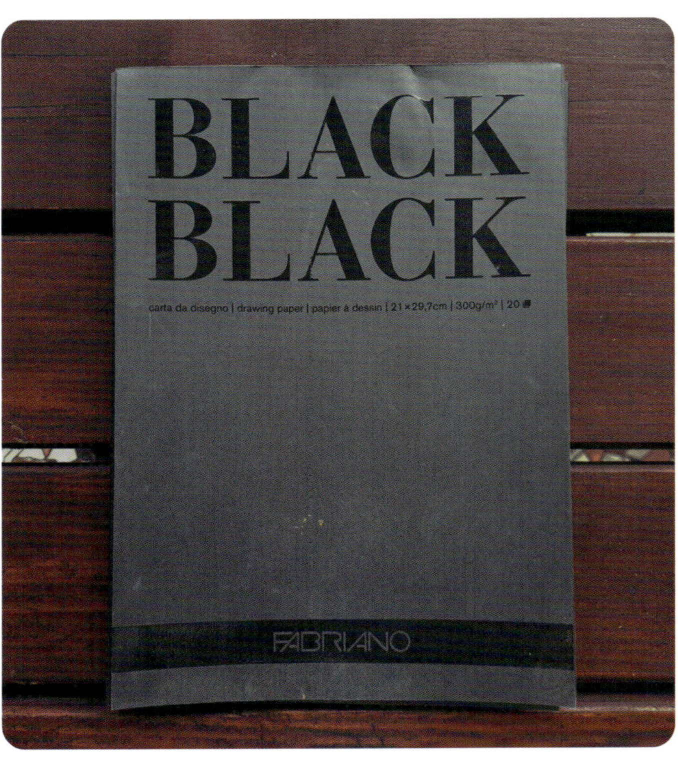

01b. Fabriano Black Black paper in 300 gsm (21 × 29.7 cm or A4 size)

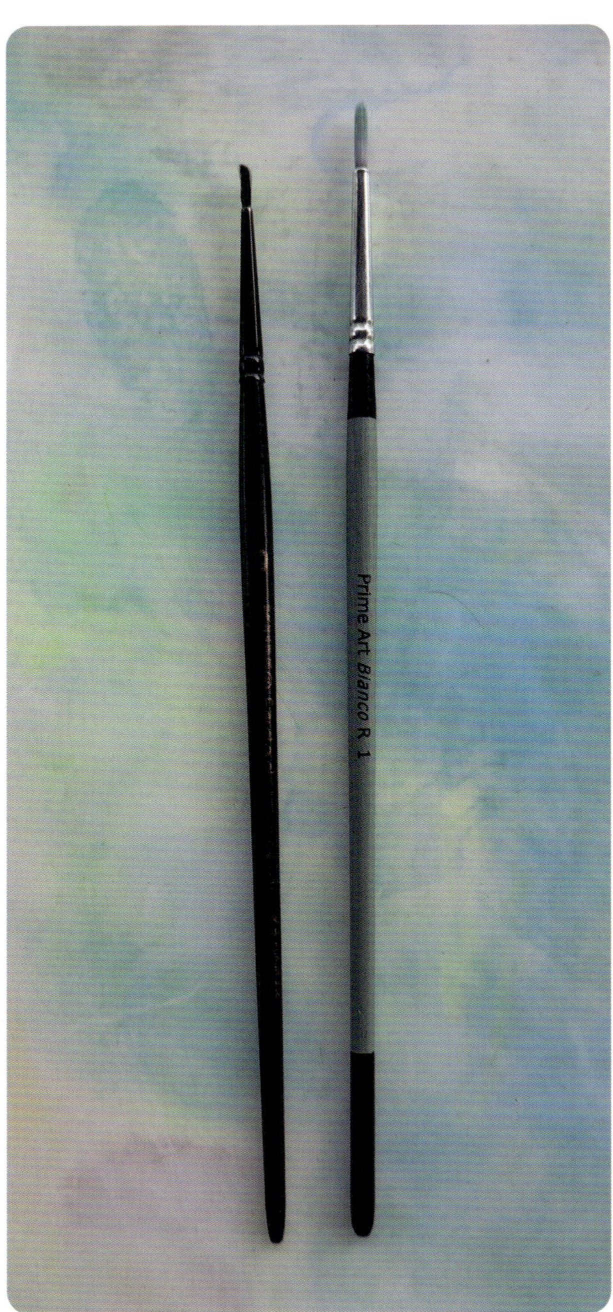

01a. Round brushes in sizes 0 and 1

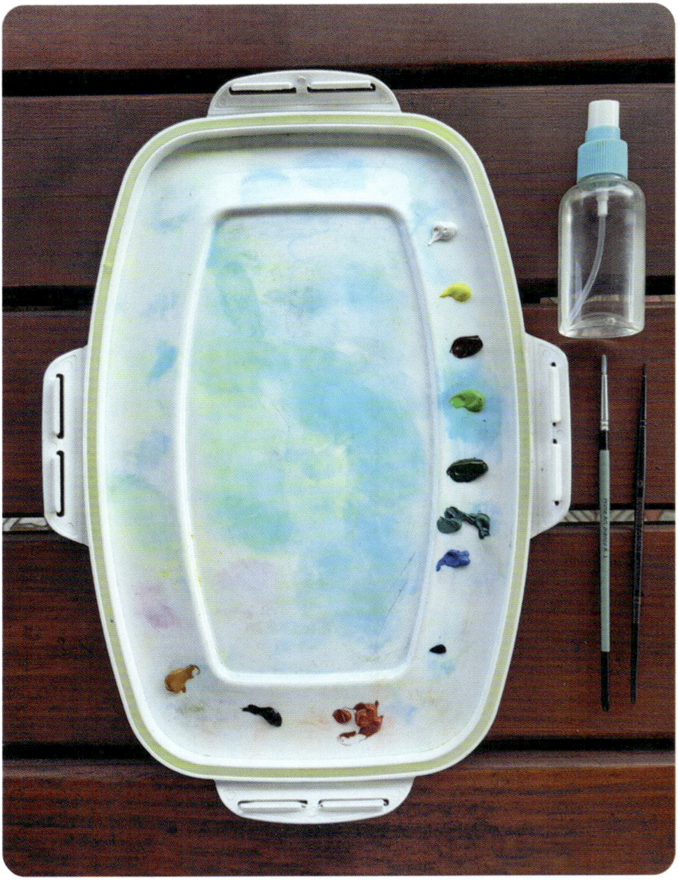

01c. A plastic palette for mixing colours

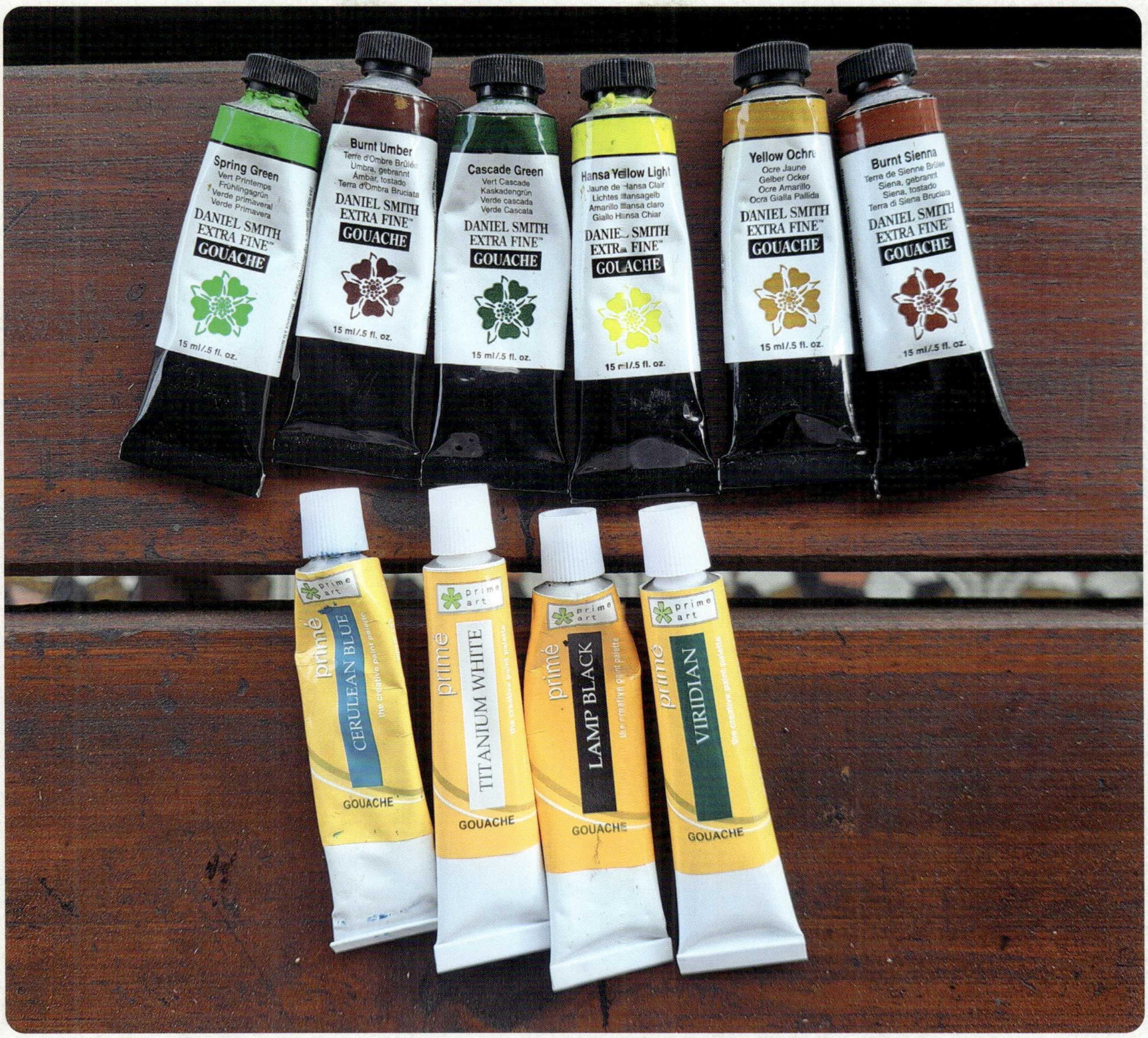

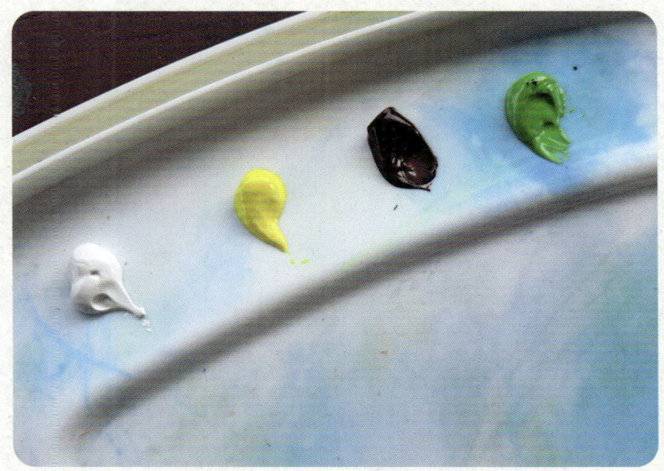

02a. The range of gouache paints used for this project

02.

Before you get down to the actual painting, you should plan the colours you'll use. This will prevent you from getting overwhelmed by all the hues that paint has to offer, and from mixing muddy colours. It will even help you to tell a better story in your painting. Plan your colours based on the lighting in your scene and the mood you want to create. This tree portal will have an atmosphere of mystery, curiosity, and wonder – a scene that a wanderer has stumbled upon and can't help but gape at. There will be a blue portal on the 'shadow side' of the tree, and warm greens and yellows on the 'sunny side'.

02b. Titanium White, Hansa Yellow Light, Burnt Umber, and Spring Green

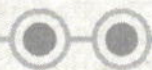

03.

The first step is to draw a rough idea of the tree design and where the primary light source would be coming from. There are a few ways to translate a sketch onto black paper. You can draw with pencil directly on the black paper, but this might be challenging and messy because it's hard to see the lines. Plus, if you need to erase, erasing on black paper can leave a lot of marks. Instead, I use a much easier method. I start by drawing the sketch on regular white printer paper, using a Prussian-blue coloured pencil to indicate the primary light source.

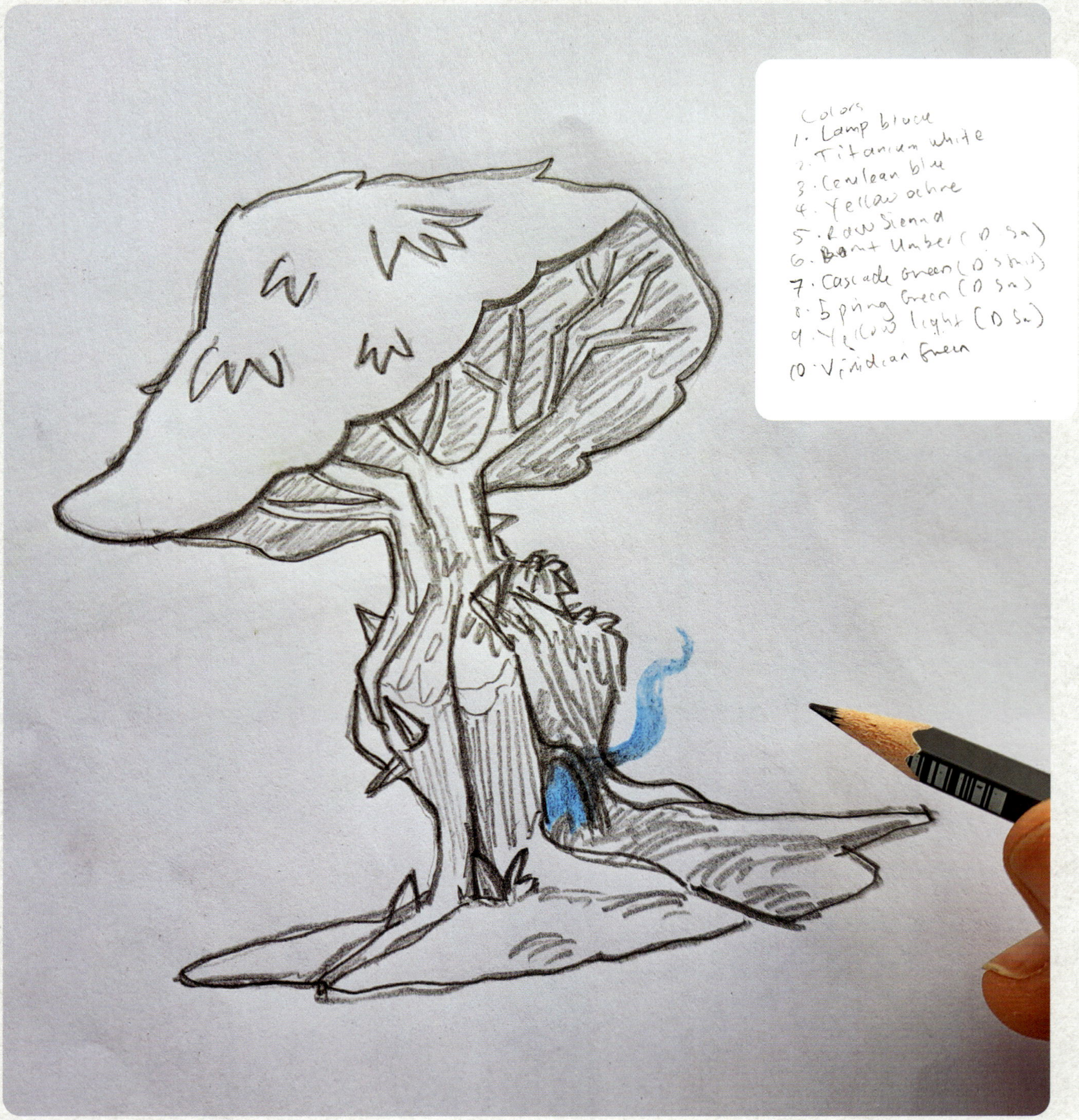

03. Planning the tree design on white paper first; this sketch is made with an HB pencil and blue coloured pencil

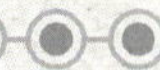

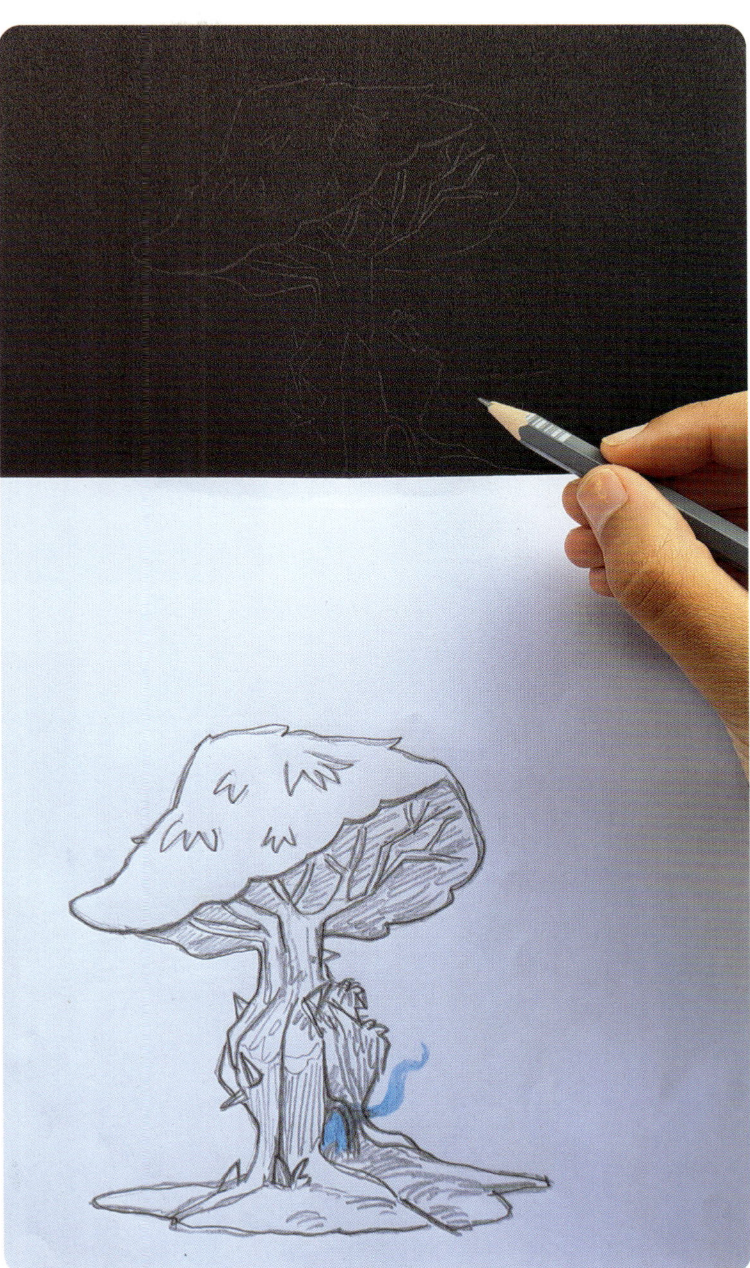

04. Create a 'transfer page' and transfer the sketch by drawing firmly on it

04.

Now the pencil sketch can be transferred from white paper to black paper. The pencil sketch doesn't need to be extremely refined because you can still decide which lines you want to keep as you do the transfer. On the reverse side of my sketch page, I use the HB pencil to entirely shade the area directly behind the drawing. I try to cover the area thoroughly and make it as dark as possible. This basically creates a transfer sheet with a smooth layer of graphite on one side and the pencil sketch on the other side.

Next I get my black paper and place the white paper over it, with the sketch side facing up towards me. I am careful to position the white page so that I'm satisfied with where the drawing will be transferred (in this case, centred on the black paper). I then use a pencil to carefully yet firmly retrace the lines on the sketch. Make sure to hold your paper firmly and not move it around, otherwise the transfer will get messed up. When you have drawn over all the lines, carefully lift the white paper and set it aside. You should see the lines you have traced lightly transferred onto the black paper.

05.

The transferred outline will be a guide for refining the sketch on the black paper before I begin painting. I use the HB pencil to draw over the traced lines with a steady hand, rectifying any errors or places I missed, and brightening any of the lines that aren't visible enough. You can compare against your original white-paper sketch as a reference. Avoid erasing on the black paper! If you make a mistake, you can cover it up with paint later.

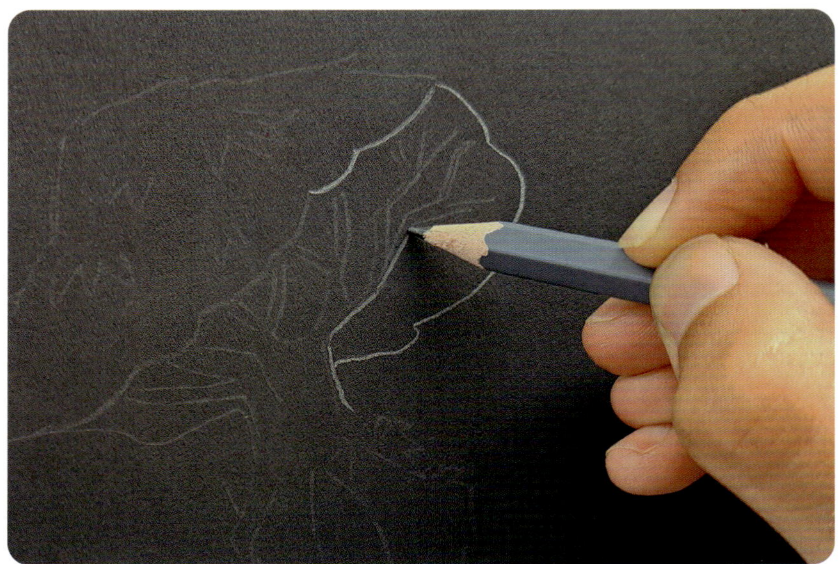

05a. The final sketch should be a clean, simple guideline for the next step: painting

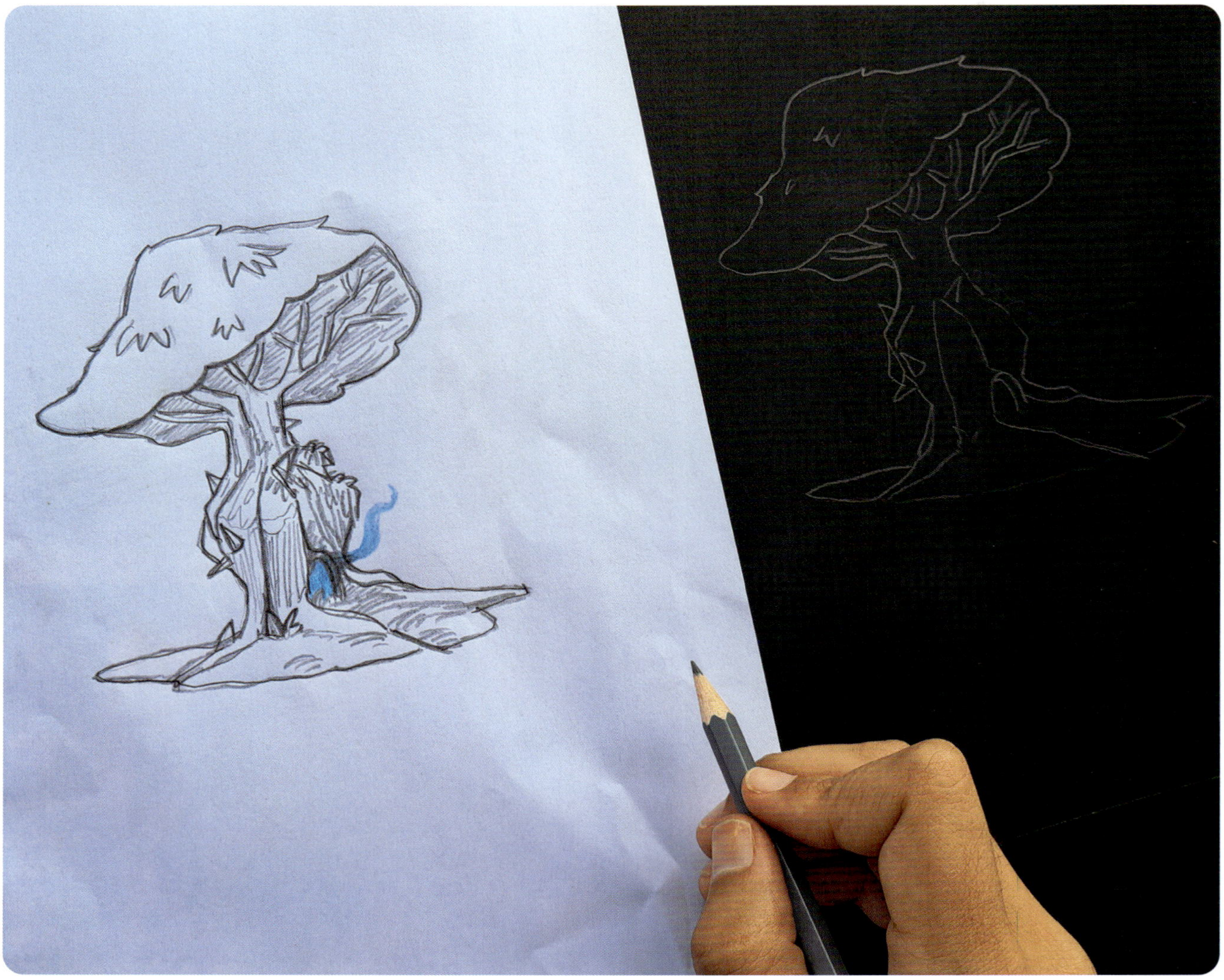

05b. Use your original sketch as a reference for refining the copy

SWATCHES

A colour looks very different on a white palette compared to on black paper. With this in mind, it's often a good idea to dab a quick paint swatch onto a separate piece of black paper, or onto an unused edge of your page, and let it dry to see how the colour will look before adding it to your work. If you plan on using black paper regularly, you might want to invest in a black mixing palette.

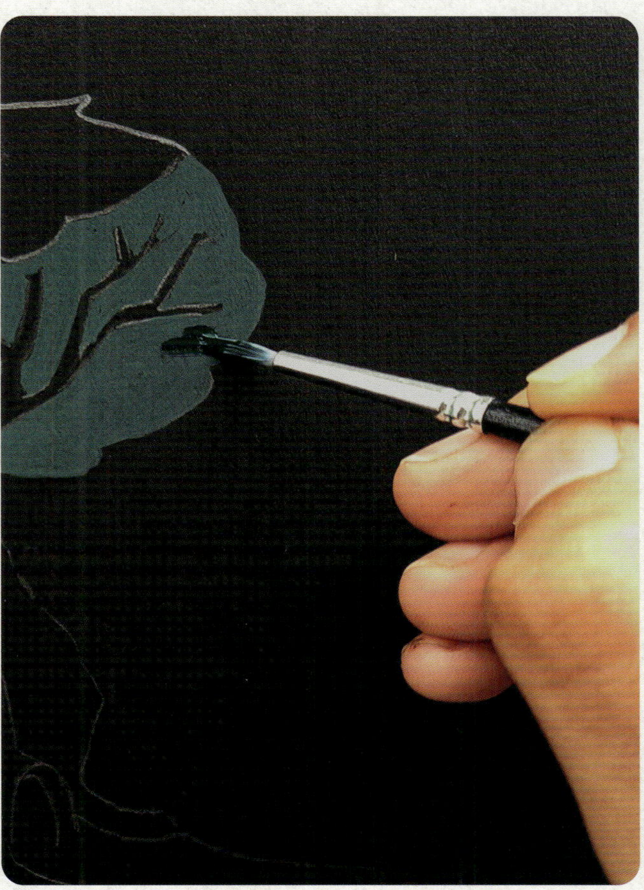

06. Paint the foliage underside a dark, blue-toned green

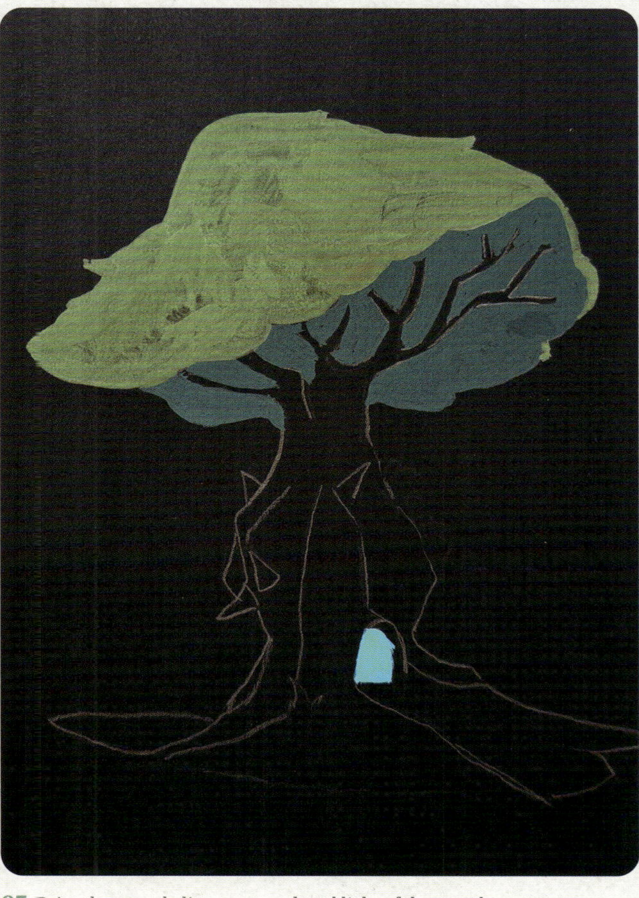

07. Paint the warmly lit canopy and cool light of the portal

06.

Now I finally get to the exciting part: adding paint. I start by painting the underside of the tree. This part should be dark green, but it's also facing the portal. Any part of the tree that's facing the portal (lower-right corner) will have more Cerulean Blue mixed into the colour, and any part facing the sun (upper-left corner) will have more Yellow Ochre. So, for the underside of the canopy, I mix Cascade Green, Viridian Green, Burnt Sienna, and Lamp Black to make a dark green shade, and then add a bit of Cerulean Blue to make it fit the scene. I like to use Viridian Green for painting these magical forest scenes because it makes the perfect gradient between Cascade Green and Cerulean Blue.

07.

In this step, I'm going to establish the colours for the lit areas. For the upper part of the canopy that's facing the sun, I put down a warm olive-green mixed from Cascade Green, Spring Green, and Burnt Sienna. This indicates the warm secondary light source. Then I mix a small amount of light, bright blue using Cerulean Blue and Titanium White and use it to paint the portal. This is the cold primary light source. Remember: because the surface you are working on is extremely dark, anything you paint on it will look brighter on the paper than on the palette, and therefore stand out or 'pop' off the page.

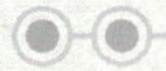

08.

Now I can continue the 'blocking in' part of the painting process – placing the base colours for different areas of a painting without getting into too much detail. I start with a mix of Burnt Sienna and Yellow Ochre for the light parts of the bark and tree trunk. These are any parts of the tree bark that are facing the sun and being lit up by warm light. Then I use a mix of Burnt Sienna and Burnt Umber for parts of the bark that would be in shadow, such as the roots and the branches beneath the canopy. Finally, I mix a little bit of Cerulean Blue into the Burnt Sienna and Burnt Umber mixture. I use this for the parts of the bark that are closer to the portal but not directly facing it. Painting the colours this way is going to help create a smooth transition from one light source to another.

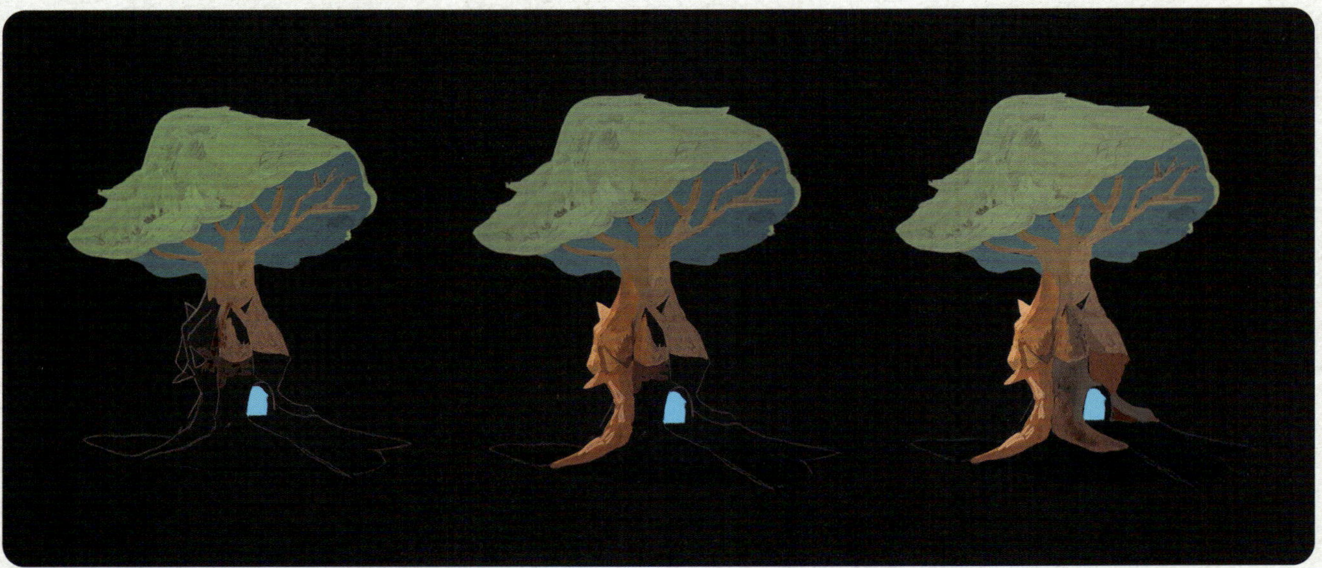

08a. Roughly block out the differently lit dimensions of the trunk

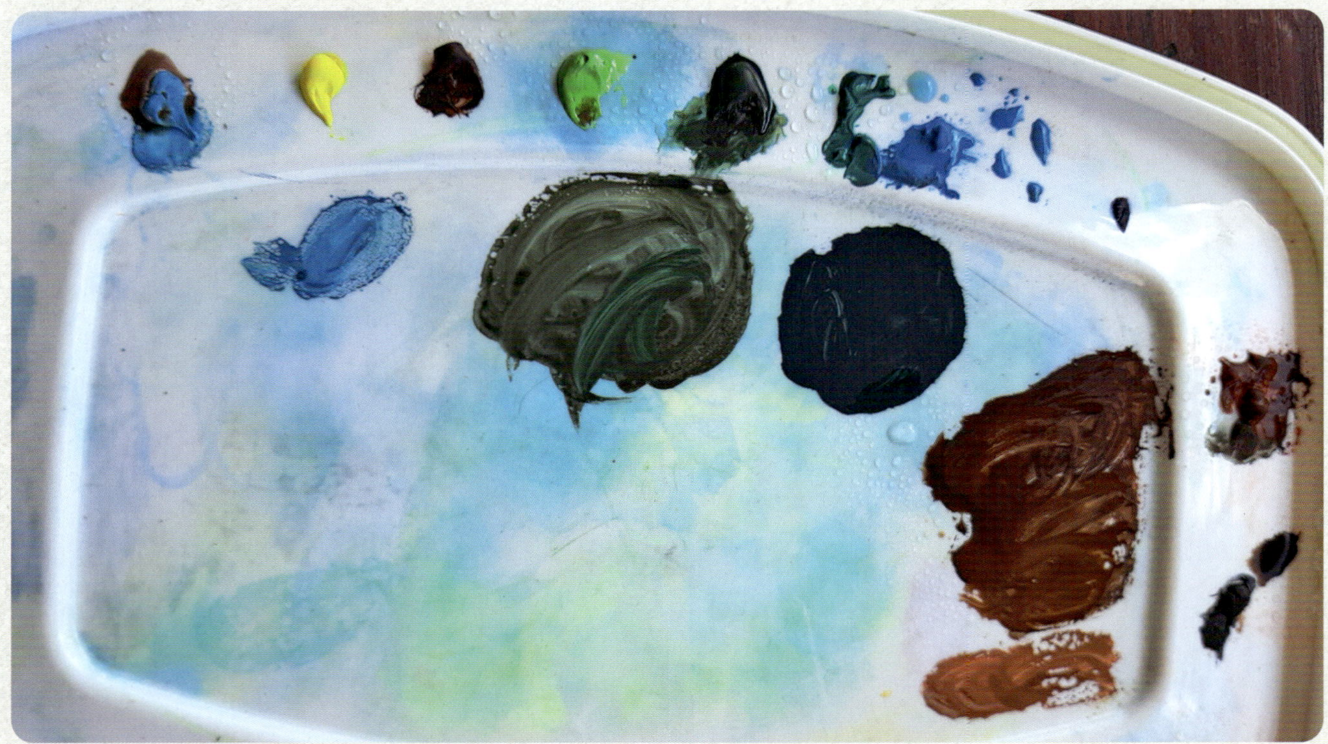

08b. Mix different shades of brown to paint the trunk

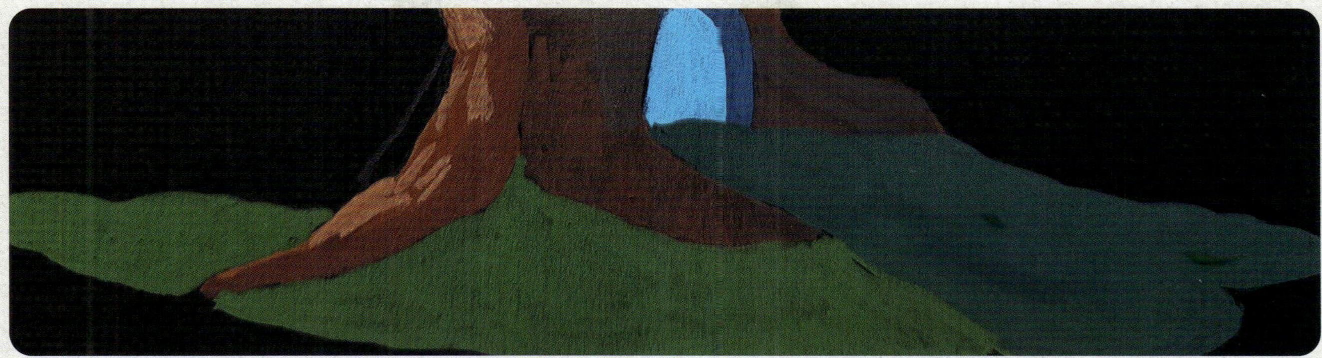

09a. Use two shades of green for the ground under the tree

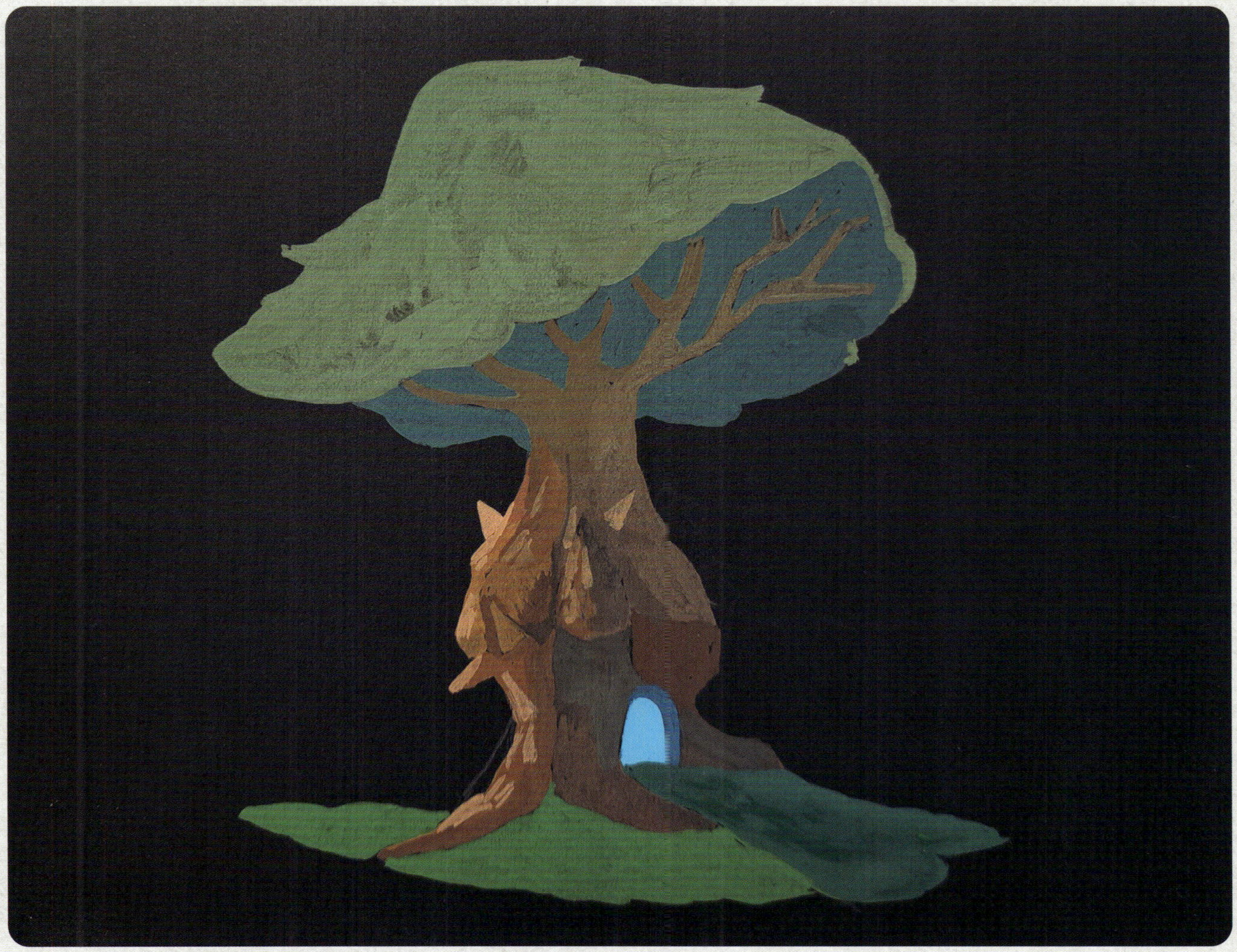

09b. The major lit areas of the scene are now blocked in; wait for the ground to dry fully before the next step

09.

This step is similar to the previous step, but I'm blocking in the basic colours for the grass on which the tree is rooted. Imagine the ground here in two parts: the first part is the grass on the 'warm' side (towards the left) and the second part is on the 'cold' side (towards the right).

I mix a warm olive-green colour using Spring Green, Cascade Green, Burnt Sienna, and Yellow Ochre, and use it to paint the warm side. Then I mix Viridian Green and Cascade Green and paint the cold side. Let all these colours dry fully before moving on to the next step.

10.

The next steps involve pushing the contrast between the warm side and the cold side, and creating a gradual transition between the two. Contrast refers to the difference between the darkest colour and the lightest colour. I can start pushing the contrast by painting bright, warm highlights on the tree leaves and the grass. I mix Spring Green and Yellow Ochre, then hold my brush loosely and create impressions of leaves by placing shapes with this light-green colour against the dark green. Don't try to blend the two colours on the paper – the aim is to create more texture by placing colours side by side instead.

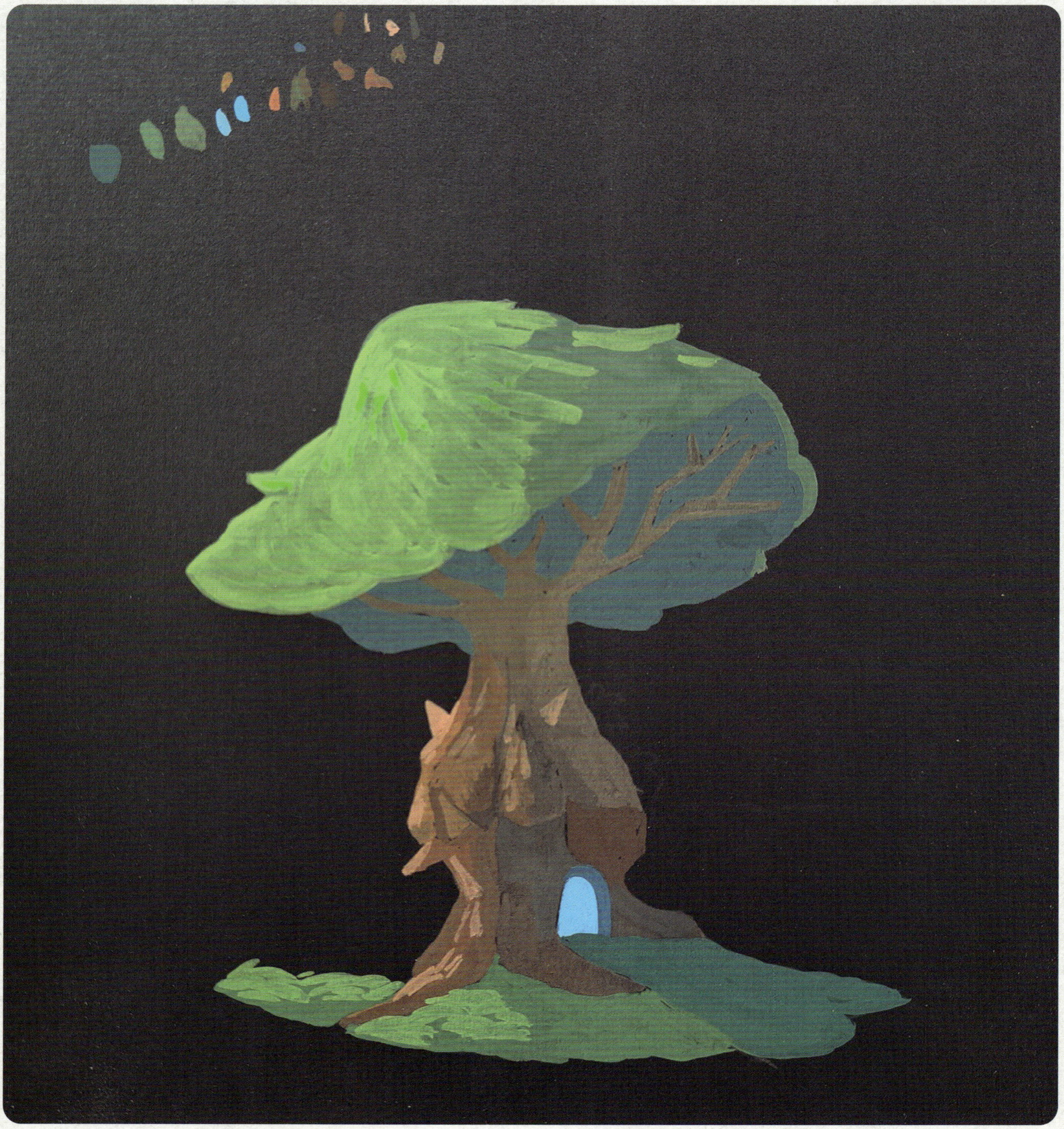

10. Bring in a light, warm green to create more contrast

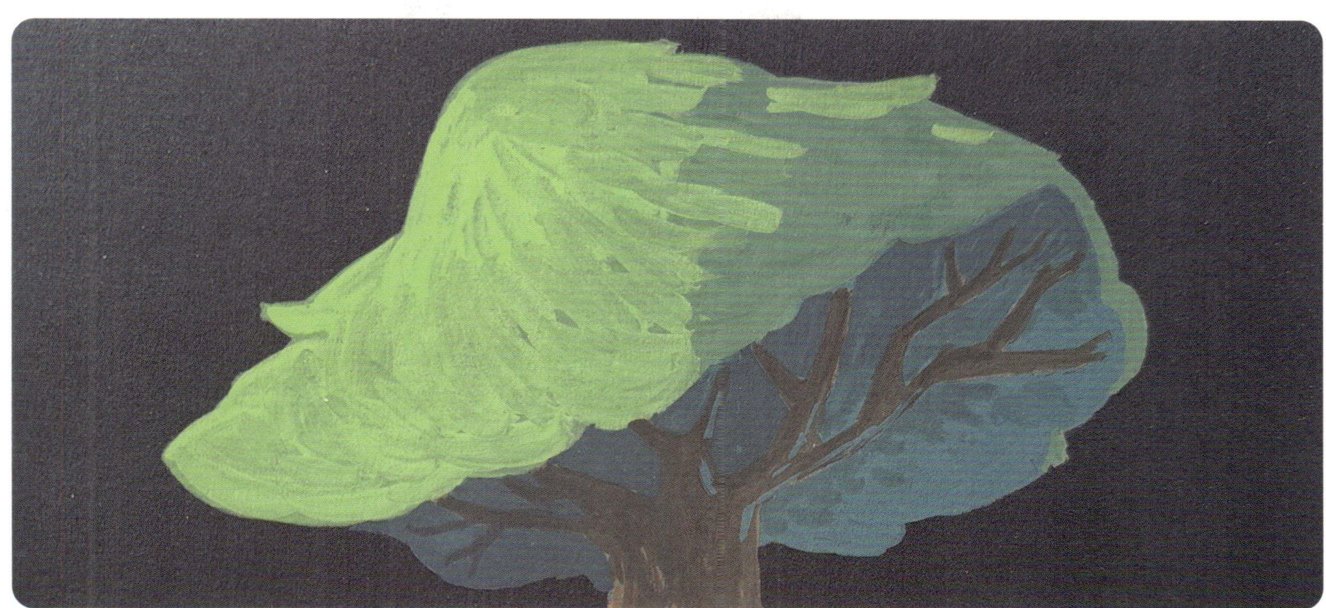

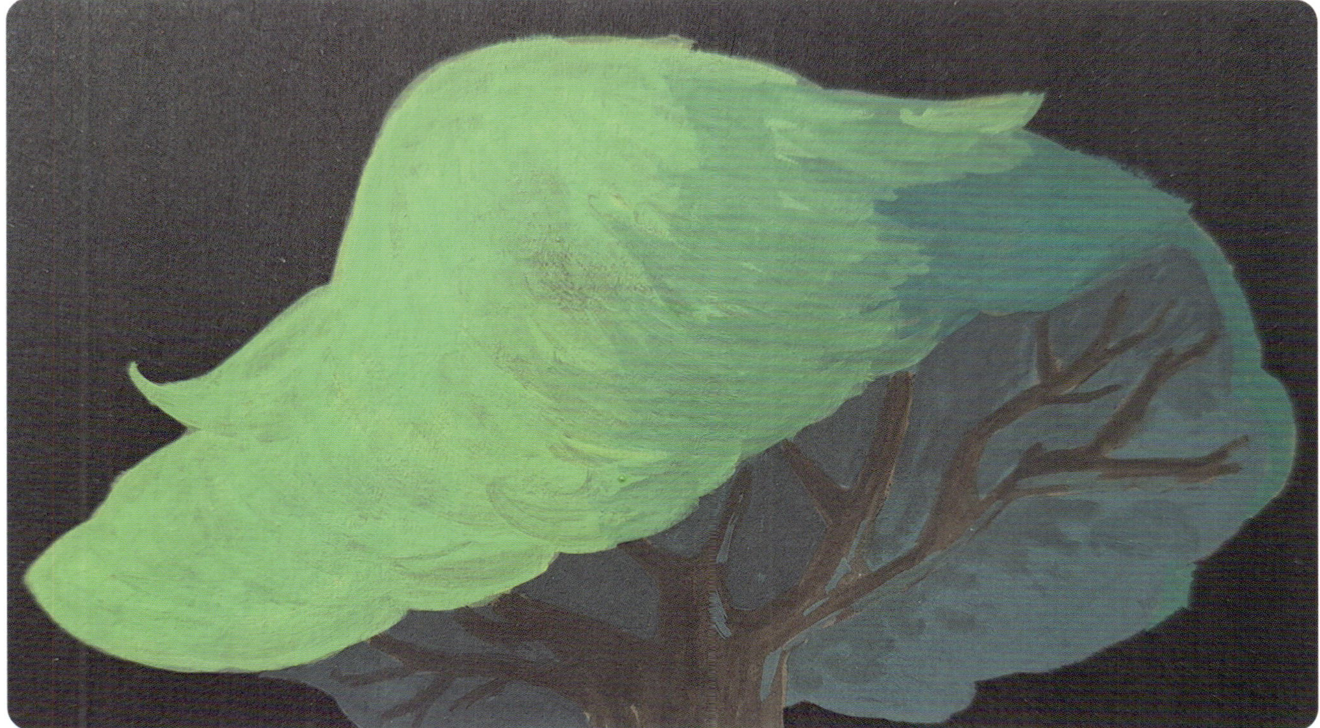

11. Build up the colour and contrast of the leafy canopy

11.

To push the contrast even further, I'll make the highlights brighter and the shadows darker. The darkest part of the tree portal is going to be the underside of the tree canopy. To better express this, I mix a dark green-blue using Cerulean Blue, Cascade Green, and Lamp Black. I use this to start painting the parts on the left side of the canopy's underside. This area should have the darkest shadow because it's directly below the leaves that are blocking the sun. This creates a beautiful contrast, adding more interest and dynamism to the illustration. I then mix Burnt Umber, Cerulean Blue, and some Lamp Black, and use this to paint the branches and parts of the bark that will be in shadow from the canopy.

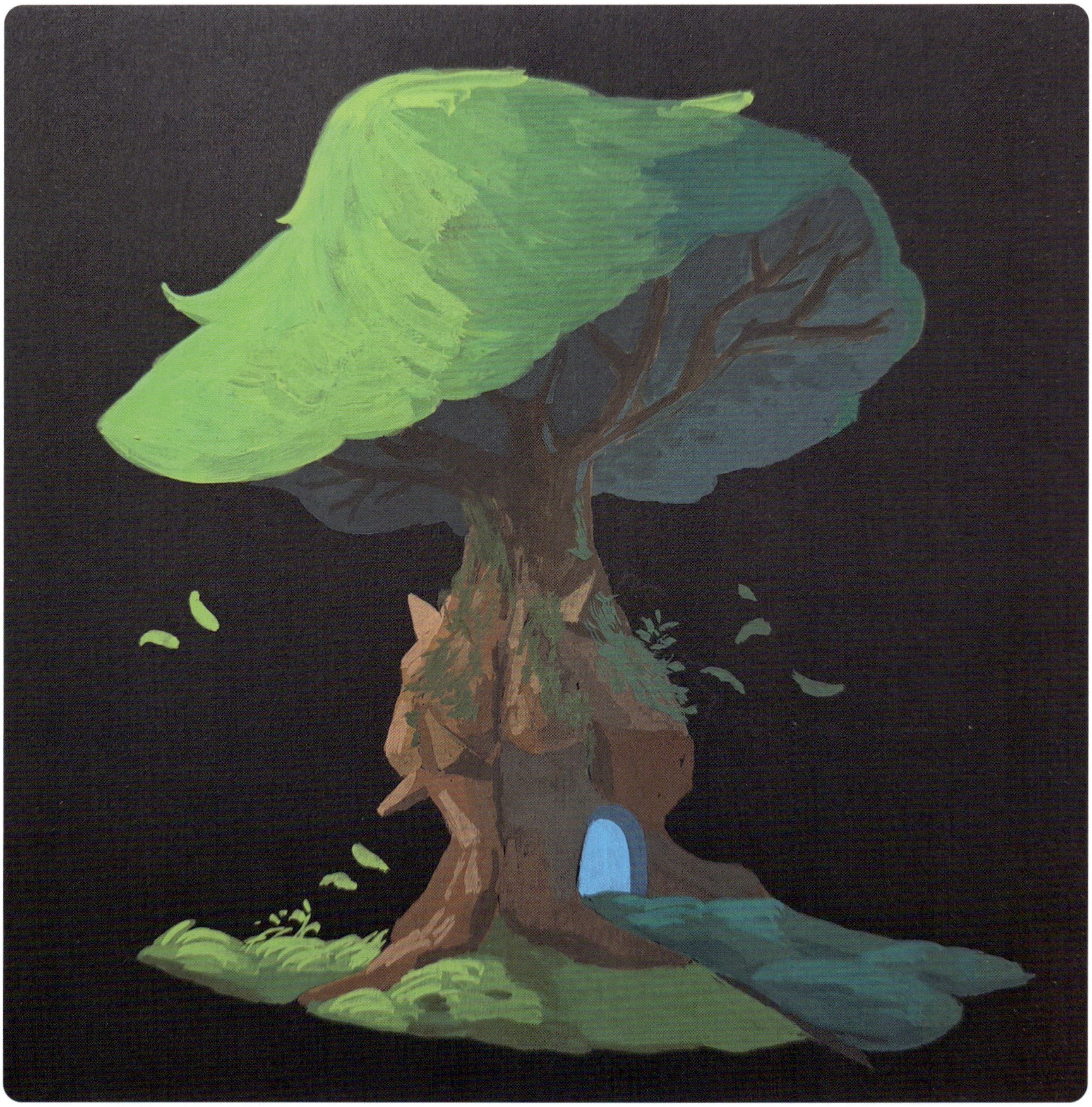

12. Drifting leaves add extra life and magic

12.

This might be the most fun step in the process! Now I get to bring the illustration to life with little details that brought me here in the first place. I start by painting highlights on the grass near the portal. To do this, mix some Viridian Green and Cerulean Blue, and move the brush over the ground in small curves to indicate small hills. The ground in a forest is never flat, but you can't paint every single detail without taking away from the main focus of the painting (the portal).

Instead, I recommend painting impressions of the forest's details with the right shape and colour. For the moss on the tree trunk and roots, I use the warm olive-green colour mixed in Step 07 (Spring Green, Cascade Green, and Burnt Sienna). One of my favourite details to add is the 'runaway leaves' – I imagine they're either captured mid-fall or blowing in a breeze. These are simple spots created with a single brushstroke using my round brush 0.

13.

In this step I'm going to add highlights to the moss and leaves, and paint a subtle transition on the grass that forms the 'middle ground' between the sun and the portal. For the moss highlights, I mix Hansa Yellow Light and Spring Green. This is the brightest colour in the illustration. I use simple downward strokes with a round 0 brush to paint the grass. Then I mix Viridian Green, Cascade Green, and some Yellow Ochre for the grass that is neither in the sun nor in the portal's light. I use the same brush technique for this grass: small curves. Here and there you can even indicate stems of a plant and its leaves sticking up out of the ground.

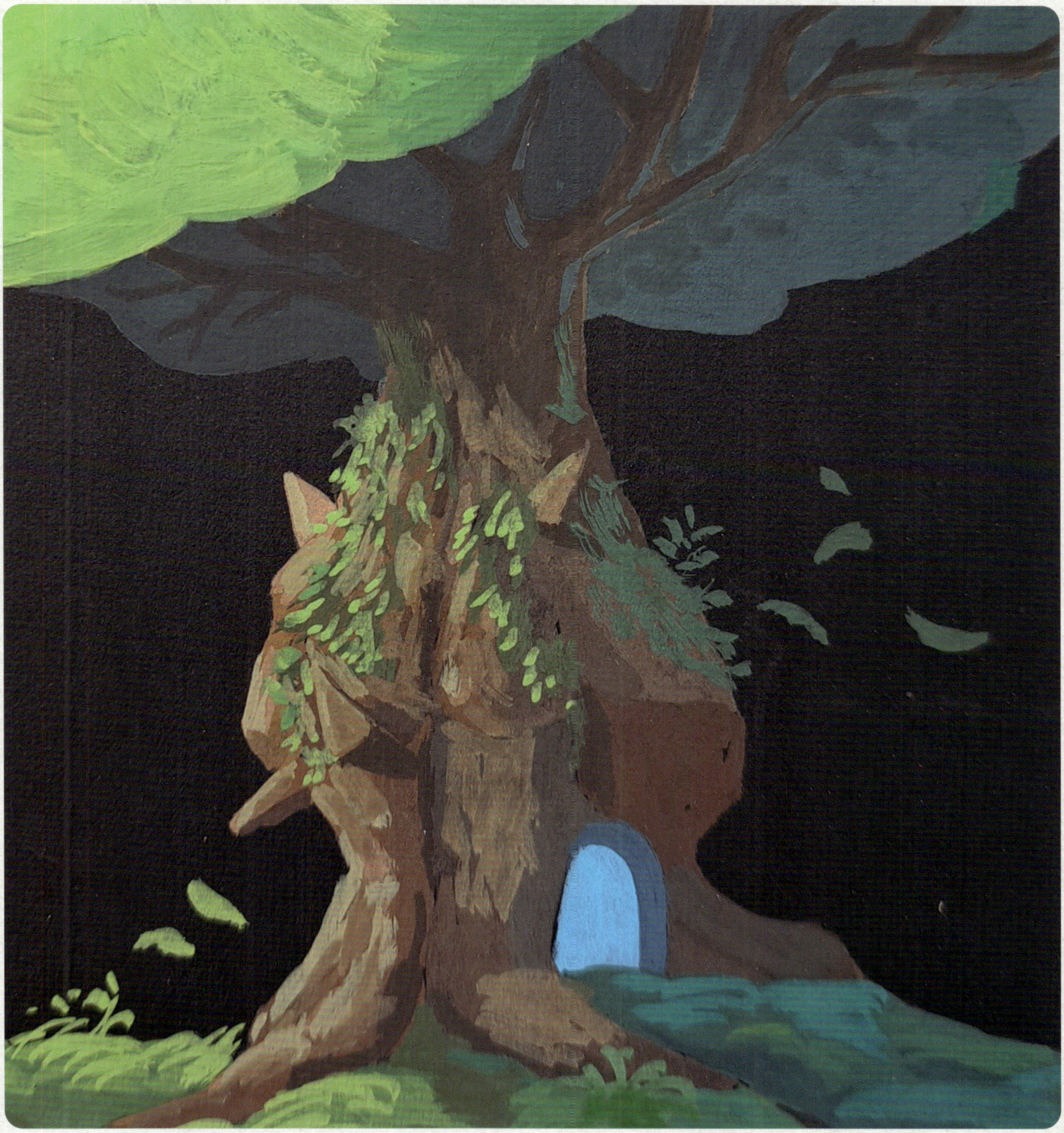

13. Strokes of lighter green add depth to the foliage and grass

14.

Now I can begin to add smaller highlights and details to parts of the grass, bark, branches, and roots. I love to paint some sticks or twigs using Burnt Umber or even plain Lamp Black against a bright colour. You can create a more gradual transition between the light sources by mixing more Cerulean Blue into any part of the tree closer to the portal, and Yellow Ochre to any part closer to the sun. I use a mix of Viridian Green and Cerulean Blue to add some leaves on the underside of the canopy that could be catching the portal's light.

To create extra focus around the portal area, I use the Cerulean Blue and Titanium White mix to highlight some blades of grass, flying leaves, and the rim of the bottom part of the tree canopy. I begin adding a few sunny leaves to the canopy, but then change my mind – I want to make some revisions to the canopy shape, so I leave those strokes to dry and will come back to them later!

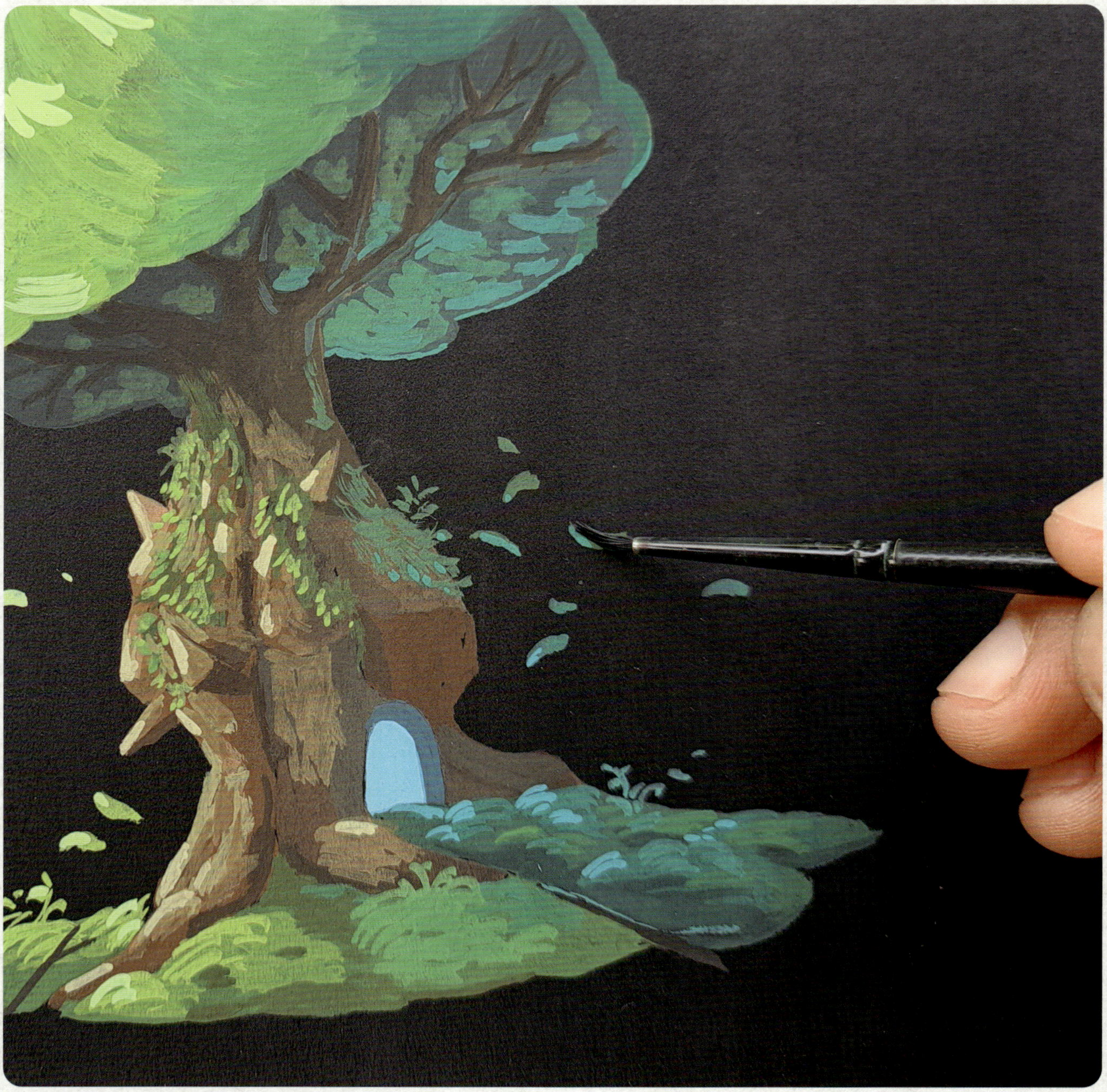

14. Pick out details to highlight and emphasize the blue light source of the magic portal

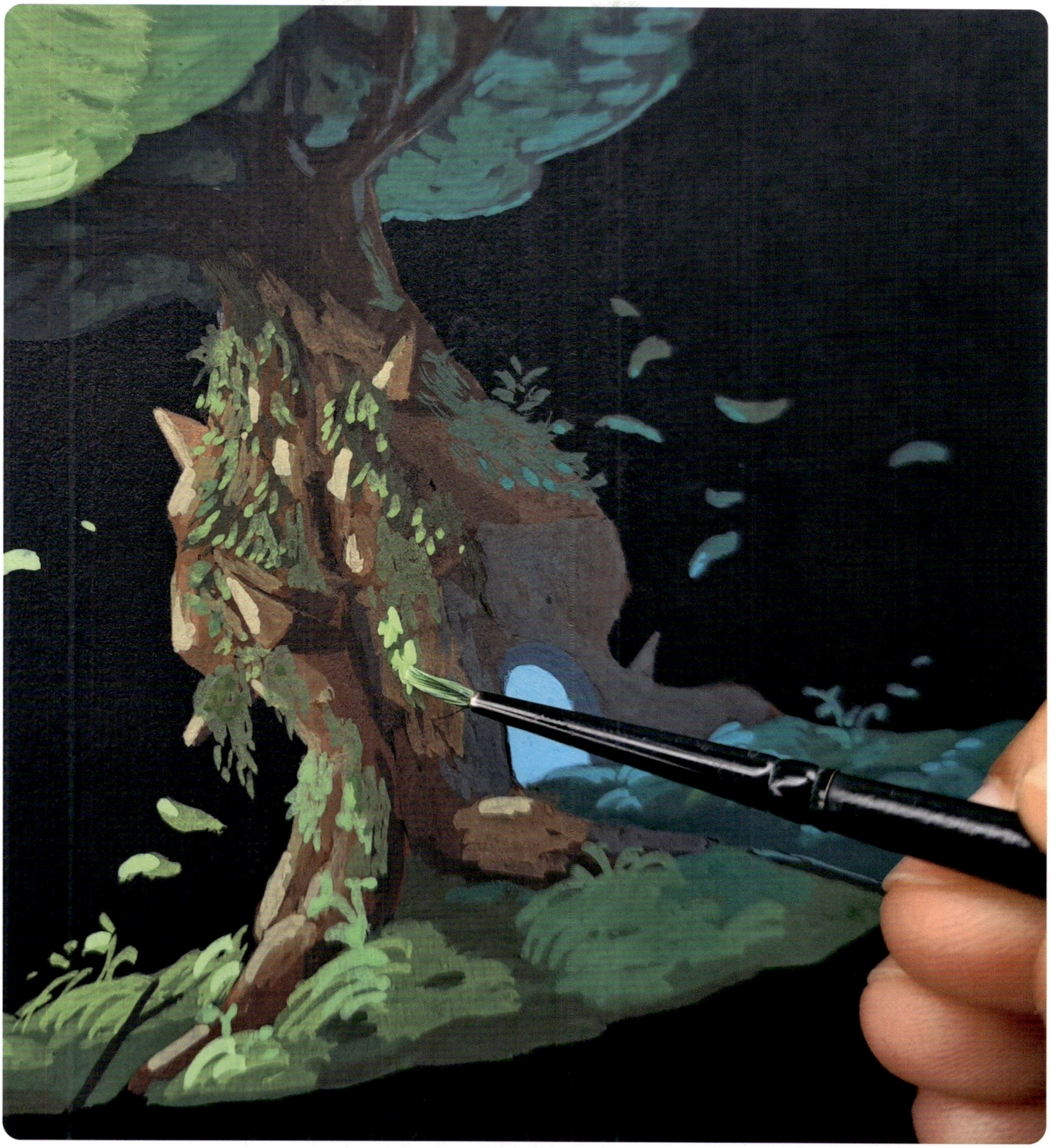

15. A few final warm and cool highlights make the greenery and trunk extra vibrant

15.

Now for the last few highlights on the trunk and lower parts of the scene. I mix Spring Green, Hansa Yellow Light, and Titanium White and use the round brush 0 to add delicate bright-green moss details on the trunk. I use a mix of Cerulean Blue and Burnt Umber to highlight the parts of the tree roots that would be getting more light from the portal. The closer the trunk is to the portal, the more Cerulean Blue is needed in the colour mixture.

16.

Black paper is a challenging surface to paint on, so after taking a step back you can better identify what needs reworking to finish a painting. I decide I want to repaint some parts of the treetop to add more visible texture and clumps of leaves. Luckily, gouache makes it easy to repaint something until you're happy with it! Just let the paint dry thoroughly, so it doesn't get reactivated, and use single brushstrokes to avoid damaging the layer beneath. That's what I do here, redoing the gradient and then painting leaf shapes using the pre-mixed greens from the previous steps. I use the round brush to

apply the paint in 'oval' shapes that create the effect of chaotic leaves sticking out of the canopy and striking the light. The final effect gives the impression of more detail and layers of texture.

Underneath the canopy, I use a mix of Burnt Umber and Lamp Black to add some extra contrast and smaller branches for detail. Keep in mind that branches are thicker closer to the trunk, and get narrower the further out they go. I also add a few more runaway leaves because I can't help it. Feel free to add your own unique finishing touches!

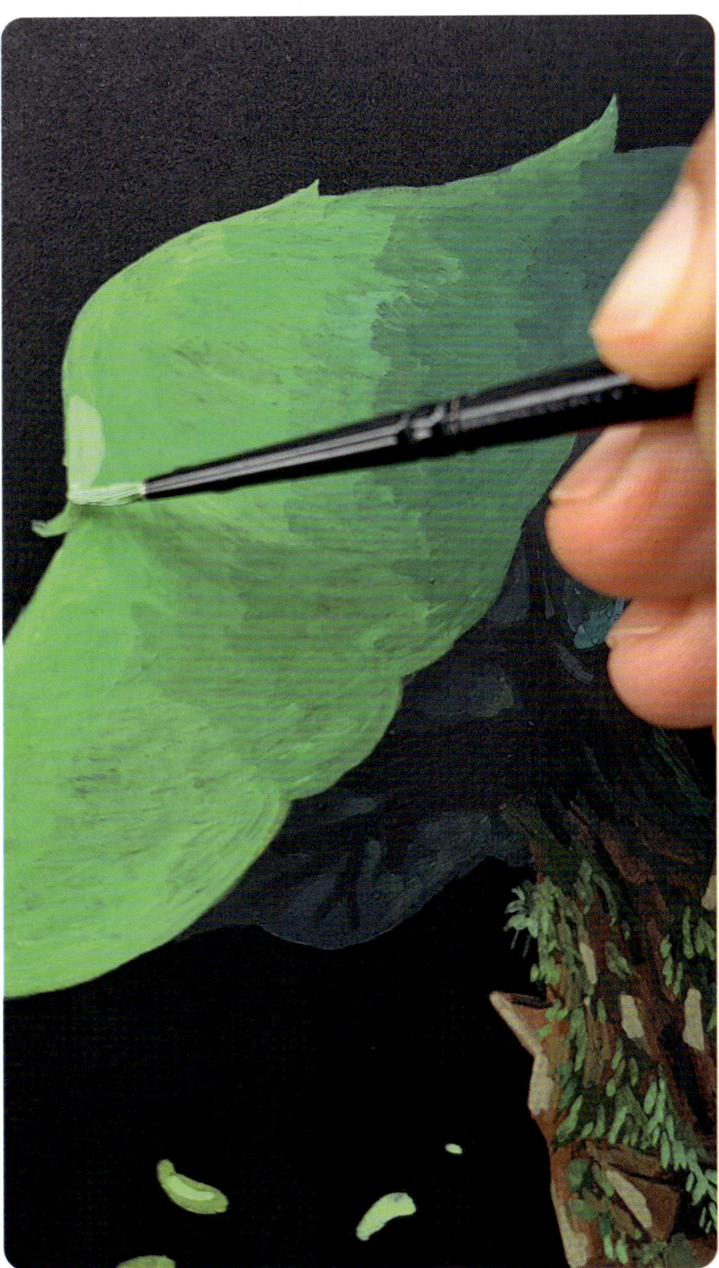

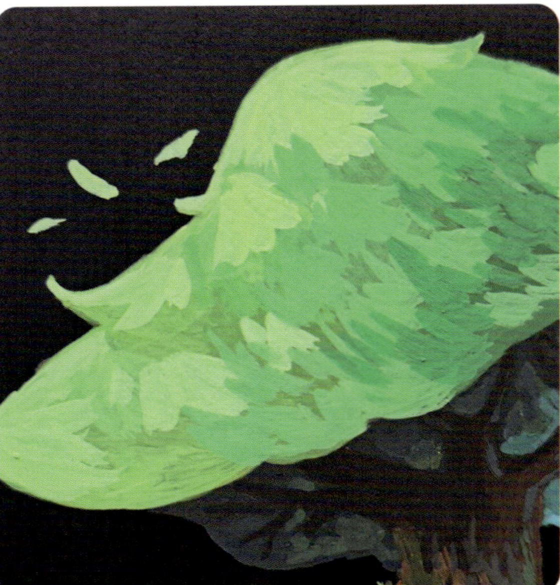

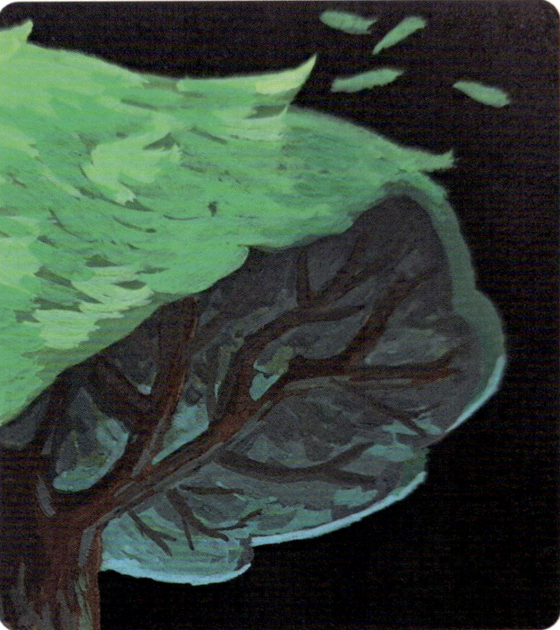

16. Gouache is a forgiving medium for revisions and adjustments

Final image © Kiara Maharaj

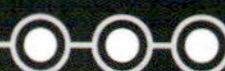

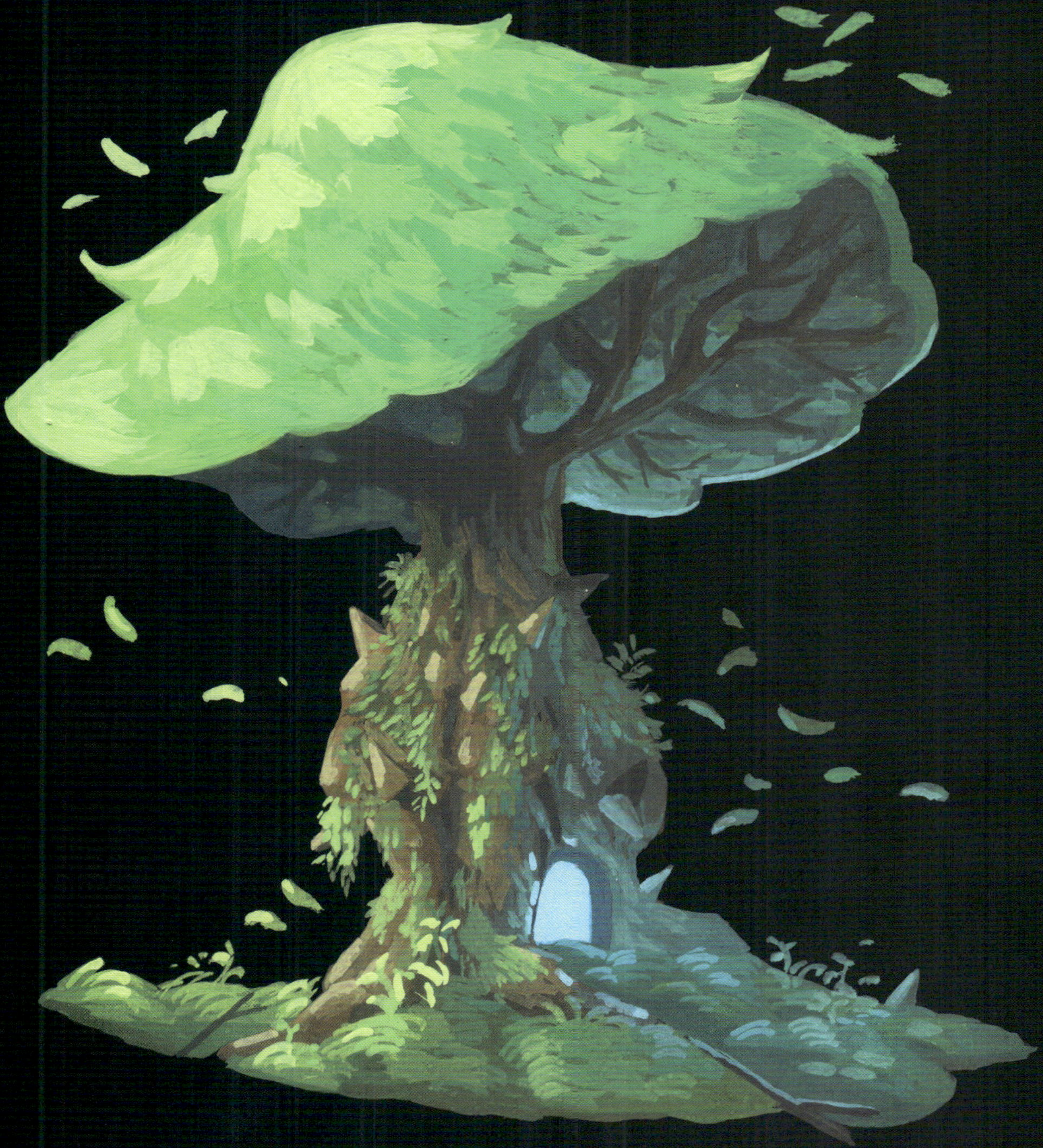

CONCLUSION

And there you have it: a beautiful tree portal with dynamic lighting, and some hints of mystery and adventure. Now go forth and create more fantasy forest scenes like these! Remember, you don't only have to use warm yellow and cold blue light sources. You can also use any of your favourite colour combinations, such as pink and purple, green and red, or orange and blue.

I also encourage you to experiment with your black paper like a scientist. What do different mediums look like on black paper? Which mediums can you mix together? What effects can you create? How can you use the black page to tell more stories? Try it out and make some magic.

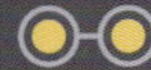

Final image © Maddy Bellwoar

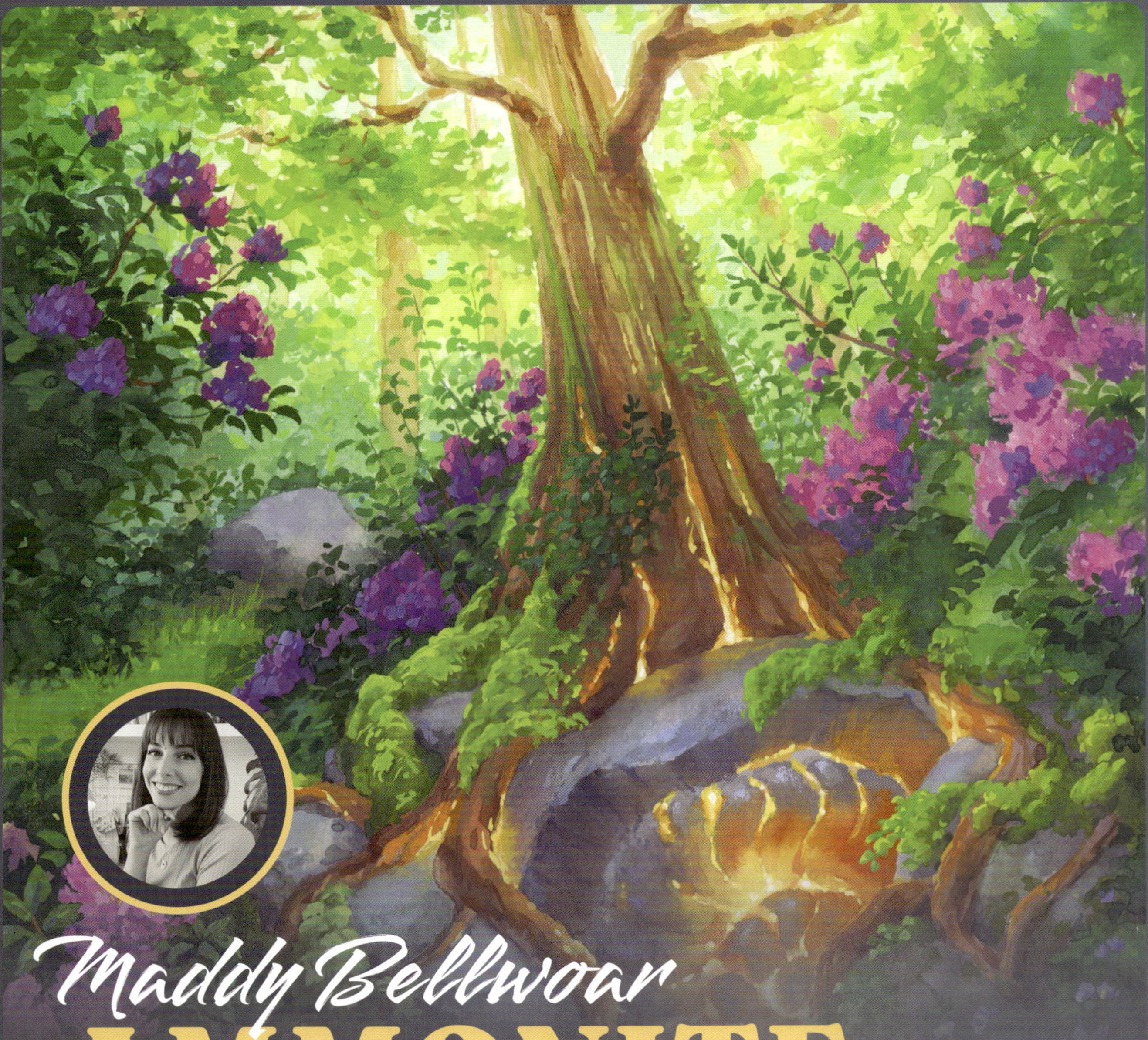

In this tutorial, I'll paint a magical forest scene with a large tree and light streaming through its branches. The tree will sit on a large boulder cracked open to reveal a giant, glowing ammonite fossil. I'll show you how to use gouache to create beautiful lighting effects including glowing leaves, sun rays, and soft gradients. I'll share how I use different amounts of water in my paint mixture to create a variety of effects and maximize the versatility of gouache. I'll also discuss the role of colour and value in painting a luminous scene.

TOOLKIT

- **Arches cold-pressed paper**
  300 gsm (110 lb)

- **Palette** (white ceramic palette or dinner plate)

- **Pencil**

- **Jar of water**

- **Paper towel**

- **Painter's tape** (for clean edges)

- **Spray bottle of water**
  (to keep paints wet)

BRUSHES

Hake brush
(to wet the paper first)

Quill mop brush
Size 2 or 3

Round brushes
Sizes 2, 4 & 8

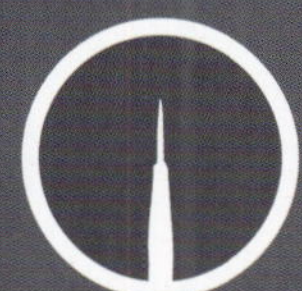

Thin rigger brush
(for fine lines)

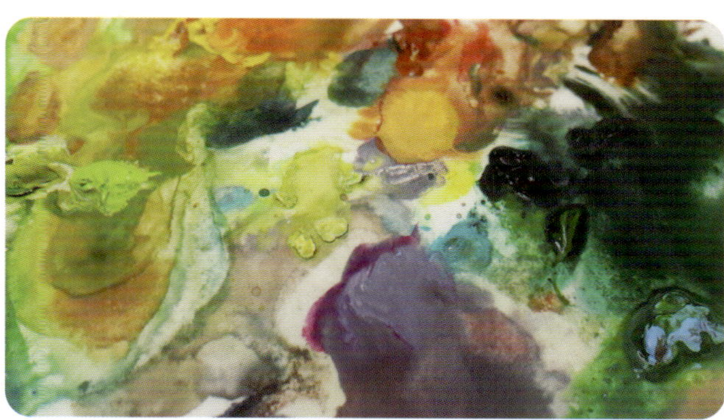

My colour selection includes four greens for convenience, but if you don't have these – especially the Holbein Irodori greens – you can also mix greens from the primaries. I like Holbein's primary set, which comes with cyan, magenta, and yellow, because I can mix brighter, more saturated colours than with a blue, red, and yellow primary set.

COLOUR LIST

Primary Magenta

Primary Yellow

Primary Cyan

Primary Black

Primary White

Ultramarine Deep

Aqua Blue

Leaf Green

Dark Green

Evergreen (Holbein Irodori 'Summer' set)

Bamboo Green (Holbein Irodori 'Summer' set)

Burnt Sienna

Burnt Umber

01.

I like to begin my paintings with a watercolour-style approach, so I use plenty of water in my paint mixture. I make a light pencil sketch on the paper, and then use the wide and flat hake brush to wet the surface evenly with clean water. Next, I add paint to the paper and allow the colours to blend. This method, called wet-on-wet painting (see page 67), can create beautiful soft transitions and gradients. I always begin with the areas that I want to appear lightest and most 'glowy'. I have propped up my painting at a slight angle, which encourages the paint to flow downwards and gives more control.

02.

Next, it's time to paint the base layer of the tree. I'm using a lot of water in my paint mixture, so the gouache looks similar to watercolour. While the tree is still freshly painted and wet, I add greens and yellows to the brown bark. The colours mix on the page to create natural, earthy-coloured gradients. My goal is to create this kind of 'base layer' for every element in the painting. I will avoid painting details until the entire scene has base layers painted, with no white paper remaining.

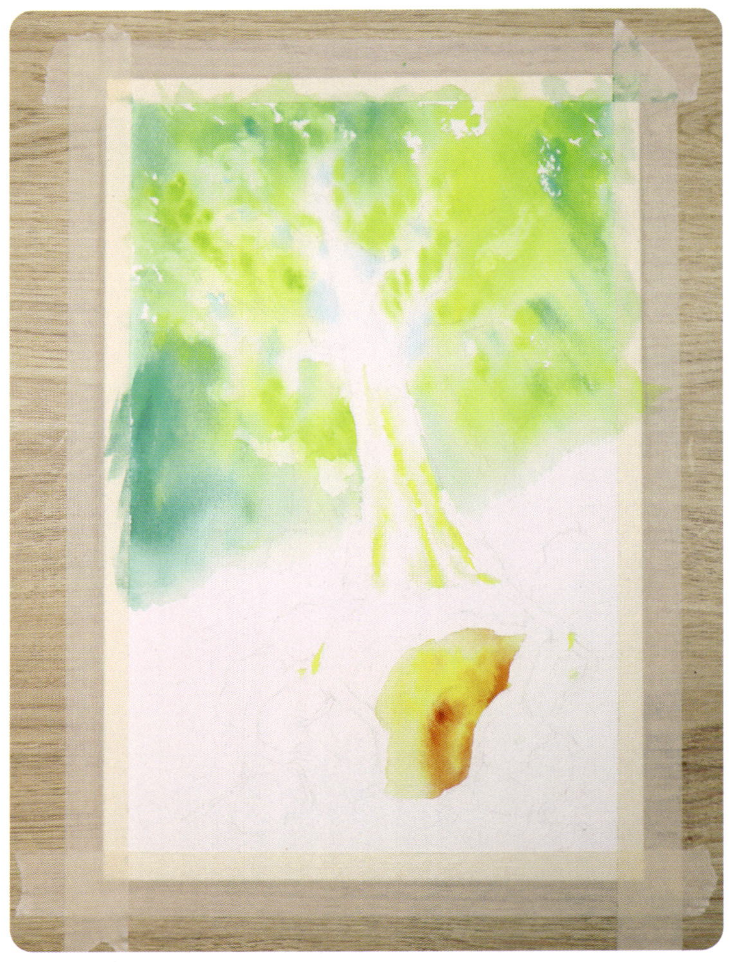

01. Use a mix of diluted colours to paint the base sunlit forest colours

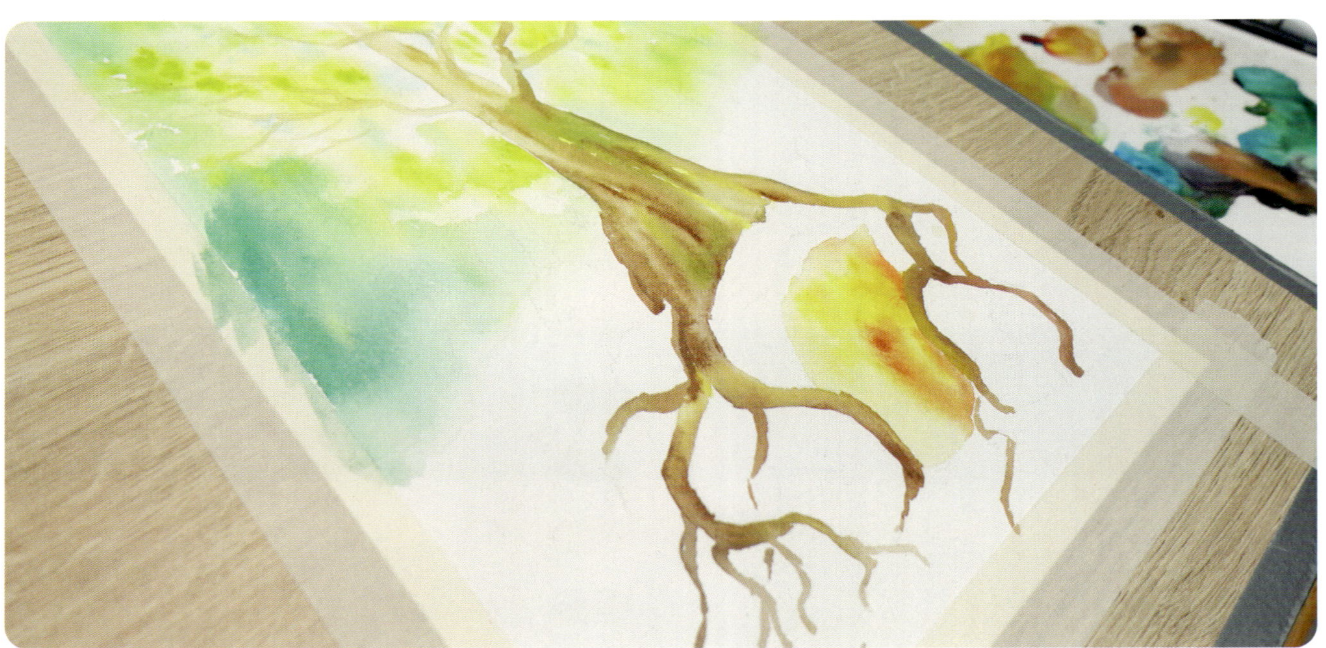

02. Paint the base colour and shape of the tree trunk and roots

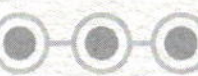

A NOTE ON BRUSHES

The majority of this painting will be made using quill mop brushes, which are great for holding water, and round brushes, which are a staple brush type for watercolour and gouache painters. Try testing out your brushes on a separate piece of paper to get a feel for the different strokes you can make with the sizes you have. I'll also be using a Kumano fude – a Japanese round brush I like for foliage painting – but this tool is optional and a round brush can be used in its place.

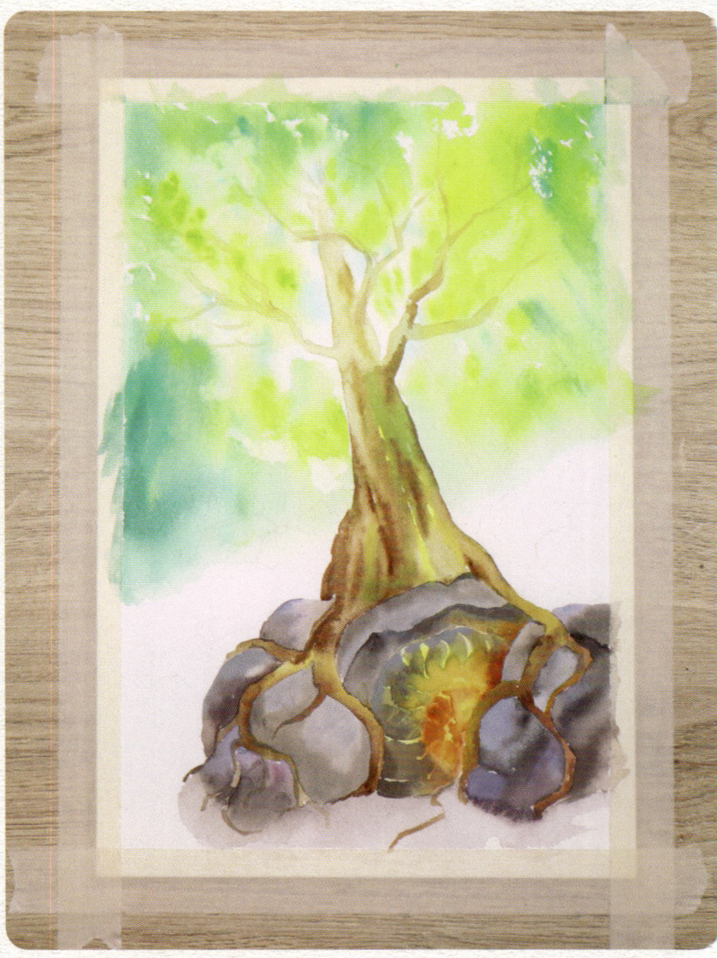

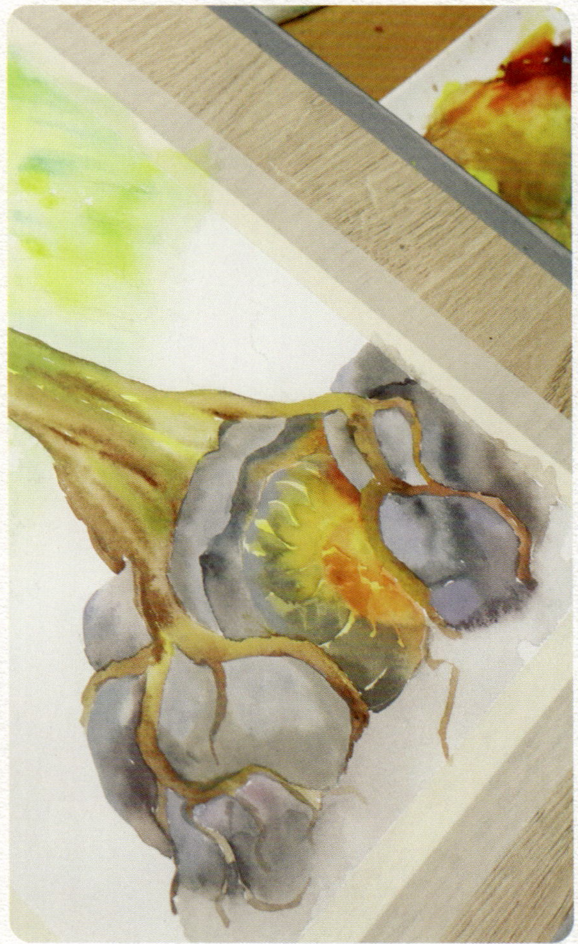

03. Paint the base of the grey rocks and glowing fossil

03.

After the tree, I move on to painting the base layer of the rocks and fossil. As I paint the rocks, I try to think of them as three-dimensional forms and paint the upwards-facing sides in a lighter colour. I add hints of blue and purple to the rock because cool bounce-light from the sky can cause this effect, and it complements the warm glow from the fossil painted in yellow and orange.

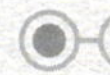

04.

The next step brings us to the distant tree trunks. I want to exaggerate their perspective, so I paint them wider at the base and thinner at the top. The trees nearest to the glow of the sun are painted in warmer colours and the trees farther away are shifted cooler, to give an effect of distance and atmosphere. It is important to keep background elements lighter in relation to foreground elements. This makes the background feel further away and pushes our eye towards the focal area, which will be painted darker and with more contrast.

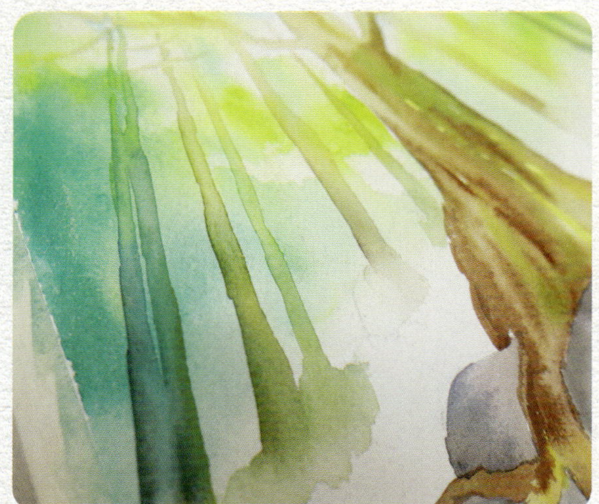

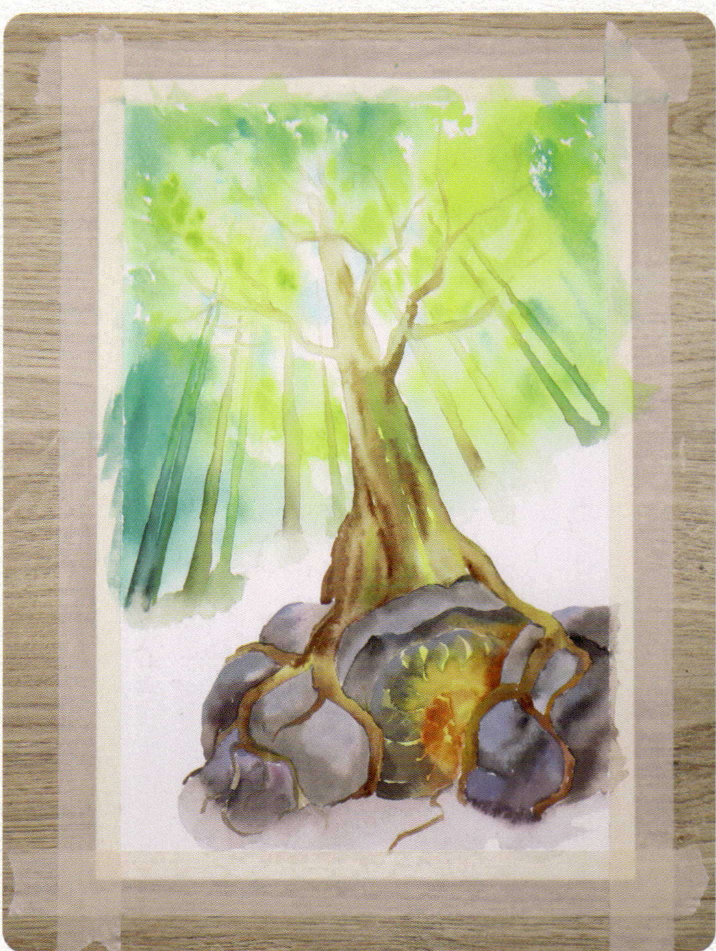

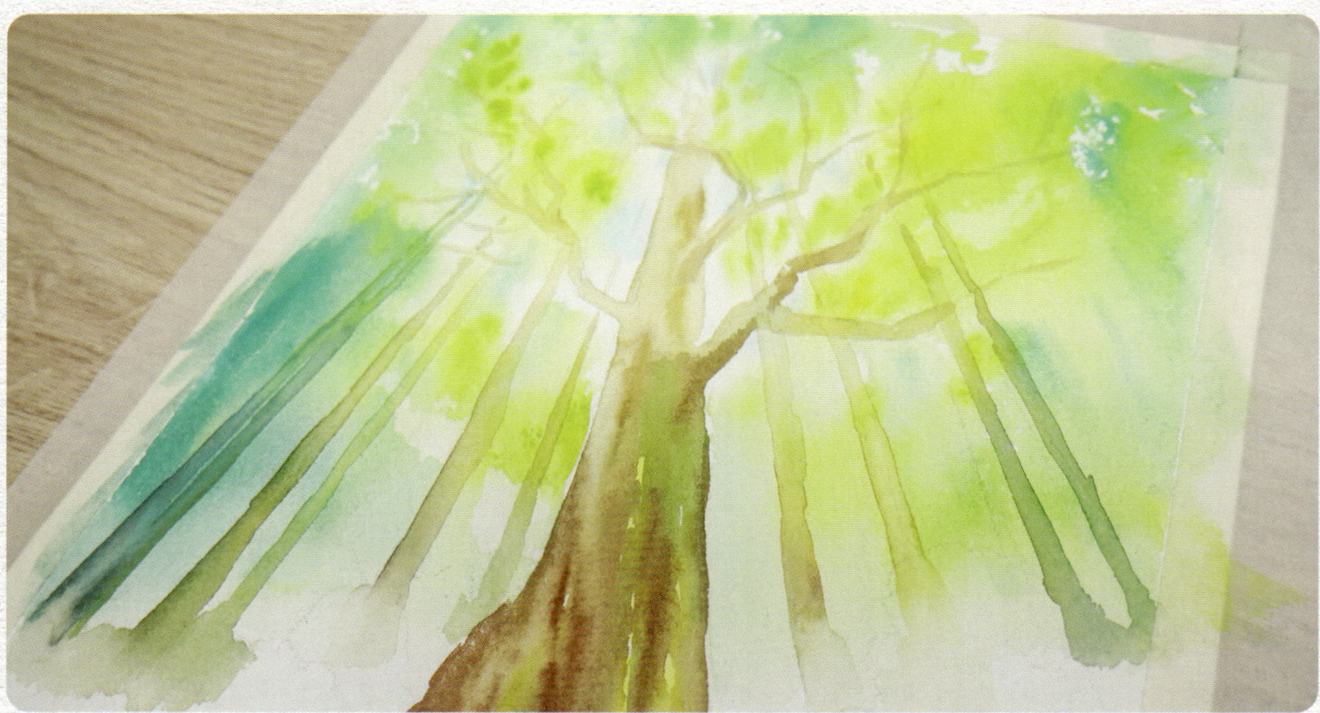

04. Add background tree trunks with diluted golden-browns and greens

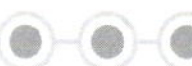

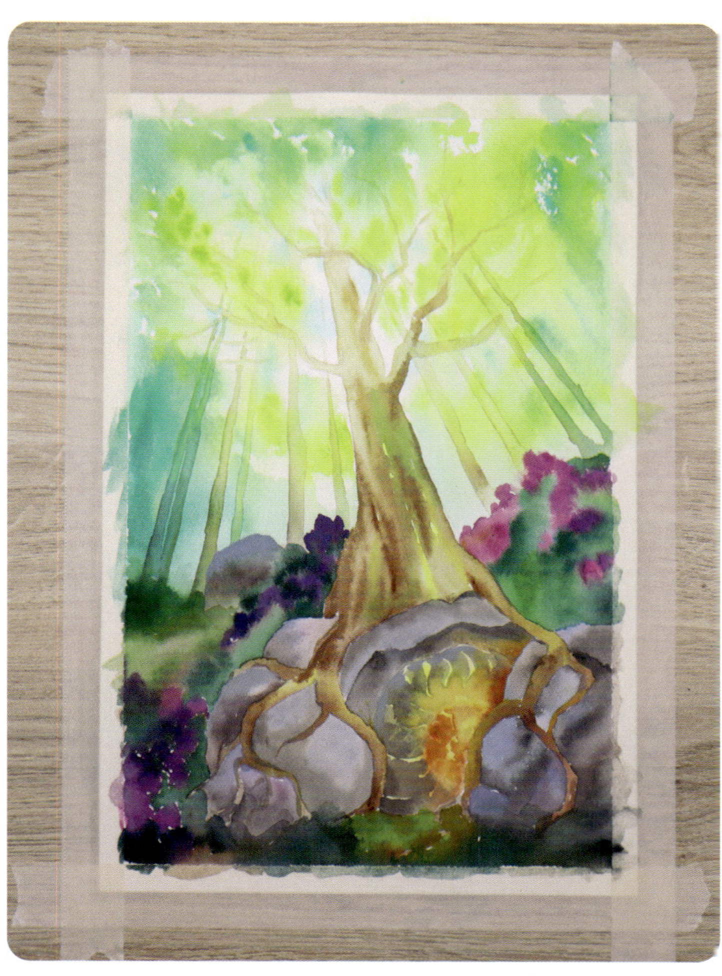

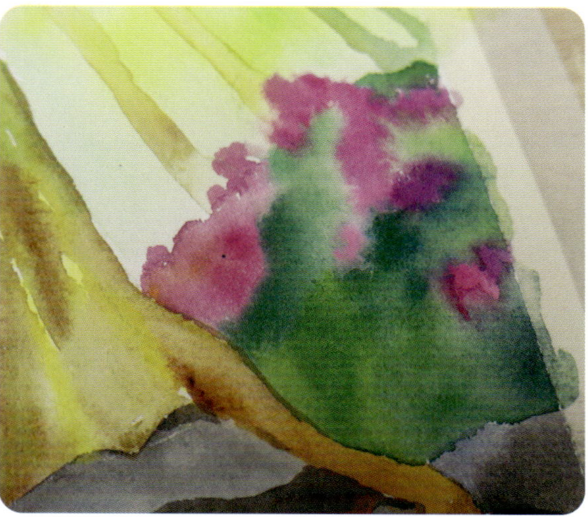

05.

For the foreground foliage, I use clean water to wet the remaining white area of the paper, carefully avoiding the tree and rocks. Then I paint groupings of purple and magenta shapes that will later become rhododendron blooms. While the paper is wet, I paint in between the blooms with different shades of green, allowing the colours to touch on the page and create soft edges. I think of this early painting stage as a 'blurry version' of the final painting.

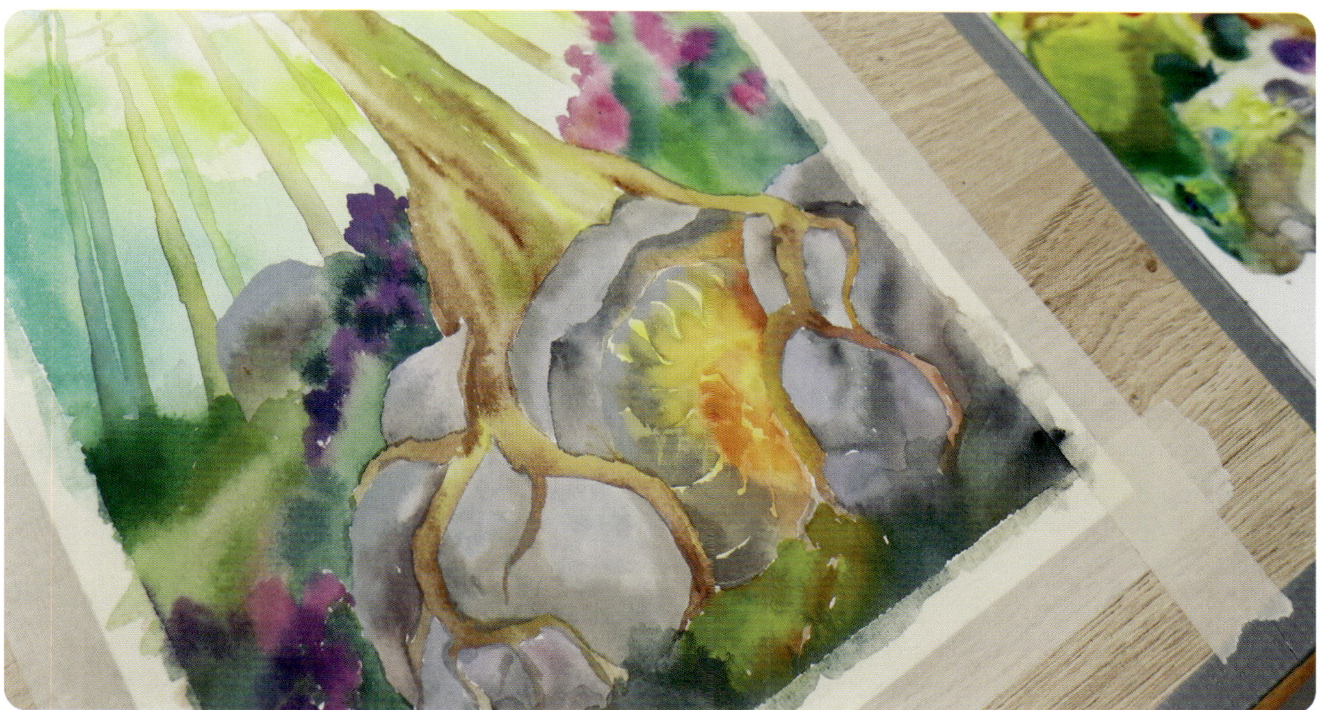

05. Wet paper creates a soft blur when painting the bushes and flowers

06.

Next I add a second layer of paint to the foliage of the tree canopy. I'm still using a lot of water in my paint mixture during this step. Transparent layering offers a beautiful, luminous effect that can mimic the look of light shining through layers of leaves. I make an effort to paint groupings of foliage in different shapes and sizes for a more natural, organic look. Looking at reference images while I work helps me to make more natural decisions as I paint, and to represent things more realistically.

USING REFERENCE

Reference is helpful, even when painting fantasy scenes. For example, a basic setting can be taken from reference and fantasy elements or creatures can be added. This helps guide your choices for colour, lighting, and value, so your scene feels believable even while part of it may be fantastical. Here's a photo I took in the forest that I used as a starting point for this painting.

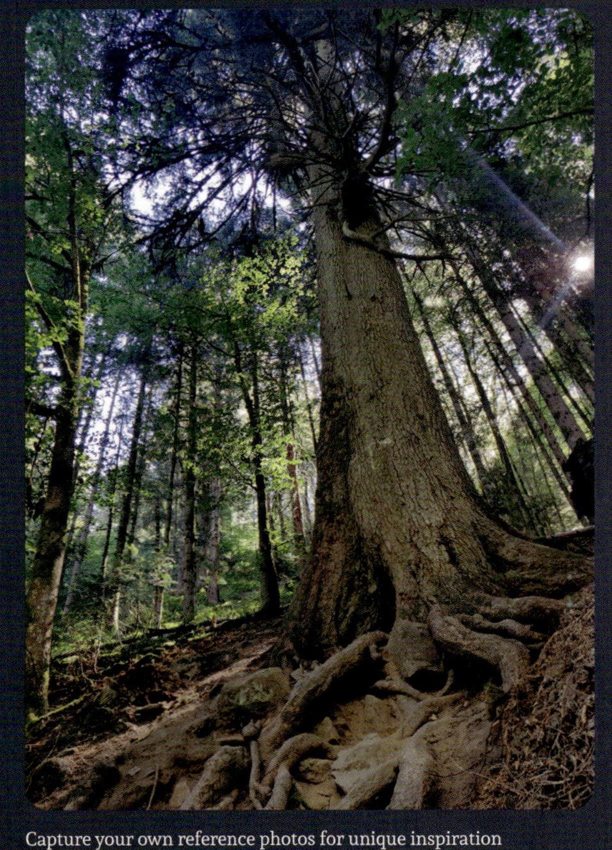

Capture your own reference photos for unique inspiration

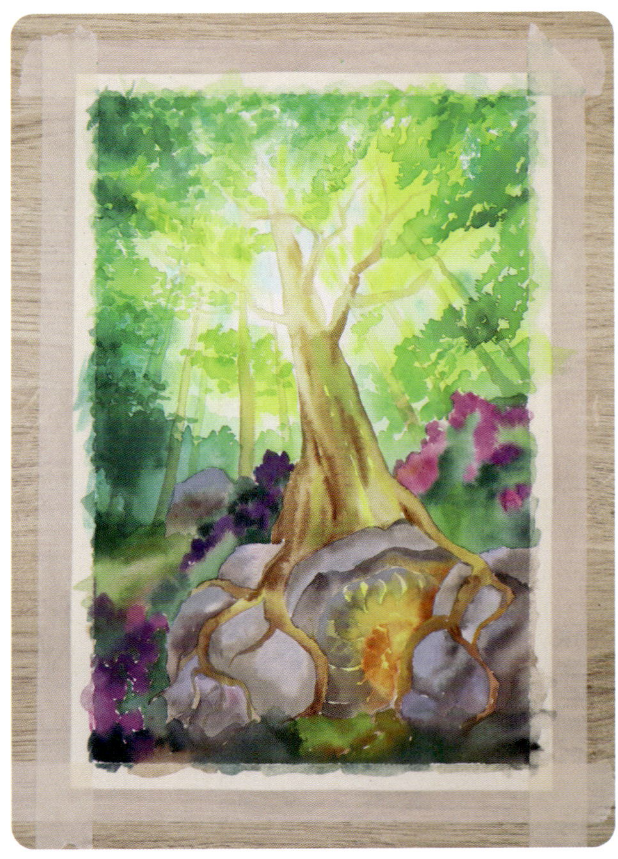

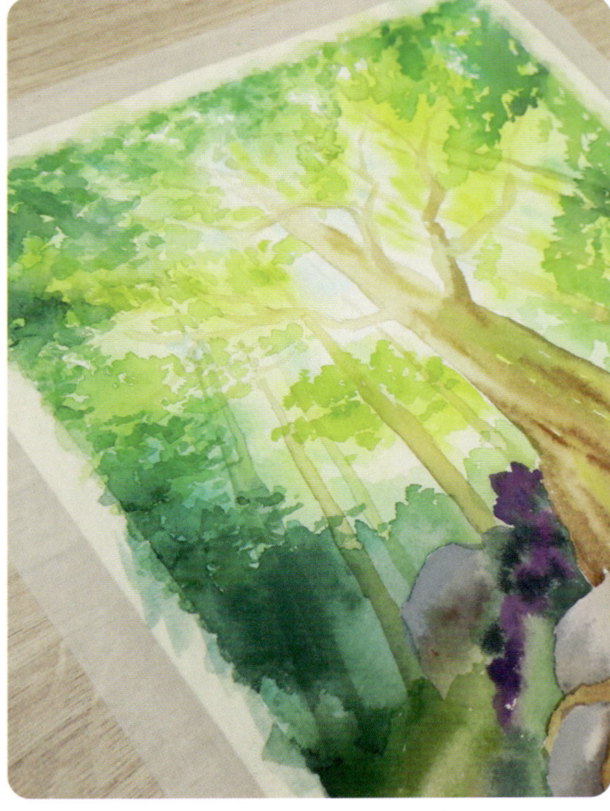

06. Use diluted hues of green to add layers of see-through foliage

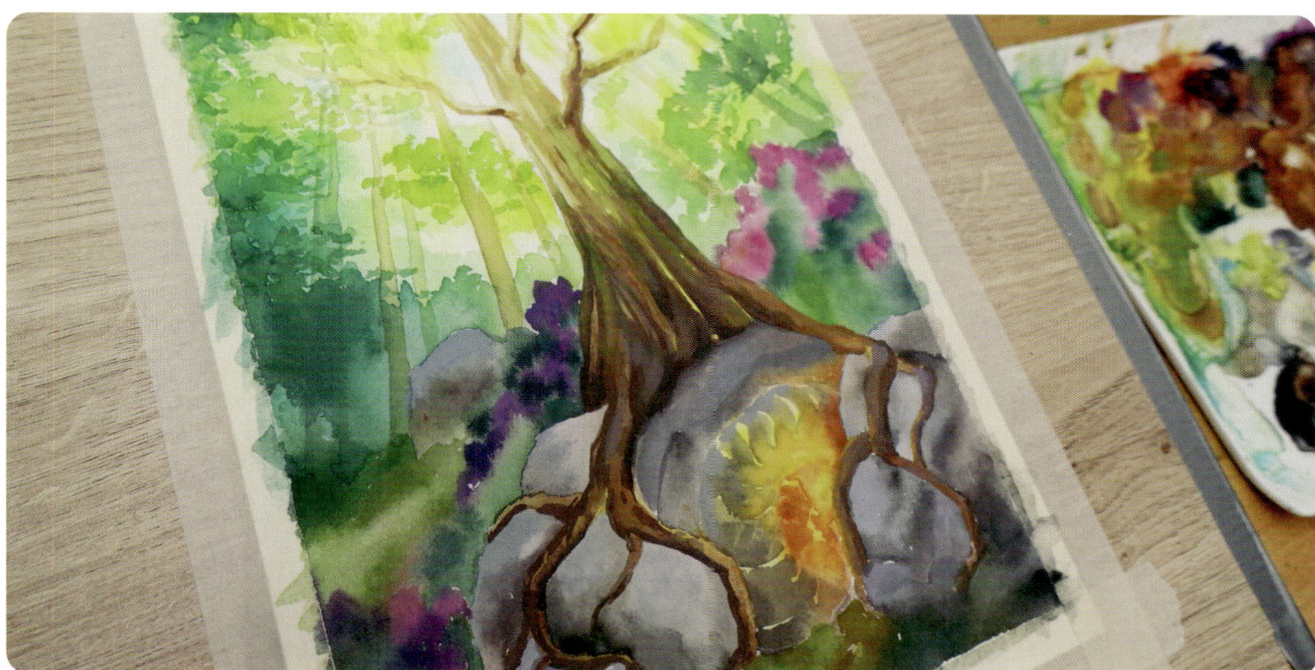

07. Darken the tree's base using a thicker consistency of paint

07.

With this step, I use less water in my paint mixture and the consistency changes from watercolour to melted ice cream. I begin layering paint onto the base of the tree, darkening the values and adding detail. I want the effect of light glowing on the tree, so I allow the warmer, lighter colours from the base layer to show through in some areas.

08.

Here I lay the groundwork for a new layer of foliage. It can be helpful to begin with the stems and branches when painting plants. This gives a base structure on which to arrange leaves and leaf groupings more naturally. Branches can be used to create motion in a scene or lead the eye towards a focal area.

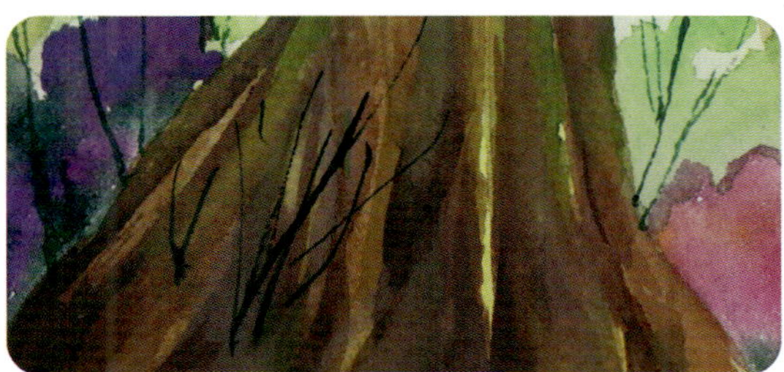

08. Add darker twigs and stems with green and brown tones

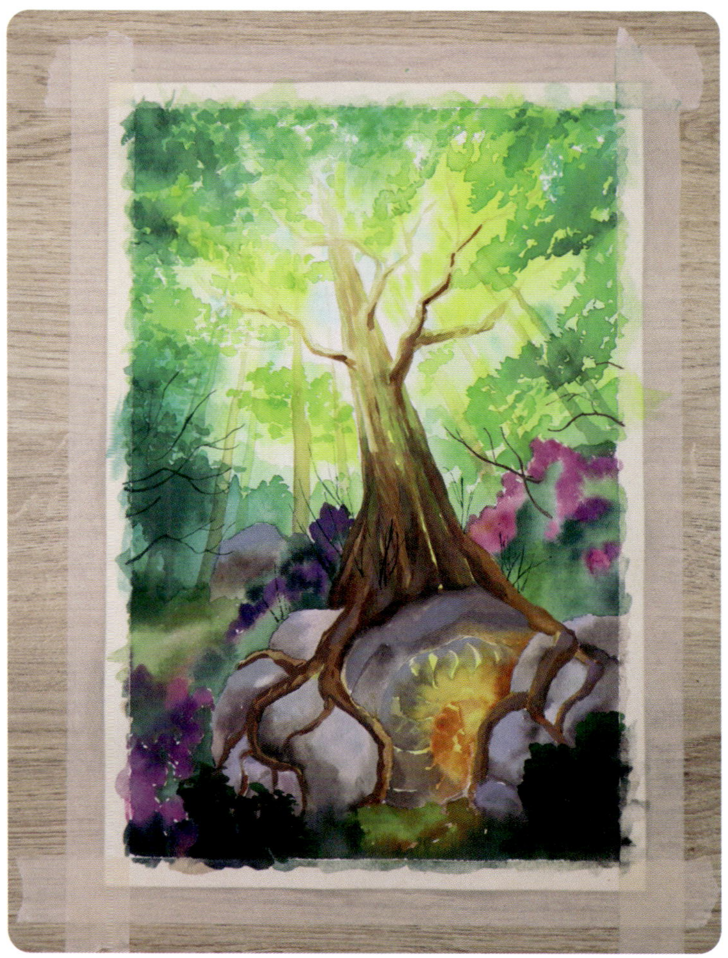

09.

In this step, I add another layer of paint to the central rock and the surrounding foliage. My goal is to darken the values and begin adding details such as individual leaf shapes. I'm paying attention to the balance of the dark and light in the image, focusing on creating a gradual shift from darker values in the foreground to lighter values as the foliage fades into the distance.

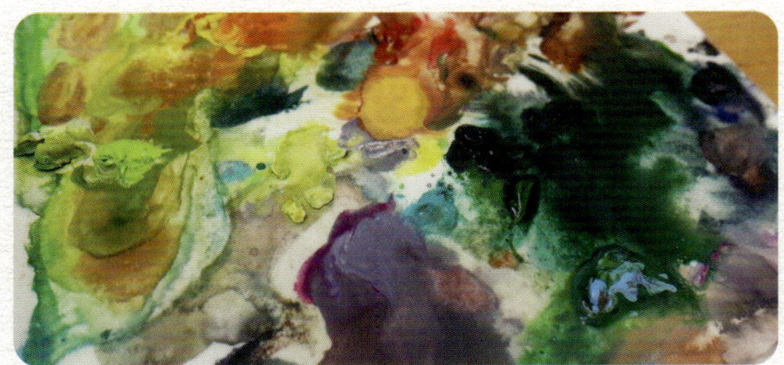

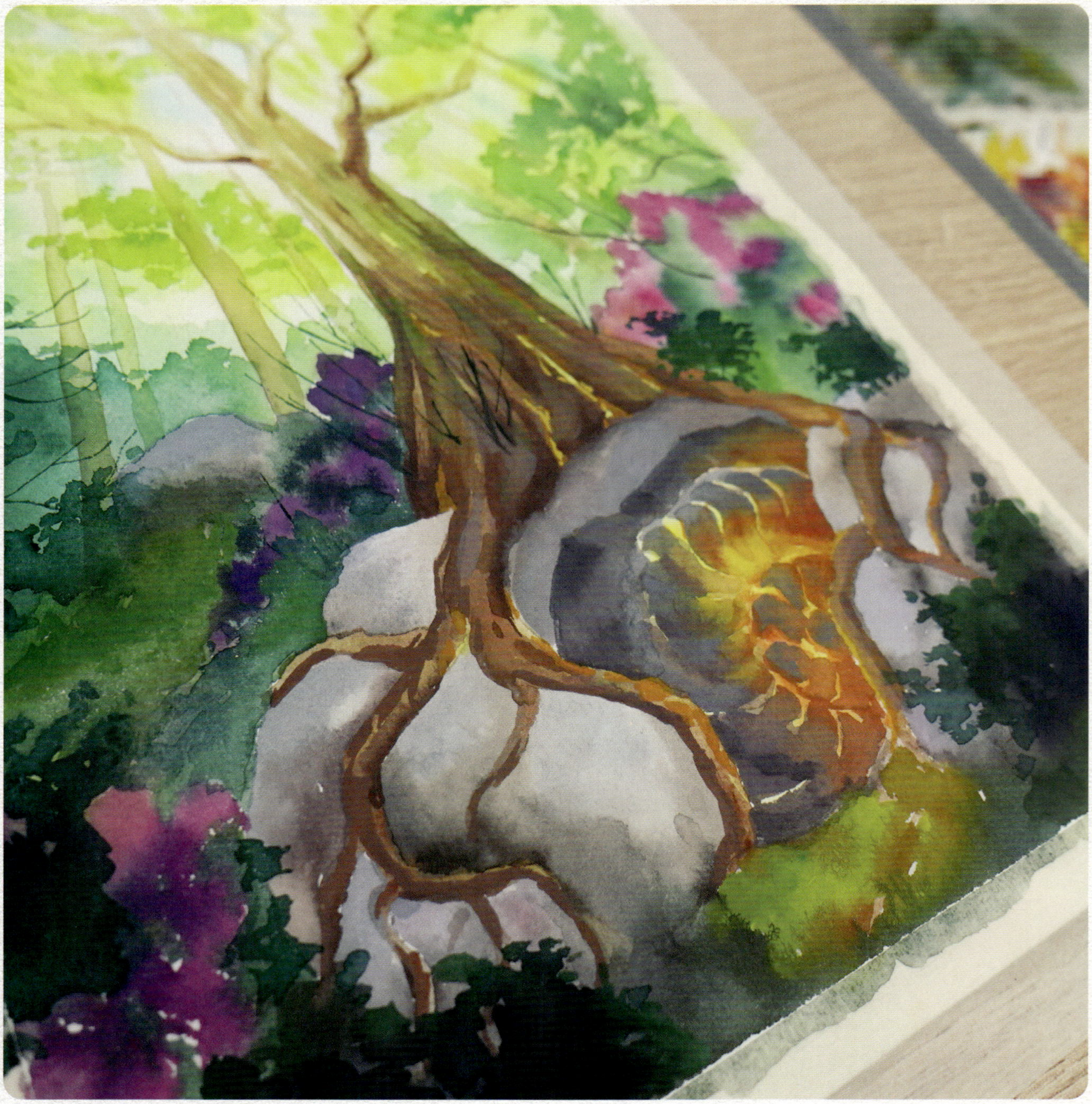

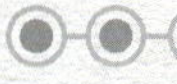 **09.** Build up the focal rock and smaller bushes around it

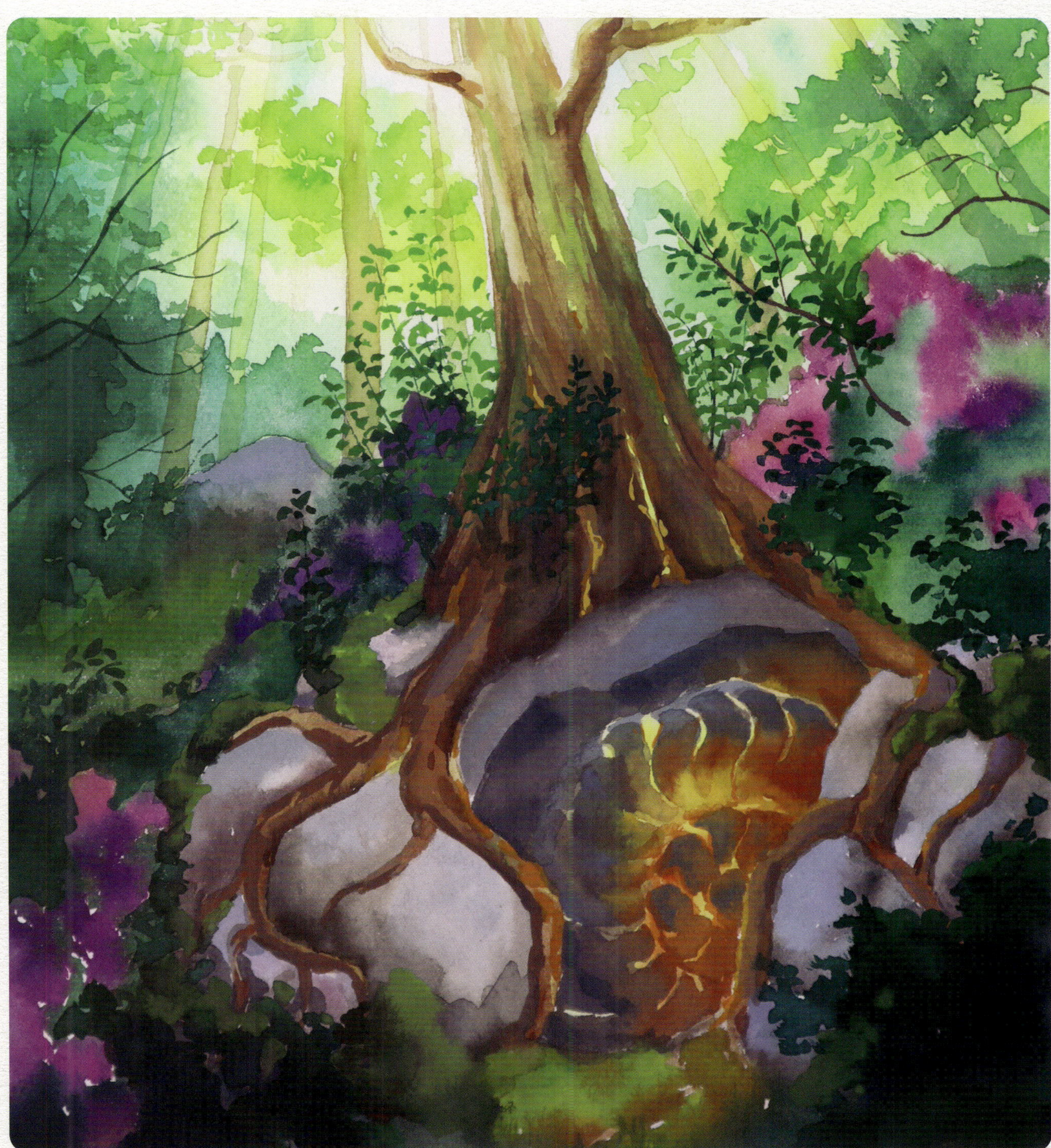

10. Add small leaves to the stems and moss to the rock and roots

10.

Next I add leaves to the stems and branches. I try to vary the size of the leaves and the direction they face to make them appear more organic and realistic. It helps to think about how the leaves may naturally reach towards the sun, and also how gravity may affect them. Leaves that reach upwards in front of the light source can be painted a lighter colour to create the illusion that light is shining through them. I also add other details here, such as moss, choosing a warmer olive-green that will stand out against the blue-green foliage.

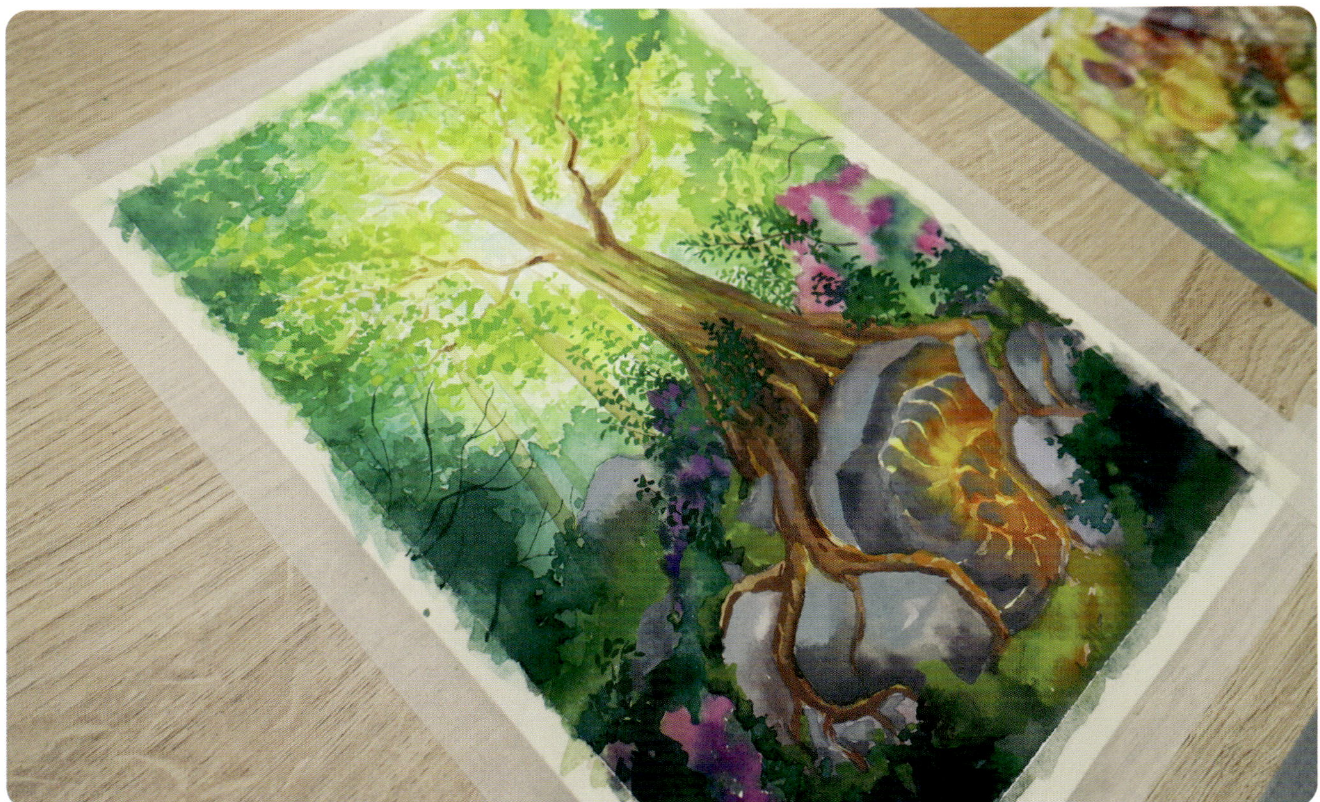

11. Build up the fossil contrast and add more canopy leaves

11.

At this stage of the process, I'm constantly thinking about values and checking to see if the lighting feels convincing or if anything can be improved. I decide to add another layer of blue-grey gouache to some of the lighter rocks to darken them. Darkening these surrounding elements will help the glow of the fossil appear brighter in comparison. I also continue work on the tree canopy, using a paint mixture with the melted ice-cream consistency.

12.

Now I focus on adding detail to the rhododendrons. Looking at reference images gives an understanding of what the leaves and blooms look like from various angles. By painting the upper-left rhododendrons as if we're seeing them from below, it gives the impression that the plants are higher up on a hill, and that the viewer is taking in the scene from a lower vantage point. Blooms that receive more light are painted in magenta, and blooms that are located in the shadows are shifted to a cooler purple.

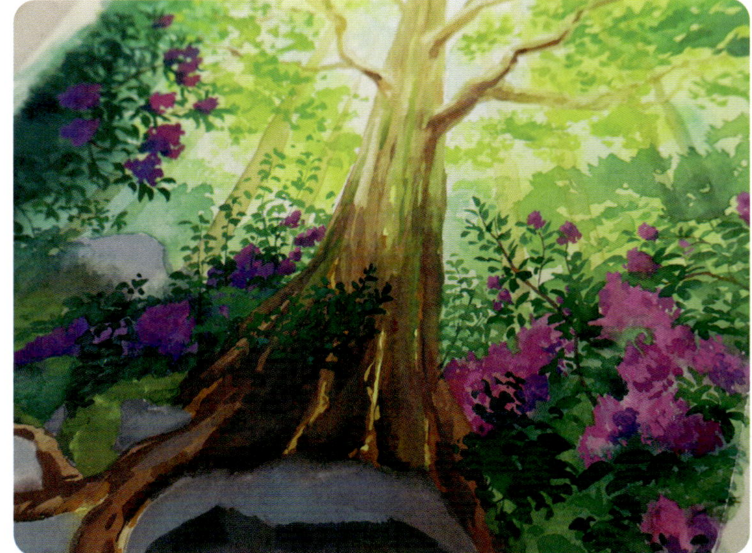

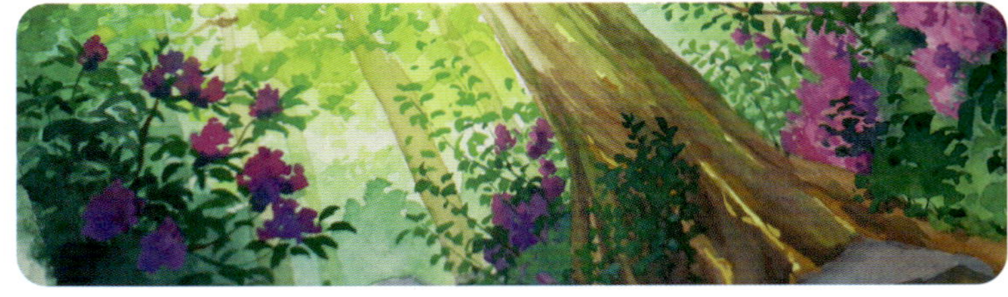

12. Add detail and colour variation to the rhododendron blooms

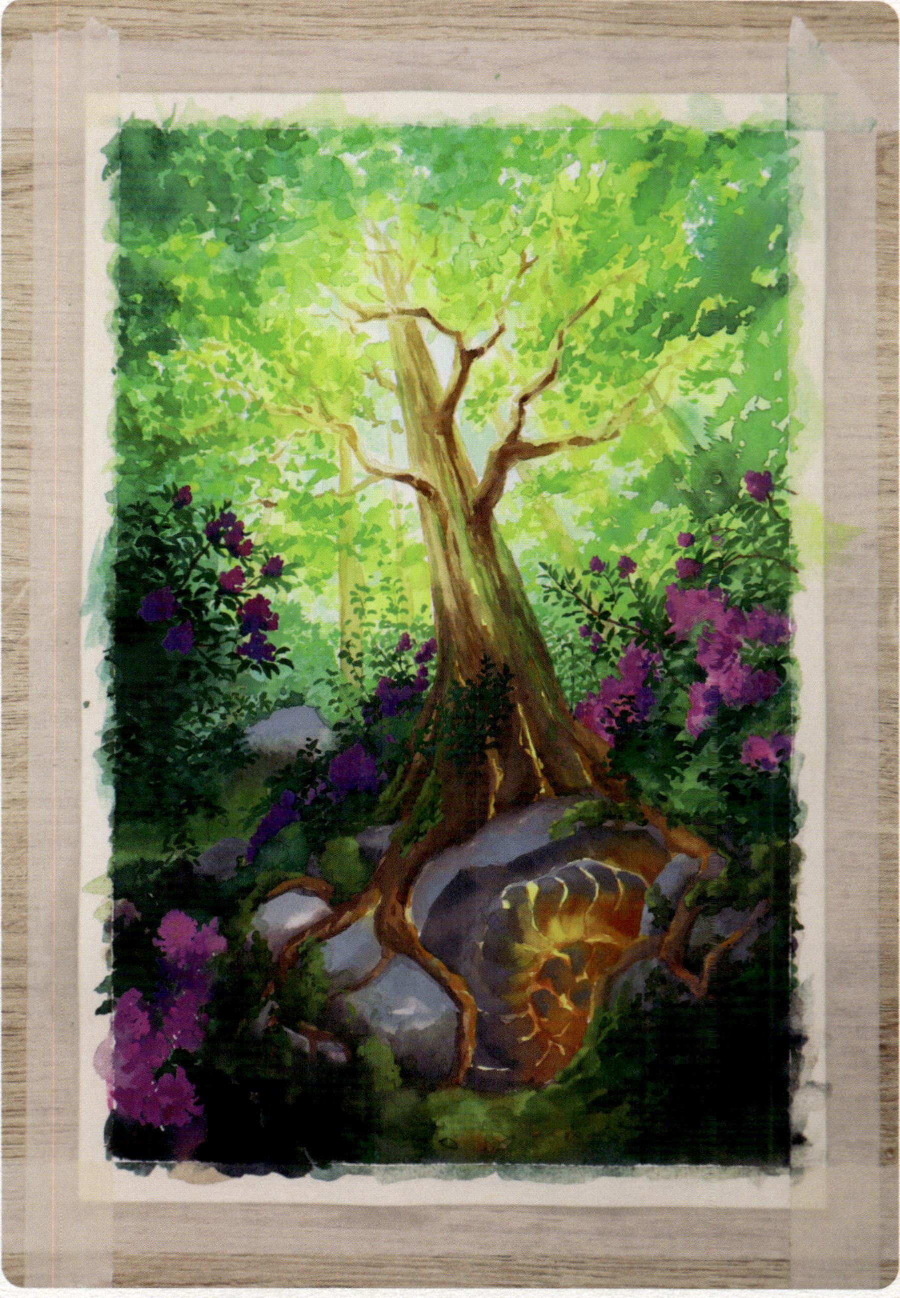

13.

Here I add another layer of moss to the rocks and roots. I want this place to feel hidden and ancient, and moss makes it look like things have gone undisturbed for a long time. As I paint the moss, I think about what direction light would be coming from. I paint each patch of moss with a lighter, warmer green on the side facing towards the fossil. This gives the illusion that the fossil is glowing and shining light on the plants and objects around it.

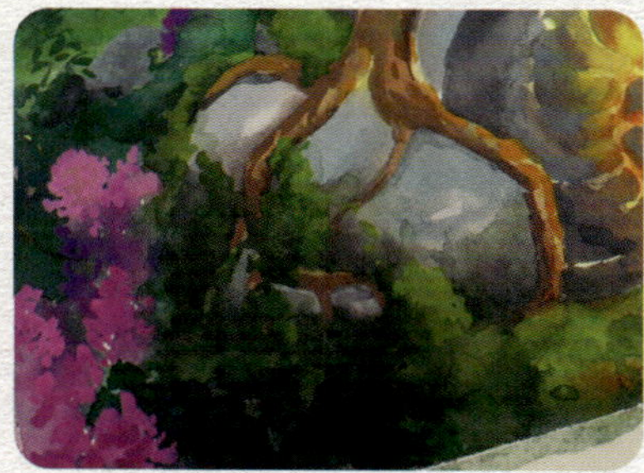

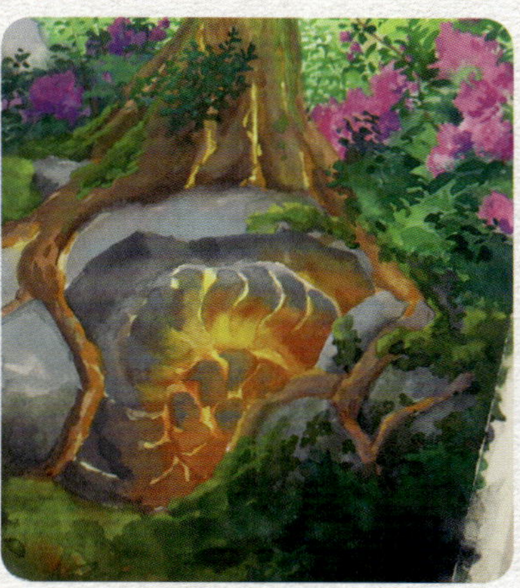

13. Add more moss and illuminate it with light from the fossil

FIXING MISTAKES

I use two methods to fix mistakes with gouache. The first method is to paint over. Make sure the area is dry, then use an opaque layer of gouache to paint over the mistake. A second method is to 'lift' the mistake. Use a brush with clean water to wet the problem area and scrub lightly. Use a paper towel to blot and remove the paint. Then, when the paper is dry, repaint the area.

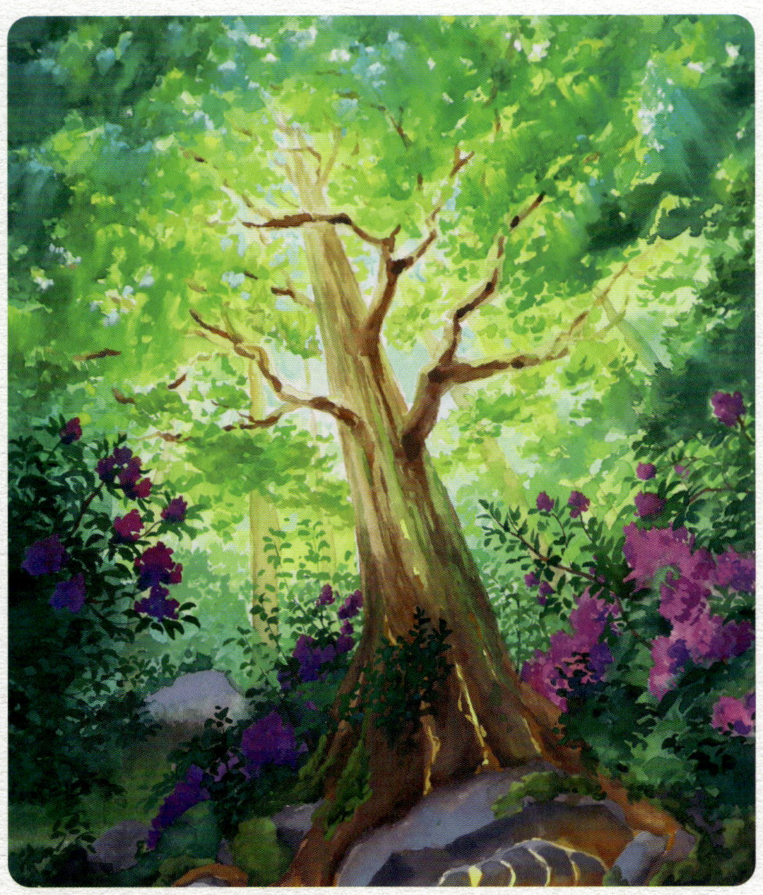

14. Use wet-on-wet to paint soft rays shining through the leaves

14.

Next I'll add rays of light shining through the branches. I want to use a wet-on-wet technique but the paper has dried, so I need to re-wet the areas I want to work on. I choose to re-wet some leafy patches in the tree canopy with green paint.

While the paint is wet, I take a light cyan and dot in some colour at the top of a leafy patch. Then I drag the brush downwards, pulling cyan through the wet paint, creating streaks. If done without re-wetting the paper, the streaks would appear very bold. Wetting the paper gives the light rays soft, diffused edges.

15.

In this step, details are added to the tree trunk and to the magical lighting effects. I paint the fossil's magical currents with dots and dashes rather than solid lines, as this method creates a more glittery look. As I add detail to the tree trunk, I'm careful not to bring the darker brown colour up too high. It's important that the tree stays lighter at the top to give the illusion of distance and the feeling of warm light from the sun.

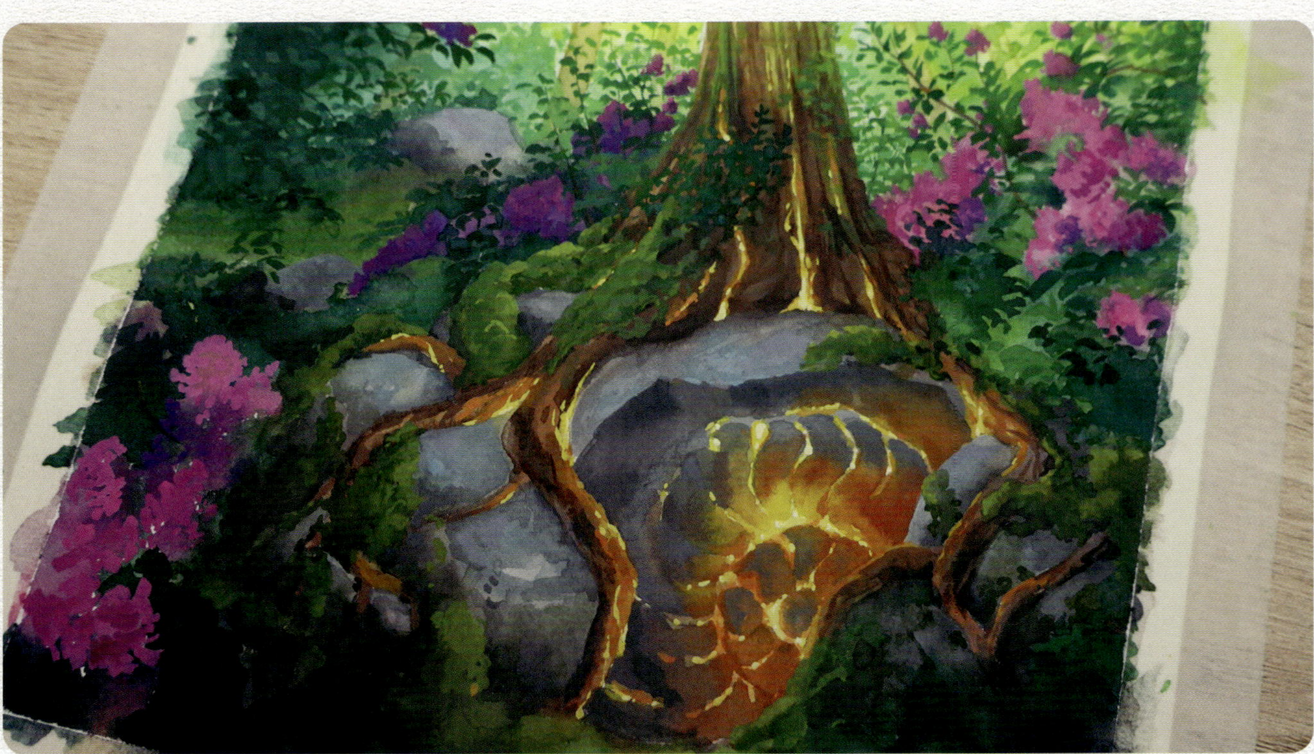

15. Enhance the lower trunk with darker browns and the fossil with dots of light

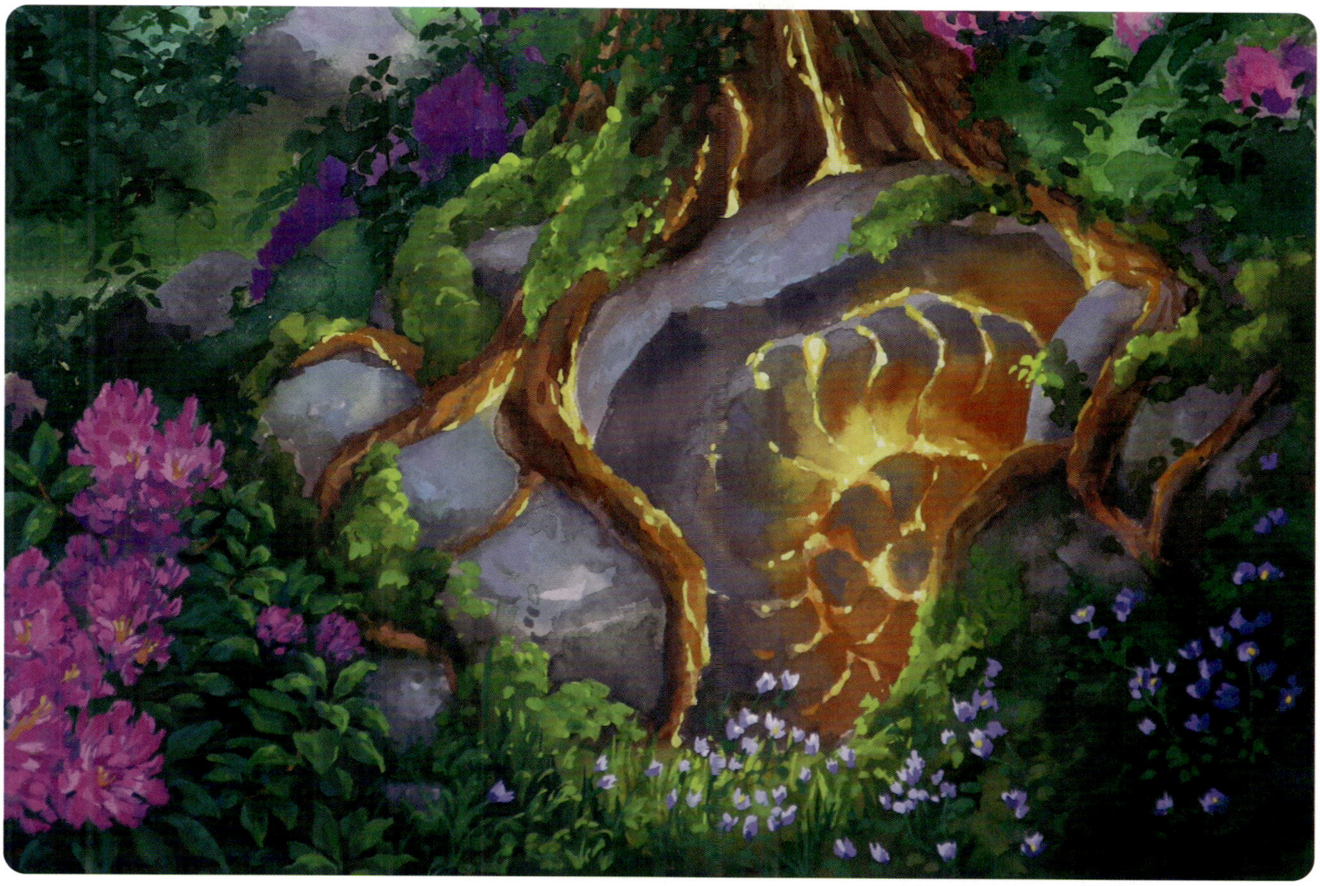

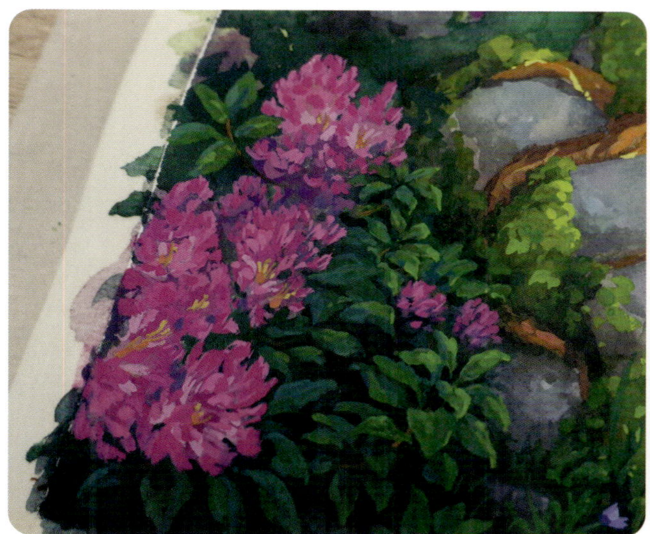

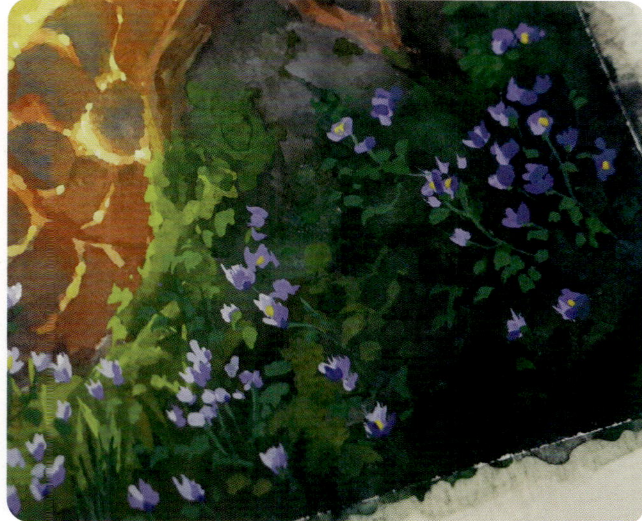

16. Take time to build up the foreground leaves and little wildflowers

16.

Finally it's time to focus on the foreground. I want the feeling of an over-the-top lush fantasy forest, so I take my time adding lots of detailed leaves and flowers. I angle the wildflowers so they appear drawn towards the magical light. I keep in mind the direction of light on the leaves, grasses, and wildflowers, so they reflect light from the glowing fossil. Flowers in front of the light source are painted lighter, and the flowers in shadow are painted a deeper purple.

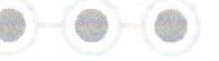

17.

I move around the painting adding details and fixing issues that catch my eye. I add darker details to the canopy and upper branches, keeping that area lighter overall, but adding a bit more balance with the busy lower half of the image. I add more details to the rocks, moss, and rhododendrons. Adding yellow to the rocks near the magical currents makes it look like they cast a warm glow. I'm very happy with how the glowing effects look and how lush the forest feels.

CONCLUSION

I've had so much fun working on this painting! I hope in your next painting, you'll feel empowered to explore dramatic lighting scenarios. Remember to use reference when needed and to pay attention to the values in your painting. Take advantage of the versatility of gouache and experiment with different amounts of water. Don't be afraid to try new things and make mistakes – that's the best way to learn, make new discoveries, and explore your style!

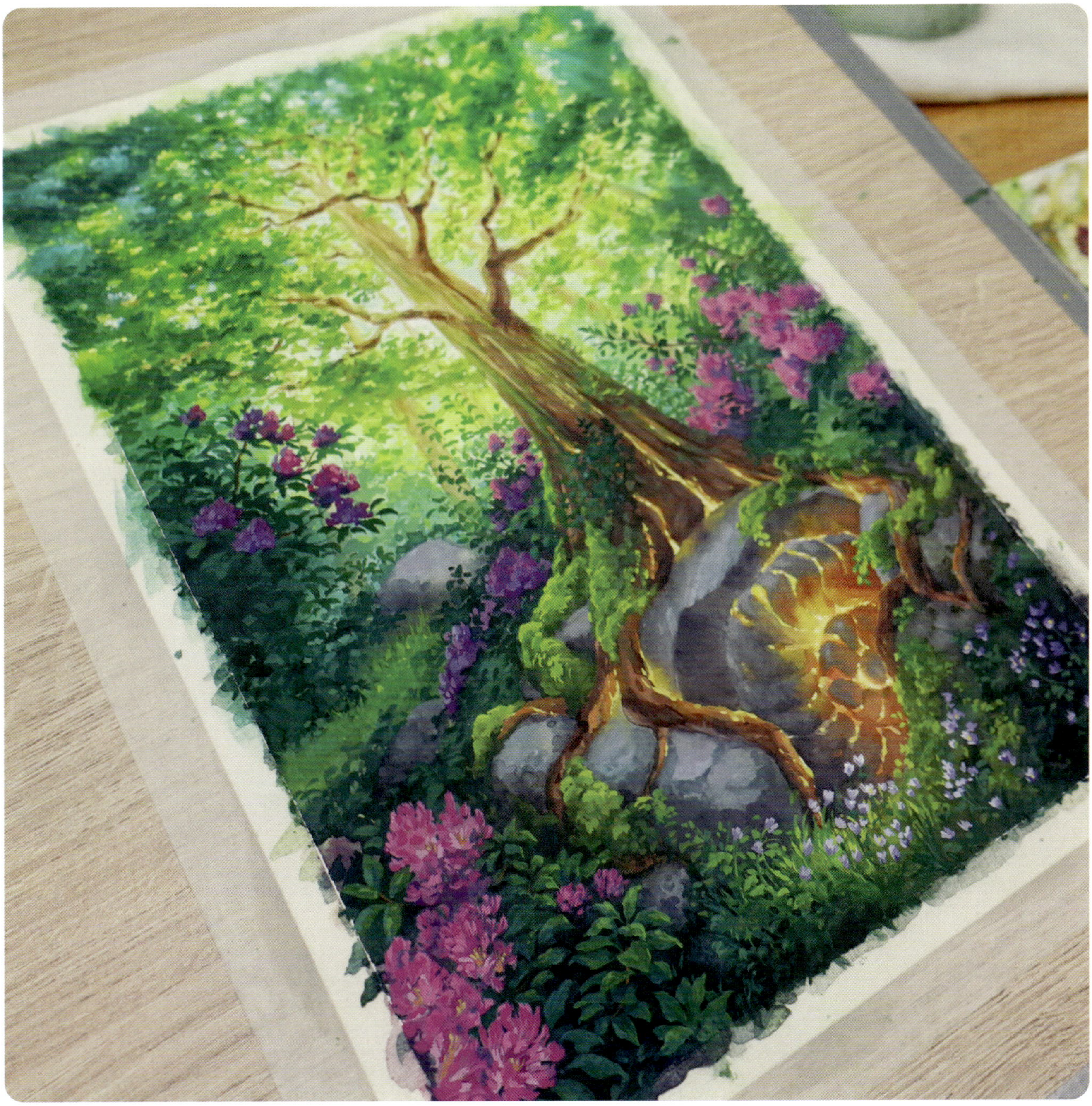

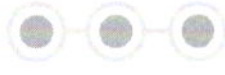

17. Check over the painting one last time for final tweaks

Final image © Maddy Bellwoar

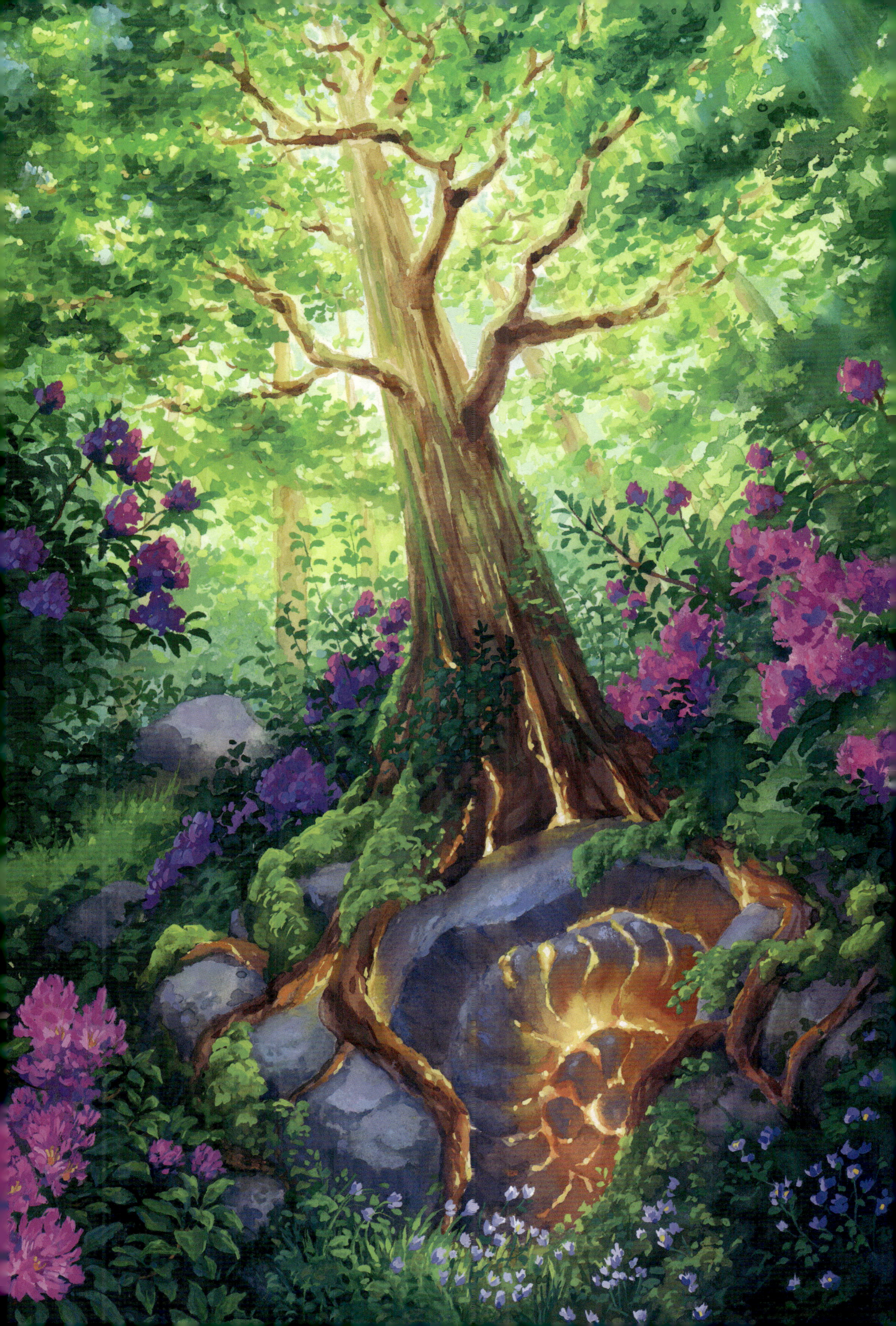

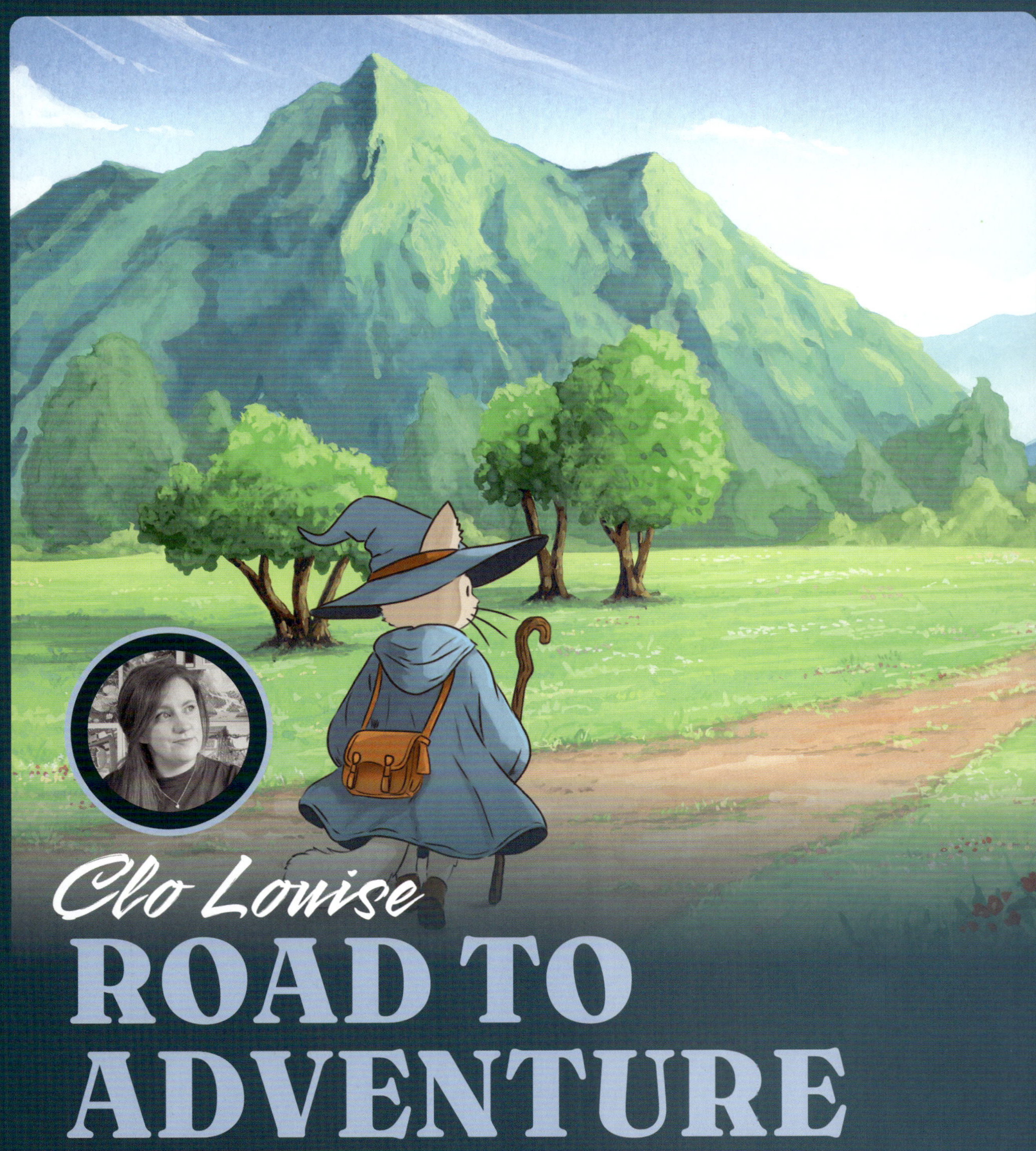

Clo Louise

ROAD TO ADVENTURE

In this chapter, I'll guide you through simple yet effective techniques for painting a sweeping fantasy landscape, complete with elements like mountains, clouds, and trees. My inspiration often comes from video games and anime, so we'll use a few stylistic touches to give our scene that animated, cinematic feel while still touching on fantasy aspects. We'll start with a simple digital sketch and build up atmosphere using a limited gouache colour palette, keeping details subtle but impactful, creating an environment that's a perfect location for an adventuring character. I hope you find the process easy to follow and feel confident in giving it a go yourself.

TOOLKIT

- **Hot-press watercolour paper**
  A4 size, 300 gsm (140 lb)

- **Pencil**

- **Digital painting software**
  (for rough sketches and adding
  an optional character)

- **Cloth or paper towels** (for cleaning)

- **Mixing palette**

- **Jar of water**

- **Painter's tape or water-activated
  tape** (for clean edges – see page 135)

BRUSHES

Flat wash brush
½"

**Japanese
calligraphy brush**
(optional, similar to a
large round brush)

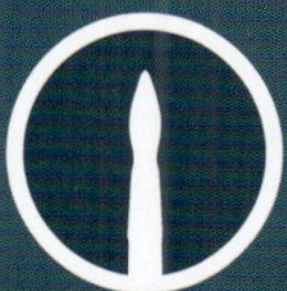

Round brushes
Sizes 4 & 8

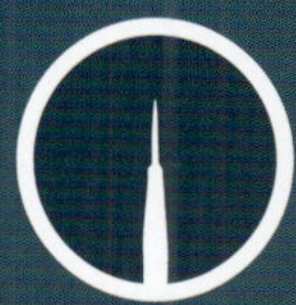

Fine detailing brush
Small size, e.g. 0 or below

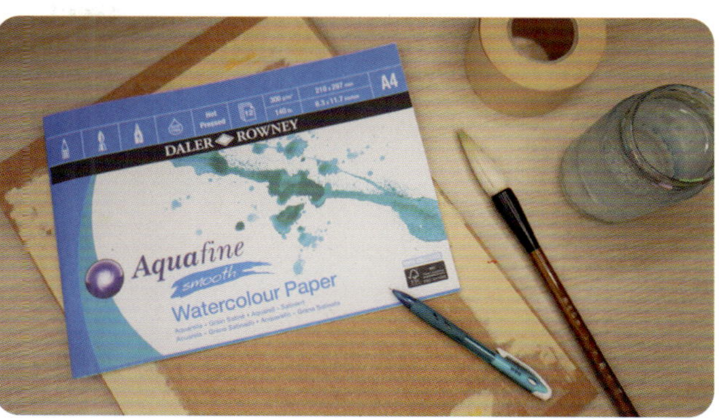

I will be using a range of 'poster colours' by the Japanese brand Nicker. These are smooth, opaque paints often used by professional anime background painters. However, if you can't access these, you can use any brand of artist-quality gouache colours. You may notice that I haven't included black – I never use it! It can be tempting to use black when darkening a colour for shadows, but I highly recommend avoiding it. Black often feels too harsh, flattening your painting or drawing attention to areas unintentionally due to its strong contrast. Instead, try experimenting with colour mixing. Blues can deepen greens, browns, and even create rich greys, while reds can be used to mix deep purples. These blended shades will create more natural-looking shadows compared to simply adding black.

COLOUR LIST

- Sky Blue
- Cerulean Blue
- Prussian Blue
- Viridian
- Light Green
- Lemon Yellow
- Yellow Ochre
- Burnt Sienna
- Carmine Red
- White

01.

For my landscapes, I like to keep my sketches simple – I'd rather add detail with my brush and paint than with a pencil. I start with a horizon line across the centre of the page, then sketch overlapping mountains above it. Next, I add bushes and trees along the horizon and foreground. Finally, I draw a curving pathway leading to the horizon, followed by a grassy bank right at the front of the landscape, and a rune-covered stone to complete the sketch. The mountains, foliage, and grassy bank will help us to create distance perspective in the finished landscape. I often use my tablet to work out colour palettes for my landscapes – I find this process allows to me start a painting with a clear vision in mind.

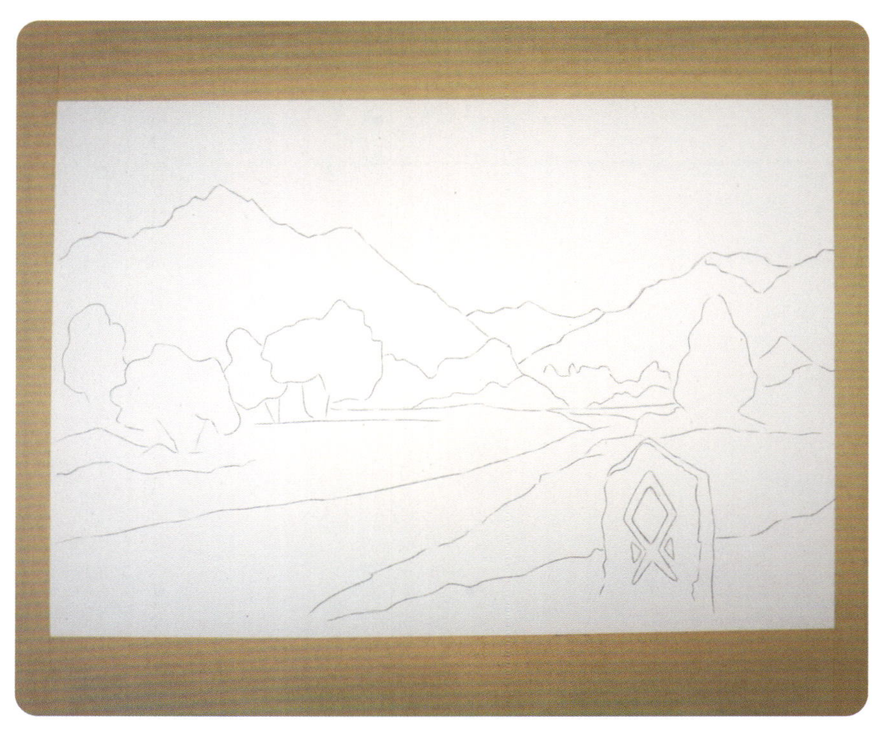

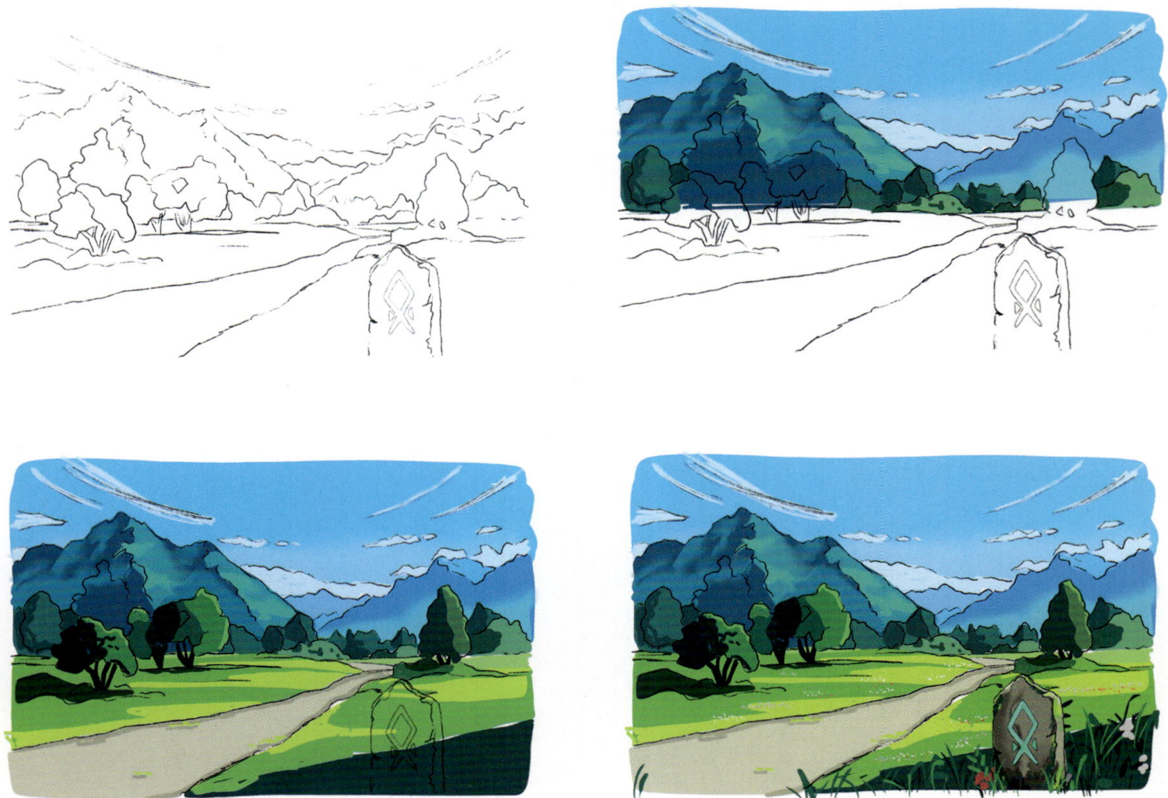

01. Plan a composition and palette in digital software, then sketch the outlines onto your prepared paper (see the tip on the right)

STRETCHING ART PAPER

I love using gouache in varying textures. Stretching my paper helps when I want to use a paint consistency with higher levels of water and want to avoid the paper buckling. To do this, I brush water over both sides of the paper, tape it to an untreated MDF board with water-activated tape, and let it dry fully. Unlike masking tape, this tape isn't removable, and needs to be cut off. You'll need to plan your painting's borders carefully before taping it down.

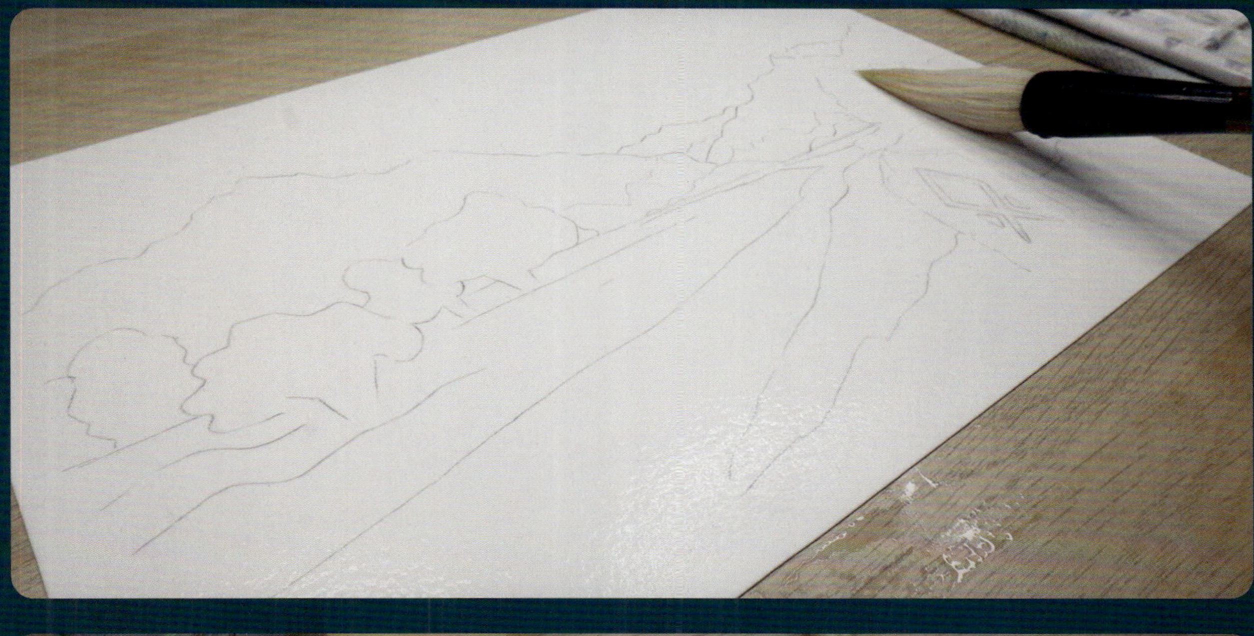

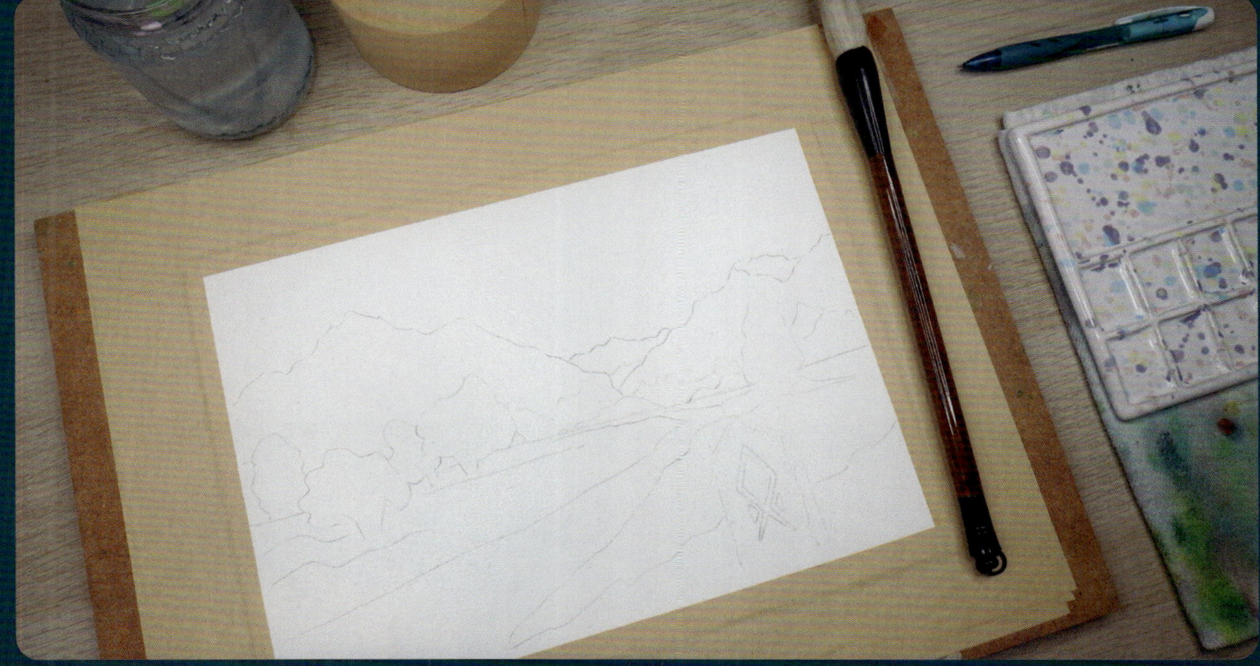

Water-activated tape goes sticky when wet and dries very securely, so these borders will need to be cut off rather than peeled

02.

To create a soft gradient for the sky, you can use a wet-on-wet technique (page 67) to blend Sky Blue into white. Using a ½" flat brush will also help to keep your paint strokes even. Start by diluting both colours with enough water to achieve the same consistency – this will help them blend seamlessly. Begin at the top of the page with Sky Blue, using horizontal strokes as you work downwards. Then, switch to white and blend upwards using the same motion. Be sure to clean your brush each time you switch colours to keep the transition smooth. Let the sky dry before the next step.

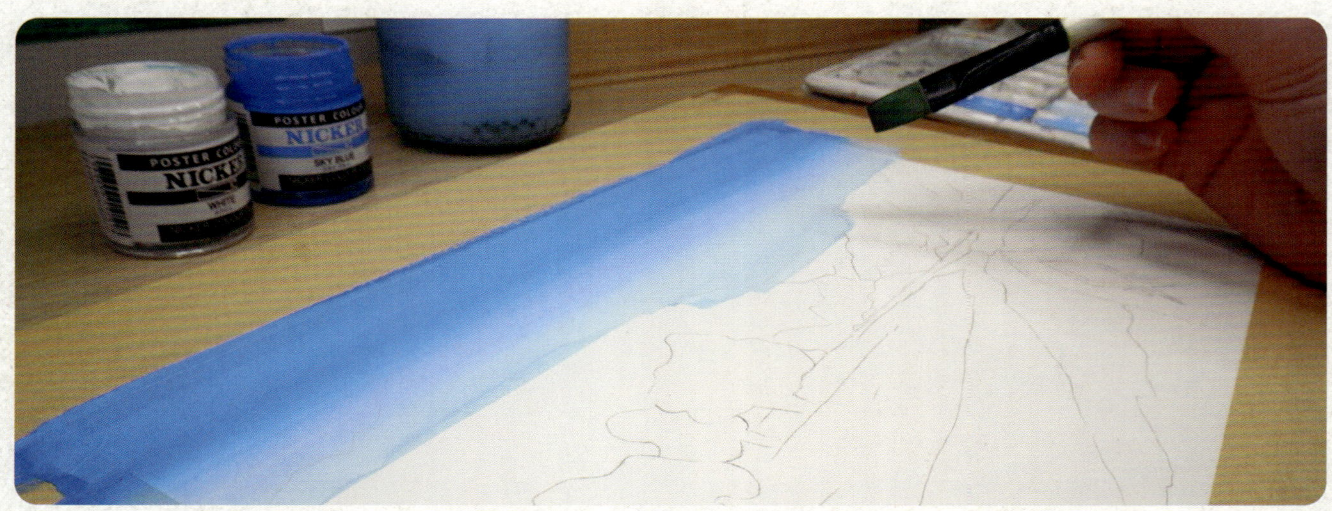

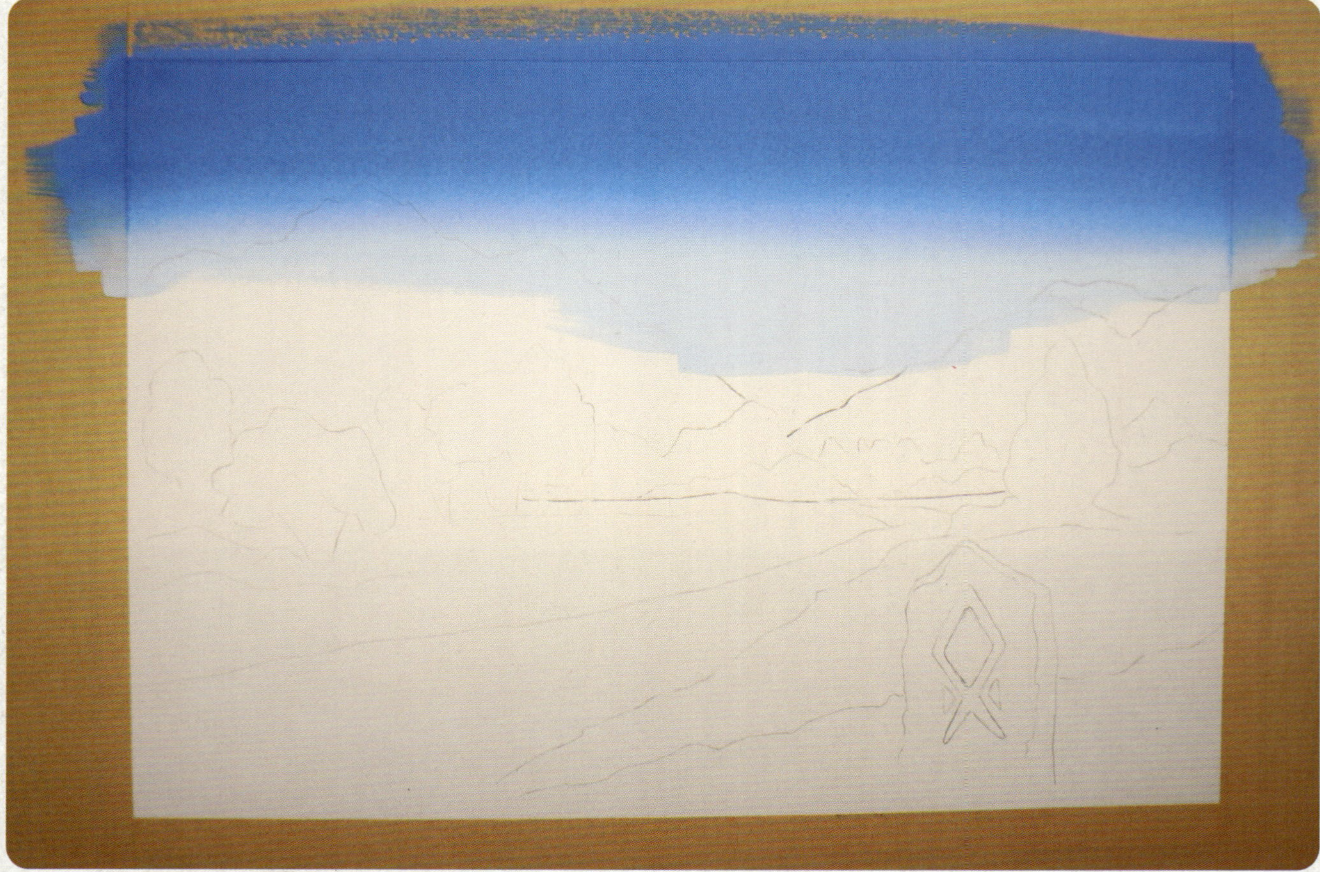

02. Paint wet gouache onto wet paper to create a smooth sky gradient

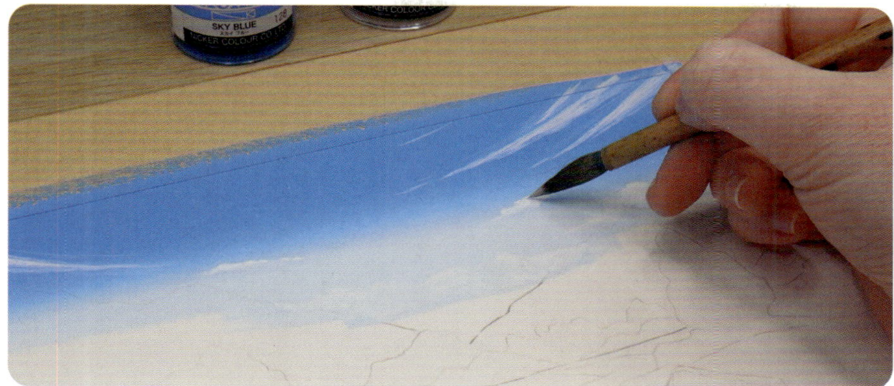

03. Use a round brush and blue-white mix to paint clouds

03.

For the fluffy clouds, swap over to a smaller round brush, and mix a small amount of Sky Blue into a larger amount of white to create a very pale blue. Use this to paint clouds along the tops of the mountains. For the sweeping clouds along the top of the sky, wipe most of the white paint off your brush with a cloth, then lightly sweep it across the page for a soft, translucent effect. Once the first layer of paint is dry, add more details to both types of clouds by layering additional paint, gradually increasing the amount of white for more depth and dimension.

PICKING THE CORRECT BRUSH

Some brushes can make certain painting techniques easier, like using a flat wash brush for smooth sky gradients or a small detail brush for fine lines. But when it comes to the rest of a landscape, the best brush is simply the one with which you feel most comfortable. Personally, I love using a Japanese calligraphy brush because it holds plenty of water and paint. I also like its versatility – I can use the tip for details while still being able to cover larger areas with the body of the brush. If you're a beginner, a round brush in size 4 or 8 is also a great option.

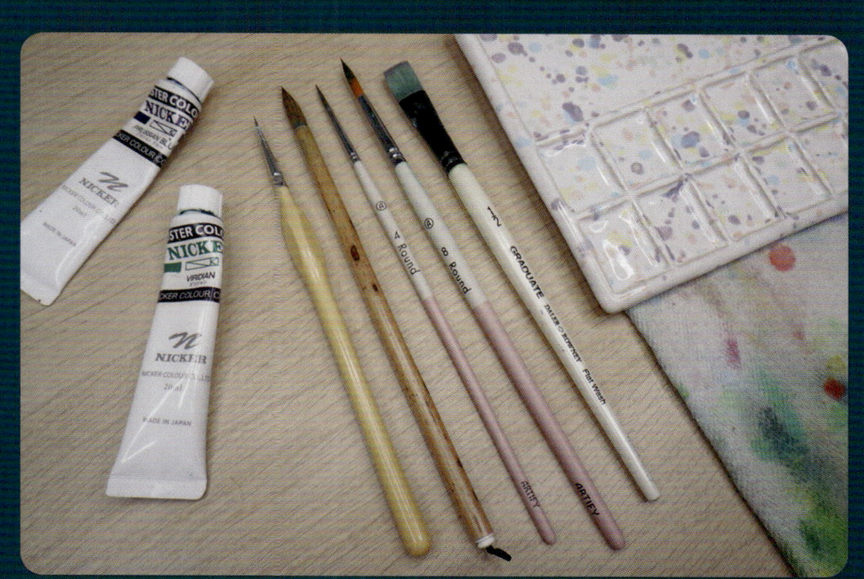

My detail brush, calligraphy brush, round brushes, and flat wash brush

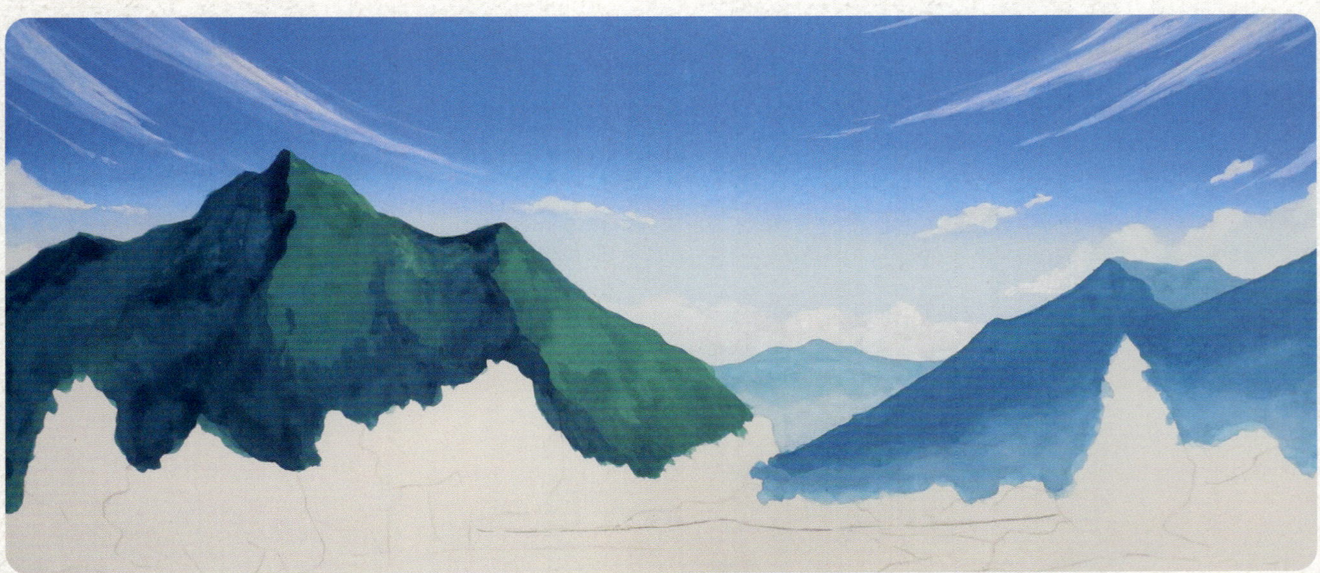

04. Use cool blue and green-blue shades to fill in the mountains

04.

For the mountains, mix Sky Blue with a touch of Prussian Blue and Viridian to make a cool, green-blue base shade. Create a light and dark variation by adding white for the lighter shade and more Prussian Blue and Viridian for the darker one. Begin with the lightest colour, blending it into white as we did for the sky gradient. For the next mountain, on the right side, use the base shade and blend it into the light colour we just used. Finally, use the darkest shade to block in the closest mountain on the left. Add highlights to the right side of each peak by mixing the dark shade with Viridian and white.

05.

When painting landscapes, I follow a 'rule of four': a dark, a medium, a light, and a highlight shade, with the highlight often introducing a warmer tone. The mountain already has dark and medium shades, so next, mix more white into the medium Viridian green for a lighter shade. For highlights, add Lemon Yellow and white to create sunlit details, focusing on the right side of each peak, as we imagine our light source for this landscape is coming from the top right. Keeping these more detailed highlights only on the front mountain enhances depth, making the other mountains feel farther away.

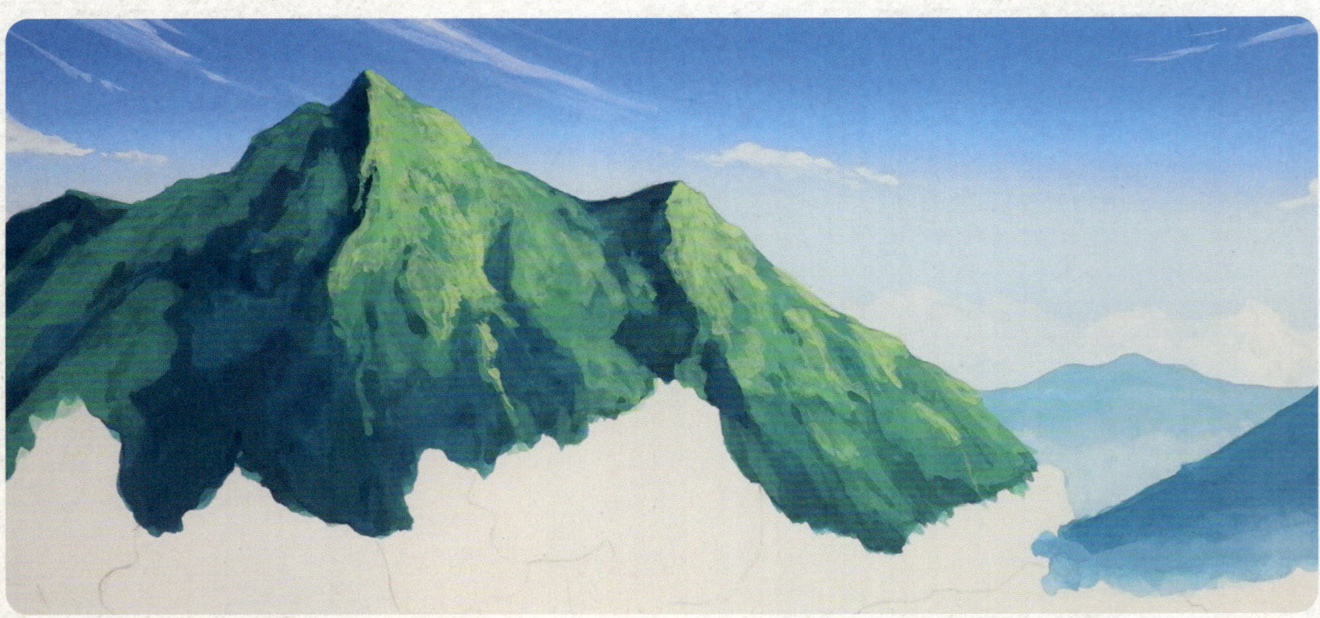

05. Add depth and warm lighting to the mountains

06.

For the horizon foliage, I start with a base mix of Viridian, Carmine Red, Lemon Yellow, and a touch of white to get a cool, medium-toned green. Then I tweak it, adding more red for a darker shade and more yellow and white for a lighter one. Using these three tones, I paint in some simple tree shapes along the horizon, focusing the lighter shade on the right side of each tree shape. Next, I mix a similar warmer green with less Viridian and more yellow and red. I use this to paint a simple hedge, adding a bit more yellow and white to create a nice highlight shade.

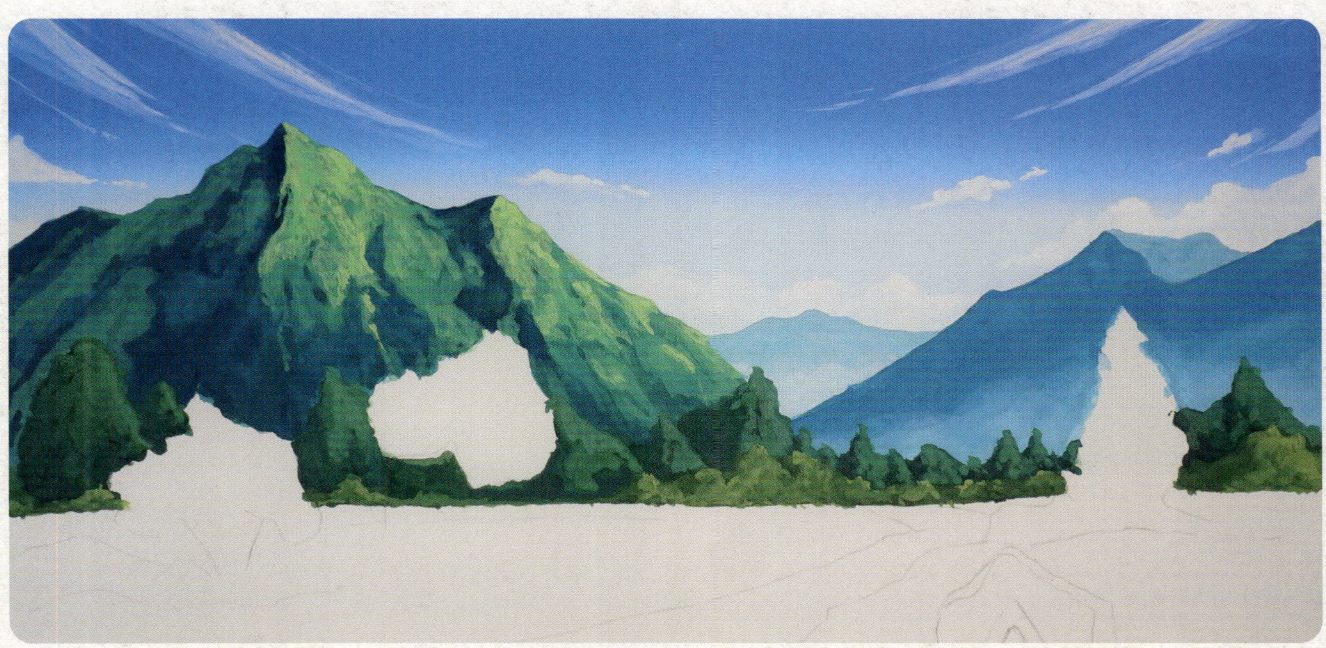

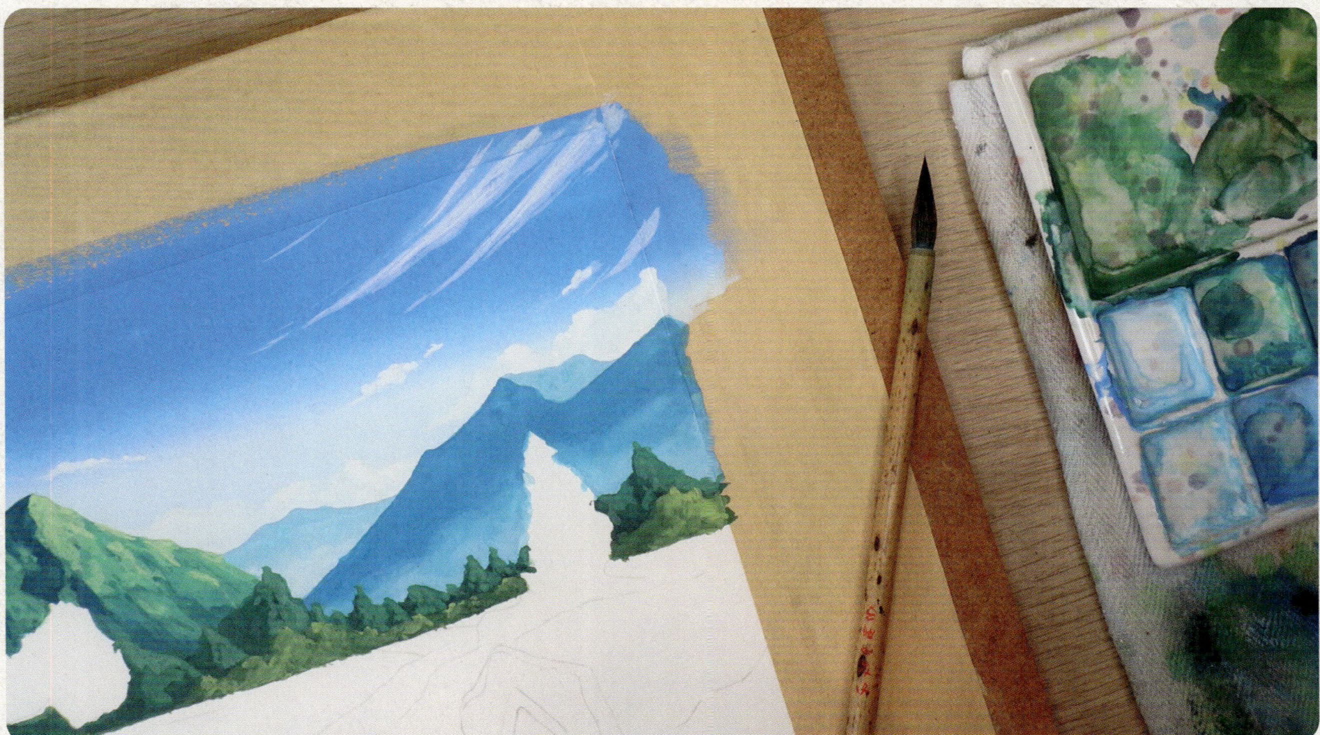

06. Start filling in the most distant trees and foliage

07.

Next, I'm blocking in the grassy meadow. I'm mixing Viridian with Lemon Yellow and just a touch of Carmine Red to get a more natural-looking green. I'm also using any leftover greens on my palette to cover the whole grassy area. I keep the lighter shades closer to the horizon and deepen the colours in the shadows under the trees (which I'll paint later). At the front of the painting, I add a much darker grassy mound by mixing Viridian with red and a tiny bit of yellow for warmth. Don't worry about painting details – this step is just about laying down a base colour.

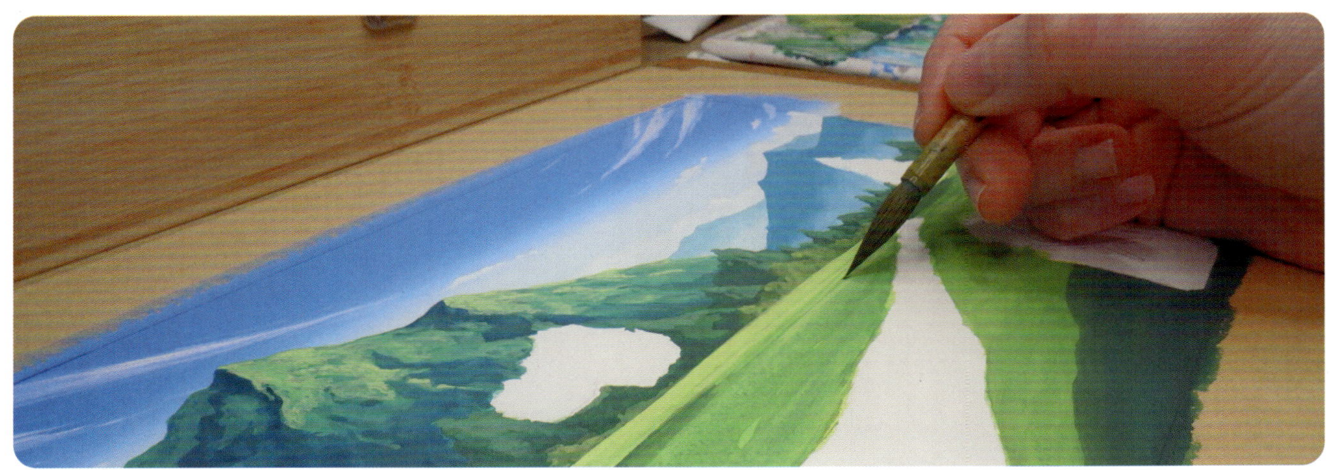

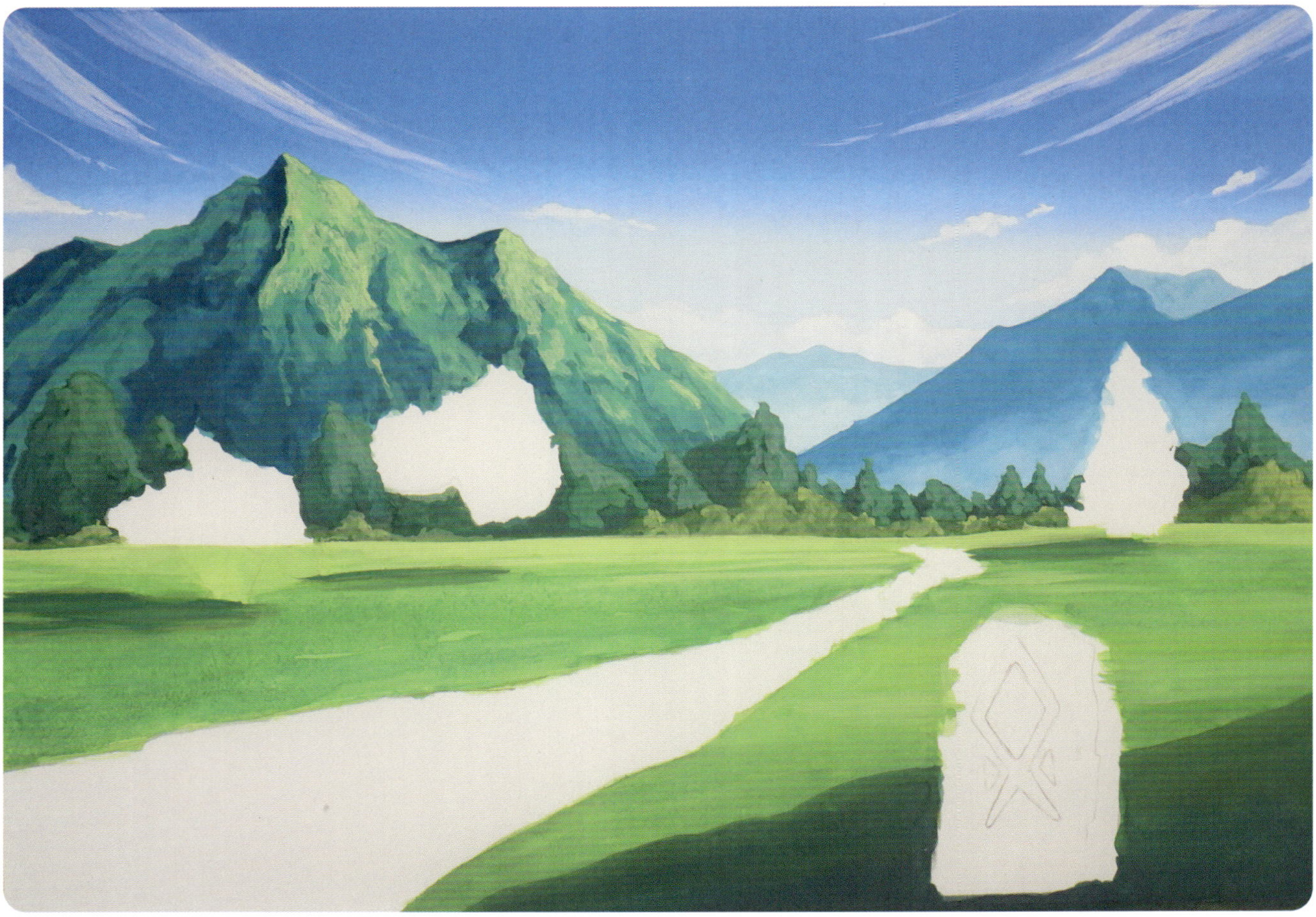

07. Use up a range of greens to fill out the grass areas, leaving out the treetops, path, and foreground stone

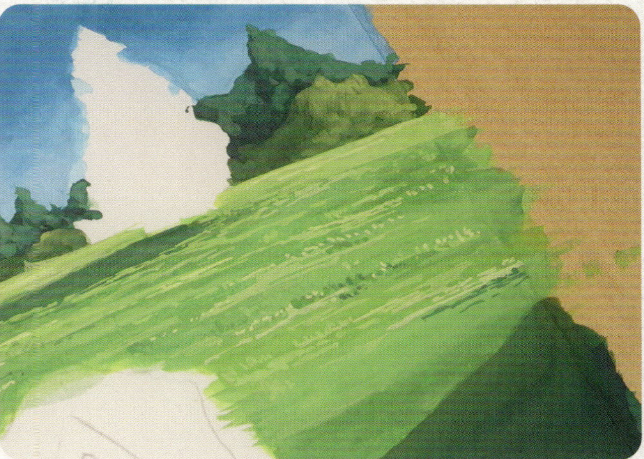

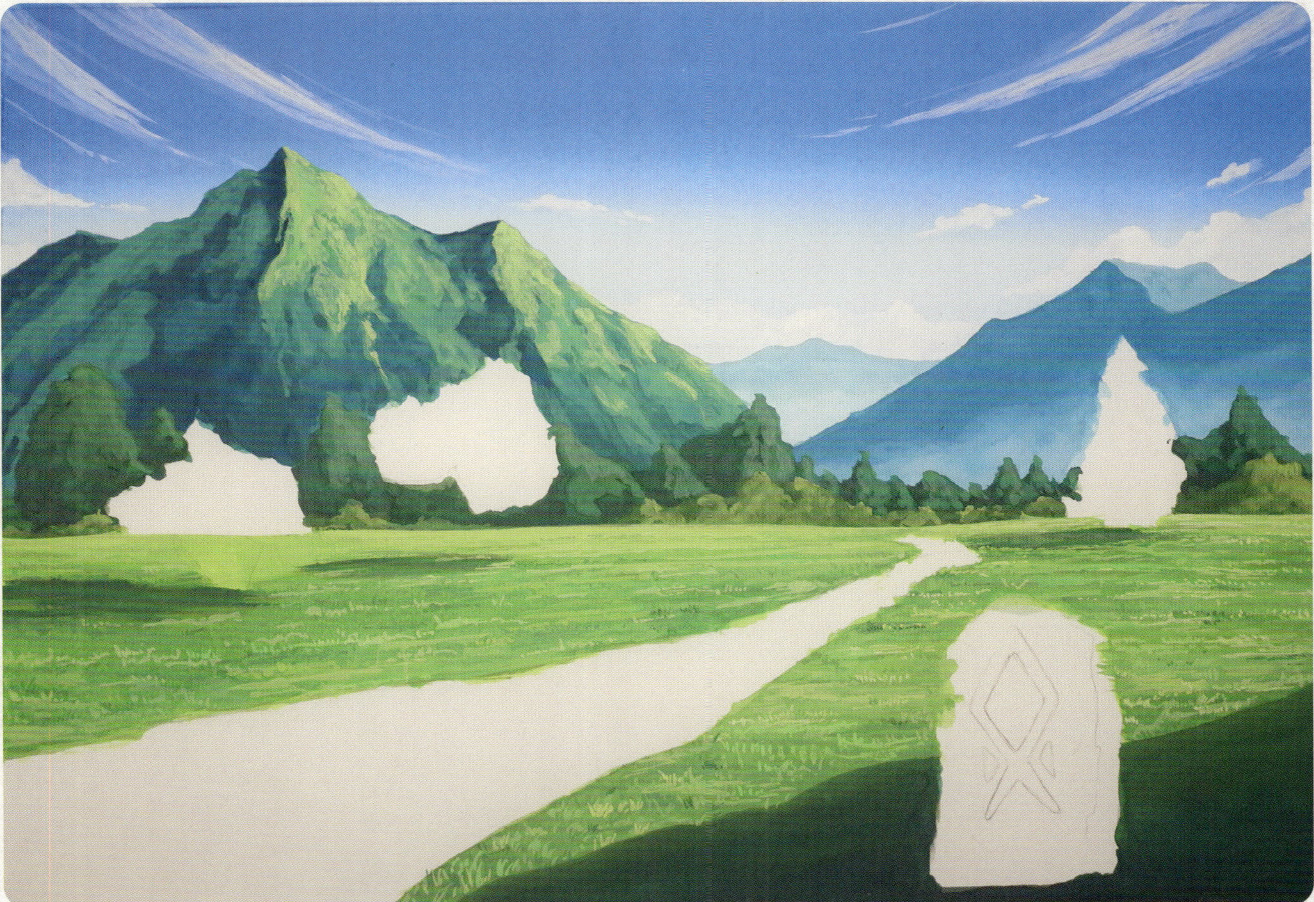

08. Switch to the detail brush to add texture to the grassy meadow

08.

Now, let's add some texture to our grass. I'm switching to a fine detail brush and using any leftover green paint on my palette. In the foreground, I create grass by painting short, vertical strokes in small clusters and rows. As we move further back in the painting, we want less detail to create a sense of depth. To achieve this, I like to pretend I'm scribbling tiny, nonsensical words and dots across the page. This creates a soft, textured effect that looks like distant grass without being overly detailed. Layer lighter colours on top of darker ones, and vice versa, to create these details while still maintaining the shadow placements.

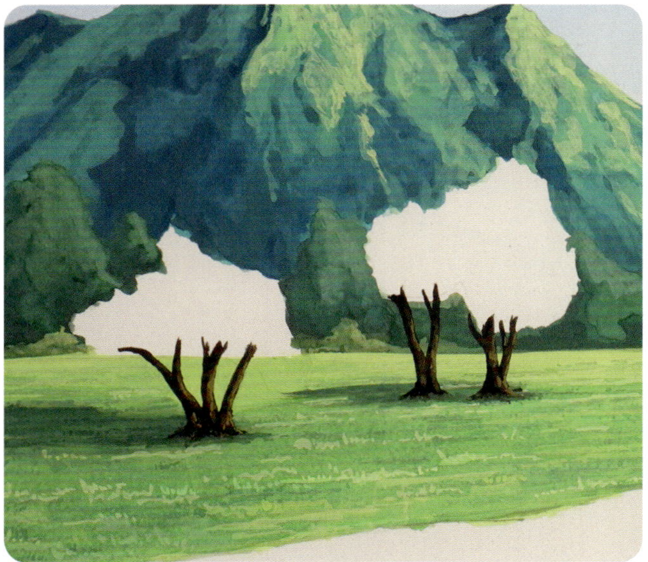

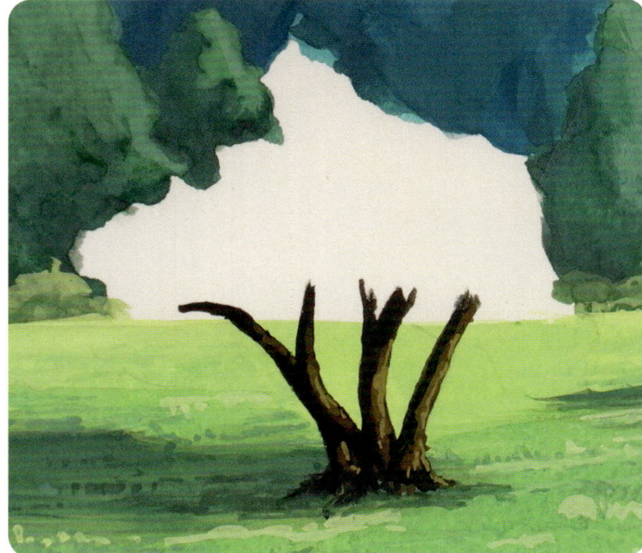

09. Start painting the trees by filling in the trunks first

09.

We're going to keep the foreground tree trunks simple by using just three colours: a dark, medium, and light warm-toned brown. To mix the medium shade, combine equal parts Burnt Sienna and Prussian Blue. For the darker variation, add more Prussian Blue, and for the lighter one, add a touch of Lemon Yellow. Start by painting the entire trunk with the medium shade, then add shadows on the left side and base using the dark shade. Finally, add subtle highlights along the right edge of the trunk. At this stage, you might also want to use a dark green to add some grass details, helping to blend the trunk into the grassy field.

10.

For the foreground trees, I'll use the 'rule of four' technique again, but this time, I'll adjust the base colour by adding a touch of Carmine Red and a bit more Prussian Blue to create a richer green. Start on the left side of the tree with the darkest shade, then gradually work towards the right, blending in the medium and light shades. You can blend while the paint is wet for a softer look or let each layer dry before adding the next for more defined shapes. Once all layers are completely dry, apply the highlight shade to give your tree a soft sunlit glow.

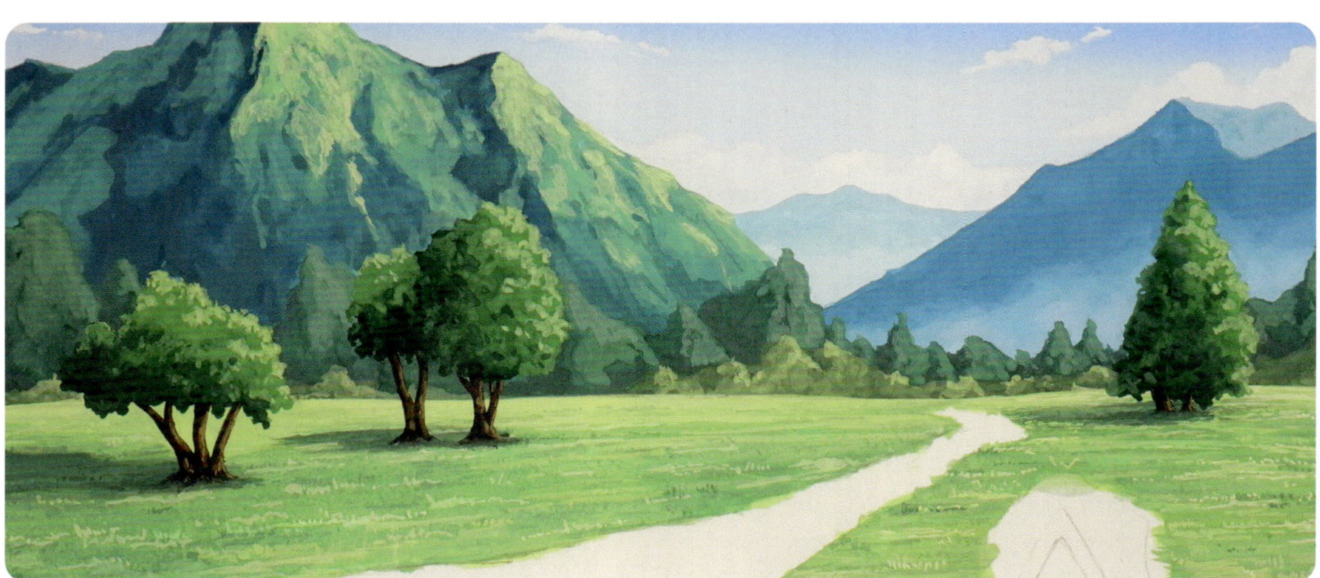

10. Use four shades of green to paint the tree foliage

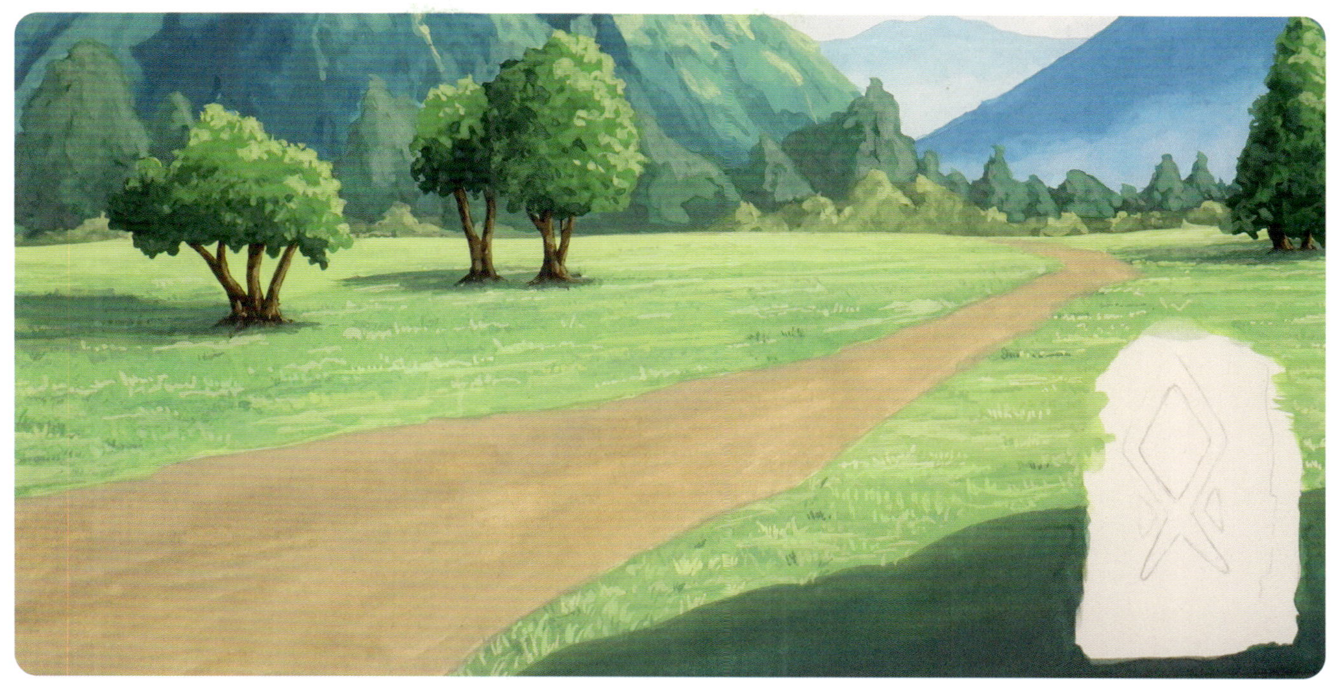

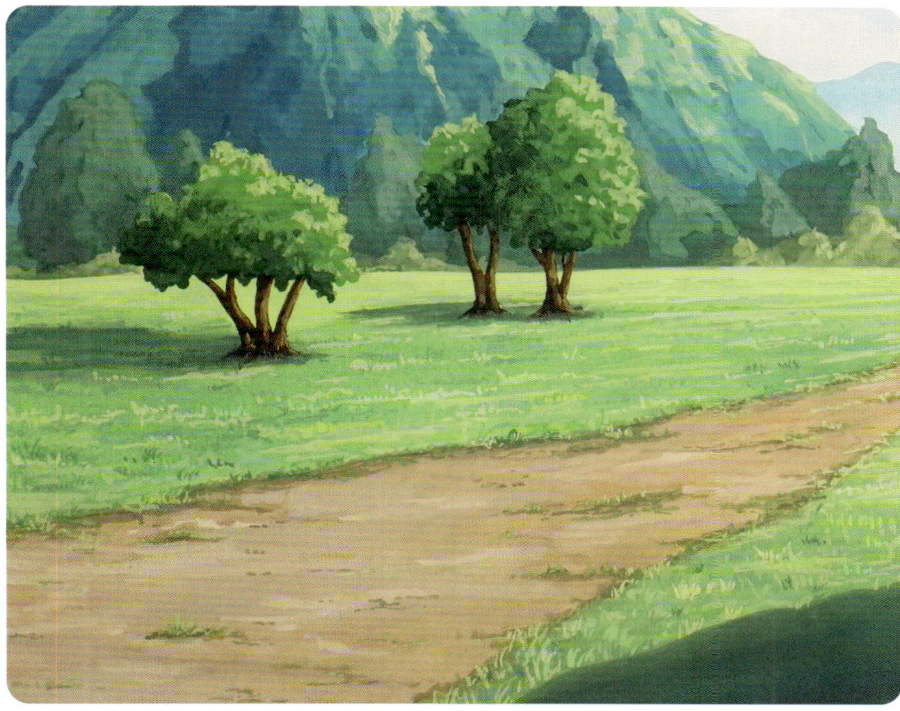

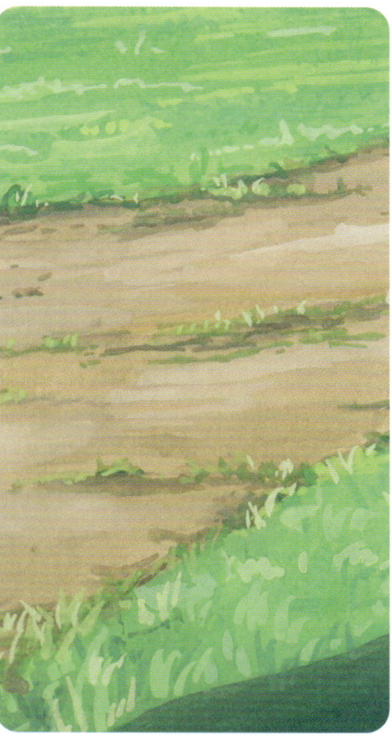

11. Mix a sandy brown to paint the path through the meadow

11.

For the pathway, start by blocking in a base colour made from Burnt Sienna and Yellow Ochre, mixed with a generous amount of white to create a light sand tone. Apply this across the entire path. Next, deepen the colour by adding Prussian Blue and more Burnt Sienna, using this darker mix to create shadows along the edges and scattered patches across the path for texture. To blend the path into the surrounding field, add patches of grass along the edges and through the centre. Finally, introduce subtle variations of lighter and darker shades of your base colour to enhance the texture and depth.

12.

We'll be reusing some of the pathway colours to paint our weathered rock. Start with a medium base shade by mixing Burnt Sienna, Yellow Ochre, and white, then add a touch of Prussian Blue to deepen it. Use this to block in the rock's shape. Next, create a darker shade by adding more Prussian Blue, and use it to add fine cracks and build shadows at the rock's base. To enhance the texture, apply a lighter shade along the edges of the cracks. Since the right side of the rock faces the light source, lighten your brightest shade with extra white to create a strong highlight on that side.

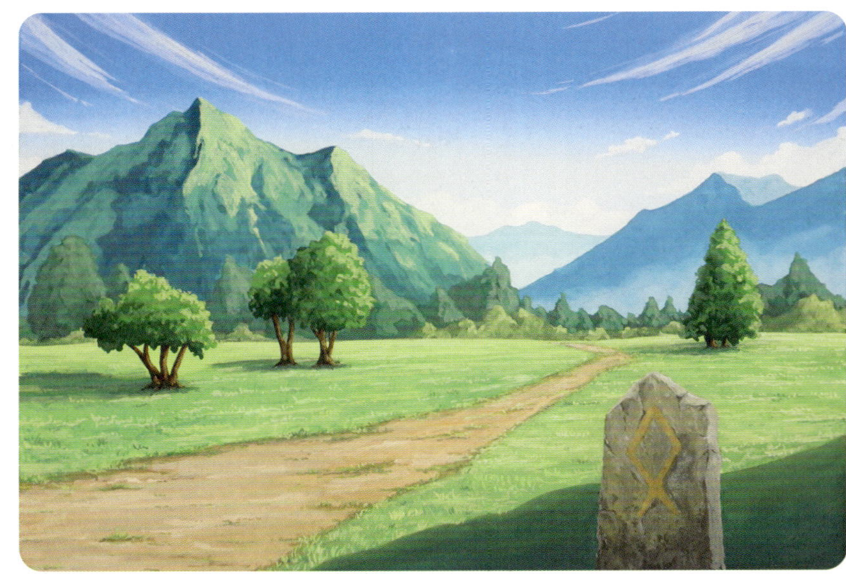

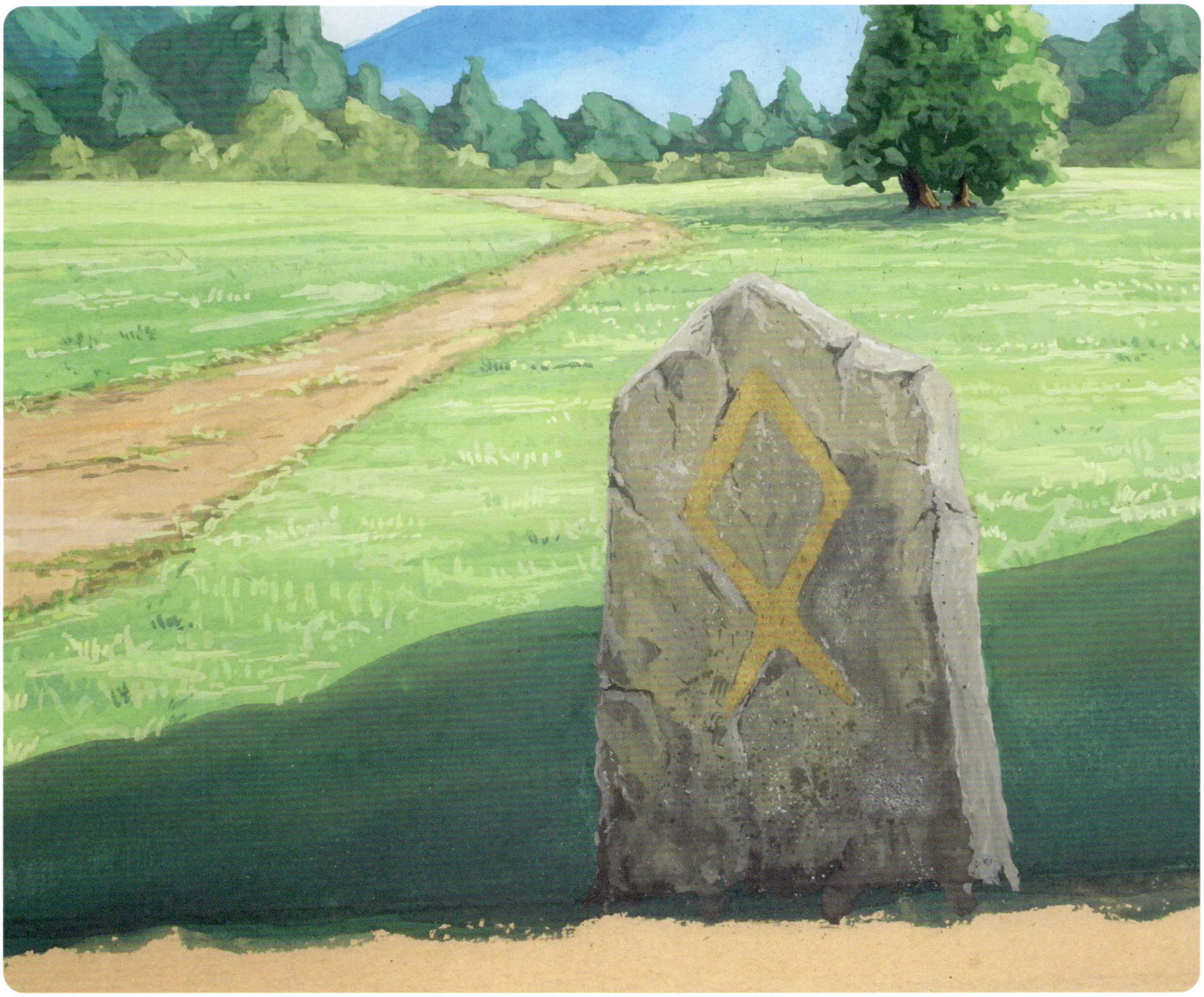

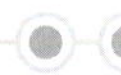

12. Mix shades of grey-brown to create variation in the weathered stone

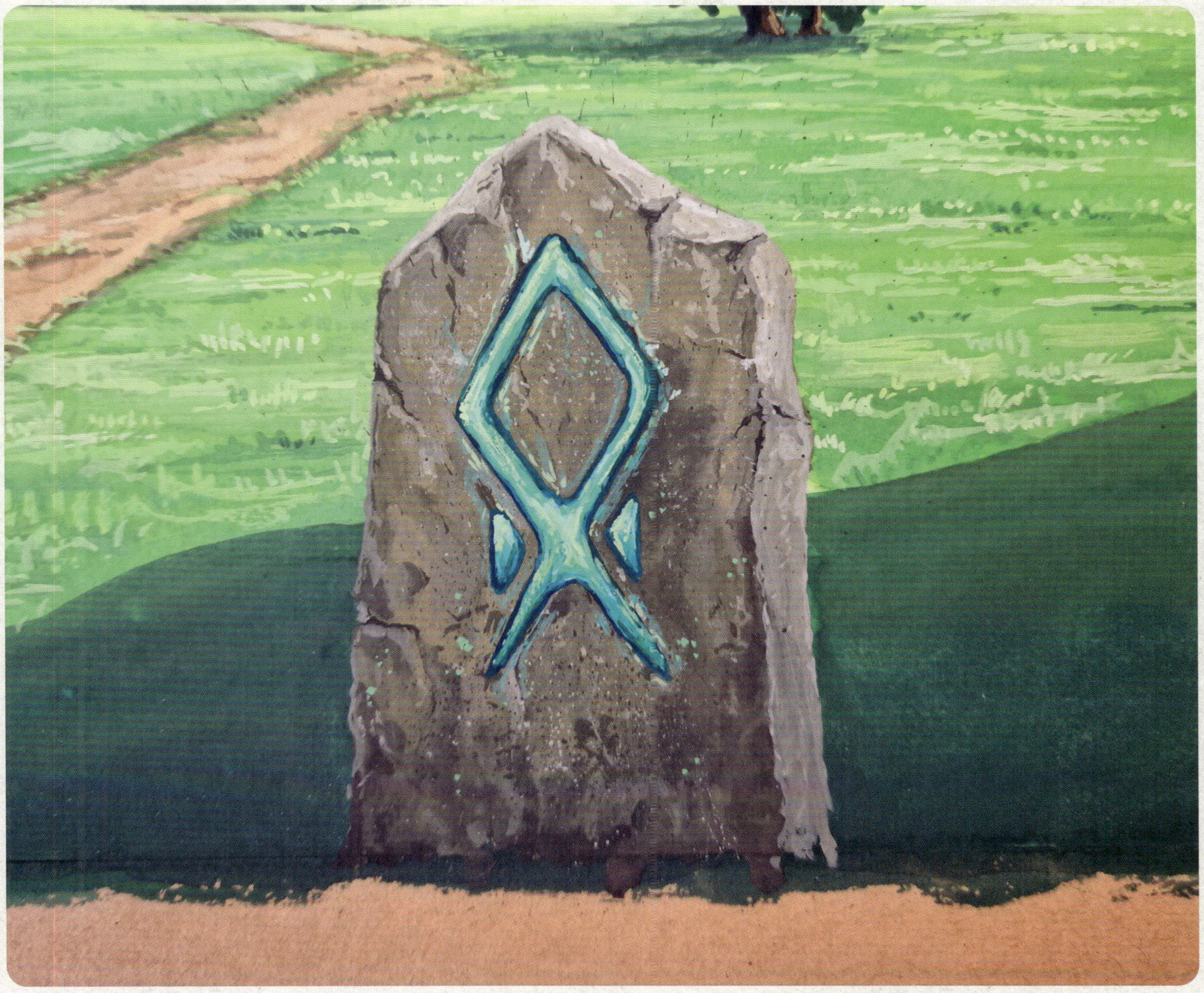

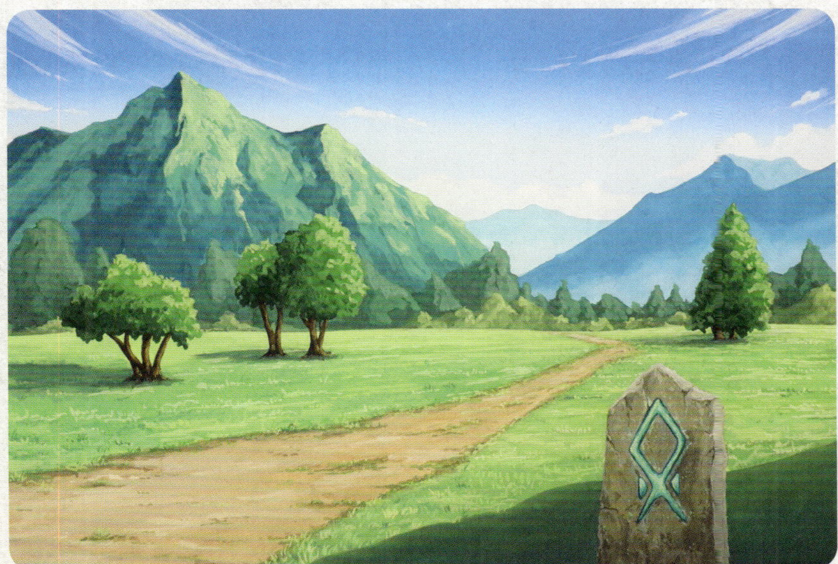

13.

For the glowing glyph, start with a base of Cerulean Blue mixed with a touch of Light Green. Fill in your glyph design with this colour, then gradually build up layers by adding more green, white, and a hint of yellow. Focus these brighter tones towards the centre of the glyph to create the effect of an inner glow. To enhance the glow, use a nearly dry brush to lightly apply small patches of these colours onto the rock surface, giving the illusion of light reflecting off the stone.

13. For a glowing effect, make the inner parts of the glyph the brightest

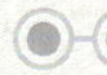

14.

Build up a variety of grass stalks and leafy foliage in the shadowed foreground, experimenting with different shapes and sizes for a natural look. Start with a deep grass green and gradually layer lighter shades, working up to a medium green. To blend the carved stone into the scene, add a touch of moss, letting it soften the transition between elements. Have fun with this step – use a small round brush to explore different strokes and create organic, flowing leaf shapes.

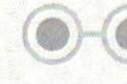

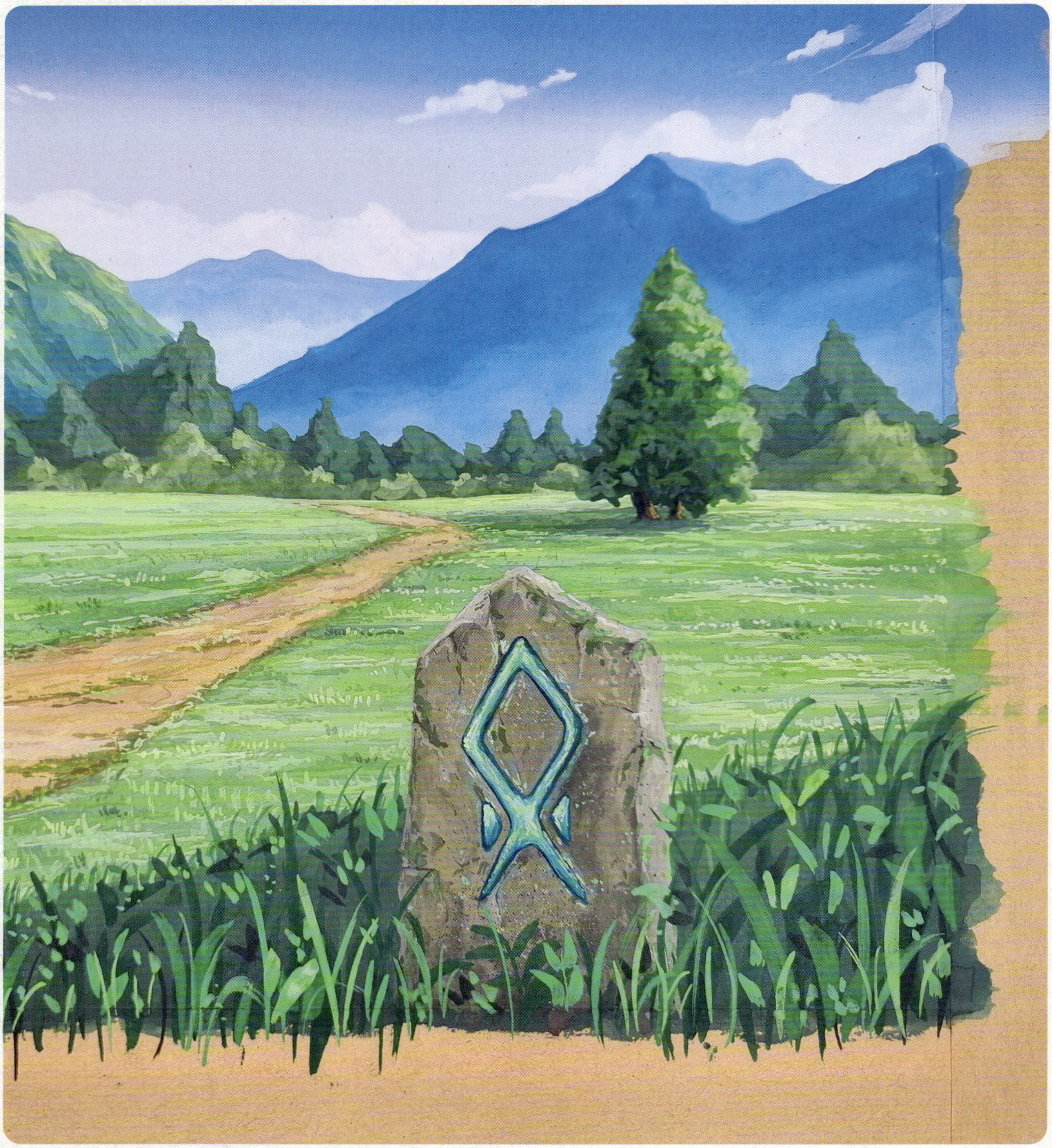

14. Use a range of greens to detail the foreground with lush grass

15.

I love adding a few wildflowers for extra charm. Using the fine detail brush, scatter small specks of paint in the distant grass – feel free to choose your favourite colours for this step. As you move closer to the foreground, gradually increase the size of the specks to enhance the sense of depth. In the shadowed patch of grass at the front, paint larger, more detailed flowers. To create the effect of shadow, mix a touch of Prussian Blue into your chosen colours for a richer, deeper tone. To finish off your painting with some extra narrative and

fantasy, try incorporating a magical character digitally! Simply scan or photograph your finished painting and add the character using a tablet or picture-editing software. This method gives you more flexibility, as you won't have to worry about altering the original landscape if you want to tweak the character's design. Don't forget to add a shadow under your character's feet to make them feel grounded in the scene. Clean lines and simple shading will give your character a look that evokes 2D animation.

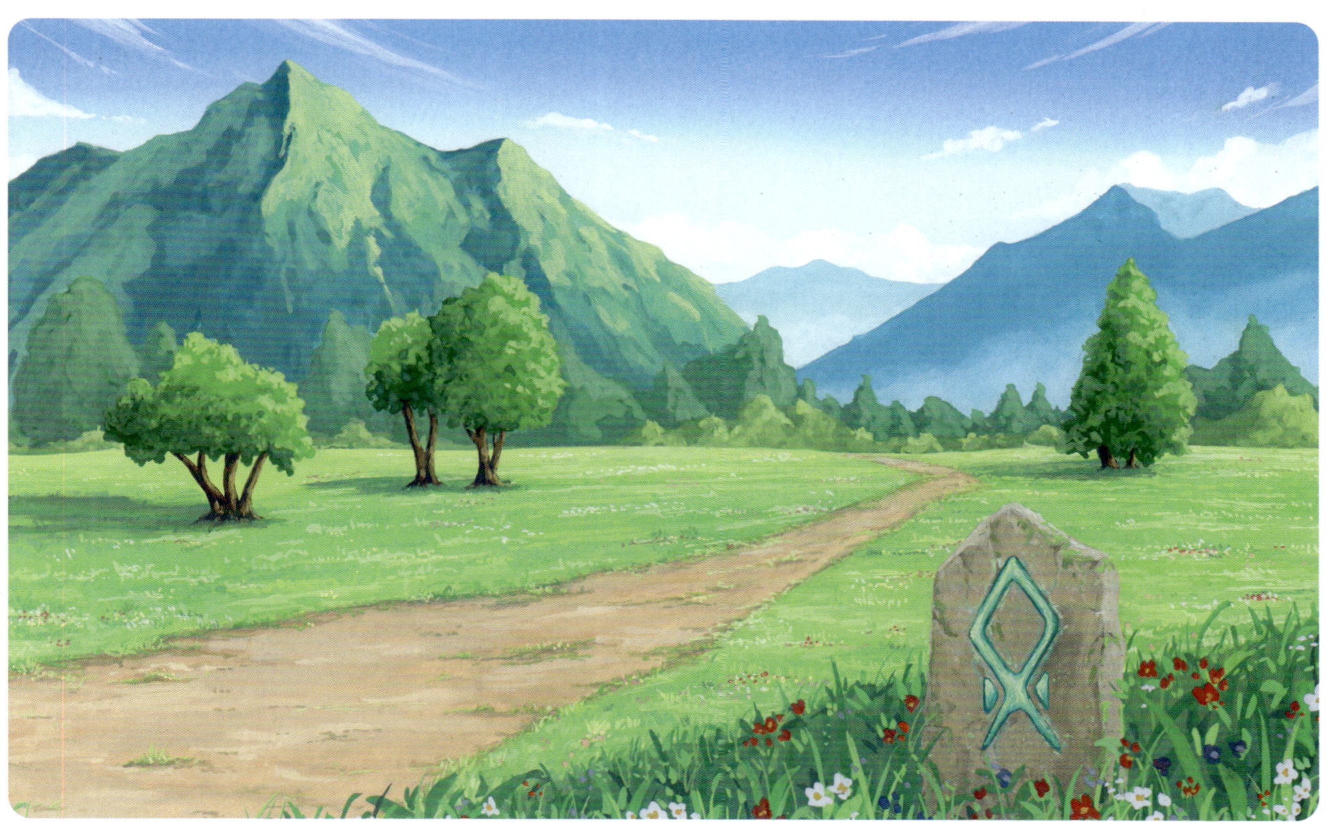

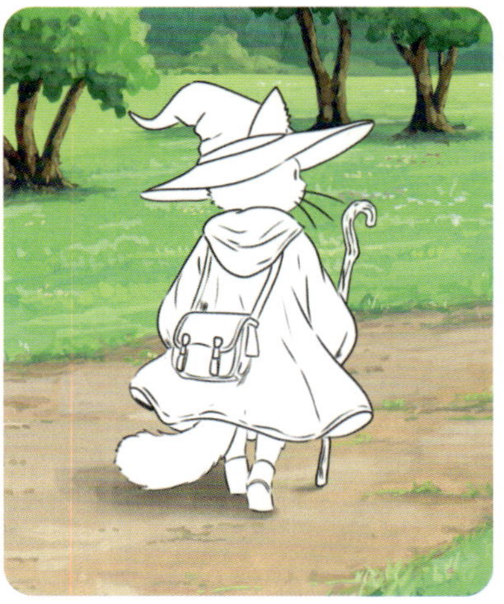

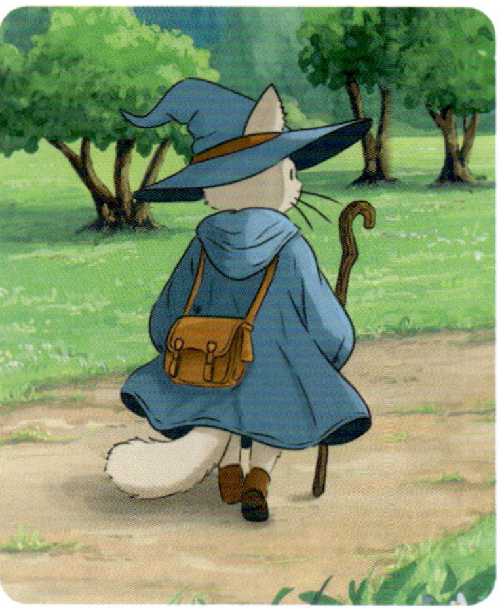

CONCLUSION

Creating this painting was such a calming experience. At first glance, it may seem like an ordinary landscape, but if you look closer, you'll notice the glowing stone – a quiet guide leading us down the path and deep into the mountains beneath the serene blue sky, where magic awaits our plucky animal magician. I hope you give this tutorial a try and find it just as soothing and enjoyable. Happy painting!

15. Combine a digital character with a traditional landscape for an animated look

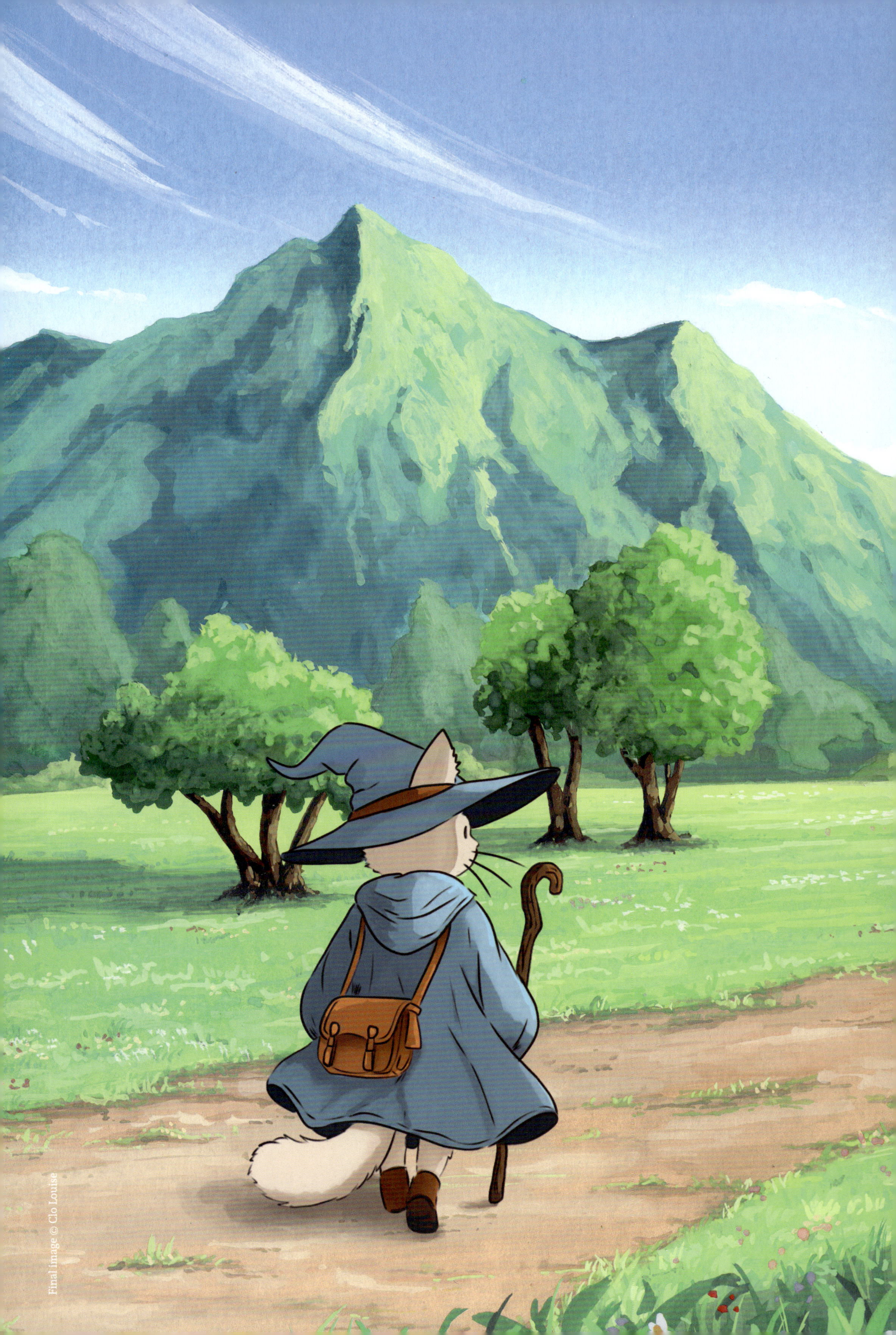
Final image © Clo Louise

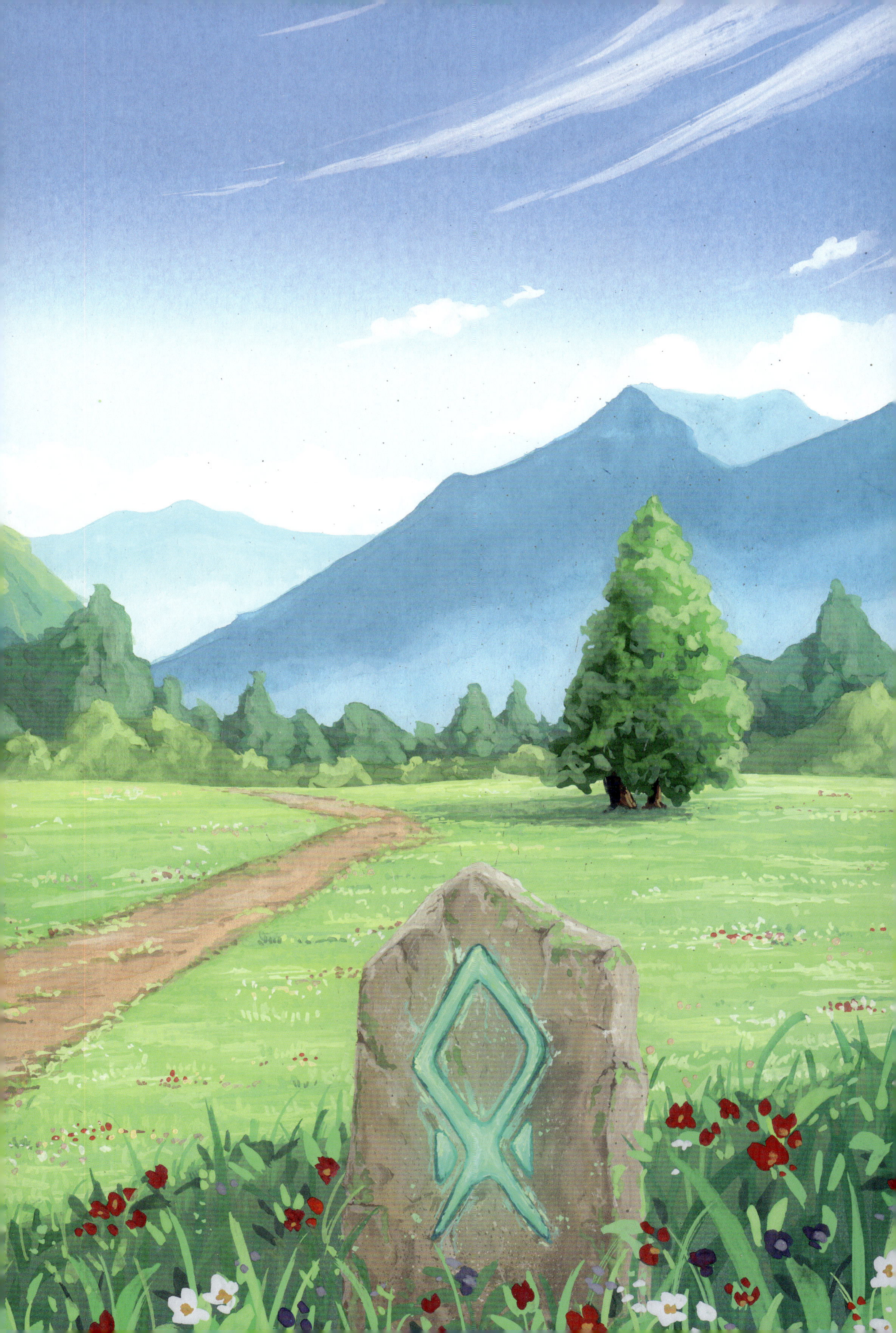

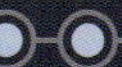

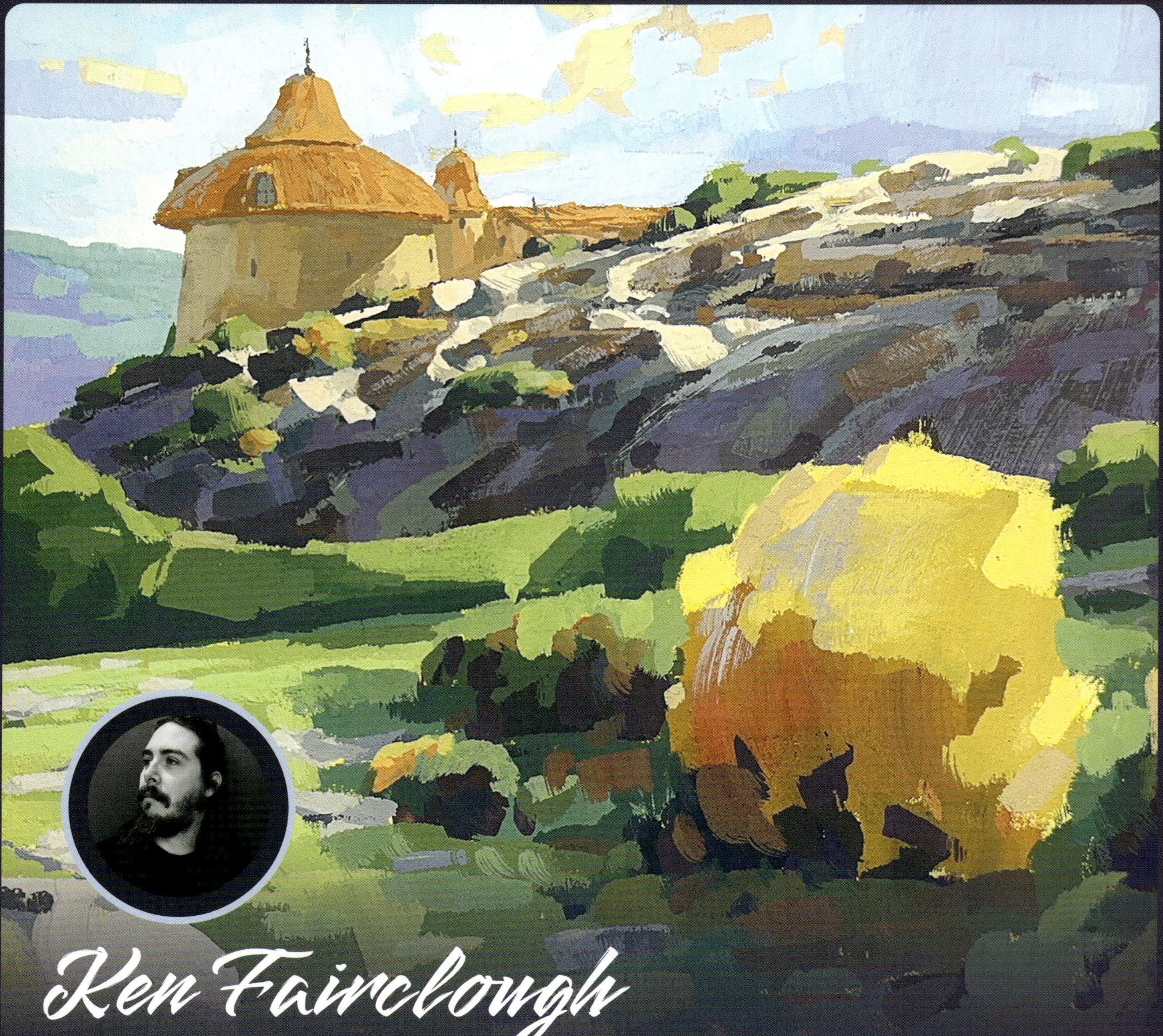

Final image © Ken Fairclough

Ken Fairclough

HILLSIDE CASTLE

In this chapter I will walk you through my process of completing a fantasy painting using traditional landscape and plein-air techniques. In my day job as a concept artist, I spend much of my time designing fictional worlds and locations with an emphasis on human-made objects. While working on personal paintings, I prefer to focus my attention on elements of nature and the inherent beauty of landscapes. In this tutorial I will create a painting that focuses on nature and a fictional structure built in harmony with the surrounding landscape, using an impressionistic approach. I prefer to paint from observation when given the opportunity, so I have chosen a location I've previously painted 'en plein air' as my main inspiration. I hope you enjoy the process of painting with gouache as much as I do!

TOOLKIT

- New York Central 140lb hot-press watercolour block (7" × 10")

- Transon paint storage palette

- Water container

- Creative Mark butcher's tray palette

- Scrap illustration board or white matte board

- Paper towels

- Spray bottle

- Masking tape

- Pencil

BRUSHES

Artegría oval wash brush
¾" (19mm)

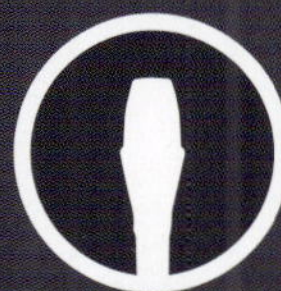

Princeton Aqua Elite stroke brush
¾" (19mm) & ½" (12mm)

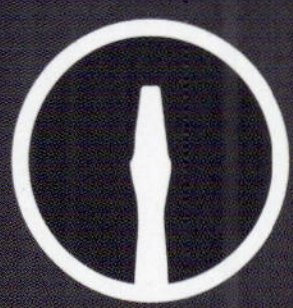

Silver Brush Ultra Mini® lettering brush
No. 5/0

I recommend artist-quality paints like Holbein or Winsor & Newton. While more costly than student-grade paints, artist-quality paints are more opaque with better coverage. It's worth noting that most colours can be achieved using only a set of primary colours, so don't worry if you don't have some of the subtle colour variations shown here. Regardless of which quality or brand, make sure to have plenty of white. You will go through more white than any of your other pigments, so having larger tubes will come in handy.

COLOUR LIST

- Permanent White
- Lemon Yellow
- Permanent Yellow Deep
- Linden Green
- Yellow Ochre
- Marigold Yellow
- Orange Lake Light
- Burnt Umber
- Venetian Red
- Spectrum Red
- Opera Pink
- Magenta
- Permanent Green Middle
- Prussian Blue
- Ultramarine
- Sky Blue
- Cobalt Turquoise Light

01.

When beginning to paint in gouache, it is easy to get overwhelmed by different materials and techniques. I, however, believe the most fundamental stage in beginning your painting journey is the act of observation. While it's challenging in its own right, try to focus less on achieving certain results and more on the joy of the process. Get outside and connect with nature. Learn to observe the elements that speak to you and focus only on capturing those details. With time, as you paint from observation, your personal affinities will guide many of your creative decisions and allow your voice to come through in your work.

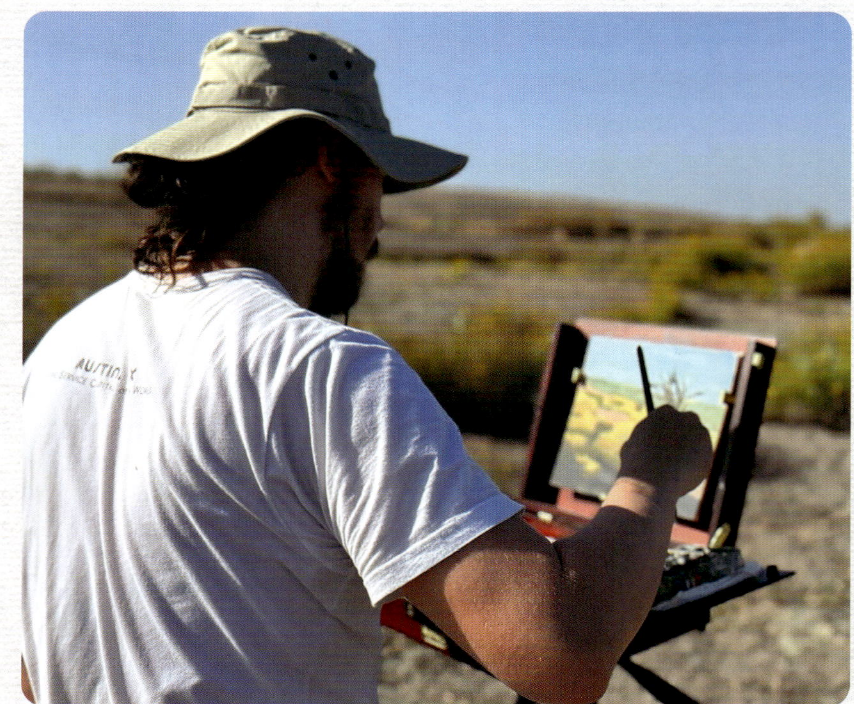

01a. Learn from nature and enjoy the process

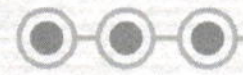

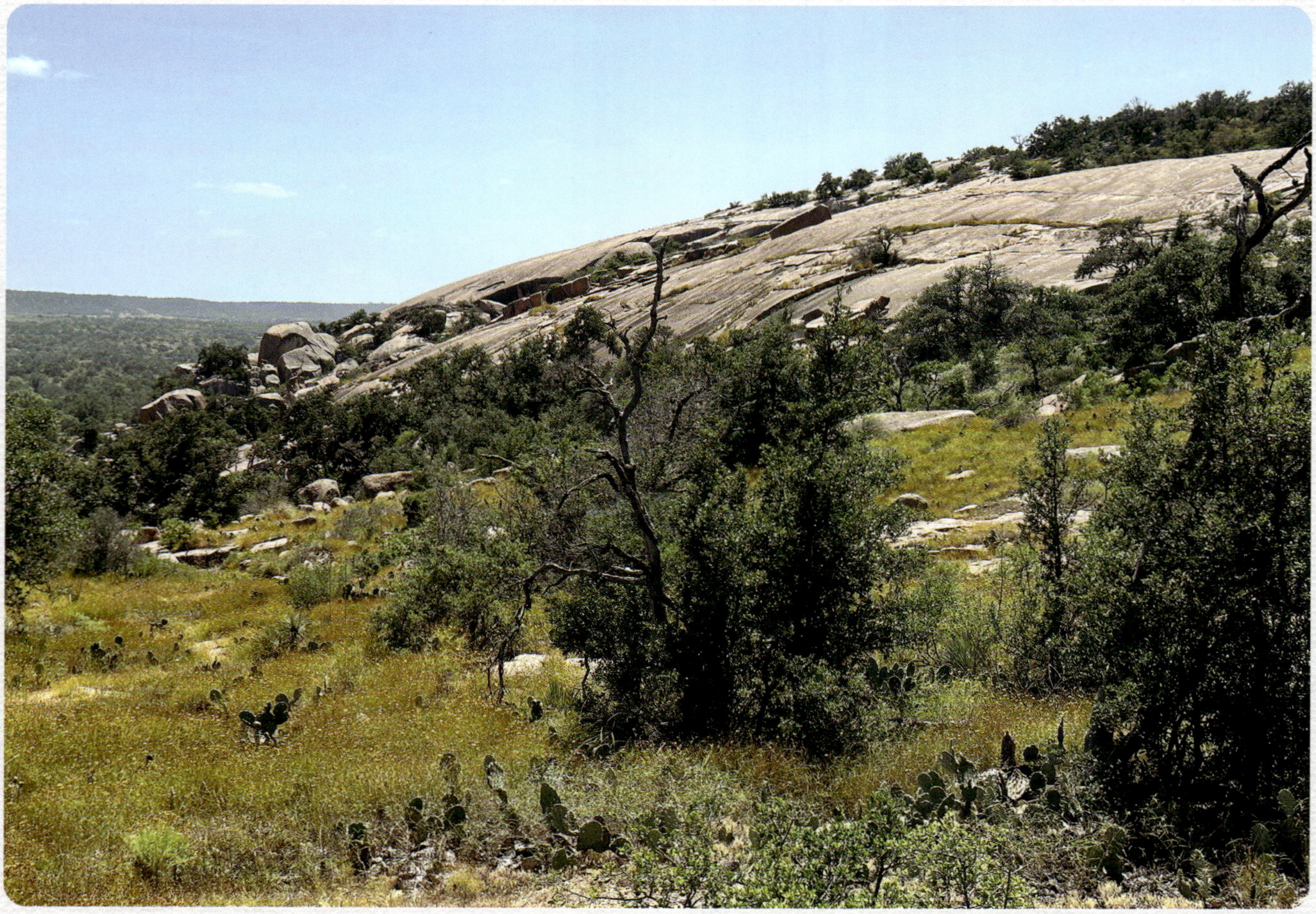

01b. The real location that will inspire the setting for a castle scene

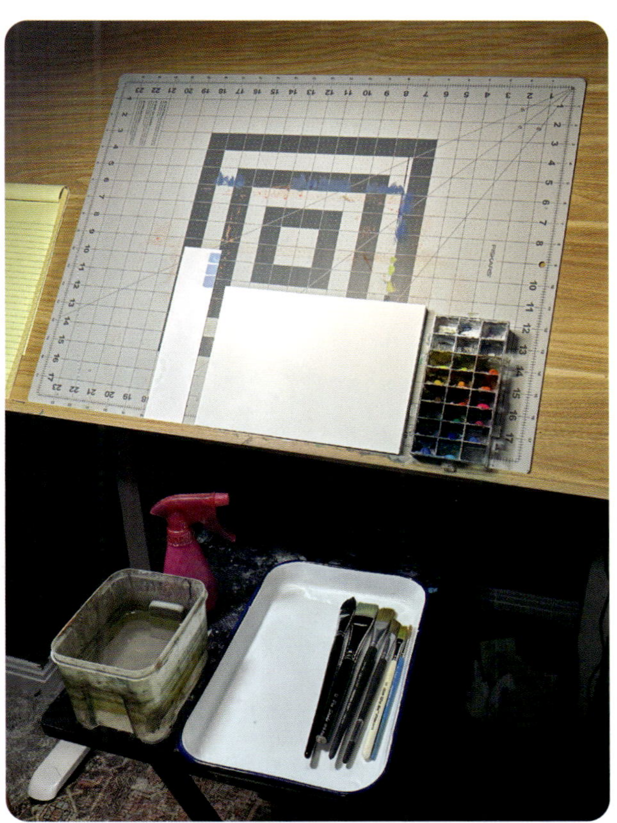

02. My workspace set-up for this project

02.

Aside from the obvious (paints, brushes, and paper), the few things that I consider essential are a decent storage palette, scrap illustration board, and a spray bottle. Storage palettes are compact ways of keeping your chosen pigments organized and easily accessible, whether you are painting at home or outdoors. The scrap illustration board is useful for testing the viscosity of your paint mix and matching previously used colours, which I'll demonstrate in later steps. Much like watercolour, gouache can become tacky and dry out after some time. Having a spray bottle is useful for keeping your paints easy to sample from your palette and mix.

03.

I always start a new project by sketching out ideas before committing to a final design. This is my chance to experiment with the placement of elements, focusing on the broad, simple shapes that make up my composition. I want to achieve a composition that draws the viewer into the scene. I have the idea of a trail leading the viewer along a winding path to the reveal of a quaint structure built into the landscape. It's important not to get caught up in details and remain focused on the arrangements of shapes, prioritizing readability and balance.

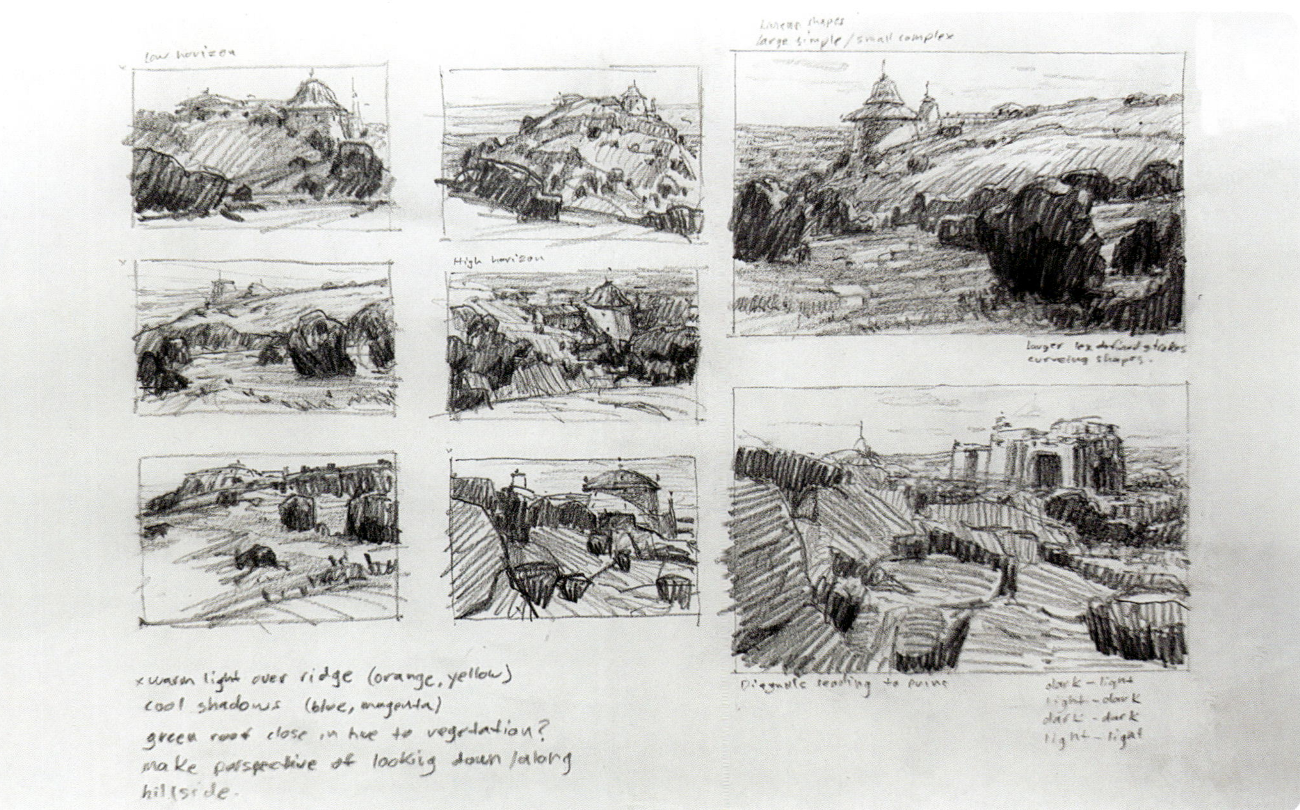

03. Small pencil sketches help to plan the composition

PLANNING VALUES

While planning your painting, it's important to think about its value structure. Values are the range from light to dark that will establish readability and reinforce depth in your image. While picking colours may seem higher priority, it's important not to neglect your values. You have some freedom with choosing colours, but without a strong value set-up your image will lack the structure needed to read properly. I suggest planning your image in three values: lights, darks, and midtones.

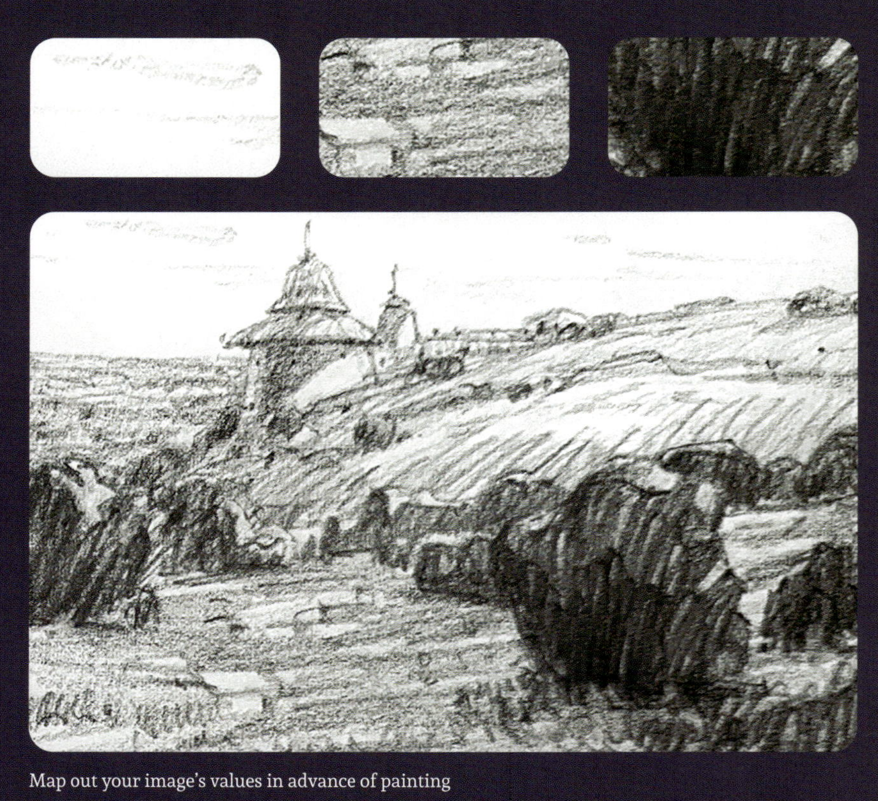

Map out your image's values in advance of painting

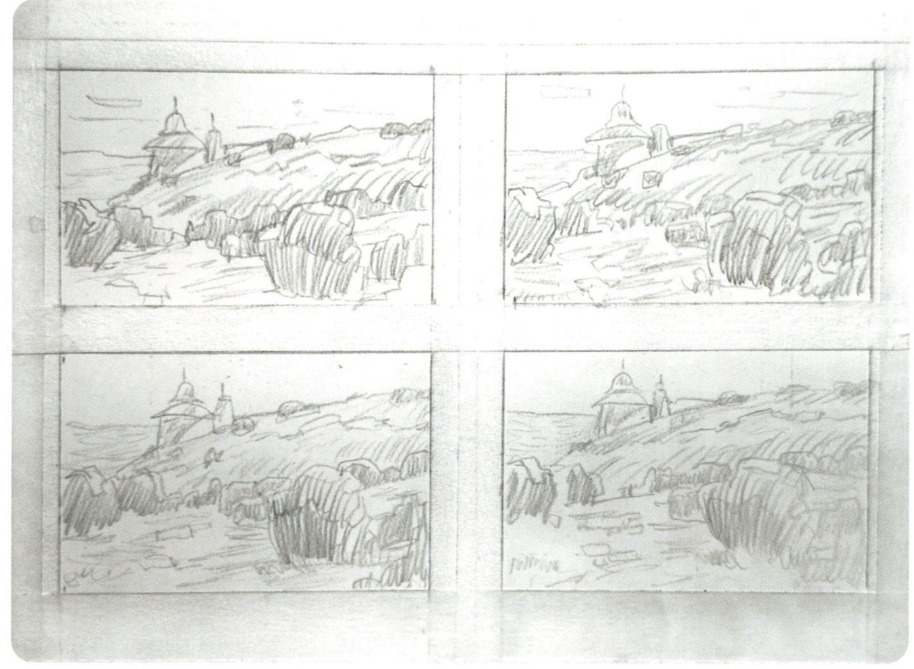

04a. Make larger pencil sketches for testing out colour palettes

04.

After landing on a composition I like, I transfer my sketch to watercolour paper to do quick colour sketches in gouache. Much like the previous step, this stage is for me to experiment with colour before committing to the final design. Choosing colours can sometimes be intimidating, but I've found that keeping palettes as simple as possible will ultimately lead me to a better result. I try to think of complementary colours that convey different moods and go from there. Painting from observation will hone your ability to choose evocative and naturalistic colour palettes.

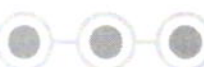

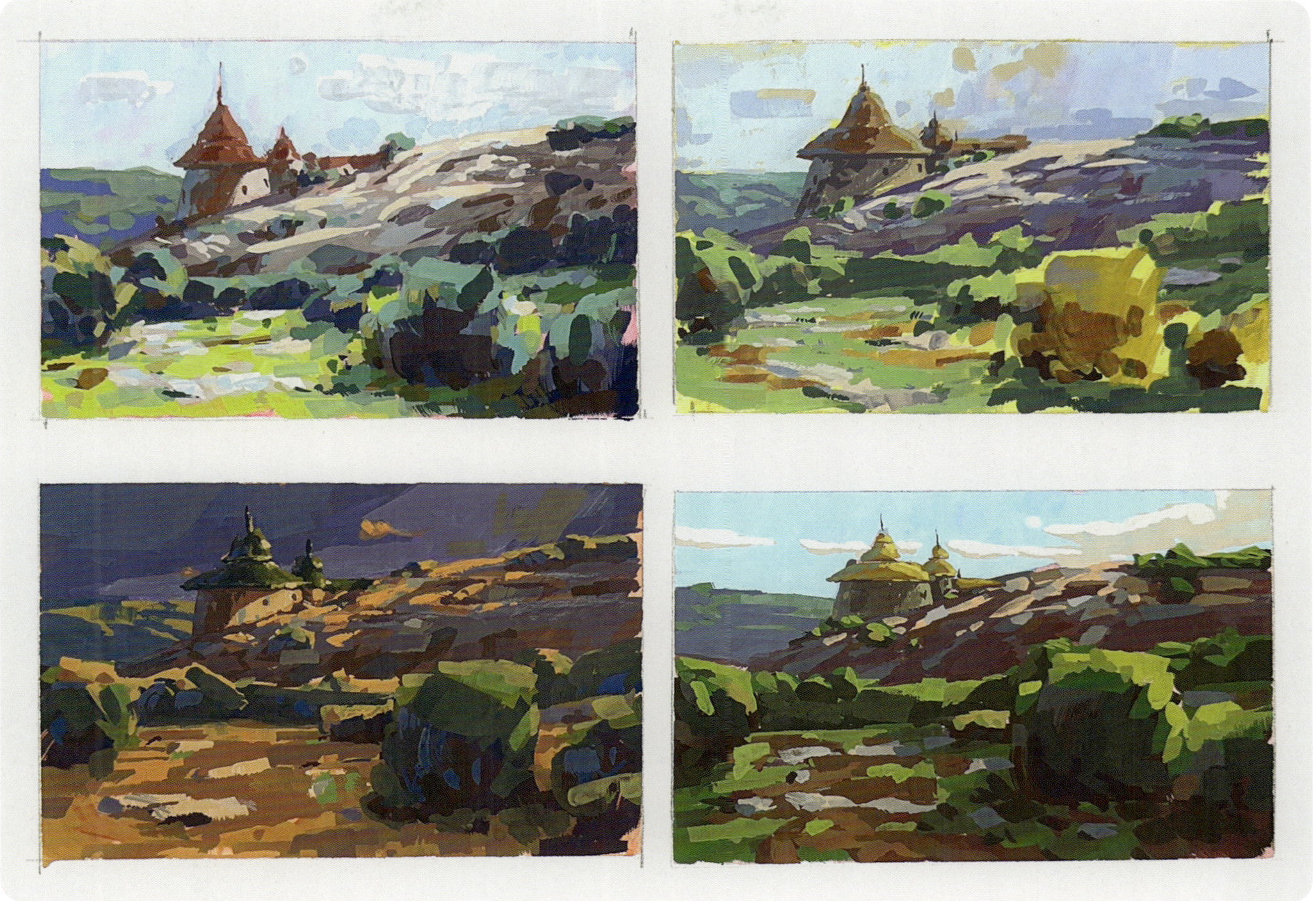

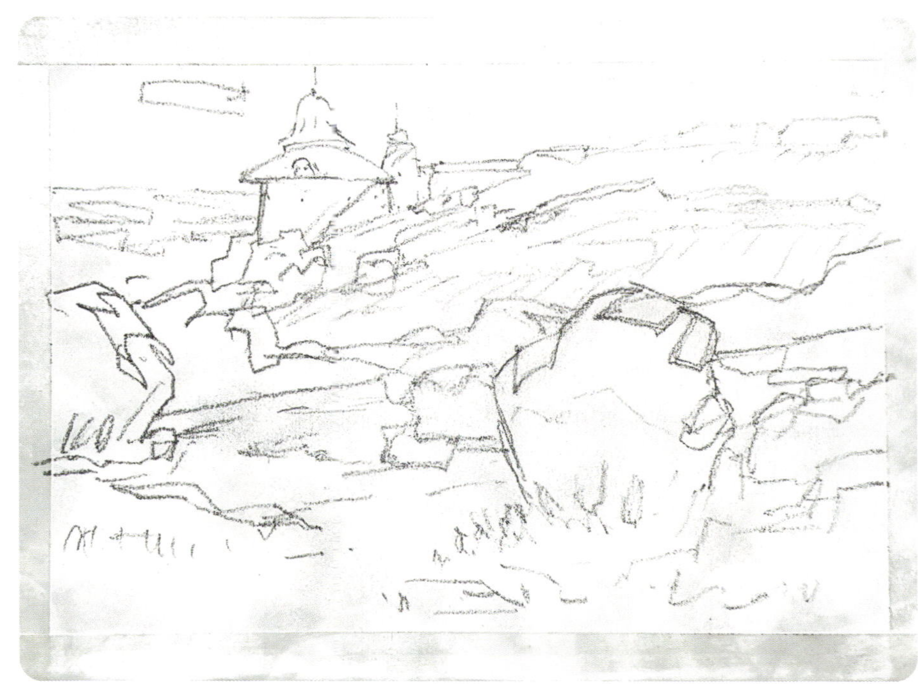

04b. Sample colour palettes painted over the pencil sketches

05.

Now that I've chosen a suitable colour palette (the top-right option), I transfer my sketch once more to the final painting surface. When I'm redrawing my initial sketch I intentionally simplify the shapes of individual elements, as well as light and shadow shapes. My goal when painting is not to capture or recreate reality but create an *impression* of reality. It's an exciting challenge to simplify shapes in nature to tell the story you are trying to tell. Through the simplification of the elements in my images, I can also reinforce the composition by creating a more appealing hierarchy of big, medium, and small shapes.

05. The full-sized sketch on hot-press watercolour paper

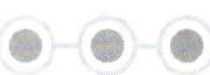

06.

Before laying down any definitive strokes, I prefer covering my surface with an underpainting. I choose a complementary midtone that will interact well with the colours I lay on top, and in some areas show through, harmonizing the colours. In this case, I use an oval wash brush to apply a diluted yellow that allows the pencil sketch to show through. Starting with an underpainting gets rid of the stark white of the paper and makes it easier for me to gauge my values. Painting on top of a complementary midtone is also very satisfying. There is something about making marks of contrasting hues on top that brings immense joy during the process. It's important to find joy in all stages of making art, even in seemingly simple acts.

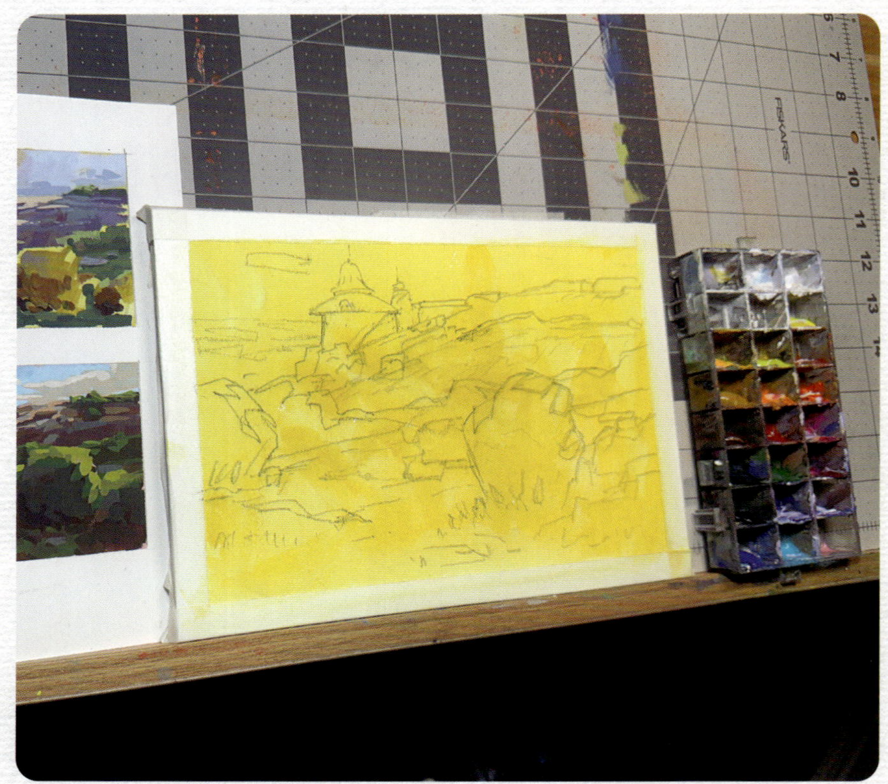

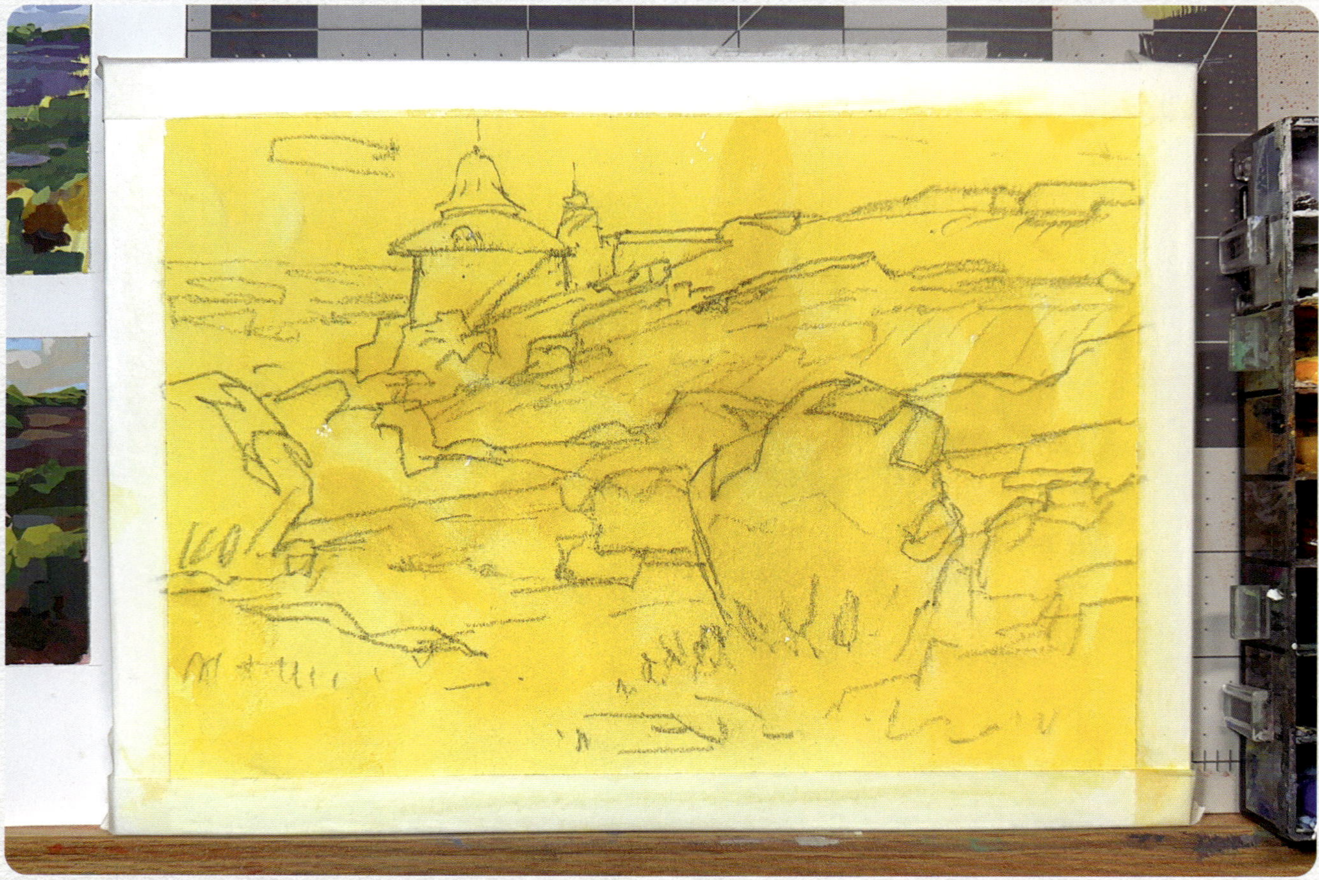

06. The translucent yellow underpainting forms a strong base

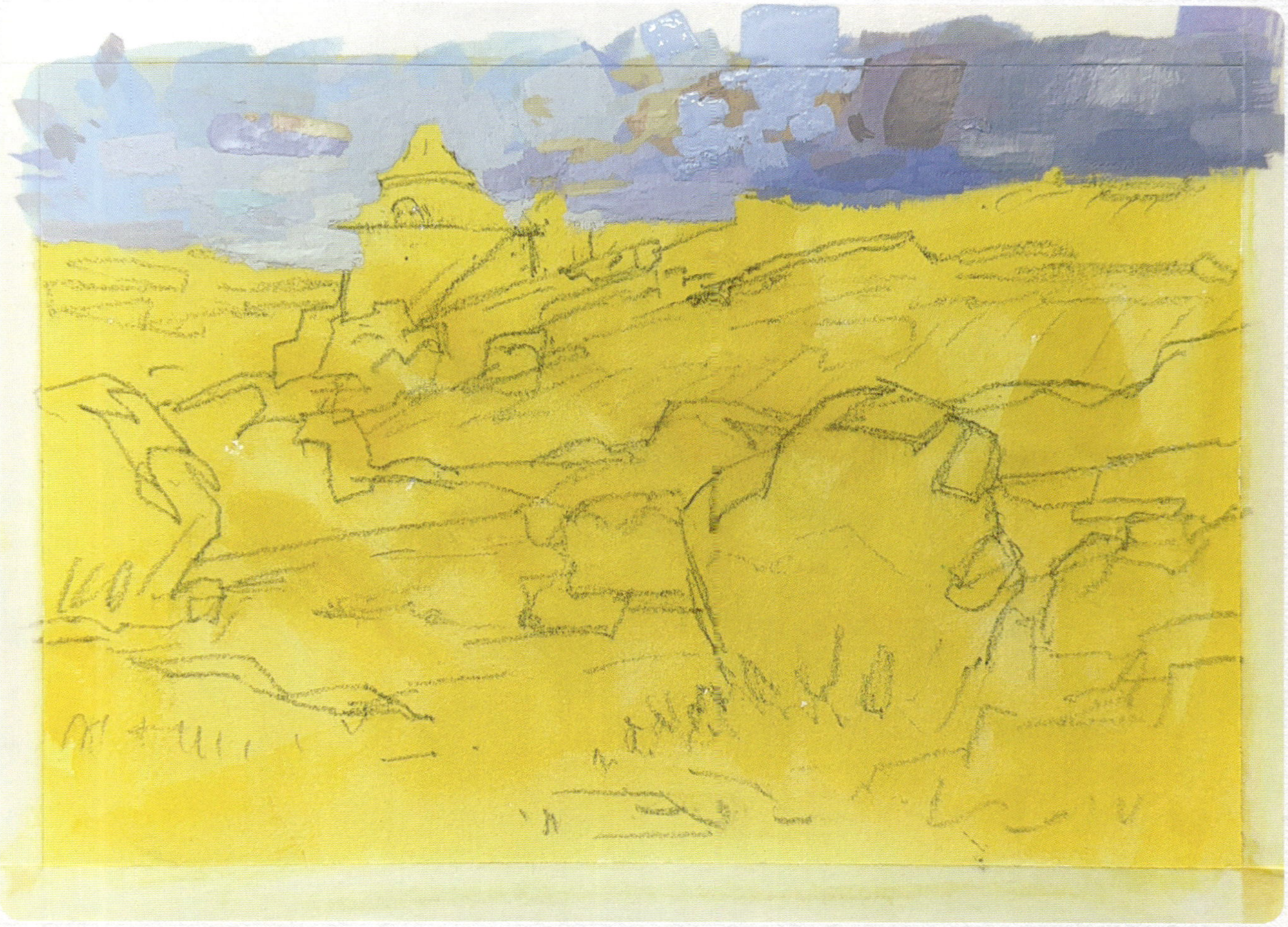

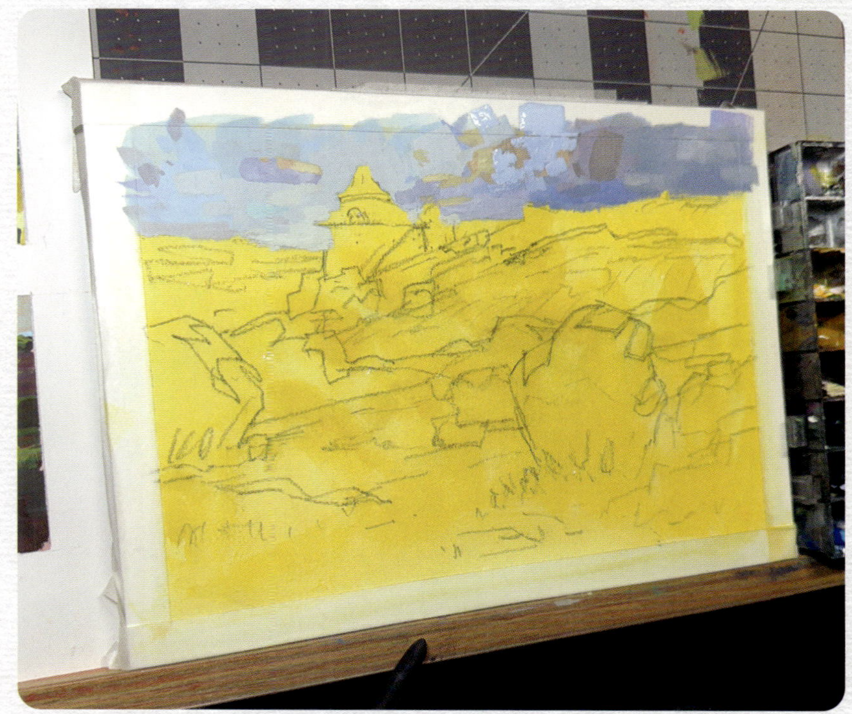

07.

I switch to the 3/4" stroke brush and mix light blue, purple-blue, and pale yellow hues to begin blocking in the sky with quite thick, opaque marks. When blocking in colour, I always start with the sky because it will interact with all other colours going forward. It's important to block something in relatively fast and move on. Getting too focused on detail too early in the process is an easy trap to fall into. Overworking areas this early can stunt your momentum and stifle the energy of the image. It is better to have an underworked painting than an overworked painting. You can always come back to these areas later to refine them.

07. Block out the sky colours with thick, rough strokes

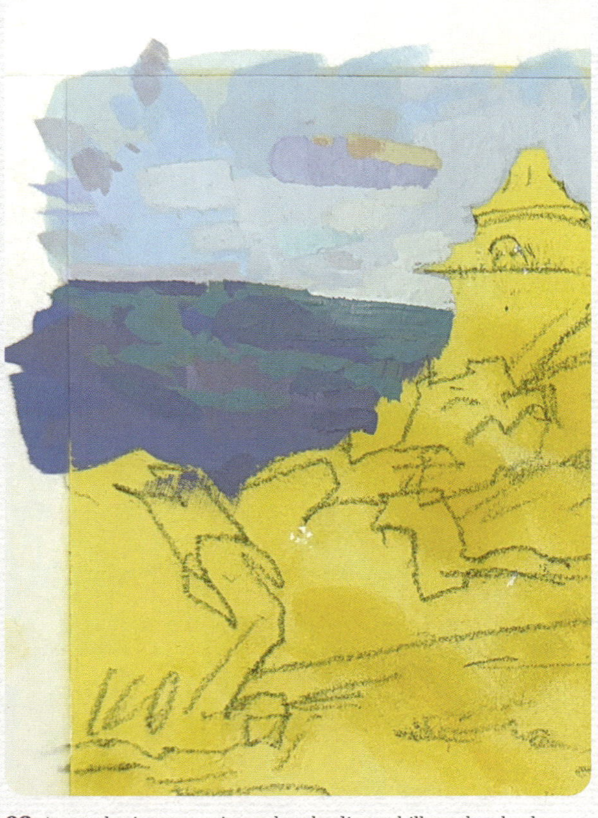

08. Atmospheric perspective makes the distant hills cool and pale

08.

Continuing from the sky, I block in the background terrain. To imply depth I need to indicate atmosphere in front of the distant hills. This is the most apparent instance of the sky colour interacting with other colours. Atmospheric perspective tends to desaturate colours and decrease their contrast. When mixing colours, I try to keep things organized and clean my palette throughout the process. I find it helpful to mix more of a colour than I may need at any given moment, so I can easily mix lighter/darker and warmer/cooler variations. In this case, I have plenty of sky colours left, and use them to mix slightly darker purple and blue-green tones for the distant hills.

09.

Once I've established the background, I move on to blocking in my darkest darks. I use warm and cool greens, yellow-browns and red-browns, and hints of purple in the darkest shadows. I now have close to my lightest lights in place alongside my darks, which allows me to better gauge my value relations going forward. These values also give structure to an otherwise flat image, allowing me to better recognize the three-dimensionality of the scene. From this point it becomes easier to imagine how light and shadow will affect the objects and keep a consistent lighting direction.

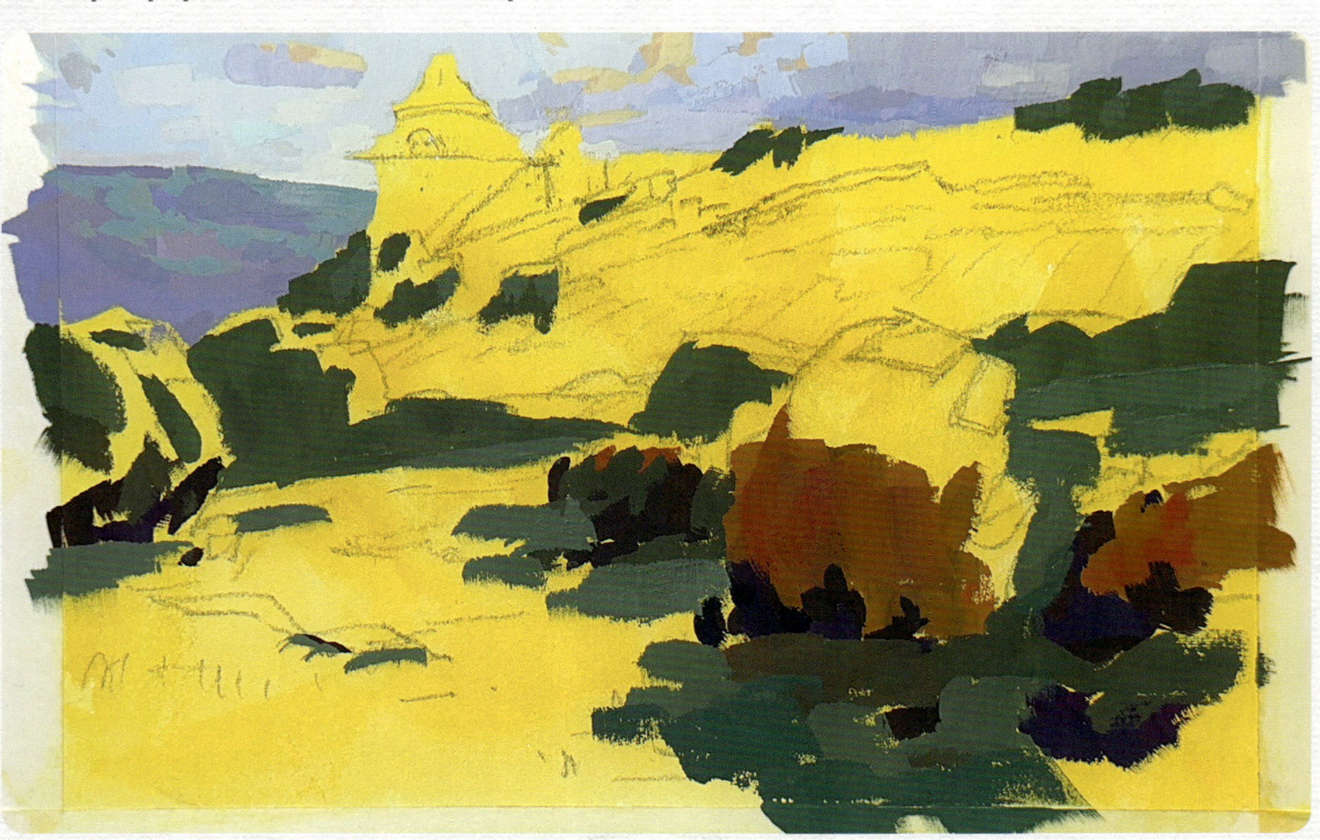

09. Add depth to the scene by blocking out shadowed areas

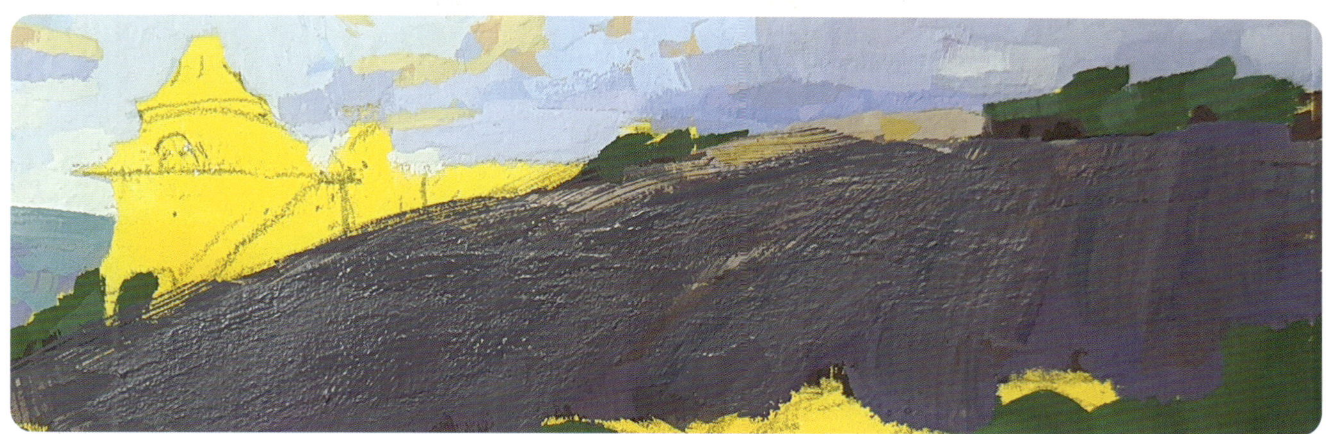

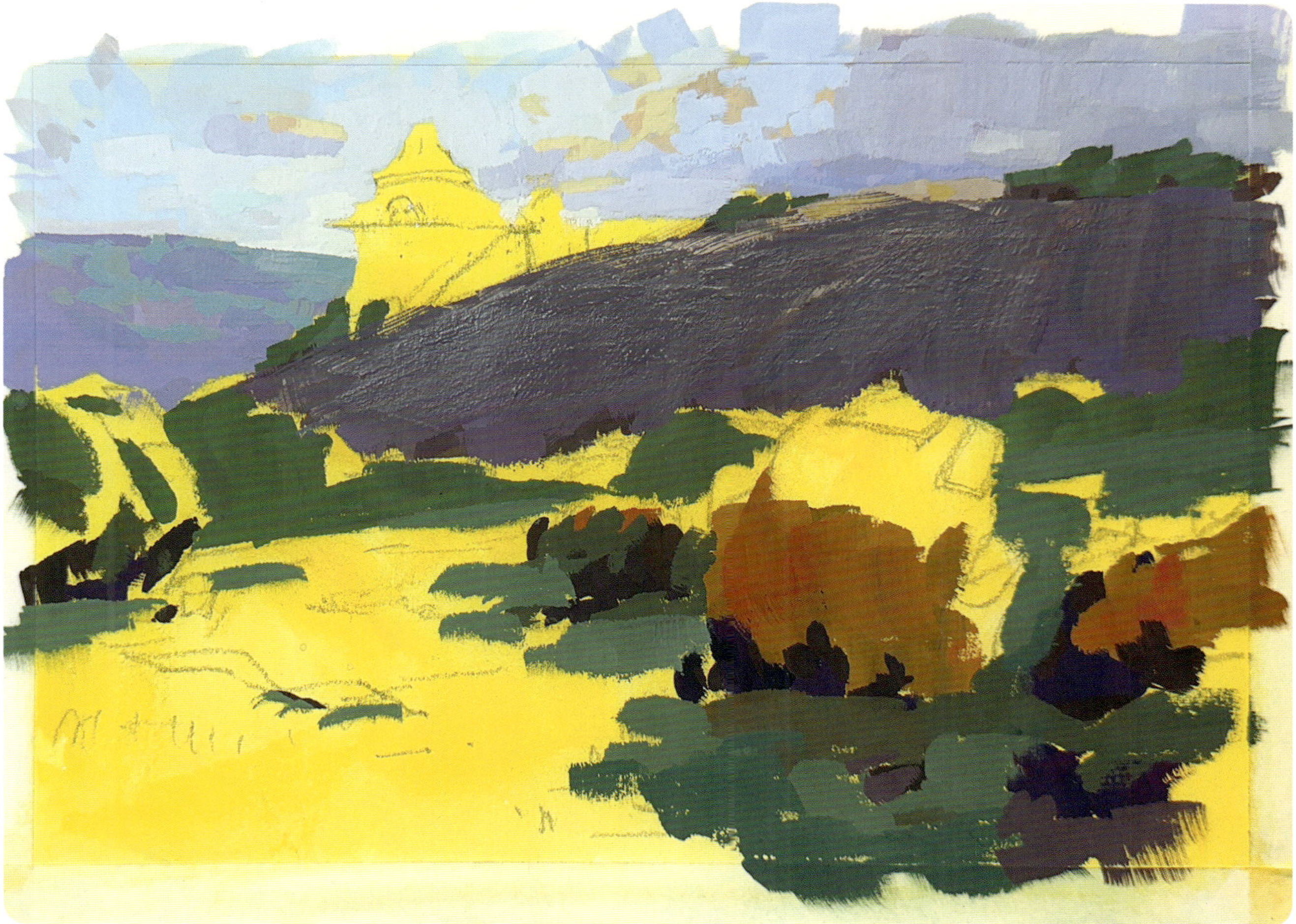

10. Begin filling out the landscape with solid colour

10.

Continuing blocking in the dark areas, I start making progress covering the underpainting with a complementary medium-purple tone. Occasionally I will fill in an entire area with one solid colour and paint areas of light on top, but typically I prefer painting around, carving light and shadow shapes. In the areas that will have large shapes of solid colour, I try to imply texture and visual interest by allowing other colours on my palette to mix in. As long as the colour variations are close in value, subtle shifts in temperature will result in streaks of colour, giving texture to flat shapes.

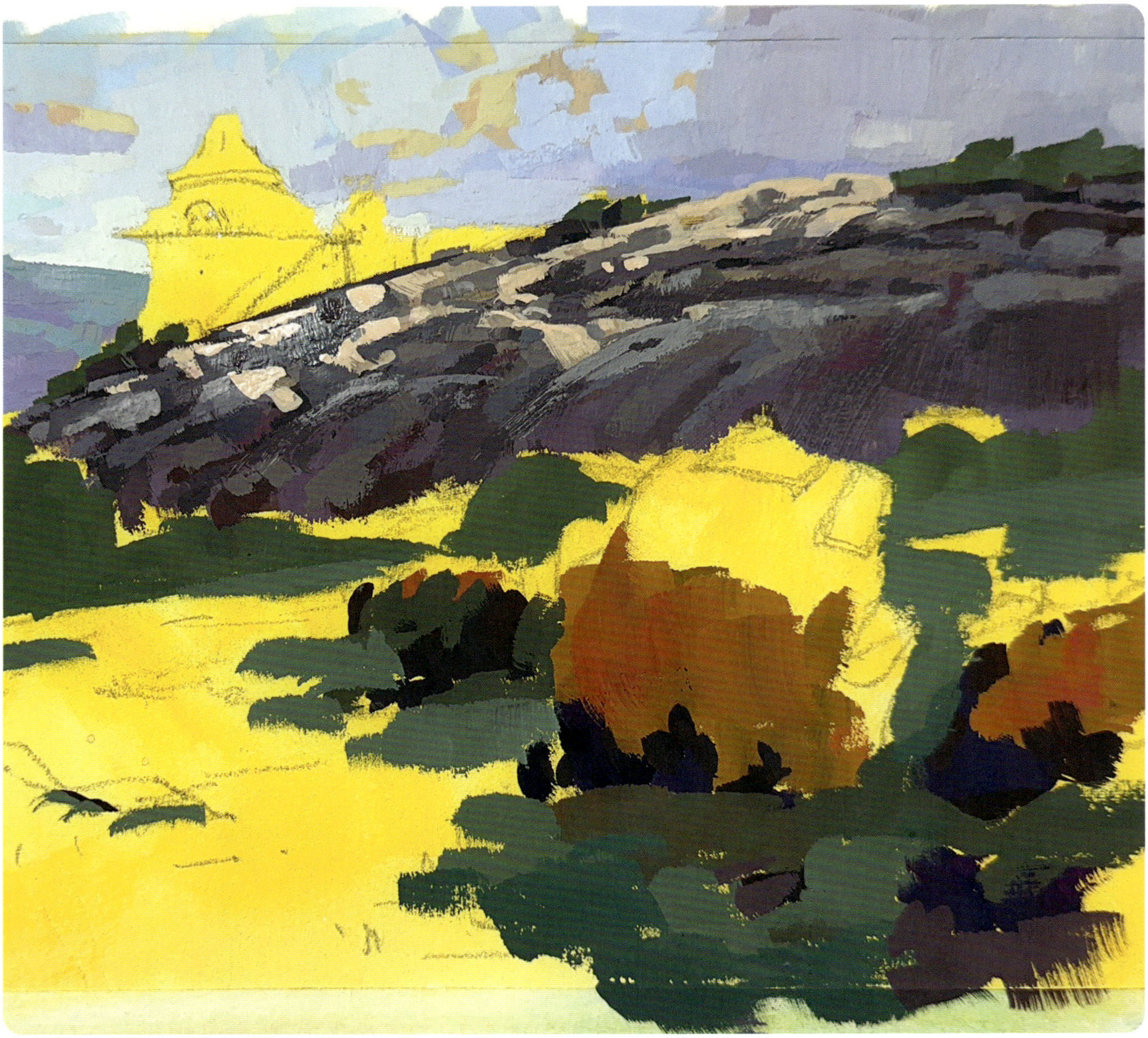

11. Use a dry-brush technique to create textured strokes

11.

Once I've blocked in the solid base for the middle-ground rocks, it's time to add definition and volume. I reference back to my earlier sketches to ensure I am maintaining consistent lighting. I want to imply the light is just making its way over the cloud coverage and raking across the rock faces. When emulating texture, utilizing a technique called dry-brushing can be very effective. Using your scrap illustration board, test out the viscosity of your paint until it's just right to gently brush over existing paint layers. If your strokes follow the form of the object they can help reinforce its dimensionality. These coarse strokes, in shades of lighter blue-grey and cream, create the effect of sunlight hitting the rough, organic surfaces of the rocks.

12.

The light and shadow shapes of foliage are specifically challenging to simplify. Foliage can seem complex when focusing too much on individual details. Instead, combining masses into simple faces of light and dark is a more effective approach for creating the impression of foliage. Try to keep in mind the overall composition when simplifying these shapes. Interior shapes of simplified objects can create lines leading to your focal point or interesting overlap of light and dark. When thinking about the design of individual shapes in this way, you can create an appealing rhythm throughout your painting.

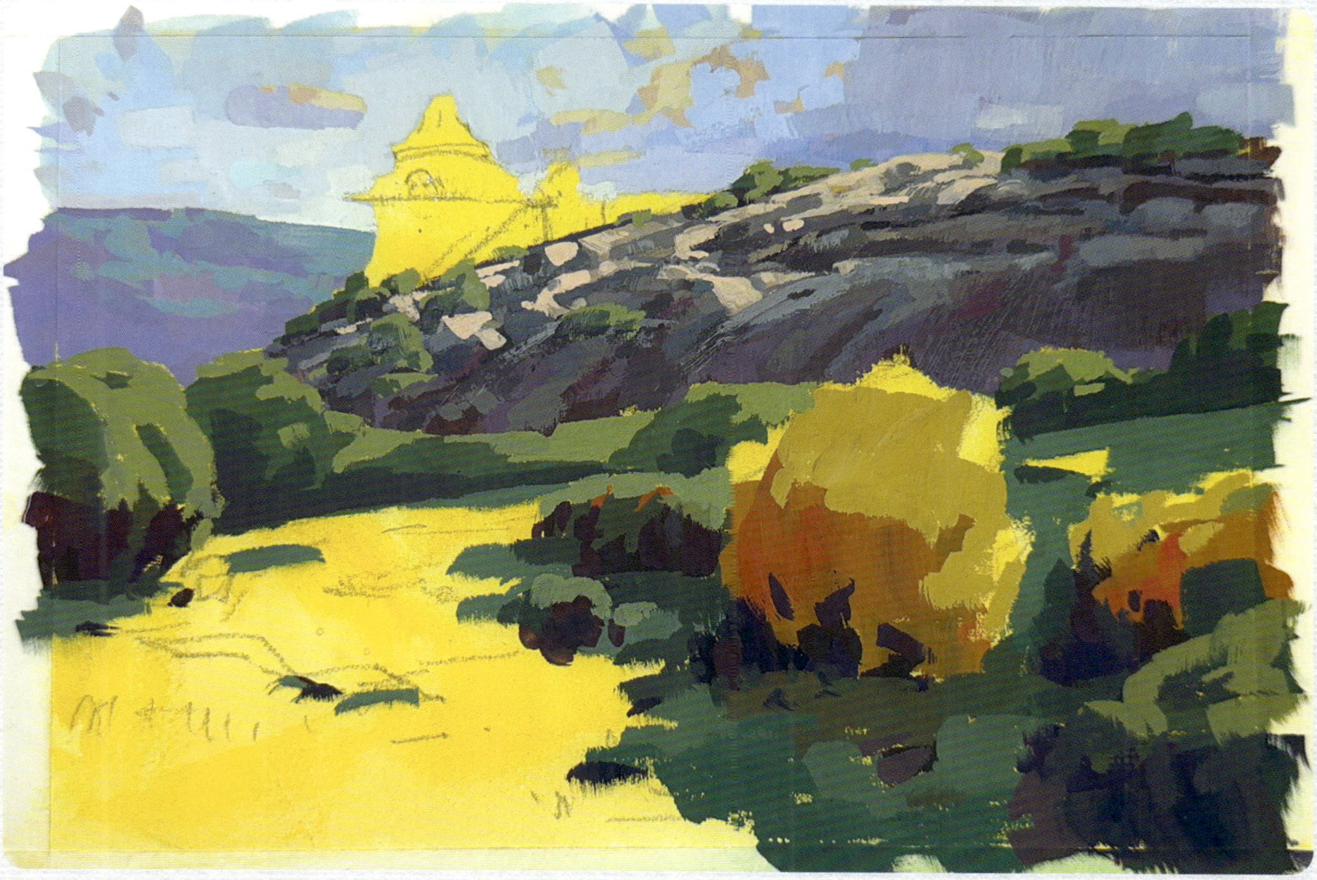

12. Keep foliage simple by focusing on light and dark faces

TESTING COLOUR

I recommend using a scrap piece of matte or illustration board to test out your colour mixes and paint viscosity. Often you may want to retouch areas that have already dried, and realize that matching hue and value can be challenging. A quality that's unique to gouache is that lighter colours dry darker and darker colours dry lighter. Having a swatch to test out your paint mix and compare wet versus dry colours can help immensely when reworking previous areas.

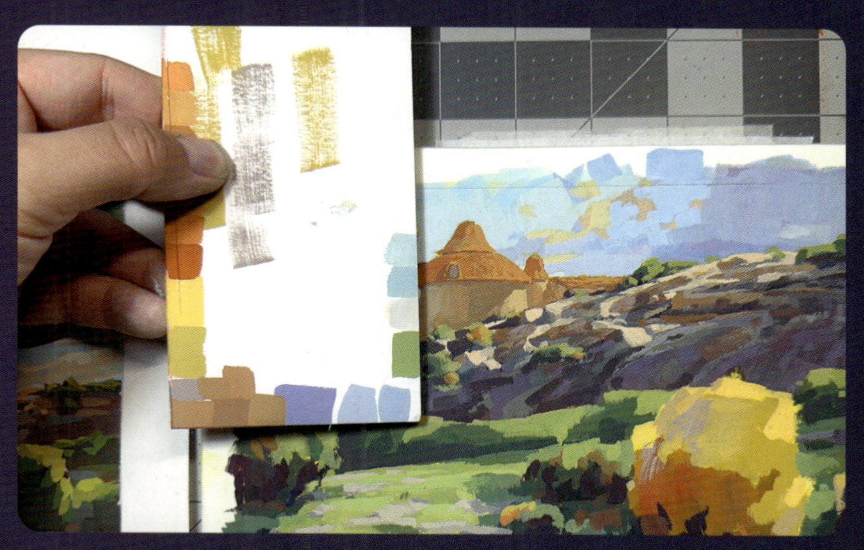

Keep a piece of scrap board handy for colour testing

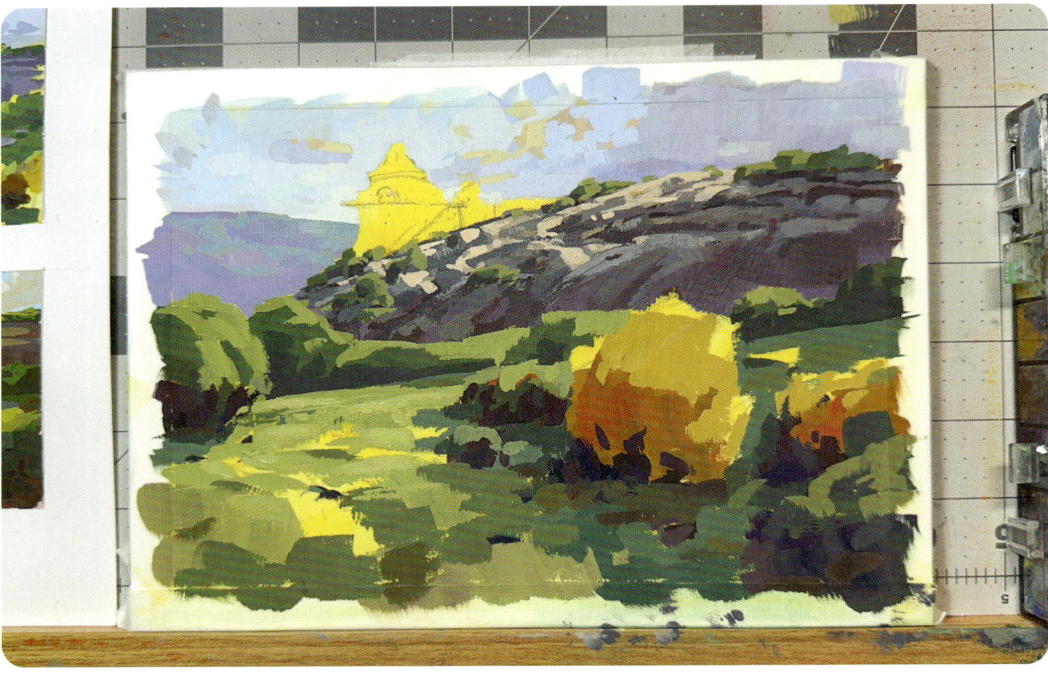

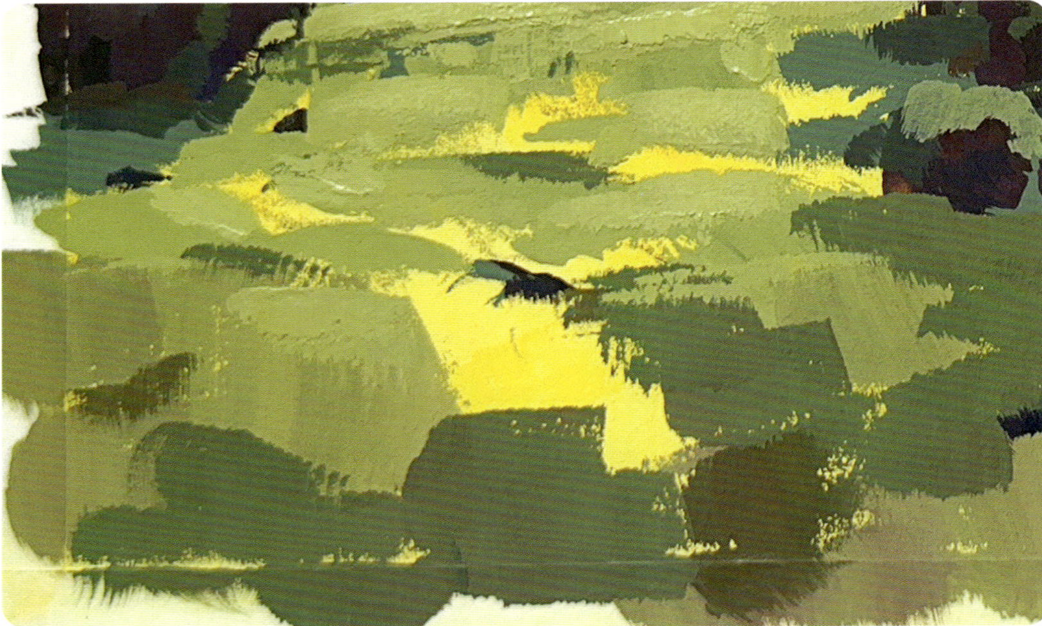

13. Fill the foreground with shades of green

13.

Along with atmospheric perspective, the scale of your brushstrokes can also help emphasize depth and draw the viewer's attention to the focal point. If your focal point is in the background, like mine, the elements may be smaller and more precise as they recede into the distance. Areas near the periphery and closest to the foreground can be rendered with broad and simple strokes. This contrast will help draw the viewer into the scene. You can also create contrast by intentionally placing simple, broad shapes next to small details. Regardless of the type of contrast, our eyes will naturally be drawn to where two opposing elements meet.

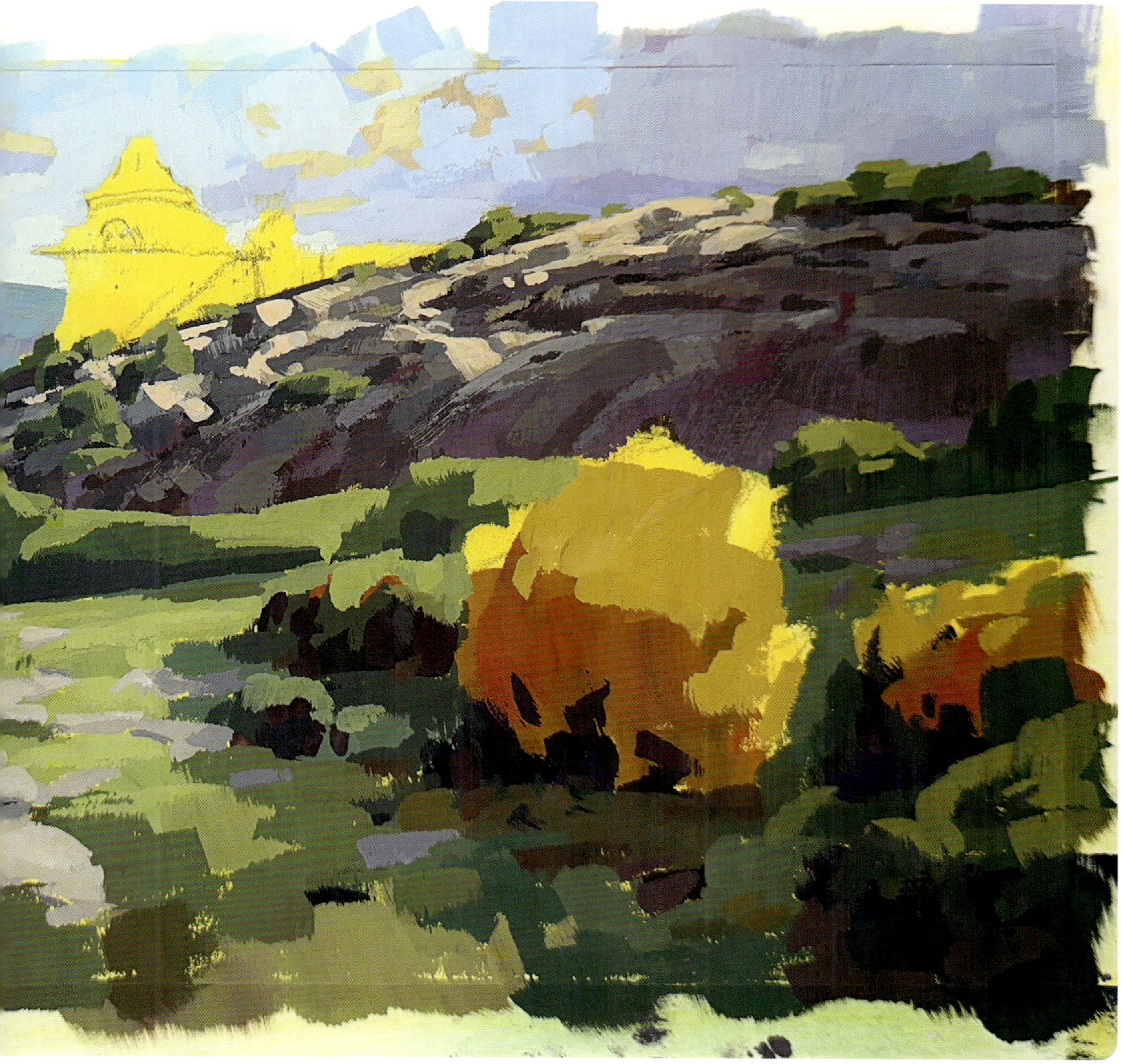

14. Fill out the rest of the terrain with ground-level elements

14.

In many of my works I try to paint from points of view typical to human vantage points. I enjoy exploring while hiking and I have found that including details reminiscent of trails, or other things you would expect to see from eye level, tends to ground the scene with relatable scale. Try adding details to your paintings that give an impression of a world that extends beyond the confines of your painting surface. This sense of wonder and curiosity is one of the many reasons why both painting and viewing fantasy scenes are so enjoyable. Here the yellow midtone underpainting is almost fully covered by light grey rocks on the ground.

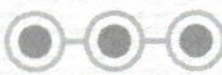

15.

I leave the architectural elements in the painting until last, because I want this area to have contrasting qualities to the rest of the image. Having the surrounding areas painted beforehand ensures I have something to compare with my intended contrast. It's important for this building to have much sharper, linear lines, so I make sure to take my time using the flat edge of my 1/2" stroke brush to lay in flat, even strokes. Keeping in mind the curvature of the structure, it's important to have subtle ambient light from the sky on the shadow-facing edges.

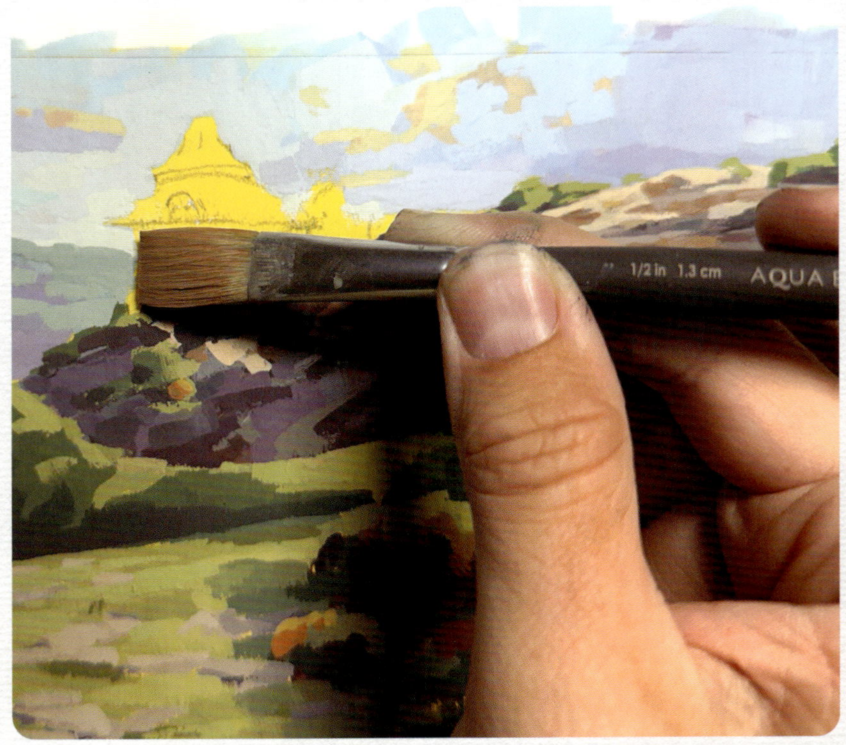

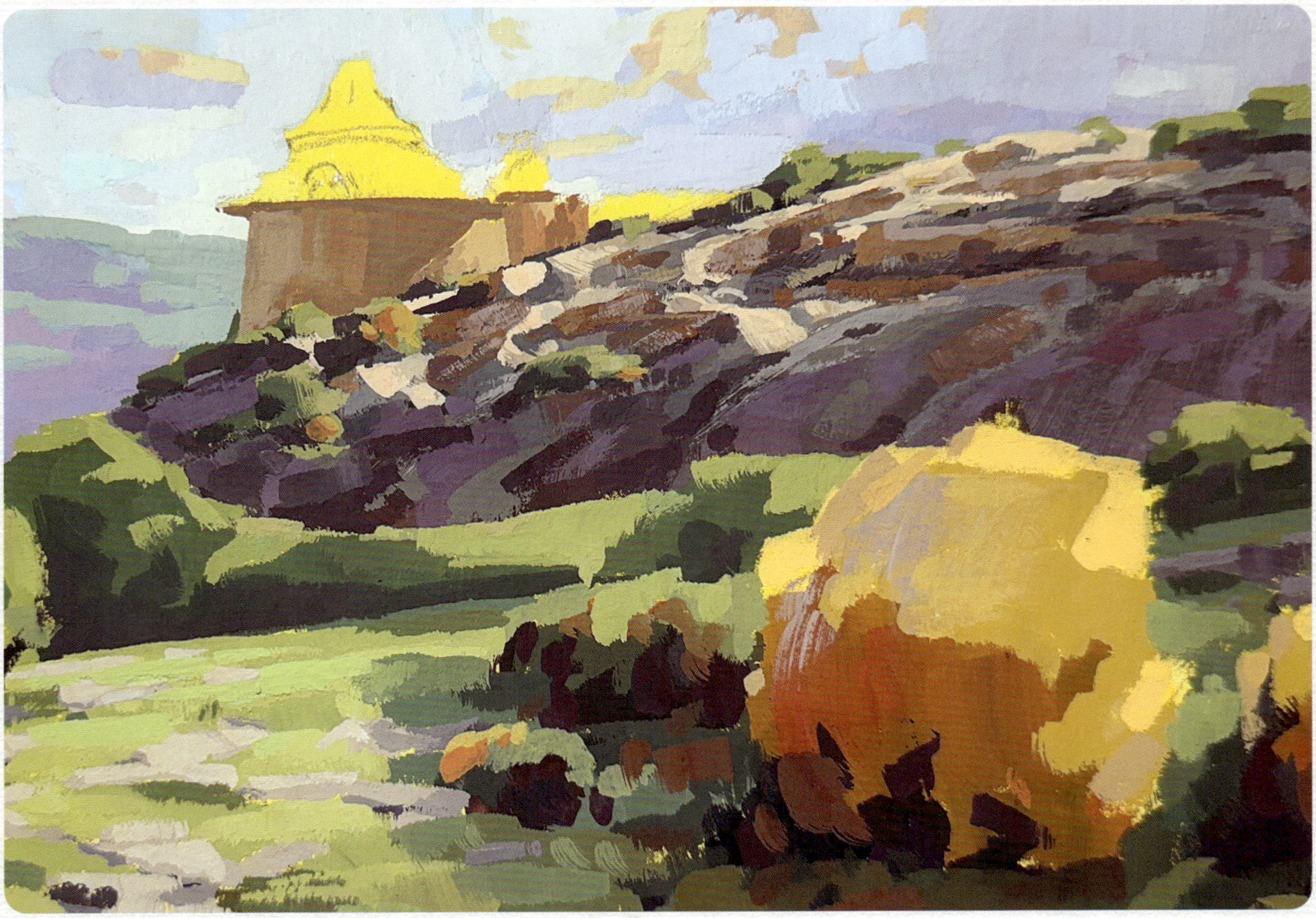

15. Keep in mind the castle's rounded shape

16.

Last of all are the roofs and final architectural details. Switch to the smallest brush for the finest details, such as windows and spires. There are only a few of these – it's easy to overwork a painting and I prefer the gestural and impressionistic quality of a 'loose' style. It's worth noting the various forms of contrast working together to effectively make the building the focal point. The line directions of objects and brushstrokes create subliminal arrows leading you into the image in an organic manner, and culminate in the meeting of perfect vertical and horizontal lines near the focal point. The contrast of dark-on-light values also helps draw attention. Lastly, the most significant temperature contrast is found around the focal point.

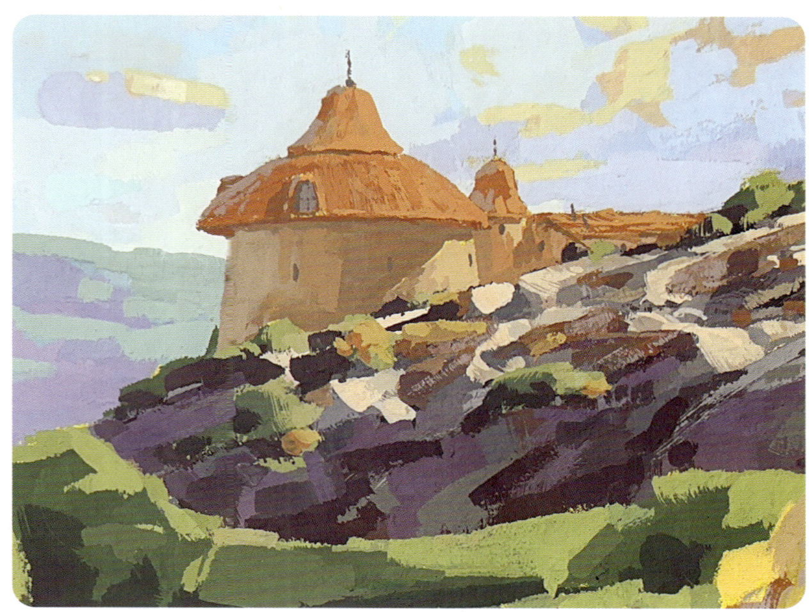

16. Save the smallest details for last and use them in moderation

CONTRAST CHEAT SHEET

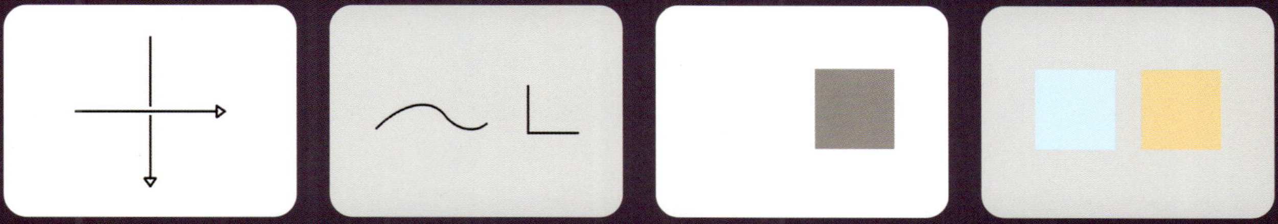

Line **Shape** **Value** **Temperature**

Several different kinds of contrast are used in this scene, all working together to draw the viewer in and direct them towards the focal point of the castle. When painting, keep these different contrasts in mind and make sure you are using them with intention.

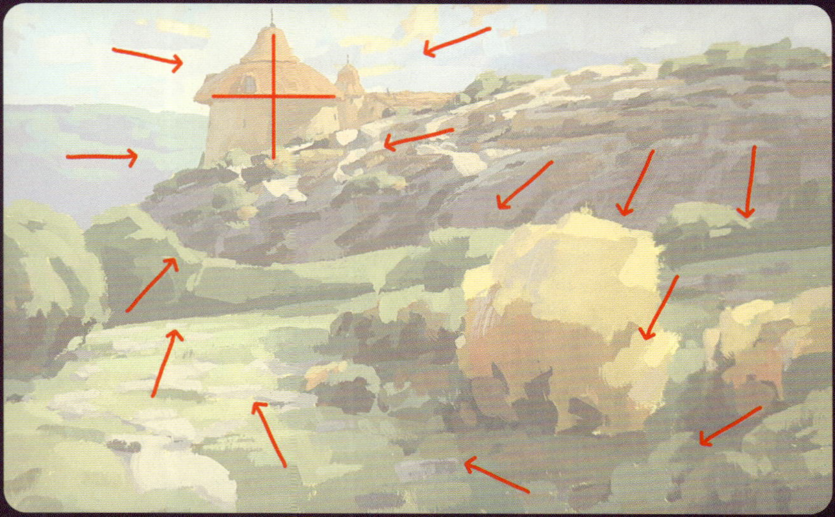

Strengthen your composition with different contrasts

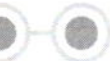

CONCLUSION

The thing I enjoyed most about this painting was referencing a real-life location I have visited, and altering the composition and lighting to tell the story I wanted to tell. I love thinking about the design and composition as a puzzle to solve. Coming up with creative ways to assemble the pieces, manipulate contrast, and create an image with intention is deeply fulfilling. I hope you feel inspired to get outdoors to paint from life and discover the things that speak to you most about nature.

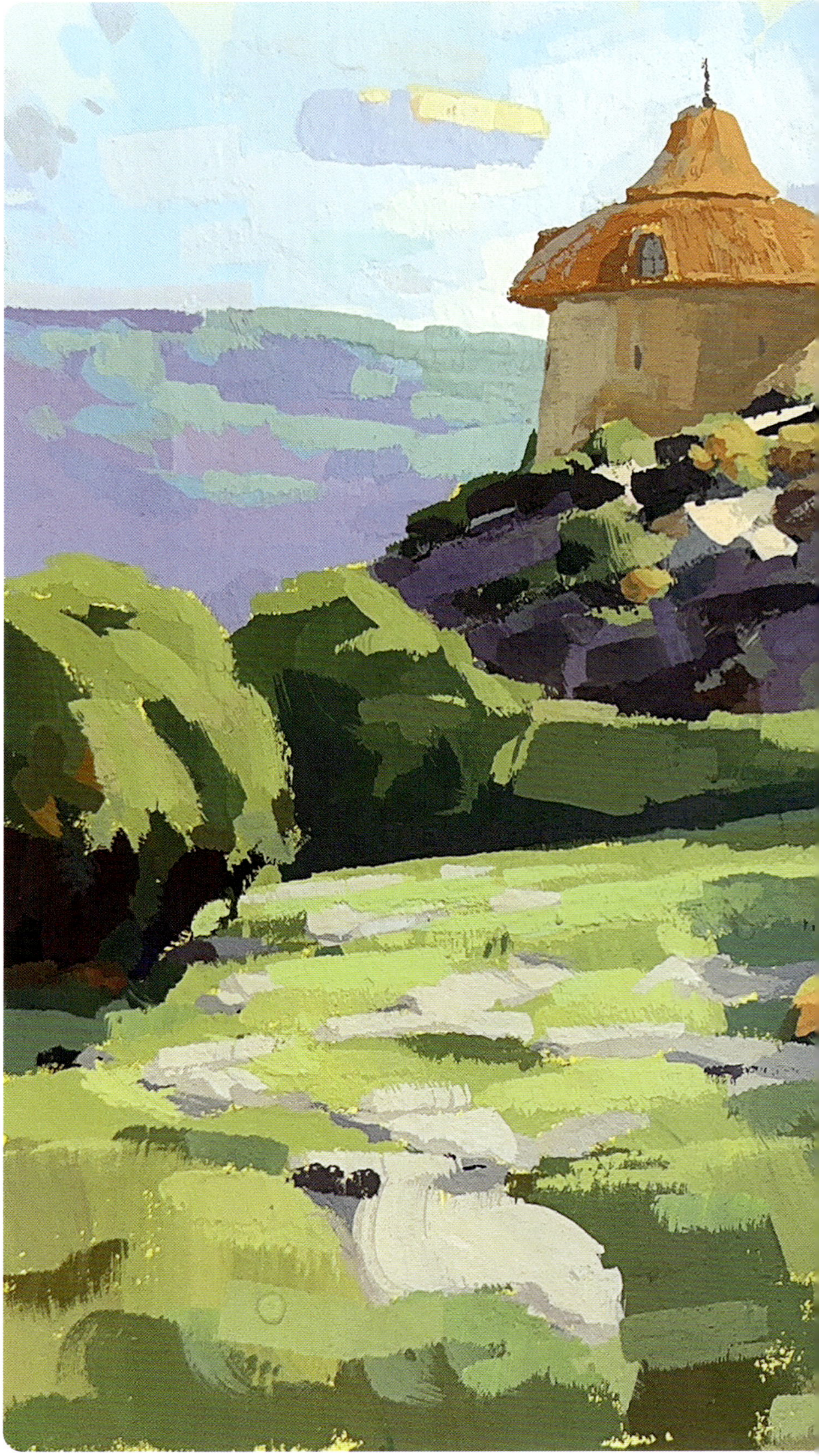

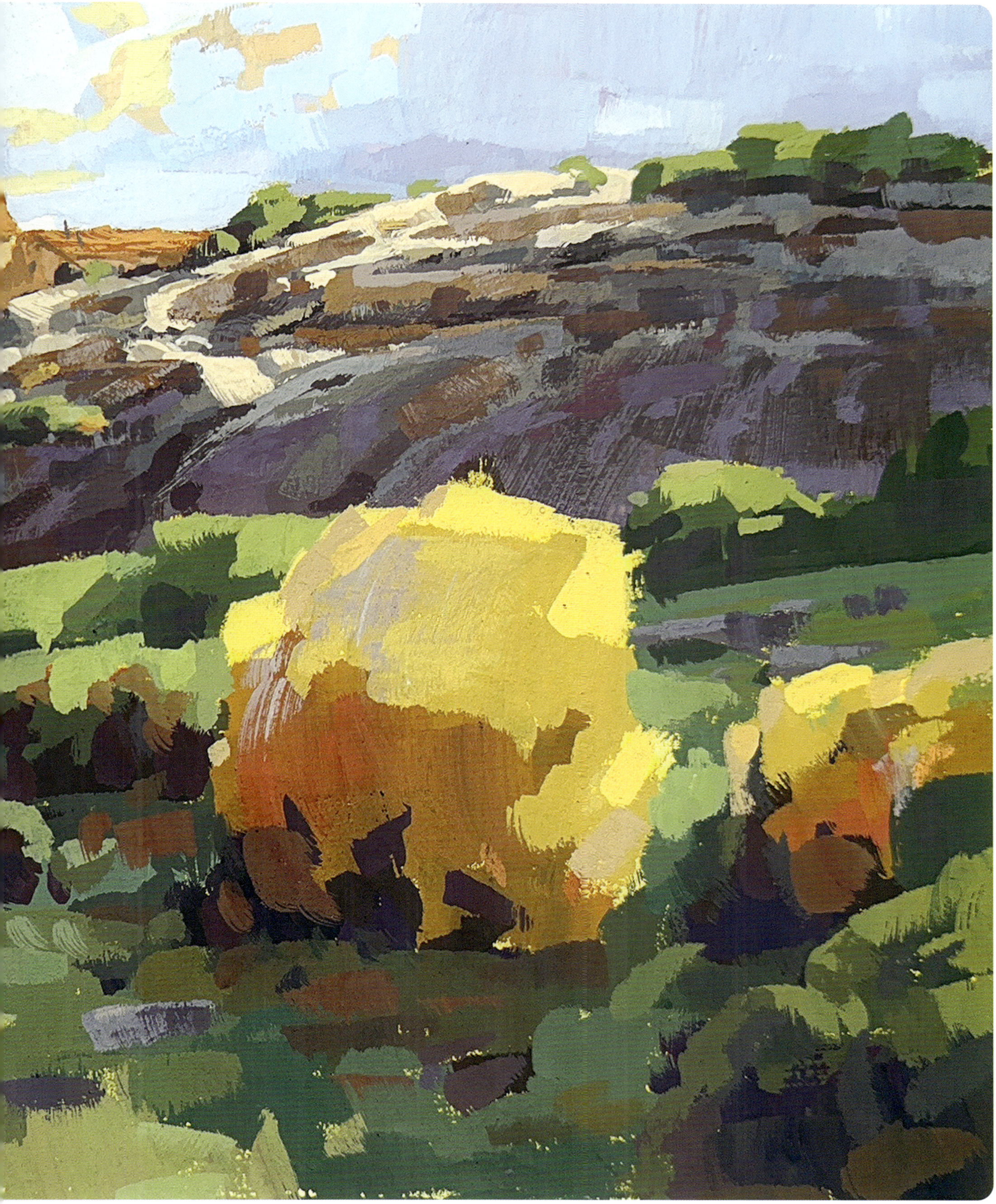

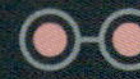

Final image © Accorvio

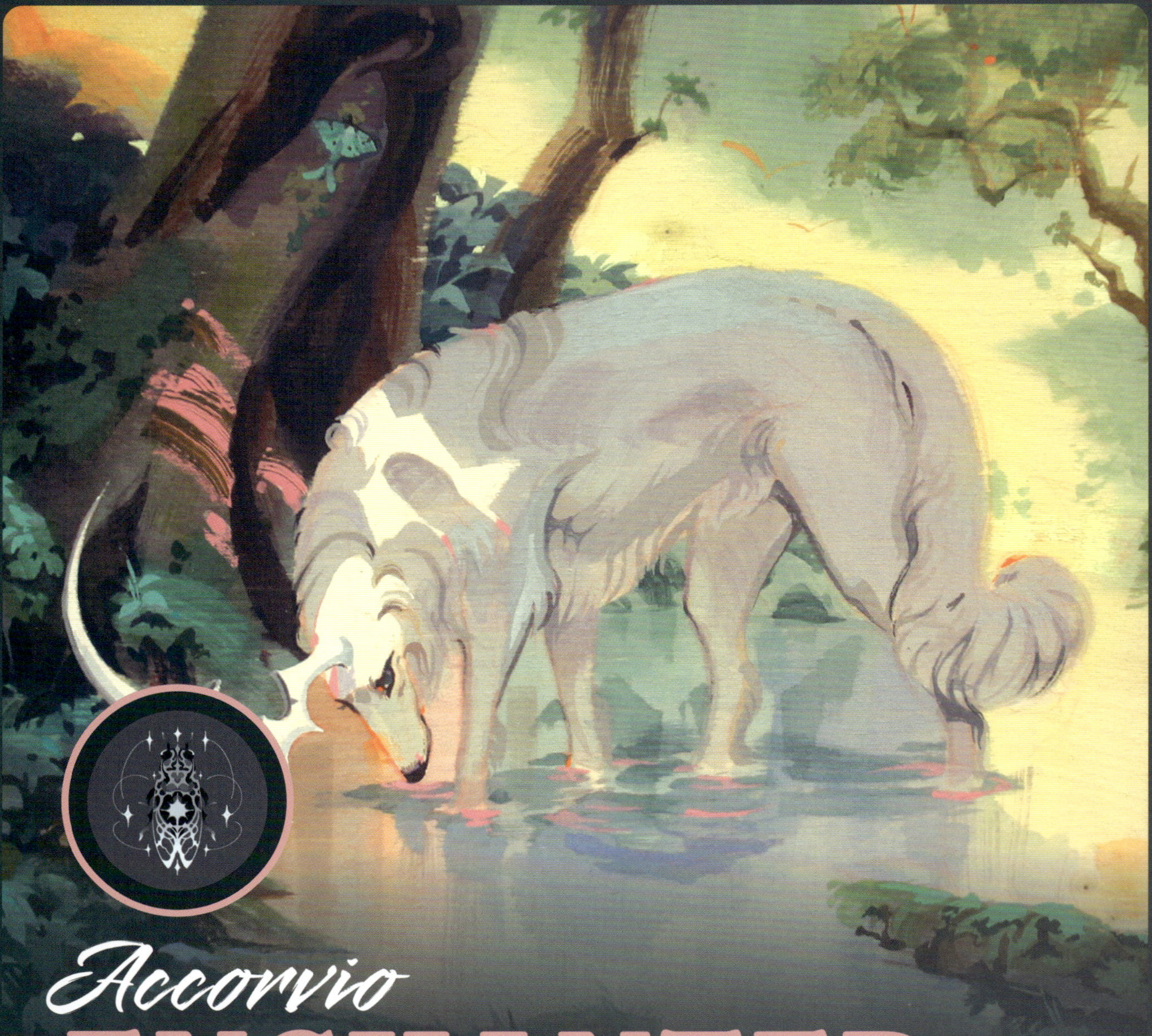

Accorvio

ENCHANTED FOREST

As someone who grew up with the Appalachia on their doorstep, I have a deep affection for tangled thickets, unruly creeks, and feral creatures. Although dense and diverse foliage is a stunning feature of forests, it can be quite challenging to tackle in a painting. In this tutorial I'll be showing my approach to creating woodlands inspired by the complex flora and fauna of my childhood.

TOOLKIT

- **Cradled wood panel**
  (18W × 12H × 1D inches)

- **Palette**

- **Coloured pencil**
  (I use red)

- **Spray bottle of water**

- **Jar of water**

- **Paper towel**

- **Ruler**
  (for straight lines while sketching)

BRUSHES

Flat wash brushes
¾" (19mm), ⅜" (9.5mm)
& 1½" (38mm)

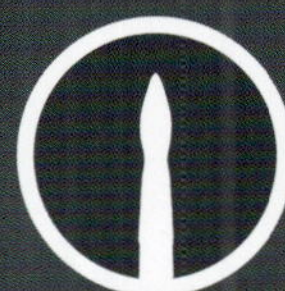

Round brush
Size 1

I use a stay-wet palette where I have my most frequently used paints pre-squeezed from the tube. Hence I have a lot of colours, which I instinctually pull from at least once or twice to create hue variations. Listed on the right are the pigments I use multiple times throughout this project, but you may prefer to narrow the selection down to use fewer greens or yellows, for example, or to incorporate some of your own favourite 'magical' hues. You can mix almost anything you'll need using primaries and white.

COLOUR LIST

- Alizarin Crimson
- Quinacridone Crimson
- Phthalo Blue
- Ultramarine Deep
- Smalt Blue
- Turquoise Green
- Chromium Oxide Green
- Cyprus Green
- Dark Green
- Sap Green
- Linden Green
- Brilliant Pink
- Lilac
- Opera Pink
- Spectrum Violet
- Lemon Yellow
- Permanent Yellow Deep
- Yellow Ochre
- Orange Lake Light
- Burnt Sienna
- Vandyke Brown
- Burnt Umber
- Permanent White

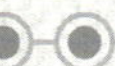

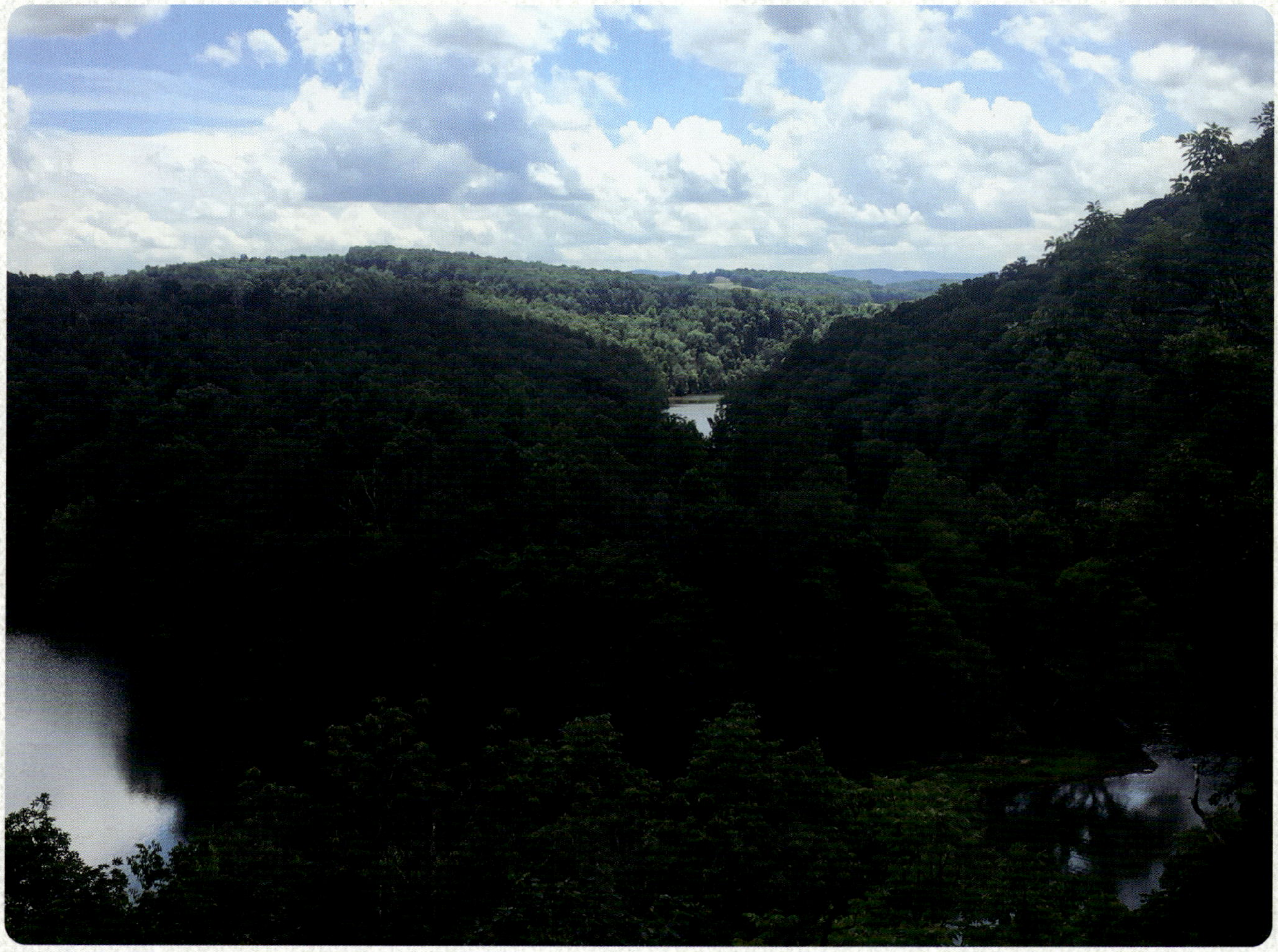

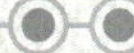

01. The real-world forest that will inspire my fantasy scene

01.

When you close your eyes, what type of forest do you imagine? Are the trees imposing and sturdy or short and spindly? Has winter blanketed the ground with snow or do spring flowers bloom? Flora and fauna can vary drastically from place to place; a familiar forest to one person might be a stranger to another. Before you start sketching, it's good to set the scene by having an idea of how you want your forest to feel. For this painting, I'm taking inspiration from the Appalachian region but I'm also adding flora not native to the region, such as crocus flowers. While there should be some logic to the plant life populating your forest, it's your world to make the rules in.

02.

I typically start with a pencil and my sketchbook, messily sketching concepts that pop into my head – often with notes – until one makes an impression. My thumbnails usually start completely illegible to anyone other than me. When an idea grips me I detail it out more and more until I end up with a rough sketch, which I then repeat as a rough value sketch, like the one shown here. I try to keep colour in mind while sketching, so if I have an idea I'll write it next to the sketch to remember later.

03.

For this painting I will be using a wooden panel with a 1" cradle as my surface. While you can ignore the cradle – the supporting wooden frame that forms the panel's outer edge – I want to utilize it as a space for decoration, adding a storybook feel to the painting. When sketching symbols and ornamentation, I try to be exact with the measurements in my sketches to minimize surprises when I go to paint on the wood itself. Since the cradle sides measure 18" × 1" and 1" × 12" respectively, I use the gridded paper of my sketchbook to create proportionate templates.

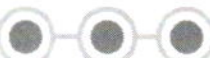

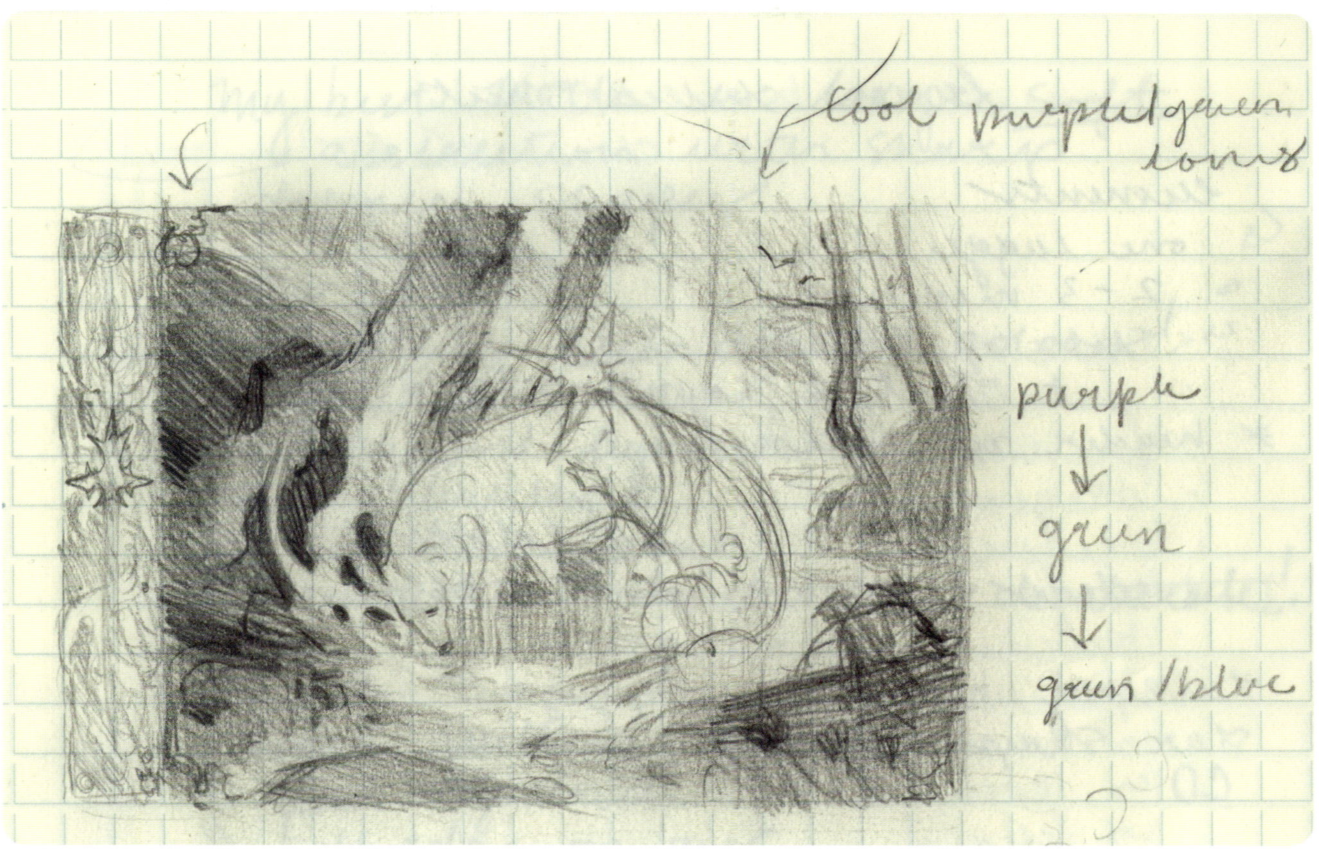

02. The rough value sketch with notes on the colour palette I want to use

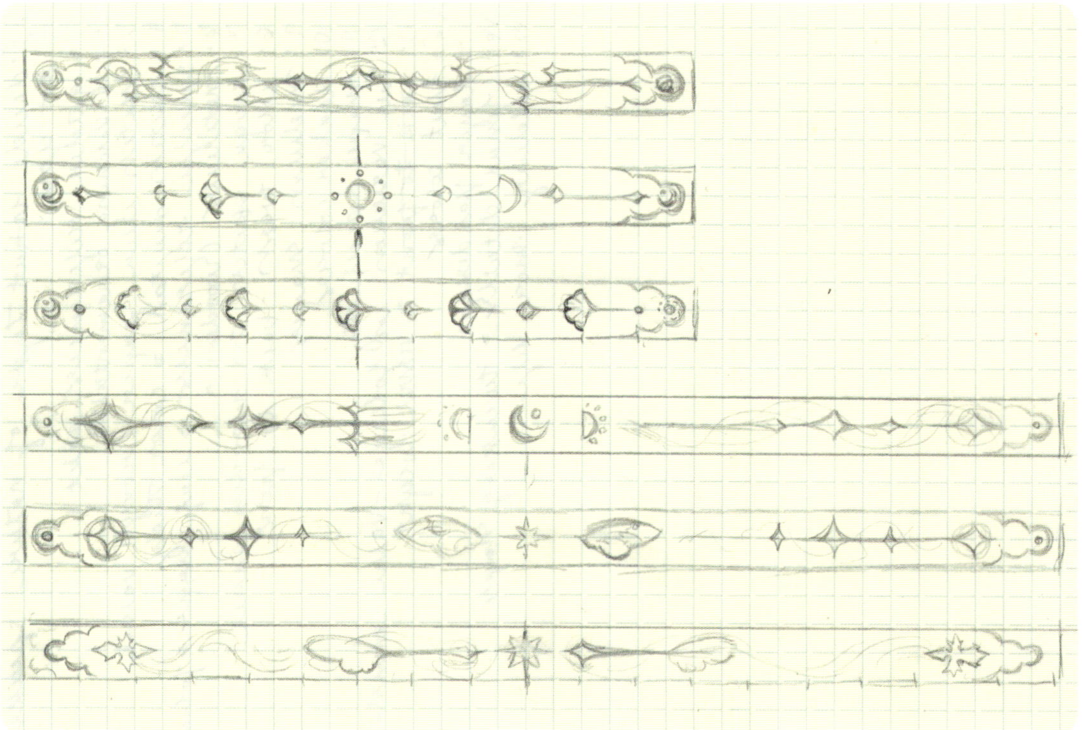

03. These designs will go around the outside edge of the wood panel

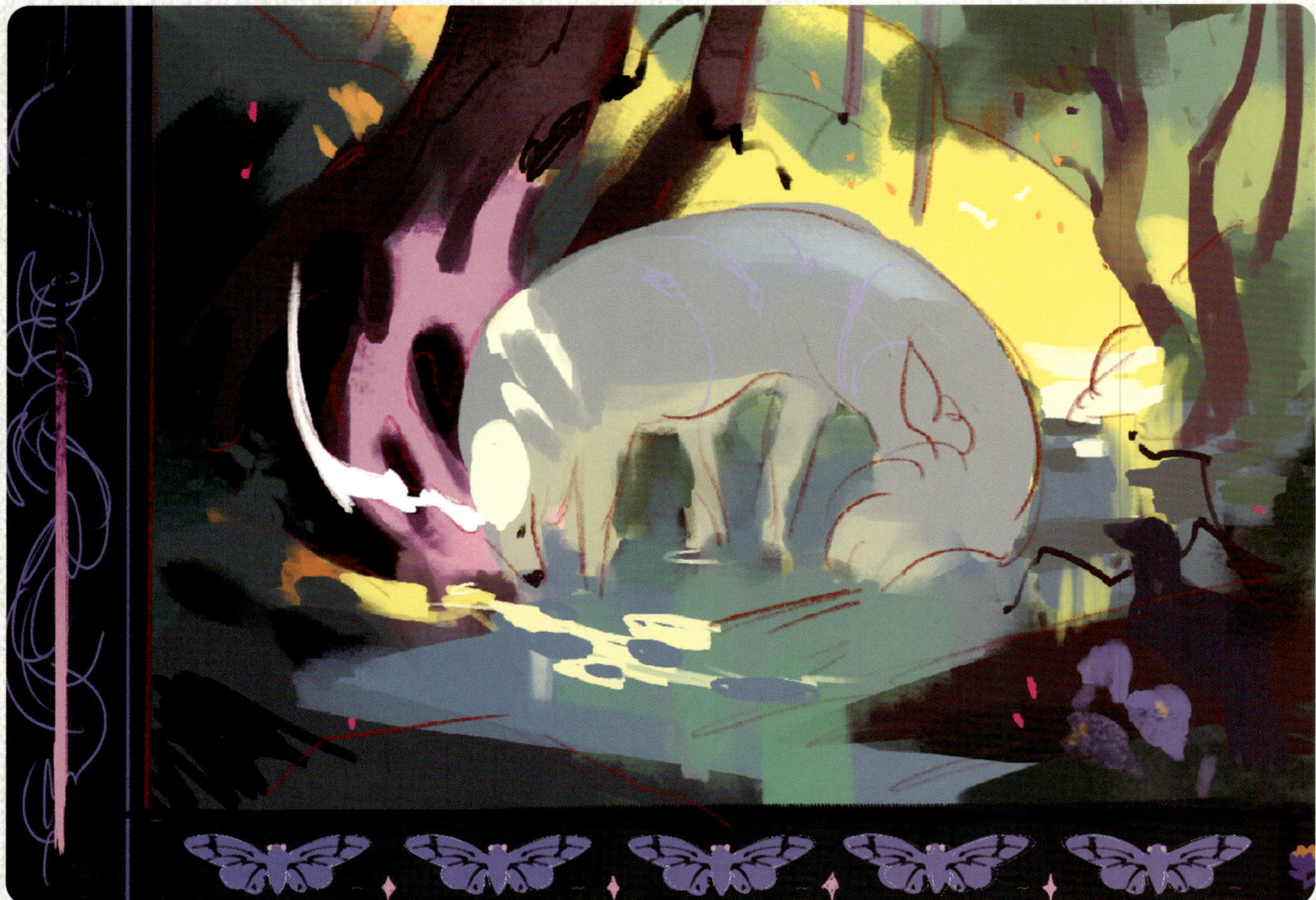

04. A rough colour study painted in the iPad software Procreate

04.

When painting digitally, it's easy to layer colours without worrying about paint reactivating and colours mixing, or how the thickness of your paint will influence your colour. As I work on my colour studies, usually in Procreate, I try not to fall into the trap of thinking about colour in a 'digital' way. I try to imitate how I would paint in gouache instead. When planning colours for a gouache painting, I try to think first in washes. I lay my lightest colours first and gradually get darker and more nuanced. The colour study is not an exact guide but a rough aid and test for the final painting.

05.

Having a large breadth of reference photos of different types of plants will help greatly in painting foliage. You might think you know what leaves look like, but as they twist and turn, interact with other leaves, and weave through underbrush, they create their own unique shapes. When I am out and about, I always try to take lots of reference photos, resulting in a sizable body of images for me to pull from. When I want to draw plants and animals I don't have access to, I take from a variety of online images.

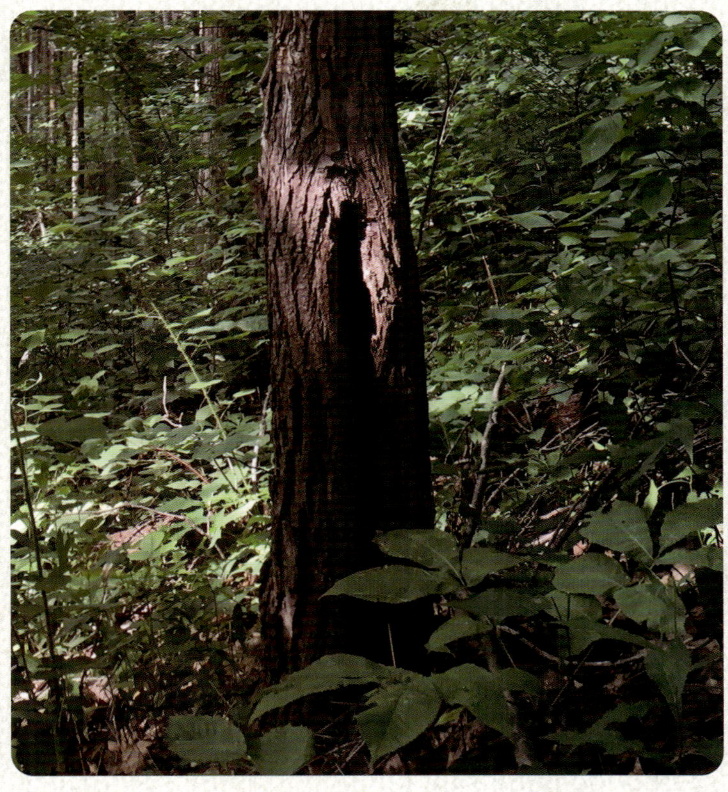

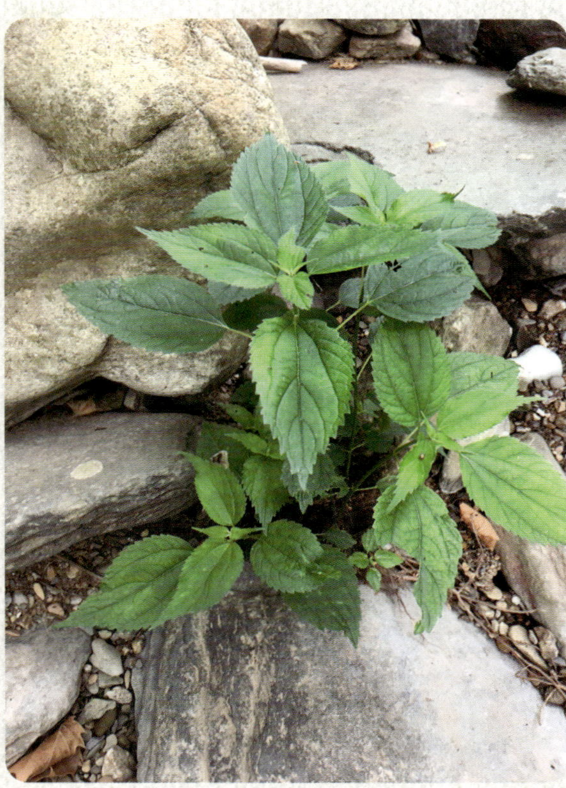

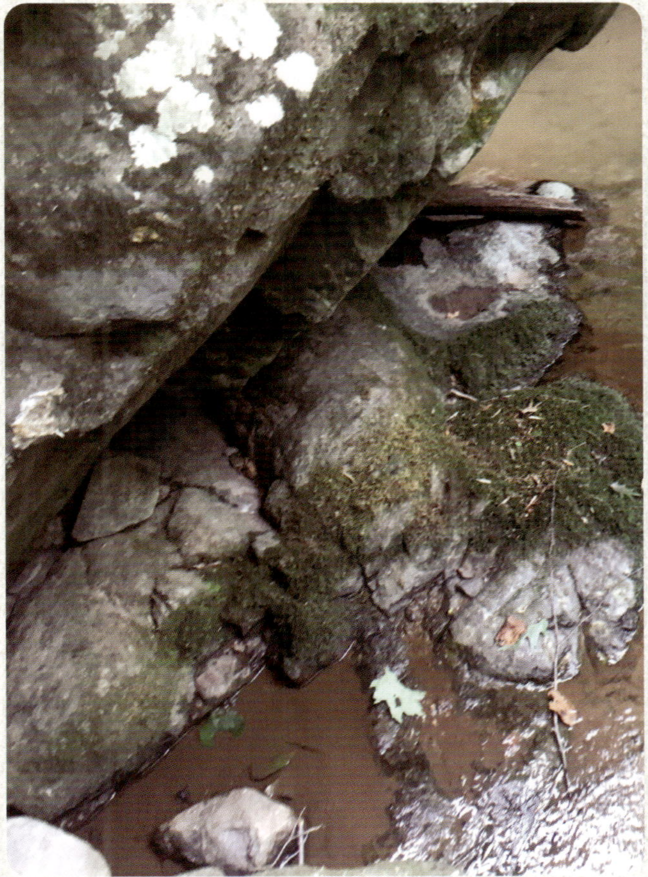

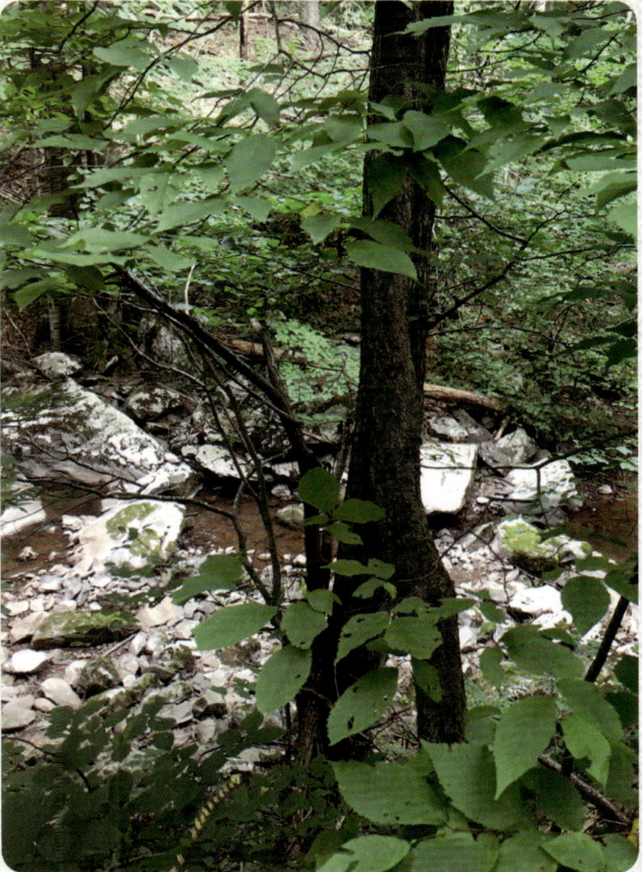

05. A range of my own photographs that I will use as references

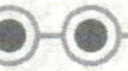

06.

Painting on wood is very different from painting on paper. It is possible to prime wooden panels, but ultimately I find it just fine to paint directly onto the wood. I enjoy the texture of the wood grain and will choose a panel based on the best grain pattern available to me. Things to note about painting on wood: watery gouache will bleed in the direction of the wood grain; you need more paint as the wood is more porous (the cradle sides are even more porous than the top panel); and if you really, really mess up, it is possible to wash off thick paint and try again.

07.

Now I sketch out the image on the wooden board. I default to a red coloured pencil for sketching but will sometimes use other colours depending on the painting. The idea is that I can comfortably see the pencil through a light wash without the colour detracting from the painting. Try to maintain a rough and loose sketch for this stage – block out the large shapes and leave the smaller shapes for the painting process.

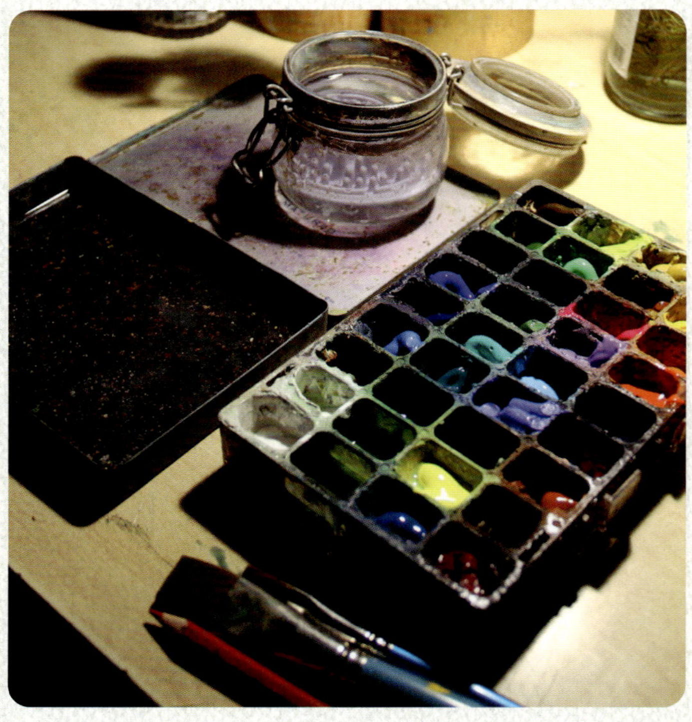

06. I use an old cigarette tin for mixing, but I recommend you use a proper palette!

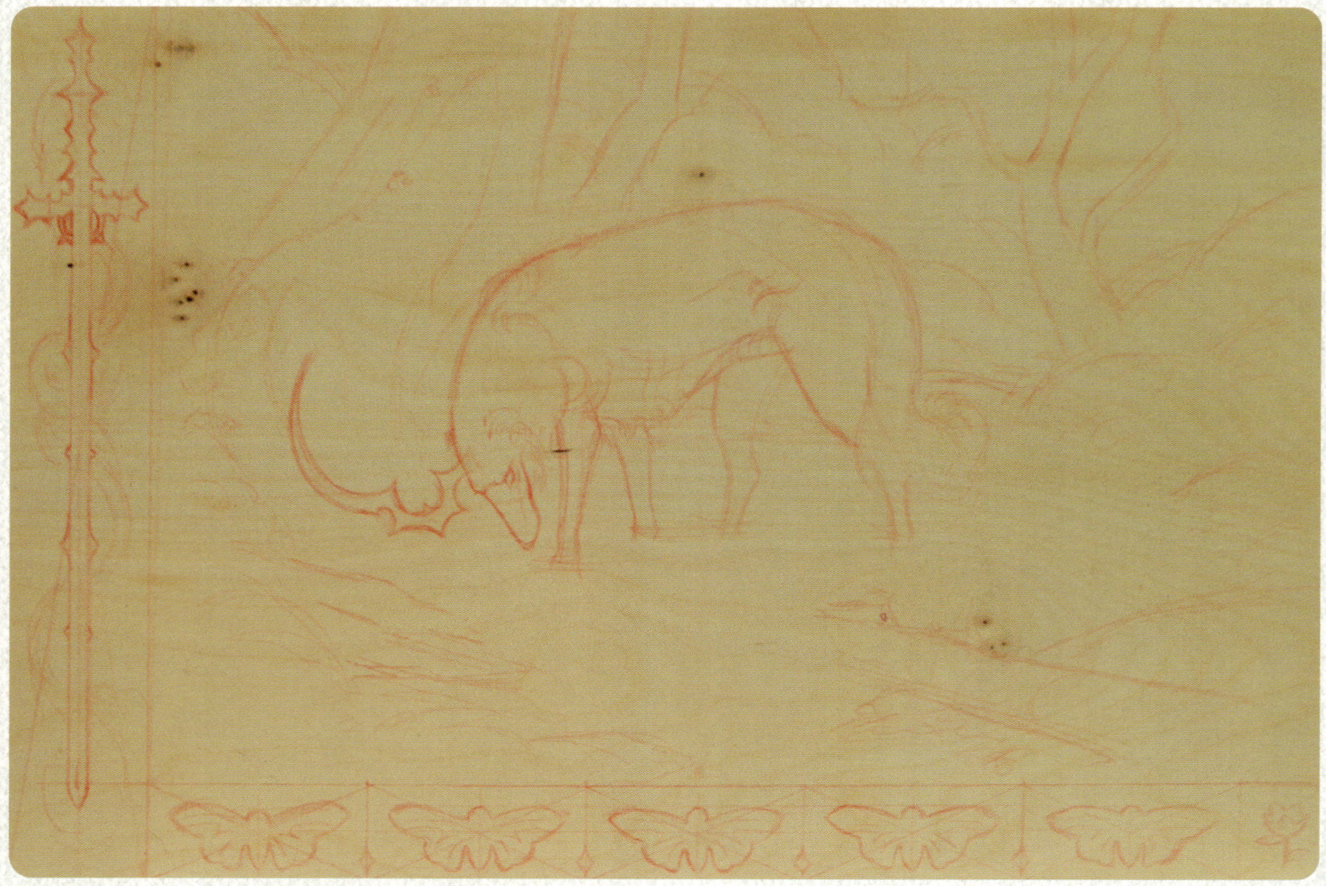

07. Use a coloured pencil for better visibility of the sketch

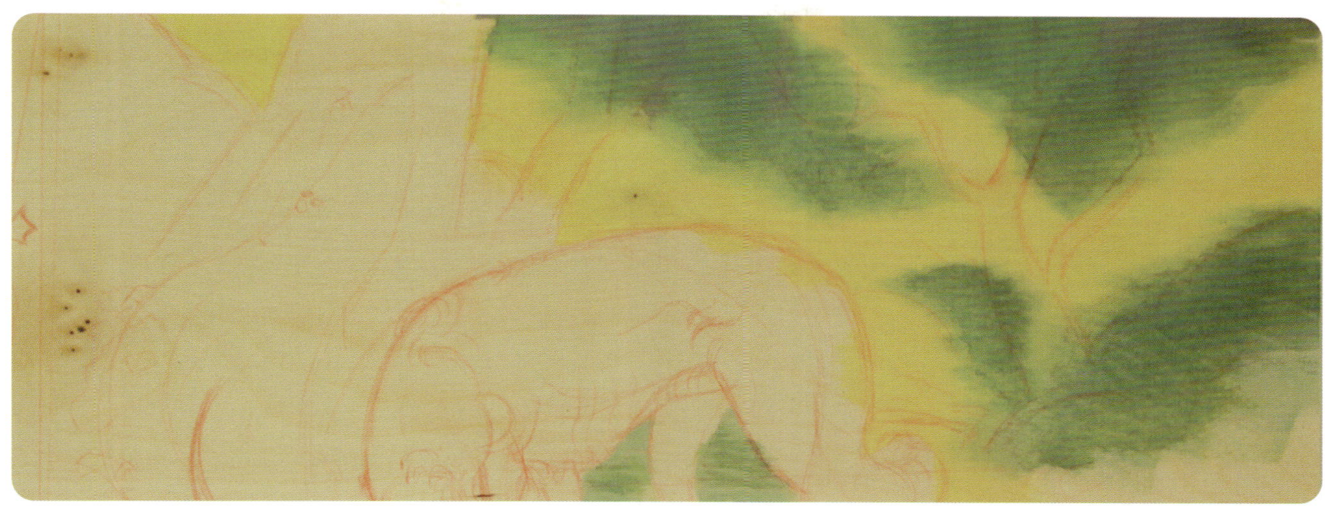

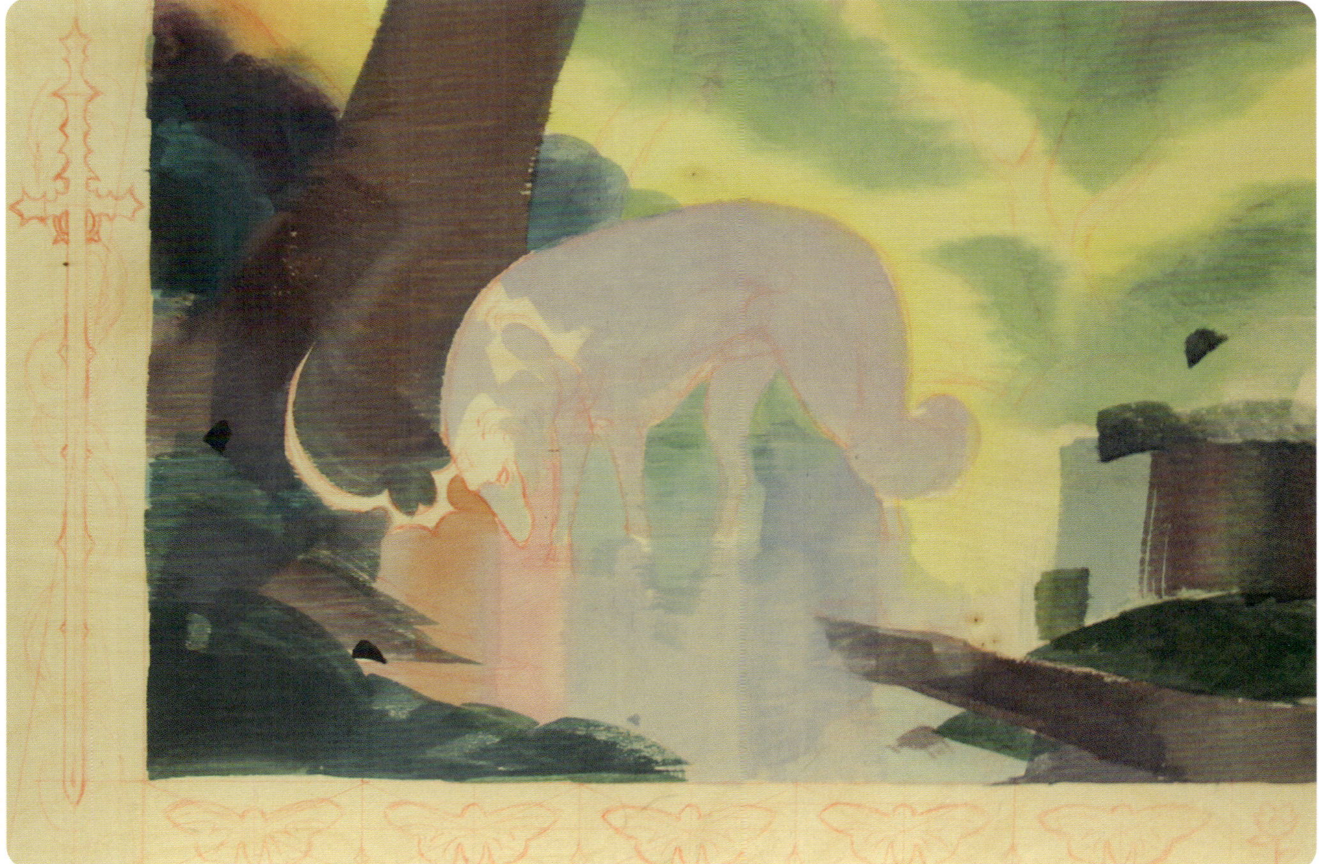

08. Start by painting the large background shapes of the forest

08.

I typically start my paintings with a large wash of colour in order to quickly fill the canvas and block in large shapes. Spray the panel with water and paint with a large wet brush to allow for broad softer strokes, starting with the yellow and green patches in the background. The colour study becomes important here as I have to work confidently and quickly before the wash dries. To me, part of the fun of working with a water-based medium is the opportunity for unpredictability in edges and colour interactions when the wet paints mix together.

09.

After blocking in the large shapes with the light wash, I block in the medium shapes. These are the cooler-toned brown and green shapes of the trees and undergrowth, and a mauve-grey base for the dog, leaving some empty patches for highlights. I use downward stripes of peach and blue tones to block out the pool of water. At this point, be less concerned about the details and more focused on mapping out the painting. Working from large to small allows the larger shapes and colours to guide the smaller ones. This helps you maintain the balance of the painting without getting lost in the minutiae.

10.

Begin adding shadows and leaf shapes to the trunk and undergrowth on the left. Although painting foliage seems daunting, the process can be simplified. I don't look to paint every individual leaf but instead to give specificity to the leaves I *do* paint. The mind is constantly looking for patterns, so carving out specific shapes in a mass will allow the brain to fill in the rest on its own. This is where having curated references is very important. Instead of painting generic leaf shapes, you can lean on your references to help carve out unique shapes that give life to the foliage.

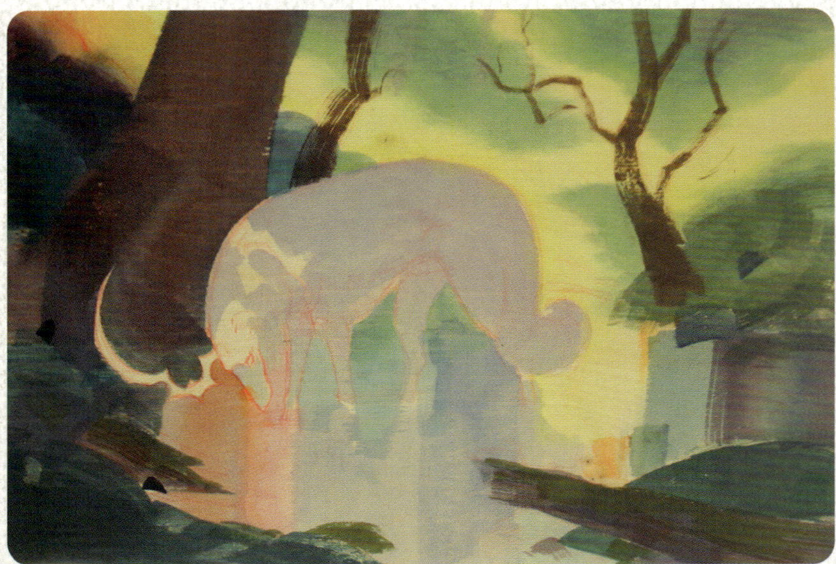

09. The middle- and foreground foliage is cooler and darker

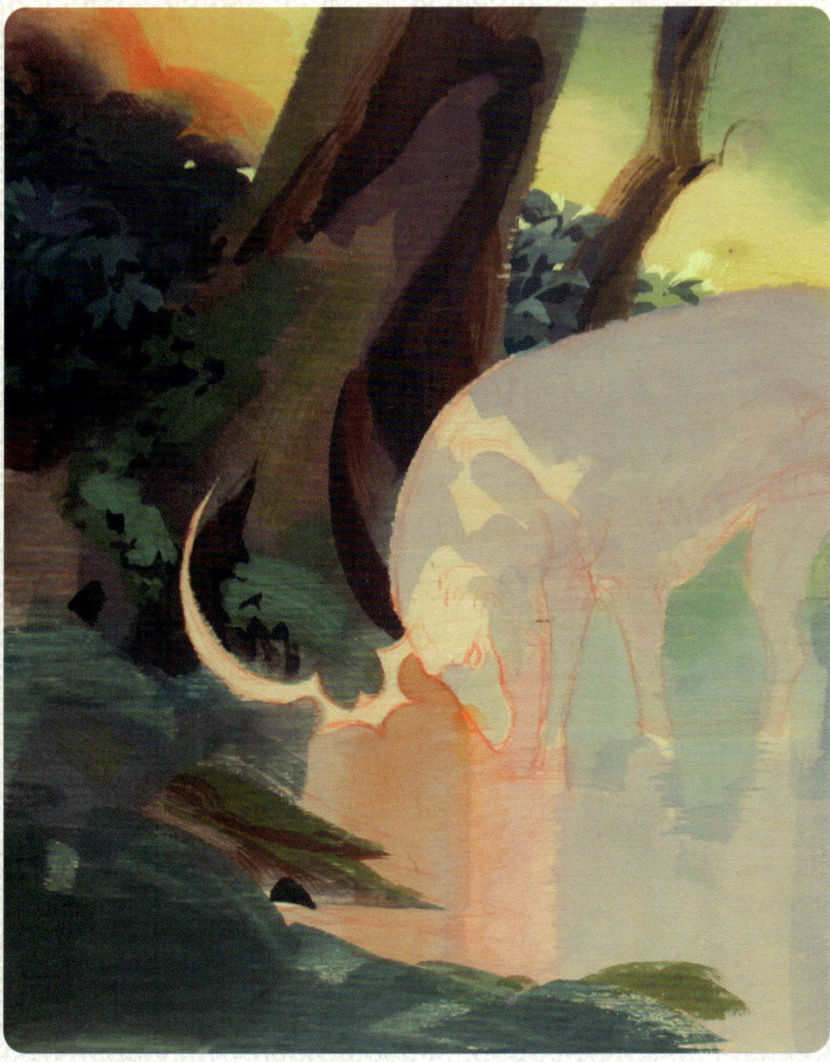

10. Checking references will help you create the impression of detail using simple strokes

CHECKING VALUES

Do your values feel unbalanced? There might be too much contrast in your foliage. Take another look at your leaves – they may be too light in value. It's common to see the lightest value of green on foliage as lighter than it actually is. Squint at your reference; the values should appear more condensed and simplified. If you are still having trouble assessing the value of the foliage, turn your reference to black and white or compare it to a simple value scale.

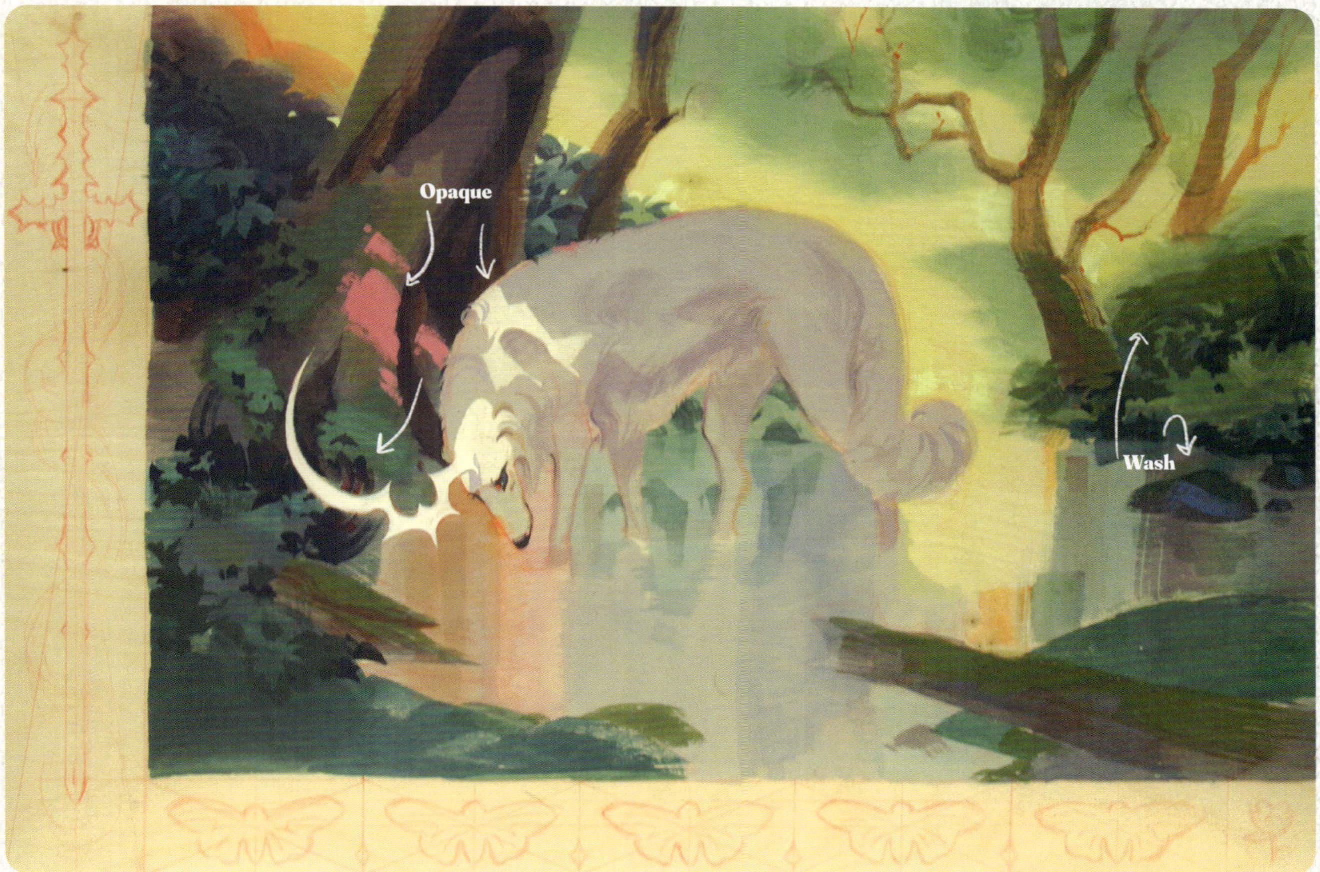

11. Key areas are detailed with opaque strokes and less important areas with thinner washes

11.

I continue working towards the foreground, adding more foliage shapes and shadows to the dog, and some strong focal highlights in pink and cream hues. As I narrow down the shapes, I use both darker and more opaque brushstrokes to slowly carve into my painting. While I tend to paint light to dark, I also enjoy the freedom gouache gives me to layer lighter values on top of darker ones, like the pink light on the tree trunk above. To get solid light values on top of dark hues, paint thickly and opaquely with very minimal water. The less water on the brush and the fewer strokes used, the less likely the paint underneath is to lift and muddy your intended colour.

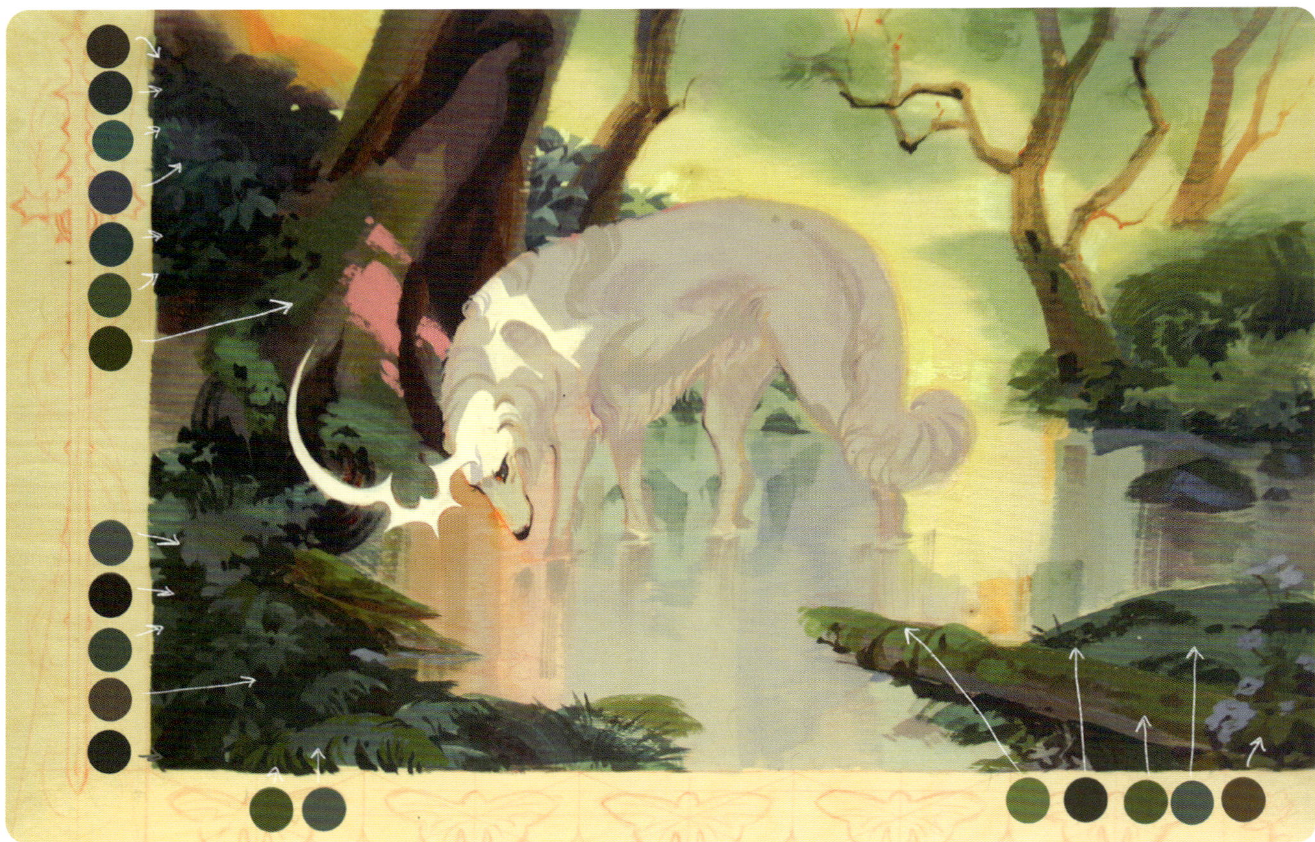

12. Here you can see how many subtle variations of green and brown I've used

12.

Hue variation can breathe life into a painting in a subtle but effective way. While painting the foliage, I vary my greens into warmer and cooler hues. It's important to note that while I am varying the hues, I am not changing the values. It's key to maintain a clear value structure in order for hue variation to be most effective. When mixing subtle changes in hue, try to mix directly onto the previous colour on your palette; this aids in maintaining a sense of harmony between colours and allows for easier value control. Try this out when painting the leaves, moss, and grass in the foreground.

13.

Maintaining visual weight is an important aspect in creating balance and harmony in a painting. After stepping away and looking with fresh eyes, I see that the top-right corner looks too bare compared to the dense foliage on the left side. I elect to add more visual interest by painting foliage on the previously bare trees. Always allow yourself breaks when you start to feel fatigued, in order to find and address problems in the painting with fresh eyes. I find that walking my dog refreshes and re-energizes me when experiencing painting fatigue.

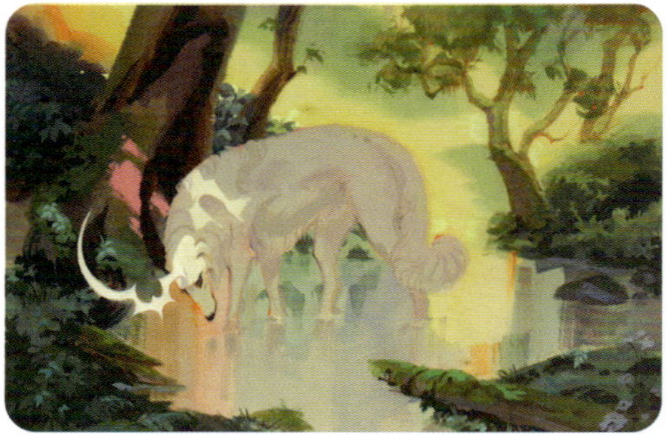

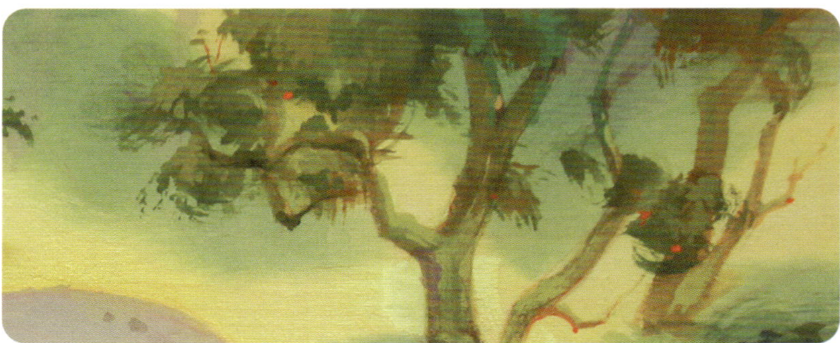

13. Take occasional breaks to help refresh your view of the composition

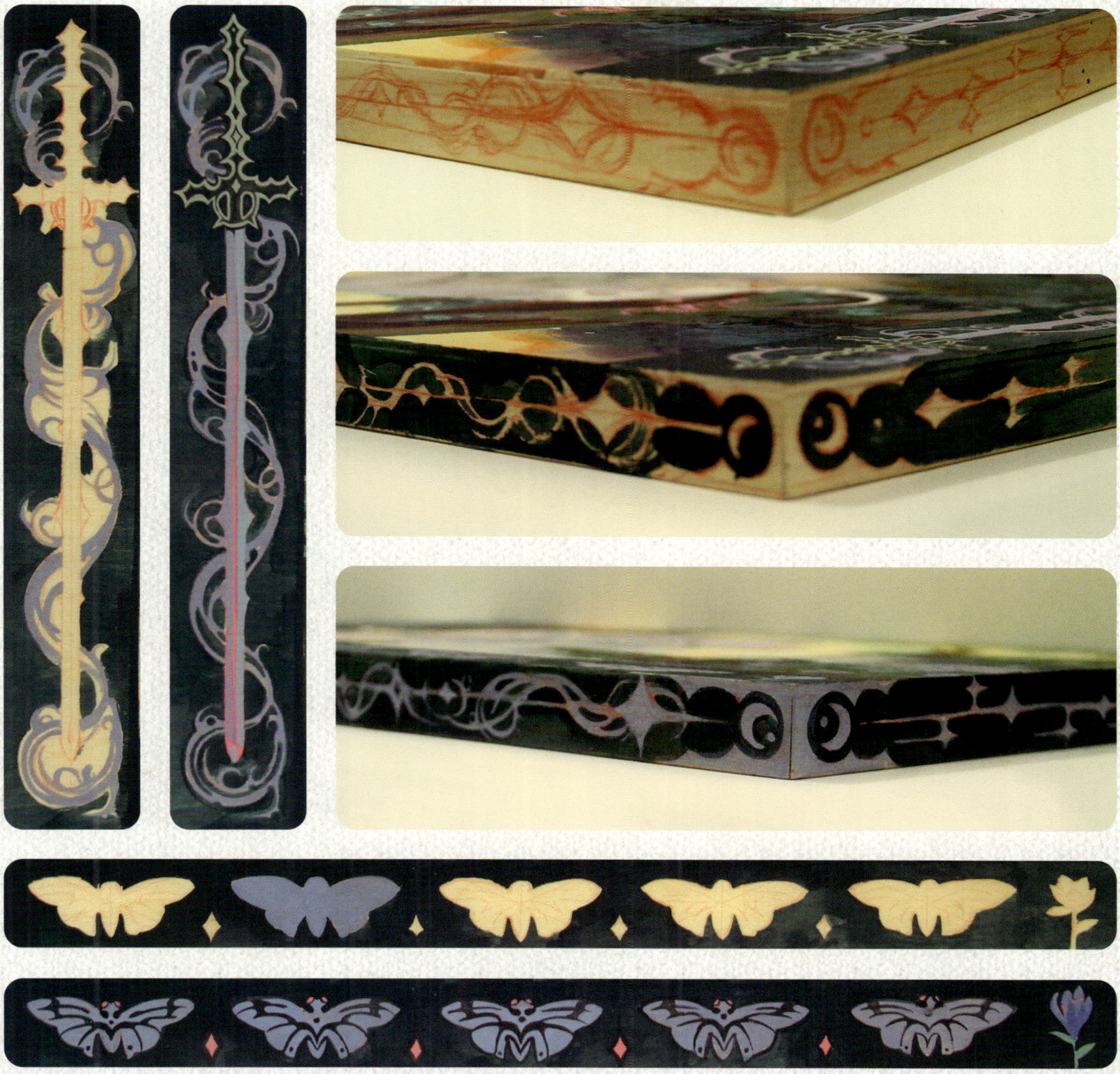

14. Paint the edge decorations, going around the details and filling those in last

14.

The patterns and ornamentals have been saved for this later stage, as a way to frame and clean up the edges of the painting, as well as to prevent cross-bleeding from the forest scene into the design. Paint these in three layers: first the flat colour for the background, second filling in the shapes, and third going back in with the background colour to clean up the edges. I find this method to be the most forgiving and it allows me the most control when I'm painting.

15.

When painting any sort of environment, it's common to over-focus on the plant life and main characters present in a scene. However, forests are not just full of diverse flora but contain a multitude of fauna as well. I enjoy populating my paintings with bugs, birds, and other such creatures in order to bring life to a painting. It's a similar concept to making a home feel 'lived in' by adding personal belongings or wear and tear; adding more fauna to a scene will make a forest feel 'lived in' by the plants and creatures that inhabit it. Try adding some insect or bird life to your scene, looking up extra references if needed. They should be subtle additions that don't distract from the main focus.

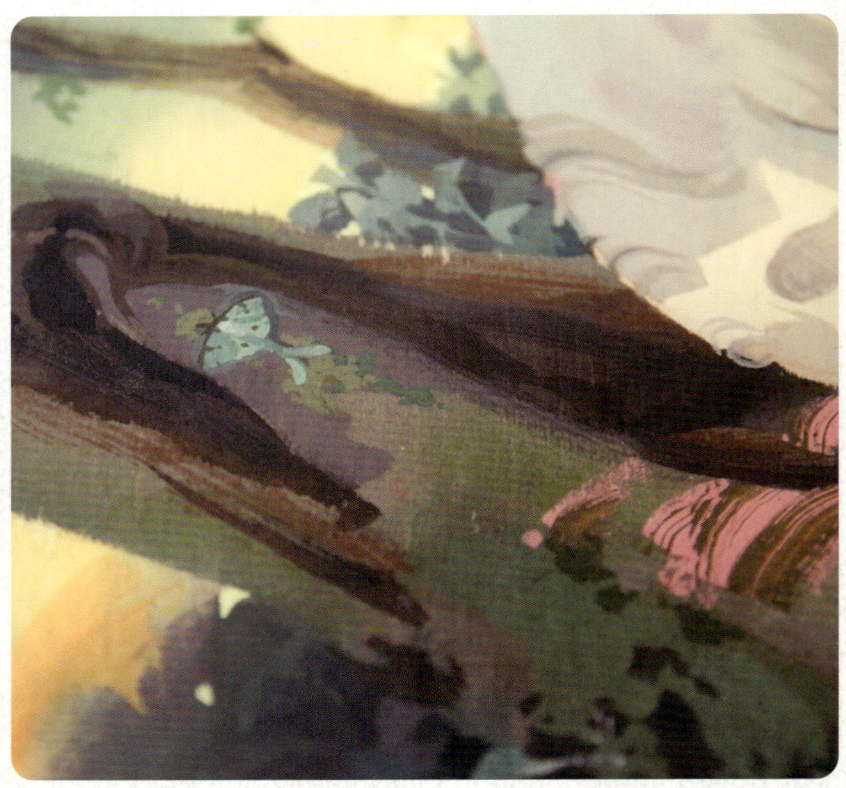

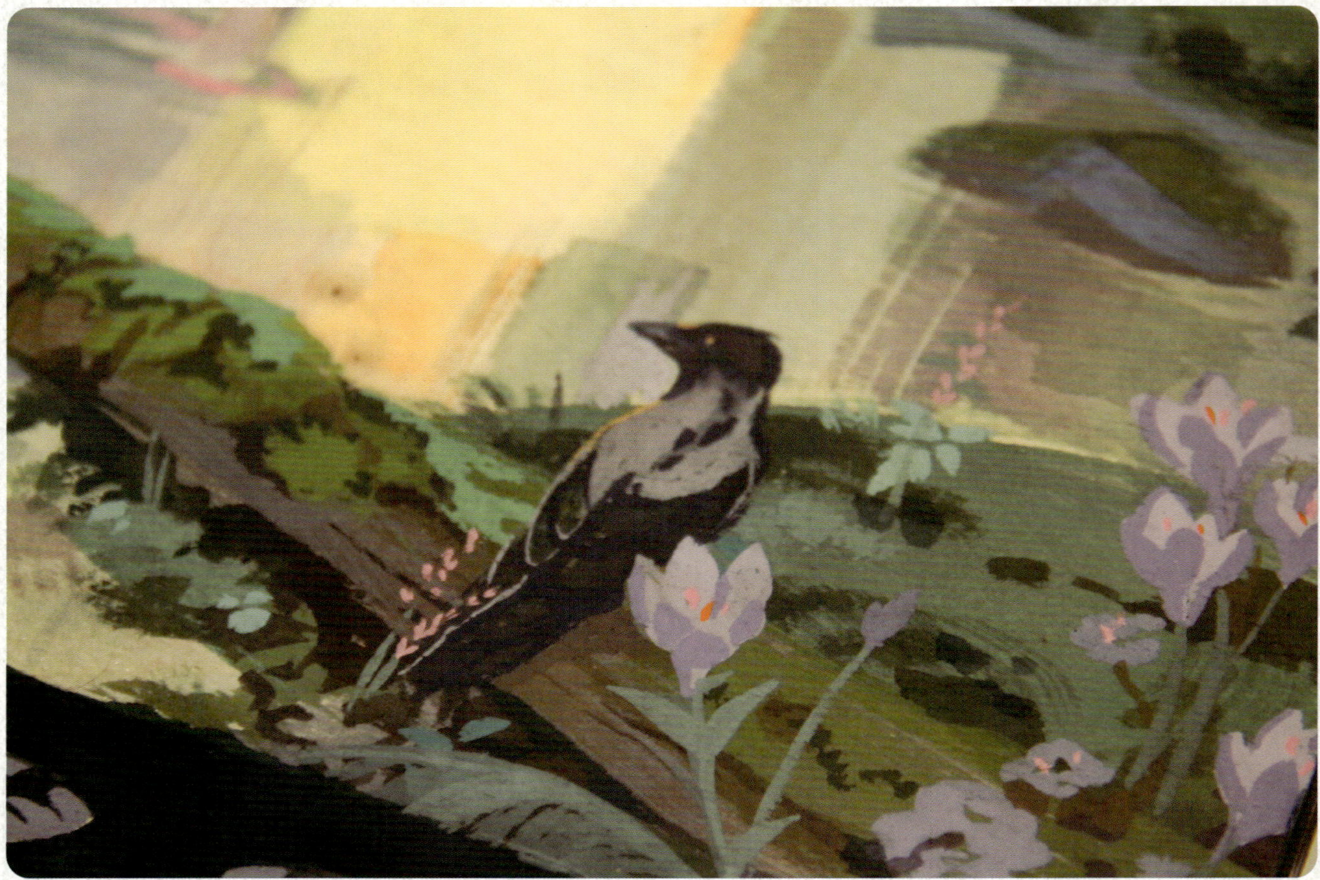

15. Small creatures such as birds and insects make the forest come alive

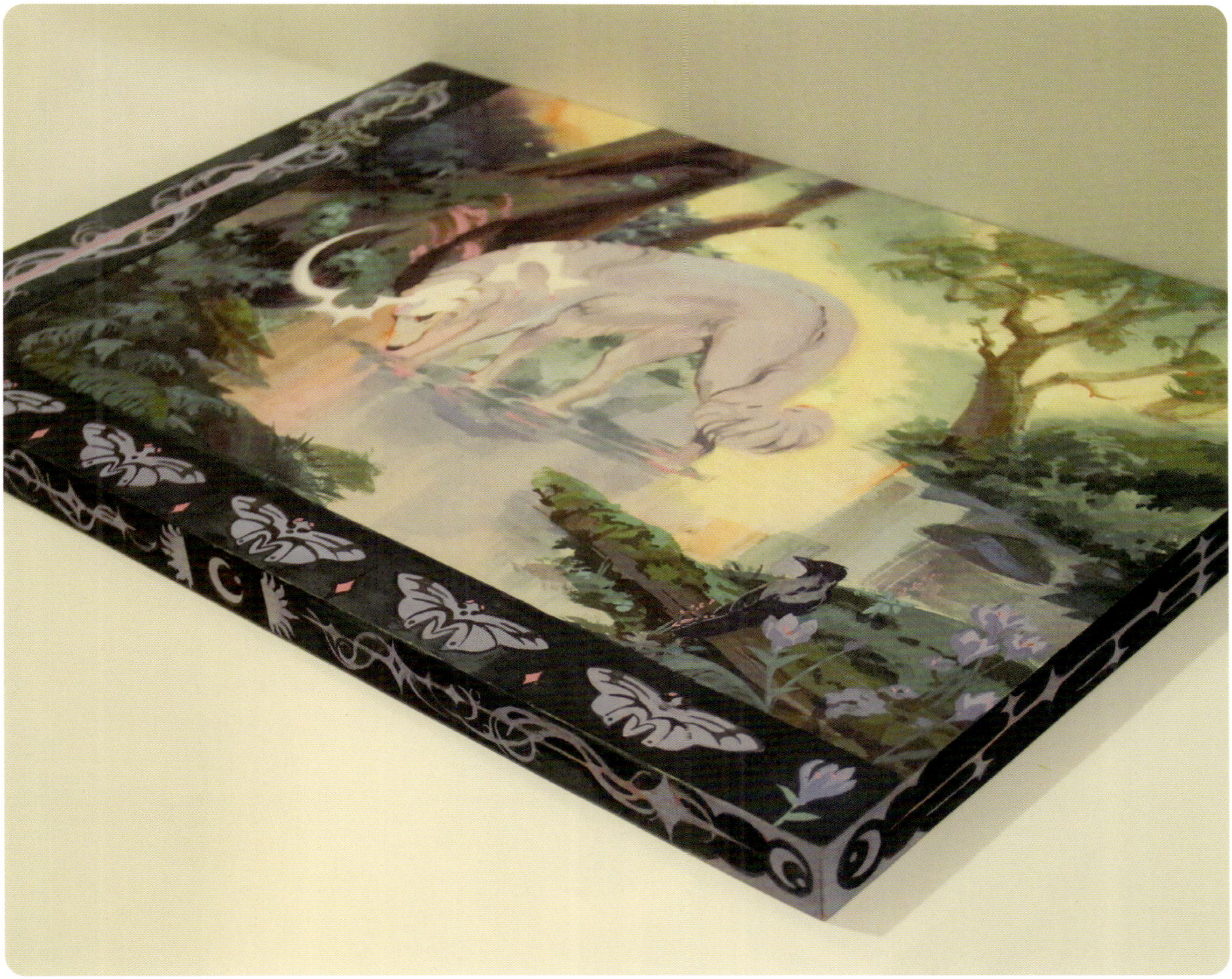

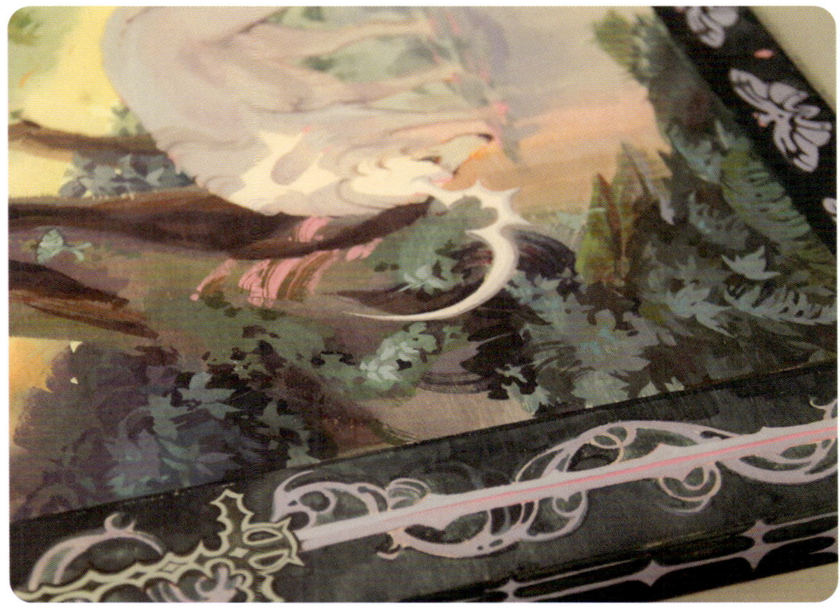

16.

This final step is the opportunity to solve any remaining issues and bring the painting all together. I tweak shapes, add darker and lighter values where they are needed, and add visual interest where the painting feels bare. Specifically, I add darker values to the dog and tweak the foliage shapes in the foreground and back tree. If you are feeling stuck, step away and take a walk or ask a friend for their opinion. Painting is never a linear process for me and I experience quite a bit of back and forth.

16. Check over the piece, get second opinions, and make small corrections

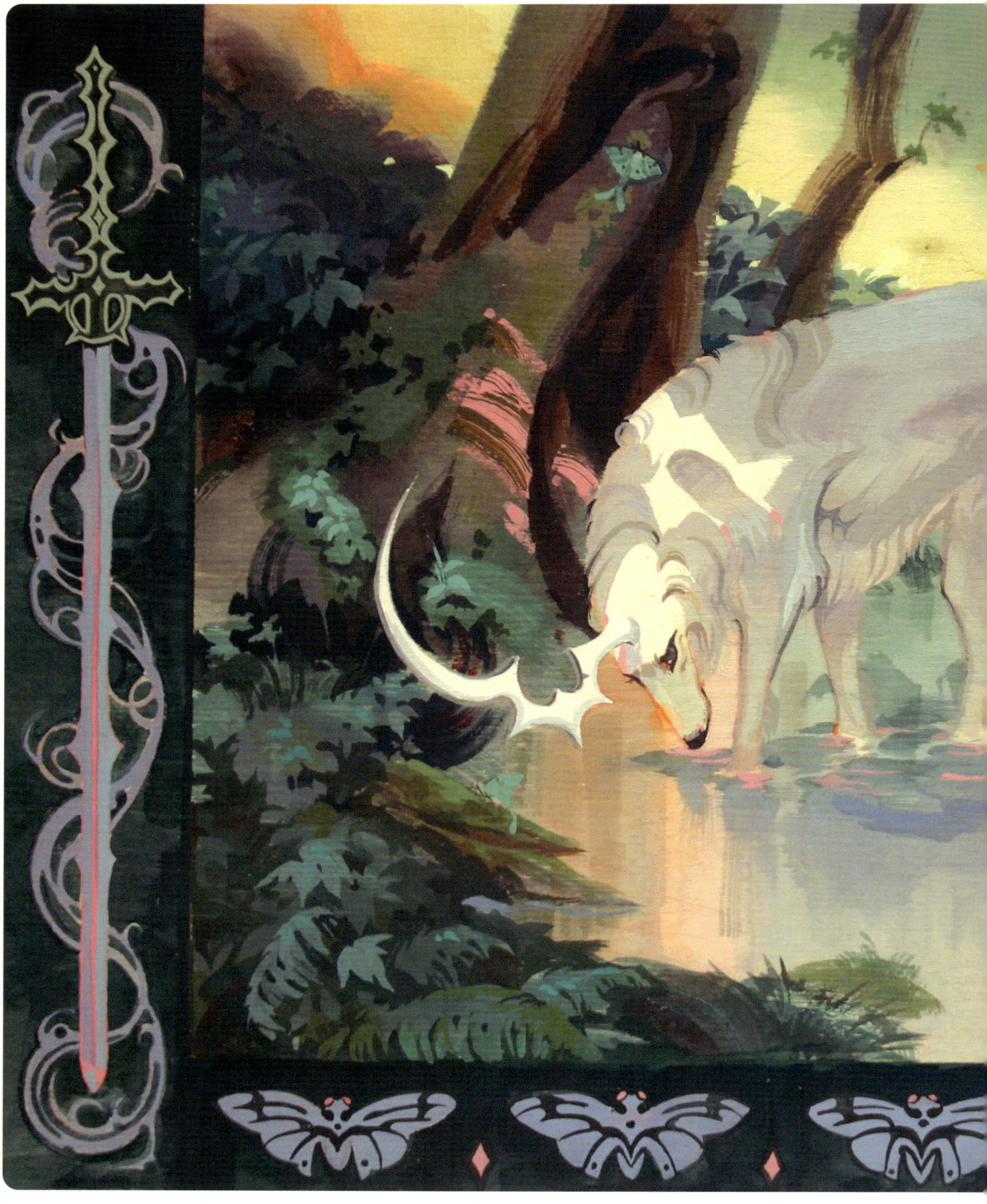

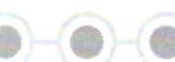

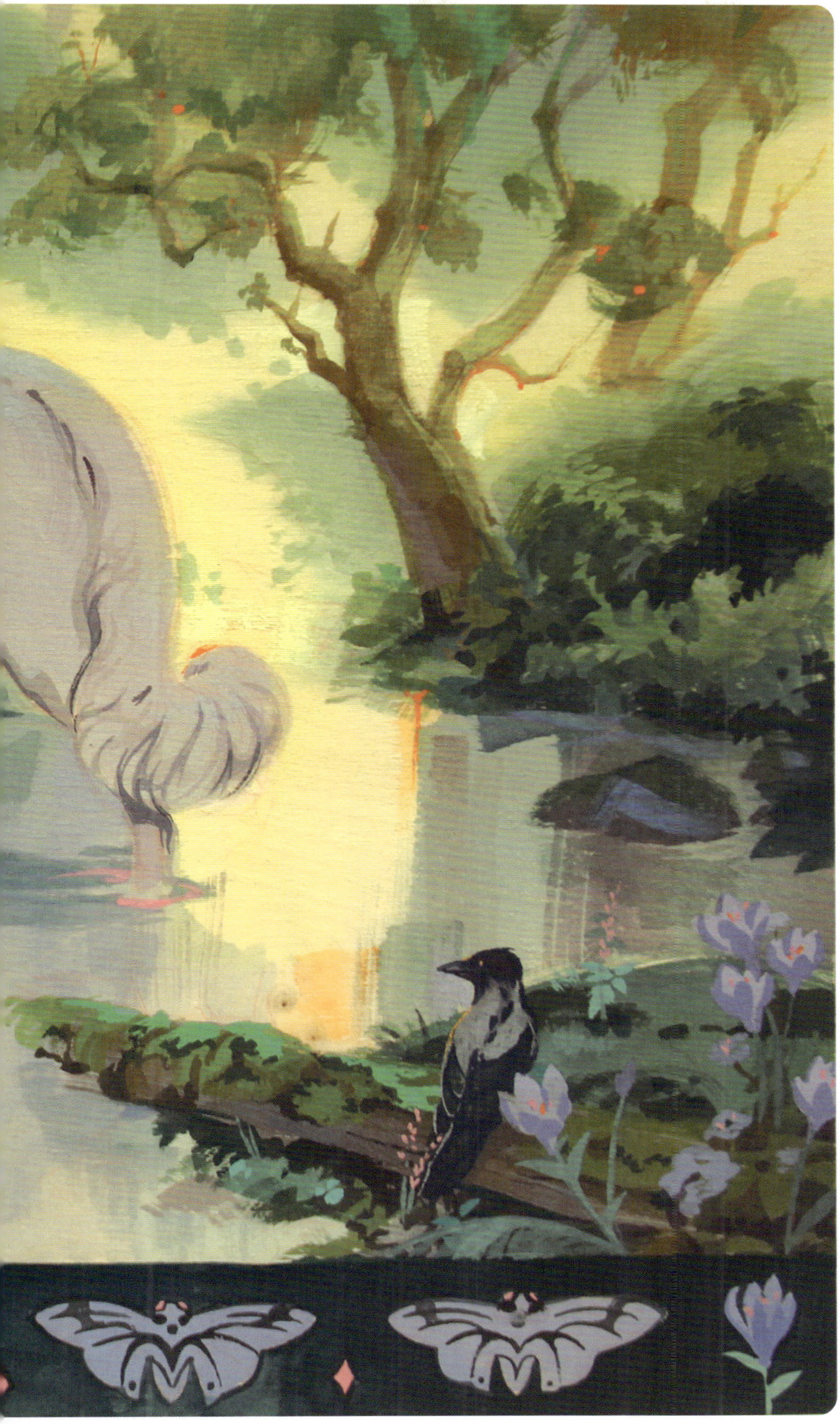

CONCLUSION

I encourage anyone interested in painting nature scenes – fantasy or otherwise – to go spend time outside in your local environment. What helped me far and away the most in my painting journey was to begin painting from life. If you're intimidated, start small by painting bouquets of flowers at home, then venture out into your local gardens or parks. Nature is a wonderful teacher, full of intricate shapes, stunning compositions, and hue variations. Translating these aspects into a world of your own imagination is deeply fulfilling and I hope this tutorial will aid you in doing so.

Final image © Accorvio

The GALLERY

In this section, we explore the portfolio pieces and personal gouache works of our talented tutorial artists: a selection of enchanting nature paintings, stylized studies, and magical scenes that will inspire you to pick up a paintbrush.

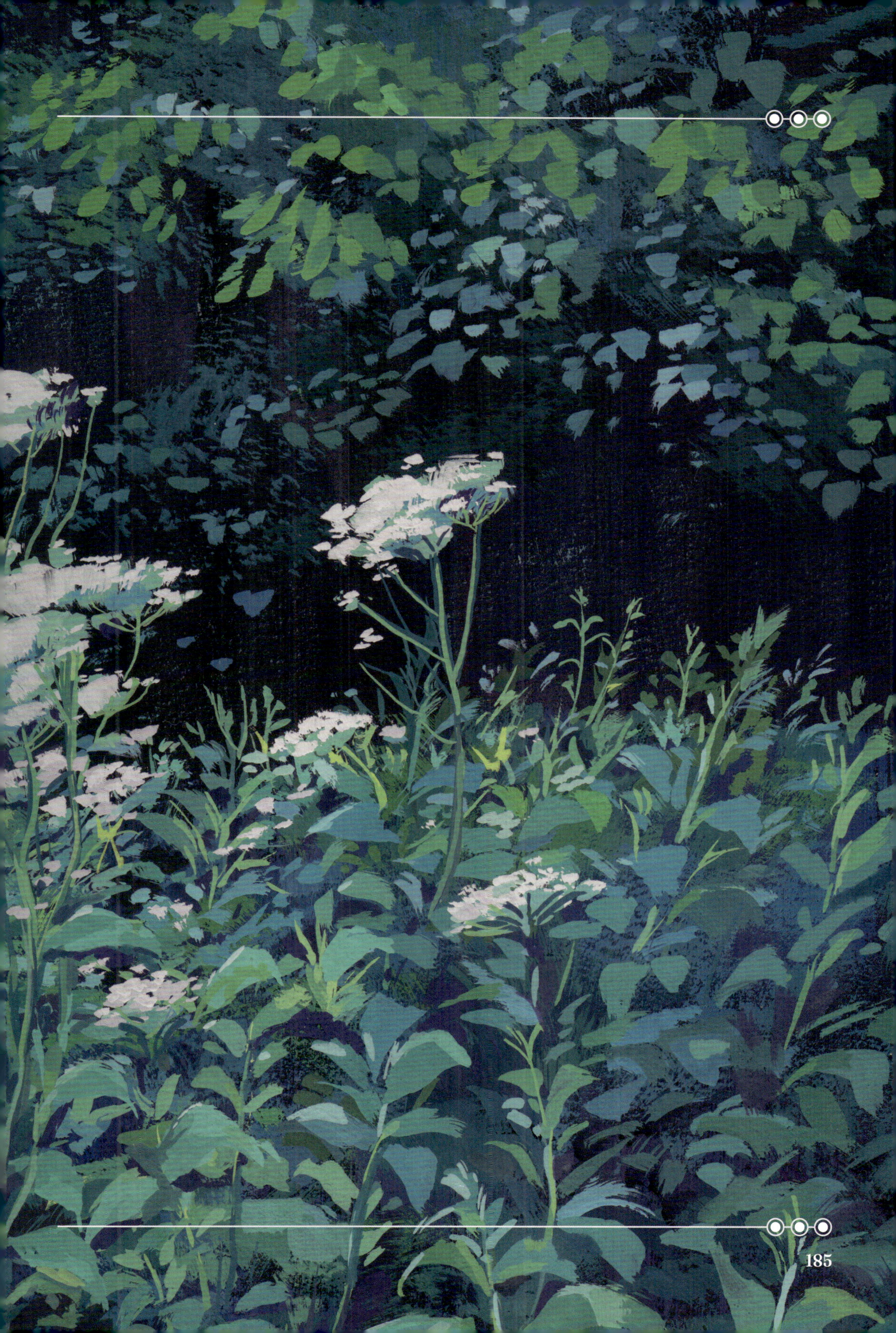

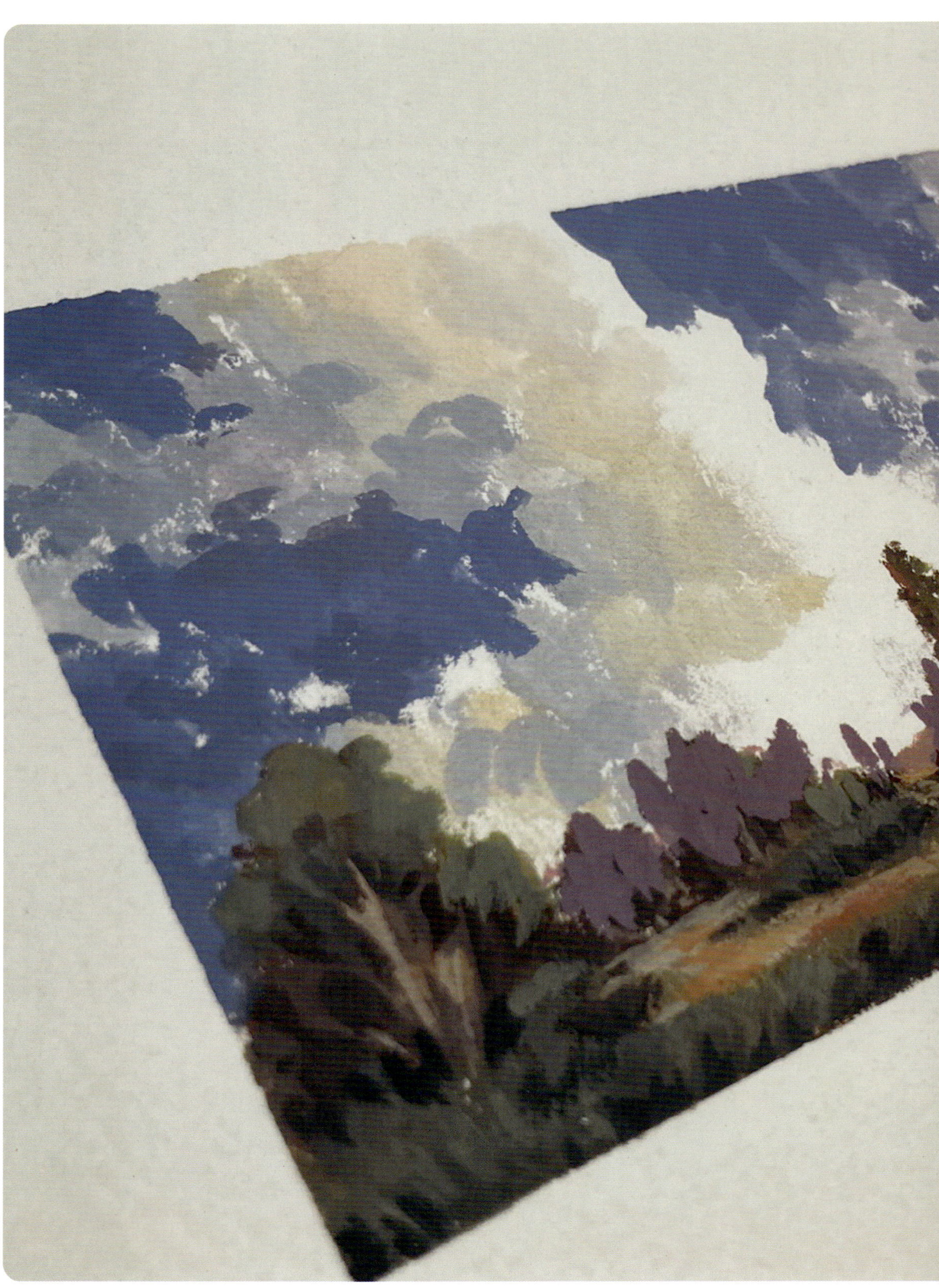

Fatima Mandouh

Cloud Study If you've seen my digital work, you'll know I'm a fan of painting cloudscapes.
The purpose of this study was to learn about organic cloud forms using gouache.

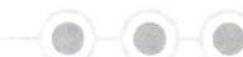

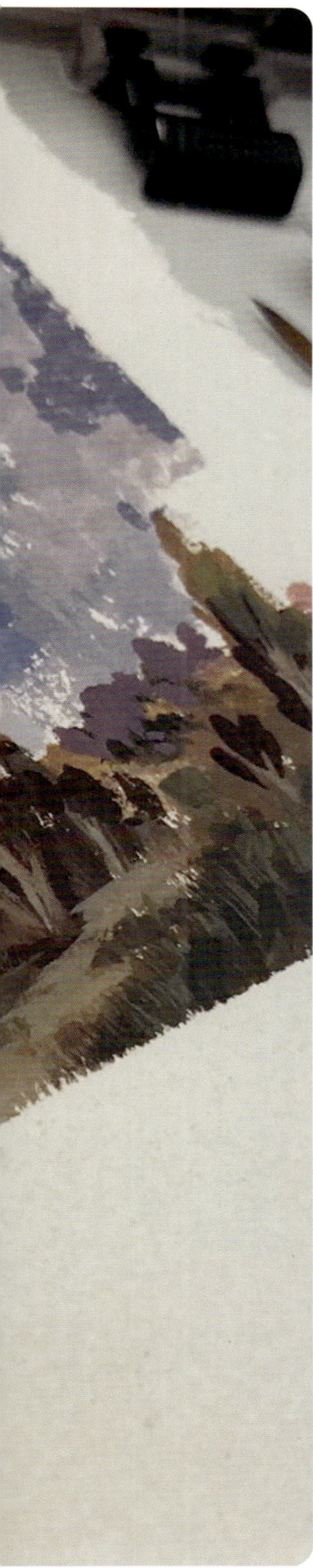

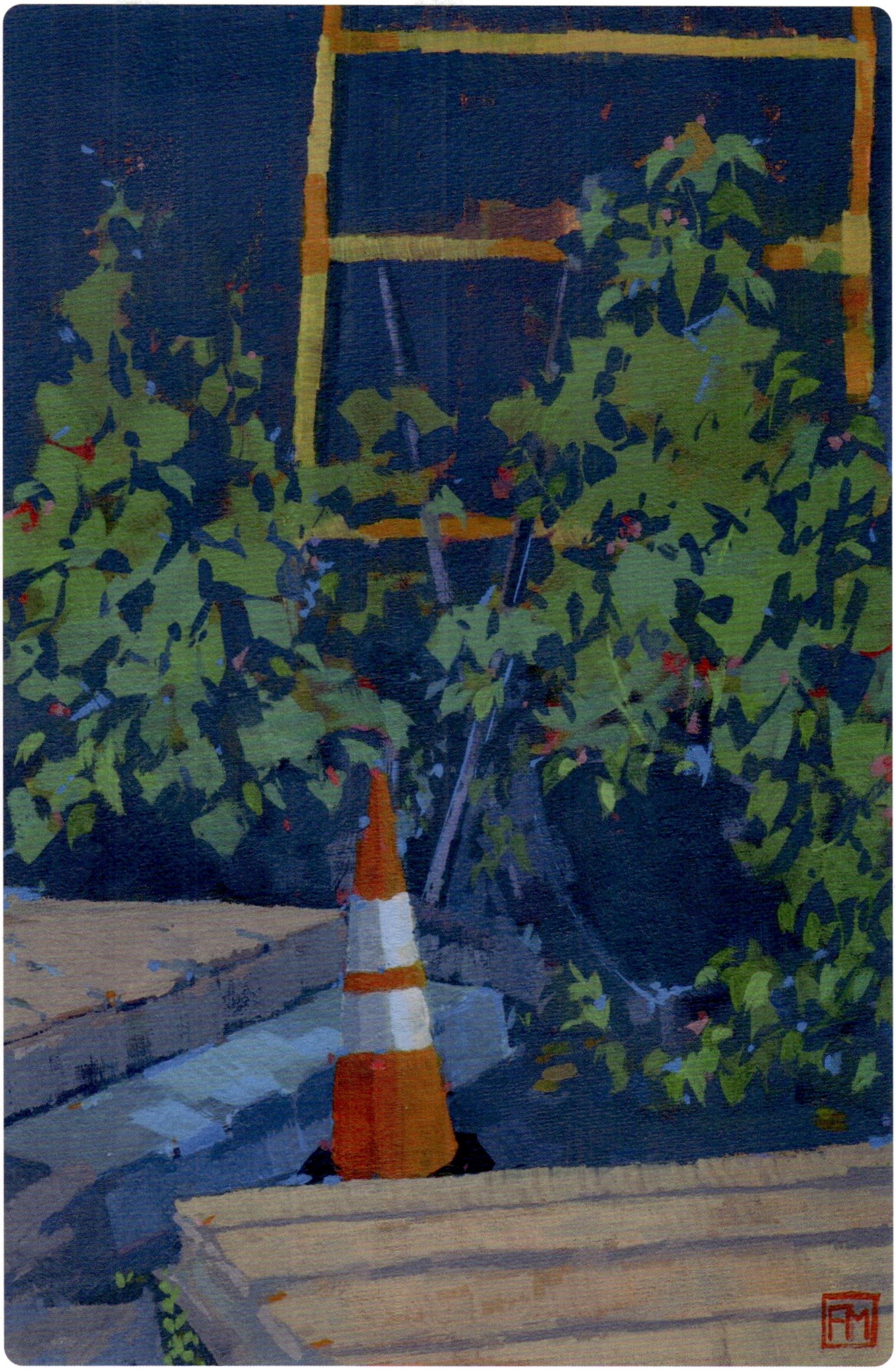

Tucked Away A piece I painted for a gallery show. It represents those small and mundane parts of life in which we can still find beauty.

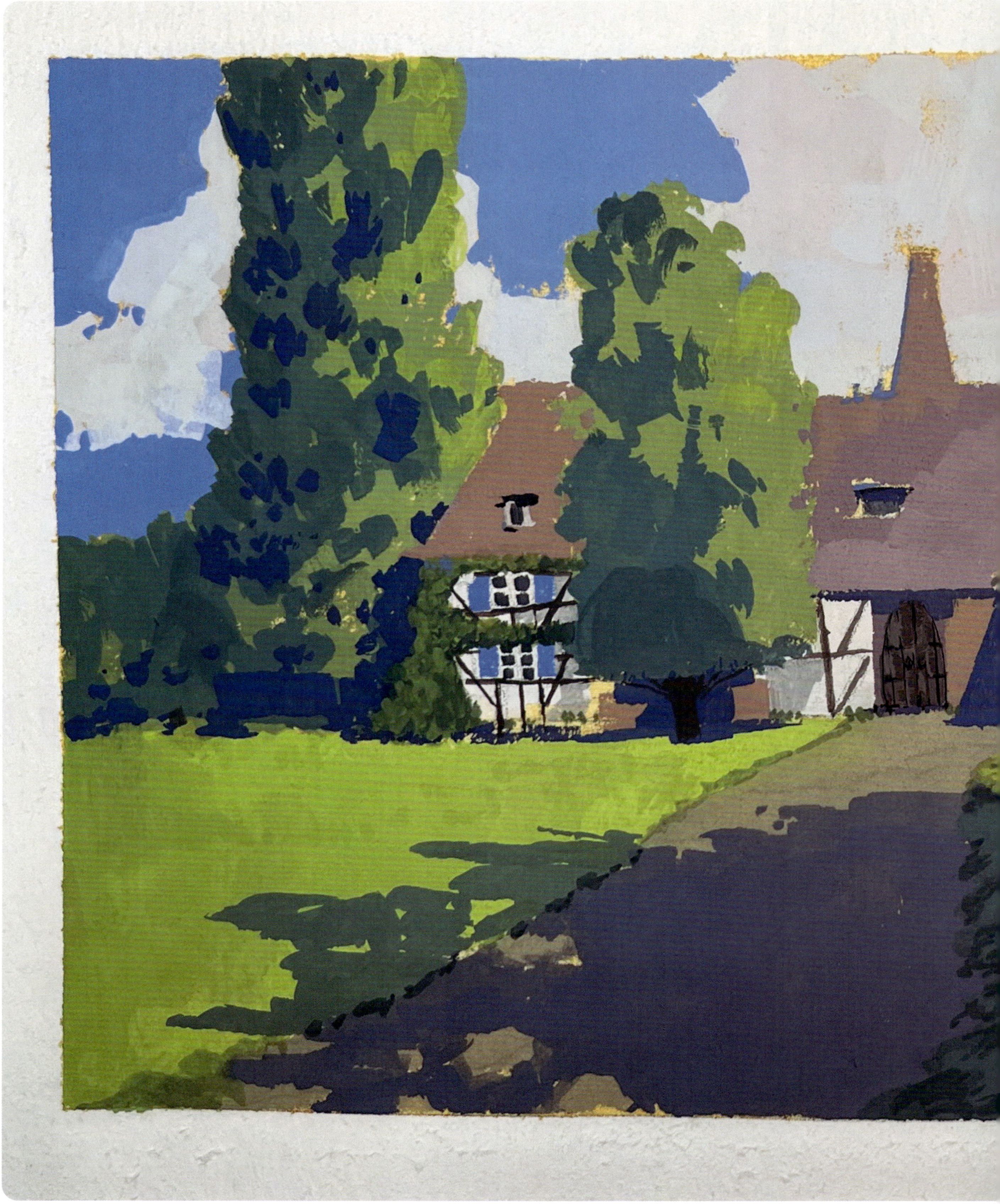

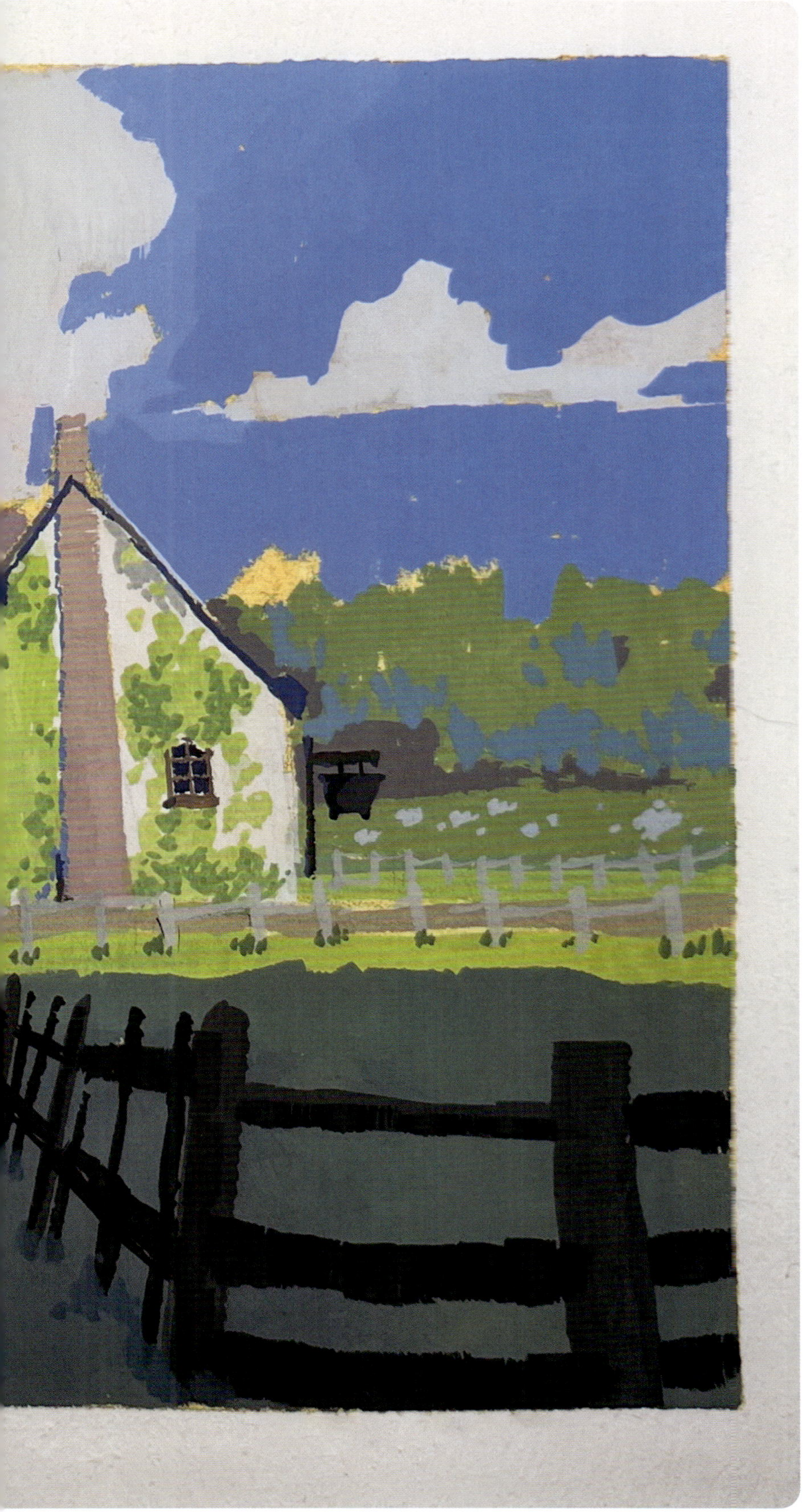

Cozy Witch's Home
The charming home of
the village witch. I had
so much fun putting this
composition together
– it's made up of some
of my all-time favourite
colour combinations.
If only I could paint
trees and skies all day!

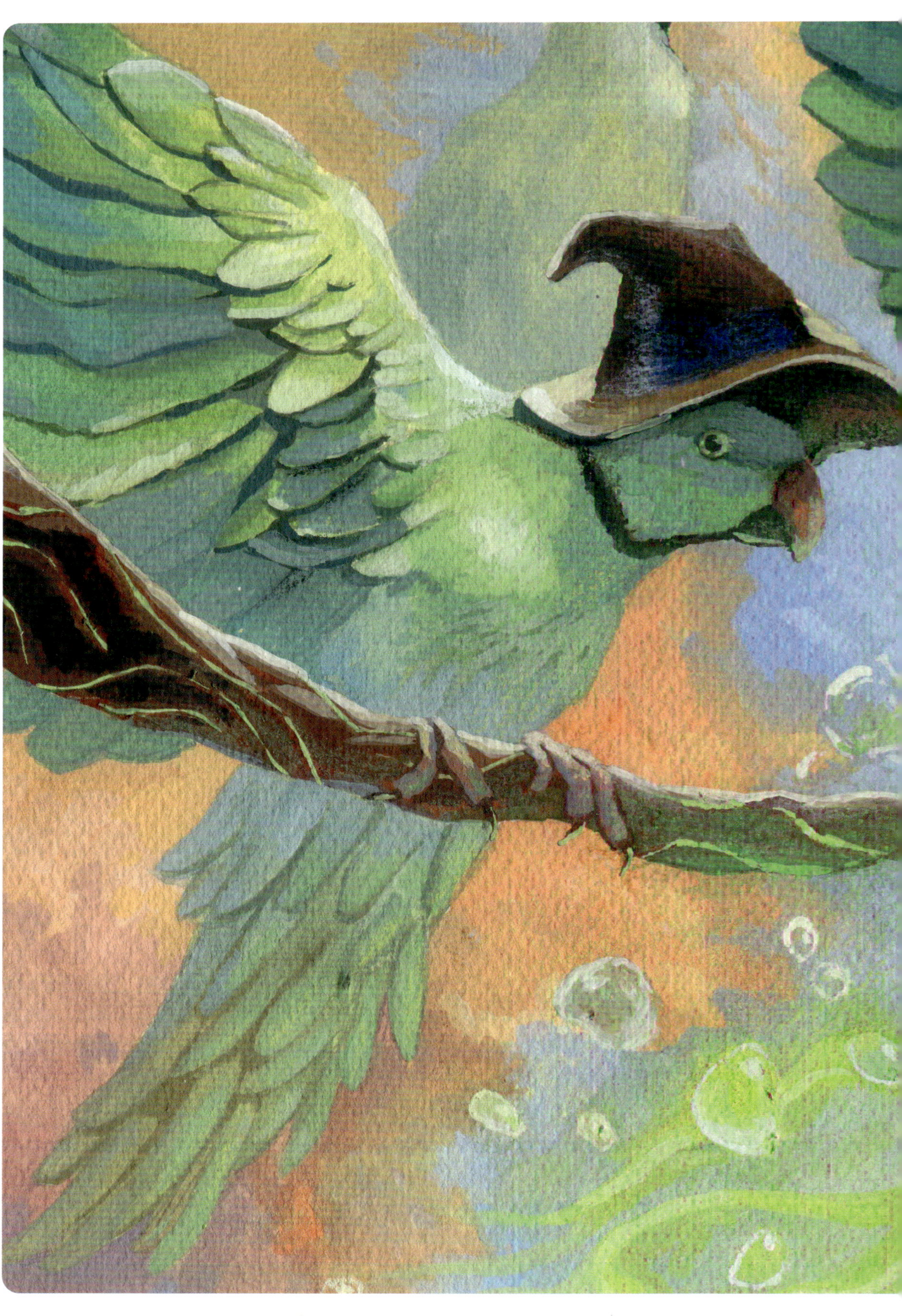

Kiara Maharaj

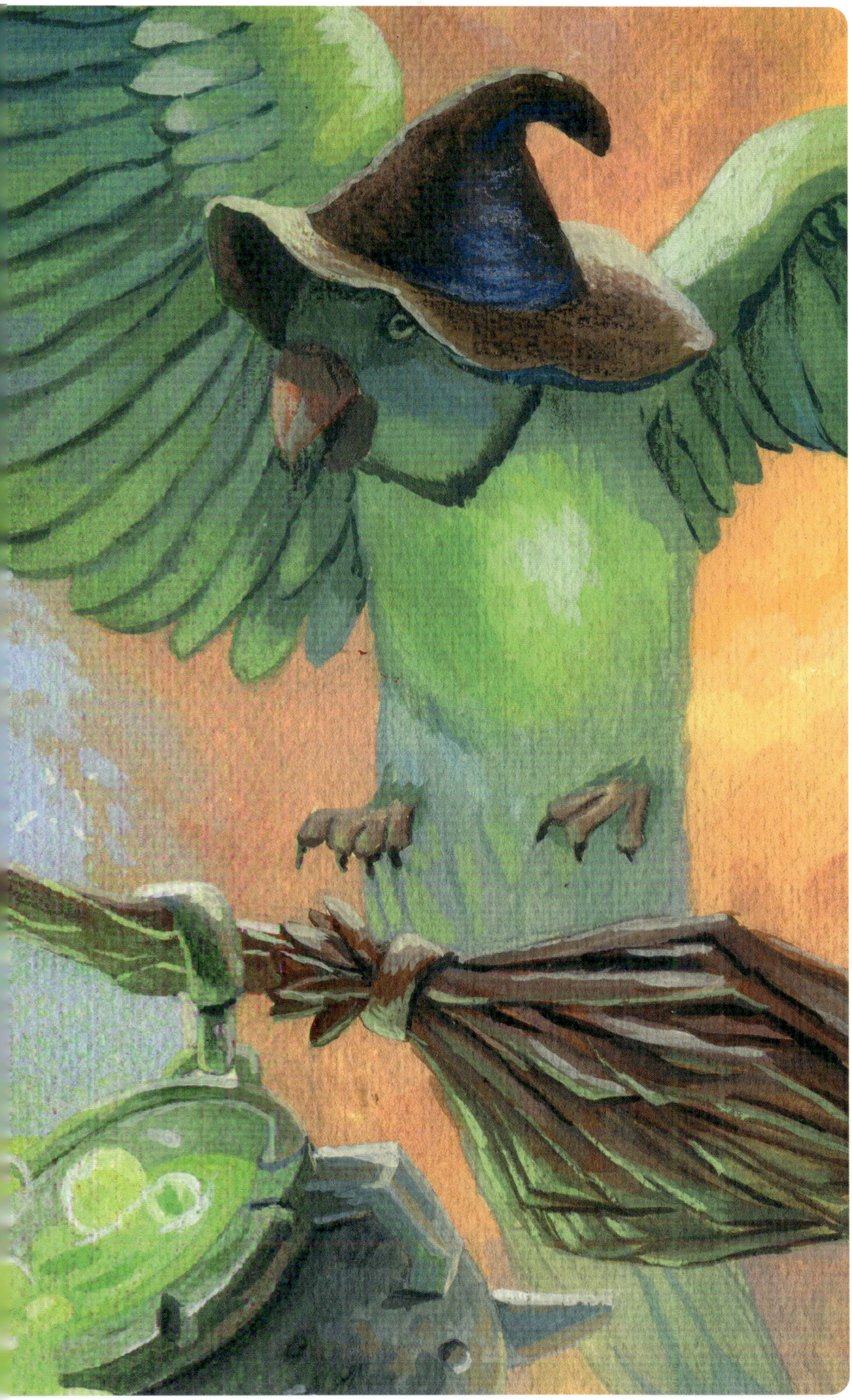

Parrot Apprentices

Parrot apprentices zipping across the sky on a rogue broomstick, inspired by my mischievous ring-necked parrot and his shenanigans. The potion may or may not be harmless, and will definitely land on unsuspecting citizens.

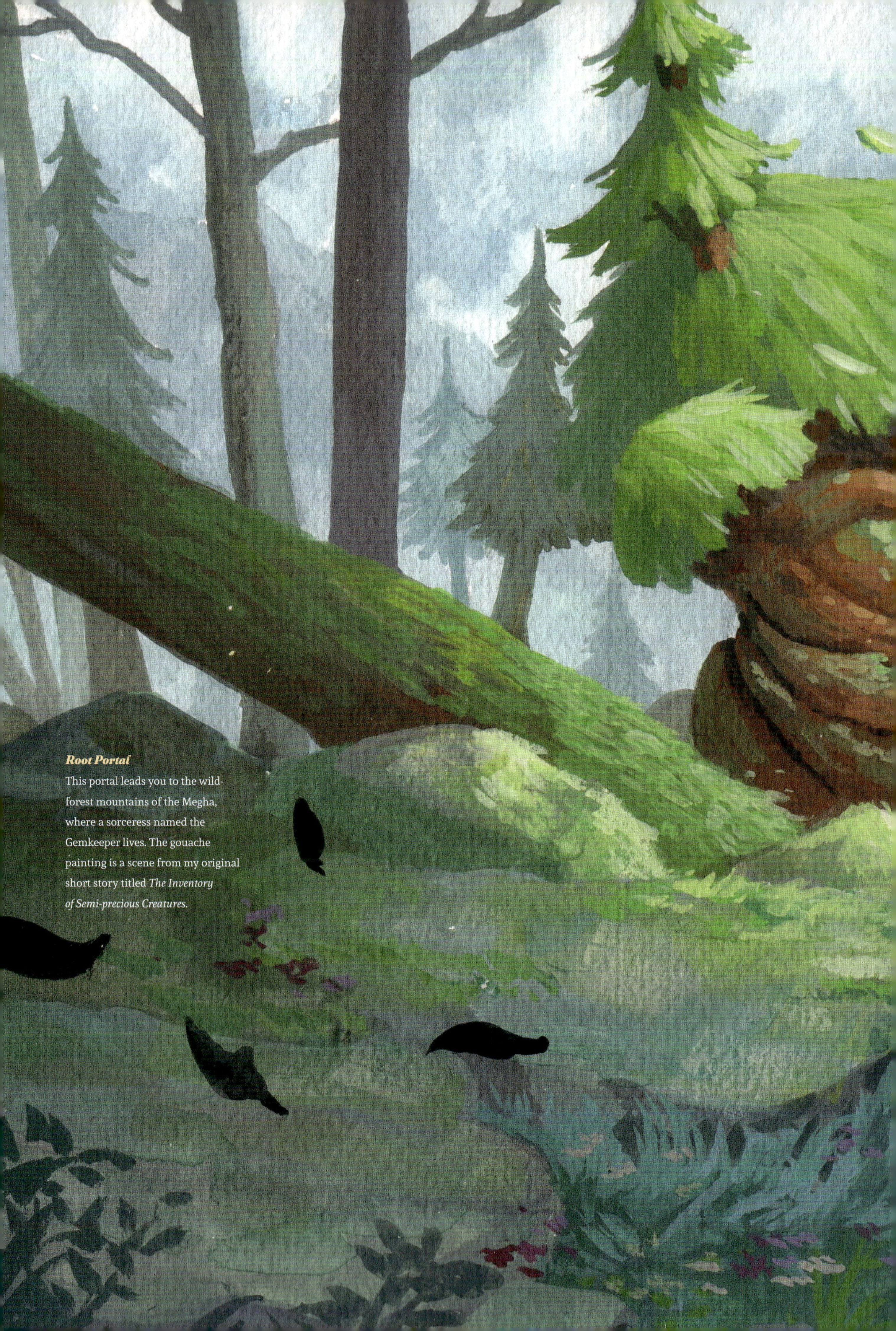

Root Portal
This portal leads you to the wild-
forest mountains of the Megha,
where a sorceress named the
Gemkeeper lives. The gouache
painting is a scene from my original
short story titled The Inventory
of Semi-precious Creatures.

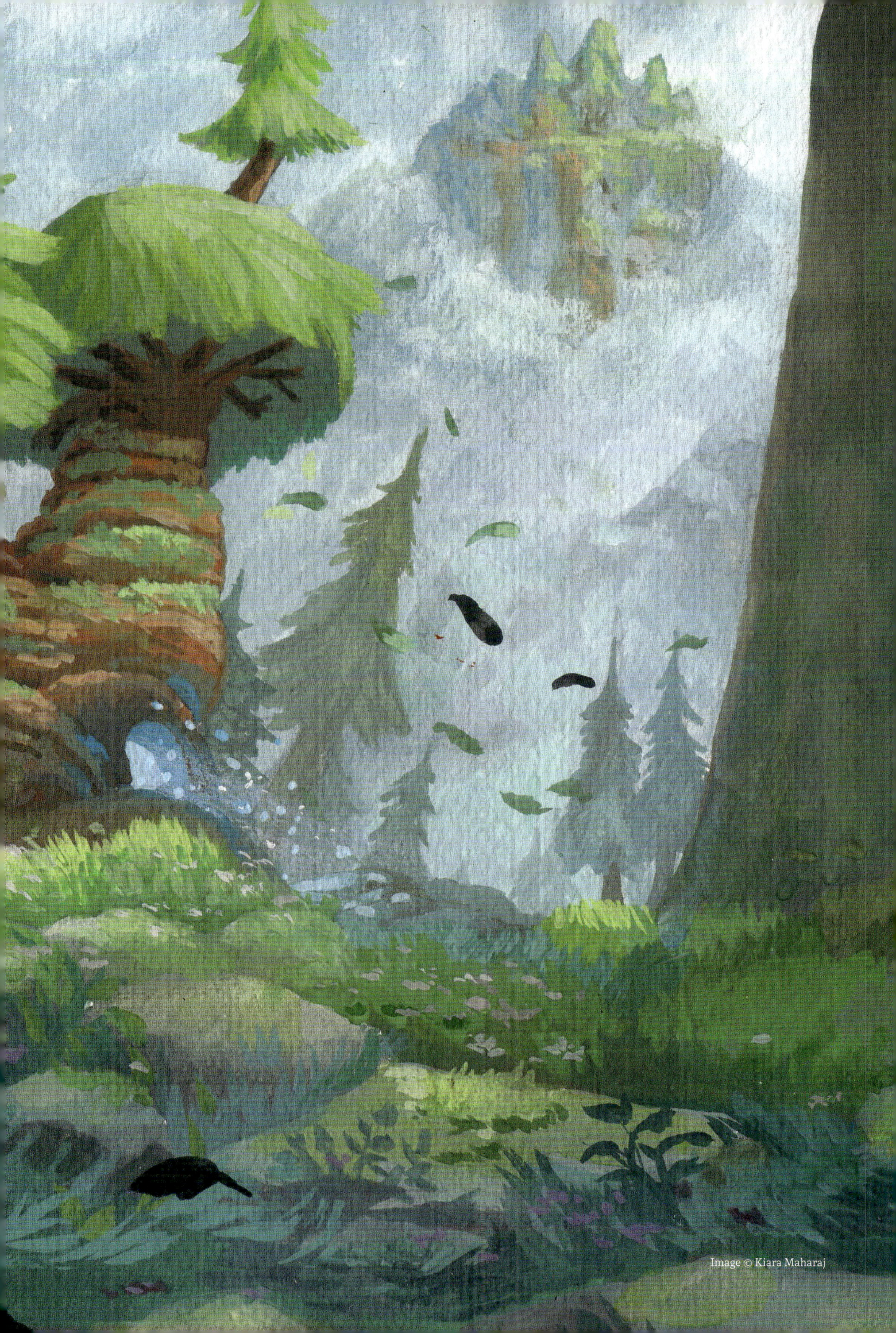
Image © Kiara Maharaj

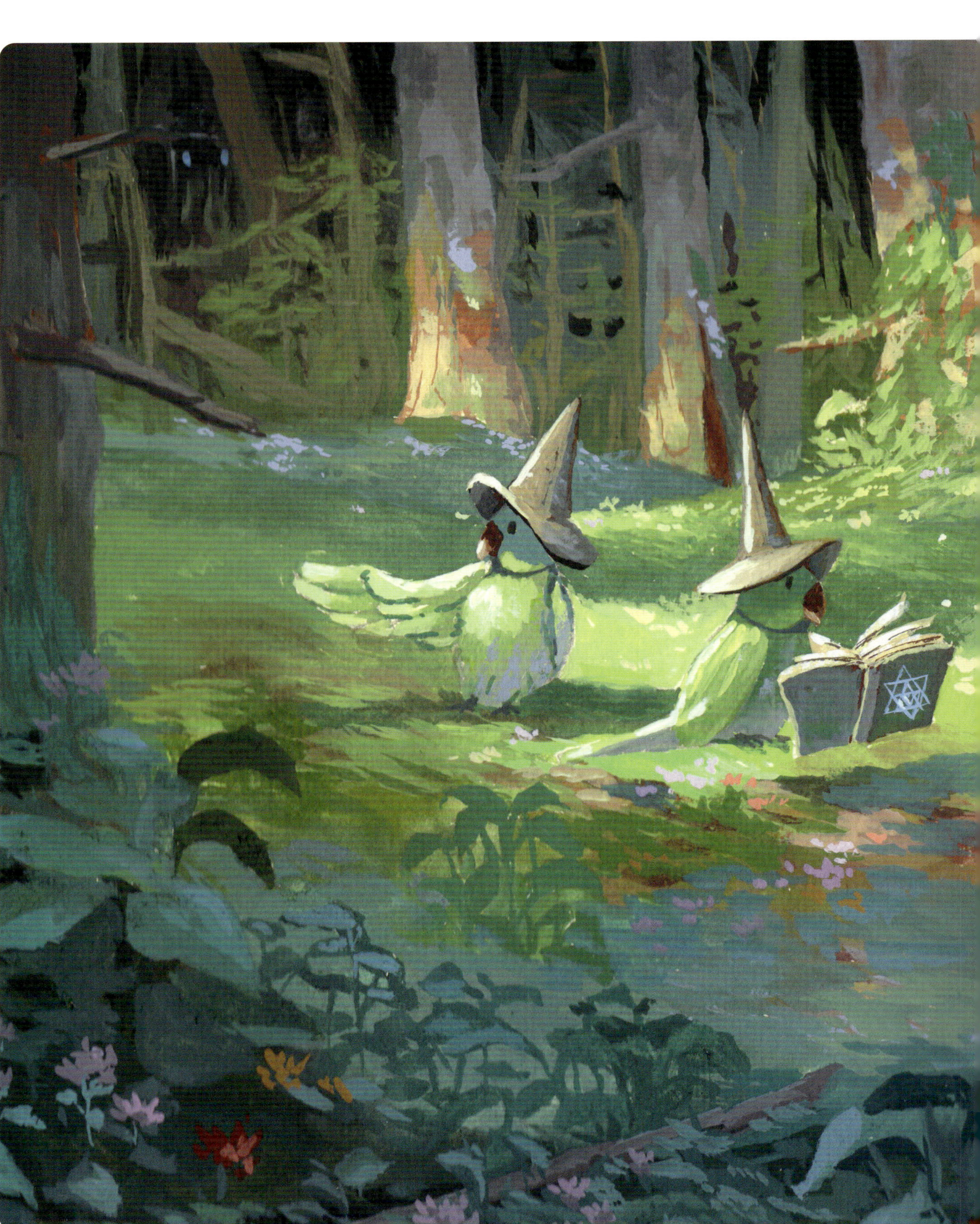

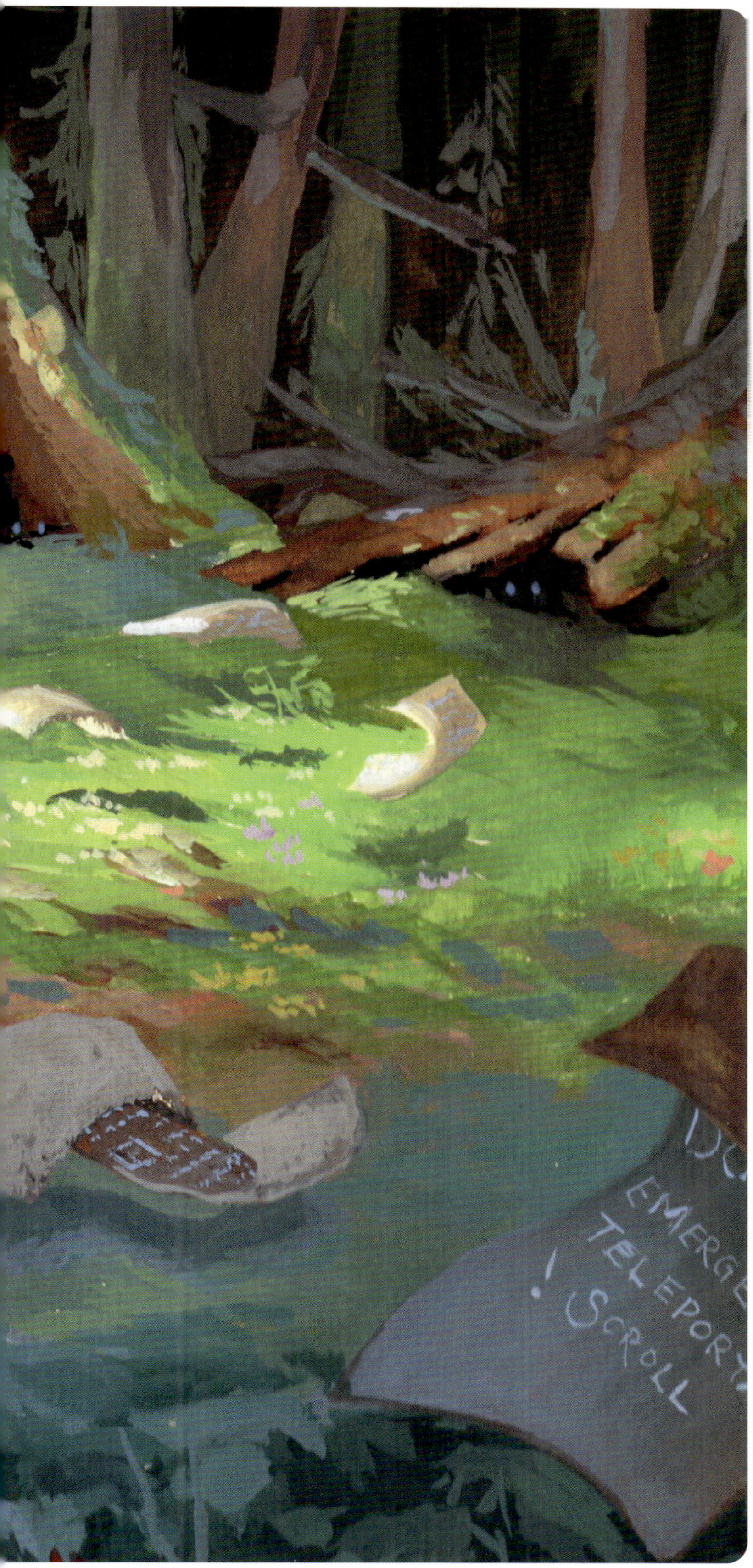

Parrot Spellbook

My favourite gouache
painting from 2024.
Parrot apprentices messing
with a spellbook, their
much-needed incantation
scrolls slipping away …

Maddy Bellwoar

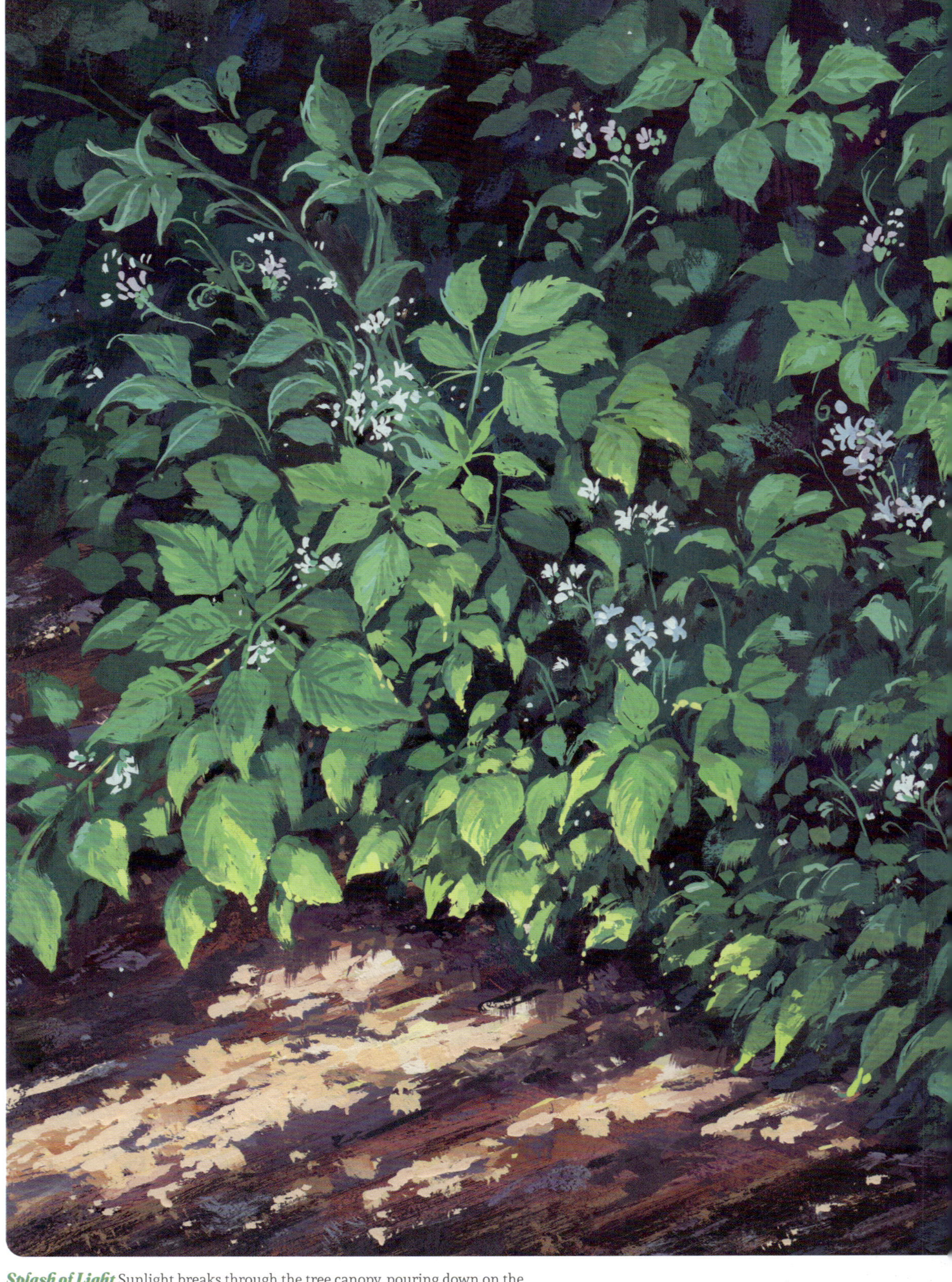

Splash of Light Sunlight breaks through the tree canopy, pouring down on the leaves below and splashing them with golden light. (Part of the *Lush* series.)

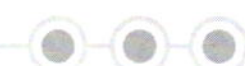

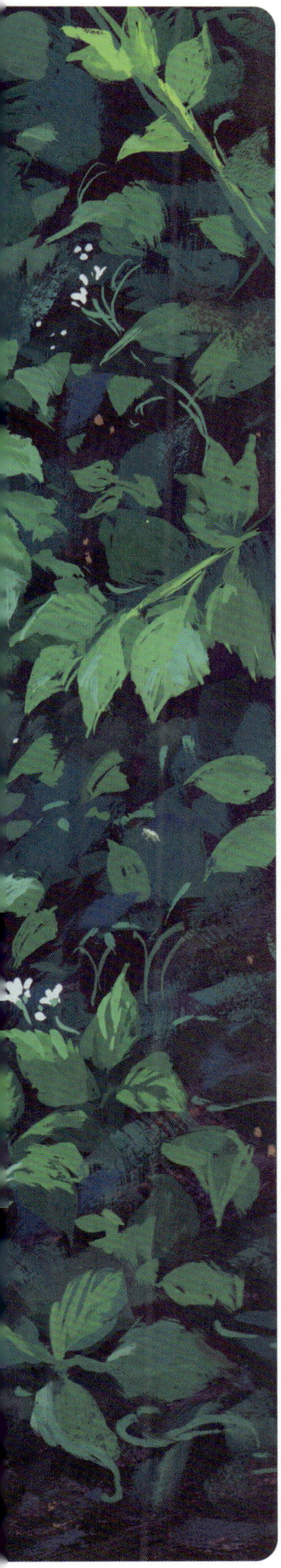

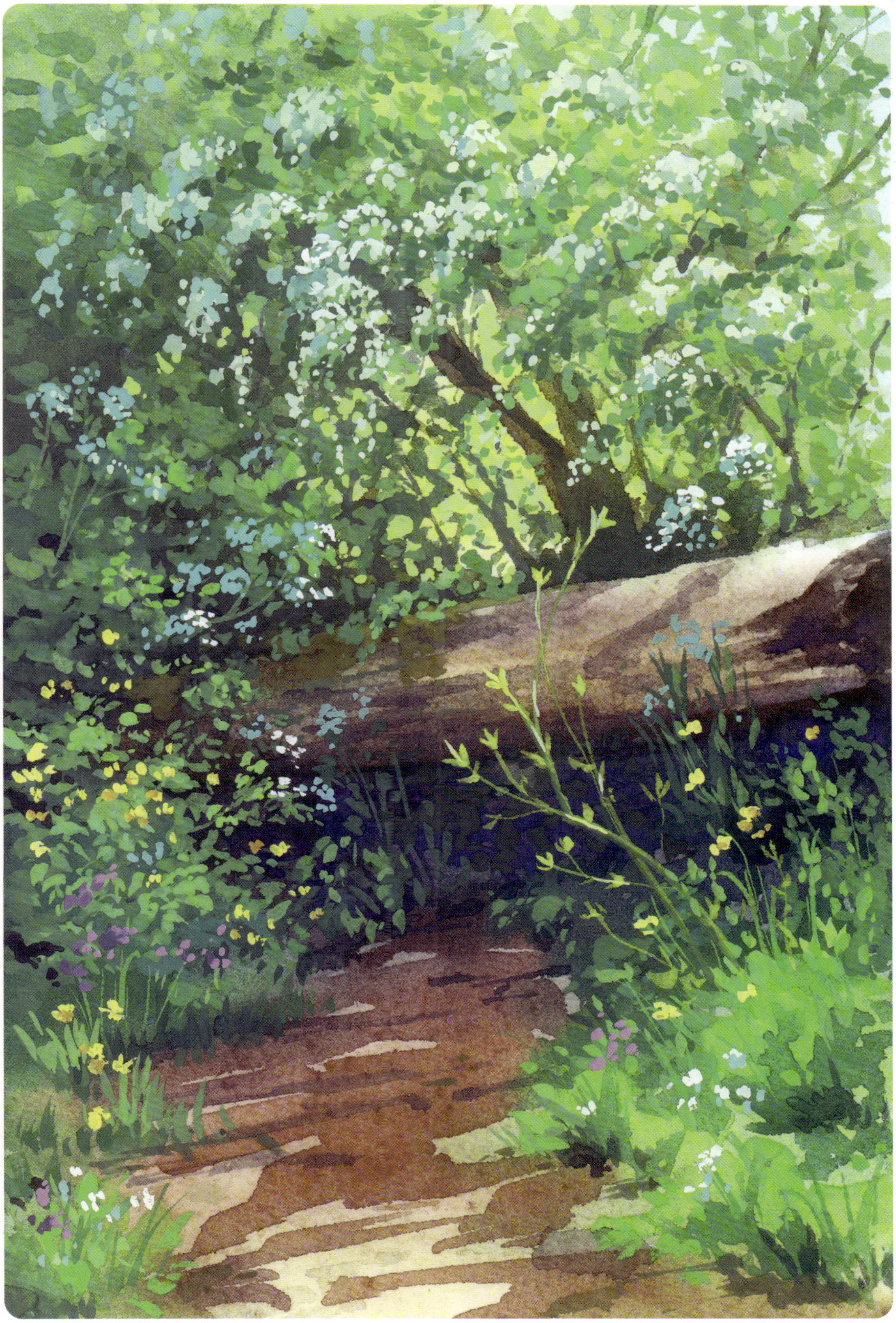

Fallen Tree with Wildflowers A fallen tree is surrounded by life in this springtime painting. A variety of plants and wildflowers have found their new home.

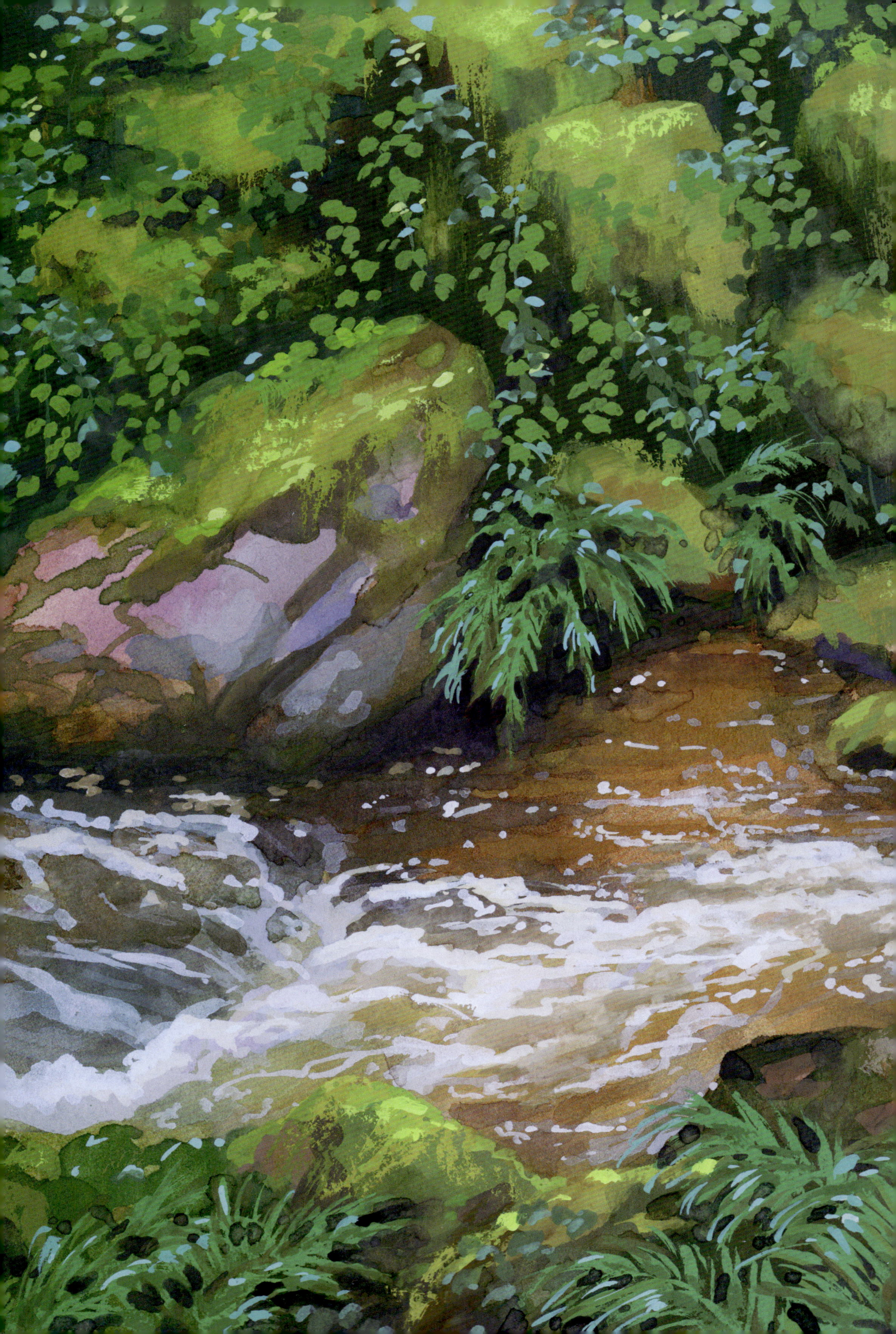

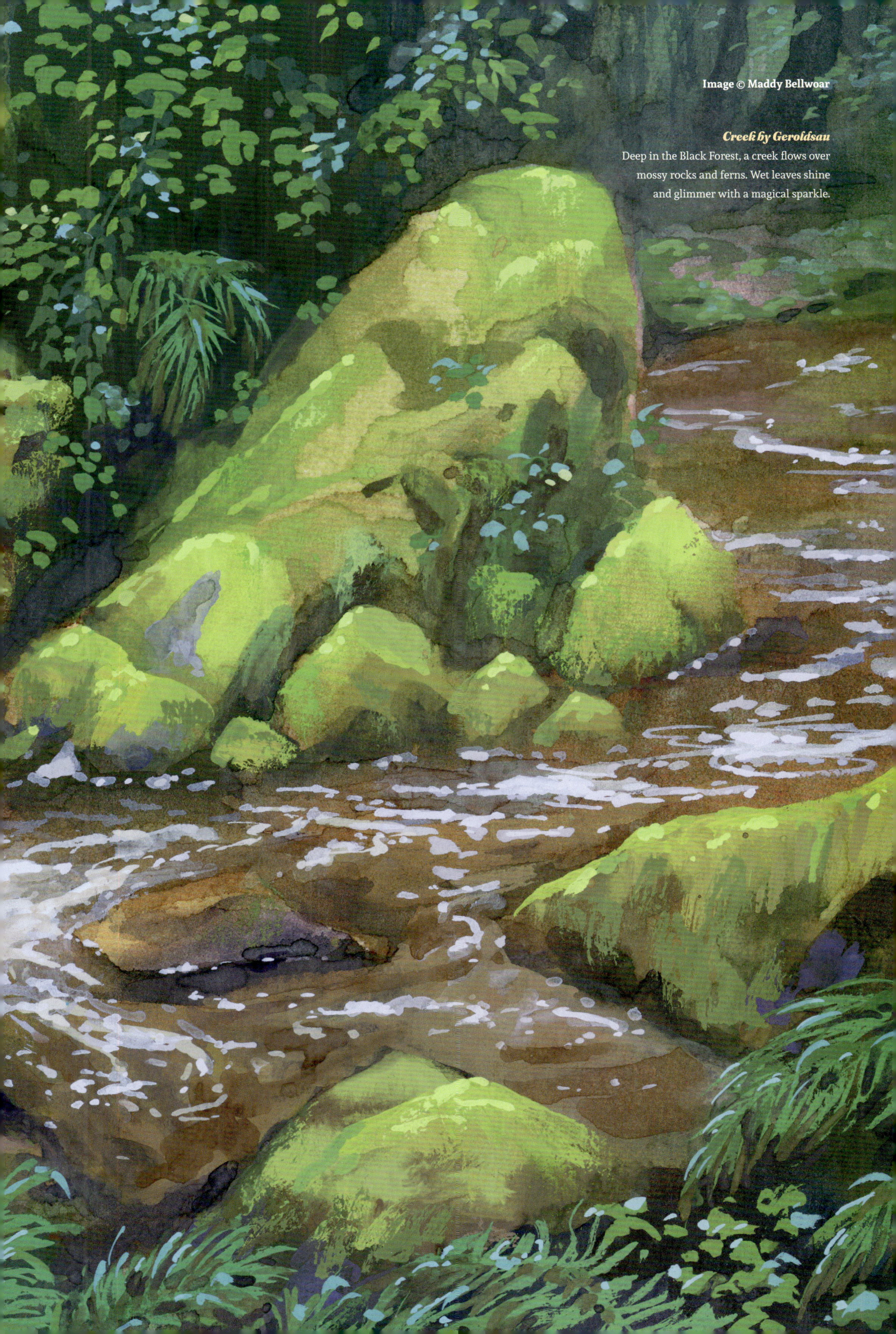

Creek by Geroldsau
Deep in the Black Forest, a creek flows over mossy rocks and ferns. Wet leaves shine and glimmer with a magical sparkle.

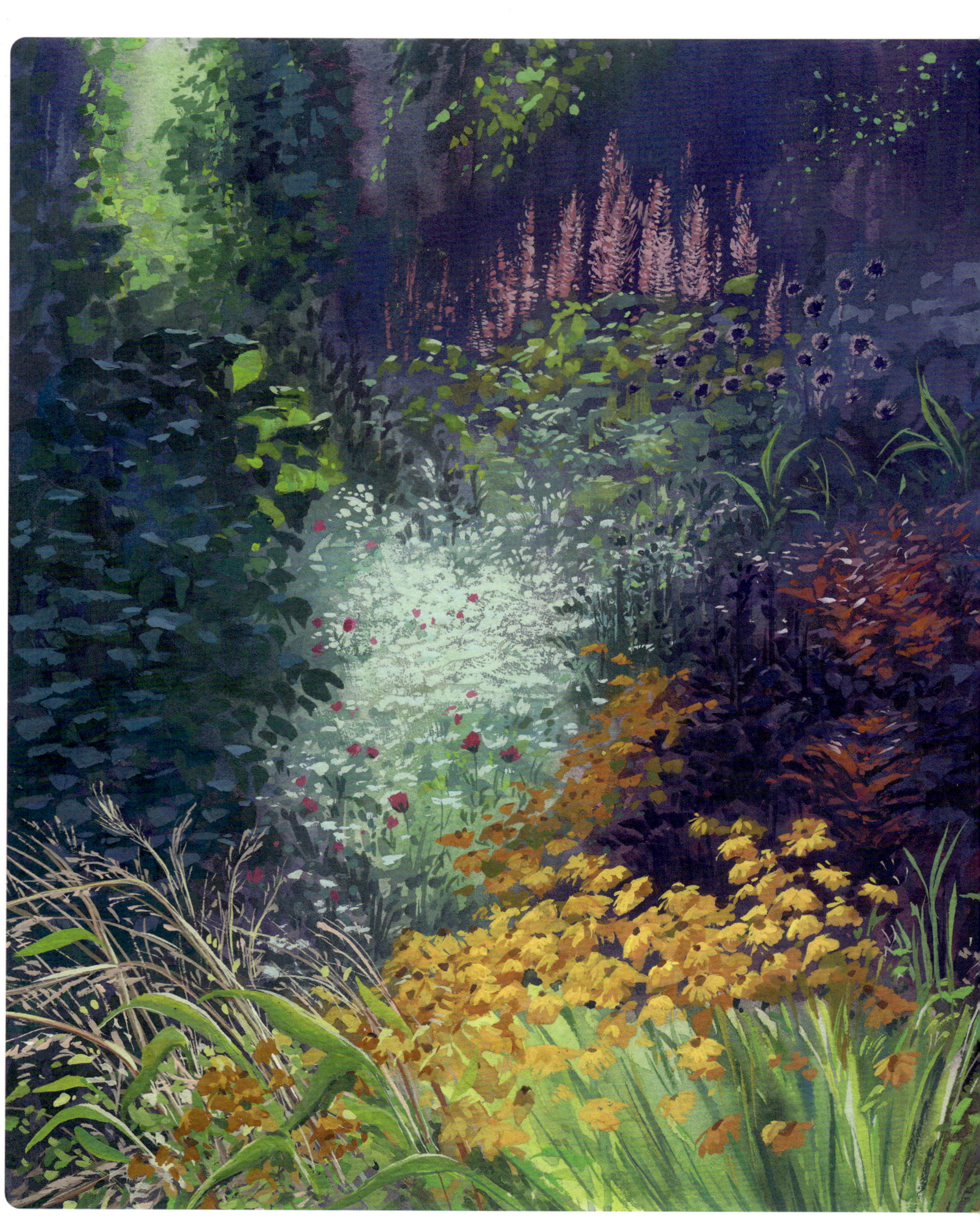

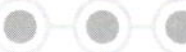

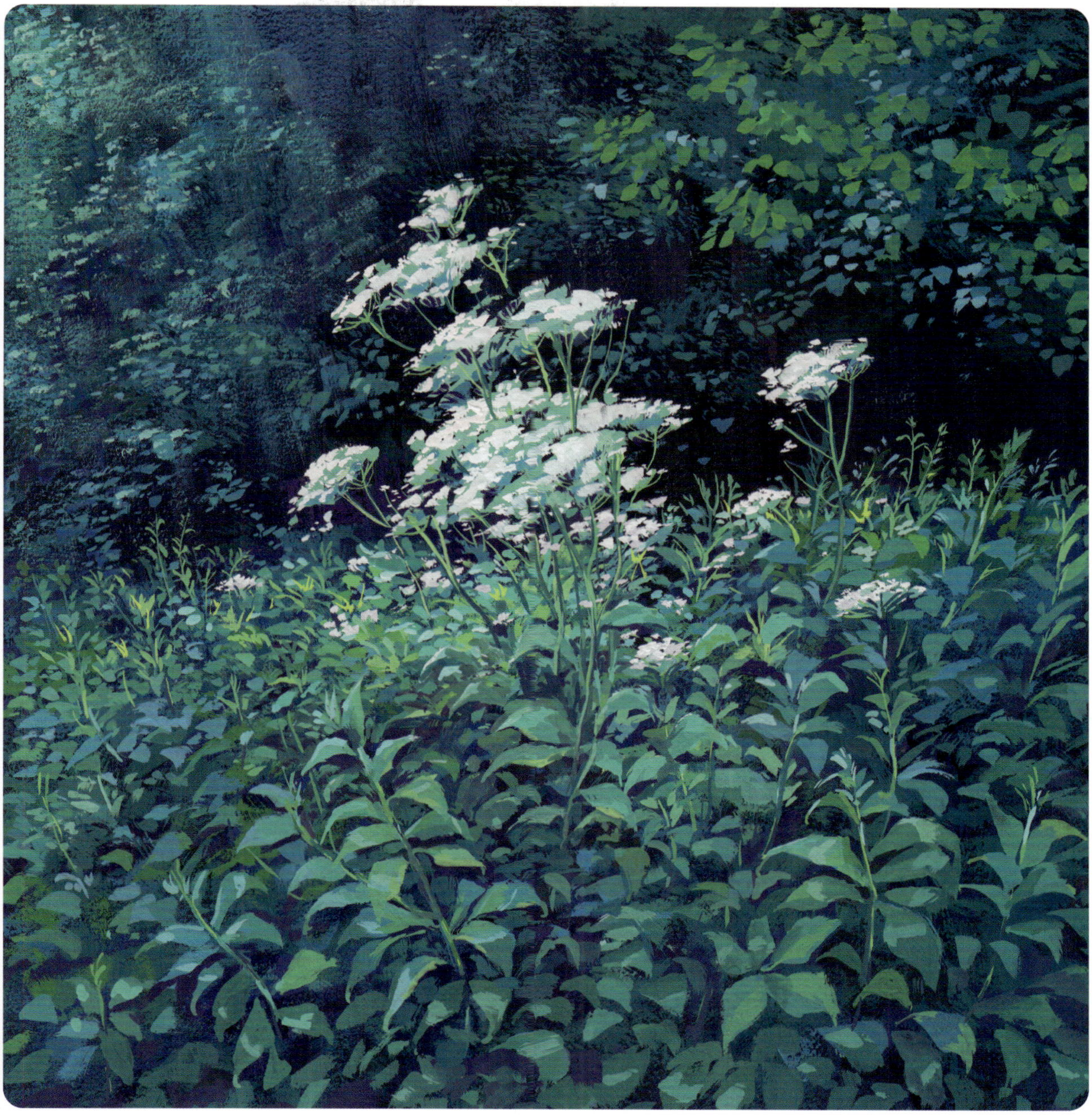

Moonlit A poison hemlock plant is surrounded
by a field of nettles. Its delicate flowers are
illuminated by moonlight as they reach
upwards towards it. (Part of the *Lush* series.)

Secret Garden Painted at the start of
autumn, *Secret Garden* honours the quiet
beauty of a lush garden in its final days
of the year. (Part of the *Quiet* series.)

Clo Louise

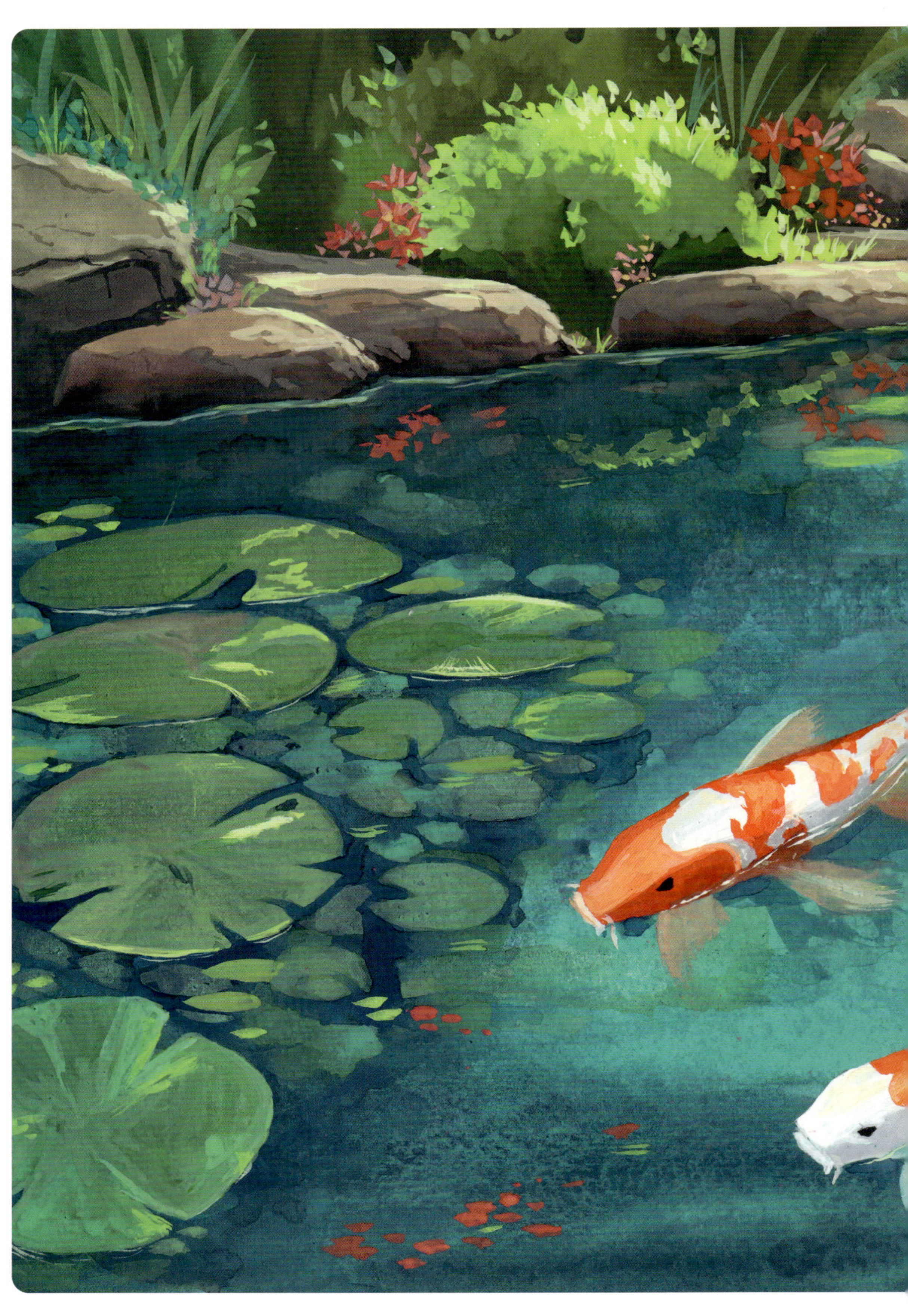

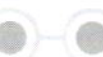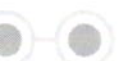

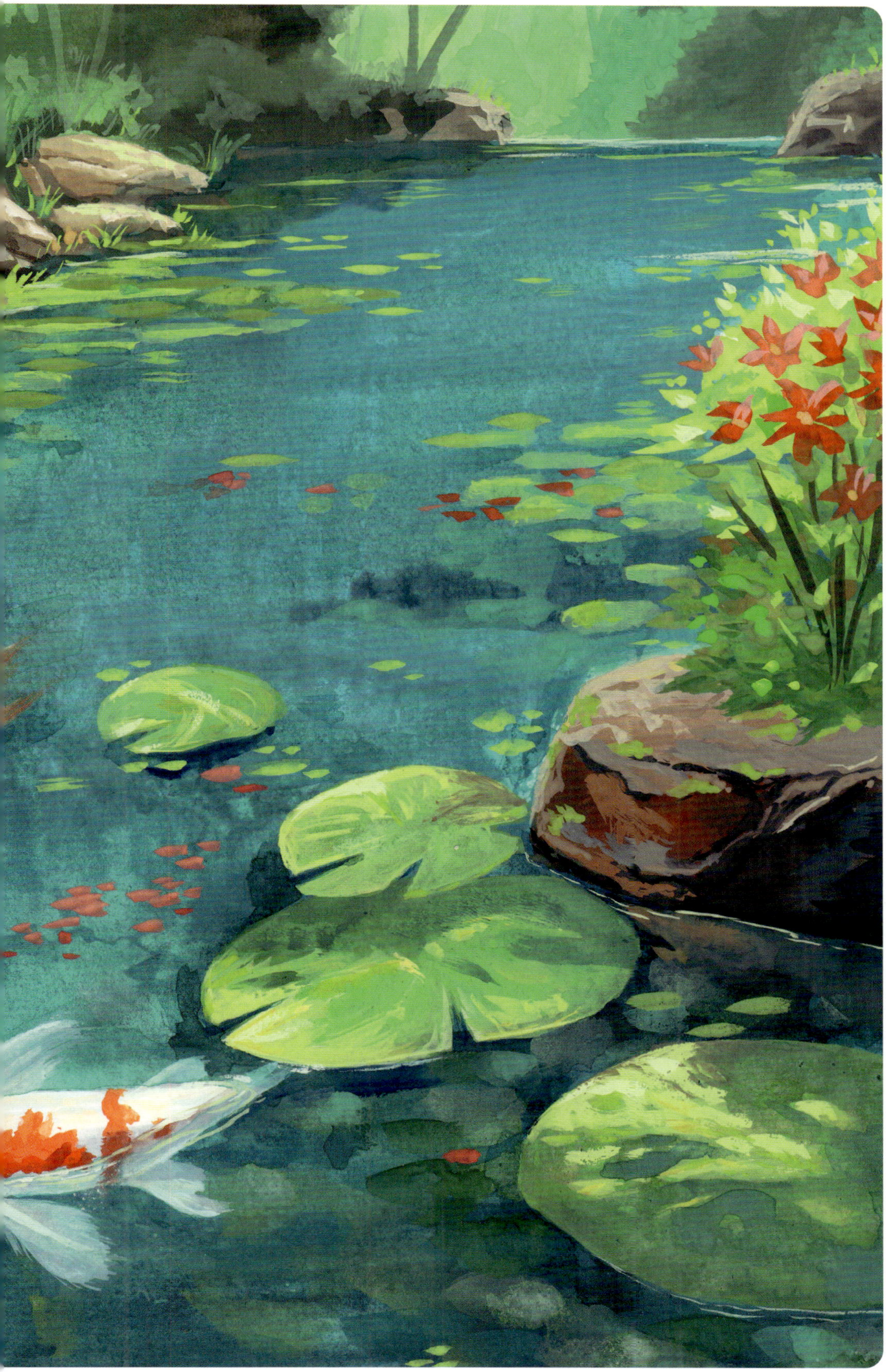

Koi Pond

A tranquil koi pond glows with rich turquoise hues, dappled with lily pads and vibrant flowers. Two koi swim nearby finishing off this serene, harmonious scene.

Image © Clo Louise

Lost Kitty

A little orange cat rides a boat through a dense lily-pad forest. Hues of lush green are reflected both in the water and the surroundings.

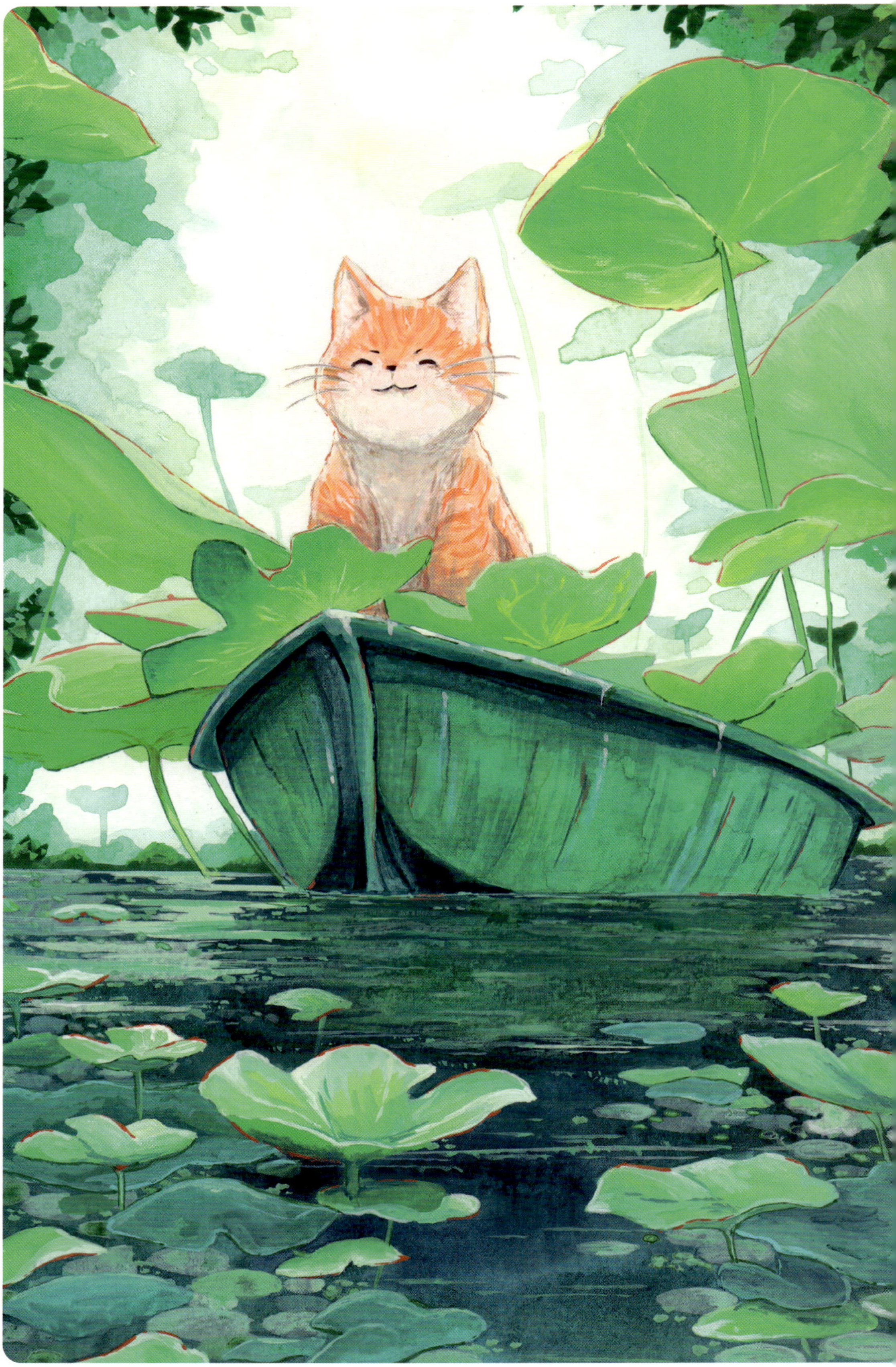

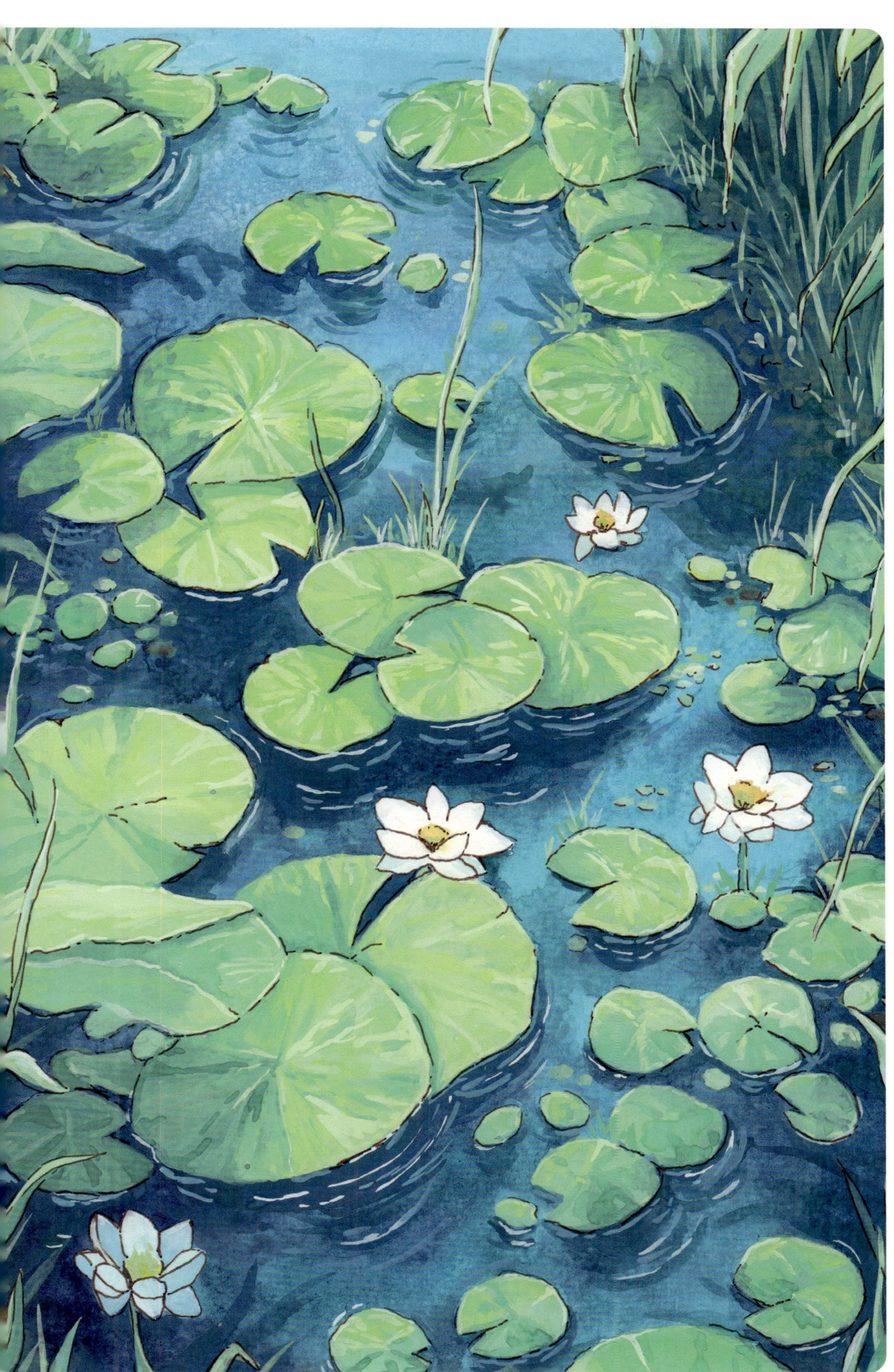

Lily Pond

A delicate lily pond rich with blue hues. Gentle fairy-like lily flowers float delicately surrounded by dense grassy banks.

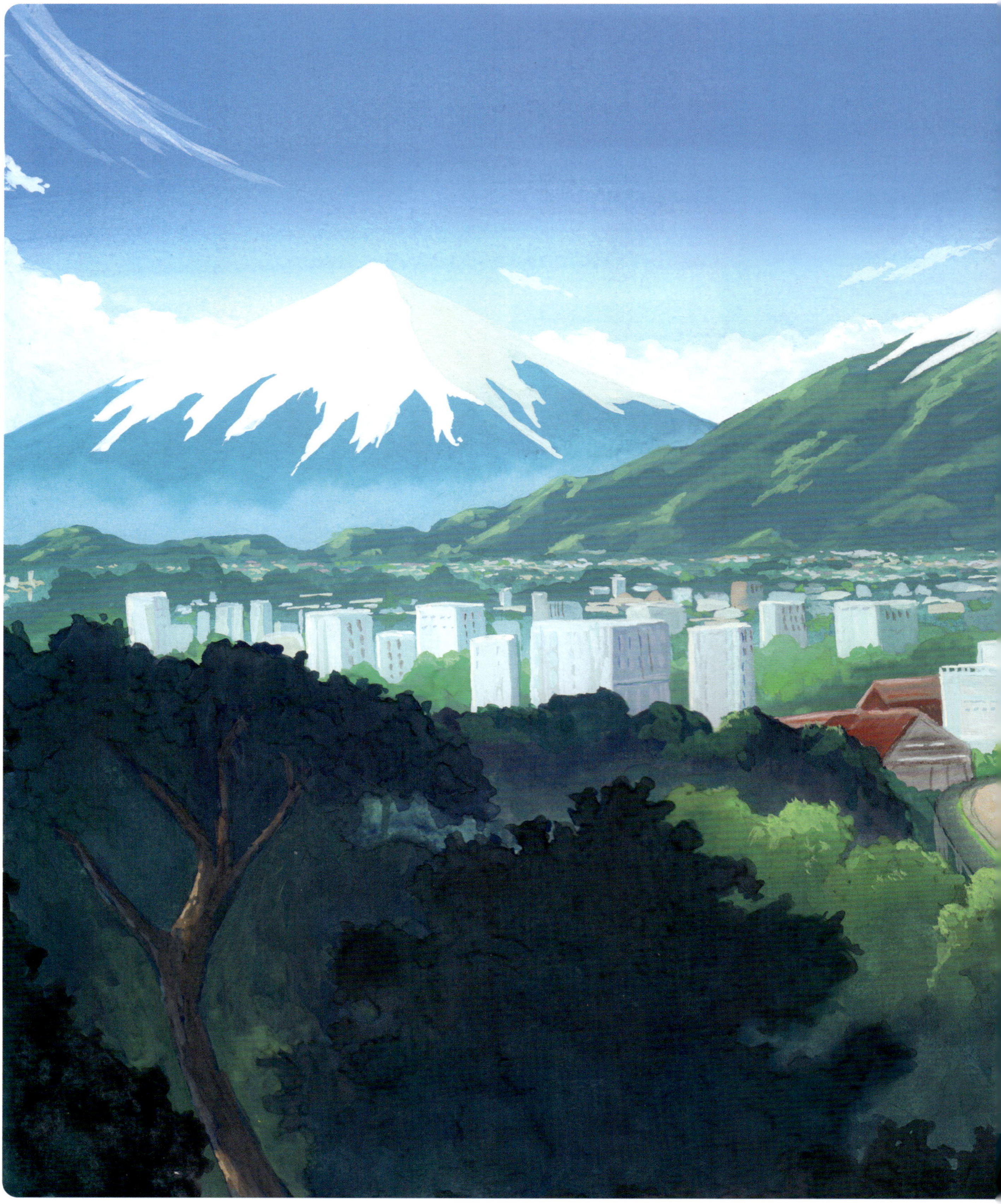

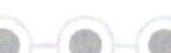
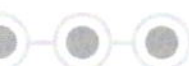

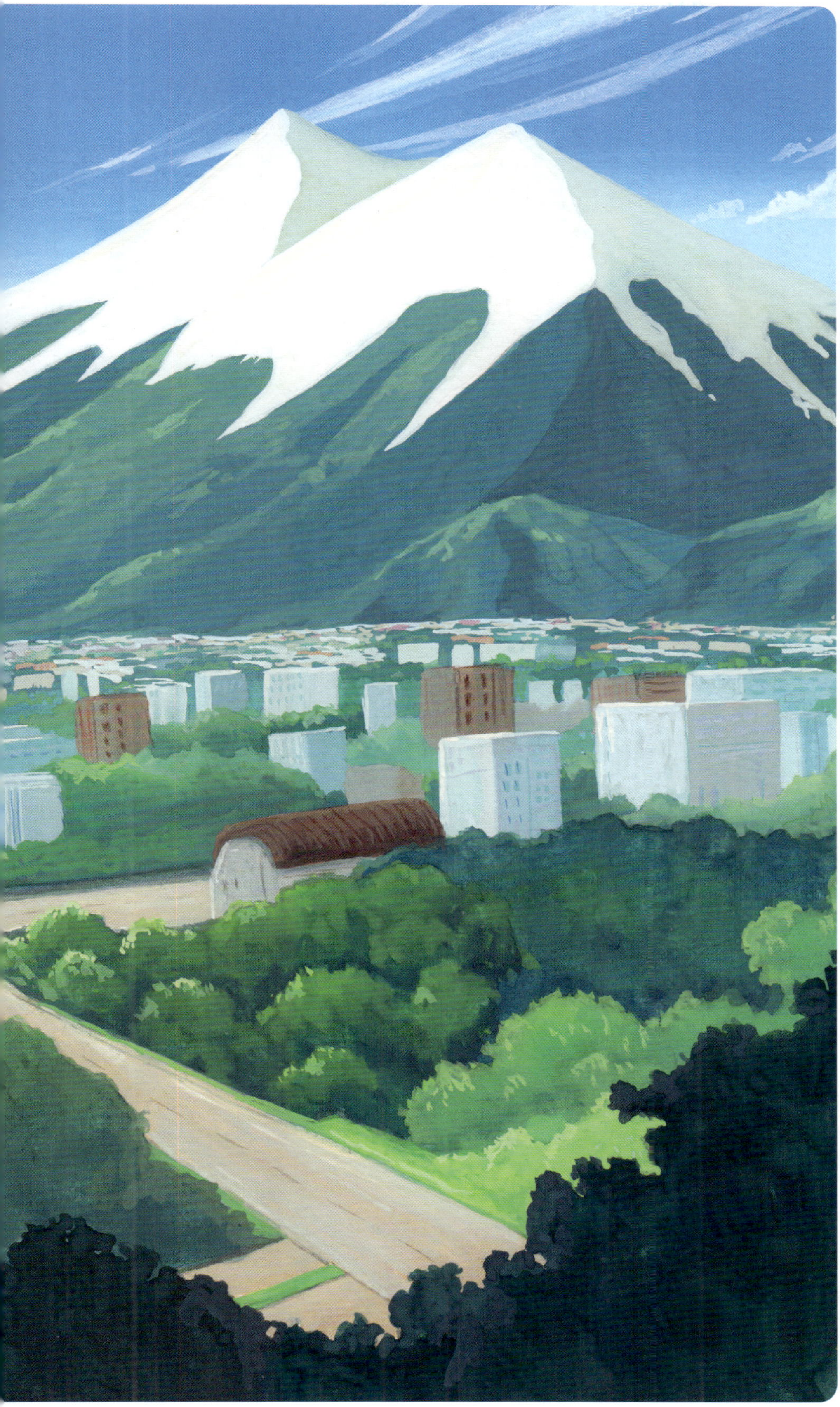

Mountains in Japan

Snow-capped mountains overlook a small town in the Japanese countryside. Crisp blues are painted next to warmer yellows to convey a chilly winter morning but with the promise of warmer days to come.

Image © Clo Louise

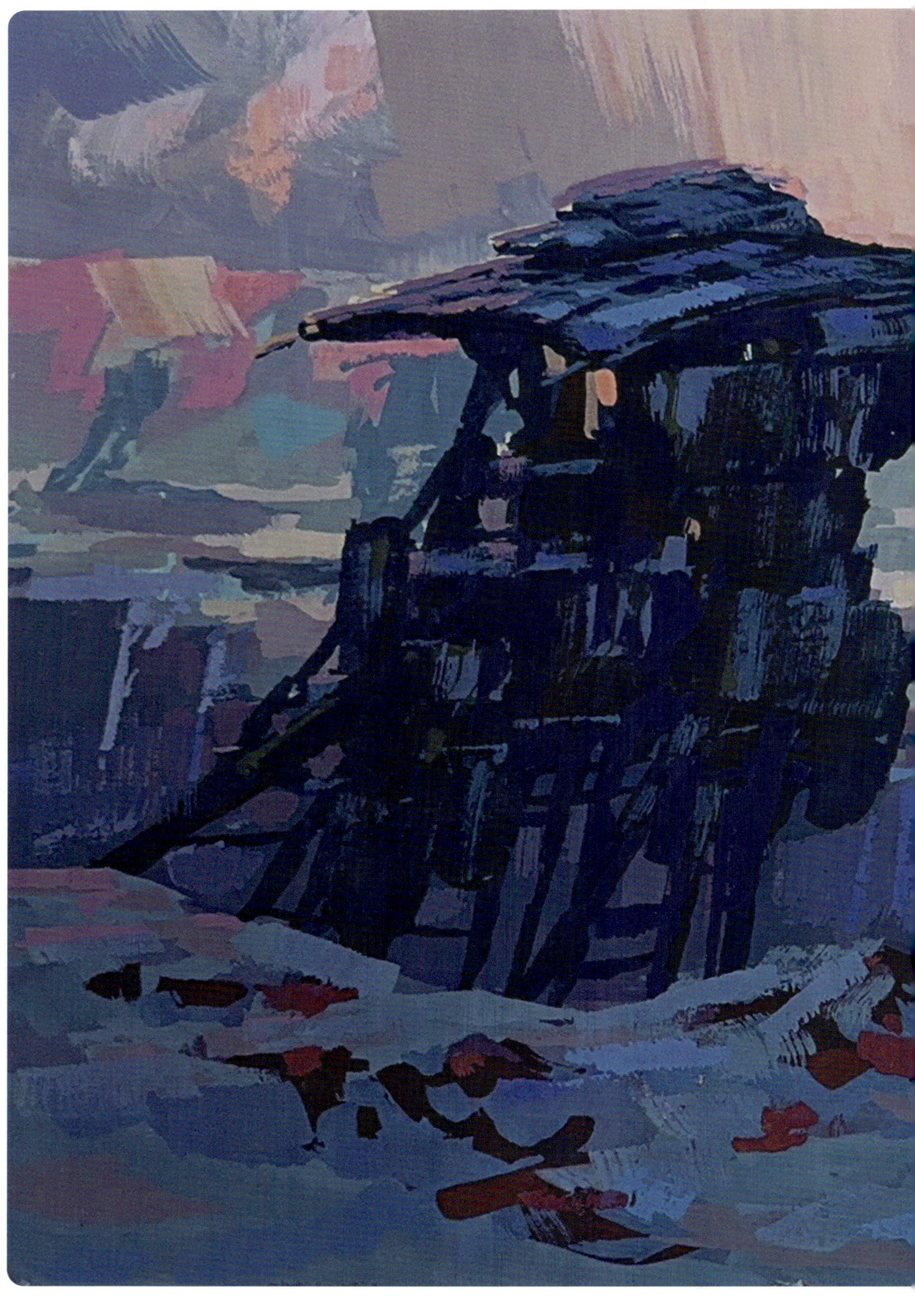

Ken Fairclough

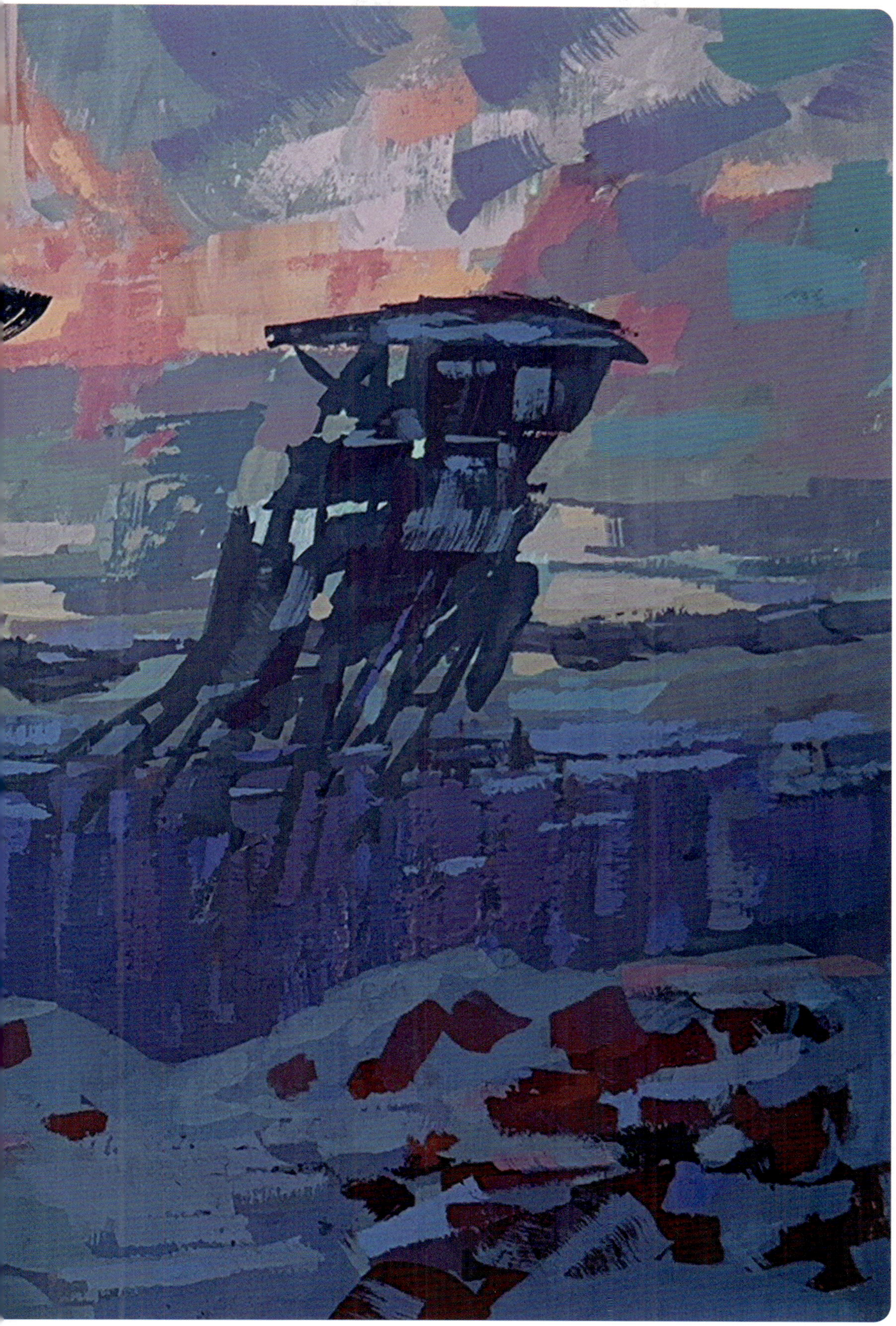

Ice Towers

Fantasy structures built into giant ice crevasses.

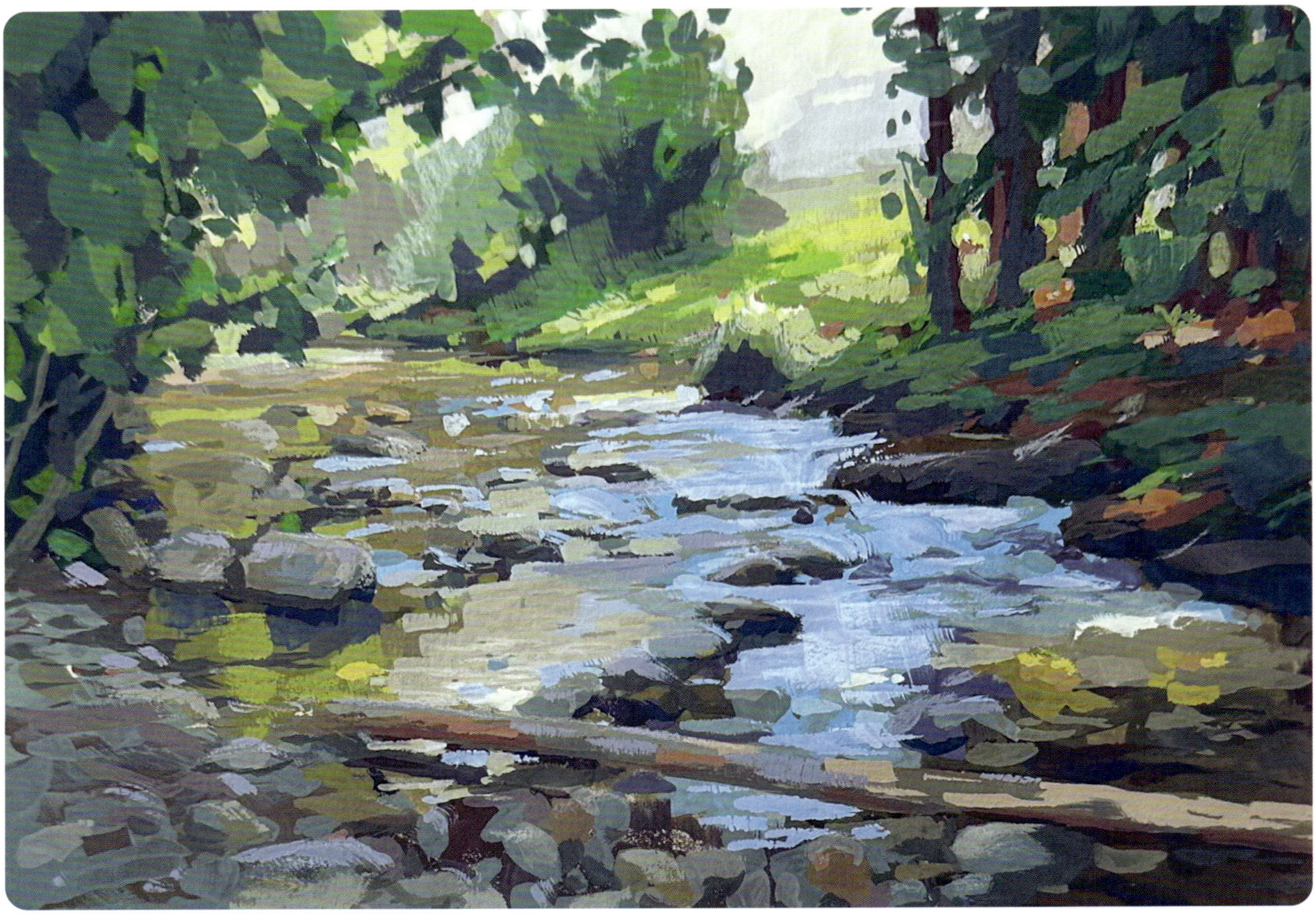

Rocky Stream Rocky Keystone
stream with dappled light.

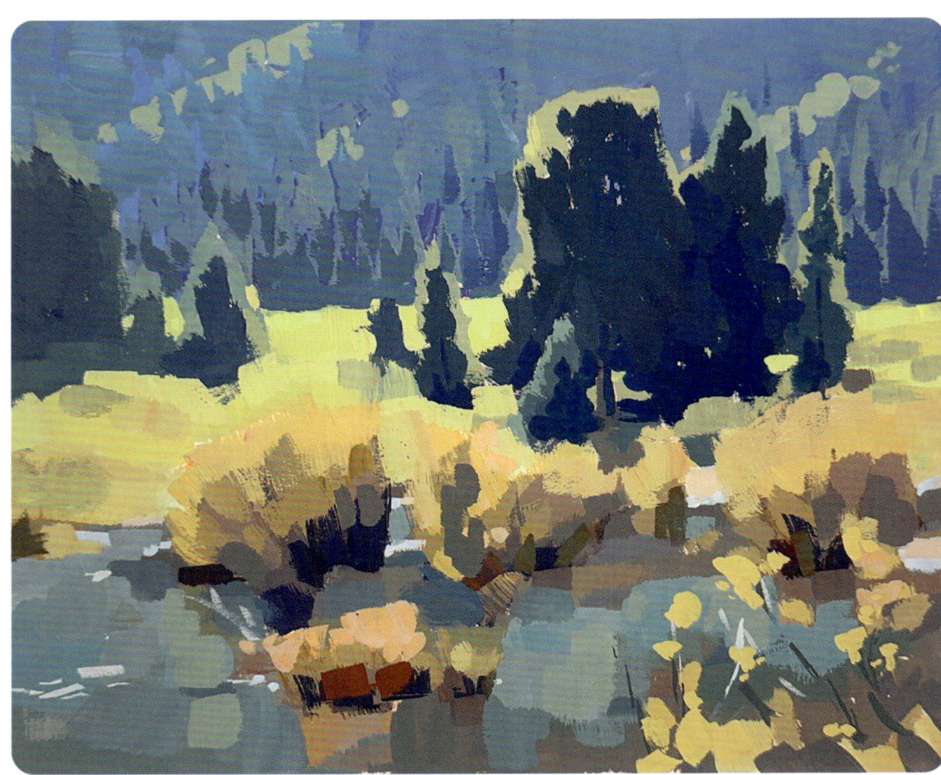

Keystone Trees Spruce
in the Colorado sun.

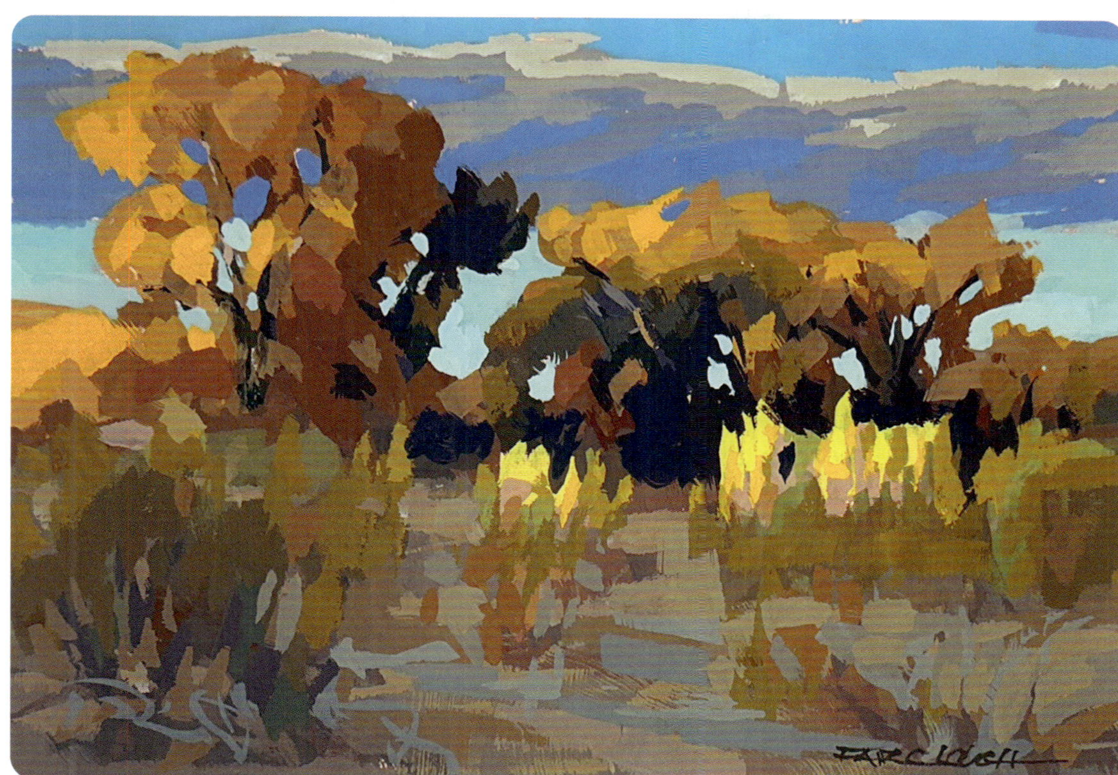

Texas Tree Glow
Sunset glow on
Texas cedar.

Fall Summit
Mountain summit
during the fall in
New Hampshire.

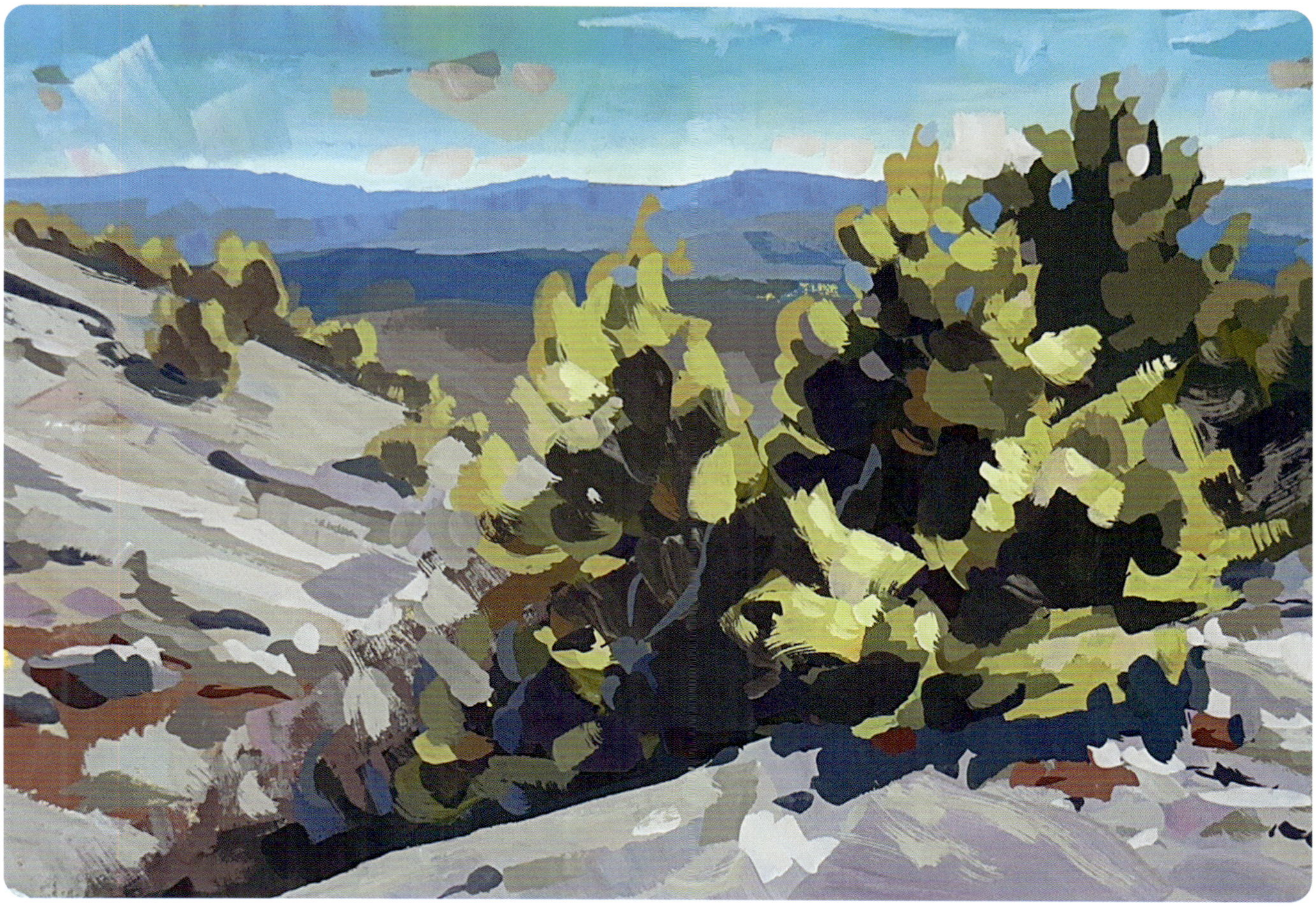

Accorvio

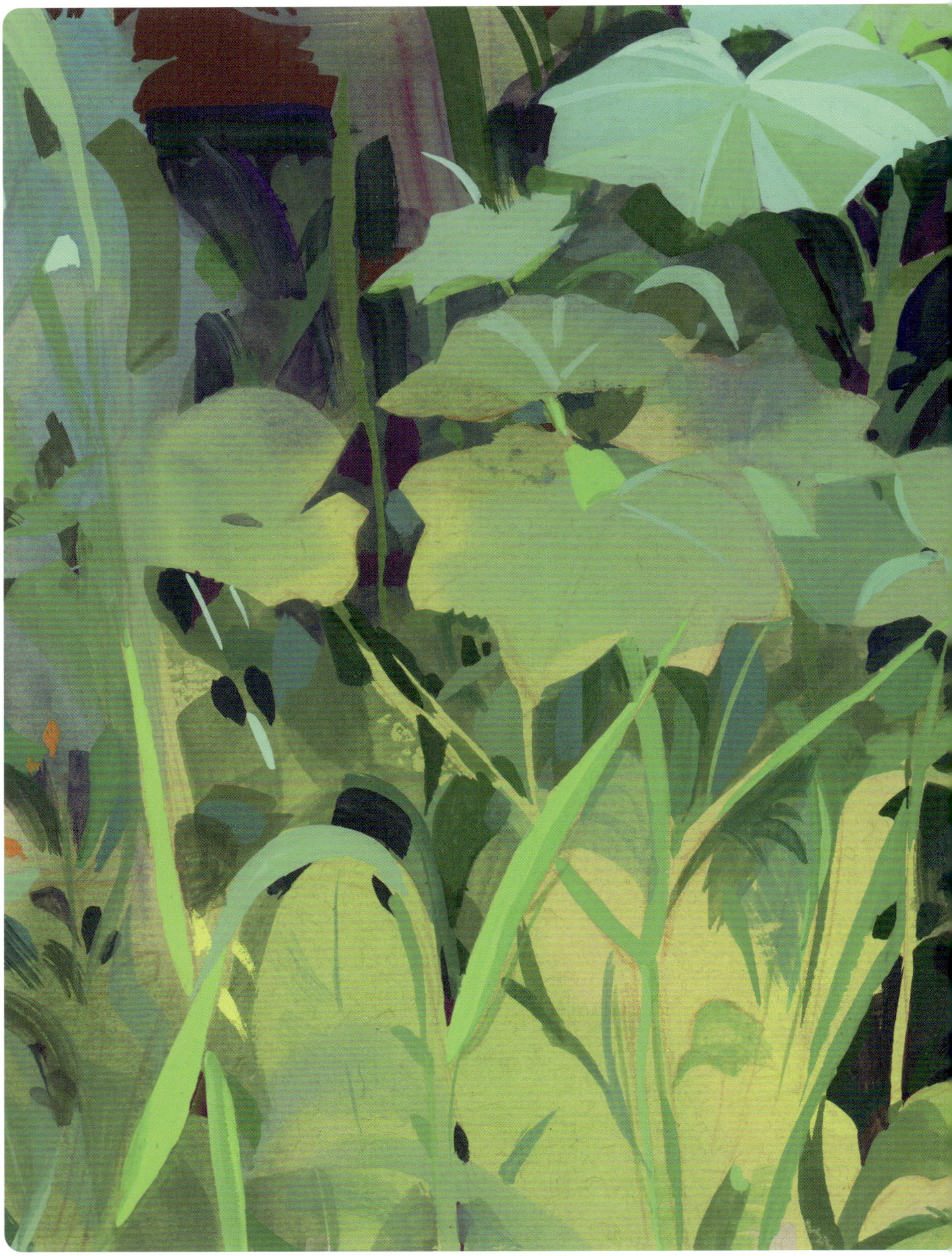

Dog Walks While walking my dog, I stumble upon
many beautiful scenes of foliage reacting to the morning
light. Those small moments inspired this painting.

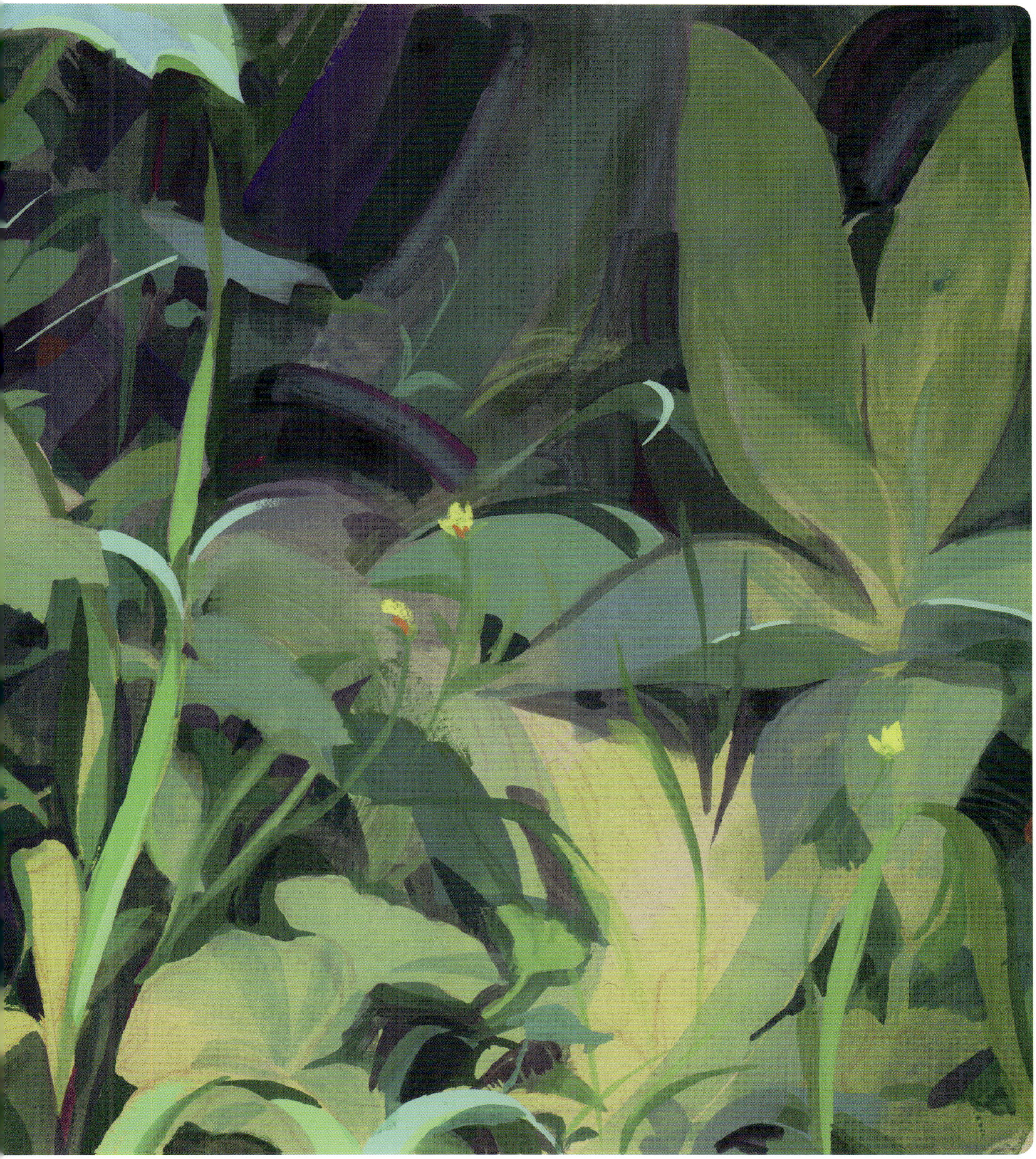

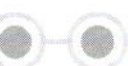

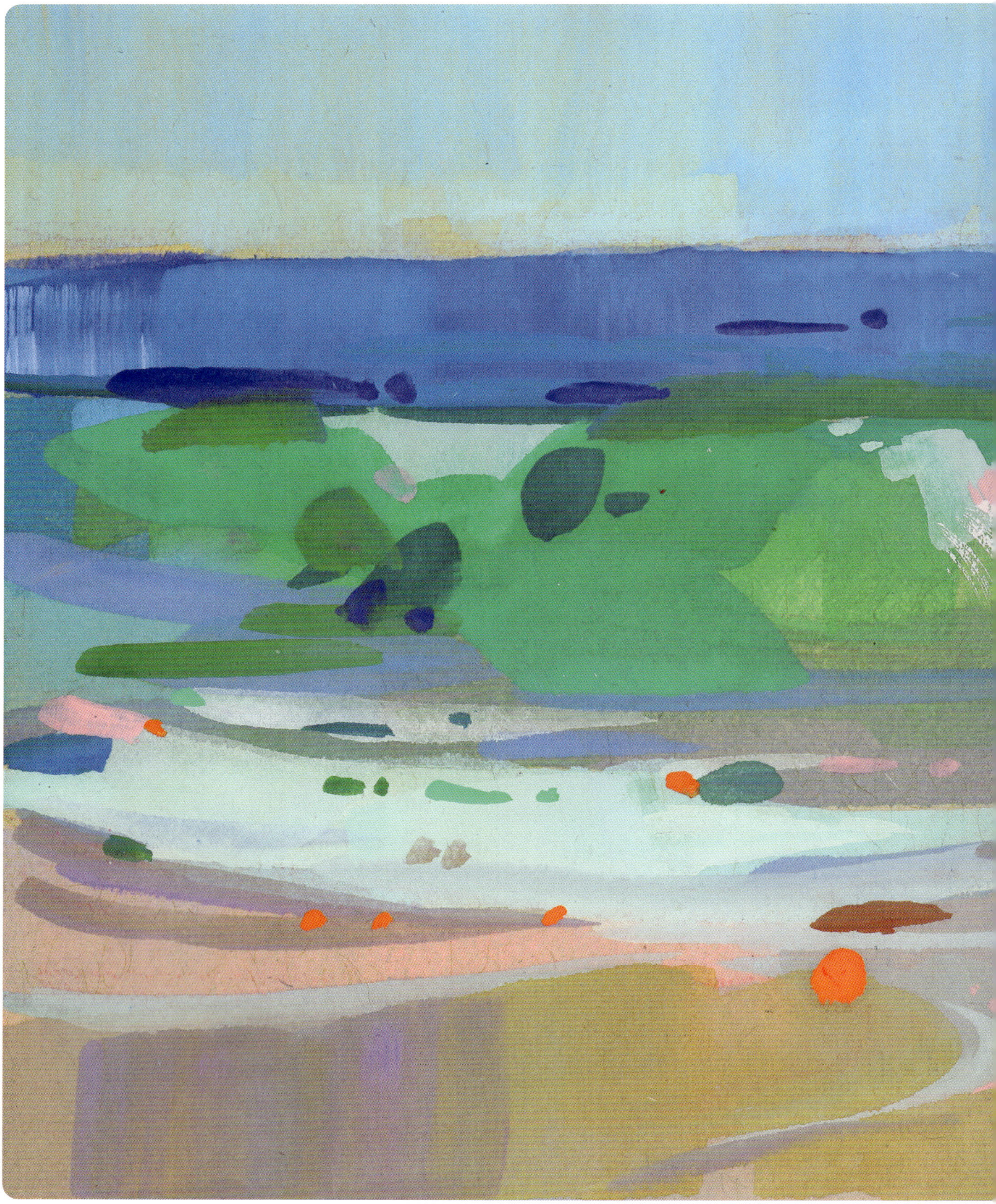

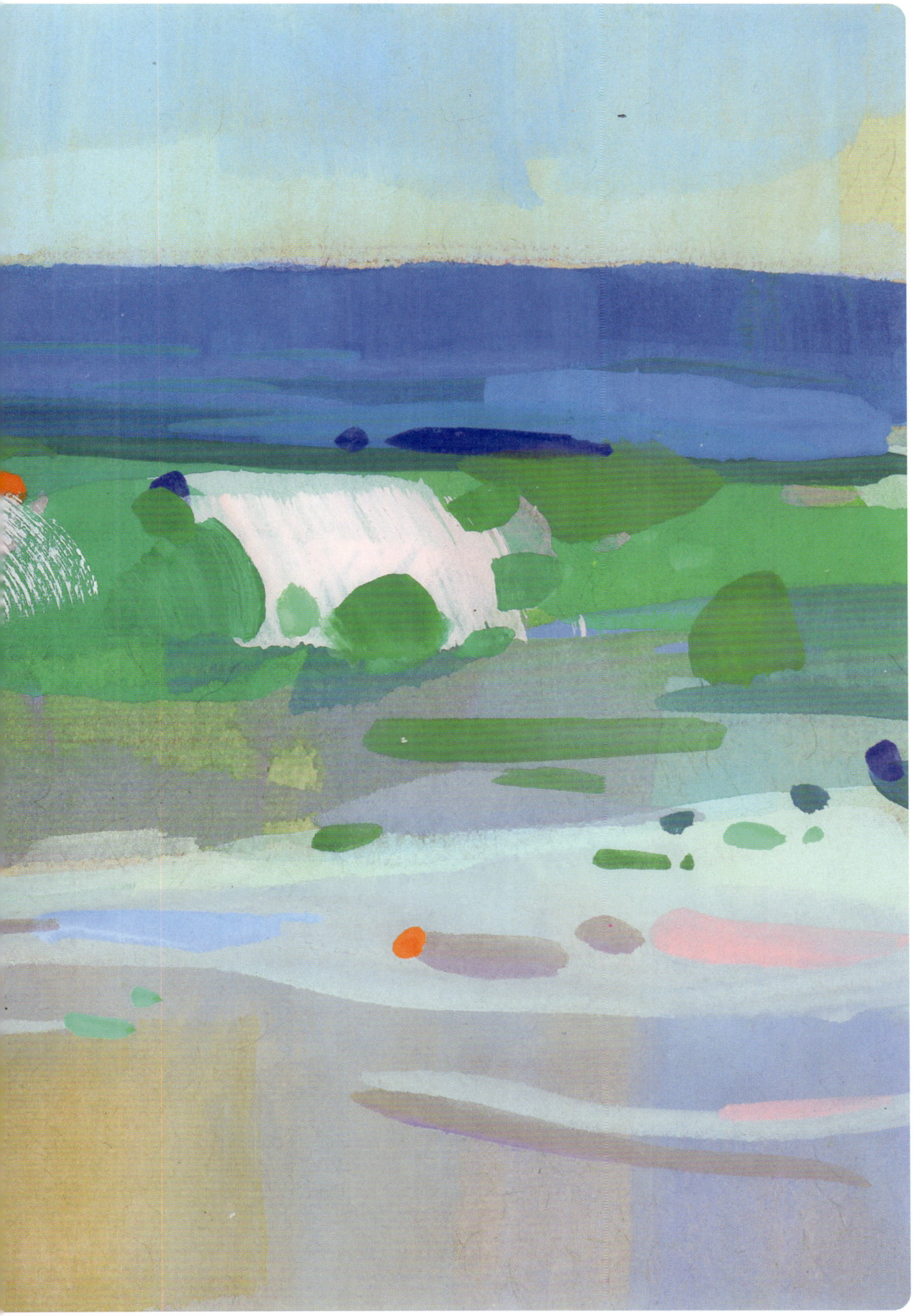

Simmering
A small painting to
remember a short
moment on a hot
summer day.

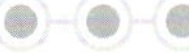

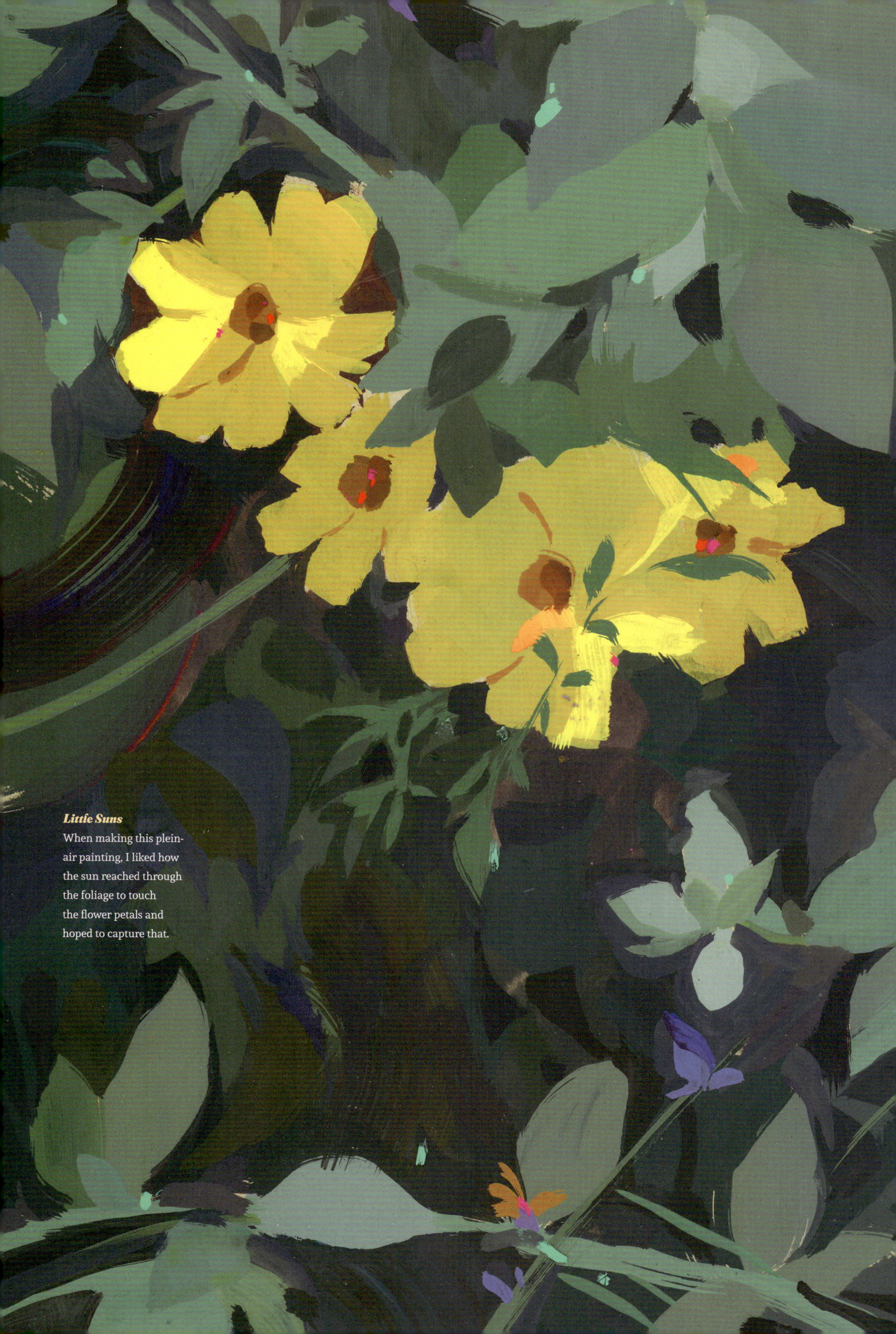

Little Suns
When making this plein-
air painting, I liked how
the sun reached through
the foliage to touch
the flower petals and
hoped to capture that.

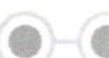

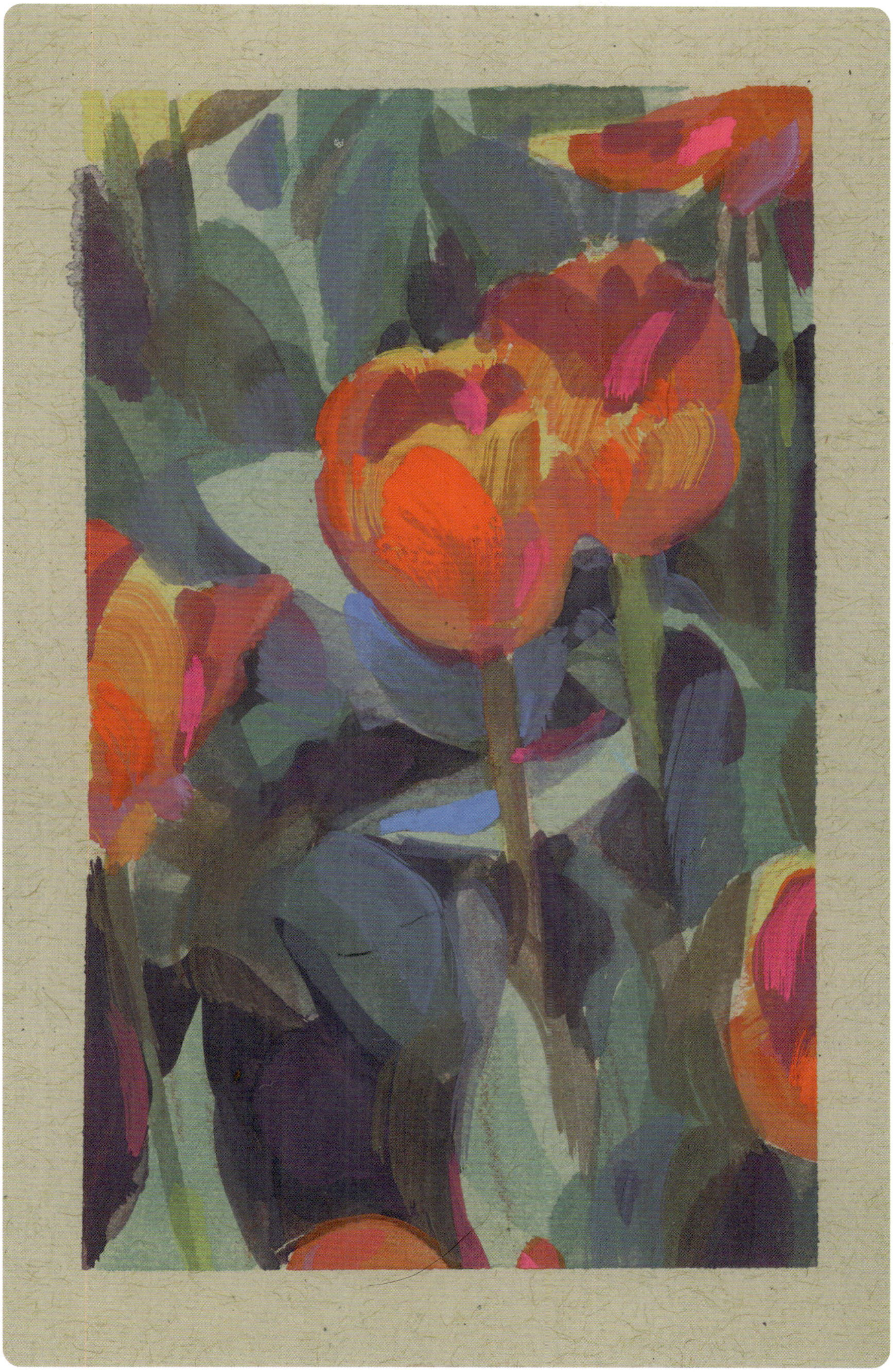

Tulips A painting I made during #PleinAirpril (an online painting challenge) of tulips found in the local gardens.

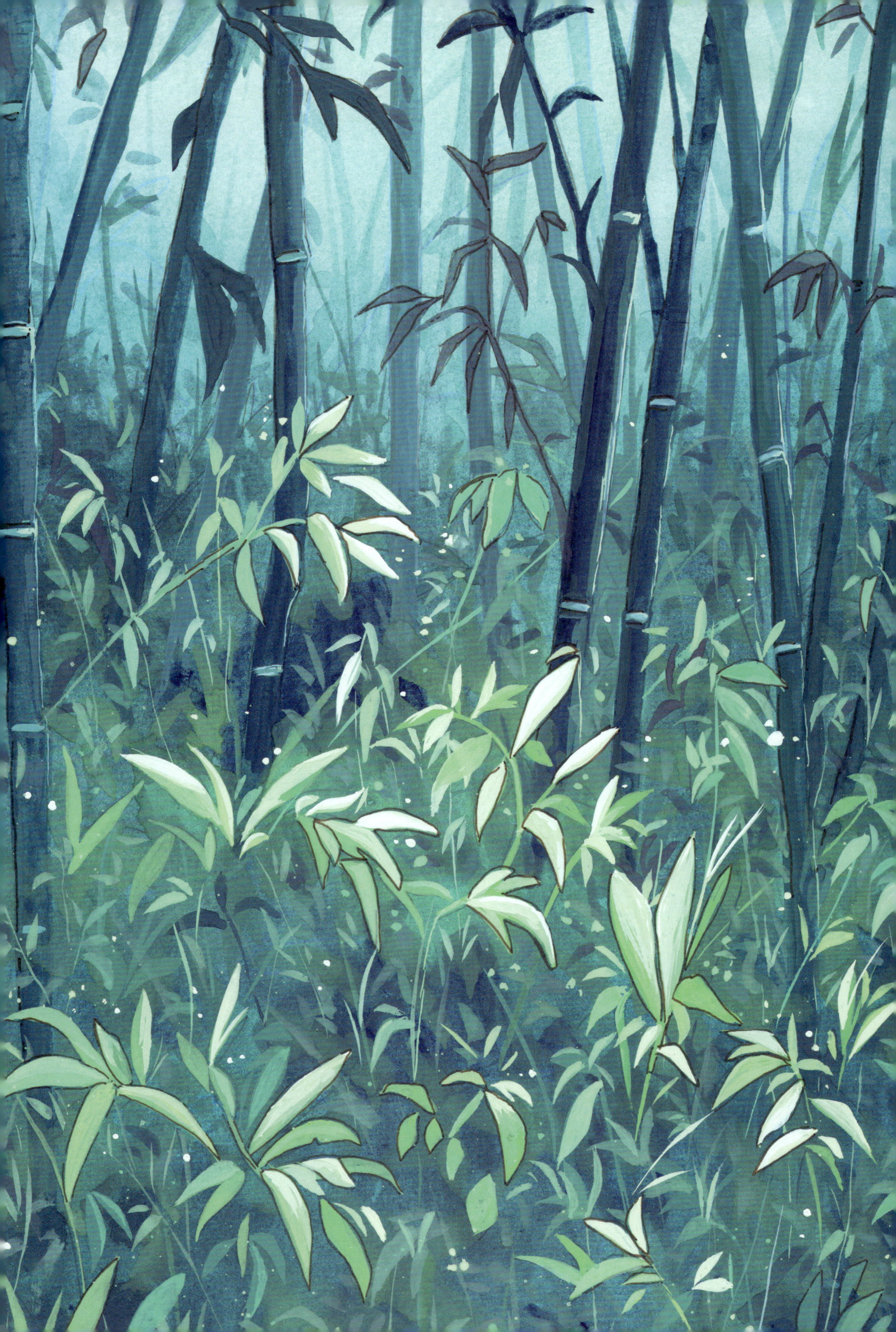

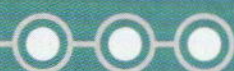

The GLOSSARY

ARTIST-QUALITY PAINTS

Many major brands offer an 'artist quality' or 'artist grade' range of paints. These are more expensive than paints for students and beginners, but offer better pigmentation and ingredient quality.

COLD-PRESS PAPER

Paper that is manufactured by pressing the sheets with cold metal rollers. This creates a coarse surface that is highly absorbent, ideal for painting with lots of water and texture.

COTTON PAPER

A high-quality, durable paper type made with cotton fibres. It can be hot- or cold-pressed in texture.

CRADLE

In painting, a cradle refers to the wooden frame that supports the back of a panel or canvas. A cradled surface is more stable to paint on and keeps its shape better over time.

DESIGNERS' GOUACHE

Many major paint brands offer a gouache range that is aimed towards professional designers. This usually offers a wide choice of refined, attractive colours to save the user time on mixing.

HOT-PRESS PAPER

Paper that is manufactured by pressing the sheets with hot metal rollers. This creates a smooth surface that's less absorbent than cold-press, but is ideal for painting fine details.

HUE

The general 'family' to which a colour belongs. For example, lime green and olive green are both green hues.

OPACITY

If something is opaque, it is a solid, non-translucent colour. Gouache straight from the tube will have high opacity. As it is mixed with water, it becomes less opaque and more transparent.

PAPER WEIGHT

Paper thickness is measured in 'weight' such as pounds (lb) or grams per square metre (gsm). Everyday printer paper is around 20 lb or 75 gsm; watercolour paper would be around 140 lb or 300 gsm.

PIGMENT

A natural or synthetic substance that gives paint its colour. High-quality gouache typically has a high 'pigment load', which means it is more concentrated and opaque, but some colours are naturally lower in pigmentation.

PLEIN AIR

Plein-air painting, or painting 'en plein air', is the practice of painting outdoors. It is valuable for studying landscapes and natural lighting conditions, and for learning how to paint efficiently.

SWATCH

A small sample of a colour or material, for reference or to test its effect.

VALUE

The lightness or darkness of a colour, with white having the brightest value and black the darkest.

WATER-BASED PAINT

A type of paint that is created with water, pigment, and a binding agent. Gouache and watercolour are both water-based paints, as opposed to oils, for example, which are oil-based. Water-based paints dry relatively fast and are easier to clean than oil-based.

The **CONTRIBUTORS**

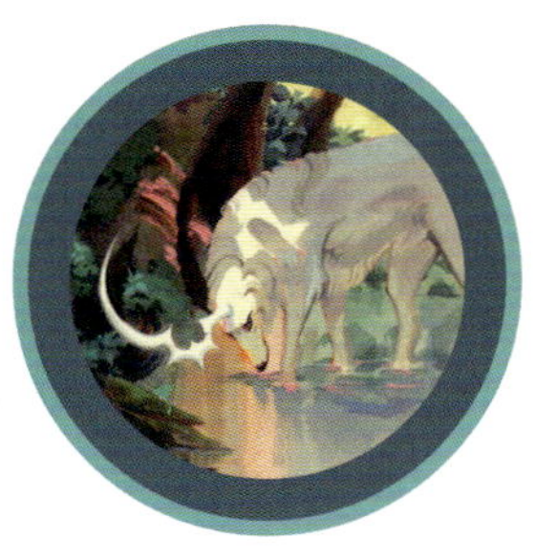 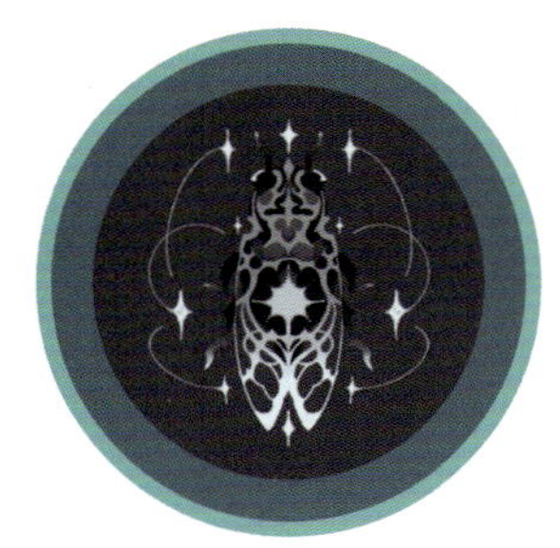

ACCORVIO

gracenicoletti.com

Accorvio is an illustrator and painter from Virginia, USA, who is most at home when playing in the rain and mud. Their previous clients include Dwarf Animation Studio, Psyop, and Bethesda Games.

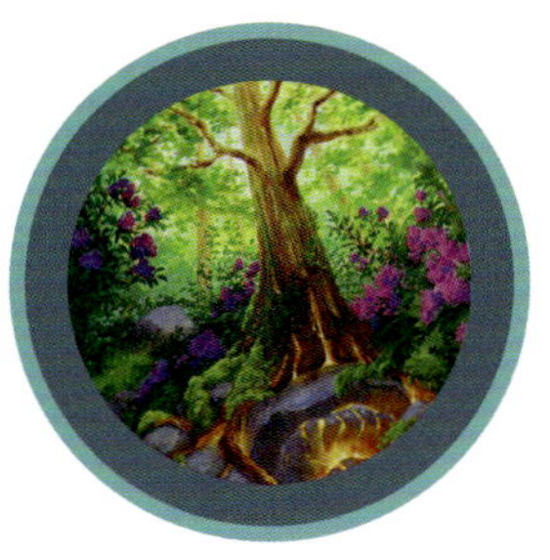 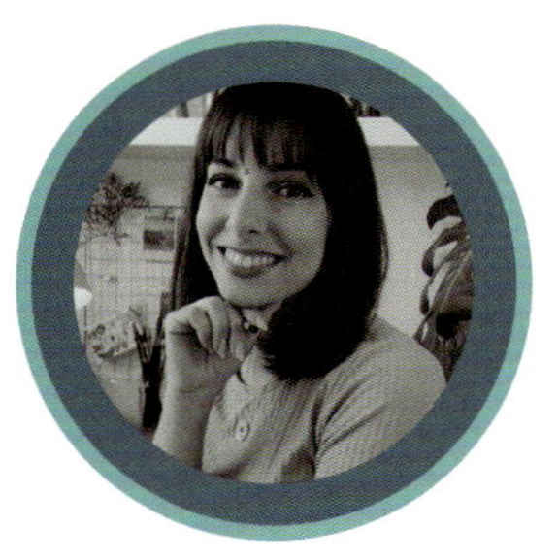

MADDY BELLWOAR

maddybellwoar.com

Maddy Bellwoar is an environment artist based in the Netherlands. Her work explores the beauty of the natural world through light, colour, and texture, in both digital and traditional mediums.

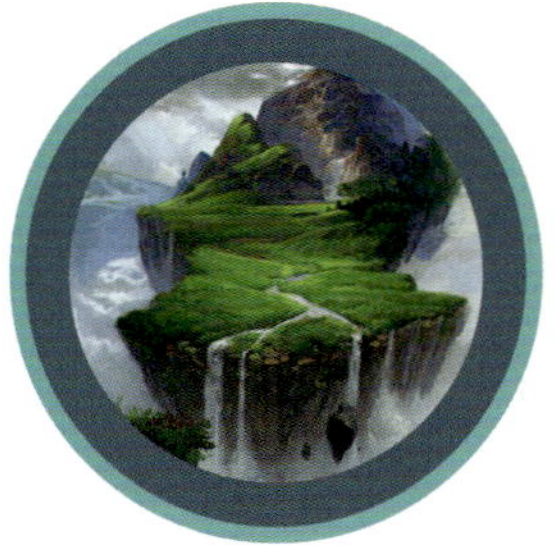 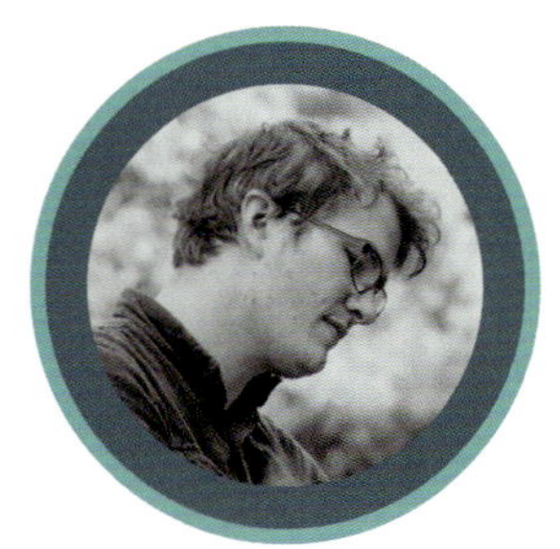

JUSTIN DONALDSON

justindonaldsonart.com

Painter and art-educator Justin Donaldson creates beautifully lush landscapes from his home base in South Carolina, USA. He finds inspiration in peace and tranquillity. In the hunt for these qualities he traverses forests, fields, and rivers, and takes his paints to the far reaches of nature. He works primarily with gouache and oil.

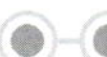

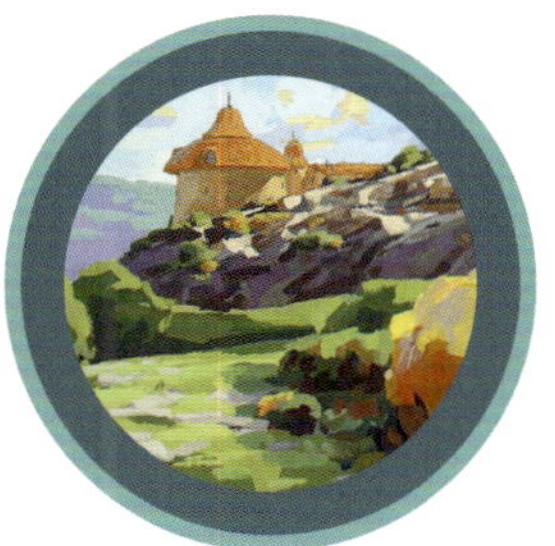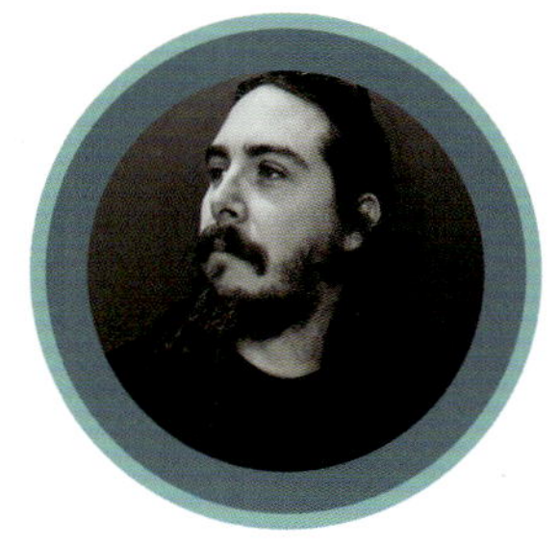

KEN FAIRCLOUGH

artstation.com/kenfairclough

Ken Fairclough is an avid plein-air painter and professional concept artist for the game industry. His work features in multiple publications and games such as *Mass Effect*, *Anthem*, and *Star Citizen*. He received his MFA at Bowling Green State University and has taught multiple online courses. He currently resides in Austin, Texas.

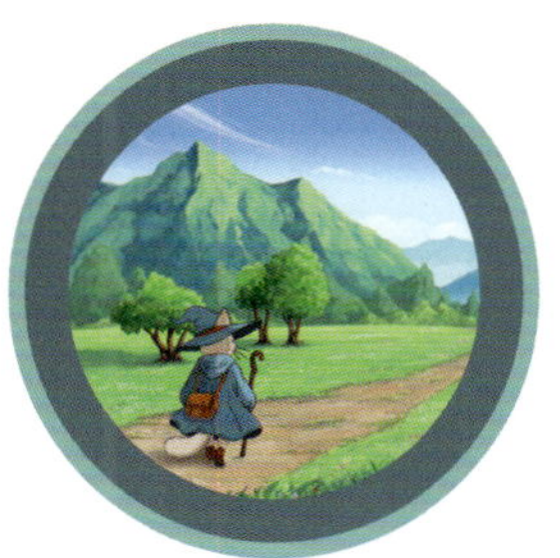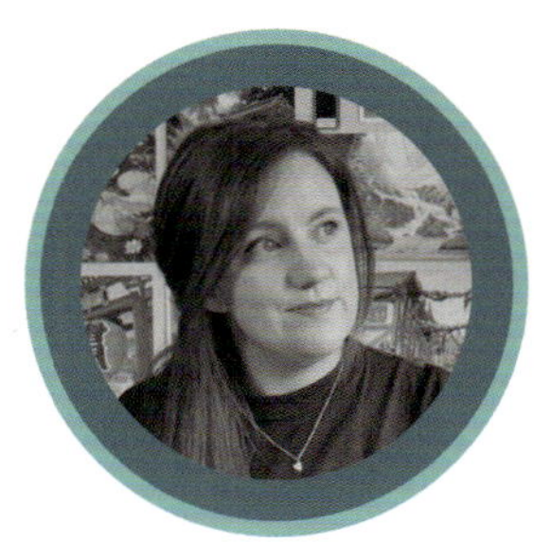

CLO LOUISE

instagram.com/clolouiseart

Clo Louise is a UK-based gouache artist who paints whimsical, vibrant landscapes. Inspired by anime and video games, she shares beginner-friendly tutorial videos on her social media to help others to learn to paint with confidence.

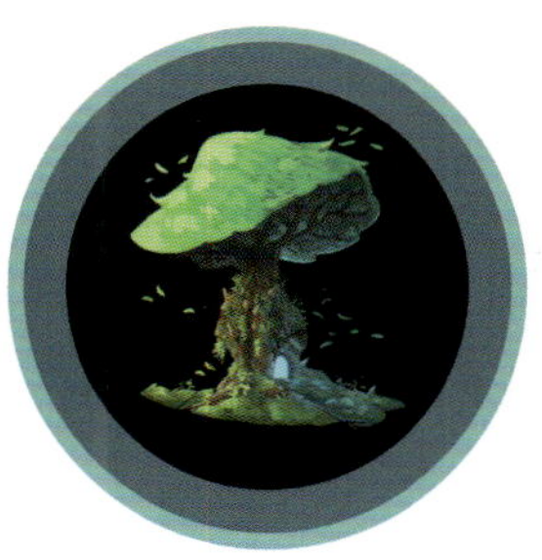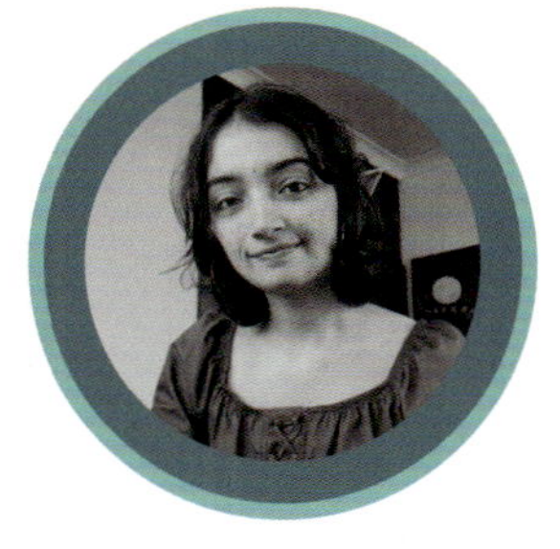

KIARA MAHARAJ

kiaraintheforest.com

Kiara Maharaj is a fantasy writer and artist from South Africa. She spends most of her time in her sketchbooks, creating other worlds, tree portals, and adventurous characters.

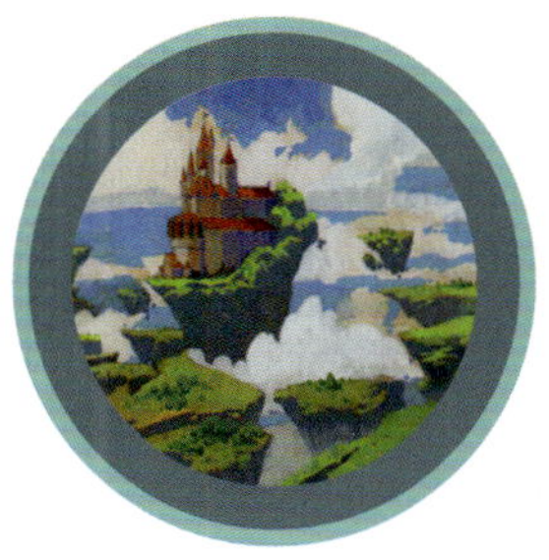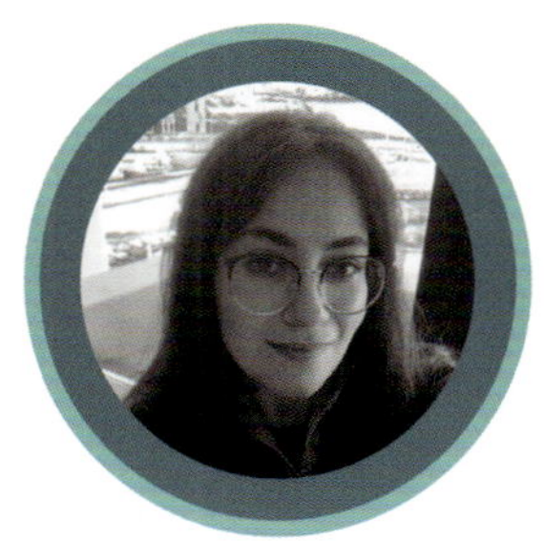

FATIMA MANDOUH

instagram.com/jigglybrush

Fatima Mandouh is a self-taught artist working in animation and games. Based in Ohio, USA, she has contributed to multiple galleries and projects with Sony Pictures Animation, thatgamecompany, and more.

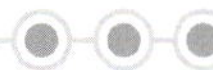

Talented French illustrator and character designer Sibylline Meynet shares her beautiful artwork, exclusive tutorials, and step-by-step techniques in her first published artbook. Through its pages, Sibylline also shares her experiences working in the art industry, juggling work commitments with exhibiting, and offers a peek into her workspace and influences. *Rêverie* is a must-have for artists and illustrators in need of career inspiration and a creative reboot.

Image © Sibylline Meynet

Available now at
store.3dtotal.com

ARTISTS' MASTER SERIES

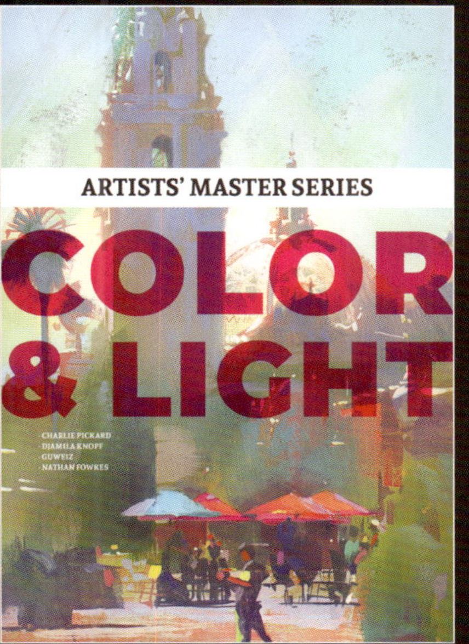

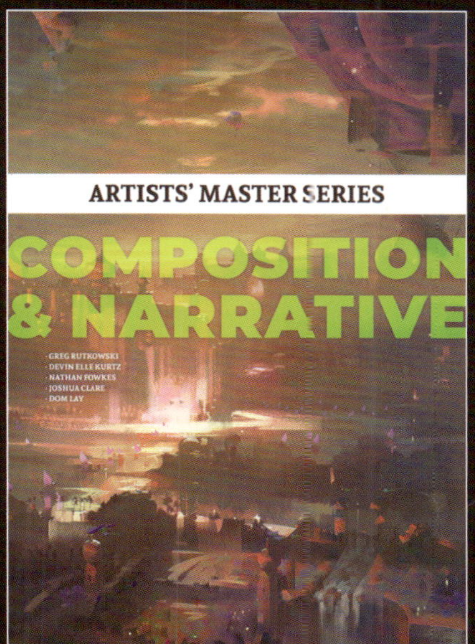

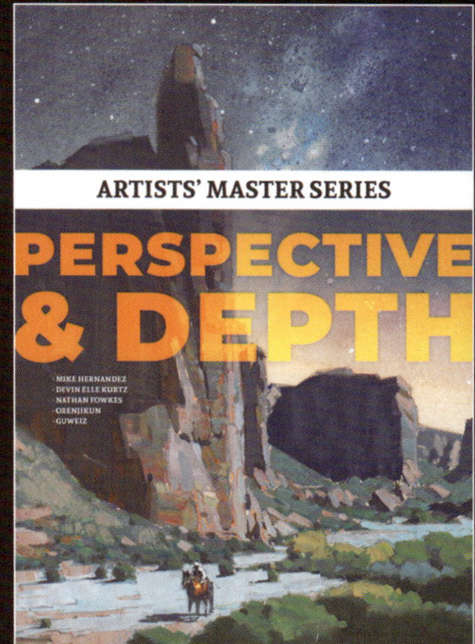

Learn from industry experts in the *Artists' Master Series*, which comprises three in-depth volumes packed with theory, tutorials, and inspiring art. Essential for artists of any skill level or medium, each book thoroughly unpacks art theory and practice, drawing on veteran artists' wealth of knowledge and experience.

The acclaimed first book, *Color & Light*, is a deep dive into these foundational subjects, presented in impressive detail by artists including Guweiz, Nathan Fowkes, and Djamila Knopf.

The second volume, *Composition & Narrative*, explores the mathematical rules and storytelling power of composition, featuring Greg Rutkowski, Devin Elle Kurtz, Joshua Clare, and more.

Perspective & Depth completes this impressive trilogy with insights from Mike Hernandez, Orenjikun, and more, making the *Artists' Master Series* a comprehensive, fully rounded education for any visual artist's shelf.

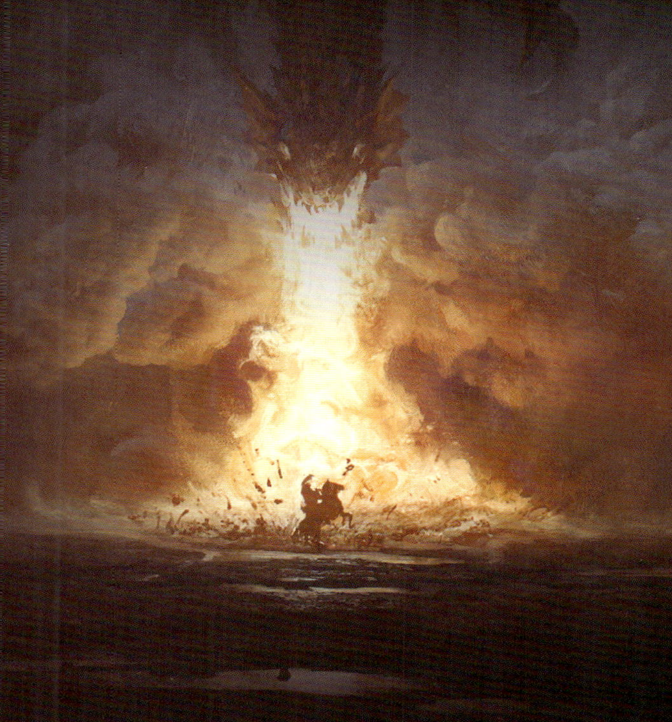

Image © Greg Rutkowski

3dtotalPublishing

3dtotal Publishing is a trailblazing, creative publisher specializing in inspirational and educational resources for artists.

Our titles feature top industry professionals from around the globe who share their experience in skillfully written step-by-step tutorials and fascinating, detailed guides. Illustrated throughout with stunning artwork, these best-selling publications offer creative insight, expert advice, and essential motivation. Fans of digital art will enjoy our comprehensive volumes covering Adobe Photoshop, Procreate, and Blender, as well as our superb titles based around character design, including *Fundamentals of Character Design* and *Creating Characters for the Entertainment Industry*. The dedicated, high-quality blend of instruction and inspiration also extends to traditional art. Titles covering a range of techniques, genres, and abilities allow your creativity to flourish while building essential skills.

Well-established within the industry, we now offer over 100 titles and counting, many of which have been translated into multiple languages around the world. With something for every artist, we are proud to say that our books offer the 3dtotal package:

LEARN · CREATE · SHARE

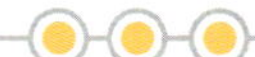

Visit us at store.3dtotal.com

3dtotal Publishing is part of 3dtotal.com, a leading website for CG artists founded by Tom Greenway in 1999.